More Notes from a Different Drummer

SERVING SPECIAL POPULATIONS SERIES

BOOKS FOR THE GIFTED CHILD

CHALLENGING THE GIFTED
Curriculum Enrichment and Acceleration Models

CREATING PROGRAMS FOR THE GIFTED
A Guide for Teachers, Librarians, and Students

HIGH/LOW HANDBOOK
Books, Materials, and Services for the Teenage Problem Reader

MORE NOTES FROM A DIFFERENT DRUMMER
A Guide to Juvenile Fiction Portraying the Disabled

NOTES FROM A DIFFERENT DRUMMER
A Guide to Juvenile Fiction Portraying the Handicapped

PARENTING THE GIFTED
Developing the Promise

SERVING PHYSICALLY DISABLED PEOPLE
An Information Handbook for All Libraries

SERVING THE OLDER ADULT
A Guide to Library Programs and Information Sources

More Notes from a Different Drummer

A Guide to Juvenile Fiction Portraying the Disabled

by Barbara H. Baskin
and Karen H. Harris

R. R. Bowker Company
New York and London • 1984

With love—
Louis, Julie, and Amy

Published by R. R. Bowker Company
205 East Forty-second Street, New York, NY 10017
Copyright ©1984 by Barbara H. Baskin and Karen H. Harris
All rights reserved
Printed and bound in the United States of America

Library of Congress Cataloging in Publication Data

Baskin, Barbara Holland, 1929–
    More notes from a different drummer.

    Includes indexes.
    1. Children's stories—Bibliography. 2. Handicapped
in literature—Bibliography. 3. Physically handicapped
in literature—Bibliography. 4. Mentally handicapped
in literature—Bibliography. 5. Emotions in literature—
Bibliography. I. Harris, Karen H., 1934–   .
II. Title.
Z1037.9.B36 1984 [PN1009.Z6]   808.06'8   84–12283
ISBN 0-8352-1871-6

Contents

Contents

Illustrations

Preface

The long-awaited thrust for including children with impairments into the educational mainstream has begun its uneven but forward movement. A major challenge to schools has been to ease integration by creating a climate in which pupils with exceptional needs would find acceptance and nonimpaired students would discover the responsibilities and advantages of living and working in a pluralistic society. Some educators have focused their efforts on preparing children with impairments, who had received instruction in separated settings, for movement into the less protected classrooms and corridors of public schools. For many the proposed placement seemed to offer as many dangers and drawbacks as opportunities. These youngsters generally had come from specifically adapted environments where their differences had not set them apart, and they were being placed in settings that potentially held very high social and academic risks. Although it was important to help these children learn skills and techniques to aid their adjustment, it quickly became clear that the responsibility for the success of mainstreaming did not reside with the disabled youth. They were numerically a small group, individually vulnerable, lacking the ability or power to control the situations in which they found themselves. It soon became equally obvious that although adaptions in the materials of instruction and pedagogical methodology would be needed and alterations in instructional routines would be required, the academic problems would be amenable to solution if there were adequate faculty and administrative support.

The major barrier to successful mainstreaming lay in classrooms where attitudes of rejection left disabled youngsters isolated even while surrounded by their peers. Consequently, many in the educa-

tional community redirected their energies toward shaping the perceptions, beliefs, and behaviors of nondisabled students vis-à-vis the newcomers to the school. Addressing this aspect of the problem meant
restructuring the mainstream to make it more hospitable and accepting. Years of segregation had insured that most pupils in regular
schools would be unacquainted with persons sustaining serious sensory, intellectual, physiological, or behavioral deficits and predictably
would be without appropriate strategies for interaction.

Teachers and librarians concerned about removing obstacles to
positive interaction often included literature as a source of information, attitude formation, and modeling in their programs. Books were
recognized as being plentiful, relatively inexpensive, and potentially
powerful agents for promoting understanding. Stories could be
adapted to a limitless variety of situations; used with individuals,
small groups, or entire classes; read in their entirety; or have relevant
segments extracted. Books could be skimmed, studied, reread, discussed, dramatized, interpreted in a variety of media, or used as a
stimulus for private contemplation.

Notes from a Different Drummer, the predecessor of this volume, was
written to assist educators addressing this issue who needed access to
juvenile fiction on impairment. This earlier book identified, described,
and critiqued works written between 1940 and 1975 that contained
disabled characters. *More Notes from a Different Drummer* extends that
first effort—examining juvenile titles written during the early critical
years of the mainstreaming experiment and containing characters with
impairments. The first volume used the word *handicapped* in the subtitle, because of its greater familiarity to nonspecialists and because of
the obvious echoing of the name of the landmark legislation, P.L. 94–
142, The Education of All Handicapped Children Act. Technically, a
"handicap" is a situationally bound restriction. The terms *disability*, or
disabled, used in this work are more precise for our purposes since they
refer to the reality of a condition, rather than the limitations placed on
opportunity or functioning by social convention. A disability, then,
need not be a handicap, and it was our intention to identify all instances of impairment in juvenile fiction whether or not they impacted
on achievement. The word will be used interchangeably with "dysfunction," "impairment," "special needs," and the more general term
"exceptionality" to provide variety of expression.

More Notes from a Different Drummer restricts its field of inquiry to
works of fiction addressed to a juvenile audience. Books written for a
readership ranging from infants to adolescents are included. Picture
books containing a story, therefore, are part of this study, as are junior
novels. Lines demarcating the upper limits of this spectrum from ma-

ture novels have become blurred in recent years, but it is our intention to bypass those works intended for an adult audience.

Fiction, we believe, is the genre that permits the widest latitude for expression of an author's perceptions and values. Separating this category from other literary forms posed several difficulties. Biographies, a category outside our current interest, blend into fictionalized biographies, then into biographical fiction—the latter designation properly within our scope. Nonfiction, an ostensibly excludable genre, is not precisely distinguishable from those heavily didactic works that contain considerable quantities of information embedded in story form. Those quasifictional endeavors with a coherent, viable, if often uninspired plot, have been included in this compendium.

One area of subliterature, publishers' formula romances, such as *Wildlife, First Love,* and *Sweet Dreams,* are interesting as an industry phenomenon but clearly stand outside any examination of legitimate literature. Folklore is specifically and deliberately excluded. Although its role in forming and expressing social perceptions and attitudes is of major interest, a comprehensive report and analysis of myths, legends, and folktales would require a separate, extensive volume. Stories written for academic purposes, such as complements to basal readers, were considered outside our scope.

Books written in foreign countries but distributed domestically have been considered within our purview if their U.S. copyright date is within the span of years encompassed by this work. Such novels influence attitudes here and are part of the American literary scene. Out-of-print books are likewise considered important since many can be found in children's collections where they may continue to affect readers for many years.

One category of fiction has been purposefully excluded. Those novels issuing from sectarian presses that expound a particular religious belief and should most properly be considered supplements to Sunday School curricula are outside our concern. Although many of these publications include disabled characters, the role of impairment, as that of all other conditions and incidents, is to provide evidence of a particular interpretation of divine intent. Discussion of these works would involve theological debate rather than literary criticism and would more properly take place in an arena we did not wish to enter. However, books that feature religious characters or settings as a natural aspect of the story are a part of this collection. Stories we believed were adapted from other formats, such as plays or television dramas, have also been considered beyond the range of this work. Titles such as *No Other Love* were reluctantly omitted.

The extent of disability a character manifested in order to have it considered eligible for inclusion here was another issue. Stories describing mild forms of an identified impairment have been included when either rehabilitation and adaptation or exploration of attitudes was a major concern. A number were not annotated despite the authors' use of disability labels when the appellation and the characters' described behavior were incongruent. Conversely, stories with characters not labeled but who displayed behaviors consistent with standard clinical definitions were added to the collection.

Chapter 1 addresses the mainstreamed society, looking at areas in which disabled persons are moving toward fuller participation, chronicling and interpreting key successes and failures. Chapter 2 examines the mainstreamed school, reporting on changes in the academic environment as it imperfectly attempts to accommodate formerly excluded groups of students, and attempts a macrocosmic analysis of juvenile books on disability, identifying patterns and trends, highlighting differences between this corpus of works and ones appearing before 1976, and noting persisting themes as well as new directions. It is Chapter 3, An Annotated Guide to Juvenile Fiction Portraying the Disabled, 1976–1981, in which each book is individually assessed, that forms the heart of this work. Titles included in Chapter 3 contain child or adult characters who have special needs by reason of intellectual, visual, auditory, speech, orthopedic, neurological, or cosmetic impairments; specific learning disabilities; emotional dysfunction or such special health problems as diabetes, asthma, or cardiac disorders. Books having temporarily injured characters, especially where rehabilitative problems are not a significant part of the story, or those containing characters who suffer terminal ailments are omitted (if we believed the focus was essentially on death) unless there is someone else in the narrative who fits one of the designated categories. Books containing handicapped animals have been rejected unless they also feature human characters with disabling problems. Again, we are aware of gray areas that allow for different interpretations as to whether an individual book should have been incorporated into the collection.

In *More Notes from a Different Drummer*, we have attempted to define and examine a field of inquiry, describe its contents, organize our findings, and provide both a qualitative and quantitative analysis. To accomplish these goals, labels must be used in order to tally, to report on disorders receiving extensive treatment as well as those garnering little attention, to draw conclusions, to identify subsets within a category as well as to analyze the genre in its entirety. Eschewing identifiers would be a disservice to readers seeking literature on a particular disorder since some users have specified they wish particular rather than global references. Headnotes for each title list the category of impairment exhibited by special needs persons within that story and the analysis specifies the particular disorder when it is known. Although there is some professional controversy regarding the propriety of using labels when referring to persons sustaining impairments, we have elected to employ them in this work. We have, however, assiduously avoided suggesting that anyone should be perceived solely or primarily in terms of this or any other descriptor. Too often labels have provided a barrier instead of a shortcut to understanding. In addition, disability labels describe areas of loss or malfunctioning, leading to a focus on deficits rather than strengths. In an effort to circumvent conceptualization of characters in such terms, annotations are deliberately not grouped by impairment and descriptions center on behavior rather than on etiology. Specific disorders, deliberately chosen as a focus by authors, are critical elements in our analysis and it must be assumed, have particular meaning for many of the readers of this study.

Locating books to be included in *More Notes from a Different Drummer* was in some ways easier, and in other ways more difficult, than for our first volume. Standard reference sources and card catalogs of the numerous libraries we used had far more entries under disability headings than were found during the search for titles in our preceding work. Contemporary reviewing journals were our prime source of usable citations, and we discovered that reviewers were more apt to note the presence of disabled characters than they had prior to 1976. Specialized bibliographies, such as those printed in library science, special education, or rehabilitative journals and textbooks, developed and distributed by professional, advocate or government agencies, or assembled for bibliotherapeutic purposes, were helpful in identifying but not necessarily for evaluating the quality of the stories; ironically, some of these bibliographies praised titles with clear-cut biases or inaccuracies. There was considerable overlap among these specialized lists, however, and the same, often outdated titles tended to reappear. In addition, definitions of disability were perceived as sufficiently elastic for some compilers to include shortness, obesity, economic hardship, fractured familial circumstances, and other such conditions outside conventional designations of impaired populations. Complicating the task of identifying appropriate titles was the awareness of some authors that disability was a topic of growing public interest and so increasing numbers of writers included characters with impairments in roles of little significance. As was entirely proper, their presence was often not indicated in even comprehensive reviews, so uncovering these titles posed a major challenge. When the exceptional person served no particular purpose other than to provide a balanced cast of characters, we ignored the title; when the exceptional person was a vehicle for the transmission of attitudes or fulfilled a symbolic function, we added the title to this collection.

With the help of many sympathetic friends, teachers, librarians, and students, and after following both false clues and serendipitous leads, and by looking for the works of authors who had previously demonstrated an interest in this subject, a sizable number of relevant books not on any standardized lists were unearthed. Inevitably some pertinent works were overlooked. Certain out-of-print titles were not available through network or other interlibrary loan facilities. Some foreign titles, enjoying limited distribution in this country, eluded our search; others undoubtedly were simply bypassed and for these omissions we apologize. Our search did turn up books in every major genre and interest area, including contemporary, historic, and science fiction as well as fantasy, romance, sports, animal, and mystery stories. Interestingly, those works purporting to be realistic in tone were not necessarily the most forthright, accurate, or honest about disability. Such sought-after qualities existed independent of genre and were found in every prose category.

It seemed important to us to include a plot summary in each annotation since it is this aspect of a book that is of most interest to the potential reader. Our synopses tend to concentrate disproportionately on those aspects of the narrative that revealed attitudes or conveyed information about impairments because this topic is our prime concern. This caveat should be kept in mind when reading the annotations.

The second component of each discussion is the *Analysis*, which evaluates how impairments are treated as well as the literary qualities of the title in question. Evaluation of the treatment of the disabled characters focuses on the accuracy and honesty of the depiction, plausibility of reported psychological, rehabilitative, and social responses to the impairment, the role of the affected character in the story, and the tone and attitude expressed toward difference. We are especially critical of patronizing, pitying, or romanticized depictions. We comment extensively on mixed messages—those works that seem to be calling for compassion but, on another level, emphasize distinctions, real and hypothesized, between the disabled and the rest of society.

However admirable the intent of an individual work, it ultimately succeeds or fails on the basis of literary merit. Literary criticism is inevitably a highly personal art, so we have tried to include specific examples from the text that are representative of the author's style and that reveal elements we have found laudable or censurable.

Illustrations, particularly in books for the very young, carry a significant portion of the book's impact, directly or subtly communicating attitudes or information about impairment. Oddly enough, it is not unusual for illustrators to omit representations of difference, even in characters with obvious, visible anomalies. Such omissions are themselves expressions of attitudes. Pictorial representations, therefore, have also been assessed in the annotation.

Many individuals helped to bring this book to fruition. The task of locating books was made considerably easier by the efforts of the staff of the Emma S. Clark Memorial Library of Setauket, by Ann Stell of the Smithtown Library, and by Kathleen "Kit" Sheehan of the Suffolk County Cooperative Library System of New York. We want to also acknowledge the help of Amy Spector in tabulating data reported in Chapter 2. In addition, we want to thank Linda Van Den Akker and Becki Davis of the New Orleans Public Library and we are indebted to Gayle Barclay, Evelyn Chandler, and Bob Heriard of the Earl K. Long Library of the University of New Orleans for whose patience and resourcefulness we are grateful. To those authors who have used their skills to illuminate aspects of the lives of disabled persons and demonstrated that the mainstream can and must find room for all, we offer our most profound admiration.

1

Disabled People in Contemporary Society

In 1776 a new nation was conceived, dedicated to the noble proposition that all its citizens were entitled to equal rights and equal protection under the law. Even so, in concert with the conventional, restricted thinking of the period, some groups were exempted from such benefits. Over time, however, more and more of the previously excluded segments of American society successfully obtained access to those educational, occupational, social, and legal perquisites enjoyed by others. But some groups did not. Despite an impressive expansion of full citizenship, some people remain outsiders, ineligible for opportunities, not covered by safeguards, excluded from activities—not for lack of ability, but by custom and convention. Why?

Why, for instance—despite their significant number and obvious problems—have the needs of the disabled been so consistently ignored? Why has the rest of American society felt that it has the right to determine where, and even if, the disabled will live, work, and go to school? Why have public officials exhibited no compunction about verbally abusing the disabled? Why have political journalists felt free to use stereotypes about disability, seemingly indifferent to the pain they cause? Why have states allowed such anachronistic and egregious practices as "freak shows" to take place in state fairs? Why do federal officials institute policies that sabotage the welfare of disabled adults by withdrawing essential financial support and undermine newly won educational rights of impaired children by attempting to eviscerate the body of benefits defined in the legislation passed in 1976?[1] Why is it that two centuries after a mighty declaration establishing a nation that embraces the ideals of political equity—with the implication of social parity—the rights of disabled people are still in doubt?

1

In an effort to find answers to such questions, the persistent issue that society must confront is whether the forces of enlightenment and public commitment will prevail over those who, by design, neglect, or thoughtlessness, prevent the disabled from access to the privileges enjoyed by others.

The Right to Life and Learning

In the first century and a half of this nation's existence, response to those Americans who sustained serious impairments moved from ignoring their considerable needs to establishing accommodations that excluded them from the rest of society. In the absence of a national mandate or guidelines, wide diversity existed in the type, scope, quantity, and quality of assistance that a disabled person could expect. States and local communities exhibited great inconsistency toward those whom they identified as eligible for assistance or protection. Religious and other charitable organizations founded institutions, schools, and centers for the disabled, which were often based on individual agency's interests and were directed toward the pursuit of variously defined, narrow goals. Predictably, need and response did not automatically match. In many instances, families of those unserved were without adequate resources, guidance, or support and had to maintain their members under conditions that mitigated against development of even the most modest skills. Although many individuals with exceptional needs received loving support from their families during that period, instances of neglect, abuse, and exploitation, from which there was no protection, could be found in abundance.

The dominant pattern for disabled people in the early nineteenth century was the residential school where isolation from nonimpaired populations and inadequate stimulation inevitably resulted in lifelong dependence and low levels of functioning. Although the better custodial centers of that period did protect residents from mistreatment and provide instruction in academic and vocational skills, their policies—as well as their location in remote areas—had the effect of separating adults, youngsters, and even infants from family and community. On a personal level, this frequently led to severe emotional distress; on a community level, it legitimized the belief that it was appropriate to segregate disabled persons from the rest of society and that responsibility for responding to their particular requirements was a matter for professionals or other caretakers specially employed for that purpose. In other words, average citizens did not need to concern themselves directly with this segment of the population. Moreover, this practice formalized the prevailing attitude that the costs of specialized services should be borne by those agencies willing to accept the obligation, by the relatives of those involved, or, to a limited extent, by the state.

The establishment of day schools in the last half of the nineteenth century and their growth during the following decades was an ameliorating force in the lives of disabled youngsters. Many of them, although still educated apart from their peers, could now retain closer family ties and be spared the trauma of separation as the price of an education. The commitment by public school systems to the education of once-rejected youngsters meant that more attention could be focused on particularized instruction. Specialized training programs for teachers were established, and the use of special texts, supplementary books, adapted materials of instruction, and conpensatory equipment conspicuously increased. However, educators were still free to exclude entire categories of students: Those who exhibited behavioral disorders, for example, were frequently inadequately served; and those with specific learning disabilities were often completely ignored. In addition, schools could bar a youngster from a public education on the basis of idiosyncratic interpretations of the severity of the child's dysfunction. For example, school boards could decide that they would accept responsibility for educating only mildly or moderately retarded youth, while refusing admission to severely impaired children. Residential settings were often the only option for those who required multiple interventions, extensive adaptions in the physical environment, or were judged incapable of responding to academic instruction or of learning self-maintenance skills. Whether special schools, institutions, or combinations of the two were used, the standard response of academic establishments included segregation in some form. The essential difference was one of degree: Disabled children were either separated from their peers for parts of the day, for the whole day, or sometimes for their whole lives.

Protection under the Law

The *Brown* v. *Topeka Board of Education* decision by the Supreme Court (1954) articulated the doctrine that separate facilities invariably mean unequal ones—a decision that was to play a critical role in the argument for the inclusion of disabled persons (as well as minorities) into the mainstream of American life. Subsequently, advocates for the disabled, calling on congressional and judicial support, pressed for full access to the rights of citizenship in the same settings, under the same conditions, and with equivalent safeguards as those enjoyed by nonimpaired citizens.

The Architectural Barriers Act of 1968 initiated a deluge of federal legislation that dramatically extended opportunities and provided protections for disabled persons: the Urban Mass Transportation Act of 1970; the Federal Aid Highway Act, the Rehabilitation Act, the Department of Transportation Appropriations Act—all 1973; the Developmental Disabilities Assistance and Bill of Rights Act, the Education for All Handicapped Children Act, the National Housing Act Amendments—all 1975; the Rehabilitation Comprehensive Services and Developmental Disabilities Amendments of 1978; and the Social Security Disability Amendments of 1980. These laws marked a watershed period for this once-ignored constituency. And, late though they were, they acknowledged the role of the national government in establishing minimum standards, providing funding, and prohibiting de facto as well as de jure discrimination. Furthermore, these laws served as models for states to use in enacting their own statutes.

Although most states moved quickly in response to the federal model, much of the resulting legislation was only declaratory, for it asserted the rights of disabled persons to entitlements or embodied statements of philosophy or intent, but it did not set up machinery for implementing specific programs or procedures. It soon became evident that it was premature to feel optimistic about the national scene, since statutes that articulate standards, establish procedures, offer direct services, and seem to imply permanent guarantees can be eviscerated by underfunding, administrative sabotage or bungling, or by management personnel committed to limit applicability and enforcement of key provisions. The recent cuts in social security services, for example, so drastically tightened requirements for disabled applicants that some terminally ill persons were denied continuation of services, and others, due to the nature of the disorders that originally made them eligible for service, were unable to take advantage of the appeal process.[2] The posture of the office providing benefits was that those whose names were removed had the responsibility to prove their right to continuation. This action might be considered deliberate, callous, and/or politically motivated. At the very least, it demonstrated a colossal lack of fundamental knowledge that those charged with the administration of such programs ought to possess. Abuses were so flagrant that public outrage necessitated congressional interdiction of this edict. Victory in this instance obviously should not be regarded as final.

Barrier-Free Living

The most visible, readily accomplished adjustment for disabled persons has been the removal of architectural barriers. In some areas of the country, appropriate accommodations are so commonplace as to be the norm. Elsewhere, however, changes have been vigorously protested on such bases as prohibitive cost, damage to aesthetic sensibilities, or possible interference with the functioning of nonimpaired persons. Much of this resistance could be charged to the unwillingness of some people to accept even minor alterations in their world, but, in other cases, it is clear that fear, ignorance, and hostility against people who are obviously "different" have been salient factors. Parenthetically, it is interesting to note that many of the vehemently protested adaptions have made access to facilities easier for those with movement restrictions for other, often temporary reasons—pregnant women, toddlers, the aged—without causing inconvenience to others. Once in place, most modifications of physical facilities soon become the norm and are no longer a matter of contention.

Progress in one area tends to highlight corollary needs. For example, barrier-free buildings that are newly accessible to disabled individuals inevitably suggest the necessity for modified transportation services, but successful responses to this problem have been rare. The use of "kneeling buses" and other adapted mass transportation vehicles has been plagued with difficulties. Design defects and inadequate maintenance practices have caused frustration among disabled would-be passengers, who find themselves delayed or even stranded because of malfunctioning vehicles. These provisions anger some members of the general public, who condemn as wasteful of tax dollars expensive adaptions that are used by few individuals. In addition to the complaint of excessive cost, it is said that such vehicles are a poorly conceived solution that fails to address such a basic problem as how disabled users can get from a departure point to a destination if either is located a considerable distance from a regular stop. Clearly, problems remain when only some of the vehicles are adapted, because disabled riders must then wait while unadapted buses pass them by. Hazards increase when passengers' travel plans require transferring from one line to another, especially during inclement weather. But despite its inherent inadequacies, this approach nonetheless signals a municipality's acceptance of responsibility for the transportation of impaired citizens. At the very least, such acceptance sets precedents that open the way to more useful proposals.

Some communities have experimented with such accommodations

as minibuses, "handicabs," and other direct approaches that, while unintegrated, appear to offer more personalized service, overcome some of the deficiencies of public transportation, and provide assistance to more severely impaired travelers.

Accommodations for disabled automobile owners can be accomplished with little inconvenience to the rest of the community. Reserved parking spaces adjacent to places of employment, public buildings, stores, restaurants, shopping center entrances, recreational facilities, and the like are now commonplace. Although in too many instances there is neither compliance with nor enforcement of such regulations, these beginnings have value.

Certain religious groups have been aggressive in adapting their activities to include disabled parishioners. Yet while many religious organizations have established hospitals, schools, and rehabilitation programs for persons with impairments, mainstreaming practices have not always been assertively endorsed or widely practiced within houses of worship. Constructing barrier-free buildings and providing simultaneous signed sermons for the hearing-impaired have rarely been standard procedures. Now many institutions are moving toward accessible physical plants, and such specific guides as *Accessibility Audit for Churches*[3] provide guidance for new construction and suggestions for modifying existing facilities. The importance of religious authorities welcoming disabled persons into the general community cannot be overstressed. Theological leaders can provide a moral force, high visibility, and establishment endorsement of the ethical validity of such integration.

The Challenge of Deinstitutionalizing

Of all the changes that have taken place within the mainstreaming movement, deinstitutionalizing has generated some of the most dramatic and challenging problems. Institutions for the disabled were conceived for the purposes of medical treatment and containment rather than rehabilitation and return to the community. It is now abundantly clear that the policy has been counterproductive and has resulted in widespread tragedy. Institutionalization was based on the assumption that the removal of certain populations from public life served the needs of both society and the disabled. Residents were perceived as requiring a level of supervision beyond that which a family could provide, and it was believed that they were an excessive burden or even, depending on the disability, a potential danger. Many facilities offered little more than custodial care, which was viewed as a practical response to hopeless circumstances.

Related factors only lowered the quality of attention most residents received. Institutions, as noted earlier, were typically located in sparsely populated areas, remote from public scrutiny and supervision. Too often administrators were not held accountable for the welfare of their inmates. Moreover, the rate and extent of rehabilitation of residents in institutions were rarely the prime concerns of academics, politicians, or the media—except when incidents too scandalous to be ignored focused public attention on long-festering abuses. Burton Blatt's exposé of the horrendous conditions endured by occupants of institutions for retarded individuals created a sensation at the time.[4] Of his return ten years later, Blatt reported:

> while everything has changed, nothing has changed. There's more schooling, there's more programming, there's more sensitivity to problems, but there remains nothing to do there; institutions are not normal environments. There are still many unfortunate things that occur in these places; there are too many accidents, there are too many medical errors, there is too much restraint.[5]

In contrast to the medical institution model, the developmental model proposes that environmental changes can promote higher levels of functioning and that habilitation programs offer valid and appropriate alternatives for those receiving solely custodial care. Thus, a return to the mainstream is not only the proper response to improved performance, it is a process enabling those with hitherto low performance to expand their capabilities for greater achievement. It should have been clear, however, that former residents of institutions could not function in society without a comprehensive support program that focused on the development of skills in organizing daily living tasks, developing and maintaining work habits, finding and keeping jobs, establishing community contacts, seeking recreational, medical, and legal guidance, undertaking management of finances, and the like. Unfortunately, too many programs were characterized by an abdication of responsibility for such broad-scale preparation and supervision, combined with underfunding or the utilization of inadequately trained personnel for these critical roles.

Breaking Out to What?

Typically, administrators who faced budget crises often succumbed to pressures to deinstitutionalize without providing adequate—or, in some instances, any—support services. Advances in psychopharmacology have made it possible for some patients with severe psychiatric problems to function at higher levels than were once thought possible. It seemed fortuitous that drugs to control or diminish psychotic episodes became available at the same time that rapid dein-stitutionalization was being undertaken. However, Thomas summa-rizes the tragic result of the overly optimistic expectation that the chemical breakthrough offered a full-fledged remedy:

> On the assumption that the new drugs made hospitalization un-necessary, two social policies were launched with the enthusiastic agreement of both the professional psychiatric community and the governmental agencies responsible for the care of the terminally ill. Brand-new institutions, ambitiously designated "community mental health centers," were deployed across the country. These centers were to be the source of the new technology for treating schizophrenia, along with all sorts of mental illness: in theory, patients would come to the clinics and be given the needed drugs, and, when necessary, psychotherapy. And at the same time, orders came down that most of the patients living in the state hospital be discharged forthwith to their homes, or lacking homes, to other quarters in the community. . . . The term "breakthrough" was used over and over again, but after a little while it came to be something more like a breakout. The mentally ill were out of the hospital, but in many cases they were simply out on the streets, less agitated but lost, still disabled, but now uncared for. The community mental health centers were not designed to take on the task of custodial care. They could serve as shelters only during the hours of appointment, not at night.[6]

This "breakout" resulted in a national scandal as former residents, unable to adjust to the pressures of surviving in a technological, mo-bile, individualistic society, joined other homeless wanderers visible in every large city, living marginal lives, sometimes even failing to sur-vive. Such drastic changes could produce stress in persons with no serious problems; for people with little or no preparation and few coping abilities, the situation has frequently been catastrophic. As in the transportation issue, administrative response has been character-ized by inadequate planning and funding, and by what appears to be a monumental inability to see the complex ramifications of the problem or to conceptualize it in ways that would address the needs of the individuals involved. Although his assessment is not universally ac-cepted, Thomas argues:

> But it is becoming plain that life in the state hospitals, bad as it was, was better than life in the subways or in the doorways of

downtown streets, late on cold nights with nothing in the shopping bag to keep a body warm, and no protection at all against
molestation by predators or the sudden urge for self-destruction.[7]

The Search for Options

The only alternative to the streets, however, should not be a return to institutions, where the quality of life cannot help but be drastically inferior to what can be offered in such other settings as family or
foster family placement, group homes, or supervised apartment facilities. With these options, it would be unconscionable to return to the
brutal and demeaning conditions that existed in most centers where
impaired persons were warehoused.

Despite overwhelming evidence that those who live outside institutions can make far better adjustments and function at higher levels,
there remains considerable community resistance to this solution.[8] The
general public, for the most part, harbors a great deal of misinformation,
holds strong negative stereotypes, and demonstrates irrational hostility
toward and fear of people known to have been institutionalized. Even
though impairments range from modest to severe, when someone who
returns to the community is labeled behaviorally dysfunctional or mentally retarded, too many people assume that disorderly, even criminal,
behavior will inevitably ensue. Protests are common from fearful home-
owners and neighborhood associations that project declines in property
values or question the safety of their families in emotion-filled meetings.
Ironically, acts of violence are far more apt to be initiated by neighbors
than by those scheduled to move into hostels or group homes. Efforts to
transfer former residents of the Suffolk Developmental Center on Long
Island, New York, into the community resulted in several cases of arson
and other acts of vandalism that necessitated posting security guards to
protect the proposed sites.[9]

Responses to Mainstreaming

There is no way to supervise every aspect of statutes, to monitor
every implementation, to scrutinize every situation where the intent,
as well as the letter, of the law should apply. Ultimately, the success of
the mainstreaming movement depends on the long-term cooperation
of the government and the industrial, commercial, and private sectors.
Responses to this challenge have ranged from hostility and implacable
resistance to imaginative, enthusiastic, intelligent support.

In those cases where advocates have been able to secure the active support of respected community organizations, acceptance of impaired populations has been made easier. In one instance, an advocacy group worked diligently to welcome the male residents of a hostel into the community, and in cooperation with the staff, a Christmas party was planned.[10] The president of the local Rotary Club was invited to attend and make a contribution to the party. He agreed to do so, despite the fact that some of his colleagues had been signatories to a lawsuit to eject the hostel from the community. This simple event precipitated his involvement and his organization's support, which thereafter funded the recreational activities of the hostel's residents. Such endorsement from the business community is a gratifying example of concern and neighborliness, a counterbalance to the lawsuit, which subsequently was denied by the court.

Perhaps the most outrageous example of noncompliance involved an employee of a government agency charged with overseeing a critical aspect of the mainstreaming movement. *Newsday* reported the case of a multiply disabled worker at the Architectural and Transportation Compliance Board, who, following a series of disagreements with his supervisor, was punitively transferred to a work area where he was "forced to scurry into a fast-closing elevator, then press a floor button with his nose, then scurry out of the elevator and walk almost a city block" to his desk.[11] That a federal agency whose mandate includes monitoring work areas to guarantee that they are barrier-free should permit an employee to be stationed at a totally inaccessible work site demonstrates how even the best laws can be undone by the negative attitudes of those who implement them.

Elevators adapted for passengers with visual impairments are a well-intentioned accommodation, but too often they are so poorly designed as to be useless. In one New Orleans hospital, for example, only one of the three "adapted" passenger elevators has braille numbers that identify signal buttons. There is no audible clue to indicate the floor to the riders. To learn location information, a blind rider must reach through the elevator's open doors, find the plate on the outside frame, tactilely read it, and quickly retract his or her arm before the doors close! Again, an attempt to address a problem was made without careful conceptualization.

Many other modifications are, fortunately, more practical and less challenging. Election boards now notify voters with impairments of arrangements that can be made to enable them to exercise this most basic right. Many commercial establishments, realizing the potential of an untapped market, motivated by a sense of civic responsibility, or both, have expanded product lines, adapted purchasing procedures, modified physical plants, or offered entirely new services specifically designed for disabled customers. In New York, impaired drivers may request full service at gas stations while being charged the lower self-service price. Some newspapers now use the disability logo to indicate listings, such as barrier-free restaurants, that offer facilities for persons with impairments. The publisher Houghton Mifflin of Boston has underwritten a project by the National Braille Press to produce children's braille book club selections, which can be purchased at the same prices as their print equivalents.

The responses of museums, libraries, and other cultural centers to the needs of patrons with impairments range from merely providing physical access to instituting a whole array of services. Some libraries have installed teletype phones to facilitate communication for hearing-impaired patrons; others have made Kurzweil machines available to blind users for instantaneous translation of print to synthesized speech; and still others have purchased special collections, prepared bibliographies, initiated outreach services, and the like.[12]

Advocacy Groups

Three major changes in the nature of advocacy groups for the disabled have occurred in recent years: The number of such organizations has grown significantly since the 1970s; their membership, composition, and roles have altered; and the causes to which they dedicate their resources, the means they choose to pursue goals, and their political strategies are being transformed. Although there are more disabled persons now living in America than at any time in history,[13] their total number remains small, and their needs are diverse, highly specialized, and sometimes completely peculiar to the individual. Certain organizations, speaking for a homogenous subset of similarly disabled persons, are more knowledgeable about specific needs and can direct their energies toward clearly defined objectives. Others work through umbrella groups, exercising more political clout because they claim a larger constituency.

Persons with impairments are moving from client status to peer or management positions in many of these advocacy organizations. These members are no longer merely passive recipients, but more and more frequently act as policy makers, managers, consultants, and co-planners, bringing their special expertise to the decision-making process.

Until recent years, the most visible advocacy group activities involved pleas for charitable contributions to be used primarily for medical research or rehabilitation programs. Among some of the older, more traditional direct-service groups, this type of public plea, which relies on arousing feelings of pity, guilt, or compassion, is still widely practiced. But many of the newer groups are more assertive, even confrontational. They insist on recognition of their basic civil rights and access to the opportunities and privileges enjoyed by nonimpaired citizens.[14] Instead of holding telethons, they engage in political lobbying, develop public awareness programs, and demand guarantees of equal access to employment, education, recreation, transportation, housing, and the like. And if they are met with implacable resistance, they do not hesitate to file lawsuits. The Human Policy Press poster slogan "You gave us your dimes. Now we demand our rights" captures both the substance and the style of the new movement.

A critical example of the direction that advocacy groups have chosen is the movement toward independent living. As the focus shifts from impairment to an emphasis on intact abilities, the image of passive and dependent disabled people often held by the general public is being transformed into one of assertive competence. The Special Olympics can attract spectators who come, not to pity, but to celebrate achievement. The Very Special Arts Festival, offering an arena for nourishing the talents of exceptional children, underscores participation, effort, and recognition of creative accomplishments. While it is important that *Science* magazine has made its issues available on audio format for the visually impaired, it is at least equally significant that *Bride's* magazine contained an article featuring weddings for the disabled.[15]

Publications such as *The Mainstream, The Bridge,* and *The Disabled Writer's Quarterly* offer outlets for the literary and journalistic talents of exceptional people. The *Detroit Free Press* runs a weekly column on disability topics. And sports organizations for athletes with impairments, travel clubs, and such hobby groups as clubs for disabled computer hackers, are organized primarily on the basis of common interest rather than shared disorder. Another key development is the participation of disabled individuals in activities with ablebodied people. Such organizations as the Boy Scouts of America now include integrated as well as special troops. Even such chaotic celebrations as Mardi Gras now contain students in wheelchairs moving along with other high school band members in parades. The best news about these events is that they are no longer newsworthy.

Pressures For and Against

The dramatic advances that have occurred since the early 1970s have been made possible, in part, because of changes in the awareness and perceptions of the nondisabled population. Although there are now many more opportunities for people with impairments to be integrated into the mainstream, there are still many areas of resistance: Advances are both hard won and sometimes only temporary. The tremendous push for civil rights for the disabled has coincided with difficult economic times for the country as a whole. In addition to traditional resistance, taxpayers have expressed hostility to any unprecedented expenditures to support the needs of this newly vocal group, even though it can be clearly demonstrated, in many instances, that net costs would ultimately decrease. Administrators have often been resistant to changes, inept in managing them, dedicated to the most peripheral ones, or bogged down by bureaucratic considerations. Even though there is tremendous pressure to deinstitutionalize in New York State, for example, facilities have been built by the issuance of bonds, and the indebtedness remains even if the buildings are abandoned. Also, not surprisingly, the approximately 55,000 union members employed in such settings have a vested interest in their continuance.[16] While official policy may favor alternative arrangements, other influences—equally strong, if not always obvious—are likely to interfere with their implementation.

For every advance toward mainstreaming, there have been powerful forces in opposition. If the law could not be swept off the books or its accomplishments reduced by administrative resistance, then debilitating amendments, underfunding of the agencies charged with monitoring enforcement, or revisionist judicial interpretations were still real possibilities. Considerable controversy has raged over the government's role in extending accessibility in the environment. Conservative voices argued for "voluntary compliance" with minimum guidelines. Enforcement efforts have been branded as government interference, although widespread apathy or unwillingness to make the workplace barrier-free necessitated the law originally. Court decisions favoring settings that do not comply with Section 504 of the Rehabilitation Act on the grounds that conforming would cause "undue administrative or financial burdens," known as the "reasonable accommodation" rule, are condemned by DeJong and Lifchez, who warn:

> Implicit in the reasonable-accommodation rule is a cost-benefit consideration: Are overall costs reasonable in the light of anticipated benefits? One should be cautious, however, about shaping disability policy solely on the basis of cost-benefit analysis. In the extreme there are instances where taking cost-benefit criteria to their logical conclusion would entail withholding essential life-support systems. . . .
>
> The increasing preoccupation with cost-benefit analysis also betrays the degree to which society hesitates to make financial out-

lays on behalf of disabled people. The current outlook on disability issues would change materially if it were clearly understood. . . . that much of the cost is the product of society's success over the years in saving and prolonging the lives of millions of Americans, often at the cost of a long-term residual disability. This success has its price, and it is a price that must be paid.[17]

This humanitarian position is not supported by the Office of Management and Budget, which proposed that administrators base their responses to the needs of disabled clients on "the value of the accommodation to society, taking full account of the potential contributions to society of handicapped persons."[18] The implications of such a policy are appalling if government agencies are allowed to prophesy the extent of a child's potential contribution to society and apportion assistance on the basis of bureaucratic guesswork.

Such reasoning appears to be part of a backlash response to the modest extension of rights so arduously achieved by disabled people. The Heritage Foundation, a conservative think tank, has offered a rationale for withholding support for the disabled, blaming youngsters with special needs for what they perceive as a failure of American education. The Foundation claimed that academically rigorous curricula were modified to respond to the needs of "special interest groups," including the "handicapped," who allegedly were favored "at the expense of those who have the highest potential to contribute positively to society."[19]

Emotional Barriers

The tearing down of emotional barriers remains a very serious impediment to the success of the mainstreaming movement. Perceptions that link impaired persons with sickness, laziness, villainy, dependence, lack of social utility, and threats to health still abound. They are manifest in everyday idiomatic language, superstitious beliefs, media portrayals, social conventions, and in the books that children read. Efforts of advocates to improve the image of the disabled and to replace ignorance with information have, however, led to some improvements. American attitudes toward impairment are currently in a state of flux: Knowledge, compassion, and understanding coexist with misinformation, indifference, and enmity. Beliefs and behaviors associated with past centuries can still be found with little effort. Exhibitions of exceptional people for public amusement would seem to be an outdated event, embarrassing to a modern society, yet such spectacles remain a feature of some state fairs. The Long Island *Newsday* headline

"Farmers, Freaks, Fun: The 142nd State Fair," heralded the 1983 event. The newspaper reported: "At the entrance to The Great Sutton's Circus Sideshow, there's an old thin man, about 3 feet tall. Then, there's Otis the Frog Boy, a middle-aged man with deformed nonfunctioning legs and hands. An animal freak show has a dog with 5 legs."[20] The state advocate's office ignored complaints about such exploitive and dehumanizing treatment.

Popular language is replete with evidence of contempt, or at least disregard, for people with impairments. Arizona Assistant Attorney General Rogers was quoted as bragging that "We're destroying Arizona's reputation as the bastion of the lame, lazy and incompetent."[21] Linking impaired mobility with a lack of character and/or competence is not only unconscionable, it is grossly inaccurate, a marvel of irrelevance. Even so prestigious a magazine as Smithsonian is guilty of the casual, insensitive slur. In an article on the creation of fake foods, it notes the utility of these products in ordering meals for those who cannot translate a menu printed in a foreign language. It describes the items as "a surprising phenomenon that brings relief to the famished foreigner who suddenly realizes that ordering a meal is possible even for the linguistically lame."[22]

Thomas and Wolfensberger note that even those who speak for disabled persons often employ language suffused with negative connotations. In "The Importance of Social Imagery in Interpreting Societally Devalued People to the Public," they condemn the title of a program about severely retarded persons, "The Others," which they claim suggests vast differences rather than the similarities between the viewers and the people who were the subject of the program.[23] Obviously, such imagery is more apt to inhibit than to foster positive identification by members of the public regarding intellectually impaired people. Thomas and Wolfensberger propose that a more suitable title might have been "Just Like Us," emphasizing similarities and proposing positive images.

The joining of disabilities and inadequacies is so common that the offense generally fails to excite public outrage. Newsday printed a cartoon intended to demonstrate the duplicitous behavior of Philippines president Ferdinand Marcos in the official investigation of the murder of Aquino, his political rival. Five men with dark glasses and Seeing Eye dogs, one of whom holds out a cup with pencils in it, are pointed to by a Marcos henchman, who says: "They're just the panel to investigate Aquino's death, boss. Not one of them has a tie to government."[24] Although entirely irrelevant to the political intent, the artist nevertheless perpetuates stereotypes about blind people as beggars who are docile, manipulatable, and ignorant of the world. In another example, a major greeting card publisher saw nothing offensive in a card that said: "It's your birthday! Would you like me to fix you up with a blind date? Or maybe you'd rather have a deaf prune? How about a disfigured avocado? A maimed eggplant?"[25]

Media Influence

Media representations of disability reflect attitudes manifest in society. As a major component of popular culture, they are mirror and model, revealing and shaping perceptions while offering standards for emulation. Of all the media, television has the most profound influence on American lives. Elliott and Byrd estimate that "99.5 percent of all Americans have a television set. The average child spends 50 percent more time viewing television than going to school. Television is easier to absorb than most media due to its convenience and auditory and visual impact."[26] In addition, for most people, TV exposure begins in infancy and remains a pervasive presence all through the formative years. Its impact on attitudes has been the subject of innumerable studies, and considerable concern has been generated over the images it promulgates of women and minorities and its unrestrained depiction of violence. Not surprisingly, advocates for the disabled have also shown continuing interest in the depiction of impairment on television. There are three major areas of study: the quantity of presentation—how much air time is devoted to situations involving people who are disabled, the types of depictions to which viewers are exposed, and the quality of those presentations.

Although it is difficult to obtain definitive figures on the frequency with which disabled persons appear on TV, it is clear that impairment is a topic of interest to program writers. There is a drastic imbalance, however, in the attention that various disorders receive. Elliott and Byrd report that "the majority of portrayals of disability deal with mental illness and primarily occur on dramas and other programs utilizing suspense."[27] Wahl and Roth concluded that "almost one-third of all prime time shows involved material of some kind related to mental illness. There are probably few other topics, apart from crime and love, which get such frequent mention on television."[28] Cassata, Skill, and Boadu found that emotional disorders were "the number one specific health-related problem in the soap opera world."[29]

Television Treatment of Disability

The Regional Rehabilitation Research Institute on Attitudinal, Legal and Leisure Barriers has identified four basic categories for grouping television treatment of impairment: real disability, fictional disability, real disabled person, and fictional disabled person.[30] The first two, which its researchers found dominate the medium, describe situations in which the dysfunction, not the person sustaining it, is the focus of interest. "Real disability" includes programs featuring the accomplishments of actual persons, such as those found on "That's Incredible," "Real People," or "PM Magazine." On some occasions, the subjects of their vignettes have accomplished some feat of true significance; more often, the achievement would be unremarkable if an able-bodied person were involved. Interest in such behavior is often the result of public ignorance about the capabilities of people with impairments, so that what may be only unusual or not commonly known seems to be extraordinary. The "fictional disability" category is found primarily in dramatic shows in which events centering on impairment generally precipitate a plot crisis. The "crazed killer" is a popular manifestation often seen on police action shows. The essential ingredient in these productions is violent or threatening behavior by an unstable, unpredictable character.

Both the real disability and fictional disability categories offer possibilities for exploitation. Too frequently, in addition to presenting misinformation or creating misleading impressions, they depersonalize the real or fictional characters involved. Such persons are seen as though their impairments were the only salient factor in their lives.

The "real disabled person" designation includes such musicians as Itzhak Perlman and Stevie Wonder, actor Gary Coleman, or comedienne Geri Jewell, whose impairments are peripheral to their status as entertainers. Programs on which they appear offer an arena for their considerable talents, and they would be equally welcome if they were without their disabilities. Although Jewell alludes to her cerebral palsy in some of her routines, it is merely part of the material in her repertoire and not the focus of her act. Perlman briefly discussed his impairment on "60 Minutes," but it was a minor component of the wide-ranging interview, of considerably less interest than Perlman's wit and charm. His use of braces and crutches are treated naturally in his concert performances. They are merely devices he needs to walk to center stage, where his musical gifts soon overwhelm any other consideration.

"Fictional disabled people" are those who exist as real characters who happen to have a disability. Roles may be minor, as that of the anonymous wheelchair user seen in some newsroom scenes on "Lou Grant." The Institute considers such portraits to be of particular importance "because these are precisely the types of people we are more likely to encounter on a day-to-day basis."[31]

The quality of any presentation can be gauged by its honesty, accuracy, comprehensiveness, and freedom from stereotypes. The children's television shows "Mr. Roger's Neighborhood" and "Sesame Street" consistently present excellent programs about people with special needs. In some early precedent-setting shows, Mr. Rogers introduced disabled people in positive roles, allowed them to reveal admirable character and personality attributes and express concerns and aspirations with which his audience could identify. With great sensitivity, he had them demonstrate adaptations that had been made to facilitate function and even explored some anxieties that children commonly hold about impairment.

"Sesame Street" routinely schedules disabled people as featured actors or as child participants in on-stage activities. Linda Bove, of the Little Theatre of the Deaf, is a regular visitor who, among other functions, instructs viewers in signing. It is the stated intention of Children's Television Workshop, the parent agency of this popular program, to "foster the positive self-image of disabled children and render certain Sesame Street curriculum goals more accessible to mentally retarded children."[32] In addition, the program's statement of goals mandates that it will provide "awareness and interaction strategies for the non-disabled child."[33] Special attention is paid to children who are retarded or who have sensory deficits. Attempts are being made to structure "the more active and visible inclusion of physically disabled children . . . [utilize] more disabled adult role models . . . [and investigate developing] animation which would include disabled children and adults."[34]

There are obvious quality differences between public and commercial television's treatment of impairment. Commercial representations are more apt to be unrealistic, either exaggerating the efforts of dysfunctional conditions or ignoring corollary circumstances. The paraplegia of the title character in "Ironsides" or Mary's blindness in "Little House on the Prairie" are little more than stage props.

Summarizing the literature on how commercial television portrays persons with impairments, Byrd and Elliott conclude that such characters are often "regarded as objects of pity," are passive, dependent, of low social status, apt to be victims, and generally viewed only in terms of their disability, instead of as fully formed individuals.[35] Although there have been some efforts to treat the problems of disabled people seriously—such as the exploration of educating a deaf child according to oralist practices rather than total communication procedures on a "Lou Grant" episode—the approach is too often simplistic, emotion-laden, and naive.

Of all the categories of disorders, emotional dysfunction seems to fare the worst on television. Negative stereotypes, misinformation, and distortion of characters so identified are standard practice in this popular medium. Wahl and Roth found that such characters typically are:

> identified . . . only by their mental illness. Almost three-fourths . . . had no family connections. Almost half of them had no specified occupation. . . . Moreover, the image of psychiatric patients as frightening and dangerous came across clearly in television portrayals. Mentally ill persons were shown to be active, confused, aggressive, dangerous and unpredictable. They tended also to be males, which gives them extra strength and, therefore, menace. Such an image is inaccurate: mentally ill persons, in general, are much more likely to be withdrawn and frightened than violent and aggressive; they are more likely to avoid than to attack others; they are as often female as male.[36]

Some Breakthroughs

There have been some important, honest, and insightful plays and films in recent years concerning people with exceptional needs. *Children of a Lesser God, Whose Life Is It Anyway?*, and *Born on the 5th of July* dealt with some of the profound, sometimes devastating crises faced by people with impairments. *The Elephant Man* (play and film), *Ordinary People,* and *Coming Home* were sensitizing dramas—more subtle and effective than any merely didactic work could be. The linkage between the exceptional characters and the audience was obvious, fostering identification rather than magnifying difference. *Best Boy*, an Academy Award–winning film about an intellectually impaired middle-aged man, offered an affectionate, sympathetic, honest portrait that showed familial adaptations and pressures and the opportunities available in a group home environment.

Parenthetically, it should be noted that while some newspapers now use the symbol of access to indicate that theaters are accessible to the physically disabled, few make accommodations for those with auditory impairments, and would-be viewers occasionally still report attitudinal barriers.[37]

It is precisely this roadblock that the National Advisory Committee on the Handicapped sees as the key problem preventing integration of disabled people into the mainstream of public life. In their 1976 annual report, the Committee stated: "The crucial central issue goes far beyond optimum pedagogical practice or research or funding or the mechanics of moving youngsters into different settings. The overriding issue in this and all other provisions affecting the handicapped is the matter of attitudes."[38]

Education the Key

Although a mainstreamed society is the overriding goal of advocates, schools will prove to be the pivotal site in which people, no matter what disabling conditions they sustain, learn to relate comfortably as peers of those without impairments. If adults with special needs are to function effectively in society, they must develop appropriate academic, prevocational, and social skills during their formative years. If their childhood is spent in a segregated setting, by the time they reach maturity, patterns of differential adaptions are already set. Likewise, these conditions could cause able-bodied children to view separate facilities as proper, and they would be predictably resistant to restructuring their expectations or behavior toward people with impairments when they reach adulthood. It is clearly best to shape perceptions in the growing years rather than try to alter ones that have already crystallized.

Mainstream schools are essential for even more basic reasons. Without a precisely detailed mandate, too many exceptional children in the past were either poorly served or denied services altogether. The National Advisory Committee on the Handicapped reported that prior to passage of P.L. 94-142, 45 percent of handicapped children in the country up through the teen years did "not receive an education comparable in quality or comprehensiveness"[39] to their nonimpaired peers. One in every eight of these youngsters had no educational provisions made for him or her whatsoever. If, as is generally believed, a good education is the sine qua non for success in America, then the most basic opportunities were closed to those with exceptional needs. Some critics have asserted that gaps continue to exist even with the implementation of P.L. 94-142.[40]

Professionals in special education have long argued for extended schooling, claiming that the traditional span of years is inadequate for some of these youngsters. If, for example, profoundly deaf children are not taught communication skills long before kindergarten, it is almost impossible to undo the damage that delay has wrought. However, many school boards are unwilling to accept responsibility for instruction outside the standard range of years.[41]

Despite the compelling arguments favoring mainstreaming, serious and not entirely unreasonable reservations were voiced. School boards worried that their newly formulated responsibilities would strain budgetary and other resources beyond what could be accommodated. Building administrators viewed the entire process as disruptive and were cynical about the actual support they would receive for their efforts. Regular classroom teachers, librarians, and other faculty feared that their jobs would expand to include responsibilities for which they were unprepared and were concerned that their new charges would be disruptive. They also suspected that administrators would use the law to justify such cost-cutting measures as increasing teacher–pupil ratios. They expressed cynicism about in-service institutes held on what should have been their free time, predicting that such brief, jerry-built, intermittent meetings could not compensate for the lack of formal, structured, sequenced instruction that special education teachers typically received in certified programs. Others were skeptical that the sums spent for specialized equipment and materials would be able to compensate in significant ways for individualized attention from highly trained teachers.

Special education personnel were afraid that their pupils would be turned over to others who were inadequately prepared and frequently unsympathetic or even overtly hostile. Parents of students in regular classes worried that the newcomers would usurp the teachers' attention, might be discipline problems, and would lower academic standards—fears they often passed on to their children. Parents of exceptional youngsters worried that their hard-won gains would be nullified as their children returned to an environment that had proven unresponsive and, in some instances, even unsafe in the past. Youth with special needs were fearful of the reception they might face in regular classes, sometimes unconvinced that the trade-off would be to their advantage.

Unfortunately, in too many situations, these fears were realized. Moreover, the timing of the movement was not propitious. Two circumstances, unrelated to mainstreaming, vastly complicated the changes required for implementation. A severe economic recession squeezed school districts, hard-pressed for fiscal relief, into adopting desperate measures. The mayor of New York City, for example, identifying special education as a high-cost program, announced the city's intention to drastically reduce services.[42] There were concerted moves to reclassify large numbers of exceptional children so that fewer were eligible for adapted education. It appeared that these youngsters' learning problems would no longer receive special attention, since the students had been defined out of existence as a group needing supportive services.

The other issue that caused tremendous difficulties was the nation's growing awareness and increased anxiety about the unacceptable quality of education in general. There was a sudden vociferous demand for instantaneous resolution of problems that had been festering for decades, such as declining college board scores, widespread illiteracy, and inadequately trained high school graduates. Special children were often the victims of political moves to remedy these problems in a highly visible, if not always well thought out, manner. Competency testing and the implementation of a single standard to measure eligibility for promotion, graduation, or entry into particular programs inevitably imposed impossible demands on youngsters who needed adaptations if they were to succeed. In New York State, developmentally disabled high school youngsters were refused diplomas upon completing their specialized studies.

Advocates will need to be alert to combat attempts to dilute gains earned after many years of arduous struggle. It is too soon for a comprehensive assessment, but it should be noted that a social change of this magnitude inevitably causes dislocations and places disproportionate burdens on some of those involved. While various forces have united to undermine the experience for some children, for others, mainstreaming has been liberating, preparing them like nothing else has before for an integrated adult life, demonstrating to the nondisabled that the disabled must be considered peers.

There is no turning back—nor should there be. Despite the difficulties and abuses, mainstreaming offers the best hope that the majority of disabled youth have of participating in the bounty of American society. Those schools and systems that have committed adequate resources to the task have watched graduates enter fields and enjoy relationships once believed impossible. The availability of a plethora of instructional materials, the acquisition and refinement of equipment that compensates for deficits, improvements in diagnostic tools and techniques, and better, more individualized, prescriptive instructional methods are beginning to be used to circumvent learning difficulties, maximize intact abilities, and offer opportunities.

The role of school personnel involves vigilant, aggressive protection of the rights of special-needs youngsters and firm resistance to those practices that can subvert the intent of P.L. 94-142. In addition, energies must be devoted to the creation of an atmosphere of acceptance, an acknowledgment that schools must be for *all* children. When citizens hold the philosophy that difference does not exclude individuals from public rights and benefits, the beneficial effects of mainstreaming will be apparent.

In a 1980 report, the director of a preschool that served blind children gave this account of a field trip: "The teacher took the children down the block to visit Santa Claus. While they were waiting in line, they overheard a person . . . say, 'They shouldn't bring those blind children here—it spoils Christmas for everyone.' "[43]

Until advocates can eliminate such attitudes, there is still an enormous task ahead for all of us.

Notes

1. Wolf Wolfensberger, "How to Exclude Mentally Retarded Children from School," *Mental Retardation* 13 (1975), 30–31.
2. Bob Wyrick and Patrick Owens, "The Disability Nightmare: The History of a Crackdown," *Newsday*, March 21, 1983, pp. 4, 22–25.
3. United Methodist Church, *Accessibility Audit for Churches* (Cincinnati: General Board of Global Ministries, 1983).
4. Burton Blatt and Fred Kaplan, *Christmas in Purgatory: A Photographic Essay on Mental Retardation* (Boston: Allyn and Bacon, 1966).
5. Thomas M. Stephens, "An Interview with Dr. Burton Blatt," *Directive Teacher* 2 (Spring, 1980), 7.
6. Lewis Thomas, *Late Night Thoughts on Listening to Mahler's Ninth Symphony* (New York: Viking, 1983), p. 98.
7. Ibid., p. 99.
8. Frank J. Menolascino and John J. McGee, "The New Institutions: Last Ditch Arguments," *Mental Retardation* 19 (1981), 215–220.
9. Robert Fresco, "Hostility Worries Judge in Retarded Case," *Newsday*, March 10, 1982, p. 17.
10. Ronne Cosel, "Minutes," Awareness Coalition of the Exceptional, December 14, 1981, and January 7, 1982.
11. Patrick Owens, "A Poignant Federal Controversy," *Newsday*, December 23, 1982, p. 4.
12. Barbara Baskin and Karen Harris, *The Mainstreamed Library* (Chicago: American Library Association, 1982), pp. xi–xvii.
13. Gerben DeJong and Raymond Lifchez, "Physical Disability and Public Policy," *Scientific American* 248 (June 1983), 43.
14. Tom Bannon, "Deaf Are Shortchanged on Medical Care," *Long Island Deaf News* 4 (Spring 1984), unp.
15. Anon., "Weddings and the Disabled," *Bride's* 48 (June–July 1981), 68.
16. Stephens, "An Interview."
17. DeJong and Lifchez, "Physical Disability," p. 49.
18. "Restrictions Are Under Way in Aid for Handicapped," *Times Picayune/The States Item*, April 7, 1982, p. 5.
19. George Will, "A Morally Repulsive Argument on Help for the Handicapped," *Newsday*, June 23, 1983, p. 83.
20. Mary Brady, "Farmers, Freaks, Fun: The 142nd State Fair," *Newsday*, September 5, 1983, p. 13.
21. "Disciplinary Duo Disdainfully Dumps Inept Employee," *Times Picayune/The States Item*, October 20, 1981, Sec. 1, p. 3.
22. Carol Simons, "Costly Cuisine, But It Has a Long Life," *Smithsonian* 14 (March 1984), 130.
23. Susan Thomas and Wolf Wolfensberger, "The Importance of Social Imagery in Interpreting Societally Devalued People to the Public," *Rehabilitation Literature* 43 (November–December 1982), 357.
24. M. G. Lord, untitled editorial cartoon, *Newsday*, October 13, 1983, p. 78. For another example, note the *Orlando Sentinel's* cartoon by Dana Summer, which prominently displays President Reagan's hearing aid as he says to his distressed adviser: "Troops to the Mideast? I thought you guys advised me to send some soup to Ed Meese," September 13, 1983.
25. "It's Your Birthday," American Greetings Corp., Cleveland, Ohio, 1974.

26. Timothy R. Elliott and E. Keith Byrd, "Media and Disability," *Rehabilitation Literature* 43 (November–December 1982), 350.
27. Ibid.
28. Otto F. Wahl and Rachel Roth, "Television Images of Mental Illness: Results of a Metropolitan Washington Media Watch," *Journal of Broadcasting* 26 (Spring 1982), 604.
29. Mary B. Cassata, Thomas D. Skill, and Samuel O. Boadu, "In Sickness and in Health," *Journal of Communication* 29 (Autumn 1979), 76.
30. "Disabled Portrayals on TV Evaluated," *The New York State Advocate*, August 1981, p. 7.
31. Ibid.
32. Barbara Kolucki, "Sesame Street Challenges Secrets That Shouldn't Be," *The Directive Teacher* 2 (Summer/Fall 1980), 5.
33. Ibid., p. 6.
34. Ibid., p. 29.
35. Elliott and Byrd, "Media and Disability."
36. Wahl and Roth, "Television Images," pp. 604–605.
37. Dawn Moody, "Letter to the Editor," *Disabled USA* 2 (1983), 31. This writer reports trying to enter a movie house but was told she would be "a fire hazard. I assured them that I hadn't burst into flames for at least a year, but to no avail."
38. National Advisory Committee on the Handicapped, *Annual Report* (Washington, D.C.: United States Office of Education, 1976), p. 3.
39. Ibid.
40. Jonathan Smith and James W. Fawney, "Compliance Monitoring: A Dead or Critical Issue," *Exceptional Children* 56 (October 1983), 119–127; K. Charlie Lakin et al., "A Response to the GAO Report 'Disparities Still Exist in Who Gets Special Education,' " *Exceptional Children* 50 (September 1983), 30–34.
41. Anon., "Gallaudet Comments on PL 94-142 Regulations," *Gallaudet Alumni Newsletter* 17 (March 1983), unp.
42. Project R.E.E.D. (Resources on Educational Equity for the Disabled), *Creating a New Mainstream* (New York: Non-Sexist Child Development Project, Women's Action Alliance, Inc., 1982), p. 3.
43. Anon., "The Special Education Spirit," *New York Times*, January 26, 1984, p. A22.

2

The Disabled
in Literature

Although few professional educators are philosophically opposed to mainstreaming, not many agree on what administrative structures, teaching methods, and educational materials would prove the most efficient and effective in achieving this goal. Traditional research tries to isolate a single variable and test its impact in a controlled situation. Although useful in the laboratory, this method has obvious limitations when transferred to a complex, dynamic setting such as a school where personal, social, and academic objectives are varied and often conflicting. In addition to the primary goal of guiding intellectual development, schools have been given responsibility for helping youngsters to mature emotionally, learn social skills, build character, and function as responsible members of their families, community, state, and nation. Concerned faculty, then, need to regard schools and classrooms as ecological systems, aware that any alteration, no matter how benign, may ultimately affect other aspects of the environment.

The specific intent of mainstreaming is to integrate children who are exceptional into academic life. However, care must be taken to employ tactics that enhance the entire school experience. An often overlooked approach, capable of supporting all of the above-named goals, involves the use of literature featuring disabled characters.

Intervention Strategies

Since mainstreaming is just one of many imperatives that schools must incorporate into their agendas, every proposal should be examined to determine how the maximum effect can be achieved with a minimum of disruption to in-place programs. The following listing identifies the basic standards for assessing an intervention strategy and describes how these are met through the use of juvenile literature.

Criteria for Selection of Intervention Strategy	Capability of Literature to Meet Criteria
1. *Cost.* The intervention should be inexpensive. Poorer school districts have needs as equally urgent as those of more affluent ones, but have fewer resources for accomplishing identified tasks.	1. Many appropriate titles are already part of the school library's holdings or can readily be included in acquisition plans. Financially pressed districts can borrow titles from local libraries or through networks.
2. *Training time.* Intervention managers should be able to employ the selected strategy without a great deal of time spent on training.	2. Certified teachers will have already been trained to use literature in the classroom. In addition, school librarians have particular expertise in this area.
3. *Match.* The program must be sufficiently large and varied to allow for continued interaction based on felicitous combinations of materials and methods with user needs and interests.	3. The ever-increasing body of juvenile books that contain disabled characters includes works on every ability level with a sufficiently wide spectrum of topics to appeal to the most varied interests.
4. *Flexibility.* The intervention should be adaptable for use in a variety of settings, alone or as a supplement to other interventions.	4. Books are limitlessly flexible, allowing application in many educational and prosocial situations. They can be employed either as the primary instructional tool or in conjunction with other materials.
5. *Ease of use.* Considering heavy demands on teacher time, it is unlikely that any intervention will be consistently employed if excessive staff effort is required.	5. Books can be read by individual children without teacher involvement or can readily be incorporated into standard classroom procedures.
6. *Compatibility with scheduling limits.* Because of the rigidity of many school schedules, interventions that mean extensive time adjustments are unlikely to be welcomed or frequently used.	6. Teachers can fit stories or story fragments into any time frame or assign out-of-school readings. Discussions can easily be extended or limited.
7. *Curriculum interface.* The intervention should be part of or complementary to the curriculum. Decisions to award attention to the	7. Educators perceive literature study as a central component of the curriculum. Some juvenile titles support such other academic goals

selected intervention should be justifiable as academically sound and appropriate.

8. *Intensity of interface.* The intervention should allow adequate opportunity for exposure and contemplation, such as staring, imagining, questioning, role playing, and discussion.

9. *Individualization.* Assignments relevant to the intervention should be adaptable to the particular needs of individual students.

10. *Identification promotion.* Nondisabled students should be able to see similarities between their life circumstances and those of persons with impairments. Such shared concerns as dealing with siblings, finding work, developing social relationships, achieving a measure of independence, and so on, foster recognition of likeness.[5]

as developing character, examining values, and promoting citizenship. In addition, carefully chosen works, even those containing descriptions of neglect, abuse, or discrimination, can enhance the study of various historical periods or geographical regions and may sensitize students to injustice toward disabled persons.

8. Although reading is an inherently interactive process with high potential for emotional involvement, its effect can be intensified by encouraging close examination of pictures and narrative, such as staring,[1] reinterpreting or extrapolating from the text,[2] assuming the identity of selected characters or rehearsing encounters between those described as disabled, and others.[3] Ensuing activities are likely to be lively, yielding myriad opportunities for examination of concerns.[4]

9. Youths experiencing adjustment problems or insufficiently knowledgeable about the implications of disability in a friend or relative can learn more about the situation and discover that they are not the only ones to experience certain concerns and reactions. Other students may use literature to find ways of thinking about and preparing themselves for future encounters with disabled peers.

10. The process of identification with and development of empathy for literary characters who share similar human needs, aspirations, and hopes is a situation familiar to librarians and teachers who have observed their students reading. Freeman and Algozzine contend that "a productive means of alleviating negative attitudes or ratings of

[mentally retarded] children . . . may be accomplished by altering or embellishing the characteristics of those children."[6] Books may reshape perceptions and point out positive attributes within all categories of disability. In addition, disabled students, confronted with realistic portrayals of characters with impairments, may observe how their fictional counterparts cope with particular situations and problems.

11. *Accuracy and comprehensiveness.* Information needs to be honest, accurate, and extensive. It is especially important that the disabled population is seen as limitlessly varied and multidimensional, with interests and attributes in addition to their disorders.

11. Carefully selected books can be a prime source of reliable information in a palatable, comprehensible form. While the scope of any individual title is limited, a well-designed reading program is able to provide depth and breadth.

12. *Duration.* Intervention should extend over a child's academic life.

12. There are many different titles on the same subject available for students of varying maturity and ability levels. Readers' understanding of disability should keep pace with their developmental and intellectual growth.

13. *Modeling capability.* Children should be exposed to constructive examples of how disabled and non-disabled persons interact.

13. Books allow vicariously interactive experiences, permitting readers to see themselves in new situations and shape their own behavior to emulate admired characters.

Books as mainstreaming aids have not been used as extensively as would seem logical or appropriate. Although no single reason for this lack is apparent, several may be considered. Of ten recent (1979–1983) introductory texts in special education, only two mentioned the use of books to facilitate integration. One devoted only three lines to the subject; the other listed forty-five fiction titles in its appendix. However, the mean publication date of works in that bibliography was 1965, so the average book was fifteen years old at the time the text was printed! It must be concluded that these textbook authors, all of whom endorsed mainstreaming, were oblivious to the vast numbers of valuable books in print or unaware of the efficacy of literature as an agent of change. They clearly had not made the connection between the power of books to influence beliefs and the necessity of employing these agents deliberately and habitually in ways that would refute stereotypes and construct positive images about disabled persons in the consciousness of the reader.

Reading—The "Messy" Variable

The impact of reading is a messy variable for researchers to measure. Because of the impossibility of isolating this experience from other influences and due to the idiosyncratic nature of reader response and latency of effect, it is an elusive behavior to assess—a difficulty compounded if change in attitude is the outcome being tested. Frank denies that books alone can channel moral development, but thinks that when they reinforce perceptions gleaned from other sources, their impact can be critical:

> If we cannot look to books—or to any single device—to remake our children's characters, we can yet rely on books to do what books have always done: to open doors to ideas, to challenge thought, to give form to aspirations, and even eloquent expression to ideals. Boys and girls may even find in certain books stories that crystalize in precept what the home has taught by example.[7]

Smith argues that books play a key role in cognition, that information learned from them is not compartmentalized, but is synthesized with data from other sources to generate a new level of understanding:

> Thinking is the process of working with elements or parts and combining them in such a way as to constitute a pattern or structure *not clearly there before.* This requires a recombination of parts or all of a previous experience with new material, reconstructed into a new and integrated whole. Applied to reading, this means that ideas acquired from a reading selection are combined with ideas or information acquired elsewhere in a purposeful search for a new product, pattern or structure.[8]

Changing Attitudes

Fiction, in particular, has qualities that make it a potent agent for attitudinal change. It has the power to foster insight into the nature of the human condition, revealing both the universality and the uniqueness of experience. That sense of isolation, so often injurious to the healthy development of social ties, can be sundered by literature. Although often thought of as promoting solitude and being an unsociable act, reading can provide identification and a feeling of connectedness to others. Parr explores this critical faculty:

> By giving students an awareness that they are part of the larger human community, literature reassures them that they alone do not carry the burden of certain thoughts, ideas and feelings. By demonstrating to them that the dilemmas of their own lives have precedents, it further reassures them that they alone need not reinvent whatever metaphorical wheels their lives require. By leading them to empathize with others, it brings them the first step toward assuming responsibility for others.[9]

This "assumption of responsibility" has been reported in research studies of children who listened to or read stories about the aged, women, and minorities.[10] Morse claims that books have equivalent utility in promoting empathy toward persons with impairments.

> In depicting the human dilemma, a literary account is often more vivid than even our everyday experiences because essentials are winnowed from the ephemeral and highlighted. We are left with the human essence, which carries a meaning far richer and more poignant than one sees in the helter skelter of fortuitous observation. The artistic gift is the revelation of psychological meaning in context. If this is correct, the way to human understanding is to be found in creative literary writing. . . . One excellent way to know [persons who are disabled] is to experience their lives drawn taut by the sensitivity and insight of the masters.[11]

Purely informational books, although useful in expanding the depth and scope of knowledge about disability or refining the quality of data that readers possess, generally have only a modest influence on attitude formation. Novels, however, exhibiting both cognitive and affective appeal, can translate objectively defined societal problems into subjectively realized experiences, creating characters with whom readers can identify, whose emotions they can vicariously share, whose behavior they can imitate, and whose perceptions and judgments they can embrace or reject. Those encounters that the child may be psychologically unprepared for in real life may be tried out safely through the written word in a selected, distilled, focused, compressed, intensified form. This is because, paradoxically, fiction simultaneously provides distance and intimacy. As Shrodes explains:

Being at once both phantasy and reality, it permits the reader to be both participant and spectator. As participant in the action of a novel, he will move about in a symbolic world which is inaccessible to him in life. As spectator, he will bring to bear upon the fictional situation his predispositions, the circumstances of his life, his unique perspective, and in adding them up in relation to what is given, he may be compelled to reevaluate his own experience.[12]

Rather than providing an escape, good literature offers resources for understanding, altering, or judging one's own behavior. Probst contends that through books "some part of the reader's conception of the world is either confirmed, modified or refuted, and that changes the reader."[13]

Although it is difficult to ascertain changes effected in a private, unstructured reading program, there is a growing body of evidence that deliberate use of books, followed by discussions or other exploratory activities, has a measurable impact on attitudes. Monson and Shurtleff[14] used filmstrips supplemented by fiction and informational books with nondisabled children in an attempt to alter perceptions about persons with impairments. An analysis of the youngsters' artwork after the year-long intervention showed constructive change. The group showing the greatest gains had read or listened to several books during the period of the experimental study. Baskin and Becker[15] reported on reactions of six- and seven-year-old students to stories containing characters with disorders. The youngsters included these fictional people in their drawings, showing one in a wheelchair and another with zigzag-shaped legs, an obvious attempt to represent the gait of a character with cerebral palsy. Their teacher's tape of their discussion revealed considerable interest in impairment. One child asked: "How could the deaf boy's parents know he was deaf if he was still a baby and couldn't talk?" Another wondered: "How could the girl go to the bathroom if she's in a wheelchair?" Although the majority of the respondents primarily asked pragmatic questions and drew literal representations of events in the stories, a few reacted more dramatically. Some illustrations revealed negative feelings, such as disabled characters enclosed in boxes, placed behind walls, or obviously separated from the artist's self-portrait. Others depicted cooperative interactions—playing catch with a child in a wheelchair, holding hands, or showing a balloon with the message "I love you" addressed to a disabled child. It was clear that the stories had the capacity to elicit strong reactions.

This experiment was replicated in 1982 by Becker, Baskin, and Lennox,[16] with similar results. Youngsters spoke enthusiastically about the fictional characters as though they were real people, proposing scenarios involving positive encounters. It is precisely this capability of imaginatively entering into the universe of a story that allows a child to react profoundly to the literary experience.

Hagino[17] reported that fiction was successfully used in kindergarten to introduce the idea of exceptionality, and Melton[18] described its utilization with preschoolers. Mauer concluded, after a study involving four- to seven-year-olds, that "meeting disabled children in books and discussing them with teachers or parents who wish to effect this change would appear to be the best preparation for actual experiences and socialization with the disabled."[19] Salend and Moe, reporting on their empirical study using quasi fiction to influence attitudes, concluded: "Children's books about handicapped individuals, when combined with activities to highlight the critical information . . . is an effective and economical method of promoting positive attitudes toward the handicapped."[20] Dewar and Policastro and Di Angelis all report similar positive results with grade-school youth.[21] After extensive field testing, Cohen developed "A Curriculum for Fostering Positive Attitudes toward the Handicapped."[22] The English section, containing poetry, drama, biography, and fiction accompanied by discussion guides, is useful for readers in middle and secondary school. Bower[23] indicated that the inclusion of literature in a university-level course on psychology offered special insights beyond those provided in the text.

The Obvious Weaknesses

All books, however, do not succeed as literature. Although most of the works intended for a juvenile audience are well-intentioned, in too many the message overwhelms the narrative. Some authors, calling on personal experience, lack the gift of being able to communicate anything but their own anguish. Others, dominated by a zealousness to convert unaware readers to their cause, produce lifeless prose, closer to tract writing than to literature. In general, the more earnest their endeavors and extravagant their claims, the less palatable is their product. Johnson, Sickels, and Sayers have affirmed this observation:

> A just cause is not enough. All the ramifications of that cause must have been experienced by the writer, not necessarily in actuality, but by the grace of a powerful and involved imagination; it must have become his own life, transmuted into art, before the revelation is apparent. The key word is revelation as opposed to putting over a point of view.[24]

Some organizations with an advocacy function have sponsored the publication of books on disability. With few exceptions, they engage "authors who are more anxious to write a story that will support a cause in which they, as adults, are interested, rather than tell a story for the sake of the pleasure it will give a child."[25]

Despite the failure of this approach, preaching and hortatory appeals continue to be promoted by reformers, who, using literary characters as their stand-ins, generate heavy-handed sermons about their favored topics. Books, however, are not effective pulpits and the use of literature to instigate social transformations has had limited success. Collinson claims didactic approaches fail to make the crucial connection between the objectives of writers and the receptivity of youthful audiences:

> Didacticism in children's books is quite rightly frowned upon, for the harmful thing about didacticism is not that the writer has some clear convictions himself and is anxious to communicate them, but that he does not help you discover that truth for yourself, he doesn't stimulate your imagination in such a way that you exclaim, "Yes, of *course*, that's it!"[26]

Alan Garner, a highly respected contemporary juvenile author, endorses that dictum, saying: ". . . the writer's task was 'not that' [pointing an admonitory finger], 'but this' [opening his hands in display]. You don't tell young readers what's what, you demonstrate what life's about."[27] Isaac Bashevis Singer articulates this fundamental precept: "Fiction can entertain and stir the mind; it does not direct it. If a preacher like Tolstoy could not help his people, we are not going to be helped by a lot of little preachers."[28]

A literary weakness that almost always attaches to the didactic story is shallow characterization. As in the inspirational children's books of the nineteenth century, certain features of characters are inflated to serve the missionary purpose of the work. Such distortions drastically diminish the credibility of events. The more exaggerated the manipulation, the less convincing the characters and their behaviors become. McDowell asserts: "The central character . . . must be created in the illusion of fullness, roundness—must be shown as a complete human being."[29] It is primarily in the creation of believable characters that the difference can be seen between accomplished writers of juvenile fiction like Thrasher and Bridgers, and hacks capable only of manufacturing cardboard cutouts.

Reflections in the Literature

Although the theme of any single work of fiction may be original, even unique, an overall look at the books within any category inevitably reveals identifiable patterns and trends. If a single author expresses a bias or purveys faulty information or reveals a distorted perspective, that writer's work may be dismissed with little fanfare. If, however, the same erroneous statements, misunderstandings, superstitions, or mystical beliefs repeatedly surface, this indicates a situation that needs further examination. In looking at juvenile literature on disability published in the six years following the passage of P.L. 94-142, it is worth noting which elements show continuity with previous years and which have been added or have disappeared. While certain features can generally be said to characterize the genre, the statements of minority voices are frequently significant. They may reflect latent, even suppressed perceptions, signal anachronistic ideas or future interests, or speak to a special, limited audience.

The single most obvious development in the field of children's and adolescents' books about impairment is the dramatic increase in the quantity of new titles. *Notes from a Different Drummer*,[30] the predecessor to this publication, covered 36 years and identified 311 relevant works. The half-dozen years examined in this volume produced 348 books that meet the same criteria. Since children's literature reflects adult concerns and the recent past has demonstrated an impressive growth in awareness about disability, this phenomenon is not surprising.

Types of Disorders

In *Notes*, one out of every three identified disabled characters exhibited an orthopedic disorder. Although this is still the most common category, the proportion has decreased to about one-quarter of the total, and polio has all but disappeared as a causal agent. Since 1976, many more books include victims of accidents and wars. Severe forms of impairment, such as those necessitating wheelchair use, are again seen more frequently than milder disorders, indicated by a limp, a prosthesis, or crutches. The most unexpected development is the increased presence of dwarfs in these stories. No clear reason is evident since these characters serve a variety of functions and play diverse literary roles. Atlas, the court fool in *In the Time of the Bells*,[31] is simultaneously foil and prophet in this medieval drama. Cantú, an ex-law student in the historical novel *The Captive*[32] and its sequel, *The Feathered Serpent*,[33] evolves from being the hero's mentor to being both manipulator of events and victim of the political intrigue of others. Musket in *Westmark*[34] and Seed in *Footsteps*[35] are colorful characters who are provided with outrageous situations in which they engage in clever, witty, and provocative dialogue. *Little Little*,[36] a black comedy, fields an extensive cast of "diminutives," who expose the absurd values and limitless talent for self-delusion of contemporary society.

The second most frequently recorded category of impairment in this collection is emotional dysfunction. Almost 17 percent of these special fictional characters either carry specific clinical labels or exhibit patterns of destructive, irrational behavior, including depression, compulsive and/or obsessive actions, suicide-proneness, or frequent delusional episodes. Autism and anorexia nervosa are included in this grouping, even though some professional controversy exists over the most appropriate designations for them. Next in frequency are visual impairment, intellectual impairment, auditory impairment, special health problems, neurological impairment, speech impairment, and cosmetic impairment. Although there is little change among the ranking of major categories, there are noticeable shifts within categories.

Some specific, once-popular disorders have declined in literary interest, while others have more recently attracted the attention of a number of writers. These shifts in focus can generally be attributed to two factors. First, books to a great extent reflect the society that produces them. Infantile paralysis, once an unchecked scourge, has all but disappeared since the development of effective vaccines. Formerly seen as a major cause of disability, it is now found mostly in period pieces set before 1950 or is manifested in older characters. Anorexia nervosa has been the subject of numerous magazine articles, television dramas, and news reports. Interest in this affliction, observable in juvenile fiction in five recently published works, was not evident previously.

Second, the "popularity" of certain disorders can be ascribed to their usefulness in allowing writers to comment in a dramatic manner on issues of interest to them. In *Notes*, the common appearance of blind characters in stories about blacks permitted the delivery of some pointed messages about "color" blindness—an approach that has virtually vanished in more recent titles.

Antiwar Themes

One significant development in the present collection is the inclusion of many more antiwar books in which physically and psychologically damaged characters symbolize the destructive consequences of military action. The horribly disfigured, reclusive veteran in *The Foxman*,[37] the tormented veteran of the war in Vietnam in *Where the Elf King Sings*,[38] the shattered, totally withdrawn ex-fighter in *What's the Matter, Girl?*,[39] and the debilitated flyer in *Red Flight Two*[40] personify the terrible price paid by combatants. Even in novels that imply armed conflict was unavoidable, such as *Pack of Wolves*[41] and *Lori,*[42] the hero-ism of the soldiers is less important than their suffering. Casualties also include innocent bystanders and those philosophically opposed to war, for example, the victim of the Holocaust in *Alan and Naomi,*[43] and the wounded conscientious objector in *The Beckoner.*[44] Some authors stress that war wounds are not subject to ready healing, and part of the survivors' burden is the inability to find support from those who did not share their experiences. The father in *Where the Elf King Sings*[45] begins his recovery only when he joins other vets in a mutual support group. The soldier who returns from the Boer War becomes an object of pity in *The Aimer Gate,*[46] and the alcoholic and severely depressed former soldiers in *One More Flight*[47] find themselves outsiders, unable to readjust to the society for which they fought. As Sontag[48] suggests, illness (and disability) is frequently employed as a literary metaphor.

Expressing the Realities

In the real world, there are more disabled males than females, and this situation is reflected in juvenile fiction. In every classification except emotional dysfunction and special health problems, male characters out-number females. The most extreme imbalance occurs in stories about characters with learning disabilities, which depict four times as many boys as girls. There are over twice as many males as females in fiction featuring persons with intellectual, orthopedic, or speech disorders.

As might be expected, the majority—nearly two-thirds—of char-acters with impairments in this collection are children or adolescents. Older adults appear frequently, making up almost 10 percent of the disabled characters; this change represents a major shift in interest in these juvenile stories. Approximately 30 percent of the disabled adult characters are married; slightly more than half of the adults with im-pairments are portrayed as having no marital relationships; and the remainder are divorced, widowed, or abandoned.

Whether the writer's theme is subtly developed or is only a thinly disguised sermon, attitudes expressed toward persons with impair-ments are generally benign, a finding that differs from the situation in adult fiction.[49] There are, however, several titles in this collection that project mixed or even hostile messages concerning disability. In most, language or situations revealing pity, contempt, or disdain are ap-parently inadvertent; in others, the negative intent is clear. The heroine of *Unleaving*[50] is repulsed by Molly, a child with Down's syndrome—a repugnance shared by the disabled girl's father, who expresses the wish that his daughter were dead. Patrick, her brother, questions the

wisdom and motives of doctors who worked to save Molly's life. Although he loves her, the boy, made desperate by his sister's circumstances, pushes his sibling over a cliff to her death—an act that, he
rationalizes, frees her from an intolerable destiny. The heroine informs
Patrick that she witnessed the murder, but loves him nonetheless.
Molly's mother mourns briefly, but relief soon supplants her grief. The
child, initially referred to as "it," is described in contemptuous terms
and treated as object and obstacle throughout the narrative. The protagonist in *Clunie*[51] allows the central character to drown since he concludes that retardation dooms her to a tormented existence. The author
obviously condemns the persecutors, but he seems, albeit regretfully,
to endorse the hero's decision.

In *The Wind Eye*,[52] the child's hand and arm, damaged through the
stubborn, foolish actions of her irreligious, rationalist father, are
miraculously restored by a saint. The implication that such remedies
are available to the sufficiently devout, while dysfunction and disfigurement are linked to agnosticism, is most unfortunate.

In some stories, death and disability, most commonly blindness,
are also linked in mystical ways, a conjoining that is irresponsible and
inexcusable. The father of the blind child in *The Seeing Stick*[53] single-
mindedly mourns his daughter's inability to see. Until she learns to
interpret events through the development of her tactile sense, she is
shown dressed in white, shroudlike clothing. Although the narrative
stresses the improvement brought about by her rehabilitation, her
father's funereal demeanor, abetted by the illustrations, creates an irresistible connection between blindness and death. The title character in
The Dark Princess[54] at long last finds someone who truly loves her even
though she is blind. To demonstrate the sincerity of his ardor for the
skeptical young woman, the court fool, her would-be suitor, willingly
sacrifices his own sight, then plunges over a precipice to his death,
followed immediately by his beloved. The eponymous hero of *The
World of Ben Lighthart*[55] is advised, "If death can be a loving friend,
blindness can certainly grow to be a good companion."

Other disabilities are also frequently tied to superstition. In many
instances, however, these naive ideas are seen as the result of immaturity, or lack of education or sophistication, or as products of a prescientific society. The disabled heroine of *The People Therein*[56] lives in rural,
turn-of-the-century North Carolina. She explains her malformed foot as
a result of her mother's having seen an anomalous calf while she was
pregnant. A child in *Devil by the Sea*[57] thinks Dotty Jim's clubfoot is a
cloven hoof, and the foolish villagers convince themselves that an adolescent's birthmark is evidence of Satan's presence in *The Diary of Trilby
Frost*.[58]

Disabled characters are shown both as victims and, especially when they exhibit emotional problems, as perpetrators of violence. Rape, a more common occurrence in this volume than in its predecessor, is seen as an act perpetrated on impaired women, which produces disabled progeny and/or precipitates permanent psychological damage. The intellectually impaired title character in *Clunie*[59] is the intended victim of a high school bully; Bedelia, in *A Striving After Wind*,[60] "spoke only in rhyme" before she was raped and was mute thereafter; the woman who stutters in *Between Dark and Daylight*[61] gave birth to retarded twins after an incestuous rape; Mad Moll, of *Encounter at Easton*,[62] scorned by her neighbors after being attacked by soldiers, becomes a homeless recluse who is tormented by delusions. In *Song of the Pearl*,[63] a tale of convoluted morality, the asthmatic adolescent is raped by an uncle whose forgiveness she must seek if she is to find happiness.

Characters with impairments are apt to be violently rejected by their communities—beaten, sacrificed, or killed. The limping hero in *A Way of His Own*[64] and the disfigured boy in *Manwolf*,[65] presumed by their neighbors to have evil powers, are driven from their homes; Reetard in *Let a River Be*[66] is shot at, then fatally rammed by a boat; Hanno, almost totally blind, is chosen to be martyred by the corrupt priests in *Divide and Rule*;[67] the retarded character in *The Doomsday Gang*[68] is fatally stabbed; the child with Down's syndrome is pushed to her death in *Unleaving*;[69] Dimsy, a boy who is brain-damaged, is drugged and falls to his death in *Fike's Point*.[70] The title characters in *About David*[71] and *The Dark Princess*,[72] as well as the grandfather in *Grandpa—and Me*[73] and Tammy in *Flames Going Out*,[74] are among the impaired characters who end their own lives.

Disabled characters are likely to experience inadequate familial, social, and romantic relationships. Her father deserts the family when Gerry returns home from an institution in *Welcome Home, Jellybean*;[75] the overprotectiveness of Mary's father in *The View beyond My Father*[76] and of the mother in *Father's Arcane Daughter*[77] conceals shame at their children's disorders; Gary's adventitious paraplegia so distresses his friends that they can no longer find ways to relate to him in *Winning*,[78] and the romantic relationship in *Passing Through*[79] between a boy with cerebral palsy and an unimpaired girl is abruptly terminated as both decide to return to "the real world," implying that a romantic relationship between such a pair is "unrealistic."

Vocational choices and experiences of disabled characters show much variability. Although there continues to be an abundance of unusual depictions, particularly of those who have special powers—kings or shamans—or who work alone, such as hunters, others have more ordinary professions and work with people who accept them, for example, as an aide in *Alice with Golden Hair*.[80]

Although many writers present a balanced, informative, authentic view of the ramifications of dysfunction, others are guilty of distortion, unwarrantedly exaggerating or minimizing its impact. The mother of the disabled child in *Laura's Gift*[81] is depicted as so burdened by the responsibilities of caring for her daughter that she has no life of her own. Despite Laura's regular school attendance, her parent is reported as having "no time for fashion," a deprivation as unlikely as it is trivial. Students are upset when their paranoid teacher is threatened with dismissal in *Belonging*.[82] Even though the woman has become punitive, vindictive, and irrational, the unflaggingly understanding youngsters see her supervisor's actions as repressive. The problem is inappropriately presented in political rather than psychiatric terms.

The proposition that psychological trauma is a likely cure for speech disorders or even mutism can still be found in books like *Mirror of Her Own*[83] and *The Spuddy*,[84] and writers continue to exaggerate the role of will power as a remediative agent. Serious distortions occur in *Sally Can't See*,[85] in which it is reported that blind people "see blackness" and it is implied that blind youngsters need levels of supervision more suited to much younger children. In *Season of Discovery*,[86] compassionate instruction allegedly so improves the functioning of a severely retarded adolescent that he moves from barely being able to recognize his twin at 12-and-a-half years old to memorizing a prayer in a foreign language a mere six months later.

While some authors are misinformed, others are reporting, not endorsing, the misperceptions of their characters—a distinction that is not always clear even to careful readers. Clunie's father attributes his daughter's retardation to his drunkenness at the time of her conception, and the heroine's pregnant mother in *Between Friends*[87] avoids a child with Down's syndrome, afraid the encounter could affect her unborn child—foolish ideas that are not adequately countered by the writers.

The most befuddled message in this collection is to be found in *The Boy with Two Eyes*.[88] The story concerns a two-eyed resident of a planet where one-eyed people are the norm. His anomalous condition results in an unhappy childhood, but all ends well when he marries and has a "normal" baby with only one eye. Although the authors claim that their purpose in writing the book was to support the rights of handicapped children, they paradoxically seem to be saying that deviant appearance is a barrier to self-fulfillment and social acceptance.

In a discussion of the differences between adult and juvenile fiction, McDowell[89] condemns cynicism and misanthropy as inappropriate elements in children's books, claiming that immature readers have not yet sufficiently developed positive values or confidence in their own beliefs to resist such arguments. This collection, however, contains a few stories that depict a world devoid of hope and stripped of traditional mores. *Fike's Point*[90] is a tale of unrelieved moral corruption featuring a heroine whose route to happiness entails betrayal of trust and premeditated murder; in *The Ennead*[91] and *Divide and Rule*,[92] Mark proposes exploitive societies from which artists and nonconformists must inevitably be outcasts. The role of disabled people in doomsday scenarios is of special concern. They are consistently seen as victims, often the object of brutality, frequently dying a violent death. While their function generally is to underscore a caustic social commentary, the secondary message may inadvertently have the effect of devaluing persons with impairments.

It is necessary to distinguish between fiction that promotes anxiety and despair and that which explores serious, even somber topics, in an honest and developmentally suitable manner. Townsend argues:

> Books that superficially are unpleasant may in fact be richly rewarding to the reader. They may offer him a more satisfying sense of human possibilities, a deeper awareness of the human predicament. But *the more painful the subject matter, the greater the literary art needed to make it acceptable.* Where art is insufficient, the result will merely be depressing.[93]

Protecting youngsters from knowledge of the darker aspects of human experience may leave them more vulnerable than a reasonable, balanced exploration would. Edwards concludes that "it is a disservice to a young person, who must live dangerously, to acquaint him only with good, innocuous people in ideal situations."[94] Pollyanna perceptions of impairment, instantaneous cure, easily restructured familial and social relationships, while not totally unprecedented, depict an improbable world. Such an untenably benign view is becoming less common in children's fiction, surviving primarily in lesser literary efforts like *Breakaway*,[95] in which an adventitiously deaf youth is able to overcome his communication problems by reading books and watching soap operas on television, or in such missionary works as *A Pebble in Newcomb's Pond*,[96] in which megavitamin therapy is proposed as a panacea for the heroine's problems.

Although most of the novels in this volume are serious in tone, there are more instances of humor than in prior years. Unfortunately, some writers still see situations arising from hearing loss as a source of mirth. The deaf farmer in *Down in the Boondocks*[97] is ludicrously portrayed as totally oblivious to his surroundings; the shopkeeper in

The Bookseller's Advice,[98] incorrectly interpreting his customers' requests, gives strange counsel that inadvertently turns out to be fortuitous; the hearing-impaired lady in *Otto Is a Rhino*[99] thinks every remark is a request for a cup of coffee. This patronizing mockery is as tasteless as it is misguided and a poor substitute for funnier, more imaginative situations.

In other novels, the humor is on a higher level—more sophisticated and far more amusing. *Anastasia Krupnik*[100] exhibits a gentle, tongue-in-cheek wit; *Ox under Pressure*[101] intersperses explorations of profound issues with hilarious vignettes, and *Return to Treasure Island*[102] combines literary parody with slapstick. *Little Little*[103] is the most cosmopolitan, satirical work. In this absurdist drama, characters with impairments are central to the humor but never its victims.

Role Shifts

There has been some shift in the literary roles played by disabled characters in recent years. The use of exceptional people as portents—the blind seer, for example—has all but disappeared outside of novels set in prehistoric or classical times. In addition, the inclusion of an animal with an impairment as a model and inspiration for similarly involved human characters appears to be declining in popularity. When a severely impaired person has the central role, much of both internal and external action remains focused on situations arising from the disorder—medical and rehabilitative regimens, adapted familial and social relationships, self-image problems, and the like. More new books, however, feature severely impaired protagonists for whom the impairment is only one of a host of attributes that affect their lives. In other words, they are seen as interesting people engaged in varied activities whose behavior is complicated but not determined by their special needs. Lester in Slepian's books, Sorrow in Callen's series, and Sam in *Do Bananas Chew Gum?*[104] are typical.

Of special interest is the growing casual treatment of minor disabled characters as though they were simply a natural part of the passing scene, a phenomenon endorsed by numerous advocates. The two disabled people who adopt puppies in *A Bag Full of Pups*[105] are unexceptional among the ten other new pet owners. One child in *My Best Friend Moved Away*[106] wears a leg brace, observable in the illustrations but not noted in the text. Cousin Thomas, in *The Bassumtyte Treasure,*[107] accommodates his orthopedic impairment with notable casualness.

There are more disabled villains in this collection than in *Notes*.

Some few still carry identifying stigmata: a pirate's eyepatch or a criminal's disfiguring scar. More prevalent is the psychotic killer, a popular figure who has rescued more than one poorly plotted story. There are also more female villains, typically portrayed as emotionally disturbed and quite often as child abusers.

Stories in this collection, like most juvenile works, generally employ omniscient narrators. A few use a sibling or other relative to provide a compassionate perspective. On rare occasions, events are revealed as seen through the eyes of a disabled character. Some of the action of *Secret Dreamer, Secret Dreams*[108] is described by autisticlike Caroline, a bold and, in this instance, successful literary approach. Lester, the adolescent with cerebral palsy in *The Alfred Summer*[109] and *Lester's Turn*,[110] describes himself with wit that is both acerbic and poignant in Slepian's superior novels.

Revealing Titles

Titles often reveal the attitudes, beliefs, and approaches that authors display toward impairment. Some are neutral, offering no clue to perspective or even, occasionally, to subject matter, while others suggest their focus through connotative, literary, or ironic cues. Such straightforward, blunt titles as *The Rose-Colored Glasses: Melanie Adjusts to Poor Vision*,[111] *A Boy Called Hopeless*,[112] and *Me and Einstein: Breaking through the Reading Barrier*[113] announce quasi-fictional works more interested in informing than entertaining. Both subject matter and style are clearly revealed by books named *My Sister's Silent World*[114] and *More Time to Grow*,[115] which promise little in the way of originality. *Apple Is My Sign*,[116] *Triple Boy*,[117] and *The View beyond My Father*[118] more obliquely allude to the disabilities that are the concerns of these books.

The Seeing Stick[119] and *The Seeing Summer*,[120] each featuring a blind central character, are remnants of a coy approach to naming books that has diminished in popularity in recent years. The excessively melodramatic *What If They Knew?*[121] and the obvious use of disability to signal villainy in *One-Eyed Jake*[122] seem curiously anachronistic and are, happily, rare in this collection. Others continue to employ romanticized titles that perpetuate unacceptable connotations, such as *The Dark Princess*,[123] alluding to the heroine's blindness. Some titles are ironic, as *The Best Little Girl in the World*[124] and *The Right-Hand Man*,[125] offering clues to both the central problem and the tone in which the story will be told. Others hint at desires reflecting common juvenile obsessions, for example, *Just Like Everybody Else*[126] and *Belonging*.[127] A felicitous trend is the appearance of titles like *Do Bananas Chew Gum?*[128] and *Keep*

Stompin' Till the Music Stops,[129] which suggest that serious topics will be balanced by humor. A greater proportion of titles in this new collection are neutral in tone.

Occasionally, a derogatory label forms part or all of a character's name—One-Eyed Jake, Cap'n Smudge, and Dimsy are prime examples. When the story borrows from folkloric sources as for King Crookback in *Dream Weaver*[130] or takes place in a pretechnological society as does *Claw Foot*,[131] use of appellations follows established custom. In a contemporary realistic setting, such epithets as "Crazy Charlie" and "Loony Clunie" demonstrate taunting and rejecting behaviors. Reetard, in *Let a River Be*,[132] has no other known name. Through the author's exemplary skill, this terrible descriptor changes from a term of contempt to one that is neutral, then finally to one infused with tragic irony.

Illustrating the Theme

Illustrations in juvenile books in this volume vary in quality from wonderfully sensitive renderings to pictures that are deficient in composition, line work, perspective, color usage, and, most critically, choice or treatment of subject matter. The visual treatment of disabled characters is a critical component of an illustrated book's message concerning impairment. Cullinan observes: "Illustrations that . . . make disabilities indiscernible by concealing them or inaccurately depicting what was truthfully detailed in the text contribute to the inauthenticity of a book and detract from its honesty."[133] Although an aesthetic analysis is beyond the scope of this work, instances of superior art that enhance a title's impact or inferior illustration that diminishes it receive comment.

Artists whose works are represented here include some of the most prominent in the field today. Lillian Hoban is found in Rabe's *The Balancing Girl*.[134] Tomie de Paola, among the most popular and prolific of illustrators, has two titles in this volume: *Jamie's Tiger*[135] and *Now One Foot, Now the Other*.[136] Joe Lasker's distinctive style is evident in *Nick Joins In*,[137] and Glen Rounds's artistic skill is displayed in *Blind Outlaw*.[138]

A full spectrum of media, including photography, is seen in this collection. Artistic styles range from highly representational works to more suggestive, impressionistic ones, although detailed, naturalistic pictures predominate. Works of quasi fiction are generally far more interested in information than aesthetics and consequently typically use either photographs or simple, uncluttered drawings that clearly depict prostheses, adapted or specialized equipment, medical or diagnostic procedures, or modified environments. *My Sister's Silent World*[139] and *Jamie's Tiger*[140] are handsomely illustrated exceptions that focus on the problems of self-doubt and social isolation that can result from profound hearing loss.

The overwhelming majority of illustrations are adequate—if undistinguished, offering images no more memorable than those found in most classroom texts. They provide some design balance for the lines of print, but fail to imbue characters with special identity or elicit much real interest; they only decorate instead of inviting involvement. Some few titles include unacceptably poor drawings. The pictures in *Becky*,[141] for example, are particularly unattractive—muddy and unappealing. Characters' features change drastically, making it difficult to ascertain their identity.

Many illustrations in these books are valuable. They not only present an accurate view of the physical aspects of impairment, but also honestly depict the familial, educational, and social responses that characters with the special needs experience. These pictures allow readers to stare unreprimanded at people and objects, a behavior generally unacceptable in real life. They provide a stimulus that caring adults can use to initiate discussion, solicit questions, probe feelings, and answer concerns in a nonjudgmental situation.

Some impairments are more readily represented in pictorial format than others: Many orthopedic and neurological disorders result in specific deformations; sensory losses may necessitate the use of hearing aids, special lenses, and the like. Other dysfunctions have no readily identifiable physical manifestations: A person with a specific learning disability, a cardiac disorder, diabetes, or many forms of intellectual impairment, for example, may be visually indistinguishable from the general population. A special problem for the artist is to depict a character with particular identifying characteristics (as one with Down's syndrome), maintaining individuality while avoiding stereotyping. Some artists' efforts to circumvent this challenge altogether have yielded ludicrous results. The retarded child in *A Special Kind of Sister*[142] is never clearly seen; views of him are all partially obscured even though he is a major character and every other family member is clearly portrayed.

In books for younger children, illustrations are as important as the narrative. Ideally, in addition to being informative, they should present characters with whom readers can identify, demonstrate appropriate interactive behaviors involving the disabled person, and set a positive emotional tone. DiGrazia's pencil drawings for *My Friend Jacob*[143] meet all these criteria. He depicts a warm, close, mutually satisfying relationship between two boys who are far apart in age and intellectual poten-

FIGURE 1.   From *My Friend Jacob* by Lucille Clifton. Illustrated by Thomas DiGrazia. Reprinted by permission of E. P. Dutton.

tial. The handsome, sensitive pictures are free of condescending or patronizing components, showing the adolescent without any identifiable disorder, but with a visage more open, innocent, and trusting than one would expect (see Figure 1).

Among the dozen dog lovers agreeing to adopt the appealing animals in *A Bag Full of Pups*[144] are two with sensory impairments. They receive no special attention in either narrative or illustrations; they, like their sighted and hearing neighbors, are an unremarkable part of the community. The middle-aged blind man has a slightly rumpled look and wears a hat that has seen better days, but this does not distinguish him from his neighbors. It is the lack of emphasis—the ordinariness of his inclusion—that is an important feature of this book (see Figure 2).

Hoban's considerable talents are admirably displayed in *The Bal-*

FIGURE 2.   From *A Bag Full of Pups* by Dick Gackenbach. Copyright ©
1981 by Dick Gackenbach. Reprinted by permission of Ticknor &
Fields/Clarion Books, A Houghton Mifflin Company.

ancing Girl.[145] Her pictures of lower elementary school youngsters perfectly capture their movements, postures, and expressions. The young
heroine is shown with leg braces and in her wheelchair, a self-assured,
competent child but, most significantly, an integrated member of her
class (see Figure 3).

Few novels for older readers contain illustrations, so the book

FIGURE 3.   From *The Balancing Girl* by Berniece Rabe. Illustrated by Lillian Hoban. Reprinted by permission of E. P. Dutton.

jacket is of special interest. It should give potential readers an honest representation of the contents and be attractive enough to excite interest. For instance, the wraparound cover of *Apple Is My Sign*[146] features a pensive but alert youngster set against a rustic turn-of-the-century backdrop, and except for his dated clothing, the boy with a hearing impairment looks as though he would fit easily into a lively contemporary classroom.

The jacket for *The Alfred Summer*[147] shows the two disabled heroes running awkwardly toward the reader (see Figure 4). The physical

FIGURE 4.   Reprinted with permission of Macmillan Publishing Company from *The Alfred Summer* by Jan Slepian. Jacket illustration by Tom Allen. Copyright © 1980 by Jan Slepian.

manifestations of Lester's cerebral palsy can readily be seen in his stance and the position of his hand. Alfie's hands, one holding tightly to his friend, the other curled against his chest, and his unguarded, ingenuous expression suggest the nature of the boy's disorders.

It can be concluded from all these observations that literature about disability is plentiful and varied. Some books intentionally or inadvertently deliver derogatory messages about people with impairments; others combine inspired, insightful writing with honest, accurate presentation (often accompanied by quality illustrations) to produce an abundance of valuable materials that can be used to facilitate the mainstreaming process. In its 1976 annual report, the National Advisory Committee on the Handicapped asserted: "The crucial central issue goes far beyond optimum pedagogical practices of research or funding or the mechanics of moving youngsters into different settings. The overriding issue in this and all other provisions affecting the handicapped is the matter of attitudes."[148] Books are among the most potent tools available for promoting attitudinal change.

Notes

A short form of reference is used for works cited fully in Chapter 3.

1. Gerald L. Clore and Katherine M. Jeffrey, "Emotional Role Playing, Attitude Change and Attraction toward a Disabled Person," *Journal of Personality and Social Psychology* 23 (July 1972): 105–111.
2. Sidney G. Becker, Barbara Baskin, and Shelley Lennox, "Young Children's Reactions to Disability as Depicted in Their Drawings of Disabled Fictional Characters" (State University of New York at Stony Brook, Stony Brook, N.Y., 1982).
3. Margie K. Kitano, Jim Steil, and Jack T. Cole, "Role-taking: Implications for Special Education," *Journal of Special Education* 12 (Spring 1978): 59–74.
4. Roger Haney, Michael Harris, and Leonard Tipton, "The Impact of Reading on Human Behavior," in *The Implications of Communications Research*, ed. by Melvin J. Voigt and Michael H. Harris, 6th ed., Advances in Librarianship Series (New York: Academic Press, 1976), pp. 140–216; Jacob Jaffe, "Attitudes of Adolescents toward the Mentally Retarded," *American Journal of Mental Deficiency* 70 (May 1966): 907–912.
5. Tordis Ørjasaeter, "The Handicapped in Literature," *Bookbird* 18 (1980): 3–6, 21–25; Gary N. Siperstein and Alice C. Chatillon, "Importance of Perceived Similarity in Improving Children's Attitude toward Mentally Retarded Peers," *American Journal of Mental Deficiency* 70 (May 1966): 907–912.
6. Sheryl Freeman and Bob Algozzine, "Social Acceptability as a Function of Labels and Assigned Attributes," *American Journal of Mental Deficiency* 84 (May 1980): 589–595.
7. Josette Frank, *Your Child's Reading Today*, rev. ed. (New York: Doubleday, 1969), p. 125.

8. Richard J. Smith, "Using Reading to Stimulate Creative Thinking in the Intermediate Grades," in *Creative Reading for Gifted Learners: A Design for Excellence*, ed. by Michael Labuda (Newark, Del.: International Reading Association, 1974), p. 52. Emphasis added.
9. Susan Resneck Parr, *The Moral of the Story: Literature, Values and American Education* (New York: Teachers College Press, 1982), p. 23.
10. Phyllis L. Schneider, "The Effects of a Literature Program of Realistic Fiction on the Attitudes of Fifth Grade Pupils toward the Aged" (State University of New York at Buffalo, Buffalo, N.Y., 1977); Patricia B. Campbell and Jean Wirtenberg, "How Books Influence Children," *Show-Me Libraries* 32 (August 1981): 18–24.
11. William C. Morse, Forward, in *The Handicapped in Literature: A Psychosocial Perspective*, ed. by Eli M. Bower (Denver: Love Publishing, 1980), p. vi.
12. Caroline Shrodes, "The Dynamics of Reading: Implications for Bibliotherapy," in *The Special Child in the Library*, ed. by Barbara H. Baskin and Karen H. Harris (Chicago: American Library Association, 1976), p. 138.
13. Robert E. Probst, *Adolescent Literature: Response and Analysis* (Columbus, Ohio: Merrill, 1984), p. 21.
14. Diane Monson and Cynthia Shurtleff, "Altering Attitudes toward the Physically Handicapped through Print and Non-print Media," *Language Arts* 56 (February 1979): 163–170.
15. Barbara H. Baskin and Sidney G. Becker, "An Investigation of the Affective Responses of Primary Grade Children to Handicapped Literary Models" (joint paper presented at the New York State Convention of the American Association of Mental Deficiency and the Council for Exceptional Children, Rochester, N.Y., November 16, 1979).
16. Becker, Baskin, and Lennox, "Young Children's Reactions."
17. Janice L. Hagino, "Educating Children about Handicaps," *Childhood Education* 57 (November/December 1980): 97–100.
18. Gary B. Melton, "Preparing 'Normal' Children for Mainstreaming," *Journal of Special Education* 16 (Winter 1980): 198–204.
19. Ruth A. Mauer, "Young Children's Responses to a Physically Disabled Storybook Hero," *Exceptional Children* 45 (February 1979): 326–330.
20. Spencer J. Salend and Laura Moe, "Modifying Nonhandicapped Students' Attitudes toward Their Handicapped Peers through Children's Literature," *Journal for Special Educators* 19 (Spring 1983): 27.
21. Randy L. Dewar, "Peer Acceptance of Handicapped Students," *Teaching Exceptional Children* 14 (March 1982): 188–193; Margaret M. Policastro and Carla Di Angelis, "Storytelling: Teachers and Children Developing Positive Attitudes toward the Handicapped in the Regular Classroom (paper presented at the national convention of The Council for Exceptional Children, Detroit, Mich., April 8, 1983).
22. Shirley Cohen, "A Curriculum for Fostering Positive Attitudes toward the Handicapped," in *Fostering Positive Attitudes toward the Handicapped*, ed. by Shirley Cohen, Proceedings of the New York State Network of Special Educational Instructional Materials Centers, 1975, pp. 127–142.
23. Eli M. Bower, ed. *The Handicapped in Literature: A Psychosocial Perspective* (Denver: Love Publishing, 1980).
24. Edna Johnson, Evelyn Sickels, and Frances C. Sayers, *Anthology of Children's Literature*, 4th ed. (Boston: Houghton Mifflin, 1970), p. 755.

25. Margaret A. Edwards, *The Fair Garden and the Swarm of Beasts*, rev. ed. (New York: Hawthorn, 1974), p. 74.
26. Roger Collinson, "A Sense of Audience," *Children's Literature in Education* 10 (March 1973): p. 38.
27. Alan Garner, quoted in Roger Collinson, "A Sense of Audience," *Children's Literature in Education* 10 (March 1973): 38.
28. Isaac Bashevis Singer, quoted in Paul Gray, "Singer's Song of the Polish Past," *Time*, July 3, 1978, p. 60.
29. Myles McDowell, "Fiction for Children and Adults: Some Essential Differences," *Children's Literature in Education* 10 (March 1973): 57.
30. Barbara H. Baskin and Karen H. Harris, *Notes from a Different Drummer: A Guide to Juvenile Fiction Portraying the Handicapped* (New York: Bowker, 1977).
31. Gripe, *In the Time of the Bells*.
32. O'Dell, *The Captive*.
33. O'Dell, *The Feathered Serpent*.
34. Alexander, *Westmark*.
35. Garfield, *Footsteps*.
36. Kerr, *Little Little*.
37. Paulsen, *The Foxman*.
38. Wolkoff, *Where the Elf King Sings*.
39. Brochmann, *What's the Matter, Girl?*
40. Dank, *Red Flight Two*.
41. Bykov, *Pack of Wolves*.
42. Goldreich, *Lori*.
43. Levoy, *Alan and Naomi*.
44. Jones, *The Beckoner*.
45. Wolkoff, *Where the Elf King Sings*.
46. Garner, *The Aimer Gate*.
47. Bunting, *One More Flight*.
48. Susan Sontag, *Illness as Metaphor* (New York: Farrar, Straus & Giroux, 1977).
49. Trenton Batson, "The Deaf Person in Fiction—From Sainthood to Rorschach Blot," *Interracial Books for Children Bulletin* 11 (1980): 16–18; Leslie Fiedler, *Freaks, Myths, and Images of the Secret Self* (New York: Simon and Schuster, 1978).
50. Walsh, *Unleaving*.
51. Peck, *Clunie*.
52. Westall, *The Wind Eye*.
53. Yolen, *The Seeing Stick*.
54. Kennedy, *The Dark Princess*.
55. Ter Haar, *The World of Ben Lighthart*.
56. Lee, *The People Therein*.
57. Bawden, *Devil by the Sea*.
58. Glasser, *The Diary of Trilby Frost*.
59. Peck, *Clunie*.
60. Johnson, *A Striving After Wind*.
61. Thrasher, *Between Dark and Daylight*.
62. Avi, *Encounter at Easton*.
63. Nichols, *Song of the Pearl*.
64. Dyer, *A Way of His Own*.

65. Skurzynski, *Manwolf.*
66. Cummings, *Let a River Be.*
67. Mark, *Divide and Rule.*
68. Platt, *The Doomsday Gang.*
69. Walsh, *Unleaving.*
70. Britton, *Fike's Point.*
71. Pfeffer, *About David.*
72. Kennedy, *The Dark Princess.*
73. Tolan, *Grandpa—And Me.*
74. Platt, *Flames Going Out.*
75. Shyer, *Welcome Home, Jellybean.*
76. Allen, *The View beyond My Father.*
77. Konigsburg, *Father's Arcane Daughter.*
78. Brancato, *Winning.*
79. Gerson, *Passing Through.*
80. Hull, *Alice with Golden Hair.*
81. Jacobs, *Laura's Gift.*
82. Kent, *Belonging.*
83. Guy, *Mirror of Her Own.*
84. Beckwith, *The Spuddy.*
85. Petersen, *Sally Can't See.*
86. Goldreich, *Season of Discovery.*
87. Garrigue, *Between Friends.*
88. Garcia and Pacheco, *The Boy with Two Eyes.*
89. McDowell, "Fiction for Children."
90. Britton, *Fike's Point.*
91. Mark, *The Ennead.*
92. Mark, *Divide and Rule.*
93. John Rowe Townsend, "Dark Dreams," review, *New York Times,* June 23, 1974, p. 8. Emphasis added.
94. Edwards, *Fair Garden.*
95. Hallman, *Breakaway.*
96. Dengler, *A Pebble in Newcomb's Pond.*
97. Gage, *Down in the Boondocks.*
98. Breitner, *The Bookseller's Advice.*
99. Kirkegaard, *Otto Is a Rhino.*
100. Lowry, *Anastasia Krupnik.*
101. Ney, *Ox under Pressure.*
102. Judd, *Return to Treasure Island.*
103. Kerr, *Little Little.*
104. Gilson, *Do Bananas Chew Gum?*
105. Gackenbach, *A Bag Full of Pups.*
106. Zelonky, *My Best Friend Moved Away.*
107. Curry, *The Bassumtyte Treasure.*
108. Heide, *Secret Dreamer, Secret Dreams.*
109. Slepian, *The Alfred Summer.*
110. Slepian, *Lester's Turn.*
111. Leggett and Andrews, *The Rose-Colored Glasses: Melanie Adjusts to Poor Vision.*
112. Melton, *A Boy Called Hopeless.*
113. Blue, *Me and Einstein: Breaking through the Reading Barrier.*

114. Arthur, *My Sister's Silent World*.
115. Grollman, *More Time to Grow*.
116. Riskind, *Apple Is My Sign*.
117. Carlson, *Triple Boy*.
118. Allen, *The View beyond My Father*.
119. Yolen, *The Seeing Stick*.
120. Eyerly, *The Seeing Summer*.
121. Hermes, *What If They Knew?*
122. Hutchins, *One-Eyed Jake*.
123. Kennedy, *The Dark Princess*.
124. Levenkron, *The Best Little Girl in the World*.
125. Peyton, *The Right-Hand Man*.
126. Rosen, *Just Like Everybody Else*.
127. Kent, *Belonging*.
128. Gilson, *Do Bananas Chew Gum?*
129. Pevsner, *Keep Stompin' Till the Music Stops*.
130. Yolen, *Dream Weaver*.
131. Witter, *Claw Foot*.
132. Cummings, *Let a River Be*.
133. Bernice E. Cullinan, "Literature and Children with Special Needs," in *Literature and the Child*, ed. by Bernice E. Cullinan, Mary K. Karrer, and Arlene M. Pillar (New York: Harcourt Brace Jovanovich, 1981).
134. Rabe, *The Balancing Girl*.
135. Wahl, *Jamie's Tiger*.
136. de Paola, *Now One Foot, Now the Other*.
137. Lasker, *Nick Joins In*.
138. Rounds, *Blind Outlaw*.
139. Arthur, *My Sister's Silent World*.
140. Wahl, *Jamie's Tiger*.
141. Hirsh, *Becky*.
142. Smith, *A Special Kind of Sister*.
143. Clifton, *My Friend Jacob*.
144. Gackenbach, *A Bag Full of Pups*.
145. Rabe, *The Balancing Girl*.
146. Riskind, *Apple Is My Sign*.
147. Slepian, *The Alfred Summer*.
148. National Advisory Committee on the Handicapped, *Annual Report* (Washington, D.C.: U.S. Office of Education, 1976), p. 3.

3

An Annotated Guide to Juvenile Fiction Portraying the Disabled, 1976–1981

This chapter contains individual descriptions of 348 books of juvenile fiction published between 1976 and 1981. The annotations are presented alphabetically by author's name, but access can also be obtained by consulting the Title Index and the Subject Index under particular impairments. Each annotation consists of a plot description and, when appropriate, excerpts from dialogue or narrative. The plot description is followed by *Analysis,* commentary that encompasses both interpretive and literary treatment, as well as some discussion of illustrations when pertinent. Since the focus of this book is on the treatment of impairment, this issue will receive the most attention, sometimes exaggerating its importance in the narratives. Stories are coded for reading level as noted below.

Reading Level Designations

YC (young child); approximately 5–8 years old or in grades K–3. These children will need guidance in comprehending meaning and interpreting stories. They are relative newcomers to literature and have had limited personal experience. They may read simple stories by themselves but are dependent on pictures to carry part of the literary message. They may confuse fiction and life and believe that characters in books are real people.

MC (mature child); approximately 9–12 years old or in grades 4–6. These children have the ability to read more mature books. They have wider experiential backgrounds, both personal and vicarious, and are able to read books of over 100 pages, keeping plot line and characters straight. Character identification is frequently strong and loyalties to particular authors, genres, or content areas often develop. Their response is frequently excessive and approved models are inflated to heroic proportions. Children at this stage can begin to understand dissimilar life patterns.

YA (young adolescent); approximately 13–15 years old or in grades 7–9. Young adolescents have the ability to read more mature books. They have developed some sense of chronological time, so books of historical fiction can have meaning. They understand and are interested in boy/girl relationships and can perceive subtleties in human behavior. They are caught in the conflict of needing to conform to peer pressure while simultaneously developing their unique identities. By this stage, it is possible for them to understand and enjoy books using more sophisticated literary techniques, such as flashbacks, subplots, and nonomniscient perspectives.

MA (mature adolescent); approximately 16–18 years old or in grades 10–12. These readers can understand novels of considerable complexity. They are potentially responsive to ambiguities of human behavior as expressed in literature, to paradoxes, to multiple levels of meaning, and to philosophical, as opposed to pragmatic, approaches. They usually see themselves as mature and are interested in concerns of the adult world.

Any designation of reading level must of necessity be arbitrary. Obviously, children in any particular grade or age level will display tremendous variation in intellectual, social, and emotional maturity. We feel, then, that maturity level may be a better guide than chronological age to the ability of a child to understand a book. Approximate age and grade designations are included, but they are only general suggestions. It is entirely possible for a child reading on an eighth-grade level to exhibit maturity traits and interests of a fifth-grade or younger child. Conversely, extensive background information in combination with high interest can substantially elevate the level on which a child can comfortably read.

Following the reading designation is the *impairment designation*. If several impairments are listed with initial capital letters, all play a central or critical role in the novel. Those disablements of secondary importance are noted in lowercase letters; those of peripheral significance are noted in lowercase letters and are separated from the main designation by a semicolon and introduced by the word "also." Some impairments are of such minor importance that they have been omitted from the *Disability* heading but may be mentioned in the text of the annotation. Most impairment groupings are self-explanatory except for Special Health Problems, which is a miscellaneous collection including unspecified impairments and illnesses such as cardiac disorders, rheumatism, and so on. The ten disability designations are: Auditory Impairment, Cosmetic Impairment, Emotional Dysfunction, Intellectual Impairment, Learning Disability, Neurological Impairment, Orthopedic Impairment, Special Health Problems, Speech Impairment, and Visual Impairment.

Adler, Carole S. *Down by the River*. New York: Coward, McCann & Geoghegan, 1981. 206 pp. Reading Level: YA/MA
Disability: Neurological Impairment

Marybeth Mason and Peter have been going together since the sixth grade. When Peter first met her younger sister, who has cerebral palsy, he wondered if the girl was retarded. "It annoyed Marybeth when anyone assumed Lily was retarded just because of her slurred speech and lumbering walk. Even Doris, their mother, used to think Lily was retarded until Marybeth made her sister work so long on the tongue exercises the doctor gave her that Lily began speaking clearly enough for Doris to understand her."

Marybeth has always assumed that she and Peter would marry one day, so when he becomes part of a fast crowd in high school, she is jealous. He pressures her to become more intimate but at the same time makes it clear that he will be less attentive and seek experiences and adventures outside their relationship and beyond their staid, unexciting little community.

Marybeth frequently baby-sits for her neighbors, the Fraziers. When Laura Frazier walks out on her husband and children, Garth, their father, relies on the willing teenager to help him out. Soon after, he is able to persuade his Aunt Florence to stay with his youngsters, but the older woman is lazy, incompetent, and a chronic complainer. The final straw occurs when young Lise Frazier's arm is severely injured as Florence pushes the child across the room. Garth is summoned from work and immediately takes his daughter to the emergency room of the local hospital. There the distraught man reveals to Marybeth that he just learned his aunt has been drugging his son so that the boy will be too lethargic to demand attention from her. The desperate father is relieved to know that once again Marybeth can be counted on to see him through this latest crisis. Her kindness, loving nature, and obvious affection for his children attract him, and despite the difference of almost ten years in their ages, he begins to date her. Mrs. Mason's disapproval of Peter is now transferred to Garth, whom she feels will keep her daughter confined to their backwater town. But Marybeth shares neither her mother's frustrations nor ambitions, and after Peter leaves without a backward glance, she marries Garth and settles down to what is an unexciting, sedate, but, for her, fulfilling life as a mother, wife, and homemaker.

Analysis. This low-key examination of the maturation of a gentle, kind, unexceptional young woman is enriched by several well-drawn characterizations. The portrait of Lily as a sensitive, shy, but astute youngster who vicariously participates in her older sister's romances is expertly developed. The girl's disability is presented as a factor in her relationship with others and as a determinant of her aspirations. Lily is not totally realistic in assessing its impact—as when she proposes a career as a professional singer—but her self-assessment is no more out of line than that of many starry-eyed youngsters. Marybeth's affection and loyalty are introduced in her relationship with her sister and then naturally extend to Garth's children. Adler, using this central character's perceptions, depicts Lily in a positive manner and places her disorder in perspective. The girl's successful accommodation, effected through considerable effort and smoothed by maturation, is of special interest: "Marybeth looked at her sister. Lily wasn't a little girl anymore. She had slimmed down some and showed breasts and a waist. It was hard to tell she had any handicap, she covered it so well. She spoke as clearly as anyone now, and her limp was only evident when she tried to hurry."

Albert, Louise. *But I'm Ready to Go.* Scarsdale, N.Y.: Bradbury, 1976. 230 pp. Reading Level: YA
Disability: Learning Disability

Fifteen-year-old Judy Miller, eldest of four children, is jealous of her sister Emily, who is bright, pretty, and clever. Except for English class, which Judy enjoys, she does poorly in school, finding difficulty both in following discussions and in concentrating on her lessons. Her classroom gaffes, her inadequate social skills, and her clumsiness contribute to her isolation and make her the butt of jokes and pranks. The adolescent's one real friend is a boy named Larry, who attends a special class for students with learning disabilities. Despite Judy's poor academic record, one counselor suspects that she may have more ability than has yet been demonstrated. Testing reveals that the counselor's hunch is correct: Judy is an intelligent young woman who has a disability that interferes with school achievement. Arrangements are made for the teenager to enroll in a special school where her specific problems can be addressed properly. However, Judy is unhappy about the transfer since she believes such places are for "weirdos," despite Larry's attendance at one.

Judy has a good singing voice and hopes to use this talent professionally. She frequently fantasizes about a successful audition that will launch her into instant stardom. Discouraged by the other developments in her life, the adolescent decides to take fate into her own hands, and she sets out to pursue her longed-for show business career. She travels alone to New York and, after considerable difficulty, finds a recording company she hopes will cut her first record. Judy is told, however, that she must have an appointment for an audition, which will be granted only if a demonstration tape, submitted in advance, is favorably reviewed. Exhausted and disheartened, she returns home. Emily finds her sister crying in her room, and although the two have been estranged, the younger sister's obvious sympathy is eagerly accepted. Emily generously offers to provide guitar accompaniment for the required tape, the two plan to rehearse together, and it is clear that the rift between them is ready to be bridged.

Analysis. Albert pictures the academic, familial, and social stresses that could create problems in the life of a student with undiagnosed learning disabilities. Although she is intelligent, the heroine's difficulties in drawing inferences, attending, responding appropriately, processing arithmetical concepts, combined with her clumsiness, immaturity, and undeveloped social savvy mark her as a likely failure in school. Her consequent poor self-image and inappropriate compensatory behaviors cause trouble in the other areas of her life as well. The author's account of the jealousy that arises between siblings when one child makes inordinate demands on parental time and attention is the best-developed aspect of this work. The heroine's revulsion at being labeled, her self-protective rationalizations, her use of food as a pacifier, and her retreat into daydreams for the satisfactions she lacks in real life are likewise convincing. Nonetheless, the story is basically flat and uninvolving: characters speak and move but are only intermittently vital. In addition, the didactic content tends to overwhelm the literary quality.

Alexander, Lloyd. *Westmark*. New York: Dutton, 1981. 184 pp.
Reading Level: MC/YA
Disability: Orthopedic Impairment; also auditory impairment,
speech impairment

After his beloved daughter's disappearance and presumed death,
King Augustine plunged into a state of abject despair. The monarch's
apathy has permitted the evil Cabbarus to consolidate his power, resulting in ever-increasing repression of the people of Westmark. Publishing has been added to the growing list of seditious acts, and when
young Theo, a printer's apprentice, tries to prevent the destruction of
his employer's press, a melee ensues and the king's emissary is hurt.
Theo and his master prudently leave town, but the printer is killed,
leaving the orphan boy at a loss about where to seek refuge. In flight,
he meets Musket, the fellow who originally commissioned the out-
lawed printing. "A riding coat swept to the little man's boot heels, an
enormous cocked hat perched on the side of his head. He stood, hat
included, no higher than the middle button of Theo's jacket. In swag-
ger, he took up more room than half a dozen taller men."

Musket's master, Count Las Bombas, dissuades the naive youth
from turning himself in to the authorities. The reluctant lad thereupon
joins his new acquaintances, aghast as he watches his mentor change
names as he works his scams in many towns and hamlets. When Theo
complains of their employer's rascality, Musket defends him, recalling
with gratitude his purchase from a "beggar factory":

> But you've never wondered why there's no shortage of first-rate
> paupers, lame, halt, and blind. But half your noseless, or legless,
> or hunchbacked—they've been customtailored for the trade.
> Youngsters bought or stolen, then broken past mending, sliced
> up, squeezed into jars to make them grow crooked. Sold off to a
> master who pockets whatever charity's thrown to them. . . . I was
> lucky. I was born like this, no adjustments required.

A waif named Mickle, who is amazingly skilled in ventriloquism
and mimicry, joins the company. The count, shrewdly intuiting great
commercial possibilities, advertises Mickle as a medium and sets up
many profitable performances. During the day, Theo spends many
happy times with the orphan girl. He teaches her to read and write,
and in exchange, she instructs him in a form of sign language she
learned from a man she thought of as her grandfather, whose lack
of speech and hearing necessitated having to devise some mode of
communication.

Theo grows increasingly troubled by the count's fraudulent

schemes and about the intensity of Mickle's persistent nightmares about drowning that disturb her sleep. Prodded by his conscience, Theo leaves the troop, finding protection with Florian and his small band of revolutionaries. The charismatic leader sets the youth the task of repairing a small press on which he intends to reveal to the populace the truth about the printer's death.

News arrives of the count's capture, and Florian employs Theo to create a diversion and rescue his imprisoned friends while he leads a charge against the town arsenal. The two adolescents are reconciled, but Theo is still disturbed by his role in the deceptions. Their interlude of freedom is short for they are soon recaptured and taken to Cabbarus's quarters in the castle. The wily prime minister promises them he will drop all charges if Mickle, who resembles the lost princess, will persuade the king to abdicate in favor of their captor. When the girl (who actually is Princess Augustine) recreates the scene of her attempted murder at the hands of the very man who seeks royal power, her father recognizes the truth of her tale. The villain at this point flees to the tower, followed by the hero, who saves his life. Later, the lad successfully pleads that the criminal be exiled instead of put to death. The compassionate boy subsequently receives an unsigned note, presumably from Florian, informing him, "My child. You did well. Perhaps you even did right."

Analysis. In this typical Alexander extravaganza of unbridled wickedness, courage, morality, derring-do, and romance, the disabled character has a minor, albeit colorful role. Musket adds measurably to the performances, exploiting the charitable impulses of the crowds by his physical appearance and challenging them with his bravado. His accounts of the deliberate mutilation of helpless youngsters is horrible, but not without some historical foundation. The grandfather's disorder is heard about secondhand, but the skills he acquires to compensate for this loss allow the development of some specific acts that advance the story. *Westmark's* literary qualities—wit, tight plot, masterful language—get top marks, but readers are also exposed, in unsubtle ways, to matters of ethics, loyalty, and personal responsibility.

Allen, Mabel E. *The View beyond My Father.* New York: Dodd, Mead, 1977. 192 pp. Reading Level: YA
Disability: Visual Impairment

Restless under the excessive restrictions imposed by her autocratic father, Mary tries to exercise some independence. The rules of the Angus household, however, are applied with the utmost stringency to their blind daughter. Although nearly 15, she is treated more like a girl half her age; consequently her knowledge about the world is fragmented, limited, and unsophisticated. Her father, refusing to enroll her in the school that houses "cripples, and blind children, and imbeciles," employs a tutor and unstintingly satisfies her material needs. Nevertheless, it is clear that he and the rest of the family are embarrassed and ashamed of having a child so obviously impaired and different. Mary continues her relationship with some of the girl friends she had before she became blind, but she takes special pleasure in her friendship with 15-year-old Dennis Weston. He and his family deal in the most direct, straightforward way with her vision loss, noting her badly neglected but considerable intelligence and speaking to her as if she were an adult. Mary's intellectual boundaries expand enormously as she listens to discussions about politics, religion, and the exciting technological breakthroughs that seem to characterize the changes taking place in the early decades of this century. She is astounded at how Dennis interacts with his parents in a manner that contrasts so sharply with her subservient role.

Mr. Angus is skeptical when he first hears that an operation has been developed that might partially restore his daughter's vision. Mary is both hopeful and afraid, yearning desperately for the return of some sight. The surgery is indeed successful, and after a long convalescent period, she returns home with vision adequate for some independent mobility. Corrective lenses allow her to read print again, to her great delight. When she discovers that their maid's father is missing in a mine accident, she accompanies the young woman to Wales, aware that this action will enrage her father. After hearing that the entombed men have no hope of rescue, she leaves the bereaved family and returns home to face her parent. The adolescent is aware that the most restricting aspect in her life has not been her loss of vision but her family's insistence that she remain childlike and dependent. Mary clearly understands what her confrontation with her father and the management of the crisis means: "That I had seen so far beyond my father I had somehow become free. And he knew I had. No doubt there would be troubles in the future, but he would never really be able to dominate me again." She now feels confident of her ability to pursue a career as a writer and to demand respect as a competent human being.

Analysis. Allen provides an historically accurate picture of the medical beliefs and practices surrounding the treatment of cataracts during this period. More concerned with character development than dramatic incident, this work, although slow moving, sustains reader interest easily. Mary is a determined, admirable, and intelligent young woman who must contend with a loving, but suffocatingly repressive paterfamilias who has contempt for women and demands obedience to his orders, no matter how arbitrary. The heroine's adjustment to years of blindness, then her wonderment in the recovery of her vision are movingly depicted.

Amdur, Nikki. *One of Us*. Illus. by Ruth Sanderson. New York: Dial, 1981. 133 pp. Reading Level: MC
Disability: Visual Impairment

Nora, new in school, has not yet made any friends. She reluctantly takes the only available seat at lunchtime and initiates a polite but cool conversation with Jerry, the "blind kid" in school, worried that "everyone would know that the only friend she had was someone no one else would even talk to." Impulsively she invites him to visit her on the weekend to see the rabbit she has been promised for her birthday, an invitation that marks the beginning of their friendship. Jerry encourages her to enter an essay contest on citizenship, pointing out that if she wins she will be noticed by other students and so find making friends easier. As predicted, Nora's paper is chosen for a special prize, after which a girl to whom she had spoken earlier invites the newcomer to join her group for lunch in the cafeteria. Elated but loyal to her first friend, Nora brings Jerry along, pleased to find he too is welcomed by the other girls. When one acquaintance reports she may have to attend summer school because she is failing math, Jerry generously offers to tutor her for the next exam. He confidently asserts that if a serious attempt is made, she, like Nora, will succeed.

Analysis. The narration is meant to be breezy and casual, but the effect is unconvincing. Characters, events, and particularly conversations and monologues are contrived. Although the heroine gains some self-insight, Jerry is shown as an outcast whose self-esteem is apparently unaffected by the isolation he experiences and who is so benevolent that he guides his only friend into acts to find other companions who could replace him. His lack of anger, frustration, or other such expected attitudes diminishes dimensionality and thus undercuts his portrayal. Jerry's depiction as a loner is contrasted to his easy acceptance by Nora's new female acquaintances, a situation clearly separating him from the usual companionship that boys his age seek.

Anderson, Margaret J. *In the Circle of Time*. New York: Knopf, 1979. 181 pp. Reading Level: MC
Disability: Orthopedic Impairment, Visual Impairment

Robert and Jennifer enter the circle created by the ancient Stones of Arden in rural Scotland and are catapulted into the twenty-second century. They are surprised to find, instead of a highly technological society, a simpler one dependent on human labor and total economic cooperation. The two strangers meet Karten, a boy their own age who initially mistakes them for the Barbaric Ones, raiders from across the sea who are trying to enslave his people. As the children talk, they are discovered by one of the invaders. Two escape, but Robert, hampered by his polio-weakened leg, falls and is captured. Karten loyally returns to stay with his new friend, and the two boys are held prisoner. From the cave where they are confined, the captives can observe boats anchored offshore, which will be used to take them to the land of the Barbaric Ones. Hoping to create a diversion, Robert slips out of the enclosure and into the sea, where he cuts free a boat. The water therapy he undertook after his illness turned him into a strong swimmer, and he experiences little difficulty in accomplishing his mission. In the confusion that follows his departure, the captives, joined by Jennifer, escape. Karten acts as a scout through a dangerous swamp. The children pass through safely, but their pursuers are trapped. Karten is disturbed by this occurrence, since harm befalling his enemies because of his particular actions violates the passionately avowed nonviolent tenets of his people.

The visitors are introduced to Vianah, an elderly, much-revered member of their commune, who is blind. She alone had encountered other time travelers, and the children fervently hope she can help them return to their own era. The relentless troops follow the escapees, and in their flight, Robert and Karten are accidentally returned to the present, again leaving Jennifer alone. After some further adventures, an exchange is made at last with each of the displaced children and they are restored to their concerned families.

Analysis. Robert's disability involving a limp and muscle weakness is relatively minor, but it provides an excuse for his capture and is the instrumentality of his newly found companion's escape. Vianah's blindness establishes her credentials as a wise woman.

The book's pacing is uneven and the preparation for events is inadequate. As a result, the plot appears to be characterized by excessive and unnecessary commotion. The benefits to be garnered by a passive and pacifistic society are presented in a didactic manner. The commune members are a kindly and saintly lot who do not even resist enslavement, hoping thereby to convince the invaders that their lifestyle is too nice to be destroyed. A corollary to this message, and one frequently repeated, is the evil of heavy dependence upon technology.

Anderson, Margaret J. *Searching for Shona.* New York: Knopf, 1978. 159 pp. Reading Level: MC
Disability: Learning Disability

In an effort to save them from Nazi bombing raids, many children are being evacuated from Edinburgh, Scotland. Two of the refugees are Marjorie Malcolm-Scott, heading for resettlement with unknown relatives in Canada, and Shona McInnis, who is preparing to travel with other orphans south into the countryside and comparative safety. During the ensuing turmoil, the two girls meet by chance and impulsively agree to trade places. Shona instructs Marjorie that for the rest of her journey she must take responsibility for Anna, a young frightened child who will need to be comforted and reassured. Shona sets sail, excited about her new identity, while Marjorie, with Anna in tow, boards a train to a part of Scotland she has never seen. When they arrive, they are billeted with two middle-aged, unmarried sisters, Morag and Agnes Campbell. The youngsters attend the local school, where Marjorie excels, but Anna has persisting difficulties in basic academic subjects:

> Anna was nine, but she had been put back to Primary One at school because of her reading. "The baby class," she called it, angrily. She had trouble with writing too. She kept getting her letters backwards. Marjorie had noticed that Anna's printing often came out like mirror writing, and she thought it rather clever, but Anna's teacher wasn't impressed. She scolded Anna, telling her to start over again, and Anna became more and more discouraged.

The girl is labeled "backward" by the school authorities because of her problems with reversals, her trouble with directionality, and her inability to deal well with spatial elements. Her strong verbal skills, her clever repartee, and her excellent memory are discounted. Anna's future is shaped by her teacher's lack of awareness that her learning disabilities mask considerable intact abilities. "There were ways in which Anna was smart, but most people overlooked them, and Anna hadn't learned a thing in all those years at school." Marjorie refuses to accept the school's assessment of her young friend. The seeming inconsistencies in the child's behavior and her obvious intelligence, despite her poor academic record, pique the older girl's curiosity, causing her to consider a medical career as a means to help others with similar problems. During the girls' stay, the women come to love their charges, and Marjorie contentedly experiences a sense of family for the first time. The older girl discovers some information about Shona's real family and, when the war is over, tracks down her counterpart. Returning to the residence she once occupied, Marjorie is astonished to discover that Shona has become a haughty snob who insists that the girls retain their false identities. Marjorie is more than willing to comply since she has traded a wealthy but loveless existence for one in which her surrogate family provides both affection and a strong sense of security.

Analysis. This simple, slow-paced story is filled with a potent sense of place and time. Although only a secondary element of the plot, Anna's difficulties, arising from improper assessment of her abilities and lack of remediation of her disorder, are fairly presented. The sad consequences of misdiagnosis of the girl's learning problem are clearly depicted in this historically valid presentation.

Anderson, Mary. *Step on a Crack.* New York: Atheneum, 1978. 180 pp. Reading Level: YA
Disability: Emotional Dysfunction

Sarah is frightened by her recurring nightmares, in which she tries to kill her mother, and is simultaneously puzzled since, when awake, she honestly feels exceptionally close to the woman. After her terrifying dreams, the girl is under strong compulsion to steal inexpensive and apparently useless items, an action that dissipates her stress. The teenager's father travels extensively, and her only other close relative, Aunt Katrin, is a peripatetic bohemian phantom, who occasionally sends postcards from around the world keeping them apprised of her artistic activities.

On the last day of the term at her exclusive New York high school, the 15 year old says goodbye to Josie, the school "brain," who thanks Sarah for being her only friend and says she will always be around if "she ever needs to talk to someone, sometime." Sarah has been too embarrassed to tell anyone about her problem but has tried on her own to discover its causes, control her reactions, and identify a pattern in her thefts. Her distressing behavior is further extended as she begins to sleepwalk after hearing of an impending visit from Aunt Kat. The woman arrives, bound for an art show in Chicago featuring her works, but delays her departure when her sister breaks an ankle. Josie tells Sarah that she has observed her steal, and at first the girl denies it, but when matters seem to be worsening, she calls on her friend for help. The two hypothesize wildly about what the cause might be, and Josie ultimately intuits that her friend's behavior has something to do with a secret, clues to which, she guesses, are hidden in their basement. When their search is unsuccessful, Josie drags Sarah, protesting all the while, to a psychic, who sees a grave like the one in Sarah's dream, which is "near in space . . . but far away in time." The two friends dash off to the New York Historical Society, where their frantic research suggests a site near Grant's Tomb that sounds identical to a place in Sarah's dreams. Actually seeing the grave is extremely traumatic, and heretofore repressed associations flood back to overwhelm the girl. When she returns home, the women confirm the accuracy of her memories, confessing that Katrin is her natural mother and the woman she now knows as her mother is actually her aunt. The scene she experiences in her dreams replicates one from her infancy in which Katrin abandoned her. She is told that Kat is a victim, too, but Sarah is too angry to deal with that idea or to forgive the woman who hurt her so cruelly. Josie is put on restriction for playing amateur psychiatrist, and Sarah is scheduled to begin therapy when the summer ends.

Analysis. The story's strongest quality is its presentation of the proposition that people have many sides to their character and are motivated by complex, often conflicting needs. Much of the tension is developed from the heroine's need to see the world in blacks and whites and the reality of many human acts falling into gray areas. Its major weakness is its facile, contrived explanation of a very complex problem. Sarah's difficulties are treated compassionately, and her rising panic is effectively communicated. Josie is established as an admirable character. Unfortunately, she is dealt with in stereotypical terms. "Josie's rather plain looking and thin, with glasses so thick they must be *trifocals.* That's because she spends all her time reading." The story interweaves such predictably popular themes as a wealthy attractive heroine in distress, psychic communication, hidden identity, and exotic emotional disorders into a fast-paced but shallow junior novel.

Annixter, Jane, and Paul Annixter. *The Last Monster.* New York: Harcourt Brace Jovanovich, 1980. 84 pp. Reading Level: YA
Disability: Orthopedic Impairment

Ron lives a contented life in the Montana Rockies with his father, Nat Seldon, who maintains a small farm and exploits its isolation by spending his time writing. Ron angrily remembers that his father's skill as a sportsman was cut short four years ago in an encounter with a grizzly. "What the bear left of him was a 130-pound cripple, with a sideways limp that hurt and angered Ron whenever he saw it."

The 16 year old becomes anxious one night when his dog fails to return, and he finds evidence that a bear is in the area. The next morning, Blaze is discovered badly mauled. Ron's Indian friend, Jim Blindwolf, treats the animal's injuries, but predicts the pet will be lame. At his father's insistence, the high school junior leaves for his aunt's house, where he stays during the week so he can attend school, only returning to his mountain home for weekends. Pressures of the classroom and the presence of Rhea, an attractive girl, offer some distractions from his growing obsession with the marauding bear. When he sees both his father and the dog limping, he becomes infuriated and decides to kill the grizzly. Jim tries to dissuade him and speaks of his respect for the magnificent creature, warning the impetuous youth: "He own that mountain." Undeterred, Ron takes his rifle and sets off to track the bear he is convinced is the same beast who injured his father. Although frightened of the encounter, the boy interrupts his quest with a quick swim in a mountain stream. His worst fears are realized as his quarry suddenly appears, watches him briefly, tears apart his shirt, then, apparently concluding that the naked, unarmed boy poses no threat, disappears into the forest. This narrow escape awakens Ron to the validity of Jim Blindwolf's attitude that one must live in harmony with all of nature.

Analysis. The often-repeated message of this slow-moving, easy-to-read story is delivered with a notable lack of subtlety. The narrative is burdened with anthropomorphic thinking, simplistic language, choppy sentences, and stereotypes of women and native Americans. The disabled father, although having made a phenomenal adjustment, nevertheless inspires feelings of guilt and a desire for revenge in his son. The man's literary function, while neither credible nor interesting, provides the motivation for what little action there is.

Arthur, Catherine. *My Sister's Silent World.* Photog. by Nathan Talbot. Chicago: Children's Press, 1979. 31 pp. Reading Level: YC
Disability: Auditory Impairment

The narrator accompanies her younger sister to the zoo, where the eight-year-old child enjoys watching and sometimes petting the animals, but "Heather doesn't hear the sounds that the animals make. Heather is deaf." The child's hearing aid amplifies sounds, but not enough so that she is able to differentiate words. To compensate, the youngster receives special training in sign language, speech reading, and speaking. Heather's sibling bemoans the insensitivity of the neighborhood children and their lack of understanding about hearing loss since she is convinced, given the chance, Heather could be a good friend and companion.

Analysis. The obvious didactic intent of this work dominates the fragile story line. Some basic information is conveyed by the awkward text; however, the excellent photographs more than compensate for the choppy writing, featuring portraits of an appealing child and her supportive, loving family.

Arthur, Ruth. *Miss Ghost.* New York: Atheneum, 1979. 119 pp. Reading Level: YA
Disability: Emotional Dysfunction, Speech Impairment, orthopedic impairment, neurological impairment

Elsbeth, often called Elphie, correctly perceives that she is unloved by her mother, and this dreadful observation is confirmed when her callous parent runs off to Australia with the girl's younger brother. Elphie knows that her schoolteacher father sometimes "got moody and depressed, shut up inside himself so that I could not get near him." After his wife leaves, the man deteriorates markedly until one day he refuses to leave his bed. He is taken to a hospital, and his daughter inquires of her grandmother with whom she is now living if it is a hospital for "mad" people. The woman replies: "He's mentally ill, sick in his mind, dearie, and he needs to be taken care of in a hospital until he's better." Elphie makes friends with a boy who has ambulatory problems in the small Scottish town where she is staying, but has no other companions. The girl's sense of security is shattered when her beloved grandmother is killed in a car accident and she is sent to live in a small community as the foster child of the Tuckers.

Life at school is difficult: "My stammer was embarrassing, and the other children tended to avoid me. I soon found that having no parents set me apart, I didn't quite fit in. . . . My feeling of isolation, of odd-ness increased, my sense of not belonging deepened." None of the Tuckers likes their new charge, but Elsbeth's pleasure in caring for their baby compensates for the dreariness and loneliness of her life. A series of unpleasant events follow one after another, and the supersti-tious villagers begin to speculate that a curse has been put on the Tucker home and their little town and pointedly begin to ostracize Elsbeth. When their baby almost drowns, it is the final straw, and the Tuckers, holding Elsbeth responsible, tell the authorities to remove the shocked and disbelieving girl from their premises. She is sent to Bar-nalogie, "a very special children's home, a place where they took in children who were emotionally disturbed, children who needed time and care to recover from some shattering experience or disaster."

Despite her deliberate attempts both to look unattractive and to act aloof, Elphie is aware that the setting and the staff are helping her. She becomes curious about an abandoned room and is fascinated by a seemingly malevolent spirit she senses is present. She makes an effort to comfort and befriend what appears to be the ghost of an elderly woman. Miss Ghost becomes, in effect, her silent therapist. Soon the adolescent is able to interact with others, even doing small errands in the village. She "adopts" a young boy named Jo-Jo, who is subject to seizures and has serious communication problems, and this caring rela-tionship thaws her even further. Out one day, she encounters Pad, a youth slightly older than herself whose family she thinks of in ideal-ized terms. Tragedy still seems to haunt her when she recognizes Pad's broken bicycle on the side of the road and, looking down the embank-ment, sees his still body. The distressed girl goes for help and is later informed that her friend has a broken collarbone and leg, a back injury, and a concussion, but is expected to recover. She enjoys helping with Pad's recovery and begins to think of nursing as a possible profession. The various elements of her life begin to fall into place—her father is scheduled for brain surgery, Jo-Jo is adopted locally, and Elphie learns she will be placed as a foster child with Pad's family.

Analysis. A gothic romance is not a likely genre in which to find realistic treatment of emotional problems, and this novel provides no exception. Elphie's maladjustment is certainly mild considering she has experienced constant rejection. The author describes an idealized institution that provides a casually supervised but supportive refuge for children, employing a caring staff and a matron who understands the needs for solitude her charges may require before they can cope with the world again. Little attention is given to the heroine's stammer, a by-product of her nervousness in new situations. Some misinformation is casually offered: brain surgery is proposed as a likely "cure" for a decades-long depression, and seizures are improperly described here as "fits." The story, however, is easily read and has a quaint, old-fashioned quality in its involvement with evil eyes, hens that won't lay, abandoned towers, secret entrances, and the like.

Avi (pseud. for Avi Wortis). *Encounter at Easton.* New York: Pantheon, 1980. 138 pp. Reading Level: MC/YA
Disability: Emotional Dysfunction; also special health problems

Following common practice, John Tolliver, a landowner in colonial New Jersey, pays for the contracts of child felons so that he may benefit from a source of cheap labor. When Elizabeth and Robert escape from his employ, Tolliver's offer of a reward for their capture attracts the attention of Nathaniel Hill, who soon sets off in pursuit of the girl, unaware that Robert, captured once, has gotten free again. The boy rejoins his female companion with a horse given to him by a compassionate constable's family. The two fugitives head for Easton, a labor-poor town, hoping for immediate employment and sanctuary. Elizabeth's injured arm begins to trouble her, and the wound, unattended, starts to fester. While the boy searches for a place to ford the river, he meets Hill. The man, unaware of the youngster's identity, offers him a job caring for his horse and running errands. The man speculates wildly that his new employee could be the companion of the runaway he seeks but dismisses the idea as too unlikely. Robert becomes alarmed when he realizes how sick Elizabeth is. Their river crossing brings disaster as the mare runs away and the girl is further weakened. When the youth returns from a fruitless search for his mount, he sees an old woman standing beside the almost comatose

.girl. In desperation, Robert accompanies Mad Moll to her cavelike home concealed in the mountains. The boy notes her soiled clothing and her distracted behavior: "The woman looked at me as if sometimes she saw me, sometimes not, depending on her thoughts. All the while her eyes blinked and her mouth remained slack." The unhappy woman reveals her background, stating she was attacked by a soldier and thereafter abandoned by her fiancé and her family. An outcast, she wandered to this remote location, where she has lived for years, friendless and alone. Mad Moll, formerly known as Rachel, begins to nurse the semiconscious girl and soon believes that the child is her own daughter. Muttering to herself, she complains about her lot: "When they see me . . . they lower their eyes and look away."

Hill learns that Robert has been seen with a girl whom he deduces is his quarry. The boy suspects Hill's motives but, intent on his own concerns, does not notice that he has been followed to his friend's hideaway. In anticipation of her imminent capture, the man informs the local constable of Elizabeth's status as a felon and demands his cooperation. The youth is locked into the constable's house but breaks a window and escapes once more. Racing to the cave on a stolen horse, he tries to prevent Elizabeth's capture. In the melee, Mad Moll is fatally shot trying to flee with the girl. The runaway's body is recovered, and she and the woman are buried together on the hillside by the heartbroken lad.

Analysis. Events in the story are revealed through the testimony of Tolliver, Hill, the constable, and Robert in a hearing held subsequent to the deaths of Moll and Elizabeth. This technique gives a sense of immediacy and great tension while it simultaneously retards the progress of the tale. Readers need to be astute enough to realize the adults' statements are self-serving and not to be taken as literally true. Although the tragic climax is adequately foreshadowed, the ending seems too abrupt, not allowing sufficient time for assimilation of the action. Moll is compassionately described, her "madness" attributed to a brutal, traumatizing event and her subsequent social and familial rejection. However, she seems a shadowy character, lacking in dimensionality.

Avi (pseud. for Avi Wortis). *Man from the Sky.* Illus. by David Wiesner. New York: Knopf, 1980. 117 pp. Reading Level: MC
Disability: Learning Disability

Ed Goddard has spent a year planning the heist of a payroll worth nearly a million dollars. Using false names, he has reserved all of the seats on the small plane carrying the money and hidden a fake gun that he slips unnoticed through airport security. Alone in the pas-

senger section, Goddard puts on the parachute he packed in his suitcase, breaks into the storage compartment where the money is locked,
forces open the door on the small aircraft, and jumps out, landing near
the New York–Pennsylvania border. He has memorized maps of the
area and is confident that once he locates a road, he can find his way
into town, then to a bus stop, and ultimately to safety.

Jamie Peters is visiting his grandparents during the summer. The
11 year old spends many solitary hours watching the changing cloud
formations in the sky over the Catskill foothills. These form the stimuli
for the adventure stories the imaginative child creates. On an errand to
a neighbor's home, he is teased by Todd about his inability to read and
the special school he attends, but is comforted by Gillian, who implies
that her brother's marks in school are "probably a lot worse than your
grades." Todd dismisses the boy as "weird, standing there, staring at
nothing, like some sort of retard," but Gillian's mother had been told
that Jamie was really very smart. Unsure of which assessment to believe, the girl is puzzled by Jamie's strange preoccupation and decides
to suspend judgment while surreptitiously keeping an eye on him.

Jamie is sky watching on the day of the robbery and sees Goddard
parachute from the plane. During his fall, the man drops the money
and is alarmed to see he has been spotted by a child. Jamie runs
toward the area where he believes the stranger may have fallen,
searching frantically for the man who he fears may need help. He sees
Gillian and tells her what he witnessed, but she discredits his story and
wonders whether her brother's judgment may have been correct after
all. On her way home, the girl finds the stolen case and, yanking it
from beneath some rocks, inadvertently opens it. After stuffing the
bills back inside, Gillian heads for home but is seen by the thief, who
intercepts her and forces her to lead him to Mansfield, a nearby town.
Jamie observes the encounter and wisely decides to keep his presence a
secret. Bending over to fix his perpetually untied laces, he notices that
Gillian has left a clue. He forces himself to figure out the meaning of
the letters, dredging up every special educational technique he can
recall. Finally decoding the marks, he is able to report to his grandmother that Gillian has been abducted and reveals her destination.
Although initially skeptical, she finally calls the police, and with
Jamie's help, the thief is apprehended.

Analysis. Jamie partially compensates for his lack of success in
decoding the written word through the fantasies he creates by "decoding" other stimuli. The boy's intelligence and willpower combined with
his utilization of the instructional strategies he has been taught are the
key elements in the successful capture of the criminal. The boy's isolation and compensatory behaviors are credible, but the sequence of

incidents is farfetched and too obviously marshaled for the purpose of creating a hero of the learning disabled youngster.

Bach, Alice. *A Father Every Few Years.* New York: Harper & Row, 1977. 130 pp. Reading Level: MC/YA
Disability: Special Health Problems

Since his stepfather Max ran off, Tim has become the official family handwringer, worrying unreasonably that his mother's real estate job will not support them and that he and Margot will not recover emotionally from their sudden heartbreaking loss. In addition, the sixth-grade boy is riled by his neighbor Melanie's insistence that her new status as a high school student must drastically change their relationship. Tim is jealous of the boys she talks about and scornful of her excursions to the local shopping center.

Hemophilia has kept Joey, one of Tim's best friends, housebound. When the youth visits, Joey initiates a conversation about death, causing them both discomfort at first, but later the topic leads to a mutual revelation of anxieties and a closer bond between the boys. Joey subsequently enters a difficult period during which he regularly requires plasma. His "left arm was in a splint, a needle was taped to a vein in his right arm. Through plastic tubing Tim could follow the steady drip of the plasma, for how long nobody could predict—until the joint was drained of the blood swelling it [to] the size of a grapefruit." Although the interest of his other schoolmates wanes, Tim and a friend, Willie, loyally keep the patient up to date on homework assignments and events at school. Willie complains: "Most of the class treat him like a martian." Commenting on a class to which the sick boy was assigned, he recalls: "What burns me is that the teachers call it *special* art and the kids pass by the room and think *spastic* art. I used to wise off the worst, dragging a foot behind me, or pretending my arm was paralyzed—I was a stinker until I got to know Joey."

Obsessed with the need to locate his stepfather, Tim enlists his friends in a ridiculous campaign to try to find Max by calling every area code number around the country and asking the information operator for his stepfather's phone number. When his mother decides to go to California for a vacation, Tim refuses to accompany her, convinced that the trip is merely a cover for Margot's true intention: a search for her errant husband. The self-deceiving boy convinces Joey and Melanie that his mother and Max will return together, and they optimistically plan a big welcome home party. When the woman gets off the plane alone, Tim is finally forced to admit that his stepfather's abandonment is permanent and he and his mother must rebuild their lives without him.

Analysis. Joey is perceived as a highly valued friend. His concern with death is realistic considering the severity of his disorder and his history of precarious health. The boy causes his friends to become sensitive to issues about which they would otherwise be callous. The title is misleading, implying that the hero has had a succession of surrogate fathers rather than indicating, in his words, "the need [for] a father every few years." Characterizations and dialogue are the strongest features of this original, moving, and frequently witty story.

Baldwin, Anne N. *A Little Time.* New York: Viking, 1978. 110 pp.
Reading Level: MC
Disability: Intellectual Impairment; also special health problems

Sarah cannot resolve her ambivalent feelings about Matt, her four-year-old brother who has Down's syndrome. He "walks in jerks, sometimes very fast, but always clumsily, as if his stubby arms and legs were made of wood. . . . His face is a full-moon face, and his smile covers all of it." The ten-year-old girl feels she is the only one of his four siblings who understands him, yet is convinced that his presence in the family deprives her of the opportunity to make close friends. On the day of Sarah's party, Matt disappears temporarily, and the aftermath of this incident provides an opportunity to discuss the ramifications of his disability.

The burdens of family care exhaust Sarah's mother, who unnecessarily inflates her responsibilities by making too few demands on Matt. However, after taking classes in child development, the woman revises her initial assumptions about the capabilities of her retarded child. When she is hospitalized, family life deteriorates rapidly, and her husband, unable to manage his many new obligations, has Matt placed with foster parents. Although life is easier and more relaxed without the child, at a family conference all agree the youngster needs to be at home with them.

Analysis. Despite its low reading level, *A Little Time* confronts some sophisticated problems: the consequences of excessively low aspirations for intellectually impaired youngsters, family dislocations, social difficulties of siblings, inappropriate placements, neighborhood pressures to close a foster home for special children, and so on. This exposition is the novel's strongest feature, but the prosaic dialogue, listless story line, and anticlimactic ending detract markedly from its value. Since this novel focuses on a particular developmental disability, the careless language employed in describing that disorder is unfortunate. Baldwin's use of "Down's" instead of Down's syndrome" seems ill-advised, and jacket copy containing the term *mongoloid* is inexcusable.

Further, the author's comparison of an exceptional child with an animal is demeaning when a character describes Matt as "like Mary's puppy. He wants attention all the time."

Bates, Betty. *Love Is Like Peanuts.* New York: Holiday House, 1980. 125 pp. Reading Level: YA
Disability: Neurological Impairment

Marianne accepts a job supervising eight-year-old Catsy Kranz, even though she has heard that the girl is severely disabled. Approaching her job with some trepidation, the 14 year old discovers that her charge is a child with poor motor coordination who frequently overreacts to provocation. Catsy's mother, unable to deal with her daughter's condition, deserted the family when her daughter was a baby. As Toby Kranz explains, "Mom couldn't stand to be around Catsy. She never wants to see her." Since that time, Mrs. Johansen has been their housekeeper. In the early days of her employment, the woman had been supportive and caring; however, recently her declining health coupled with personal problems have made her short-tempered and impatient in dealing with Catsy. She tries to control the child's behavior by threatening and shaking her when she is clumsy, a response Marianne perceives to be both counterproductive and cruel. Toby, Catsy's 18-year-old brother, is staying with his father for the summer, and a romance soon develops between the two adolescents.

Failing to convince his father of the housekeeper's diminished abilities, Toby enlists Marianne's assistance in minimizing Mrs. Johansen's abuse of his defenseless sister. Marianne arrives at work one day to find Mr. Kranz at home listening to the woman's complaints about her. The girl responds by telling her employer about her accuser's punitive behavior, thereby confirming Toby's accounts. The incompetent woman is dismissed, to be replaced by Marianne's aunt. Toby subsequently leaves to return to school and to his mother's home. Both teenagers are saddened by this rupture in their relationship.

Analysis. A tepid, bland, and exploitive romance, *Love Is Like Peanuts* casually introduces erroneous information about brain damage and callously endorses insensitivity to those sustaining it. Catsy, probably the least convincing character among this pallid crew, is shown little compassion. Toby, in a rare self-critical moment, muses: "I ought to be more patient with Catsy. I ought to let her talk everything out. Anyway, it's not as bad as it used to be. I never used to want to be seen with her or have anybody know I had a brain-damaged sister. At least I've outgrown that. Now all I do is get sick listening to her." Marianne reasures him: "Well, you can't help it." The possibility that revulsion at his sister's difficulties is a less than admirable trait is never suggested by the author; in fact, this position is endorsed by her. The mother's desertion of her daughter is cavalierly treated, as though it were evidence of nothing more than an idiosyncratic character flaw. The heroine's ignorant assumption of the etiology of the child's problem is revealed in a passage where she thinks sympathetically about Mrs. Kranz: "It must be awful for her not to know what made Catsy the way she is . . . she'll never know if it was because she ate pickles while she was pregnant, or maybe because she fell and landed on her behind." This demeaning reference is typical, one of many that pass by uncriticized. Further, Toby's treatment of his sister as an object available for his convenience is not portrayed as reprehensible: The young man had impregnated a girl when he was 16, and to avoid replicating a situation where such an occurrence could be repeated, he uses his sister to perform the unwitting role of chaperon. The book is a simple-minded romance, but even so, there is no excuse for the meretricious moral vacuum in which it operates.

Bates, Betty. *Picking Up the Pieces.* New York: Holiday House, 1981. 157 pp. Reading Level: MC/YA
Disability: Orthopedic Impairment, special health problems, auditory impairment

Nell and Dexter have been friends since first grade, but now, in their last year in junior high, there are signs of an incipient romance. However, when the glamorous Lacey Dunn shows an interest in him, the inexperienced and awkward youth is unable to resist her charms. Nell shares her consequent distress with her Great Uncle Charlie—her neighbor, confidant, and unswerving supporter. Because of their relationship, the young girl has been charged by her parents with keeping a watch on her elderly uncle, supervising his daily care and generally overseeing his well-being. In mild surprise at her affection for him, she observes:

> Uncle Charlie is in the old family rocker in his front room, snoring with his mouth open, and with Ruff at his feet. Saliva's drizzling down his chin. He seems okay, but he looks awful. I mean, he really is a terrible problem, with his dentures and his snoring and his deafness and his arthritis and his stubbornness, plus the brown spots on his hands and face and the dripping saliva. How come I care about him?

Uncle Charlie is hospitalized with a mild heart attack. He is considerably weakened by the incident, and his resolve to maintain his independence is shaken. Unable to perform the tasks he was once accustomed to doing, he becomes resigned to accepting his brother's offer to make a home with him in Florida.

Dexter, now completely involved with Lacey's fast crowd, snubs his former friends. After a school dance, Nell invites some of the students to an impromptu party at her home. The gathering is invaded by Lacey's friends, one of whom grabs some car keys. The drunk and rowdy teens pile into the automobile, crashing it into an oncoming vehicle. All escape with minor injuries except Dexter, whose "leg's going to be short. And kind of stiff."

Completely deserted by his fair-weather friends, the dejected boy is supported by his old crowd, except for Nell, who remains hurt and angry over his abandonment. When Nell hears that he would like to see her, she wonders if he feels he must accept second best now that his impairment has made him undesirable in the eyes of the girl he really prefers. Finally, moved by compassion and pressured by friends, Nell visits Dexter in the hospital and at home, helping him to put aside his fears about being unable to participate in sports and being a social outcast. Dexter is upset as they walk together on the first day of high school when he notices that all the other students easily pass them by. Nell berates him: "You may take longer to get places, but you're going to get there." Buoyed by her faith in him, Dexter enters the doorway ready to face the future.

Analysis. This lightweight junior novel presents a positive, upbeat, although patronizing and superficial look at a range of disabling conditions. Uncle Charlie's reduced functioning is seen as a correlate of advancing years; the young hero's impairments are depicted as a direct consequence of his keeping bad company, especially being in a car with a drunk driver. The resultant injury separates the worthwhile people (those for whom his impairment does not matter) from those of inferior worth (those who disdain his company after the accident). Dexter is a simple, self-centered, somewhat passive boy and Nell a caring, nurturing, self-sacrificing girl—roles that seem to carry the author's approval.

Bates, Betty. *The Ups and Downs of Jorie Jenkins.* New York: Holiday House, 1978. 126 pp. Reading Level: MC
Disability: Special Health Problems

The year Jorie enters junior high school, her father, a doctor, is hospitalized with a heart attack. His slow recovery, marked by frequent setbacks, pain, frustrations, restlessness, and most of all pronounced changes in personality and attitude, are unsettling to his young daughter. Jorie's schoolwork and social life are affected by worry about her father's condition as she recognizes an urgent need to move from childlike dependence upon him to a more mature and responsible role. Initially she finds it difficult even to mention the subject of her distress, but soon she learns that family, friends, and teachers are concerned and supportive. The irrepressible youngster engineers a romance between her sister and a Cuban refugee, discovers that a boy she formerly found contemptible is really attractive, and provides her ailing parent with the support he needs when faced with yet another setback. The weakened invalid finally returns home to recuperate and begin the slow process of rebuilding his life.

Analysis. The Ups and Downs of Jorie Jenkins is a pleasant, lightweight story of a mercurial preteen who reacts to a traumatic family crisis with compassion and increasing maturity. Her exaggerated responses and chatterboxlike commentary are prime elements in the characterization of this perky, admirable, if unmemorable heroine. The easy-to-read story line and amusing dialogue make few demands on the reader, and the inclusion of peripheral events involving admiration for Cuban refugees and criticism of an anti-Japanese attitude solicit endorsement without offering any special insights. Despite a facile style, considerable information about difficulties accompanying the recovery from severe coronary damage, the personality changes that attend this, and the resultant alteration in the lifestyle of both patient and family are presented in an honest and straightforward manner.

Bauer, Marion Dane. *Tangled Butterfly*. New York: Houghton Mifflin, 1980. 162 pp. Reading Level: YA/MA
Disability: Emotional Dysfunction

Prodded by the inner voice she calls Grandmother, Michelle creates a disturbance at the wedding of her beloved brother, Robert. Her mother, adamantly denying that there is anything seriously wrong with her 17-year-old daughter, bundles her off to an island in Lake Superior "for a rest," despite ineffectual hints from her husband that what the girl needs is psychiatric help. Michelle has withdrawn over the years from her unloving mother and uninvolved father into an imaginary world dominated by both the inner voice and her own essence, which she conceptualizes as an embryo. Robert has been the only loving family member, and his imminent departure punctures her already tenuous contact with reality. She no longer seems to act as a rational person but rather like a puppet manipulated by her inner voices.

On the ferry, Michelle's suicidal actions are observed by Paul Dubois, who saves her from drowning. Her rescuer is a former teacher haunted by the memory of another troubled adolescent he was unable to save from self-destruction. He recognizes some of the same kinds of aberrant behavior in this girl. When the hotel where the mother and daughter were to have stayed is discovered closed for the season, Paul invites the two of them to remain at his house temporarily.

Paul is trying to work through his own pain and guilt and find a comfortable identity by returning to the Ojibway customs of some of his ancestors. He begins communicating with Michelle using some of the legends of his forebears and intermittently is encouraged by the positive—or at least temporarily attentive—response from his young guest. The former teacher knows her problems are too complex for him to handle and requests permission to take her to a psychiatrist. Before these arrangements can be made, Michelle stealthily takes Paul's infant daughter and the kitten he gave her to his boat, in which she sails to a lighthouse on another island. Frantic, Paul enlists the help of the Coast Guard and finally tracks them down. To his astonishment, Michelle furiously upbraids him, insisting *he* abandoned her. The man is too exhausted and angry to comprehend that this is a critical moment in Michelle's rehabilitation. The baby is wrestled away from the adolescent, who runs off in the fog. After deliberately releasing a cable car that could have killed him, Michelle, stolidly and with apparent relief, awaits the result of her would-be victim's revenge. He does not give in to her ploy to be punished and instead returns home with her. Robert is waiting to take her to her parents' house, insisting her behavior is part of a "game" she has played since childhood. Paul's wife gathers the worn-out girl into her arms and holds her in their rocking chair. Whimpering, Michelle curls into a tight ball and tries to nurse from the woman's breast. Shocked into realizing how desperately she needs help, Robert pleads: "My God. . . . Do something. Please. She's my sister." The entire family begins counseling sessions, and Michelle begins to travel the road back to a restored sense of self.

Analysis. Bauer is able to give dimensionality to her often very unattractive characters. Although the heroine's mother is cold, unpleasant, and stubborn, the woman's own childhood is seen as contributing heavily to her frigidity in her mother role. Michelle's delusions are an almost inevitable defense against the inadequate behaviors of her parents and the compensatory emotion she invests in her older brother. Needing the support, comfort, and guidance of an adult, she invents one, but in the process loses control over her own actions and substitutes thinking that is immature and magical rather than rational. Paul and his wife are credible characters, and his penchant for attracting troubled youth is forecast in the vision he experienced as part of his initiation into a tribal identity. Michelle, temporarily living with the Ojibway family during her treatment, is called their word for "butterfly." She reflects that such creatures "look delicate, but they're really quite strong. I've read that some of them travel thousands of miles back home again, too, once they leave the cocoon." The only jarring note is struck by the assurance that the child will be functioning sufficiently well to finish high school only "a year late."

Bawden, Nina. *Devil by the Sea*. Philadelphia: Lippincott, 1976. 227 pp. Reading Level: YA/MA
Disability: Orthopedic Impairment, Emotional Dysfunction, auditory impairment

Imaginative, headstrong nine-year-old Hilary and her younger brother, Peregrine, sit next to a menacing old man with "dull, dead eyes" and a "nervous tongue" at a fair. He wears a large, badly fitting coat, bites his nails, and strokes Hilary's knee. When the two observe the strange man go off with a girl who is later reported missing, the boy remembers "what he had seen . . . : the clumsy horror beneath the full concealing coat, the surgical boot, the clubfoot," and announces "He's the Devil. . . . I saw his cloven hoof." When Hilary learns the absent child has been murdered, she is convinced of the accuracy of her brother's assertion and informs her father. Although he initially dismisses this story as nonsense, her father eventually concludes that the mysterious stranger must be the killer. Unfortunately, he dies of a heart attack before he is able to communicate his belief to another adult.

The other members of Hilary's family are weak, petty, and so absorbed with their own pitiful attempts at extracting some pleasures from their sterile lives that they can summon little interest or energy in responding to the terror that has invaded the children's existence. Moreover, the grownups are mindlessly cruel to each other. Hilary's stepmother demeans her husband's aunt: "Aunt Florence would never have heard an intruder; she was deaf as a post. Intractable, old and proud, she refused to admit this failing of her senses. Although for years she had heard no sound but the ringing bells inside her own head." This inability to listen to or even hear each other is commonplace in the household, and the girl's attempts to connect the dead child and the disabled derelict go unheard.

In a terrifying climax at the fair, the suspect, believing that Hilary is responsible for the death of his bird, entices the child to his home. When a policeman intercepts the pair crossing the fields, Hilary, at the outset, declares that her companion is simply a poor old man, but she later discloses, when questioned at the police station, her knowledge about his abduction of the deceased child.

Analysis. The limping stranger is mercilessly treated by Hilary and the other children. Wally, a local youth, attempts to justify participation in the stoning of the victim, claiming, "He's mad. Sometimes, when the moon's full, he barks like a dog. I've heard him." The man, nameless except for the pejorative, "Dotty Jim," which the children use, is a homeless, lonely, cunning outcast, who is assumed to be the devil because of his malformed foot. Bawden uses the man's disability to dramatize his villainy and intensify the impact of his role as a child molester and murderer, not a bad stand-in for the devil. While many of the other characters have physical or behavioral disorders, none are described with the power reserved for the killer. The author skillfully uses other perspectives, typified in the house of mirrors, as people don masks and react, usually basely, to others' impressions of them. Bawden employs language with precision, generates a mood of terror and dread, and designs her novel with great care—superb literary elements that radically contrast with the pernicious bonding of disability and demonism.

Bawden, Nina. *The Robbers.* New York: Lothrop, Lee & Shepard, 1979. 155 pp. Reading Level: MC
Disability: Special Health Problems, visual impairment

Philip has adjusted to living with his grandmother in a castle set aside for the widows of those who gave meritorious service to the Queen of England. The information that his famous but peripatetic father is about to remarry and has sent for him causes the boy considerable dismay. This distress is deepened when Philip learns that what he thought would be only a brief visit is intended to be permanent. The unhappy youngster makes friends with Darcy Jones, a boy he initially mistakes for a burglar. Darcy takes him home to meet his father, now too disabled by arthritis to keep his job as a lockkeeper on the canal. The Joneses live on the ground floor of a decrepit apartment building so that the father can occasionally get out in his wheelchair into the garden. Philip notices "he wasn't as old as he seemed. . . . His fingers were shaky and swollen up at the knuckles but his voice and his eyes were much younger." He observes the responsibility Darcy has accepted in helping his father to the bathroom and offering similar supportive measures.

Philip's father buys some plates in a street market from Darcy's brother, Bing, speculating that the low price probably indicates that the goods were stolen. Philip suggests that if that were true, his parents are criminally implicated through their purchase. His father, embarrassed by the charge, rationalizes his action. When some bullies in Philip's class attack him, Darcy comes to his rescue, thus sealing their budding friendship. Philip invites his new companion to his grandmother's house for a vacation, but Darcy's holiday is cut short when Addie comes to tell her young brother-in-law that Bing has been arrested for allegedly receiving stolen merchandise. The man's detention places a terrible financial burden on his family, and the two youths decide they can help out with the donations they hope to receive from caroling. They sing at the home of a wealthy neighbor, who "rewards" them by showing off her many expensive possessions but gives them only a few pence. Darcy, infuriated at such callous treatment, decides to take something of hers, sell it, and alleviate some of the suffering at home. The plan backfires when an alarm is tripped. In the confusion, Philip has impulsively pocketed a memento, but when this is discovered by the police, he is merely reprimanded. Because Darcy is slightly older and his family circumstances seem less impressive, charges against him are heard in juvenile court. Rescuing Philip from his father's fury at his "unsavory" companions, his grandmother prevents the boy from being exiled to boarding school. She also hopes to arrange a singing career for Darcy with the assistance of her influential friends, so she speaks to Mr. Jones in an attempt to persuade him to permit his son to receive special training. Darcy, however, is determined to remain at home, where he feels he is now desperately needed and can best help his family.

Analysis. Although Philip's grandmother has a vision problem, this impairment is only casually mentioned as part of a general picture of the woman's diminished abilities associated with aging. As Philip explains, "It's when you can see all right, quite sharp and clear, but only a bit, straight ahead. As if you were looking through a telescope or a tunnel. Grandmother says it's like being an old horse with blinkers." Although this may be an indication of impending full vision loss as in retinitis pigmentosa, the woman has accommodated to her condition.

Mr. Jones is likewise developed very sympathetically. His special needs are central to the family's routines, and he is compassionately presented as a proud, intelligent, self-made man. The following incident typifies the matter-of-fact reaction to his infirmity: "His crippled hand shook and he spilled his tea. Addie got up from the piano stool, removed the wet rug from his knees and refilled his cup." When Philip heatedly tells his grandmother that Darcy's father is selfish, she coolly replies: "Being ill and in pain makes you selfish. Unless you're a saint." The father's impairment is presented as just one of the many burdens the family bears: Mrs. Jones has deserted them; Addie, who is intelligent, diligent, and black, can only find work as a domestic; Bing pleads guilty to the charge against him when he learns his incarceration awaiting trial on a not guilty plea would be longer than the sentence he would receive by falsely denying his innocence. Bawden has done an excellent job of depicting the conflicts of the disabled characters and the naive hero, dramatizing the varying and unequal options available to members of differing social and economic classes. The simplicity of the unadorned title hints at the multiple meanings of theft examined in the novel.

Beckman, Gunnel. *That Early Spring*. Originally published in Stockholm by Albert Bonniers Forlag, 1974. Trans. by Joan Tate. New York: Viking, 1977. 121 pp. Reading Level: MA
Disability: Special Health Problems

Mia's parents are separating, and it appears to her that a divorce is highly probable. The 17 year old remains in the family apartment with her father while her mother and younger sister move elsewhere. Mia learns that a girl friend is about to get married because she is pregnant. Recalling her own feelings when she and her boyfriend, Jan, anxiously waited to learn if she, too, were pregnant and her subsequent anger, then confusion, about their relationship, Mia is relieved at avoiding such a fate for herself.

The girl appeals to her father to bring her grandmother from the nursing home to live with them. Against her physician's advice, the elderly woman decides to accept the invitation in order to be where someone wants her. Although Mia and her father are concerned about the woman's heart condition, Gran minimizes her problems and soon becomes an important and valued person in the household. Once, coming home late from a date, Mia notices her grandmother's light on, the old woman's voice sounding "like a rattling whisper . . . her face . . . white as paper, a whiteness Mia had never seen in her life before." The frightened girl observes that pain in the woman's "chest and down her back and arm was making Gran twist as if she had a cramp." Medication relieves the pain; soon her groaning and heavy breathing subside and she slowly regains color in her cheeks. Sitting at her bedside, Mia speaks to her grandmother of life and death, a conversation that affords much relief to the sick woman and a sense of her roots and purpose to the adolescent.

Mia, now 18, is astonished and flattered when Martin, a handsome young man whom she admires, invites her to his apartment. Even though she is now using contraceptives, the hesitant girl makes excuses to avoid intimacy with him. She brings some school friends, who are working on a report on woman's role in society, to her apartment, where her grandmother, once an activist, offers an interesting historical perspective to their discussion. Subsequently, she and her granddaughter examine the changes in their lives and discuss women's evolving roles in education and politics. When Mia sees Martin again and speaks of her need for a fuller emotional life in addition to their purely physical relationship, he backs off in alarm, and she realizes their relationship will never be more than a sexual alliance. Mia's new-found sense of equanimity is shattered when she discovers her grandmother on the floor in terrible pain. Nitroglycerine is ineffective this time, and an anguished call to the doctors results in a hurried call for an ambulance. The pain is excruciating, and the damage to her heart too severe. With the two women holding hands, Gran dies. When the hurt begins to fade, Mia is able to acknowledge how much the relationship has meant to her by helping her growth in self-understanding.

Analysis. That Early Spring functions less as a story of a young girl coming of age than as an endorsement of the woman's liberation movement and a condemnation of casual sexual encounters unencumbered by commitment or responsibility. Mia's adolescent turmoil seems predictable and mechanical, although her behavior with her infirm relative shows some real warmth. The older woman, fully aware of her dangerous, potentially fatal ailment, prefers to risk an early death with her family rather than endure a lingering, unfulfilling life in an institution. The story is honest and realistic, although only sporadically involving.

Beckwith, Lillian. *The Spuddy*. Originally published in England by Hutchinson, 1974. New York: Dell, 1976 (rev.). 118 pp. Reading Level: MC/YA
Disability: Speech Impairment, Emotional Dysfunction

Abandoned by his mother and unable to be cared for by his seaman father, eight-year-old Andy goes to live with his aunt and uncle in a bustling fishing village. "When people first saw Andy they tended to exclaim admiringly: 'That's a grandlooking boy!' but when they realized he could not speak they would add: 'Ach, the poor thing's a dummy!'. . . From the time he had been able to understand the speech of adults and become aware of his own affliction, he had begun to feel excluded even from his own parents."

The boy discovers an abandoned dog at his new home, and the two outcasts become close companions. A lonely fishing skipper, down on his luck, allows Spuddy to become the ship's mascot, and the dog's skill in spotting schools of fish reverses the bad fortunes of the crew.

Andy is also allowed on board for brief periods and dreams of becoming a sailor like his father. On one occasion, the ship's crew go ashore to attend a wedding, taking Andy with them. The captain and mascot, left on board, are caught in a blizzard during which the craft is destroyed. When Andy learns that both his friend and his dog have died, in his grief he speaks for the first time in his life, calling out "no, no" repeatedly.

Analysis. The Spuddy begins as an excessively romanticized, sentimental, unexceptional dog story. Its conclusion, however, is mindlessly brutal, lacking either foreshadowing or logic to give it some semblance of literary plausibility. There are no explanations or even hints of physical or psychological trauma that would justify the central character's muteness. Rather, his inability to speak seems merely a device, like his "orphan" status, to promote pity.

Bethancourt, T. Ernesto (pseud. for Thomas Paisley). *The Dog Days of Arthur Cane.* New York: Holiday House, 1976. 160 pp. Reading Level: YA
Disability: Visual Impairment

After disparaging the beliefs of an African student at a beer party, Arthur is warned that there are consequences for mocking the religion of others. He is bewildered by this response to his comments, which were uttered more from the adolescent need to contradict than from deliberate malicious intent. The next morning, Arthur awakens to find himself inhabiting the body of "the saddest, most raggedy-looking" mongrel dog. Unrecognized by his family, he is "hounded" out of his home, narrowly escapes capture by the dreaded dogcatcher, managing just in time to catch a ride surreptitiously on a truck, which takes him from his home on Long Island to Greenwich Village. In his new guise, Arthur finds street life intriguing, develops a scam to scavenge food, and prepares himself for adventure. He makes friends with Tyree, a presumably blind guitarist, and soon takes on the function of a guide dog, an assistant, and a protector of the money his new associate collects at street performances. The musician takes his newly adopted pet home, where the dog is startled to observe:

> Tyree went over to the kitchen part of the big room and sat down at the table. The overhead lamp, when he pulled out the cord, turned out to be super bright. As I watched in amazement, he took off his heavy sunglasses. He reached into the table drawer and took out a pair of clear, thick-lensed glasses. He put them on and emptied his pockets of the money he'd made. Then under the

strong light, with his face very close to the bills, he began to examine the paper money he'd collected in the park. He could see!

Later, to his great relief, Arthur realizes the dark glasses are not a fraud and Tyree's vision is very limited. For his part, the guitarist is delighted with the fortuitous appearance of the dog since the animal's intelligence has upped his income dramatically, bringing the day closer when he will have enough money for an operation on his eyes. Unfortunately, the companions get separated one day on the subway, and after being hit by a car, having his identifying collar stolen, and being almost fatally poisoned, the weakened canine crawls onto a train. He is relieved to discover that he is on the Long Island Railroad, heading back to familiar haunts. But when he climbs out at his station, he is immediately taken by dogcatchers. At the pound, he is tenderly nursed by Finney, a student veterinarian, who conjures up religious thoughts in the dog's befuddled mind. When Arthur learns he is slated for death, he begins to reflect on his short, misspent life, regretting his callowness and insensitivity. Just as he is about to be gassed, he unexpectedly returns to human form. Nobody, of course, believes his bizarre story, and he is packed off to a psychiatrist for "help." Returning to the city one day, he discovers that Tyree's operation has been successful and the happy former musician has returned to his preferred profession as a street artist. Obviously unable to explain his past relationship to the man, Arthur buys a picture of himself as a dog that Tyree had painted based on the descriptions of friends and his deductions from his sense of touch.

Analysis. The witty and clever narrative, the marvelous evocation of the more beneficent aspects of Village ambiance, and the original and engrossing plot make this an enjoyable work, despite such deficiencies as a simplistic representation of tribal beliefs, unclear religious allusions, and the inclusion of some stereotypical minor characters. Tyree is portrayed in a very positive light; he is intelligent, realistic, calm, and mature. Arthur, in dog form, perceptively observes the reactions of sighted people toward his friend:

> It seems that normal people are perfectly willing to be entertained by a blind person, so long as he stays apart from them. As soon as he talks or tries to relate to them, they take off. I think that secretly, they feel guilty about being able to see. They realize that the blind performer isn't just a curiosity, but a real person like themselves who isn't as lucky. It makes them uncomfortable to think that they, too, could be blind.

Readers may well recognize such responses in themselves or others.

Bethancourt, T. Ernesto (pseud. for Thomas Paisley). *Doris Fein: Phantom of the Casino.* New York: Holiday House, 1981. 160 pp.
Reading Level: YA
Disability: Emotional Dysfunction, Neurological Impairment

Doris Fein, an 18-year-old detective, and her friend, Carl Suzuki, a New York City policeman, accompany Harry Grubb on his elegant yacht to a small island off the California coast. There they meet Helen Grayson, Doris's former piano teacher, to whom Harry is immediately and immoderately attracted. Not put off by the aftereffects of her mild stroke, Harry begins an old-fashioned courtship. That evening, when Doris and Carl visit the casino, a huge reflector ball falls to the dance floor, slightly injuring a patron. Carl takes charge but is soon relieved by the local sheriff, who gratefully accepts the outsider's help. The investigation reveals this seeming accident is only the latest in a series aimed at sabotaging the dance hall. Harry suggests that these destructive acts may be the work of the sheriff, whose background appears suspect. After the murder of the lawman's daughter, he was involved in several violent encounters with minority youth and left his former employment under a cloud of suspicion. But Carl defends the man, claiming the case against him is far from conclusive. Doris, finding a clue that arouses her suspicion, returns to Helen's house, where she is discovered by her former teacher, who is strangely dressed and wearing a blond wig. Helen claims she is Gracie Downs, a jazz pianist who, because she was a woman, could not get a job in the 1940s with a name band. She tells Doris she became pregnant by a famous bandleader but was ultimately forced to give up her child and has since that time nursed a deep resentment. Helen forces Doris at gunpoint to return with her to the casino, which she intends to destroy. The astute young detective tricks her captor into playing a final concert in the ballroom, after which the emotionally drained woman resumes her other docile identity and collapses as Carl and the sheriff make their presence known. She is hospitalized, but the prognosis is excellent. Harry informs his friends that the doctor is optimistic and reports: "Oddly enough, that last concert she did was highly therapeutic." Carl proposes marriage to Doris, but she declines, explaining she is too young to marry; she must first find herself and not risk the consequences of being stultified like poor Helen.

Analysis. Helen's neurological disorder does not stand in the way of her characterization as an attractive person. Even after Harry learns of her psychiatric history, his emotional support and involvement are undiminished. When Helen walks, she uses a cane and drags one leg, although sometimes she employs a motorized chair. A regimen of walking and practicing the piano appear to have strengthened her considerably. However, even given the success of her rehabilitation efforts, it seems unlikely that a 60-year-old woman could have accomplished all of the strenuous tasks attributed to the "phantom." Her physician, evidently basing his assessment more on fictional necessity than medical probability, expresses unwarranted optimism for the woman's recovery from her delusional behavior.

This juvenile detective parody is indebted to Carolyn Keene, Dashiel Hammett, and Ian Fleming. The writing is smooth, sharp, and contemporary, but the comic book psychology is exploitive, allowing an unimaginative resolution of the mystery.

Bethancourt, T. Ernesto (pseud. for Thomas Paisley). *Nightmare Town*. New York: Holiday House, 1979. 158 pp. Reading Level: YA
Disability: Cosmetic Impairment; also orthopedic impairment, visual impairment, special health problems

Jimmy Hunter, running away from the abusive uncle with whom he lives, hitches a ride with the Gaynor family. Their car develops trouble as they cross the desert. Mr. Gaynor loses control when the vehicle hits an obstacle and catapults through the air. Jimmy awakens in the cabin of a former physician, Karl Horstman, who now lives as a recluse. The slightly injured boy is informed that the two adults died. Liz, their daughter, is being held prisoner by some religious fanatics in an isolated, self-contained community nearby. All the members of this cult are severely deformed, a result, Jimmy's host presumes, of generations of inbreeding. Horstman convinces the boy that no help can be expected from the authorities and that he will not become involved either. If the girl is to be rescued, Jimmy deduces, he is her only hope. Determined to save her, the still not fully recovered youth sneaks into the town, but he is captured by the zealots, who intend to put him to death.

Despite his earlier disclaimers, Horstman enters the town and frees the captive youth. They surreptitiously gain entrance to a lead mine where a ceremony inducting Liz into the cult is taking place. Jimmy is frantic when he realizes the girl will be forced to marry the son of their leader. He is restrained from revealing his whereabouts by his mentor, who leads him on an exploration of the religious sanctuary after the members leave. They discover a spaceship that is leaking radiation, presumably a contributing cause of the innumerable deformities to which the townspeople are subject. Just as the two intruders are about to leave, they are discovered. Interrupting their capture is a gigantic explosion, after which a dazed Jimmy wanders in the desert until he is picked up near a highway and taken to a hospital. When he regains consciousness, he learns that there was an atomic blast, but Karl and Liz have survived. The girl is badly burned and has lost vision in one eye. Karl reports: "She's been disfigured, and she doesn't want anyone to see her. Least of all you." The indignant youth refuses to be put off, calls her, insists her injuries do not matter to him, and announces that he loves her.

Analysis. The extreme deformities endured by the characters in the story are posited as the consequences of exposure to both a stagnant gene pool and heavy doses of radiation. The hideous demeanor they present adds an extra dimension to the revulsion the heroes feel toward them. Paradoxically, this tying of external appearance and internal corruption is negated when the heroine, although disfigured, retains her appeal. In effect, the author of this science fiction tale has it both ways: a distorted appearance is repellent when coupled with evil; it is irrelevant when tied to goodness.

Blue, Rose. *Me and Einstein: Breaking through the Reading Barrier.* Illus. by Peggy Luks. New York: Human Sciences Press, 1979. 60 pp. Reading Level: MC
Disability: Learning Disability

Through various subterfuges, Bobby has managed to conceal his inability to read. The boy's excellent memory allows him to fake his way through many situations. When his usual coping techniques fail, he cleverly falls back on creating diversions, successfully deflecting attention of teachers and family away from his deficiencies. His fourth-grade teacher shrewdly sees through his tactics and, realizing Bobby has unaddressed needs, sends him to a special class that, unfortunately, is neither structured nor demanding. Miserable in this new placement, the frustrated boy runs away. His parents finally consult a psychologist and have him tested, discovering that he is dyslexic. The boy enters a special school, where he finds help in remediating his learning disability. During the course of a class singalong, instantaneous enlightenment occurs: "Then, suddenly, all at once, as Bobby stared at the page, the funny squiggles he had seen all his life turned into letters, real letters, and the letters came together and made words."

Analysis. The subtitle clues the reader that the work will be didactic, and, in fact, it wears only a thin fictional veneer. The author's definition of dyslexia as "a condition that gives a youngster trouble focusing on symbols on a printed page" is simultaneously inadequate, misleading, and inaccurate. The impression generated that the skills needed for comprehending reading matter come together in a flash of insight, after which this problem vanishes, is without foundation. Further, it is hard to believe that simply citing names of Albert Einstein, Woodrow Wilson, Winston Churchill, Nelson Rockefeller, and General Patton (some of whose accomplishments will be known to some adults but are unlikely to all be familiar to many nine year olds) would inspire pride of association in an elementary school child. However, the emotions of a child with learning disabilities, the sense of isolation, and the feelings of frustration and inadequacy that often accompany this syndrome are effectively communicated. Also, common strategies that a desperate child might resort to for dealing with the discrepancy between familial and school expectations and actual performance are honestly depicted.

Characterizations, however, are weak and unconvincing: the young hero is lackluster, while others tend to be unidimensional. The title is not the only ungrammatical aspect of the book: the narration unjustifiably shifts between second and third person, and such careless constructions as "Everybody raised their hand" can be found. Illustrations are unsophisticated, uninformative, and amateurish.

Bødker, Cecil. *Silas and Ben-Godik.* Originally published, in Danish by Branner og Korch, Copenhagen, as *Silas og Ben-Godik,* 1969. Trans. by Sheila La Farge. New York: Delacorte, 1978. 191 pp. Reading Level: MC
Disability: Orthopedic Impairment, visual impairment

In this sequel to *Silas and the Black Mare* (see following annotation), the enterprising and impetuous Silas and his more stable, less daring companion, Ben-Godik, seek their fortunes. The two find shelter in the loft of a woman who pretends to be deaf. Soon after discovering that she is a member of a gang of thieves, they leave her home, rescue a kidnapped boy, calm an angered and abused captive bear, outwit some robbers, and escape from a jail, finally returning to Ben-Godik's home. There they discover that Ben-Godik now has a stepfather who has also adopted Maria, a girl blind since birth.

Analysis. Ben-Godik's physical impairment provides some modest complications in the boys' adventures but does not play a major role in the story. The youngster is portrayed as a contributor to the duo's fortunes because of his good sense and money-making skills and as a stabilizing influence on his reckless, albeit admirable friend. The "deaf" woman is not really hearing impaired but uses this hoax as a disguise to get her way and conceal her nefarious deeds. Maria appears only in the last scene, in which her confidence and competence are evident. Moving from a cruel, exploitive home to a warm accepting one has outwardly transformed her, to the surprise of one of the returned travelers: "Silas walked silently over and sat down by the wall of the house again with a strange feeling that something was quite different from what he had imagined. And Ben-Godik had known it all along." Although not as engaging as the other two titles in this trilogy, this story nevertheless reaffirms Bødker's status as an outstanding writer of juvenile fiction.

Bødker, Cecil. *Silas and the Black Mare.* Originally published by Branner og Korch, Copenhagen, as *Silas og den sorte hoppe,* 1967. Trans. by Sheila La Farge. New York: Delacorte, 1978. 152 pp. Reading Level: MC
Disability: Orthopedic Impairment, visual impairment

When his mother, a performing acrobat, shows that she considers the sword swallower more important than her son, Silas runs away to fend for himself. The confident, quick-witted boy encounters a greedy horse dealer, Bartolin, and in the course of their abrasive conversations a rash bet is made: if the lad cannot ride the man's untamed black mare, he will serve without pay as stableboy; if he can, the mare is his to keep. Bartolin is astonished at the boy's success and tries to renege on their wager. The wily youth plays his flute, so agitating the other horses in the stable that the dealer is forced to give in. The boy's victory is short-lived, for Silas is soon defrauded of his animal and, after his drink is drugged, set adrift in a leaky boat. Upon awakening, he tries to take the milk from a milkmaid's pail but is diverted when he observes that the child cannot see. He tells Maria's harsh parents: "The sword swallower would like to buy Maria" since "it's her special way of being blind that matters. All she would have to do is go around in the crowd looking for her eyes. . . . Everyone can see that she's lost them, so they'll put money in the holes to comfort her . . . silver coins." Later that night, the furious girl tries to filch his flute and even considers killing him.

After leaving the village, Silas sees a passing peddler on whose wagon he tries to sneak a ride. The hysterical man assumes the boy is part of a gang of thieves and whips him, forcing him to fall from the speeding wagon. Following an uneasy rest, he awakens to find a cowherd, Ben-Godik, watching him. Injured from his fall, Silas painfully limps after his new companion, who turns on him, angrily accusing the stranger of mockery: "All the others insult me about my leg. . . . They're always running after me, laughing and fake-limping. I have a foot that's turned the wrong way and it isn't even a real foot. I was born with it." Ben-Godik confides that he hoped to become an apprentice smith or a wood carver when his father died, but the town citizens pressured the local craftspeople against the move, complaining "who else would look after their cows? No one else could be bothered to sit out there all day staring into space." The boy informs Silas that his stolen horse will be sold the next day and conceals him in a large tree overlooking the auction site. The waiting youth observes and hears a strange series of exchanges about buying and selling people and property, conversations that reveal the love, concern, avarice, lust, pride, and respect that motivates the villagers. Bartolin is enraged at the proceedings, insisting he is the true owner of the animal and tries especially to discourage the hunter, his rival in his pursuit of Ben-Godik's widowed mother, from bidding on the mare. With the connivance of the hunter, Silas jumps from the trees to the back of the mare and successfully confronts the peddler who whipped him and the man who abandoned him in the river. The intrepid youngster leaves the town astride his horse with Ben-Godik, who tells Maria that the kindly hunter would give her a good home and take care of her.

Analysis. Silas and the Black Mare is a fine example of contemporary juvenile fiction. The author's subject matter is both timeless and topical, and her style is masterful. Characterization and dialogue are skillfully managed, but the author's creation and sustaining of tension and the establishment of the appropriate mood are most impressive. The scenes of isolation and stark poverty in which impairment complicates the struggle for survival are particularly effective. The disabled boy is shown to compensate well for his physical limitations and to outwit partially those who would attempt to dominate and control him. Maria is not well developed, and although her anger is apparent, her attempt on Silas's life is unconvincing. Her suggested exploitation as an object of pity by Silas indicates a credible lack of sympathy on one level but a concern that she not be abandoned or left with uncaring adults on another level. Maria is capable of milking cows and climbing a hayloft unaided, but she is shown as essentially fearful and dependent. The abuse she endures is not markedly different from that of other impoverished girls in those harsh, grim times. The overly abrupt ending is partially compensated for by the hint of a sequel involving the two boys (see preceding annotation).

Bødker, Cecil. *Silas and the Runaway Coach.* Originally published by Branner og Korch, Copenhagen, as *Silas Fanger et Firspand*, 1976. Trans. by Sheila La Farge. New York: Delacorte, 1978. 245 pp.
Reading Level: MC
Disability: Orthopedic Impairment

The sight of a carriage out of control electrifies Silas, and instinctively he urges his black mare after it. The intrepid lad, oblivious to his own safety, with much difficulty brings the frenzied team to a stand-still. Mr. Planke, a wealthy merchant, is grateful to Silas for saving his carriage and its occupants and makes numerous generous offers to the hero, all of which seem excessive from the boy's viewpoint. Pressed, the youth agrees to stay temporarily at the Planke home, where he compares his freedom and lifestyle to Japetus Planke, a boy slightly younger than he but not nearly as worldly or carefree. The youth takes Silas on a tour through the town during which the raw country boy is amazed at the sights and awed at the sound of the organ welling up through the cathedral. His wish to explore the waterfront thoroughly prompts Silas to agree to stay with his would-be benefactors, a decision that delights Japetus. The two youths, one eager, the other worried, set out to satisfy Silas's curiosity about the barges. On one, Silas recog-nizes an old enemy, the Horse Crone, who employs Valerian, "a tiny little man . . . yet surely just as old in years as the big bony woman who ordered him around" to manage a dancing bear she owns. The villain tricks the boys, trusses them up, and searches for their coins, while, in the confusion, their horses are stolen. Fortunately for the youths, the dwarf has a kindly nature and allows his prisoners to escape.

Although now safe, Silas chafes at the loss of his mounts. In his old clothes, he makes contact with some street urchins, hoping to ferret out useful information that would help recover the stolen prop-erty. When Silas learns that the animals are being hidden on the Bone-breaker property, the ingenious lad asks Planke for some cash, slips down to Bonebreaker's yard, and sets the scene for the rescue. With the help of Japetus, Valerian, and another servant, Silas recovers the purloined animals. Equally cleverly, he convinces the townsfolk to ban-ish the Horse Crone. As the barge moves down the river, Silas is reminded of his own itch to travel. Although interested primarily in fun and adventure, the irrepressible hero has found more legitimate employment for Valerian and has loosened the oppressive hold that the merchant Planke has had on his too-sheltered son.

Analysis. Bødker has shown again that she is a first-rate storyteller in this continuation of the adventures of her sanguine hero. Her plots are filled with excitement, and her characters, although developed with a notable absence of subtlety, are original and memorable. Valerian comments on how difficult it is for one in his circumstances to obtain employment and rationalizes his work for the wicked Horse Crone: "Soon I will be an old man. I have to earn the necessities of life in one way or another and she is the only person who will have me." He adds, "I have to be careful because of my appearance. People find fault with me terribly easily, assuming that I am not a real person. They prefer to think of me as some kind of animal." Mr. Bonebreaker is aptly named since his brittle bones have repeatedly fractured. As a consequence, his legs are crooked, he is shorter than his natural growth would have dictated, he limps and frequently falls. He is treated contemptuously by his wife and apparently shares this low opinion of himself, a status more the result of weak character than of disability.

Bonham, Frank. *Gimme an H, Gimme an E, Gimme an L, Gimme a P.* New York: Scribner's, 1980. 210 pp. Reading Level: YA
Disability: Emotional Dysfunction

Dana, still in high school, has a small but lucrative business breeding and selling exotic birds. He and Katie, a newcomer to the school and also his lab partner, are attracted to each other. The girl is tormented by profound emotional problems, but she disguises her feelings and appears to be hostile. In addition to teasing the puzzled youth, Katie places fraudulent ads in the newspaper offering rare birds at ridiculously low prices. When Dana calls in response to the ads, she poses as a foreigner and gives him preposterous explanations for the absurdly low costs. She desperately hopes he will find and confront her, thus giving her an opportunity to share her fears and anxieties with him.

Katie frequently succumbs to fantasies in which she is killed and her mother appears, expressing regret at having abandoned her. Katie now lives with her weak and ineffectual father and her neurotic rejecting stepmother, who favors her own son, nicknamed Cutepig. One of the teachers is concerned about Katie's behavior and enlists Dana's help in saving her from suicide. In an outrageously unprofessional conversation, Mrs. Allen describes the girl as "on a collision course," reporting that she learned from a staff member at her former school that the girl had been in two one-car accidents. The woman encourages Dana to ask for a date so he can begin the search for "the truth about Katie Norman." Eager to help, he invites the troubled girl to the beach, where she is caught in a riptide and almost drowns. Rescued by a lifeguard, she recovers enough to return home, where her stepmother accuses her of grandstanding.

Dana discovers that Katie placed ads for the birds, resulting in a considerable loss of income for him and indirectly the death of an uncommon and valuable bird it had taken him years to breed. She admits it was a deliberate, although foolish, cry for help and subsequently tries to overdose on pills and alcohol. Her father is out of town, and Mrs. Norman, outraged, threatens the girl with "a foster home, a parolee house—a nuthouse, maybe. Or electroshock." Dana again tries to help his girl friend and arranges a date at a swimming pool where they will be alone. Katie begins to confide in him but becomes frightened and deliberately precipitates a mild sexual encounter, which she uses as an excuse to end the evening. She drives off alone, heading into the hills. Mrs. Allen calls Dana and warns him of the danger Katie is in, encouraging the boy to search for the missing youngster and talk her out of committing suicide. She suggests: "There are always alternatives to suicide. . . . How about going to the desert, staying at a motel, and pointing out her anxieties? Maybe she'll feel different after some time alone. Or she could insist that her father put her in a boarding school. Or dye her hair red." The distraught boy manages to locate her, persuading her to return to Mrs. Allen's home and seek counseling.

Analysis. Bonham's thesis that even bright and attractive people can have severe emotional problems is presented in a banal formulation: "The suicidal cheerleader? . . . It's a contradiction in terms." The designation of the origins of emotional problems, their manifestation, and the ease with which they are remediated are naive and grossly misleading. The teacher claims great success with preventing suicides, apparently using a relatively novel approach: henna therapy. Describing youngsters who are ready to take their own lives, she asserts: "They're scared and hopeless. They leave clues lying around telling us that they've got problems, hoping somebody will intervene. I've tried, and usually succeeded, when I've come across their clues." The author uses concrete imagery ("The circuitry in her mind slipped channels." "He had driven her like a truck, and she was a formula racing car.") without accuracy or restraint. Outsize print, superficially attractive characters, and an endless string of melodramatic events make this a fast and easy reading experience. It is also free of any serious insights into a profound and tragic problem.

Bova, Ben. *City of Darkness.* New York: Scribner's, 1976. 150 pp.
Reading Level: YA
Disability: Visual Impairment

It is sometime in the future, and Ron Morgan has passed exams that will determine his destiny. Angered at his father's insistence that he enter a business school instead of studying science, Ron runs away to New York City, an area off limits except for the summer season. Exhilarated by the excitement there, he is picked up by a young woman and the two are accosted by a gang of toughs on the way to the hotel. When one, Dino, pulls a knife, Ron beats him in the ensuing brawl, escaping with Sylvia. The next morning, he awakens to find she has gone and he races out of the hotel after her, where he is ambushed by Dino and some friends, who steal his clothes and belongings. Sylvia ultimately returns to take him home, promising that Al, the gang leader, will help them, but Al reveals that it was Sylvia who stole his money. The naive boy at last realizes he was set up but nonetheless accepts Al's directions to get out of the city. It is imperative that he leave immediately, or, according to the rules, he will be locked in for the winter. Sylvia stops him just before he departs, explaining that if the police find him without any identification, he will be imprisoned for life. Trapped, Ron joins Al's gang, soon becoming a valued member, keeping their equipment and weapons in excellent repair—an important role considering the scarcity of tools and replaceable parts.

The city is filled with gang warfare. Initial attempts at achieving a truce are aided by Ron, who is traded out to various groups in an effort to cool tensions. During a time of trouble he is sheltered by Dewey, an older man, one of the few adults remaining in the city. Some blacks, the first Ron has ever seen, have taken over the market, patrolling the area with guns. Dewey tells Ron to remain the night since a white youth would not be safe on the streets. The two climb ten flights to the older man's apartment, which is protected against intruders by numerous booby traps. Dewey, who is losing his sight, calmly predicts he will be blind within a year. He lives in relative luxury in his aerie, and Ron, who is never free from hunger, wants to accept the man's offer to remain there as his assistant. He returns to the gang to arrange this, but Al refuses to let him go. There is an ambush led by Dino, and most of the members of Al's gang are killed except for Ron, Sylvia, and her son, Davey. Ron steals away to Dewey for help and returns after three days to find Dino has taken Sylvia away and Davey is dead. Ron is captured and marked for death but is rescued by some black youths dispatched by Dewey. The leader of the blacks keeps Ron as a slave, exploiting the boy's mechanical skills and obliging him to teach them to younger black children. His captor reveals his intention to unite the whole city under his leadership and then attack the outside world. Sylvia is allowed to visit him, bringing news that Dino is dead and returning Ron's identity papers. Ron escapes and is about to return to the outside world when he is confronted by Timmy Jim, the black leader, who says he will permit Ron to go since no one will believe him if he reveals Timmy Jim's plans. Ron says his intent is not to reveal any plans but to return and force the complacent community to acknowledge the brutal system they have allowed to develop and force its abandonment for a more humane one.

Analysis. Dewey is an entirely sympathetic character. It is not clear what literary purpose his blindness serves unless it justifies his need for Ron to assume some of his responsibilities. His age would seem to be sufficient for this, however. He is an honorable and generally adequate person. Despite his disability, he is able to respond to and use people and conditions in a lawless, life-endangering society. The story is a heavy-handed morality tale with obvious references to the brutalizing effects of the ghetto from which escape is impossible and in which ubiquitous corruption is inevitable.

Bradford, Ann, and Kal Gezi. *The Mystery of the Midget Clown.* Illus. by Mina McLean. Elgin, Ill.: Child's World, 1980. 32 pp. Reading Level: YC
Disability: Orthopedic Impairment

While pretending to be explorers, five young friends discover a cave on the outskirts of town. Two children agree to bring flashlights to probe the dark interior the following day. On the way home, they excitedly observe circus equipment and are startled by a greeting: "The voice surprised them. They looked around and saw a man who was shorter than they were! He was dressed in a pair of jeans and a T-shirt that said 'Midway Circus.' He had a mustache and a deep voice. 'Surprised?' asked the man. 'I'm Steve, the midget. I'm a clown.' "

After inviting them to attend the show, Steve chats with them about their dusty appearance, becoming very agitated upon hearing about the nearby cave. Despite the clown's warning, the youngsters resume their adventure, elated to find a tunnel extending back from the entrance. They return in time for the performance and learn the usually reliable Steve is late. His friend Joe tells them that the former circus strong man, reputed to have owned a treasure chest, left the company "after it played here." Following Steve's second disappearance, the children return to the cave, hear moans, and ultimately find the missing man, who tells them, "I think I broke my leg." Once the limb is set, the patient explains that he thought his former associate might have hidden the chest in the cave. The youngsters report how they deduced his whereabouts, and in gratitude the circus manager invites them to join the circus temporarily and push Steve, dressed in his clown costume, in his wheelchair.

Analysis. This seemingly pointless work offers little interest and less mystery despite the title. The inclusion of a midget clown serves no particular purpose but does offer some mild reinforcement of the idea that exceptionality is appropriately displayed in a circus setting.

Brancato, Robin. *Winning*. New York: Knopf, 1977. 211 pp. Reading Level: YA/MA

Disability: Neurological Impairment, orthopedic impairment

Gary's spinal cord is injured during a football game, resulting in quadriplegia. During his first days in the hospital, the 17 year old is unaware of his prognosis: "At first it had been an ego trip having so many people come up. But after they'd seen him, some kids didn't know what to say. One group had ignored him, had just joked with one another as if it was a not-very-sad funeral and he was the dead guy. . . . Coach Hammer kept glancing away so he wouldn't have to look at the tongs, maybe?" When the boy begins to recover, arrangements are made to tutor him. His parents are reluctant to permit his doctor to tell Gary that he will never walk again, but Ann Treer, his English teacher, persuades them that their dissembling is more damaging to his morale than the truth would be. Both parents, but particularly his mother, have become suffocatingly protective. His relationship with his girl friend becomes strained as she searches for a suitable role, and he, through fear of rejection governed by a lifelong habit of keeping his feelings to himself, becomes increasingly bitter and uncommunicative.

Gary's irrepressible roommate, injured in a motorcycle accident, precedes him to Phillips Rehabilitation Institute, where they both continue therapy and learn self-management and vocational skills. Gary observes the various ways the other patients cope or fail to cope with their disabilities. One young man, rejected by his family, commits suicide; one, abandoned by his wife, suffers a brief setback but pulls his life together. Gary is depressed and discouraged and briefly considers taking his own life, but with the help of Ann Treer, and calling on the discipline and fortitude he displayed on the gridiron, decides he really has much to live for.

Analysis. The story moves quickly, and the characters, although not well developed, are appealing and involving. Readers will find considerable information about the myriad medical, rehabilitative, and adjustment problems in this single-focus work. The responses of teachers, friends, family, and therapists exhibit the gamut of probable reactions, including supportive, avoidance, and accepting responses. Sudden catastrophic trauma is posited as a complex problem, not only for the injured person, but for family and friends, as all concerned must learn new behaviors and adjust expectations. The author's emphasis on the overriding importance of attitude and emotional strength suggests that the youth's loss of physical control will ultimately be accepted. Gary is seen as having once been a determined player on the football field whose battles with his body and his future will now be even more arduous.

Branscum, Robbie. *For Love of Jody.* New York: Lothrop, Lee & Shepard, 1979. 111 pp. Reading Level: MC
Disability: Intellectual Impairment

Drought is devastating Arkansas farms, exacerbating the effects of the Depression. The future looks bleak for Frankie and her family, whose hard labor barely keeps them at subsistence level. Her parents frequently argue about her younger sister:

> I thought Pa was right about sending Jody away, though some-
> times the idea of Jody being with strange folks who didn't know
> her made me twist up, all sick-like. I know good and well Jody
> couldn't help being the way she was. I mean, when she was born
> Pa couldn't get the doctor in time and Jody was sorta messed up.
> Her body growed but her mind didn't. She was most tall as me
> now, but she was fat, soft fat, like a baby. And it nigh made me
> sick to clean her, 'cause though she was ten years old, she didn't
> even know how to use the outhouse.

The older girl knows that Jody inadvertently killed some baby animals, but Pa has advised Frankie not to distress her mother with this information since the woman is becoming increasingly anxious and irritable as the birth of a new baby nears. Aunt Bonnie and cousin Tad Lee come to stay with them, providing help with the field and house-work and moral support for the beleaguered family. Tad Lee, having matured considerably since the time when he used to tease and tor-ment his cousin, suggests to Frankie that it may be possible to devise ways in which to teach Jody some self-help skills. Pa is dubious, re-vealing that the doctor predicted Jody would probably behave like a two year old all her life. The youngsters are determined to try, how-ever, and Frankie is so encouraged when her diet management efforts result in the loss of "baby fat" by her sister that she begins a regimen of toilet training. In the middle of a sandstorm, Jody wanders off and Ma begins her contractions. Frankie and Tad Lee locate the frightened child and bring her back to shelter, while in the meantime, to every-one's relief, a healthy boy is born. Tad Lee helps his cousin sort out her antagonistic feelings toward her mother and sister. She concludes: "There was no doubt at all in my mind that I was crazy as a bedbug. For, all of a sudden, my dislike for Jody had turned to pure love."

Worried that Jody may be a danger to the new baby, everyone tries to make sure that the two are never alone, but despite their precautions, the girl, momentarily unsupervised, takes her infant brother from the house. They are discovered by Frankie and Pa, who rescue the baby unharmed. Hysterical, Ma screams at her older daughter, accusing her of willful negligence. The girl's fear that she is unloved is confirmed, and she promises to leave home. Plaintively she asks: "Why do you hate me, Ma? Is it 'cause I'm not like Jody? Do I have to be not right in the head fer ye to get me ribbons fer my hair, too?" At last Pa intrudes, explaining to his wife how Frankie has been protecting them. The mother and her older daughter are reconciled as the woman admits her guilt and frustration over Jody and over her inability to penetrate Frankie's self-protective and self-imposed isolation. Admitting to her ambivalence, she says they may someday have to decide to send Jody to an institution far from home, but they all affirm that such a decision will be based on Jody's best interests.

Analysis. The tremendous pressures that a family with a profoundly retarded child experience are compassionately chronicled in this work. With neither help nor guidance from doctors nor social agencies, caring for and educating their daughter has become the exclusive responsibility of her parents. Ambivalent emotions—love, shame, guilt, tenderness, pride, jealousy, and fear—are combined in the responses of family members. The child is seen as capable of learning and the object of much love. Unfortunately, the focus is on Jody's destructiveness, her killing of numerous small animals, and the endangering of her infant brother's life.

Branscum, Robbie. *Toby, Granny and George.* Illus. by Glen Rounds. New York: Doubleday, 1976. 104 pp. Reading Level: MC
Disability: Emotional Dysfunction

Toby was left as a foundling on Granny's doorstep in a backwoods Arkansas county. The 13 year old has lived happily with the old woman, who made a hardscrabble living as a midwife and herbalist for the folks thereabouts who did not trust the town doctors. Toby's only companion has been George, a hound who obeys her implicitly. Toby comments: "I reckoned it was just a matter of two bastards understanding each other. Besides, neither one of us had a friend. Being strange makes folks stay out of your way."

People have also been avoiding Preacher Davis's church ever since Minnie Lou drowned during her baptism. Deacon Treat has hinted broadly that the calamity was the preacher's fault and suggests in church that it is high time for a replacement. When the deacon tries to oust the community's spiritual leader, Granny forces the accuser to back down. The feisty woman then takes Toby to Treat's home to see "how bad some folks can be." They find his wife and children are almost starving while the head of the household greedily heaps food onto his own plate. The teenager is startled to see how the tyrannical man has browbeaten and starved his family in the apparent midst of plenty.

While there, Toby meets Johnny Joe, the oldest Treat boy, who gives her a squirrel as a remembrance of their encounter. He is unable to speak, although Granny informs the girl that "when he was little, he could talk as well as anybody. Then one day he just couldn't talk." Soon after their visit the deacon dies, "shot with a twenty-two right through the belly." Later Toby is shot at and the Treat baby is reported missing, a situation that rouses the men in the community, and led by Preacher Davis, they organize a search but are unable to find a lead.

Granny's youngest daughter comes visiting, and Toby learns that the stranger is her mother and intends to take her away. However, the child insists on remaining with Granny, who she now understands is her "real" grandmother. She is sent off to gather celery roots and herbs and, while harvesting these materials for the old woman, happens upon a small grave. The child seeks out the preacher the next morning, tells him she has figured out an explanation for the recent events, and the two set out for the Treat farm. There they learn that when the deacon again began to viciously beat his infant, Johnny Joe panicked and shot him. Unfortunately, it was too late to save the baby's life. Preacher Davis tells Mrs. Treat that her son will not be charged with a crime since he was only "trying to save the baby." When they later talk with the boy's teacher, she explains: "Johnny Joe had stopped talking from shock because of the deacon's meanness and because Johnny Joe was such a gentle person and all." After the excitement subsides, the community returns to its former ways except that Toby becomes a modest entrepreneur, using her wheeling and dealing skills, and Johnny Joe begins to speak again.

Analysis. Branscum writes with deep affection of the characters who eke out a bare living from the inhospitable soil. Deacon Treat is presented as a man out of control whose brutal actions have caused the death of one child and the psychic muteness of another. Johnny Joe has lost his ability to talk, but when his anxiety becomes too great, in desperation, he is able to blurt out a brief message. Granny expresses her contempt for the town doctors, who failed to recognize Treat's violent rages as evidence of emotional instability and order his confinement. Round's light and captivating illustrations are perfectly suited to this down-home tale of tragedy and hope.

Branscum, Robbie. *The Ugliest Boy.* Illus. by Michael Eagle. New York: Lothrop, Lee & Shepard, 1978. 126 pp. Reading Level: MC/YA

Disability: Orthopedic Impairment

Reb, almost 14, takes a jaundiced view of his father's career as a country preacher since it has not allowed the family to call any one place home for long. In addition to always being a newcomer, the boy's uncommon homeliness makes him the frequent object of derision and exacerbates his feelings of isolation. He observes: "Reckon if there was ever a boy made of rails and snails and puppydog tails, it was me, and I was as ugly as sin, a mud fence, and lye soap all together." However, he has his own entertainments—fishing, walking in the woods—and a healthy relationship with his folks and his young sister, Annalee. Reb's competent performance of his chores is essential to the family's well-being, appreciated by them, and although his lot is far from an easy one, the youth has an open, optimistic, albeit solitary view of life.

At their new parish, Reb meets a young boy named Jake, who informs him that he, too, is a preacher's son. The boy also meets another congregant, September, whose beauty astonishes him. He notes: "She was about my age, her hair black and shiny, her eyes big and brown. Her lips were pink and her skin was creamy white and as I looked at her the pimples on my chin suddenly started to ache and swell up big as watermelons." The smitten boy subsequently notices that she has a disfigured foot: "I wasn't happy 'cause she was crippled, but reckon I just realized for the first time I wasn't the only one in the world that there was something wrong with. Truth to tell, I felt sorta low-down inside—I mean, always griping about being ugly when ugly didn't even hurt. I wondered if September's foot hurt. It sure looked painful." She returns his interest, bids him call her Steffie, tells him her mother is dead, her father has deserted them, and she lives with her grandmother. Reb tries to forget about his appearance and finds unaccustomed joy in his days spent with the distracting and entertaining girl. On footwashing day in the church, he manages to be the one who washes Steffie's feet, hoping to save her from embarrassment, and is rewarded with her gratitude. He learns to modify his loping gait when they go out together so she can keep pace with him.

The community's suspicions about a snake cult being nearby are confirmed. The preacher is urged to interfere, but asserts that freedom to worship in one's own mode is essential to a democracy. Despite his deep concern for the safety of the "snakers' " children and his wife's profound anxieties for her own family, he, in conscience, refuses to do anything to stop their ceremonies.

One evening, Annalee wanders off to the campfire of the snake cult. When Jake sees a rattler about to strike the girl, he bravely interposes his body and is bitten instead. Reb's father carries him off to their house to nurse him back to health over the objections of the boy's people, who insist that if his faith is strong enough he will be protected from harm. In the aftermath, Reb confides in his father that he wishes they would never have to move again now that he has friends, particularly a girl who doesn't care how homely he is. The man is pleased at his son's newfound happiness, but says he must always go where he is called.

Analysis. Branscum has drawn a compassionate picture of people living in rural poverty in the South during the Depression. She implies that the times were simpler but the values richer. The story hints gently and obliquely at several paradoxes: Reb's family has drastically limited economic resources, but limitless love and support for each other; the boy's external ugliness contrasts sharply with an inner beauty; the "snakers" bring danger to the community, but the life of Annalee is saved by their preacher's son. Disability is treated as one of many factors that can complicate life, but need not overwhelm it. September is orphaned. Jake is an outsider because of his membership in a cult. Reb has never known a permanent residence. Granny Horton has been abandoned by her children, who moved to the city. These are the kinds of things that can happen; one needs to accommodate such events and carry on. The illustrations complement the text, readily conveying the author's affection for her characters and the changing moods of the story.

Breitner, Sue. *The Bookseller's Advice.* Illus. by Jane Chambless-Rigie. New York: Viking, 1981. unp. Reading Level: YC
Disability: Auditory Impairment

Simon, an old bookseller, is respected throughout the community for his wisdom. He is completely unaware that "his hearing was getting worse and worse with each passing week." When the villagers come in for advice, he misinterprets their statements, dispensing suggestions that are ludicrous. His granddaughter tries to intervene, but he brushes aside her attempts at correcting his errors. She nevertheless persists, and when Simon at last realizes what he has been doing, he rushes out to try to rectify his mistakes. To his relief, he learns that his advice was as helpful as it was misguided. He returns to his store, where his granddaughter urgently requests his help: "I'm really in a jam," she says. "A jar of jam in my bookshop," her grandfather thought. "I doubt it. . . . But come inside. I'm sure I can give you some good advice."

Analysis. The intended humor of this slight story derives exclusively from the old man's impaired hearing—a source of merriment erroneously believed to have gone out of style. Although the bookseller is initially described as a wise man, his actions reveal a stubborn, albeit lucky, fool. Young readers, with little effort, can see a connections between stupidity and deafness. Simon's intermittent ability to hear correctly what he is told is unconvincing. His comment on one such occasion, "I can hardly believe my ears," typifies the insensitivity that marks this work. The illustrations are pleasant but unexceptional.

Brenner, Barbara. *A Killing Season.* New York: Four Winds, 1981. 182 pp. Reading Level: YA
Disability: Cosmetic Impairment; also speech impairment

Allie Turner's hand and arm were badly burned in the fire that killed her parents. She now lives with her embittered older brother in a tension-filled home. The high school girl is sickened by the annual bear hunts that take place in her native Pocono Mountains. Her brother, a hunter, finds her attitude contemptible, and this difference is one more topic of contention between them. Allie meets Don Bridges, a wildlife biologist, whom she accuses of failing to prevent the destruction of those magnificent animals. He defends his work and invites the angry girl to accompany him on field trips during which the bears will be observed and information recorded about them. Allie, a crack photographer, accepts his offer and is not only able to sharpen her skills but also begins to develop a desperately needed relationship. Don warns her against becoming too friendly with the animals since contact with people makes them less wary and consequently more vulnerable. She dismisses his advice and is indirectly and inadvertently the cause of death of some of the powerful beasts. Slowly, reluctantly, she becomes reconciled to the idea that prudent management of wild animals may be the only means to preserve them.

The outdoor activity has improved her health, and her friendship with Don has increased her self-confidence. Stuttering, once a disconcerting problem, has almost disappeared. A local college exhibits Allie's pictures in a one-woman show, and the dramatic, forceful depictions of the living creatures in the wild contrasted to their skinned and flayed pelts arouse heated controversy in the community. When bear hunting is prohibited the next season, many people angrily blame Allie's photographs. She becomes an outcast and, angry at Don after seeing him with another woman, begins a reclusive existence. Soon after, he calls her requesting that she join him in trying to locate a missing bear. The animal has been killed, and they later learn that the hunter, a friend of her brother's, died of exposure after the shooting. Exhausted and emotionally drained, Allie is taken home, where her brother and his fiancée take care of her. Pleased at what appears to be a positive change in her sibling and feeling more self-assured, the young woman decides to reveal to Don her feelings of jealousy.

Analysis. This teenage romance is distinguished only by the inclusion of the hunter–conservationist controversy. Considerable peripheral information about tagging, tracking, and managing wildlife resources is presented by way of providing a backdrop for the characters. Allie's disfiguring scar and slight stutter serve to enhance her shyness. Don's straightforward reaction to the evidence of her burn is to question her, discuss it briefly, suggest plastic surgery, and then drop the subject. Through this exchange, his credentials as an honest, decent person are further validated.

Bridgers, Sue Ellen. *All Together Now.* New York: Knopf, 1979. 238 pp. Reading Level: YA
Disability: Intellectual Impairment

With her pilot father fighting in Korea and her mother working at two jobs, 12-year-old Casey is sent to spend the summer with her grandparents in a small North Carolina town. Her first companion is Dwayne Pickens, coincidentally the childhood chum of her father. Dwayne's intellectual limitations are such that he has remained preoccupied with youthful interests, especially baseball. Both the 30 year old and Casey (whom he believes is a boy) need each other's companionship, and they, like others in the 1950s, happily wile away the hours at the movies, the beach, the dime store, the baseball mound, and the stock car racetrack. It is at the track that Casey's Uncle Taylor is assaulted by some roughnecks and Dwayne rushes to his assistance. Alva Pickins seizes this example of his brother's "aggression" to try to reinstitutionalize the young man, but Casey and her family, supported by many of the neighbors, so embarrass Alva at a public meeting that he reluctantly agrees to withdraw his petition.

Two romances are woven into the story; Pansy and Hazard, a middle-aged couple who decide to marry after a 25-year courtship, and Gwen and Taylor, whose initially shallow affair gradually evolves into a more mature and caring relationship. While Casey is ill with polio, Dwayne discovers his friend is a girl. When she recovers, he realizes he has to discard his bias against girls, and he, too, reveals his ability to change. Dwayne, like every other character, comes to realize that people must be accepted as they are. As she gets ready to go home, Casey recalls with a mixture of affection and regret the wonderful summer she spent, but, sensing her incipient move into adolescence, knows her relationship with her summer friend will never be quite the same.

Analysis. With extraordinary skill and sensitivity, Bridgers tenderly explores the subtleties and contrasts between life's expectations and its actualities and in doing so has created one of the most memorable exceptional characters in fiction for young adults. Much of the novel is seen from Dwayne's perspective. While his retardation is acknowledged, he is shown as a young man with many attractive qualities: good physical skills, some self-insight (he knows he has trouble learning), and a gigantic reservoir of affection and loyalty for his friends. His affectionate portrayal reveals such limitations as a selective memory, naiveté, and lack of perceptiveness. Some in the community speak disparagingly of Dwayne, but in general his neighbors think kindly of him and are concerned for his welfare. He is one of them, as the title suggests, and they come to his support when he is threatened.

Bridgers, Sue Ellen. *Notes for Another Life.* New York: Knopf, 1981. 250 pp. Reading Level: YA
Disability: Emotional Dysfunction

Kevin and Wren have part-time parents: their father, except for brief interludes at home, spends most of his life at the local psychiatric hospital; their mother, who lives alone near her job in a distant city, infrequently and hurriedly stops by her in-laws to visit her children. Fortunately, the strong loving relationship between Bliss and Bill Jackson provides a stable, supportive environment for their two grandchildren. Wren worries about the vulnerability of her older brother, who is exhibiting exceptionally defensive behavior, afraid to risk loving or trusting anyone.

> She didn't know exactly what protection she could provide Kevin, but she offered it nonetheless. Protection against their grandparents' silent concern, against their mother thinking them less than perfect, against upsetting their father's unsteady progress with yet another situation he was incapable of handling. It was an unspoken commitment between them, bonded by their regret their father's illness had brought them and the untraversable distance their mother kept.

Wren is pleased that her brother has Melanie for a girl friend and hopes he finds some emotional strength from their relationship. Sam

Holland, 14, shows an interest in Wren, which she both wants and finds disconcerting. Unsure of herself, the 13 year old is afraid he may only be making a fool of her. Their first "date" includes his entire family, a warm and loving clan. Although she revels in the association with them, Sam's parents are a painful reminder of her own parents' deficiencies.

Wren notes a definite improvement in her father's behavior, signaling that he will soon be able to try to live at home again. As Kevin feels closest to his mother, so Wren most needs her father's love: "It was hard to explain how much [he] mattered, how important a smile became, a certain tone of voice, the grip of fingers against her own." Kevin has avoided visiting his parent, but when he finally forces himself to go, it is a heartbreaking experience. He wonders: "Was he the only true, unchanging fact in Kevin's life? Was depression, insanity, the only kind of stability he could depend on? That and [his mother's] absence?" The boy casually mentions his mother's plans to proceed with a divorce and is dumbfounded at his father's reaction, realizing too late that the man had not known his wife's intention. Tom "wrenched forward, arms limp and useless, head flung back like a convulsion." Kevin, shocked, wonders whether in telling his father he was motivated, at least in part, by the desire to hurt the man. The boy becomes even more moody, keeping Melanie at arm's length, frightened of dependence on anyone but himself. His broken wrist keeps him from tennis, his only outlet from the anxiety that controls his life. His pain becomes intolerable when he learns his mother has no plans to include him in her move to an even more distant city. The 16 year old tries to protect himself from further disappointment by taking an overdose of pills, but Bliss finds him in time and rushes him to the hospital where his stomach is pumped. Their minister consoles the family and counsels Kevin, ultimately helping the boy realize he has the power to continue despite his parents' shortcomings. The cycle continues: his mother leaves them again after another rushed visit, his father withdraws more and more each day until he is recommitted, and his sister and grandparents cope with the pain, joy, variety, and sameness in their lives.

Analysis. In an intelligent, potent, and moving novel, Bridgers shows the effect of emotional disorders on family relationships. The father's life is seen from various standpoints, including, on occasion, his own. His role as husband, father, son, and individual is perceived by those most closely involved. Although his illness is not the cause of the divorce, it is a factor in the final rupture of the nuclear family. His children, aware of other instances of psychiatric problems among their kin, fear that they may inevitably be "tainted." His mother reflects on the care she has given her only son, berating herself for an inadequacy she cannot identify. Information about hospital regimens—shock therapy, antidepressants, psychiatric sessions—provide the background against which the cycle of regression and recovery is acted out. As Kevin observes:

> His dad was better and had begun to talk, making the kind of stilted conversation available to him when his world was inside one room and nothing ever happened except that he had treatment, took medicine and saw a psychiatrist. There was little concern for existence elsewhere, no interest in the news, no worries that weren't petty, selfish ones. He knew his dad would be wrapped up in himself, a cocoon of antidepressants surrounding him as warmly as if he were a larva.

The character development is admirable, the plot original, the style thoughtful and consummately literate in this altogether excellent work.

Britton, Anna. *Fike's Point.* New York: Coward, McCann & Geoghegan, 1977. 148 pp. Reading Level: YA/MA
Disability: Intellectual Impairment, Emotional Dysfunction

After being driven from their last home, Fike's peripatetic father locates some land near the sea on which he hopes to erect the family tent. He feels confident that the recluse who owns the property will allow them to remain if he hauls stones to aid the old man's obsessive construction of a castle. His prediction proves correct, and the nomadic group resumes its casual lifestyle. Although others think the hermit is crazy and are frightened by his habit of pelting strangers with rocks, Fike is sympathetic:

> I reckoned people had been throwing things at him for years and years because he was a weirdo, so in the end he just up and threw them back. I could see him clearly, his mouth working up and down, but he looked uncertain and old, a battered sort of person.

After Fike's birth, Mary, her mother, began using hard drugs. The woman's other child, Dimsey, was born already addicted and seriously brain damaged. The boy has been his sister's responsibility and almost constant companion, and she regards him with modest affection, but holds few illusions about his abilities:

> Dimsey never really thought of anything other than what he could see in front of his nose. Anyway it made him seem almost clever. Really he was pretty dumb though. You'd send him off for the water and like as not he'd forget all about it and let the bucket

slide down to the bottom of the paddock while he looked up at the sky, his mouth hanging open. I'd find him sometimes, his arms wrapped around himself like he was frozen, even on a hot day. He'd be sitting there shivering and rocking.

Before long, the family is joined by friends from a commune and two American deserters from the Vietnam War who sell drugs. Frank, handsome and very manipulative, so bedazzles the 14-year-old girl that she becomes his courier, supplying adolescents in the nearby village with his wares. Fike leaves Dimsey alone now more than ever, afraid he might be a hindrance if she needs to flee suddenly. The teenager also wants some time alone, which she spends sneaking into empty houses, where she gazes in wonderment at the order, comfort, and cleanliness apparent in others' lives. One day she is caught inside one of the homes, but instead of running her off or having her arrested, Kate and Clarissa, who are presumably lesbians, invite her to stay, treating her as a guest and lending her books from their treasured library. She begins visiting regularly and, to her surprise, is always welcomed by Kate, who hints she could have a permanent home with them should she ever want it.

Dimsey and Fike visit the hermit in his odd residence, where the adolescent is perplexed to see the old man's photographs and his collection of intricate carvings, evidence of a once more rational life. The two play chess, and the girl concludes the lonely man is neither as simple nor as incompetent as she had originally thought.

When her brother becomes sick, Fike appeals to her mother for help, but the woman is preoccupied with a group drug orgy and she shrugs off her child's plea. The other adults are angry at Fike's interruption, but Frank gives sweets to the whimpering child to quiet him. That evening, the adolescent is awakened by strange noises, observes that her brother's sleeping bag is empty, and tracks him to the castle, too late to prevent him from jumping over the precipice. She and the old man carry the boy's broken body up the incline, but it becomes evident that there is no way to help him. When Fike staggers back to the tent, she is chased away by the adults, but not before she observes Frank engaging in sex with her virtually insensate mother while her apparently indifferent father ignores this scene of adulterous copulation. In shock from the cumulative effect of these dreadful events, she wanders off to her friends' home, where the women watch the area occupied by the squatters consumed by fire. The local authorities erroneously conclude that the hermit has been the arsonist: parrafin has been discovered around the tent, indicating the blaze was deliberately set. The outcast's mumbled speech and unconventional behavior convince the judge that the man should be sent to an institution for the criminally insane. The trial confirms that the candy given to Dimsey was laced with acid, presumably responsible for the delusional behavior that resulted in his death. Fike readily accepts a permanent home with her benefactors, regretting only that she had forgotten to move the old man's cow and calf before she lit the fatal match.

Analysis. All the major characters in this nihilistic and disturbing work have serious problems, with the possible exception of the women who give shelter to Fike. The old man, solitary and rejected, is engaged in the fruitless construction of a ridiculous, anachronistic edifice. Fike's parents and their companions have chosen or rationalized their willing embrace of a drugged and tormented existence. Frank, a sociopath without scruples or conscience, is an exploitative and willfully destructive person. It is suggested that Dimsey's condition is the result of Mary's earlier experience with mind-altering chemicals. Fike, unloved, neglected, tormented by the horrors of her existence, murders easily and without remorse. The judge misjudges and incarcerates an innocent man. Britton's acutely depressing tale offers an accidental path to some happiness, but one based on revenge and homicide.

Brochmann, Elizabeth. *What's the Matter, Girl?* New York: Harper & Row, 1980. 121 pp. Reading Level: YA
Disability: Emotional Dysfunction

His relatives begin to make plans to welcome back Arion, a veteran of World War II. No one is more anxious to see him than his niece, Anna, a 13 year old who has transformed him in her mind into a perfect, godlike creature, fantasizing about his return with mildly disguised sexual longings. Although many hints are given that something is grossly amiss, Anna refuses to listen to these innuendoes and persists in imagining an idyllic reunion. She has frequently written to Arion of the daily accounts of life on their Canadian farm and also of intimate and philosophical matters, but his intermittent letters focus more and more on death, the ravages of war, and his inability to deal with its horrors. For some time there has been no response at all, even though the war has long been over and other soldiers have returned. Tensions mount in the family as its members count the days until Arion comes home.

The veteran arrives at last, accompanied by an attendant, and Anna is devastated to see the hollow vestige of the vibrant, fun-loving companion she once knew. She feels betrayed and cannot contain her anger and frustration. Her brother shows her the letters he received from Arion after he stopped writing Anna. They reveal his diminishing ability to cope with the nightmare that his life had become. The boy tells her of a conversation not intended for his ears: "Yesterday I overheard Gramps saying they wrote him and Gran to sign papers for the cure. Uncle Barnard said Gramps never should have signed, that they butchered Arion's mind. Dad said shock therapy was a good thing and couldn't do that. Aunt Cessy said Arion tried to commit suicide—that his body didn't make it but his mind did." Unable to visit him since his homecoming, she watches "tiny Gran . . . wheeling her son-parcel Arion. . . . He sits staring west, in the direction he's been placed." Anna wants to visit him: "But not yet. I can't go there. Yet."

Analysis. One of the few junior novels examining the plight of traumatized veterans and their families, this work indirectly touches on national conflicts and the complexities of loyalty when the soldier's father shares ancestry with the German enemy. Images of death continue to haunt the soldier during his hospitalization after the war. The torn youth identifies with both sides—simultaneously denying and claiming responsibilities for the atrocities he has seen and heard about. Arion's fate is very broadly hinted at from the opening pages. Time sequences are jumbled, the soldier's communications are not only confused but confusing, and the conclusion is indecisive. Despite this, the story manages to maintain tension, and its often irritating structure reflects the turmoil experienced by the young heroine, who cannot bear to confront the incredible devastation visited on one she loves.

Brookins, Dana. *Alone in Wolf Hollow.* New York: Seabury, 1978. 137 pp. Reading Level: MC
Disability: emotional dysfunction, orthopedic impairment; also auditory impairment

A cousin who had reluctantly accepted Bart and Arnie after their mother's death now sends them to live with their widowed Uncle Charlie. No one meets the boys when they arrive in town, but the stationmaster suggests that the local tavern is a likely place to find their relative. This tip proves erroneous, and they make their way through the woods to their destination only to learn that their uncle has changed his mind after impulsively agreeing to become their guardian. The boys are further distressed to discover that the man is an alcoholic and so grief-stricken over his wife's death that he can scarcely function. Nevertheless, the youths persuade Charlie that they want to remain with him. They settle in, start school, and begin to explore the fascinating hollow near their new home.

One day in the woods they overhear an argument between Madge, a woman who worked at a local bar, and an unseen person.

Later, they are shocked to come across Madge's body. Uncle Charlie, disconsolate at the loss of this friend, resumes his temporarily suspended drinking bouts and orders the boys to return to their other relatives. He leaves money for their transportation and departs without further explanation. Bart and Arnie refuse to go back to their uncongenial cousin and plan to conceal Charlie's absence from the authorities.

A drifter is caught and charged with Madge's murder. Mrs. Bruzz, who was disabled in an accident, confides in the boys that she is sure the wrong man was apprehended. She asserts that Madge had been overly friendly with several married men and concludes that the killer was someone the victim knew. Something nags at Bart's memory until he finally realizes that Clenning, the grocer for whom he works, has information only the murderer could know. Young and guileless, the child unwittingly arouses the storekeeper's suspicions. Clenning arrives at their house, uncertain about what course of action to take but, desperate to protect himself, attempts to kill the youngsters. They are saved by a runaway from the nearby psychiatric center, a gentle giant who believes that he is a monarch from another planet and has remained hidden in the woods since he fabricated evidence of his own drowning in a local pond. Lena, an old trapper and friend of the boys, arrives after Clenning is knocked unconscious, conspiring with the children to take credit for the criminal's capture in order to keep their benefactor's existence a secret. Meanwhile, the boys run off to get help, returning with the sheriff. When Bart reveals that their attacker told him he was once married to Madge, the law officer promises to investigate and puts the man in custody. The children return home and share Christmas dinner with Lena and the self-proclaimed king.

The next morning, Charlie comes back to the house, startled to find his nephews still there. They recount their adventures, and he discloses that he sought treatment for his drinking problem during his absence. He does not promise the boys can remain, but Bart, proud of the accomplishments of his younger brother and newly aware of his own resourcefulness, is confident they will manage no matter what the future holds.

Analysis. The disabled characters play minor but critical roles in this exciting adventure story, which relies too heavily on fortuitous timing. The stationmaster, who sustains a hearing loss, is the first person the boys meet, and he provides a clue to the nature of their reception in their new home. Mrs. Bruzz, isolated by her limited mobility, becomes friendly with Arnie when he delivers her groceries. Her comments, passed on to Bart, lead to the identification of the murderer. The former psychiatric patient saves the boys and articulates a central theme of the novel: grief is the prime motivator for disordered behavior. In describing a character's suicide, he comments: "She wasn't crazy, you know. Only full of grief. That's all that's wrong with most of what you earth people call crazy." Unhappiness is likewise proposed as the reason for Charlie's alcoholism and Clenning's ungovernable aggression.

Brooks, Jerome. *The Big Dipper Marathon*. New York: Dutton, 1979. 134 pp. Reading Level: YA
Disability: Orthopedic Impairment

Fifteen-year-old Horace Zweig, who prefers the name "Ace," has had polio. His legs do not function, and his hands, despite attempts at corrective surgery, remain deformed. He resents the pity shown him at school, the constant reminders that he is disabled. His parents are filled with guilt over his condition and alternately exaggerate and minimize his abilities. A trip to visit his relatives in Chicago gives him the opportunity to prove to himself that he can be "normal." A poster on the wall of the room he shares with his cousin features a roller coaster, and Ace persuades BC to take him out to the amusement park for a ride on it. The first circuit Ace makes in the company of an attractive girl is exhilarating, but the cars of the roller coaster never slow down enough so that the youth can get out. Two trips later, he is humiliatingly forced to ask for help. Nevertheless, the experience is a breakthrough for Ace and his parents: he has a more realistic picture of what he can and cannot do, and his parents are more capable of honestly assessing their reactions to him and are at last free to allow their son the space he needs to mature.

Analysis. Like other teenagers, Ace wants to take risks and discover the boundaries of his powers. He is seen as seriously hampered in this crucial developmental need by the fears of his parents, who weigh all of his requests not in terms of respective merits but on the basis of their perceived effect on Ace, who is seen as a vulnerable disabled person. The youth yearns to be free to make his own decisions without having to conform to others' conceptions of normalcy. The synthesis he finally reaches is shown to be important and more valid since it derives from his own initiative. One noteworthy aspect of this work is the protagonist's sweeping condemnation of mainstreaming. Despite its interesting messages, the literary deficiencies of this work render it of little value. The tone is excessively emotional and the exposition heavy-handed; conversations and interior monologues appear stagey and contrived; and the author reveals an apparently boundless enthusiasm for symbols, which are simultaneously obvious and underdeveloped.

Brown, Fern G. *You're Somebody Special on a Horse.* Illus. by Frank C. Murphy. Chicago: Albert Whitman, 1977. 128 pp. Reading Level: MC
Disability: Orthopedic Impairment, Emotional Dysfunction

Preoccupation with readying her horse for riding competitions has led Marni to neglect her schoolwork, causing her grades to plummet. Her parents' decision to sell Koke, her horse, is devastating news to their daughter. She has been training her mount under the able direction of Captain Blaine, who plans to have her participate in a special program for disabled children he is initiating at the riding academy. Although dubious that she can baby-sit with Todd, a mute boy adopted by the Blaines, work with the exceptional students, and simultaneously improve her grades, Marni's parents reluctantly agree to delay Koke's sale.

Blaine and his wife, a physical therapist, have taken special training to qualify them for their proposed rehabilitation program. He tells the other team members about the usefulness of their work, adding that when their students move up from the adapted class to compete as equals with nonhandicapped riders, their rewards will come. Kevin, a physically disabled youngster, is assigned to Marni's team and begins his instruction. She soon realizes the boy's cocky manner and bold front conceal great anxiety and insecurity. When he and the other participants in this new program have gained some skill and confidence, a demonstration for parents is arranged, at which time Blaine announces his plans to hold a benefit for the disabled students: "All money after expenses will go toward buying horses, specialized tack, and insurance, and for training people. . . . And we're going to have a special class in the show for handicapped riders." The teenager represses thoughts about the imminent sale of her beloved animal, concentrating instead on helping Kevin, who confesses his concern that he will never be able to achieve independence as a rider. The girl's dedication pays off, however, when her student achieves the goals established for him. Noting the emotional as well as the physiological benefits Kevin and the other orthopedically impaired youth derive from riding, Marni predicts its therapeutic value for Todd, too. Sure enough, after a ride on Koke, the formerly silent child speaks out, expressing admiration for the horse.

Unable to manage all her activities, Marni has chosen to ignore her studies, so her parents prepare to carry out their original intention to get rid of the horse. If Blaine's offer to buy Koke is accepted, Marni will at least be able to visit her beloved animal, but Kevin's father also wants the horse for his son. In an agonizing decision, the girl acknowledges that the boy's need is greater than her own and ultimately agrees to the purchase that will remove Koke from her forever.

Analysis. Readers will be exposed to some interesting information on an unusual, although increasingly popular rehabilitation regimen, including how occupational therapists plan lessons and measure progress by evaluating joint movements, how therapeutic exercises are incorporated into riding routines, how horses are desensitized to wheelchairs and crutches, and what kinds of special equipment are employed. However, the work is replete with inconsistencies; for example, the goal of the program is to have the disabled children be mainstreamed, but the benefit will have a "special class in the show for handicapped riders." Dialogue is improbable and often carries a didactic or inspirational message, as when Kevin says "If I can learn to ride alone, I won't have to depend on people to get places. I can exchange my weak legs for Koke's four strong ones." In addition, there are some unfortunate instances of insensitivity: the children arrive in a bus that is marked with a sign reading "Handicapped People," and the youngsters are shown primarily as the recipients of charity.

Brown, Irene B. *Morning Glory Afternoon.* New York: Atheneum, 1981. 219 pp. Reading Level: YA
Disability: Emotional Dysfunction, Intellectual Impairment

Seeking relief from her irrational guilt at the death of a friend, 17-year-old Jessy moves to a small town, where she finds employment as a telephone operator. The community is run by Mayor Lombard Hale, who exercises considerable power over the populace. Jessy is troubled when she finds he has impeded her efforts to relieve the plight of some Greek orphan children living in an abandoned shack in the woods. Hale refers to them as "aliens . . . human garbage," adding that such people defile the ideals of American life. Soon the newcomer observes a pattern of violent incidents directed against minorities. Her friend Lilli explains that the Ku Klux Klan is responsible, but Jessy refuses to believe that such an organization could find support in Kansas in 1924.

Torn by feelings of wanting to help the victims of persecution, but unsure of what to do and reluctant to abandon the self-protective shell she has so carefully built, Jessy leaves town for the day to relax and think through her dilemma. She takes a horseback ride into the country, stopping at a creek to go wading. Her pleasure turns to horror as leeches attach themselves to her feet. A handsome cowboy rescues her, but although she finds Hatch attractive, Jessy turns down his social overtures.

When white-sheeted men interrupt the town's Christmas pageant, ejecting those youngsters they have branded as undesirable, Jessy can no longer remain aloof. She persuades the orphans' Uncle Julio to oversee the children's care. Their grandmother arrives soon after he agrees, a fortunate occurrence since their would-be protector unaccountably vanishes without a trace. Jessy learns that Hale is responsible for the brutal beating of a Jewish storekeeper and is plotting against Joe Cooke, a black man whose ambitions to buy a livery business were thwarted by the hatemonger. Lilli warns, "Now they'll push even harder to make this a one-color, one-religion, single-minded very dull town." Jessy's job as telephone operator enables her to overhear Hale's plans for intimidating minority citizens, and a signal is devised using the words "morning glory" to alert the intended victims of the impending danger. Cecil, the mayor's handyman, whose low functioning level has made him a social outcast, is being used by Hale to do his dirty work. Since the young woman has always been kind to him, Cecil warns her that the signal is known and explains his complicity in affairs he knows are shameful:

> Nobody ever asked me to be in a club before. I wanted to. All the time I was a little kid. They always said, "no, no, not you, you looney. . . ." Then Mr. Hale said I could belong to his club. Help our town be nice, make people good. I got to wear a sheet like the other fine gentlemen.

Julio is subsequently discovered in a shallow grave, and Jessy takes upon herself the responsibility for his death since she persuaded him to stay in the community. The young woman tells the investigating detectives about the Klan's activities but omits Cecil's name from the list of those responsible, justifying this omission on the grounds that "in his own way, the handyman would always be innocent." Upset at his latest instructions, Cecil confides in his new protector that Hale has sent him to adjust the wires at the switchboard, an act Jessy realizes could electrocute her. He further confesses his role in Julio's disappearance: he had been ordered by Hale to bury the murdered man. Jessy persuades Cecil and the mayor's daughter to reveal all they know about the irrational man over open switchboard lines. Hale arrives at the telephone office in an agitated state, seizes the headset, and broadcasts an explanation and justification of his behavior. Infuriated when he receives no support from his neighbors, he pounds on the switchboard. "Then making an animal-like sound of rage, he bolted for the door, tore it open and flung his way outside, into the street." Her friends rush to the courageous woman's support, including Hatch, whose proposal of marriage she accepts.

Analysis. The clear intent of this novel is to expose the terrible harm that individuals and a community can suffer if intolerance and fanaticism are allowed free rein. The author proposes that unscrupulous and unstable people are able to capitalize on the insecurities of others to achieve entirely selfish goals through such agencies as the Klan. Her argument is undercut by naive presumptions and a Western movie–style resolution. The uncertain and wavering actions of a 17-year-old girl are unlikely to halt the spread of violence or the exploitation of those who are vulnerable. The depiction of characters who are emotionally dysfunctional and intellectually impaired is equally unsophisticated; the former is seen as a celluloid villain and the latter as a basically decent, childlike character, readily manipulated by his nefarious employer. It is altogether too simple a view of impairment, society, and bigotry.

Brown, Irene B. *Run from a Scarecrow.* Illus. by Charles Molina. St. Louis: Concordia, 1978. 128 pp. Reading Level: MC
Disability: Emotional Dysfunction; also orthopedic impairment

On a remote patch of scrabbly Missouri land, Hank Hedin dreams of going west, being a cowboy, and for once having a male friend his age. Desperate when his mother gives birth to yet another girl, the 14-year-old youth decides to run away from home. He soon becomes hopelessly lost in a cave, but is rescued by a frightened, mute boy who pantomimes his name, Bigger Stokes. Just when a friendship begins to grow between the two, the Hedin farm is devastated by cholera and Pa decides to move his family west. Hank persuades his folks to take Bigger with them, an opportunity the lonely youth eagerly seizes. As they leave, Hank is puzzled to see an odd, thin man hovering about the newly abandoned farmstead and later on the road catches another glimpse of the stranger he has nicknamed "Scarecrow." Doubting his son's story, the farmer nonetheless accompanies Hank to where he spotted the mysterious-looking man and finds that a flash flood has wiped out the man's campsite. When they return to the covered wagon with the man's stovepipe hat, Bigger stamps on it with unexpected fierceness.

Pa becomes enthusiastic about the farming possibilities in Kansas and decides to settle there. To overcome Hank's disappointment over the curtailment of their travels, Pa tells his son about wild horses roaming nearby. Hardship overtakes the family the first year, and Hank is sent to town to find work so the family will have some ready cash. While the boy is working with the village blacksmith, Bigger disappears, and although his friend is upset, the youth is also relieved since the evil-looking stranger, Chaw Varber, has reappeared and is inquiring after the missing youngster. One snowy day, two travelers arrive, and the younger turns out to be the long lost Bigger. The boy's companion discloses that he once was a wild horse wrangler before he "got crippled." He explains his impairment resulted when he "warmed [his] feet in the ashes of [his] campfire." The coals were hot enough to "burn [his] boot soles off" and so his "feet froze." Naturally he was delighted when the silent, hardworking Bigger arrived, and ever since the two have been together. When Varber, who Hank has discovered has no thumbs, learns his quarry has returned, he attacks the lad, and in the fight Bigger calls out, speaking for the first time in years. Varber is knocked out in the scuffle, and Bigger whispers that the unconscious man killed his parents in an attempt to steal a valuable pearl they had found while clamming. He adds that the murderer set fire to his parents' houseboat. "I couldn't help—so far away. Pa and Ma trapped—I kept screaming and screaming. Leastways, I think I did. But when I stopped I couldn't say nothin', no more, after the fire." Bigger shows them the pearl he has kept with him and, unimpressed to hear it is worth a fortune, decides to stay with the family that befriended him.

Analysis. Brown has constructed a historical melodrama in which those people who are good are saintly and those who are bad are evil incarnate. The former are rewarded and the latter punished. The plot cannot bear close scrutiny since key events are neither logical nor likely. Bigger's traumatically induced mutism, essential for the progress of the story, is remedied by a comparably threatening event that nonetheless allows for a happy ending. Although the wrangler's impairment is essential to explain his need for assistance in his work, the nature of the causal incident is certainly unique. The villain's missing thumbs serve no rational purpose except possibly to add to his oft-noted intimidating physical appearance.

Brown, Roy. *Find Debbie!* Originally published in Great Britain as *The Siblings.* New York: Seabury Press, 1976. 160 pp. Reading Level: YA/MA
Disability: Emotional Dysfunction, intellectual impairment

Mr. Shepherd, a highly placed civil servant, has abdicated all responsibility for caring for Debbie, his profoundly disturbed 14-year-old daughter. His wife is physically and emotionally exhausted by the ordeal of the girl's supervision. Only Debbie's twin brother, Ian, is intermittently able to penetrate her world sufficiently to provide some love, guidance, and training. Her older brother and sister try to help, but her screaming, biting, self-mutilation, and generally violent and uncontrolled behavior leave them frustrated and defeated. Debbie's sudden disappearance one night is totally unexpected since her actions have never been sufficiently coherent to manage the sequence of steps she would have had to accomplish to leave their apartment. The police are called, and a detective who has a retarded adult son is assigned to the case. Inspector Bates lays bare the complex and ambivalent feelings the various family members have toward Debbie and examines the strategies they have used to cope with her and with their own emotions. Angry at this intrusion into his life, the girl's father informs the police superintendent that his daughter is "in good hands" and that the report of her absence is "a not untypical example of hysteria on the part of a member of his household." Refusing to give up the search, the investigator doggedly follows clues and hunches until at last he arrives at the remote home of a seriously disturbed former client of Mr. Shepherd's, where he finds Debbie's grave.

Analysis. Brown has employed the detective story structure to create a chilling, shocking, thought-provoking novel. Threaded through the basic story of the search for a missing girl is the contrast between the two sets of parents and their different reactions to living with a child with a very serious problem. The difference in the integrity of the two fathers is brought into sharp relief as Shepherd rationalizes his self-serving behavior, heaping both responsibility and blame on others, while Bates, full of self-doubts, recognizes his own weaknesses, supports his wife, who is the primary caretaker and teacher of his child, and is accepting and compassionate. The characterization of the civil servant who purports to speak for the needy in society, but whose own behavior is cowardly and irresponsible, is particularly vivid. The question of whether all would not be better off without Debbie, that is, whether her death would not be beneficial to her family and society, is raised, but the unacceptability of such a proposition is negated by the actions of the persistent and incorruptible detective. Events are primarily revealed and interpreted by Inspector Bates, an adult, a situation unusual in a novel marketed for an adolescent audience.

Brown, Roy. *Suicide Course.* New York: Houghton Mifflin, 1980. 118 pp. Reading Level: YA/MA
Disability: Emotional Dysfunction

A young man who identifies himself as David Green is confined in a psychiatric hospital following a suicide attempt that left him with a broken leg. The youth, confused and moody, suffers from memory lapses and is tormented by images of death and dying. A psychiatric assistant who becomes interested in his case visits him in his room. On one such occasion, when he is distracted by another patient, David steals the professional's keys and wallet and in the ensuing confusion escapes and boards a train to London. The young man arrives in the city but cannot concentrate and finds himself floating in and out of reality:

> The specters returned, demanding admittance, dragging in a corpse as lively as a dancing skeleton. The damned face eyed Green out of a shop window . . . and his mood plunged at once. There were times Green could master simple optical realities, but there were others when the image in glass was neither ghost nor projection, but something malevolent which would never let him go, never set him free.

Green wanders aimlessly around, going through the motions of purposeful action but unable to pursue any coherent goal. "It was as if taking any step, ticking off any item from his mental list was quite sufficient unto itself. It required no logical extension." His encounters with unemployment office personnel and a physician whose questions cause him to panic and his theft of electric equipment that is subsequently abandoned on a bus bring him to the attention of the police.

When Green impulsively calls the Samaritan Center, a volunteer support agency, Keith answers the phone and agrees to meet him. As their relationship develops, the youth speaks of Mark, his troubled twin brother, who, he claims, is a drug user and a vicious, vengeful, abusive sneak thief. After their next meeting, during which Green's behavior is even more bizarre, the disturbed youth speeds away on a stolen motorcycle that he deliberately rams into a road divider, resulting in serious but again not fatal injuries. The patient is hospitalized, then moved to the psychiatric ward. On one visit, Keith meets the boy's father, who informs him that the boy he knows as David is really Mark, who, in addition to possessing all the vices attributed to him by the would-be suicide, is actually responsible for his brother's death. Mark recovers sufficiently to be brought to trial, where he is given probation on the condition that he continue therapy. Keith receives one last call on Mark's twentieth birthday inviting him to accompany the twin and his father to the cemetery where David's ashes are. The boy is transfixed by the plaque that reads: " 'David Green, aged seventeen'—his date of birth—and Mark's—then 'There shall be no more darkness at all.' " Keith, invited to join them for a drink, refuses: "He thought of his date, he thought of his motorcycle, he thought of the bearded mask that had suddenly become David Green's face, not Mark's." The men leave and go their separate ways.

Analysis. The disturbed youth speaks of his difficulty in establishing his own identity, unable to function alone, but abusive and exploitive when with his twin. David's death, described by his father as deliberate murder, results in Mark's psychological destruction. In expiation for his crime, the young man denies his own existence and attempts to resurrect his brother through the assumption of the dead boy's identity. His untenable guilt results in an emotional disorder characterized by delusional behavior and a disassociated personality. Descriptions of a young man unconnected to reality, broken by his fears, and victimized by hallucination are credible. However, the plot of this novella is so convoluted and ultimately confusing that the sustained tension necessary for a story of suspense is dissipated.

Brown, Roy. *The Swing of the Gate.* New York: Seabury, 1978. 108 pp. Reading Level: YA/MA
Disability: Orthopedic Impairment, Emotional Dysfunction

Reporter Alan Bishop is picking out a trivial news story at the typewriter with his usable right hand when he learns of the murder of a streetwalker. The young man becomes alarmed upon hearing that his half-brother, Lennie, has escaped from the psychiatric hospital and was apparently seen in the murdered woman's apartment, which she shared with Lennie's half-sister. Ted Hendricks, the brother of Alan's fiancée and the detective in charge of the case, intends to use Alan as a source of information about the suspect. Alan begins his search for his half-brother at the psychiatrist's office, where he steals a cassette containing one of Lennie's sessions. Listening to it activates recollections of Aunt Val and Uncle Ross, shadowy ghosts from their past. Alan visits his mother, who denies seeing the escapee, adding: "Let's hope this time they'll lock him up for keeps." Alan, outraged, thinks: "You spawned Lennie, you and that old layabout. What gives you the right to shrug off all the responsibility, drowning the past like an unwanted cat?" His troubled mind forces him to attempt to unravel the family history, recalling an incident in which Lennie had killed a girl and the family conspired in a successful cover-up. The memory of Lennie's deliberate maiming of him is rekindled:

The pain . . . never such pain. Lennie must have worked it out to the second. Alan's wrist was in the right place, idly, thoughtlessly, wrapped around the iron post. There was no reason for it. They'd been playing ball in the front garden. Lennie came, giggling, raised a leg, planted the sole of his shoe on the gate and slammed it shut. When Alan screamed, Lennie giggled.

When Alan deduces that "Aunt Val" and "Uncle Ross" are his (and Lennie's) actual parents, and the woman he calls mother had merely fostered the two boys, he traces Lennie to Aunt Val's and learns that his brother is hiding in the woods with a gun. Removing the remaining weapon from its case, he goes looking for the fugitive. There is a brief fight in which Alan is slightly injured and Lennie is captured by Ted, presumably to be returned to the institution.

Analysis. Alan is depicted as a person who adjusted to his disability but who may have been irreparably damaged by the conflicts left over from a traumatic childhood. His relationship with his brother involves a mixture of guilt, resentment, anger, and feelings of responsibility. The character of Lennie is never adequately developed, and his actions remain incomprehensible. The convoluted story seems to lack purpose and never gathers momentum. As Alan confronts each member of his family with his thoughts, readers cover the same ground again and again, gaining only slightly more information and losing interest with each encounter.

Bunting, Eve. *Blackbird Singing.* Illus. by Stephen Grammell. New York: Macmillan, 1980. 92 pp. Reading Level: MC/YA
Disability: Emotional Dysfunction

An invasion of blackbirds has not only jeopardized their farm, it has worsened the tensions just below the surface of the relationship between Marcus's parents. His father watches in anguish as thousands of birds strip his cornfields, while his mother, entranced by their magnificence, tries to capture the avian horde in her paintings. This conflict had previously affected Marcus, and Dr. Kelsey Lee had diagnosed his blinking and stuttering as "symptom[s] of deep psychological problems." The boy's dysfluency reappears when his father plans, in conjunction with other farmers, to destroy the ravagers, over his mother's strenuous objections. On the recommendation of the local agricultural agent, the beleaguered farmers hire an exterminator to spray poison from a plane onto their fields. In the midst of their preparations, Marcus's mother, concerned about her son's cough, makes an appointment for him with the doctor. His father adds to her worry by suggesting that their son might be suffering from histoplasmosis, a disorder transmitted by bird droppings, rather than from a simple cold. The youngster protests: "I d-d-d-don't want to s-s-see K-K-Kelsey!" He recalls:

> I looked up at her and I felt the tears coming and then I thought I felt the blinks. I'd forgotten how awful the blinks were, but I remembered them again real fast. My eyes would begin to flicker and the kitchen would flutter around me. I raised my eyebrows and put all my force into making my eyeballs stay still, but I knew if they didn't want to, they wouldn't.

The boy is afraid that "as soon as she heard my stutter, she'd know Mom and Dad were doing badly again." He also resents the doctor's condescending attitude: "Just because I stuttered, did she think I was a dummy?" but agrees to her suggestion to see a therapist at the center.

The spraying is successful and vast numbers of birds die, but the men want to ensure that their farms are not used in future years as a stopping point on the annual avian migration. They propose to cut down the stand of maples loved by Marcus's mother. Heartbroken, she agrees to a compromise when it is discovered that her son as well as other children have indeed contracted histoplasmosis.

Analysis. Blackbird Singing attempts to present legitimate arguments on both sides of the ecology controversy. Birds are clearly endangering the economic survival of the community, and their destruction is essential if the farms are to remain viable. However, the growth of the flocks is the direct consequence of the killing of predators, and it is implied that tampering with the delicately balanced environment inevitably leads to new problems requiring ever more drastic solutions. There is a parallel drawn between the conflict on a macrocosmic level in society and a microcosmic one within the fictional family. Marcus is a victim of the confrontation between the two camps, and his distress is both physical and psychological. The boy's stammering signals the need for counseling, but the larger issue is not amenable to such relatively easy remediation. Bunting has written a moving story that encompasses a crucial theme, and Grammell's drawings are faithful to both text and mood of this valuable work.

Bunting, Eve. *Demetrius and the Golden Goblet.* Illus. by Michael Hague. New York: Harcourt Brace Jovanovich, 1980. unp. Reading Level: MC
Disability: visual impairment

The prince's most ardent wish is to experience the wonder of the underwater realm, but his parents are fearful, and Augustus, the king's adviser, warns the impetuous youth against such folly. One night, unable to resist the ocean's seductive call, the prince slips down to the shore. A voice in the darkness speaks passionately to him of the sea, and the vivid words create beautiful images in the young man's imagination. The guards identify the prince's companion—"It is only blind Stavros." This is confirmed by the elderly wise man himself, who admits: "My eyes have always been without sight. . . . But only my eyes."

Hoping to placate his son, the king orders construction of a pool, but it proves a poor substitute and hardly compares to Stavros's exciting description. In due time, the prince assumes the crown and goes looking for the blind man, but is dismayed to learn of his death. Unable to go "in the sea," the new king vows he "will go on it" and orders a boat built. From it, he observes Demetrius, a young sponge diver, whom he orders brought to his side. The ruler promises the lad that he can keep the golden goblet that will be tossed into the water if he will retrieve it from the ocean depths and report exactly what he sees. Demetrius returns exhausted but triumphant, clutching the treasure that will ensure his family's fortune. His description, however, is so mundane, so banal, that the young monarch is disgusted. Obsessed with his romanticized view, he asks the youngster if the goblet did not come to rest on "the ivory mast of a drowned galleon?" The bewildered lad replies: "Nay sire. It was stuck in the sea slime." The king's disappointment turns to insight as he claims that this episode has brought him some long overdue understanding: "I have learned that the heart sees more clearly than the eyes ever will."

Analysis. Told in the style of a fairy tale, this tedious and pretentious story reworks some familiar themes on the relationship between sight and vision and the validity of both reality and dreams. The blind seer, commonplace in literature, is given no new vitality here. The major illustrations are colorful and romantic but not notably original. The text, some of which is superimposed on the pictures, is unjustifiably hard to read.

Bunting, Eve. *One More Flight.* Illus. by Diane deGroat. New York: Warne, 1976. 92 pp. Reading Level: MC
Disability: Emotional Dysfunction

On one of his periodic escapes from a residential treatment facility, Dobby meets Timmer, a young man dedicated to rehabilitating injured or abandoned birds. The 11-year-old runaway hopes to ingratiate himself and find a permanent place of his own where someone will like and care for him. When 19-year-old Timmer reveals that he has reported the boy's whereabouts to the center, Dobby bitterly compares his situation to the chained birds. He spends the next day with the youthful birdman but is cruelly disappointed when told that Timmer's age would unquestionably disqualify him as a foster parent. Two of the birds are taken to a site where they can be released, and Timmer explains that there comes a time when a creature is ready to go off independently. That optimal moment must be carefully chosen so that the return to freedom will succeed. In an error of judgment, Timmer is hurt when an eagle is set free. Barely able to return home before collapsing, the young man must turn over responsibility for safeguarding the other birds to Dobby while he goes to have his wounds treated.

When Timmer is gone, a former Vietnam prisoner of war tries to release all the birds. Dobby yells frantically: "They'll die. It's not time for them to go. They're not ready to be free." In the ensuing scuffle, the intruder kicks the youngster in the head but is instantly remorseful. Help arrives, Dobby is cared for, and there is some discussion of finding VA help for the ex-navy flier. Timmer sadly observes: "The Jacobs guy was so busy trying to free them that he would have injured them, really hurt them bad. A crippled bird is not free." Dobby confides that he is fearful the authorities will send him to a detention home, but Timmer hints such a possibility is unlikely and suggests that the therapists might even consider his assistance at the bird farm as a form of rehabilitation. The boy reflects, "Could be. That's the kind of crap they do go for at the Center," and vows he will not run away again.

Analysis. Despite his placement, Dobby is seen in these incidents as a child who acts more out of frustration than as a result of distorted perceptions or emotional dysfunction. He is impulsive and unmindful of consequences, and the reader is obliged to assume the boy has already "improved." The center's staff is portrayed as generally sympathetic but often defeated by events outside their control. The veteran's behavior is shown to be inappropriate, disoriented, and dramatically lacking in judgment. The author implies the character's war experiences are at the root of his confusion, and although the result of his actions could have been tragic, he is depicted as misguided rather than malevolent. There is heavy-handed reliance on forced parallels between the boy's needs and those of the birds.

Bunting, Eve. *The Waiting Game.* New York: Lippincott, 1981. 56 pp. Reading Level: MC/YA
Disability: Auditory Impairment

Luther, Dan, and Griff are friends as well as teammates on their high school football squad. Dan, who is deaf, plans to attend a local junior college, but the other two students hope for sports scholarships at Ohio State. Griff does get an offer, but Luther is told he is underweight, although he may be a candidate next year if he can "get some size." Devastated by the rejection, Luther tells his family that even though Ohio State wanted him he decided to turn them down. His mother is proud of her son, convinced he made that decision so he could continue to help Dan, an erroneous interpretation she conveys to Luther's friends. Dan is incensed at the implications of what he believes his teammate has done: "Don't do it for me. I don't need . . . I'm just like you. I'm just like the rest of you guys. Just as good." Luther is ashamed when he realizes he has humiliated his friend by the insinuation that his own future has been nobly sacrificed. Confessing to his family and friends, he explains the real content of the call he received from the college recruiter. When an offer comes from San Diego State, Luther turns it down, not because of his buddy, but because he wants to remain available in case Ohio State makes him an offer the following season.

Analysis. Although both the subject matter and style are simplistic, *The Waiting Game* deals with a serious problem. A genuine friendship is contaminated when one participant allows himself to gain status by seeming to relinquish his own ambitions for the sake of his disabled friend. This ostensible sacrifice radically damages the mutuality of the boys' relationship, implying it was not one of equals. This theme is fairly subtle for a book obviously intended as a high-interest, low-ability selection. Incidental descriptions of how the hearing-impaired youth functions are included; for example, Luther communicates on the gridiron by tactile means and helps Dan monitor his speech. The simile "deaf as a dish" is a surprising inclusion considering the novel's otherwise sensitive tone. The final paragraph is ambiguous: "It was because he needed to stay free that he tore up the letter. It had nothing to do with big old Dan, Luther told himself. Nothing whatsoever." In another context, this final phrase of excessive protest would seem ironic, but such a style is rarely observed in books addressed to this presumed readership.

Bykov, Vasil. *Pack of Wolves.* Trans. by Lynn Solotaroff. New York: Crowell, 1981. 179 pp. Reading Level: YA/MA
Disability: Orthopedic Impairment

In the early days of World War II, Russian partisans, inadequately armed and led by neophytes unskilled in the arts and strategies of warfare, are betrayed by some of their own people as they struggle to combat the German forces that invaded their land. Levchuk's shoulder wound clearly needs medical attention so he, along with other disabled fighters, is sent from the front line. Eager to rejoin his unit, he is encouraged by the medic's advice: "Stick your arm in your belt and keep it there. It's nothing serious. You'll be swinging a sledgehammer in a week."

One of the evacuees is Klava, almost ready to deliver a baby whose father, a compatriot of Levchuk's, is now dead. The wounded hero, relying on his instincts, assumes command of the bedraggled group, leading his party through a swamp instead of on the road suggested by his superior officer. Despite the consequent hardships, Levchuk's plan proves fortuitous for, from the swamp, they soon hear gunfire along the proposed route. Lack of attention to his injury begins to worry the partisan: "Wet, and never properly dressed, it alternately ached dully and burned terribly as though it were festering. What would he do if he got blood poisoning?"

The weary travelers endure many hardships, finding refuge at last in a shed where Klava's child is born. By chance, some Nazi soldiers trap the Russians while they are waiting for the woman to regain enough strength for them to continue their journey. In the confusion caused by the fire the enemy sets to force them from their shelter, Levchuk manages to escape. He barely eludes his pursuers, rests briefly, then returns to the shed to learn the fate of his companions. The wounded man discovers Klava's abandoned infant, clutches it to his body as well as he can with his one good arm, and retreats hurriedly toward the swamp. The Nazis, using dogs, track him to the water's edge, unload their weapons into the marsh, and leave, assuming he could not have survived. Cradling the infant, the frenzied man laboriously makes his way out of the bog, where he meets and is helped by other partisans. He names the baby Victor after its father, entrusting him to a stranger to take it to safety. His arm is hopelessly infected and must be amputated in the field. Thirty years later, having at last tracked down the child he once saved, he goes to meet Victor, wondering what kind of reception he will receive.

Analysis. Levchuk's amputated arm is evidence of his personal suffering and symbolic of the destruction endured by his war-ravaged country. Despite witnessing the death of friends, the cowardice and perfidy of traitors, and being forced to abandon his ambitions because of his injury, Levchuk remains a proud and determined man. He has sacrificed his arm, but the courageous rescue of the infant offers promise for the future. *Pack of Wolves* effectively recaptures the horrors of war and the terrible hardships endured by an ill-equipped, unprepared, undernourished, but tenacious, indomitable people trying to fight against a seemingly omnipotent invader.

Callen, Larry. *The Deadly Mandrake.* Illus. by Larry Johnson. Boston: Little, Brown, 1978. 163 pp. Reading Level: MC/YA
Disability: Speech Impairment

Some strange occurrences have been taking place in the tiny bayou community of Four Corners where Sorrow Nix lives: a gray calf is born to a black-and-white cow; a baby hen begins to crow like a rooster; and Pinch's mother, who has always been healthy, suddenly and inexplicably takes sick. Inevitably the residents begin to talk of bad luck and evil spells. Sorrow's father claims responsibility, bragging that he has put a curse on his neighbors. Soon afterward, the man dies. Sorrow, although mute, informs Pinch of a promise she made to her father, but Sorrow will not tell her friend its substance except to say that it is somehow connected to local misfortunes. Pinch then discovers that Sorrow removed a mandrake root, presumably responsible for the evil events, from the safety of the little black box in which it had been stored.

Trouble continues to plague the rural area, and someone soon finds the deadly plant growing from Mr. Nix's grave. Instead of putting an end to the problem, Sorrow's act unwittingly assured that it would continue. Pinch is frightened because his mother's condition is worsening, and he decides to dig up the mandrake and destroy its power. He and Sorrow, following carefully prescribed procedures, uproot the weed, which is promptly devoured by the gray calf, who thereby puts an unorthodox finale to the curse.

Analysis. In this sequel to *Pinch*, Callen presents a folksy, homey story of simple times and unpretentious folk while evoking a potent sense of the unique area in which the action takes place. Sorrow, misnamed according to Pinch's mother, is a courageous, bright, and loving child. Her misunderstanding of the implications of her father's instructions was unrelated to her lack of speaking ability. Beloved by her mother, who had fruitlessly sought medical help for her, Sorrow is clearly the focus of concern of various characters and is Pinch's best friend, "as good a friend as I ever hope to have. She is so smart, I don't even like to think about it. She knows words I never heard of"—an assessment of her intelligence that is endorsed by the children's teacher. Moreover, the girl is depicted as a caring, coping person with admirable traits of perseverance and ingenuity. Sorrow's speech deficiency is compensated for with equanimity most of the time by her effective use of writing, drawing, and body language. As she observes: "I can talk . . . better than some. Making sounds is only part of talking." But during crises, she suffers greatly from her disability. She confides to her buddy: "When my paw died, I could barely hold the feeling inside me. You helped me, Pinch. Just being there. Just knowing you didn't expect me to say a single word. Telling me stories and giving me presents." Callen's characters, even those with less than commendable attributes, are treated charitably and affectionately. The central metaphor, emphasizing the need to respect innocence and the natural world, is particularly well developed in this warm and gentle tale.

Callen, Larry. *Sorrow's Song.* Illus. by Marvin Friedman. Boston: Little, Brown, 1979. 150 pp. Reading Level: MC
Disability: Speech Impairment

The Zoo Man, an itinerant animal collector, inquires about the presence of wild creatures in the area and indicates his willingness to pay for interesting specimens. When he discovers that some rare white whooping cranes may be nearby, he recruits several locals to capture one. Sorrow Nix, a mute girl, and her friend Pinch are determined not to let this happen, and they quickly devise tactics to save the magnificent birds. Since the smaller one, named Whooper by the youngsters, has a defective wing, a rescue operation, although tricky, is possible. The endangered young crane is caught, surreptitiously removed from the bayou, and hidden from the would-be captors. The two children try valiantly to conceal Whooper, who gradually and hesitantly begins to tolerate Sorrow's attempts to make friends. When Pinch's mother visits the penned creature, a copperhead silently invades the yard. Noticed only by Sorrow, the mute child tries to signal the oblivious woman, finally alerting her husband to the danger by blowing on a whistle. Before he can safely react, the crane angrily attacks the deadly snake, saving the woman's life. The local rowdies, learning of the hideout, attracted by the promised money, and anxious for some sporting action, make plans to steal the bird. Aware of their intentions, the children employ some rash countermeasures, which result in Sorrow becoming critically ill. The men are contrite—momentarily ashamed at the consequences of their greed and sincerely distressed by Sorrow's suffering. John Barrow, who considers himself a particular friend of the girl's, confides in Pinch that Sorrow

> was telling me she thought I done wrong. . . . She talked to me with those big eyes of hers. She didn't want me out hunting for the crane while she was sick in bed. . . . She saw the crane in the wagon and her eyes told me her heart was breaking. She said it better than if she'd used a bucketful of words.

As the man leaves Pinch's home, he pauses to add: "Last night I turned that pesky bird loose near the boat tie-up. It flies pretty good now, Pinch. Ain't likely somebody's going to catch it again."

Analysis. Sorrow's disability is accommodated by a community that values her highly. When the Zoo Man, a stranger, barges into the school demanding to know why the child can't speak, he learns her parents had exhausted every medical possibility before resigning themselves to teaching their daughter "to make the best use of what she had." The teacher admonishes him: "Sorrow Nix is more normal than the two of us. Don't you do anything that will make her feel otherwise." Sorrow's name seems to be not only a heavy burden to bear for a lifetime, but one that is at odds with her outlook and with others' responses to her. Although an injured bird plays a key role, its problem is not related to the heroine's disability, and the creature's function is logical and unstereotyped.

Carlson, Dale. *Triple Boy*. New York: Atheneum, 1977. 172 pp.
Reading Level: YA
Disability: Emotional Dysfunction

When Paul was six, his three-year-old brother was killed in a train accident, a tragedy their father irrationally considers the fault of his surviving son. Accepting this blame, the adolescent boy now also shoulders the burden of his mother's alcoholism, his father's failure as a husband, parent, and writer, as well as his parents' acrimonious divorce. The unremitting guilt he lives with and the anger he is unable to express have caused Paul, at 16, to develop three distinct personalities. He becomes more and more panicked over his "lost times," amnesialike episodes during which his behavior is controlled by one of the other parts of his splintered self.

A chance encounter with Dr. John Marsh, a psychiatric trainee who takes an immediate interest in his young neighbor, provides a lifeline for the desperate youth. By a remarkable coincidence, Marsh is engaged in researching Freud's interpretation of hysteria, a condition he explains to his young friend as a

psychoneurotic disorder arising from an emotional conflict in which repressed material finds an outlet through physical disturbances. In other words, if something terrible is troubling you, and your mind can't cope with it, you might go blind or become paralyzed or show the disorder of your mind in other ways.

Sensing that a relationship with this therapist may be his only chance for survival, the youngster pursues more contacts. Soon after some tentative starts at getting through the boy's defenses, Dr. Marsh is able to call up Paul's other selves at will. However, the young man's "lost times" continue, threatening his school status, friendships, and summer employment as his behavior becomes increasingly governed by the whims or demands of these other personalities. When "George" steals a ring, the incredulous, bewildered Paul reemerges to find himself in police custody. Dr. Marsh's intercession prevents charges from being pressed, but Paul's mentor now feels that the time is ripe for drastic measures. The aspiring analyst arranges for a tour through a psychiatric hospital where what are considered the most intractable paranoid and schizophrenic residents are shown to the shocked youth. Soon thereafter, therapy is initiated with Dr. Jason, a sympathetic and skilled specialist. Although told that his condition is dissimilar to that of the inpatients he has seen, Paul is distraught at this depressing glimpse of human misery. Soon after this frightening episode, the pressures imposed by his inadequate parents, the unrelieved pain caused by his guilt, and a dreadful feeling of futility prompt the youth to attempt suicide in a manner that recapitulates the death of his younger sibling. Fortuntely, an alert trainman saves Paul, and after his hospitalization, he meets, for the first time, his other personalities. Dr. Marsh convinces "Mike," the boy's bright, aggressive persona, to merge with Paul, promising him that he will have more freedom, not less. "Mike" replies: "I understand. . . . And I agree," thus eliminating one of the fragments. "George," his agreeable but immature dimension, is more resistant, but at last he too reunites with Paul, who is then able to integrate the strengths of these two fractions of himself into his own functioning. Despite this initial achievement, he still faces "years of therapy."

Analysis. This simplistic account dramatizes how multiple personalities might possibly originate and function. That Paul is able to articulate the source of his distress clearly, that alternate selves can so readily surface, that these aspects of the personality can be logically and rapidly persuaded to blend in with the core personality, that a tour through the back wards of a psychiatric hospital would be considered in any way therapeutic are insupportable propositions. The narrative is further burdened by improbably generous and compassionate characters: an employer who accepts any and all absences; an aspiring psychiatrist who devotes himself totally to the boy; unquestioning and uncomplaining teachers, coaches, friends, and so on. The excessive use of coincidence and the contrived events hopelessly undercut the novel's plausibility.

Carpelan, Bo. *Dolphins in the City.* Originally published in Stockholm as *Paradiset*, 1973. Trans. by Sheila La Farge. New York: Delacorte, 1976. 145 pp. Reading Level: YA
Disability: Intellectual Impairment

Marvin and his mother reluctantly abandon their home on Bow Island, moving to cramped and dingy lodgings on the nearby Finnish mainland. Although their friends, Nora and Johan, make the transition easier, Marvin is regularly taunted for his slowness by the neighborhood children, who are egged on by the bully, Peter. Gerda recollects early memories of her son's delayed development:

> I noticed early on that Marvin was different. . . . He didn't want to learn to walk, he was slow and late learning to talk, he sat quietly most of the time and sometimes I couldn't understand what he said.

It was very difficult. . . . You couldn't tell whether he understood. He would look at me, and I didn't know whether he saw me. The doctor said he was retarded and should be put in an institution. . . . Marvin slowly woke up and started to look around. . . . Everything made him happy. He was very slow and difficult to teach . . . but eventually he could learn. He went to Solgorden clinic when he was ten, but didn't get on there. . . . The doctors . . . told me that Marvin is like a telescope, so sometimes he sees little things very close and huge, and then sometimes everything is far away. . . . He had a hard time of it if anyone except me ever touched him. He got frightened and sometimes he couldn't utter a single word. . . . But there were rewards, and they started coming more and more often.

Gerda finds custodial work while her son takes a tedious factory job, which he is able to handle when there are no changes in the routine. His mother reports, "He works so hard he has to lie down and rest when he comes home. The warehouse boss says he doesn't see or hear, he gets so involved with his work, as if it were a matter of life or death." Although Marvin's daily existence is dreary, Christmas at Nora's provides an exhilarating interlude, and young Johan's unswerving loyalty sustains Marvin. Their visit to a library supplies him with books about sailing that give both solace and excitement to the restless young man. Gerda invites Matti, a male companion, to move into their apartment, but his lack of sympathy for her son's needs causes dissension from the outset.

The hysterical mother of a young girl who was sexually attacked wrongly accuses Marvin of the crime, shrieking that he is a madman and must be sent away. Unable to explain what happened, frustrated and frightened, Marvin bolts from his home, running toward the waterfront, where he teeters on the edge of the embankment, then falls in. Matti, who has been chasing him, dives into the water and rescues the terrified young man. Despite this demonstration of valor, his initial belief of the charges against her innocent son irreparably sours his relationship with Gerda and precipitates his moving out of her house. Withdrawn and uncomprehending, Marvin is sent to a rural residential center where, under the patient and sympathetic guidance of the staff, he begins to rebuild his self-confidence, unaware that his mother is making plans to return with him to their former island home.

Analysis. This sequel to *Bow Island* contains complex and original characters, has rich and vivid images, conveys a powerful sense of setting, and generates a memorable portrait of a developmentally delayed man as incapable as the dolphins that inhibit his dreams of surviving in a contaminated environment. Marvin is seen much like other people but in far greater need of support and protection since his skills for coping with adversity are minimal. He is the pivotal character and, because of his ingenuousness and vulnerability, elicits responses that expose flaws and strengths in others. Nora and Johan protect Marvin and seek his company out of genuine affection, not a sense of duty. Peter, a victim of parental violence, finds Marvin an easy target on which to vent his ungovernable, unfocused rage. Gerda is a loving mother who must make grave sacrifices for her son, acts she undertakes without any feelings of martyrdom but because the imperatives of maternal love make such behavior essential.

Carrick, Malcolm. *"I'll Get You!"* Illus. by author. New York: Harper & Row, 1979. 188 pp. Reading Level: MC
Disability: intellectual impairment; also visual impairment

Nine-year-old Michael lives in post–World War II London, where his father owns a factory that employs many of the neighborhood men. After Tommy Barker's father is fired, the other workers, not knowing the dismissed man is a thief, strike in sympathy. All are rehired when the facts are known, and they willingly return, except Mr. Webb, whose children are particular chums of Michael's. Rosemary lives in their community. "She's not mad, like kids say, but can't talk properly. When she opens her floppy-lip mouth, her tongue looks as if it's too big for words to pass it. She's not mad, only simple." With casual cruelty, the local boys taunt and tease the vulnerable child. Despite their mockery, Michael feels he must rescue the girl from their abuse and return her home whenever he discovers she is being victimized. When the hero asks why his friend took Rosemary's money, the boy unthinkingly replies: "She's so stupid, she hardly knew."

Mr. Barker intends to muscle in on the route of an ice cream salesman who is a friend of the neighborhood children, but a plan is devised to thwart the bully's scheme. Angry at being tricked, Barker tries to force his supplier to give him the last carton of ice cream even though it had already been purchased by someone else. Outraged at the man's strong-arm tactics, the factory owner angrily informs Barker that he is blacklisted as a vendor, a status he will ask other sellers to respect. Michael also discovers that Mr. Webb had not been rehired because of his failing sight, not because Michael's father had been vengeful. The boy is astonished to learn that his parent has arranged for medical care, which should result in sufficient restoration of vision to permit rehiring Mr. Webb.

Analysis. Rosemary is a minor character who rounds out a picture of life in this London community. She is one of the victims of the sometimes kind and sometimes cruel, obstreperous youngsters who struggle and flounder toward maturity. Michael's trip to return Rosemary's stolen purse and give her a present allow the author to express his philosophy: "Perhaps we're all just creatures together. All the same, not more or less important than a tree, nor a snake, just all, alive, on the earth." Although the ending is far too pat, the turmoil of a sensitive child as he gradually sheds some of his naiveté makes a compelling story.

Chaiken, Miriam. *Finders Weepers*. Illus. by Richard Egielski. New York: Harper & Row, 1980. 120 pp. Reading Level: MC
Disability: special health problems; also speech impairment, orthopedic impairment

The horrible news from Germany during the 1930s affects the lives of Jews in America, and Molly's family is no exception. The girl's heritage provides a comfortable structure for her life, and her Brooklyn home is a refuge and unfailing source of love. On the holidays, relatives visit, and Mordi, one of the cousins, stutters in his announcement to the others: "I'm going to b-b-be a f-f-flyer, l-like Lindbergh. . . . You don't have to t-t-talk. . . . You j-j-just fly the plane." Molly worries a great deal about her young brother, Yaaki, who suffers from asthma. Another problem Molly is struggling with concerns a ring that she finds, procrastinating in a search for the rightful owner. Aware that her mother would not permit her to keep this unexpected treasure, Molly devises a fraudulent explanation of how she came to possess it, but the woman is too distracted by worry about Yaaki's illness to question her daughter carefully. To the youngster's dismay, she learns the ring belonged to Hanna Gittel and was a gift from her father, a victim of the Holocaust. Conscience-stricken, Molly determines to return it but is unable to remove it from her finger. When Yaaki's condition worsens and he must be rushed to the hospital, the child concludes that this "punishment" is retribution for her "crime." A voice seems to scold: "On account of your sin, the whole family is being punished. And Hanna Gittel, a poor refugee girl is crying. Dirty, rotten, lousy, stinking crook!" Her shame is compounded when she discovers that Mrs. Gittel must use a wheelchair, the result of lingering injuries deliberately inflicted by her Nazi captors.

Now desperate to get the ring off, Molly pulls at it constantly, causing her finger to swell and throb. When this is noticed at school, she obtains relief from the principal, who snips the band, assuring her it can easily be mended. She arrives home to hear the news that her brother is better and will soon be discharged from the hospital.

"Molly's heart exploded with joy. She couldn't believe how quickly God had acted." The penitent girl goes to the synagogue, where she hands the damaged ring to its surprised and grateful owner; then, relieved of her guilt, she happily joins her mother for the Yom Kippur service.

Analysis. This homey, slow-moving story, with its focus on the minutiae of a young girl's life, features a heroine of surpassing innocence and naiveté. The baby's asthma is serious, but it is responded to in a reasonable, concerned manner by his loving parents. Molly believes her brother's attack is divine punishment for her misdeeds and his subsequent recovery the instantaneous reward for the mending of her ways, a misperception unfortunately not contradicted by the author. Mordi's reaction to his dysfluency is likewise immature but free of the emotionalism that permeates his cousin's responses. Mrs. Gittel's condition personalizes the writer's message about the treatment of Jews by the Nazis but also functions to accentuate the shame of Molly's offense.

Chambers, Aidan. *Breaktime.* New York: Harper & Row, 1978. 180 pp. Reading Level: MA
Disability: Special Health Problems

The worldly, cynical, and conceited Morgan challenges his companion to an intellectual joust—to refute his accusation that literature is worthless. Ditto, jealous of his friend and afraid that his charges may be unanswerable, worries about how to formulate a response. The latter's relationship with his father has been steadily deteriorating, and after a confrontation, the man collapses and is rushed to the hospital to the emergency cardiac care unit. Although troubled by feelings of guilt, his son makes arrangements to go away. He is determined to think through his family problems, prepare a rejoinder to Morgan's disturbing indictment of literature, and meet Helen, with whom he is determined to lose his virginity. During Ditto's odyssey, he encounters Jackie and Robby, who dare him to take part in an evening of unspecified adventure. Their jaunt begins at a political rally during which Robby deliberately provokes a riot. Exhilarated by the turmoil he has instigated, the youth reveals the second phase of his entertainment—to rob the house of the Labour Party speaker. Ditto, dismayed, is nonetheless goaded into going along with his newfound companions. When they are caught red-handed, it suddenly dawns on the naive, duped youth that it is Robby's father's home they are burglarizing. In the violent, animosity-filled encounter between father and son, Ditto sees echoes of his own filial behavior. Ditto continues his journey, determined to keep his rendezvous with Helen. After an awkward reunion, the adolescent has an idyllic sexual initiation.

Upon returning home, Ditto's mother gives him a letter and present from his father. The prodigal is undone to see the man's medals, received as a youth for his motorcycle racing prowess—an aspect of his father's life that contradicts the image Ditto holds. The two are reconciled, and Ditto offers Morgan an imaginatively written account of his recent adventures as a response to his friend's challenge. This account raises the hero's intellectual status, leaving his arrogant challenger the clear loser in their continuing rivalry.

Analysis. Unique, demanding, tightly constructed, *Breaktime* is a study in symmetry. While the man's heart disorder has some realistic aspects to it, the ailment is used primarily as a plot device to create a crisis between the hero and his father and to provide a rationale for the events that are about to transpire. Ditto also is faint of heart, a condition that is likewise remedied by story's end. While his father successfully holds off the Angel of Death, Ditto finds an "angel" to sponsor his initiation into sexual life. Hoping to mend the rift between himself and his son, the father gives the boy a gift of his prized medals, symbols of his once fearless and adventurous nature; Ditto, eager to regain the loving relationship they once shared and no longer a passive dreamer, recognizes in the present, evidence of a kindred spirit. The structure of the work is cleverly designed with obvious bows to James Joyce via puns and other linguistic jokes, double entendres, triple ironies, and multitudinous other literary games.

Chambers, Aidan. *Seal Secret.* New York: Harper & Row, 1980. 122 pp. Reading Level: MC/YA
Disability: Speech Impairment

Disgruntled at his family's change in summer plans, William anticipates a boring week at an isolated cottage in Wales. While exploring a road in the countryside, he meets Gwyn, an unpleasant, abrasive youth who taunts him about his lack of skill in climbing trees. William tries to respond, but, as usual, "when he lost his temper, or got nervous, he began to stutter." Gwyn cruelly mimics the English lad's hesitant speech: "G-g-go back where you c-c-came from. . . . And good riddance." William's parents are furious when they see his torn clothes and accuse him of trying to spoil their vacation. The boy is doubly embarrassed being reprimanded in front of Miss James, the owner of the cottage. Unsuccessful in her early attempts at consoling and distracting him, she finally suggests that exploring the contents of an abandoned barn might be a pleasant diversion. Without consulting him, the well-meaning woman arranges for a companion, and William finds, to his dismay, that Gwyn has been bribed to accompany him. The Welsh boy is unenthusiastic over this assignment, but in return his father, a friend of Miss James, has promised him money toward the purchase of a calf, an inducement he cannot resist. While William is trying to decide which would be worse—staying at the house with his irritable parents or going camping with the contentious boy—Gwyn persuades him to choose the latter action by promising to reveal something amazing. After the skeptical William promises under oath not to speak to anyone about what he will see, Gwyn leads him to a cave at the edge of the sea where he shows his astounded companion an abandoned seal pup. The Welsh lad has started building a wall to pen the animal in, planning to use the creature as part of a projected seal farm. He excitedly explains: "There'd be meat, you see, and skins for fur coats as well. Good profit." His outraged companion responds, " 'But you c-c-can't!' Then 'No.' He spoke firmly and without stammering, despite his churning insides. 'No, you won't.' " When William insists that he is determined to save the seal, Gwyn jeers: "You couldn't knock the skin off a rice pudding." But William vows to save the animal from destruction "in his own way. Without help from anyone," and is more adamant about this than anything before in his life.

Before dawn the next day, William drags a dinghy to the cave, where he finds he must fight the rapidly rising water as well as attacks from the terrified animal before he is able finally to force the reluctant mammal into the boat. William observes Gwyn in the distance, separated from the cave by waves, which rapidly gather force. Disregarding his enemy's angry gestures, William tries to calm the animal, but the baby seal bites him before somersaulting into the raging waters, joining at last an adult seal waiting nearby. William notes with alarm that he is being propelled toward the rocky cliffs of an island but is helpless to prevent himself from being shipwrecked. Gwyn alerts the coast guard, who rescue the injured boy. His parents are pleased at their son's unexpected assertiveness, and William treasures this incident in which he was tested and met the crisis with resolve, ingenuity, and courage.

Analysis. Chambers has written a compelling tale featuring an initially passive, overly sensitive hero, who, when sufficiently provoked, asserts himself, gaining stature in his own eyes and, less importantly, in the eyes of others. William's stammer reflects the boy's indecisiveness and disappears when he gains control over other aspects of his life, a perception of remediation often held by the lay public. His dysfluency is modest, emerging only when the boy is distressed. It is implied that in yielding to subtle pressures imposed by his impatient parents, William has turned his aggressions inward, consoling himself through such solitary, nonoral activities as reading and drawing. His stutter is seen as an outward, concrete expression of his hesitancy, and its absence when he announces his determination to save the seal foreshadows the successful accomplishment of his goal. Supporting characters in this unusual story are equally well rounded, demonstrating complex motivations and conflicting needs. The tension-filled, suspenseful work moves rapidly to a satisfying climax.

Christopher, Matt. *Football Fugitive.* Illus. by Larry Johnson. Boston: Little, Brown, 1976. 119 pp. Reading Level: MC
Disability: Auditory Impairment

Larry Shope is unhappy because his lawyer father takes so little interest in his football games. The boy has written several letters to Yancey Foote, a professional football player whom he idolizes. The last two communications have been returned with the words: "Moved— Left No Forwarding Address" stamped on them. Larry, worried about what may have happened to his hero, buys a sports magazine, which reports that the athlete was involved in a brawl with a much smaller man and may be in serious trouble.

Larry's best friend and teammate, Greg, has a severe hearing loss, which interferes only mildly with his playing. The other boys occasionally assist him, and Larry repeats or interprets when he thinks his buddy may have missed something. After a typical locker room session, Larry asks Greg: "Did you get all that?" The boy replies: "I think so. I'm not sure. Most of the time the coach doesn't open his mouth very much when he speaks, except when he sees me frowning at him. Every time I frown he knows that I'm not reading his lips very well, so he starts talking a little louder and forms the words with his lips." Larry expresses surprise that his friend knows when the coach is speaking in a louder voice. Greg responds: "I can tell. And, remember, I'm not totally deaf either."

The boys notice a stranger watching them from the sidelines. Larry tracks him down, goes to his apartment, and learns he is the missing Yancey Foote. The Green Bay Packer tells Larry he wants his father to represent him in court and will call for an appointment. In the meantime, he sends his young fan back to the coach with a couple of hot shot professional maneuvers. These plays turn the team around, and after a winning game the professional football player escorts Larry home and meets the boy's father, who agrees to defend him. The day of the trial is also the day of another big game. Thanks again to Yancey's long-distance coaching, the boys win. After the game is over, Larry is startled to see both his hero and his father, who joyfully inform him that they have won the case. In the future,

Mr. Shope promises to take an interest in his son's pursuits: "From now on I'm going to see to it that the word *lawyers* is interchangeable with *fathers*."

Analysis. There is plenty of play-by-play action in this highly improbable story of a neglected youngster, a misunderstood gridiron hero, and an inattentive father who mends his ways. The best aspect of this work is the totally natural, almost casual treatment of the youth with a hearing loss. Some accommodations must be made for his disability, but these are done without fuss or drama. Although only a secondary component of the story, it is handled with commendable sensitivity. Most of the black-and-white illustrations show football action and complement the straightforward presentation of the plot.

Christopher, Matt. *The Submarine Pitch.* Illus. by Larry Johnson. Boston: Little, Brown, 1976. 137 pp. Reading Level: MC
Disability: Special Health Problems

Reluctantly, Bernie announces his intention to quit baseball, a decision that puzzles and disappoints his younger brother, Frankie. Dave, Bernie's best pal, stops by to discuss an underhand pitch called the Submarine, which he is confident his disheartened friend can master. The former pitcher's two main supporters persuade Bernie to practice, and soon, to his surprise, the youth improves his technique to such a degree that he agrees to come out of "retirement." When the season opens, Bernie uses the new pitch, which sizzles over the plate, astonishing all his opponents. As each game is played, the hurler's control and reputation increase. During one of the contests, Bernie becomes distracted when he cannot spot Dave in the stands. He vaguely recalls that his friend has been having difficulty breathing lately, lacks energy, and tires excessively after only slight exertion. Dave shows up late but, soon after, misses a game completely. Now very worried, Bernie insists his mother call the hospital and learns his unspoken fears have been realized: Dave is in intensive care. The patient's father informs the hero that his son is desperately ill with a liver disease: "He never told anybody. He's been fighting a battle with it for the last two years. I hope he's going to get well, but Bernie, it doesn't look too good." Shocked, the boy rushes out to buy a model ship he knows his buddy coveted and which he hopes to be able to give him as a token of his gratitude and friendship.

Analysis. Despite extensive clues that Dave is seriously ill, there is no literary justification for the sudden announcement that his disorder is fatal. The use of this dramatic ploy is a transparent attempt to beef up a work whose exclusive purpose is to provide detailed descriptions of baseball action.

Churchill, David. *It, Us and the Others*. New York: Harper & Row, 1978. 119 pp. Reading Level: MC/YA
Disability: Orthopedic Impairment

Andy ordinarily spends much time alone—in the fifth form at school in England, at the orphanage, or working on his mechanical projects—but the events that take place at the river one afternoon are so bizarre that he needs a companion to talk to about them. By coincidence, a classmate speaks to him, and he spills out his disquieting tale: something tugged on his fishing line in so pronounced a pattern that it could only have been done by an intelligent being. Instead of scoffing, Jill is intrigued and agrees to accompany him to the river. Andy overcomes their transportation problem by locating a tandem bike. The girl had always wanted to ride a bike but considered it beyond her ability. She explains: "My left arm never properly grew," and she has what she calls "my little hand" below her shoulder. Andy shows his companion the dinner plate–size ring that was on his hook when he reeled in his line from the water, and they puzzle over the strange drawings on its sides. Jill guesses they represent some conflict between forces of good and evil. When they spot a beautiful but badly wounded creature beneath the waves, their contact is interrupted by the presence of two dark and ominous hooded figures.

Jill ponders the problem of how to communicate with It, finally deciding to use her own primers. She places these initial reading instruction books, paper, and pencils in partially inflated, plastic sealable bags. Andy weights them, lowers them into the water, and notices with pleasure that their offering is "accepted." The youth must return alone the next day, and It gives him a picture that seems to move. Andy is startled to see himself in the illustration holding up the ring at the water's edge while standing under a full moon. When the protagonists try to recreate the scene at night, the creature rises from the river, flies through the ring, and disappears into the dark but sheltering sky. Although It has been rescued and the nefarious, hooded figures thwarted by this courageous act, the confrontation is traumatic for Andy, who is reminded of the terrifying night when his despondent father tried to commit suicide and his mother, attempting to intervene, died instead. Unable to help himself, the distraught boy is saved from drowning by a frightened but determined Jill. After a month in the hospital, he returns to the orphanage, where he hears of an opportunity to work for a company engaged in making prostheses "for people who need them in order to live normal lives." He muses: "I've had a few ideas already, but I expect they will have thought of them by the time I start there."

Analysis. Although restrained by an overprotective mother, Jill manages to take part in most of the activities engaged in by her peers. She is depicted as an ingenious and attractive adolescent whose boyfriend is undeterred by her birth disorder. Her attitude is accepting and gently self-mocking, as typified in her assessment of her cooking skills: "Sausage roll, not easily made one-handed, hence the lopsided appearance, which you will be too polite to notice, of course." Andy matter-of-factly concerns himself with solving such practical problems for Jill as using a fishing rod and dares a "sort of joke, although [he] meant it seriously. . . .'You need a bionic arm.' " Jill "looked quickly away, and [he curses] himself for upsetting her." Inadvertently, he has touched upon a source of anxiety for the reluctant girl, whose mother has been urging her to adopt a prosthesis. Little mention is made of Andy's father's difficulties except to imply that his long-term depression has sufficiently alleviated to permit him to renew contact with his son.

The chapters, narrated alternately by the two principals, show no difference in style, tone, or point of view. The science fiction motif is not well developed: all conditions and events surrounding the supernatural creature whose distress provides the focus of the story are completely arbitrary. Nonetheless, the central characters are appealing and their adventures mildly interesting.

Clark, Margaret Goff. *Who Stole Kathy Young?* New York: Dodd, Mead, 1980. 191 pp. Reading Level: YA
Disability: Auditory Impairment

While her parents are vacationing, Meg stays with her friend, Kathy Young, who lost her hearing as an adolescent. The two girls spot a suspicious-looking couple, whom they nickname Heron and Toad. Meg takes Kathy's dog, Rusty, with her for a walk, and on the way back she sees her friend pulled into a mysterious van, which is quickly driven away. Rusty gives chase and disappears down the road in the direction of the truck. Meg dashes home to report the kidnapping to Mr. Young, who immediately contacts the local authorities. The official search gets underway, but Meg and Julian, an attractive older boy, impatiently begin their own investigation. Alongside the road, the two young sleuths discover the dog, who has collapsed, exhausted from the fruitless pursuit of his mistress. In the meantime, Kathy has been bravely but vainly trying to escape from her captors.

Meg reveals her suspicions about Toad and Heron and learns that Toad, whose real name is Morgan, had been a private detective. As Meg finds out more about the woman and begins to like and trust her, she hopes the investigator may be helpful in obtaining Kathy's release. Morgan freely offers her services to the search team. When the ransom demand arrives, Mr. Young immediately makes plans to meet all the conditions while the sheriff prepares to trail whoever picks up the money. Meg, deciding she wants to be in on the rescue too, hides in Morgan's car, which is driven to a warehouse. To everyone's surprise, subsequent events reveal that Morgan masterminded the entire kidnapping scheme. Although the sheriff's deputies surround her, the desperate criminal tries to escape, using Kathy as a shield. Meg signals the hostage in sign language to drop to the floor so the law enforcement officer will be able to have a clear shot at the kidnapper. The plan works, the heroine is saved, the felons are captured, and the innocent are cleared.

Analysis. This Nancy Drew analogue is filled with improbable events enacted by stock characters who are developed in unexceptional ways. The depiction of the hearing-impaired character is simplistic, but no more so than others in this trite, easy-to-read formula story. Using sign language to foil the villains provides an expected and unoriginal plot resolution. The term *stole,* conventionally employed in reference to objects, is depersonalizing when applied to a human being.

Clifton, Lucille. *My Friend Jacob.* Illus. by Thomas Di Grazia. New York: Dutton, 1980. unp. Reading Level: YC
Disability: Intellectual Impairment

Eight-year-old Sam narrates a brief episode in his friendship with Jacob, an 18-year-old neighbor with developmental disabilities. The young boy dismisses his mother's mild protests and hints that such a relationship is inappropriate since he knows that Jacob is kind, gentle, and loyal, while acceding that he functions on a very low level. The boys are mutually helpful, and when the younger one realizes that Jacob's habit of bursting in on Sam's family without bothering to knock on the door is an irritant, he decides to teach his impetuous friend this social skill. He is moderately successful: Jacob now remembers to knock but has not comprehended the idea that he must always wait for permission to enter.

Analysis. The older boy's limitations are accepted with matter-of-factness by his young friend. Sam's mother's anxiety is not unusual, but she is a reasonable woman and takes pleasure in Jacob's achievement, incomplete though it is. Jacob is shown as having certain skills, such as visual discrimination and memory. The central incident indicates he has learned the task but understood only incompletely the purpose, timing, and sequence required. The black-and-white illustrations are sensitively rendered and complement what is essentially a celebration of a very special friendship.

Cohen, Barbara. *Queen for a Day*. New York: Lothrop, Lee & Shepard, 1981. 158 pp. Reading Level: MC
Disability: Emotional Dysfunction

Except for school, which she views as an oasis, life in her pre–World War I Brooklyn tenement home seems unremittingly dreary to 12-year-old Gertie. The youngster's mother has been institutionalized in the Broadmere State Hospital for the Incurably Insane, and her father has deserted her, ostensibly to make his fortune out west. Gertie lives a Cinderella-like existence in her grandmother's home. The endlessly complaining old woman heaps more chores on her than on Lilly or Bereneice, her slightly older aunts, who make up the rest of the household. Mrs. Grobowitz incessantly reminds her granddaughter that the girl is only there on sufferance and that unless she is diligent and uncomplaining she will be sent to an orphanage. Frightened at the prospect of such a fate, the girl labors endlessly at her assigned tasks.

Mr. Neufeld, their new boarder, views Gertie's plight sympathetically, commiserating with her orphan status and commending her on her aptitude for learning. He coaches her in the Hebrew language and shares his love of biblical stories with the knowledge-hungry child. When he observes that her onerous workload would be considerably reduced if her aunts helped, she indicates her awareness of the accuracy of this comment and caustically remarks, "People may think my mother is a lunatic, but I'm certainly not crazy."

On Gertie's birthday, her grandmother takes her to visit her mother but warns against unrealistic expectations, observing: "People don't usually get better here." An attendant advises them to wait for the woman in the hall: "Some of the loonies'll bother you if you stay in here. Babble to you . . . or pull at your clothes." The meeting is traumatic for the child. Her mother's failure to recognize her and insistence that the baby she once had is now dead are frightening. Gertie is further distressed when the patient becomes obsessed with grabbing and eating the candy she has been given, ignoring her visitors. The girl calls out to her mother as the attendants hustle her off. "But Mama didn't hear, or if she heard, didn't pay any attention. She was still weeping over her lost candy."

When Lilly, chosen to play the lead in a Purim play, is still unprepared by the day of the performance, she fakes an illness. Mr. Neufeld convinces Gertie to step in since she has been coaching her incompetent aunt and knows all the lines. Elated by the applause she receives for her performance as the heroic Queen Esther, Gertie is disappointed when her life returns to its usual humdrum domesticity after the play. The boarder suggests she must never hesitate to grab life's other opportunities, as she did the Esther role, whenever they present themselves. Soon after, he announces he will be leaving for Chicago to accept a new job. Gertie feels she has been abandoned once more, but her faith in her new mentor is reaffirmed when she learns he has sent her grandmother money for her support and located her father and encouraged him to write his lonely daughter. She goes to visit her mother again and realizes that her mother has permanently regressed to the level of a young child and will undoubtedly have to remain a patient in the institution for the rest of her life.

Analysis. The tragic picture of institutional life in the early part of the twentieth century, complete with the hospital's chillingly hopeless name and its unsupportive, ineffectual staff, is real and credible. Although some aspects of the lives of impoverished immigrants are vividly depicted, the ethnic components receive heavy-handed, repetitive treatment. Characters are presented in two-dimensional terms, then suddenly and unconvincingly are shown to be more complex than originally suggested. The story lacks subtlety; its didactic intent overwhelms its function as fiction.

Coleman, Hila. *Accident*. New York: Morrow, 1980. 154 pp. Reading Level: YA
Disability: Neurological Impairment, orthopedic impairment

Despite her family's poverty, Jenny Melino has an upbeat view of life. She especially enjoys the roller skates her mother gave her, relishing the feeling of speed and control they provide. Adam DeWitt, an affluent fellow student, stops to chat with the attractive high school girl and her girl friend while they are skating, takes photos of her in motion, and asks her to accompany him on a motorcycle date. When the bike strikes a hole, Jenny, who had let go of Adam's waist because something had flown into her eye, falls onto the road. The frightened boy seeks help from a neighbor, who calls an ambulance that rushes Jenny to the emergency room of a nearby hospital. The family keeps a vigil there as Mrs. Melino tries to calm her son, Mike, who is furious with Adam because of his sister's injuries, falsely assuming the boy's obvious wealth has made him callous. When Jenny regains consciousness three days later, she is disoriented, has had a tracheotomy, and suffers from a partial paralysis of her right side. Her physician coolly tells her that her brain sustained damage that will prevent her from walking "until the lesions heal." She is devastated by these statements and interprets them to mean she may never walk again. It is difficult for her to converse with anyone because of her reduced attention span, distractibility, and irritability. When Adam comes to visit her, she is still befuddled. He announces that he is in love with her, but she accuses him of merely feeling pity.

Jenny is soon transferred to a rehabilitation setting and, at first, is moody and uncooperative. The prospect of not being able to control her movements depresses her, and she is suspicious of what she perceives as the "heroics" of some of the other patients. Lanie, her roommate who is in a body cast to correct scoliosis, tries to be friendly, but Jenny resists any social overtures. She disparages her rehabilitative progress and that of the other patients. The resident social worker rejects her pessimism and tries to give the girl encouragement:

> Snap out of it, Jenny. You're going to make a lot of messes before you're through. You're going to spill food, drop things, be awkward, have a million little frustrations learning how to make your limbs work. But if you don't keep at it, you will never learn. If you're lazy and impatient, you may remain crippled: If you work at it, though, your chances are better than even that you won't. It's your decision.

The woman's words are sobering, and although Jenny begins to apply herself to her physical and occupational therapy regimen, her progress is slow and uneven. When Adam visits with a photograph of her on skates that won first prize, Jenny is furious, accusing him of cruelly mocking her present immobilization. He counters that her free spirit, evident in the picture, is the quality the judges recognized. Therapy gradually brings about enough improvement to allow Jenny to take a few faltering steps and anticipate continuing her rehabilitation at home. She confides to her still angry brother that she will probably be seeing less of Adam because: "I like Adam, but I don't *need* him anymore."

Analysis. Several lessons are developed in this easy-to-read novel: maturation consists of distinguishing between the essential and the superficial; attitude is a major factor in determining the impact of misfortune; and one must accept responsibility for one's own actions. The complexities of the rehabilitation process are explored in *Accident*, as are the interrelationships of ancillary professionals in the recovery of a patient. Particularly effective is the depiction of the sharp, no-nonsense social worker who will not cater to Jenny's self-pity and apathy. The cast of characters is ostentatiously ethnically balanced, and each is generally motivated by a single persisting need or perception.

Cook, Marjorie. *To Walk on Two Feet.* Philadelphia: Westminster, 1978. 93 pp. Reading Level: MC
Disability: Orthopedic Impairment

Carrie Karns is plagued by nightmares of the car accident that required below-the-knee amputation of both of her legs. The physicians have prepared her stumps for prostheses, but unreconciled to her loss, she remains depressed, withdrawn, and irritable. Despite the urgings of her parents and medical personnel, she refuses to see neighbors or friends or to begin rehabilitation therapy. Surreptitiously, however, she learns to use her wheelchair and tries on her artificial legs. One evening she observes a robbery from her bedroom window and is able to provide the police with important evidence. Her parents are determined to leave for a brief vacation even after their daughter has been threatened with harm. Predictably, the thief enters the Karns' house but kidnaps Carrie's younger brother. There is no police response even when the adolescent girl rolls her wheelchair into the street screaming for help. Ultimately the criminal is traced to a parking lot, where he manages to elude capture and kidnap the hapless heroine. After a brief chase, the police shoot the villain as he tries to leave the car and run with the teenage hostage in his arms. This traumatic event, which takes place at the scene of the accident where she was injured, purges the girl of her nightmares and enables her to face the future with confidence.

Analysis. There is some substantive information about the rehabilitative difficulties that attend amputation—notably the nature and functioning of prosthetic devices, problems of phantom pain, the importance of attitude on recovery, and the need for emotional support from family and friends. The plot, however, is totally unbelievable, depending on unlikely and improbable events and the uninterrupted stupidity of all the major characters. The dialogue is particularly wooden, typified in this instance when the villain addresses Carrie:

> "Why you little snip," the man laughed unpleasantly.
> "Better do as he says," Carrie ordered. "Do just as he says. No one must be hurt."

Characterizations are naive and age-inappropriate. The heroine, supposedly 15, observes: "It was fun to sit on the floor. It gave a very different view of things." In sum, the literary deficiencies far outweigh the modest informational values.

Cookson, Catherine. *Go Tell It to Mrs. Golightly.* Originally published in Great Britain, 1977, by Macdonald & Jane's. New York: Lothrop, Lee & Shepard, 1977. 192 pp. Reading Level: MC
Disability: Visual Impairment, emotional dysfunction

Bella has been living in a residential school for the six months since the death of her alcoholic father. Dour old Joseph Dodd, her grandfather and presumed only living relative of the eight-year-old child, is assigned her guardianship. When he sees his granddaughter for the first time, he notes with dismay that her "eyes were wide and dark and brown, but the lids were unblinking." The child's social worker provides a background report to the suspicious and hostile old man:

> Her eyes were weak from when she was born. . . . Her mother was very young, only sixteen. She had to take the child to the hospital every week, and it must have been a strain for her because she left the child and her husband before the child's first birthday . . . when Bella was five she could see relatively well, but then she contracted measles and other childhood ailments and these weakened her system. Her sight went completely when she was six years old.

The bright, articulate, and relentlessly cheerful child is not put off by her grandda's gruff manner and adjusts readily to living in his joyless house. Dodd is angered by Bella's constant chatter and particularly her repeated references to imaginary animal companions and to a Mrs. Golightly and forbids her ever to mention them again in his presence. The reclusive and self-reliant man is reluctantly obliged to ask John, an older neighbor, to supervise Bella occasionally. The 14-year-old boy is initially dismayed at this unwelcomed assignment but is mollified as he realizes he has an attractive, entertaining, and feisty charge on his hands. As she becomes acquainted with her neighbors, Bella encounters a mysterious Mrs. Campbell, who in the course of conversation speaks obliquely of an extended illness in the past. The two enjoy each other's company, sharing such simple pleasures as walking or unhurriedly exploring the nearby village.

One day in her meanderings in the woods, the girl happens upon a helplessly trussed up man who implores her to go for aid. But when her skeptical grandfather finally follows Bella to the spot where she claims the poor wretch should have been, there is no one there and Dodd is furious, believing he has been tricked into participating in one of the child's make-believe games. Undaunted, Bella convinces John of the stranger's peril, and when they investigate, they too are made prisoners by the kidnappers and incarcerated in a cellar along with the first captive.

When Mrs. Golightly shows up to visit Bella, Dodd is astonished that the woman actually exists and is not just a figment of his granddaughter's imagination. He begins to suspect that the child's latest farfetched tale of a victim might also be true. In the meantime, John and Bella escape their prison and report the crime. The malefactors are caught and the hostage rescued. After the youngster recovers from this trying ordeal, she discovers that Mrs. Campbell, who is really her mother, plans to marry John's father. Upon due consideration, Bella decides not to live with her parent but to stay with her crusty but loving grandda since she remembers how sad it is to be all alone and she is unable to leave her dear relative in this dreadful plight.

Analysis. The myth that disability naturally confers a more saintly disposition finds expression in this absurd and cloying little novel. Except for periodic crying jags, the angelic heroine is without fault: she is kind, considerate, self-sacrificing, sensitive, cheerful, cooperative, brave, and forgiving. Even her teenage caretaker and companion compares her to the cherubs in the chapel, a likeness emphasized by her "eyes, wide, staring, sightless." The basis for her mother's psychological distress, which resulted in the abandonment of her daughter, is developed with some logic, although it is underexplained and overdramatized. No comment is offered about her proposed second marriage to a man with a drinking problem similar to that of her first husband. Characterizations and plot are equally ridiculous, and the dialogue seems borrowed from decades long past.

Cookson, Catherine. *Lanky Jones.* New York: Lothrop, Lee & Shepard, 1980. 158 pp. Reading Level: MC
Disability: Neurological Impairment

Obliged to accept the hospitality of the Everton family when their car is immobilized, Mr. Jones and his son, Daniel, also known as Lanky, soon feel right at home on the remote farm. But that night the youth is awakened by "weird, awful scream(s) followed by a groan." When Lanky opens his bedroom door to investigate, he sees Michael Everton descending from the attic with what looks like a weapon. Lanky assumes, with some shock, that the 17-year-old boy is reponsible for the bruises his sister Sally tries to conceal the next morning. Nevertheless, Lanky looks forward to accepting the Evertons' invitation to spend his vacation at their farm. The fly in the ointment is Billy Combo, obnoxious army buddy of the deceased Mr. Everton, who hopes to marry his friend's widow.

Although his mother sorely neglected him, Lanky still aches at the gap left in his life when she remarried. When she arrives at the farm to claim him temporarily for her court-sanctioned visit, the angry 15-year-old boy runs off, refusing to leave with her. Unluckily, he blunders across some men, led by the nefarious Combo, who are engaged in sheep stealing. Sally searches for Lanky, intending to inform him that his mother has finally gone away. She discovers him bound and gagged, but before she can come to his assistance, she has an epileptic seizure. Lanky is "overwhelmed by a feeling of sadness and pity," but he now understands the mysterious screams, the injuries, and the extreme limitations on the child's activities imposed by her mother: "Poor, poor Sally. That's why her mother wouldn't let her go to dances; that's why she couldn't ride." Lanky rouses the child sufficiently to report the gang's plans and convinces her of the urgency of leaving immediately, but semiconscious, she wanders only a short distance away. The drowsy, confused girl is discovered by friends and taken home to sleep off the effects of this episode. The crooks load the sheep and the youth into a van, drive to the docks, then throw the still trussed up lad into the hold of the ship, intending to dispose of him at sea. One of the crew, unwilling to be a party to murder, frees the captive, with whom he makes tentative plans to escape. Meanwhile, back at the farm, Sally awakens, accurately recalls Lanky's message, and, in the nick of time, the police are informed of the wicked plot. Although initially skeptical, they search the vessel thoroughly, locate Lanky and his new ally, and apprehend the villains. Lanky is reconciled with his now contrite and repentant mother. His father hints at plans to wed Mrs. Everton, who is at last convinced that her daughter should be allowed social contacts and opportunities for independence.

Analysis. Epilepsy is a disorder long associated with unfortunate connotations, and these isolating, denigrating stereotypes are perpetuated in *Lanky Jones*. The novel exploits this dysfunction for literary effect by treating it in highly emotional terms. Characters and events in this novel are manipulated so as to make ordinary, readily explained actions seem mysterious and menacing. Cookson exaggerates the hero's wonderment about noises emanating from the uppermost floor. By doing so, she creates the impression that someone up there is being cruelly abused. Lanky hears strange sounds, which he believes someone "demented" is responsible for, "and there came over him the most odd feeling, a terrifyingly odd feeling." When the brother is seen leaving the attic with a ruler, Lanky suspects it may have been employed as a device to insert in Sally's mouth during a seizure—a popular but now thoroughly discredited response. Some "new technique" is hinted at that is effective in the treatment of epilepsy, but what it is or how it works is never explained. Sexist attitudes are manifest both in such phrases as "[Lanky] would have screamed like a girl" and in the portrayal of excessively passive and dependent female characters. In addition to these flaws, the story line lacks imagination, with all major story elements being simultaneously contrived and farfetched.

Cookson, Catherine. *Mrs. Flannagan's Trumpet.* Originally published in Great Britain, 1976, by Macdonald & Jane's. New York: Lothrop, Lee & Shepard, 1976. 192 pp. Reading Level: YA
Disability: Auditory Impairment, special health problems

Mrs. Morley, who must spend three months in a hospital undergoing treatment for asthma, decides to send her children, Eddie and Penny, to stay with their grandmother, who lives in a small town. Eddie vehemently objects to staying with Mrs. Flannagan because of the contempt she has always openly expressed toward his now deceased father. But Eddie reluctantly agrees to his mother's wishes, realizing there are no other workable options. The move is as bad as the lad feared for the old woman's hostility toward her son-in-law seems to extend to her grandson. In addition, the constant shouting to his grandmother through her ever-present ear trumpet is disconcerting, and Eddie can never seem to modulate his voice correctly, much less communicate his thoughts to her.

Daisy, the maidservant, tells Eddie about Mrs. Van, a Belgian neighbor who collects pebbles on the North Sea beach abutting the Flannagan home. Kemp, a relative presently staying with the family, has denied knowing the foreigner, but Daisy says that Kemp is lying. Eddie speaks to his grandfather about overhearing a suspicious conversation between Van and Kemp, and the old man deduces that they must be engaged in an activity far worse than the smuggling in which so many of their neighbors take part. He decides to investigate the matter. Later, Eddie fortuitously spies Kemp dumping his grandfather's limp body in an inaccessible cove. Desperate to save the man before the tide comes in, Eddie, his grandmother, and a neighbor descend through a secret passageway down the cliff to the shore. The route is perilous, but they are able to complete the rescue, and the intended victim begins his recovery in the cavelike passage. Soon after, Penny and Daisy are kidnapped. The frightened 15-year-old Eddie reveals his suspicions to the coast guard and seeks their assistance. He and his grandmother confront Kemp with their accusations. In the ensuing fight, feisty Mrs. Flannagan smashes her hearing trumpet on the head of the villain, who falls to the floor unconscious. The youth figures out where the hideaway is and, in his brave rescue attempt, is stabbed by Mr. Van. Luckily the coast guard, having spotted Eddie, trails him to the "white slaver's" hideaway. Arriving in the nick of time, they capture Van, pull off the rescue, and take the wounded Eddie to the hospital. The family members are reunited, the kidnapping racket is sundered, Eddie is recognized as a hero, Kemp is dead, and Van is put in prison. Mrs. Flannagan belatedly announces that she was mistaken about the qualities of her son-in-law. Eddie will be able to pursue his dream to become an engineer, and he realizes that Daisy may be the girl for him. The enmity the boy felt toward his grandmother is laid to rest "for now he knew he loved his granny Flannagan."

Analysis. The treatment of Mrs. Flannagan's hearing loss is one of many unfortunate aspects of this book. The constant shouting into her ear trumpet, her ever-present complaints, and her use of the instrument as a weapon are intended to provide some mild levity. They are not successful. The woman claims: "I've had partial hearing in this ear for the past six months." She hadn't told anyone because it "served my purpose in many ways and I found out who my friends were. Anyway, what was the good of shouting about it when they told me up there it may only be temporary and I could lose it at any time again." Her personality is stiff and uncompromising, and her vacillating ability to hear adequately and consistently provides some rationale for her irritability. However, this "playing" at deafness is one of the least acceptable devices used to complicate an already overburdened plot. The writing is weak, redundant, pretentious, and cliché-ridden. Eddie considers: "in a business like this there was a string of villains, evil villains"—presumably a more nefarious type than beneficent ones. He later concludes that Kemp's death was for the best "because if he had been caught, he would have rotted in prison for years and likely gone through hell there from other prisoners, for even the worst of wrongdoers hated men who in any way harmed children." The work is unintentional satire.

Corcoran, Barbara. *Axe-Time, Sword-Time.* New York: Atheneum, 1976. 201 pp. Reading Level: YA/MA
Disability: Learning Disability

Since a freak accident in which she suffered "some kind of damage in her temporal lobe," school has been a source of incessant frustration to Elinor. Despite possessing considerable intelligence, she has not been able to learn to read or to work simple math problems. Her physician father pores over his professional journals seeking help for his daughter and, although she can scarcely tolerate the idea of another year of high school, unrealistically talks of Elinor's college career. The dissolution of her parents' marriage and the outbreak of World War II are unsettling events that offer unexpected opportunities to the sheltered young woman. Her teacher, Mrs. Jones, enlists Elinor's assistance in civil defense work. This modest experience has great importance for the girl since it provides her with objective evidence that she is competent. As the two spend time in each other's company, the teacher is able to observe her student's learning style, information she tries to translate into classroom modifications.

Elinor's father's new friend, Frau Braun, a German refugee, bluntly asks her why she is aggressively engaged in neither academic pursuits nor useful employment. At first the girl is angry and hurt, but after Pearl Harbor and the death of a friend in the war, she accepts the validity of the implied criticism and obtains a job in a defense plant as an inspector. Conscientious, skillful, and increasingly mature, she is soon offered a promotion. Her boss tells her: "I know all about your so-called problem. Ah, nuts. I couldn't read till I was eleven, and I had no excuse. You're the best inspector we have." When Elinor sees Jed, her casual boyfriend, now home on leave, he confirms his romantic interest in her, offering more evidence that others do not share her low opinion of herself.

Analysis. Corcoran has developed an accurate portrait of a girl adjusting to her learning disability at a time when medical and educational knowledge of the disorder were embryonic. The girl's academic problems are compounded by her parents' unrealistic expectations and overprotective responses. Her social problems derive from consequent low self-esteem. One parent flounders in his attempt to understand his daughter but does not adjust his aspirations for her to the reality of her performance; the other, self-absorbed and concerned with appearances, fails entirely to provide essential support. Elinor's teacher, although without training in appropriate techniques, intelligently tries to adapt her pupil's self-instructional methods to a school setting. Although the historical picture is mildly interesting, the characters fail to involve, and, as a result, the reader remains emotionally distant from the story.

Corcoran, Barbara. *Making It.* Boston: Little, Brown, 1980. 156 pp.
Reading Level: YA/MA
Disability: Intellectual Impairment

The youngest daughter of an impoverished minister eagerly awaits the return of her older sister, Charlotte, from college. Sissy is finishing her last year of high school and living at home with her parents and her brother, Harvey, who "doesn't look especially retarded, if you don't talk to him. He's not a Mongoloid type or anything. In some ways he seems almost normal. For instance, he loves music, and he knows the names of a lot of composers and pieces of music. . . . But most of the time he acts more like a little kid, and he has trouble speaking words clearly."

Charlotte makes her entrance extravagantly dressed, driving a late model rented car. Their glamorous daughter tells her parents she has quit school to pursue a career, which she hints will lead to the life of luxury she always coveted. She insists Sissy go away to school and escape from the repressive atmosphere of their provincial community. Through a fortuitous set of circumstances, the high school student is able to enter UCLA. Charlotte, who has moved to Los Angeles, generously helps her sister but tries to keep much of her life a secret. When they speak of home, Charlotte expresses her hostility for the indigent life they led and her frustration over her brother's overprotected treatment: "Something has to be done about Harvey. . . . He ought to be in school somewhere, so he can develop as far as possible. It's no good, his living at home like that with Mom always hovering over him."

Sissy is devastated when she learns her much admired older sister is a call girl who deals in drugs. When Charlotte seeks refuge to elude some underworld characters, her terrified sister, with the help of Marty, her wealthy boyfriend, makes arrangements for the fugitive to fly to Hawaii under an assumed name. After Charlotte fails to meet them at the airport, Sissy becomes panicky. Her fears are confirmed when a policeman reports the desperate woman has been murdered. A will reveals that Sissy will inherit enough money to finish college and that Harvey has been left $2,500 for a piano and music lessons. Sissy, just emerging from her protected childhood, refuses Marty's proposal of marriage, declaring she is not yet ready for another restricting relationship.

Analysis. Harvey provides just one more weak and pointless characterization in a slick and facile story that holds few surprises. The extent of his retardation is never clear; he has poor motor control, immature speech, but some musical skill and knowledge. The boy's literary function is to underscore Charlotte's basic generosity, a quality already established through her relationship with Sissy. This story of a girl's growth toward independence is never convincing and, despite some sanitized glimpses of the seamier side of life, never very interesting.

Corcoran, Barbara. *Me and You and a Dog Named Blue.* New York: Atheneum, 1979. 179 pp. Reading Level: YA
Disability: Orthopedic Impairment

Both teenage Maggie and her disabled father, Harrison Clarke, are proud, independent, obstinate characters, and the two inevitably clash over many issues. Mr. Clarke sustained an injury when he was with NATO in Germany and is now obliged to use a crutch to move about. Maggie, assuming her dead mother's responsibilities and hoping for a career as a professional baseball player, often resents the extra work that results from her father's mobility limitations: "She knew it was hard for him to get around, but sometimes he used that for an excuse. He got down to the boat all right when he wanted to, and he always managed to get to the bar with his chums . . . or to the Legion Hall." Despite these conflicts, their basic relationship is loving and supportive. Maggie, whose academic interests and effort are minimal, dreams of dropping out of high school to join a pro team in Ohio. The Clarkes' dependence on a modest government check, however, precludes having money for either travel or tryouts.

On a solitary trip to the beach, the girl sees a Jaguar with keys in its ignition and impulsively takes it out for a trial run. CoCo Rainbolt, who owns the car, instead of being angry, sees Maggie, and later her father, as fresh material for her philanthropic efforts. As Harrison Clarke explains: "She's taking us up. She wants to relate to us. She wants to establish a meaningful relationship. She's the kind of person if you say hello, right away it's an encounter session. Project Clarke. . . . A lethal woman." Despite his cynical, albeit accurate description, he allows CoCo to begin governing segments of their lives. She gives Maggie a dog, a job at her kennels, and permission to drive her car and promises further employment traveling to dog shows, which the youngster privately calculates will ultimately get her to Ohio. Maggie increasingly resents the woman's seemingly benevolent intrusions into her life, seeing her magnanimity as a means of taking control. CoCo's Lady Bountiful role currently extends beyond the girl to an exconvict who is employed in an unspecified capacity at her home and to Mr. Clarke, who is attracted to the flamboyant woman. When her jeweled watch is missing, CoCo indirectly accuses Maggie of taking it, but the former felon is discovered with the timepiece in his possession. The conflicts between the major characters come to a head on the boat trip, when Blue, Maggie's dog, drowns because of CoCo's reckless insistence on taking charge of everything. The adolescent heroine is able to see her predicament with greater clarity through the help of her pragmatic boyfriend. He cautions her against reacting perversely to the pressures other people put on her instead of looking at all of her options and choosing what is best for her—advice she now seems ready to heed.

Analysis. Corcoran has posed some provocative questions about conflicts between people that are fueled by issues of power, responsibilities, and identity in this easy-to-read junior-level novel. One of the author's most successful efforts is reflected in the depiction of the disabled veteran, who is extremely competent in some situations but petulant, demanding, and exploitive in others. His attempts to cope with his reduced abilities include carving objects for sale to supplement his meager income, supporting military-connected organizations like the American Legion to find friends and bolster his ego, and embarking on drinking sprees to obliterate the humiliations that attend the genteel poverty in which he and his daughter live. The reaction of others to his disability rounds out the picture. Maggie's boyfriend tells the astonished girl that his dad "feels guilty" about her father's disability. He explains: "Dad would have liked to go into the service . . . and he sees your dad, wearing his crutch like a medal of honor." Maggie protests: "But my father was never in a war. He just happened to fall out of a Jeep after a beer bust in Germany." Bradly insists: "Yeah, but it's the crutch that counts." On balance, Harrison Clarke is seen in a compassionate light, and his occasional pettiness, pretentiousness, and obstinacy are understandable and credible traits.

Corcoran, Barbara. *The Person in the Potting Shed.* New York: Atheneum, 1981. 121 pp. Reading Level: MC/YA
Disability: emotional dysfunction

Dorothy and Franklin are unenthusiastic about joining their mother and Ian, her new English husband, on a plantation temporarily rented in the bayou country south of New Orleans. The children become skeptical about explanations concerning the sudden disappearance of the drunken gardener, whose peculiar behavior has been the subject of considerable conjecture. Franklin discovers the man's body and rushes home to tell his mother, who promises to call the police the next morning. When the officer arrives, there is no evidence to confirm the boy's story. Ian is furious, convinced he has been made to look the fool by his hostile stepson. Searching for evidence to prove his claim, Franklin comes across a snapshot of the gardener and Jasmine, the absent owner of the plantation. Arthur, a mysterious visitor, demands the photograph and, when he is refused, threatens the boy with a gun. Fortunately, Ian appears, tackles the aggressor, and rescues Franklin. The police chief returns, reports that a body dragged from the river has been identified as the missing gardener, and proposes a reconstruction of the crime:

> Jasmine, as you know, has been in a nursing home. Her mind has slipped a bit . . . [she] crept out of the house . . . conked him on the head with a hoe and knocked him out. She saw a bottle of whiskey . . . and apparently gave Francois a hefty swig. Unfortunately it turned out to be some sort of pesticide.

Hoping to protect Jasmine as well as his own social ambitions, Arthur was obliged to conceal his mother's reprehensible behavior and his illegitimate origins. To do so, he had to get rid of Francois's body and destroy the picture that clearly revealed the romantic relationship between Francois and Jasmine, his unwed parents. Ian apologizes to his stepson for doubting his word, and the boy expresses his gratitude and admiration for the man whose bravery saved him from possible injury.

Analysis. This dull, slow-moving story works hard but never successfully to create a mystery. The setting lacks authenticity, the characters are dimensionless, and the plot stumbles along, prodded by a sequence of highly unlikely events. Having a disturbed woman as the murderer allows a resolution without a villain. It is an unsatisfying and shabby ploy.

Corn, Anne L. *Monocular Mac.* Illus. by Diane Dawson. New York: National Association for Visually Handicapped, 1977. 31 pp. Reading Level: YC
Disability: Visual Impairment

Billy's impaired vision necessitates the use of monoculars and magnifiers. He willingly shares these lenses with his older brother, Jackie, who finds them useful for examining stamps, and with a new friend, who also ignores their corrective function, enjoying instead the wonders that magnification reveals. Billy is given a new low vision aid, which he nicknames "Mac." The monocular enables him to decode such things as the words on the blackboard in school, street signs, and other environmental information.

Analysis. Corn's quasi-fictional paperback book depicts an average third-grade child whose deficient vision is maximized through prescribed aids and whose attitude toward reducing the consequences of his problem is responsible, cooperative, and optimistic. Mac, Billy's corrective device, is introduced as though it were an intriguing rather than a burdensome tool. The young hero's ordinariness and his matter-of-fact pride in his magnifiers "normalize" the use of the recommended lenses. Dawson's engaging illustrations support this healthy and useful approach.

Cosgrove, Stephen. *Cap'n Smudge.* Illus. by Robin James. Mankato, Minn.: Serendipity, 1977. unp. Reading Level: YC
Disability: Orthopedic Impairment

Long ago, Cap'n Smudge had disobeyed his father by rowing out to a dangerous part of the sea where a "fairly ferocious sea monster . . . unfortunately, and quite accidentally, bit off his leg." A carpenter made him a new one, but he was still tormented by other fishermen, who called him "Peg Leg" and "Old Wooden Toes" and who even set fire to his wooden leg. Before that time, he had been "a normal, healthy person like you or me," but now "he was so dirty and despicable that he didn't even have a real wooden leg but instead used an old mop handle with the mop still hooked on the end." That certainly made him "the dirtiest, dustiest sea captain in the world. He had gum wrappers stuck in his hair, coal dust on his nose, a filthy smile on his face and . . . on his shoulder he had a muddy, mucky mudlark."

To strike back at his tormentors, the unhappy seaman throws garbage in the waters, fouling the nets of the fishermen. His frustrated neighbors appeal to Serendipity, a friendly sea serpent, who, hearing the one-legged man's side of the story, adjudicates the dispute and presents the captain with a beautifully carved new leg as a peace offering from his enemies. Pleased, Smudge agrees not to dirty the waters any more. As the captain sails off into the sunset, readers are cautioned: "If you ever see someone different than you or me, just remember Cap'n Smudge and this tale of serendipity."

Analysis. Slick, colorful, commercial illustrations depict a piratelike central character more attractive than the person described in the narrative. The text is ambiguous: seemingly a sugar-coated but didactic narrative for youngsters about the acceptance of differences, the structure, dialogue, and underlying theme telegraph a contradictory message. Cosgrove ties disability to disobedience, provides an extended description of the physically repellent captain, employs biased, distancing language ("normal . . . like you and me"), tags the protagonist with a name like Smudge (something to be rubbed out?), includes detailed accounts of abusive, taunting behavior, all supported by a frivolous tone. No criticism is leveled at the fishermen who assault the sea captain, and this lack of comment gives support to the assumption, although seemingly opposed by the tacked-on ending, that since the victim's appearance is so unpleasant, their hostile reaction is natural. The author does not propose a change of heart for the tormentors or even depict them seeing the error of their ways. The men only seek arbitration when vengeance knocks on their own door. In the guise of a morality tale, *Cap'n Smudge* propounds an uncivilized set of values.

Cowley, Joy. *The Silent One.* Illus. by Hermann Greissle. New York: Knopf, 1981. 136 pp. Reading Level: MC
Disability: Auditory Impairment, Speech Impairment; special health problems

The infant Jonasi, brought to a South Pacific island by a sea captain, is given to Luisa to raise. No longer able to bear children, the arthritic woman welcomes the mute and deaf child into her home, bringing him up as her own. The other islanders distrust the boy because of his uniqueness. " 'It was not human,' they said. 'It would bring evil in their midst.' " When Jonasi is old enough to join the men in the ceremonial hunt for pigs, which marks a male child's rite of passage, he is rebuffed, forced to remain behind while younger, less able youth are allowed to participate. Disconsolate, he takes his raft out to sea where he discovers an albino turtle that plays companionably with him. Jonasi realizes he must keep this remarkable creature hidden from the islanders or they would kill it for its valuable shell. Despite his precautions, two youngsters learn his secret and the news soon sweeps through the village. The men devise a scheme to capture the precious turtle, and when this fails, they plot instead to use Jonasi as bait to tempt the creature. The youth is rescued by the chief, but when a hurricane damages their settlement, the superstitious people become angry and vengeful and want the boy punished. Aesake, his only friend and the chief's son, proposes that Jonasi be sent to another island to attend a school for deaf children where he will be safe.

Luisa, her youngest son, Samu, Jonasi, and Aesake board a launch that will take them to their destination. When the albino turtle is spotted, the greedy captain orders the passengers and crew to capture it. Fearful, they refuse. In frustration at the possible loss of the strange and valuable animal, the man seizes a gun and prepares to kill it himself. Jonasi quickly dives overboard, swims to his pet, redirects it away from the launch, and dives with it below the waves. The boy is never seen again, but later the crew of a cargo ship claim to have seen "two turtles swimming together. They were both white, they said, and they gleamed like stars in the dark blue water."

Analysis. Told in the manner of a legend, *The Silent One* offers an outcast hero, set apart by his disability, who finds immortality through his kinship with the natural world. The author's emulation of a mythic style precludes any literal response to the title character, but it is clear the isolation caused by Jonasi's inability to speak or hear is essential to the progress of events and the development of the theme. Brown-and-white wood engravings nicely complement the narrative.

Cummings, Betty Sue. *Hew Against the Grain.* New York: Atheneum, 1977. 174 pp. Reading Level: YA
Disability: Emotional Dysfunction, Neurological Impairment, Orthopedic Impairment

Mattilda Repass is both exhilarated and frightened by talk of secession and war. She is proud when her father frees his slaves and her brother-in-law, Jason, announces his support for the Union, but when proslavery men, led by Ray Beard, lynch Jason and murder one of their exslaves, the terrible dangers inherent in the approaching conflict become all too clear. Her older brothers leave—one to join the Federal Army, the other to fight for the Confederacy. Her sister, Sarah, alienated from her family for their loyalty to those allied with her husband's killers, refuses any contact, leaves home, and becomes active in the Underground Railroad. When Union troops move into the area, they requisition livestock and supplies and burn the house and barns. Mr. Repass, distraught over the death of his son-in-law and the destruction of his land, abandons all responsibility to others as he attends exclusively to his maps, on which he plots the progress of the battles.

After the old man apparently suffers a stroke ("One side of her father's face was drawn and one eye bulged a little, staring blindly. One arm chopped the air with every word and the other arm hung unmoving. He limped, looked like the ghost of her father"), all merely try to pacify or calm him when he becomes argumentative. One of his sons loses a leg in the war, another has a hand badly shattered in an explosion. Mattilda, now 15 and responsible for much of the heavy farm work, is surprised at the attentions of a former neighbor, who is now attached to the Southern forces. They correspond and he visits her when he can, announcing his desire to marry her after the war. One day when Mattilda is alone in the house, Ray Beard enters and rapes her. She is able to distract him momentarily, seize her father's gun, and fatally shoot him. Afraid she is pregnant, and ashamed, she tries to sever her relationship with her suitor, who steadfastly pleads with her to marry him. Although sorely depressed, Mattilda is encouraged and revitalized by her sagacious grandfather, who insists she fight to build her life by refusing to succumb to the destruction around her. As the war winds down, Sarah returns home, and Mattilda, relieved of her fears, agrees to the wedding, insisting that her father participate in his traditional role in the ceremony.

Analysis. The divisions, internal strife, acrimonious assaults, terrible carnage, death and suffering, and deliberate and intentional pain suffered by the Repass family are a synecdoche for the condition of the United States during the Civil War period. The wounds of the sons and the father's diminished abilities are simultaneously real and symbolic as the characters suggest the critical damage done to the body and soul of the nation. The youth whose leg was amputated embodies the most potent symbol: He returns from the fighting gravely wounded and seriously debilitated. After some hesitation, he chooses the wood from which to shape a crutch; then, gathering together the fragments from his life, begins to rebuild the farm and participate in the reconstruction of the family unit.

Cummings, Betty Sue. *Let a River Be*. New York: Atheneum, 1978. 195 pp. Reading Level: YA/MA
Disability: Intellectual Impairment, Special Health Problems

Ella Richards, 76 years old, is committed to saving the endangered Indian River that flows past her ramshackle boathouse. Despite an increasingly painful arthritic condition, she fills her days with writing protest letters, toting antipollution placards, monitoring local industries, and soliciting support for her cause. Although barely able to eke out a living from her environment, Ella ignores all but her most basic needs, sending whatever extra money she can scrape together to support the work of ecologists. When discouraged, she draws on the supportive memories of the life she once shared with her bright, sensual, and vibrant husband.

One day a frightened, dirty young man appears at her dock, revealing with some hesitation that his name is "Reetard." When Ivan Maxwell, the woman's nemesis in the ecology conflict, threatens to have Reetard jailed or institutionalized, Ella realizes the crude and boorish man was part of the posse that shot at the stranger while he was hiding in a nearby Florida swamp. Reetard says he is an orphan and speaks fearfully of the treatment he received as a child, alluding to a cattle prod used as a disciplinary device. Ella takes him into her home, offering protection and instructing him in the skills he needs to live off the land. Worried about what will happen to him after she dies, the elderly woman considers placing him in an institution, but a visit to the place causes her to quickly abandon that plan. She insists on knowing what name he calls her secretly, and when he answers "Mama," she is overcome with emotion and forced to acknowledge the depth of her feeling for him.

Reetard tells Ella that he saw machines working at the headwaters of the river. Fearing that developers are irremediably destroying the area's fragile ecological balance, the woman surreptitiously confirms her charge's story. Ella convinces a local reporter to accompany her to the site of the illegal activity, but they are interrupted in their quest for proof of violation of the law by the noise of Marine Patrol boats. Ivan and his partners dash to their boats, but their attempt to escape is thwarted by Ella's companion. Reetard jumps from the boat, determined to get the man who is his surrogate mother's enemy, but is deliberately run down when Ivan turns his vessel into him. Although the court decides that Reetard's death was accidental and lets the man responsible off with only a fine, public opinion over the incident is galvanized and the authorities turn the region into an aquatic preserve.

Devastated by the loss of the young man she has come to think of as a son, Ella attempts suicide. Before it is too late, she changes her mind, realizing there is still much work to be done and rededicates herself to fight for her own life and the life of her beloved river.

Analysis. Cummings has written an original, literate, and sensitive novel about people and nature struggling to survive. Reetard is both a real person and an important symbol: his violent death and subsequent immortality, achieved through community reassertion of preservationist goals, are simultaneously credible events and metaphorical reminders of the fragility and inestimable value of life. Reetard is seen initially as a persecuted, powerless victim of an indifferent and hostile world, then as a highly valued and much loved young man who brings unexpected joy and renewal to another, then, finally, once again, as victim, but one who though tragically destroyed, has achieved heroic stature.

Cunningham, Julia. *Come to the Edge.* New York: Pantheon, 1977. 79 pp. Reading Level: MC
Disability: Visual Impairment, Orthopedic Impairment, Auditory Impairment

After learning that his only friend has been adopted and his idealized father has callously rejected him, Gravel Winter escapes from the orphanage that has been his inadequate substitute for a home in recent years. In a convulsion of self-doubt, the distraught boy questions his identity and the fact as well as the value of his existence. Exhausted and without resources, the runaway happens upon the home of Mr. Paynter, a sign painter, who accepts Gravel without reservation and makes only the most minimal demands of him, while at the same time generously providing food, shelter, and training in the rudiments of his craft. The boy neither understands the man's trust nor his own growing uneasiness about his existence, and he precipitously departs this haven. Moving on to another town, he meets a wealthy blind man, a physically disabled woman, and an elderly woman who is deaf, each of whom offers him housing, food, or money in exchange for his services. Despite some mutually beneficial arrangements and the obvious affection of the women, Gravel's emotions remain frozen, and his reactions to his employers are detached and mechanistic. Hoping to enslave the boy, the evil blind man threatens to inform the police that the youth murdered a servant, an act for which he alone is responsible. The solitary, lame woman tries to remake Gravel into the image of the loving, caring son she has yearned for but never had; while the deaf woman wants him to give her the companionship she desperately craves. Unwilling to be trapped either by kindness or maliciousness, the youngster returns to the home of his first benefactor, where he is casually but warmly greeted. Hesitant to accept his good fortune, the boy is silent, although he wants to yell at his mentor:

> You fool, don't you remember that I deserted you, that I walked out and didn't care whether or not you needed me? Don't you know that I sold myself to the first people who were seeking a prop, that I shaped myself to please them so they wouldn't know what I was? Don't you know yet what I am? Nothing! Nobody!

Paynter's "eyes were now looking into his as though he were listening, hearing what the silence said." The man turns back to his work, inviting the boy to help him with the layout of a newly commissioned sign.

Analysis. Gravel is depicted as a child so battered and devastated by rejection that he finds the unaccustomed kindness offered to him unbearable. The three disabled characters are catalysts in helping him to rediscover his identity as he defiantly refuses to accept bondage, adopt a persona not his own, or even respond to an open offer of friendship that would require a modest commitment, but one beyond what his fragile personality could support. Although Cunningham's writing is fluid and rich in vivid images, its central purpose remains obscure, and the employment of specific characters and events seems arbitrary. There appears to be no defensible literary rationale for the three impaired characters who test the boy's mettle. The presentation of a villain who is blind, a blackmailer, and a murderer is excessive and unlikely, a criticism that echoes the core problem of this brief novel.

Cunningham, Julia. *Flight of the Sparrow.* New York: Pantheon, 1980. 130 pp. Reading Level: MC/YA
Disability: intellectual impairment, orthopedic impairment

Mago, a 14-year-old street urchin, rescues a waif (whom he names "Cigarette") from a Dickensian-style Parisian orphanage, taking her to live with him and his companions. These include a mortally ill girl who soon commits suicide and a "strange boy shaped like a stump, who was retarded. His name was Drollant, and sometimes he really was droll." One day, the youngster darts into traffic, is injured, and is subsequently taken to a city hospital. Fearful that his friend will be institutionalized after his recovery, Mago maneuvers to have Drollant removed to a local clinic. Desperate for money, the youth agrees to take part in a robbery masterminded by Eel, an unsavory underworld character. Cigarette becomes the model for the intended victim of the scheme, and she identifies the painting coveted by an unscrupulous dealer. Having developed an affection for the kind and generous artist who owns it, she is reluctant to proceed with the theft, but loyalty to Mago is the more powerful emotion. With the profits from the sale of the stolen artwork, Mago is able to rescue his injured friend.

Mago urges Cigarette to leave town since he believes the police are certain to arrest her if she remains. Eel intercepts the departing girl, steals her money, and reveals his plan to blackmail Mago into working for him. Frightened and desperate, the child decides to locate the artist, explain what has happened, and beg for his help. On her journey to his country home, she encounters a succession of characters who are variously generous, grasping, benevolent, or exploitive. Arriving at her destination too late, Cigarette discovers the man has returned to Paris, but his wife gives the girl train fare back to the city. There she locates Mago, telling him she intends to admit her role in the crime and turn herself over to the authorities. He dissuades her, insisting that through her he can know vicarious freedom. Eel declares he will take her to the police, and when Mago tries to intercede, he is fatally stabbed. Heartbroken, Cigarette finds a refuge for Drollant, then tracks down the artist, who rescues her from self-destruction and supports her while she recovers.

Analysis. When Cigarette first meets Drollant, she is repulsed, describing his behavior in denigrating terms: "He . . . began his blubbering kind of crying," and "[his] face was almost normal with delight. He puffed out his chest like a pigeon and nodded." Part of the establishment of Mago as a noble character derives from his selfless devotion and assumption of responsibility for his vulnerable friend. Conversely, Eel's villainy is manifest through his verbal abuse and threats toward the boy, as when he says: "Still got the idiot with you? I'd tie him to a cart and use him like a horse if he were mine." Cunningham tosses in other off-hand comments about disability: "[Eel] carried trouble on his back as surely as if a hump grew there," and no criticism is even implied about Mago teaching Cigarette to limp to extract pity, then money, from passersby.

Cunningham, Julia. *The Silent Voice.* New York: Dutton, 1981. 145 pp. Reading Level: MC/YA
Disability: Speech Impairment

When four Parisian street urchins find a 14-year-old boy in the gutter, Astair, their leader, directs the others to help carry the unconscious youth to her makeshift living quarters. She restores the health of the stranger, and Auguste, although without speech, joins her ragtag band of street entertainers, contributing significantly to bettering their hand-to-mouth existence. Astair takes Auguste to Madame Louva, housekeeper to Mr. Bernard, once a gifted mime, who now manages a children's theater school. Impressed with Auguste's performance, Bernard offers the youth a job at his house and a scholarship to the academy. The newcomer is resented by the other wealthy students, and some boys, egged on by the malicious and sly Philippe, make his life miserable.

Auguste's evident pleasure in the theater vivifies the weary man, and despite active opposition to the newcomer's presence by Philippe's mother, the sustaining patron of the school, the mime offers him private instruction. In addition to taking over some household tasks for Madame Louva, Auguste acts as secretary/choreographer for the aging manager and also manages to memorize Philippe's starring role. The other boys, prompted by Philippe's comment: "I'm tired of the master defending that walking garbage with no tongue in his head," hide the boy's pet stray cat. A melee erupts when they try to steal the medallion given to Auguste by Hilaire, his former mentor, and Raymond, pushed by Philippe, falls from a window and is hospitalized. The guilty one later accuses Auguste of the crime to the police inspector, warning the innocent boy that other witnesses could be brought to support his assertion and adding that they "will do a job on you that will leave you twisted as a crab. You'll be lucky to walk again—ever."

Astair and her willing accomplices kidnap Philippe the night of the opening performance, after which she persuades Auguste to step into the starring role. The youth gives a bravura performance, as brilliant as either of his teachers could have wished. Bernard insists he wear the medal Hilaire gave him as he acknowledges the adulation of the audience. Raymond later recovers and identifies his true assailant, thus removing the last impediment to the gifted young mime's continued success.

Analysis: This continuation of *Far in the Day* does not have the verve of the prior two titles in the trilogy, in part because the themes are familiar although replayed in a new locale. Artistry, compassion, and poverty are again arrayed against power, violence, and affluence. Auguste, wraithlike, mute, talented, and vulnerable, is contrasted to Philippe, physically aggressive, vicious, and a liar. At the climax, the hero's strength, despite his disability, is shown to be of greater potency than that of his tormentors. This positive portrayal of the central character is vitiated by the author's latent endorsement of the philosophy that the end justifies the means.

Cunningham, Julia. *Tuppenny*. New York: Dutton, 1978. 87 pp.
Reading Level: YA
Disability: Emotional Dysfunction, intellectual impairment, speech impairment

Prodded by desperation and fueled by hate, the usually stammering Jessica silently calls for help, and it comes in the form of an odd girl who calls herself Tuppenny. The stranger discomfits Jessica's parents, Mr. and Mrs. Standing, who are shaken by the newcomer's resemblance to their other daughter, Victoria, a runaway. Tuppenny wanders into the small town dominated by the Standing factory and a sinister-looking church, finally entering a cafe run by Al and Lou. Her presence also upsets the owners, who argue once more about the institutionalization of their daughter, Josie. Later, Tuppenny goes to the church, confronting Reverend Mason with the cryptic phrase: "I was chosen." Unnerved, he remarks that Tuppenny reminds him of Dorrie, his daughter, whom he once publicly condemned for committing suicide.

Impetuously, Mr. Standing invites Tuppenny, now working as the family maid, to join them for supper, during which he taunts his wife although he directs his conversation to the girl. Mrs. Standing becomes enraged and, in an uncontrollable, emotional outburst, reveals that she tried to kill Victoria, desperate to prevent her daughter from repeating her own mother's evil behavior. Then, considerably calmer, the woman claims that she feels relieved at having confessed her terrible secret.

Tuppenny leaves this conflict-ridden household and, in exchange for room and board, goes to work at the cafe. Mrs. Standing confronts Lou, who admits that she was pressured into sending Josie to a hospital for the retarded and she is now drowning in guilt and remorse. She determines to visit her child, and as she leaves the house, Al calls out: "Maybe I fathered an idiot, but now it seems I married one, too!" There is a fire in the restaurant, but Tuppenny conceals the fact that Al was drunk during the conflagration. He grudgingly thanks the girl for neither exposing his condition nor leaving him to die and then contritely agrees to Josie's return home.

Prior to this, Tuppenny has accompanied her new employers to church, where they are all dismayed by the preacher's inexplicable behavior. Reverend Mason insists on "collecting" the sins of the congregation—not for expiation or atonement, but for some mysterious, diabolical purpose, to which he obliquely alludes but for which he offers no coherent explanation. Tuppenny next encounters Victoria, who is returning to claim her share of the family fortune and to obtain vengeance for the death of her friend, the minister's daughter, who she maintains did not kill herself.

Tuppenny retraces her steps to the rectory to inform the minister and his wife that she has come to serve them. The couple accept her offer but require that for disciplinary purposes she must wear a hobble and occasionally chains, noting that their own daughter had endured such restrictions. Tuppenny overhears the minister swearing allegiance to the devil and conversations that confirm Victoria's allegations. Victoria devises a scheme to reveal the Masons' responsibility for their daughter's death, but she needs a witness. To carry out her plan, Victoria dresses like her dead friend and instructs Tuppenny to hide at the back of the church until the killers arrive. After the Masons enter the building, the disguised child begins to describe Dorrie's homicide as if it were her own, claiming she was sacrificed to Satan. This dramatic reenactment of the murder shocks the adults into revealing more details of their actions during this horrendous scene. Suddenly awake to their danger, they chase the girls to the river. The minister catches Tuppenny and begins to strangle her, while his frenzied wife babbles incoherently. Then the girl's "breathing ceased. With a cry that penetrated the depths of night, he cast her into the rough flow of the river. As she floated out of sight, a little fleet of gold and scarlet leaves surrounded the body." The Masons are arrested, "but their minds were so severely disconnected from reality, the court ruled against legal proceedings." Josie returns home, bringing joy to her family. Purged, the town begins its recovery. Jessica once again encounters Tuppenny (evidently temporarily resurrected for the meeting), who promises another reunion some day, then disappears in a "light rush of wind."

Analysis: Several themes, unsatisfactorily developed, are played out in this bizarre story. The characterizations show rigid contrasts—adults are weak, wicked, petty; children are "flawed" but innocent victims; Tuppenny, an avenging angel, comes to redress the balance. She acts as a supernatural messenger who prods adults to admit their roles and responsibilities in the tragedies involving their teenage daughters. Conflicts between good and evil, benevolent yearnings and malevolent acts, individual desires and public pressures are intertwined. Disability has a significant function in this work as excuse, explanation, or cause: Josie's ready victimization is possible because she is retarded; Jessica's speech impairment is used to justify her role as a silent observer of events; and the villainy and charismatic power of the killers are seen as concomitants of their psychoses.

Curry, Jane Louise. *The Bassumtyte Treasure.* New York: Atheneum, 1978. 130 pp. Reading Level: MC
Disability: Orthopedic Impairment, visual impairment

Tommy Bassumtyte is sent from America to his cousin's home in London when a social worker decides his great aunt can no longer be considered an adequate guardian. The 90-year-old woman, despite having to resort to a wheelchair to get about, has been managing their home with the assistance of a cousin, aged 72, who was "recently deprived of a driving license owing to failing eyesight." Preferring that the youngster be with family instead of being placed in a foster home, the cagey old women bundle him on board a flight to London, where he is met by Cousin Thomas and taken to Boxleton House. The Englishman greets Tommy, saying, "You've been long enough in coming. . . . It's been four hundred years." The new arrival notices that his cousin has a "stiff, faintly ungainly walk," the result of an unfortunate climbing accident.

All is not well: taxes and maintenance costs have left their ancestral home in financial jeopardy. A very handsome offer has been made for the residence, and Tommy is afraid that his cousin will be obliged to accept it. The American youngster recalls that his grandfather told him that there was a puzzle associated with the house, and he is convinced that it involves a treasure trove. Fearing that the estate may have to be sold before he can solve the riddle and urged on by the resident ghost, the youth resolves to unravel the mystery quickly. The enigma seems related to their family history, presumably involving one of Tommy's ancestors, a supporter of Mary Stuart. That loyalist had been implicated in a plot to free the Queen of Scots but was captured and executed. Pressures for a speedy solution instensify when it is discovered that the would-be purchaser has sent in a team of appraisers disguised as tourists to assess the value of the estate.

One of the neighbors, Gemma, discovers an incongruity in the tapestries of Boxleton House. When the original stitches are revealed, a design containing Mary Stuart's name emerges. Gemma's proposal to rip out more stitches angers Thomas, who warns her she is not to damage the embroidery. She challenges him, asking what will he do, spank her? "If that's it, it'll be a good six months before you're fast enough on your feet to catch me."

The observant Gemma finds a painting of Mary that was disguised as a family portrait to avoid Queen Elizabeth's wrath. Its value insures that Boxleton House can remain in the Bassumtyte family. A casket is subsequently unearthed containing presents from the deposed monarch and evidence that cousins Thomas and Tommy are descendants of the martyred queen. As a result of clever deduction, aided by Gemma's curiosity and persistence, Tommy is able to unlock the key to the mystery surrounding the treasure and maintain the family fortune.

Analysis. This marvelously engrossing tale interweaves a contemporary mystery with historical adventure using puns, words, and phrases with double meanings and other linguistic tricks to provide the clues for its solution. The treatment of disability is unusual and admirable: it is simultaneously important and peripheral. All three characters with impairments are brave, loyal, ingenious, and willing to defy authority for their principles—traits echoing those of their defiant ancestors. The authorities' assumption that because people are old or infirm they must of necessity be incompetent is mocked when the old women outsmart a do-gooder, make and carry out alternative arrangements, and continue to make key decisions affecting their lives. Thomas's impairment, occasionally the subject of offhand remarks, is treated very casually. When Gemma comments on his slow pace, he realistically accepts her statement, clearly implying her remark is a description, not a criticism. Later, she advises against Tommy jumping from a tree into his cousin's arms, observing with exasperation, "He's as stiff-necked as he is stiff-backed." Disabilities, as other facts of life, are neither sentimentalized nor exaggerated but ignored or accommodated as is most appropriate at the moment.

Curry, Jane Louise. *Ghost Lane*. New York: Atheneum, 1979. 151 pp. Reading Level: MC
Disability: Learning Disability

When Richard Morgan returns to his father's home in England, he becomes friends with Fan, a young girl, and Nolly, her dyslexic brother. The three are invited to the home of Mr. Drew, an elderly gentleman who owns a house crammed with fascinating treasures. After robbers make off with some of Drew's prized possessions, the astute children track down the missing objects.

While shopping for a gift for her brother's sixth birthday, Fan is startled to recognize an employee of Drew's working for a moving company, an observation she stores away for future reference. Nolly briefly disappears, turning up unexpectedly at the opera house where Richard's father works. The agitated boy tries to explain his distress through pantomime and by printing the word "Ruskeryscod," but his problem with visual sequencing makes his message incomprehensible. Nolly finally blurts out to Richard's father: "Surrydox," which is ultimately translated as Surrey Docks, the word the frustrated lad had evidently been trying to print. After everyone returns home, Nolly reenacts his adventures during his disappearance. He mimes hearing noises in the night, getting dressed, slipping out of the house and down to the river, where he discovered a hiding place obviously used by the thieves. Mr. Morgan persuades him to continue his narrative in words instead of pantomime. Swinging into that mode, he reports that some men loaded furniture in which he was hiding onto a truck and drove it into the city. Escaping from the warehouse they used as a hideout, the resourceful lad laboriously made his way to the concert hall and safety. Fan's recollection of Drew's ex-employee's association with the moving company leads to the uncovering of the burglary ring. During this time, a romance has blossomed between Richard's father and Fan and Nolly's mother, and it is now clear that the two families will be united.

Analysis. The character of Nolly is developed as an intellectually and musically gifted child with severe and extensive learning disabilities. His verbal communication problems are attributed to early emotional distress, which left him better able to convey his feelings to animals than to people: "But, do you know, I have heard him talking to birds and squirrels and our cat Alice in what sounds uncannily like their own speech." It is implied that his lack of oral language is controllable—an accusation of willful misbehavior commonly but unjustifiably leveled against learning disabled youngsters: "It's simply that he cannot or will not talk. . . . He *does* talk, you know. Or can." The youth's ability to clearly articulate "Victoria, please," yet be unable to say "no," generally one of the easiest words in a child's vocabulary, is odd. Labeling a child less than six as dyslexic is clearly contrary to accepted procedures since symptoms otherwise compatible with such a diagnosis might merely indicate a developmental delay in one so young. Further, Nolly's problem is primarily with expressive language; he has trouble with speech and copying tasks, not with reading. It is equally distorting to propose that a perceptual disorder would cause a child to scramble the letters of a word then anagrammatically reassemble them without losing a single one. Whatever slight interest *Ghost Lane* may have as an adventure story is completely invalidated by the empty promise of its title, the improbable descriptions of travel astuteness and sagacity of a perceptually impaired youngster, by his portrayal as a "nature child," and by its misleading and misinformed depiction of the behavior of a child who has learning disabilities.

Cusack, Isabel L. *Mr. Wheatfield's Loft.* Illus. by Richard Egielski. New York: Holt, Rinehart & Winston, 1981. 141 pp. Reading Level: MC

Disability: Emotional Dysfunction

Ellis Hampton's teacher claims that he is bright and explains his mutism as a result of seeing his father killed by lightning. Jesse is skeptical about this assessment: "If he's so smart, then why's he in that class for exceptional children? . . . Exceptional don't *mean* exceptional, it means—well, dumb." He adds, the "boy may be awkward, but he's not crazy." This appraisal has naturally interfered with any close relationship between the 11-year-old youngster and his stepfather.

Ellis seeks out Mr. Wheatfield, an elderly man knowledgeable about the boy's enthusiasm—racing pigeons. Their conversation is interrupted by Rosalia, a migrant worker looking after the retired man in return for board and room. Later, Ellis meets Jaime, her younger brother, whom she is trying to direct away from a life of stoop labor. The silent boy soon recruits Jaime to help him repaint and repair the old pigeon loft for the youth's prospective purchase. When the day to select the bird arrives, Ellis's mentor is called away and the excited boy goes on the shopping expedition alone. He is swindled out of his five dollars by an unscrupulous man who sells him a sick female and a male bird that is not a racer, smoothing over the fraudulent sale by declaring, "I'm not one to take advantage. . . . and especially where this here's a handicap person." The female dies almost immediately, but Partleigh, at first, lives up to his owner's expectations. When the old man comes back, he demoralizes the boy, announcing that Partleigh is not a racer and that training the bird will be a waste of time. The discouraged boy writes on the pad he uses for communicating that he loves his pet and intends to keep him anyway.

Ellis overhears his mother trying to persuade Jesse to become friendlier with their son and is stricken upon hearing her, in an attempt to be conciliatory, comment offhandedly that perhaps he is dumb. The discouraged boy further considers that Mr. Wheatfield probably also thinks him stupid for persisting in the bird's training. Unhappily, he concludes that Jaime also would prefer to have another friend if there were only another candidate about.

The two boys become closer until one day they are shocked to overhear a policeman tell Mr. Wheatfield that Jaime's sister is a prostitute. Jaime, embarrassed by this revelation, "borrows" Partleigh and runs away. Ellis is horrified and angry but finally convinces himself that his racer will be able to find its way back to Florida from the North Carolina migrant camp where he presumes the Cuban youth is headed. The police report that the runaway was in an auto accident and has partial amnesia and that no bird was found with the injured lad. Ellis still maintains a tenacious belief in his pet, convinced the bird is unquestionably en route home.

Florida residents begin to make their usual preparations when they learn over the radio that a hurricane is approaching. Paralyzed by the fierce squalls and the lightning that erupts all around him, Ellis is rescued by Jesse. Suddenly, the worried boy spots his missing bird and, in the emotional release of the moment, blurts out his pet's name. It is, presumably, the beginning of the recovery of his speech and the onset of a closer relationship with his stepfather.

Analysis. Ellis has become demoralized by the label "dumb," and when he overhears his mother use that term, he initially feels betrayed by the one person in whom he put his trust. Later, he is able to discount its pejorative meaning for her and understand the context in which she used it. He is at pains to explain in writing that he is only mute, but is sometimes worried that he is really as unintelligent as some people seem to think. The attribution of both cause and "cure" of his muteness is simplistic, and such a literary device, although once common in children's stories, is becoming as rare in fiction as it is in the record of therapists. The story is replete with stereotypes, and the introduction of a prostitute "with a heart of gold" is a jarring note in an otherwise simple work. Additionally, dialogue is more earthy than is usually found in books for this audience. For some inexplicable reason, Ellis is shown to have atrocious spelling skills, a behavior that bears no relationship to his disorder and raises some questions as to what evidence his teacher has for her laudatory assessment of her student's abilities.

Dana, Barbara. *Crazy Eights.* New York: Harper & Row, 1978. 194 pp. Reading Level: YA
Disability: Emotional Dysfunction

Unhappy with her parents, whose lives she considers shallow and purposeless, contemptuous of her sister's involvement in a loveless and demeaning relationship, and suffering with headaches and vertigo, Thelma Baldwin becomes increasingly hostile and alienated from other adolescents. After she sets fire to the building where her sister is to be married, the girl is sent to a residential school for youth with behavioral disorders. The staff understands that her defiant, uncooperative demeanor is the result of inner distress and, through mildly intrusive, nonconfrontational techniques, introduces a host of structured therapeutic experiences. In this supportive setting, the teenager learns to relate to others in a healthy manner, use meditation as a means for mastering anxiety and fear, and talk through problems with her psychiatrist and other concerned personnel. Ultimately, Thelma is able to begin discarding self-destructive behaviors, even reaching a stage where she can offer strength and succor to her suicidal roommate. When she is at last able to disown the frightening nightmare about the death of her beloved dog, a turning point is reached. No longer the helpless victim of obsessive and ungovernable fears, Thelma moves toward a restoration of her emotional stability.

Analysis. Told in the form of a memoir written at the instigation of a psychiatrist, *Crazy Eights* seems more an amalgam of case histories than a cohesive novel. This work contains one of the few positive portrayals of a treatment center for behaviorally disordered adolescents, but such grandiose claims of competence are made by the staff, including an instance of clairvoyance, that believability is sacrificed. Considering the focus of the narrative, the characters' earthy language should not be surprising, but the casual insensitivity expressed in reference to a teacher's "funny bent way of walking" and acknowledgement of a woman's culinary skill "although she has two emotionally disturbed, retarded and vicious children" is unexpected. The self-absorbed, self-pitying, infantile heroine at the story's core limits the appeal of this novel. The author's immoderate enthusiasm for extrasensory explanations and her unrestrained endorsement of meditation as a panacea for psychological dysfunction detract from the story's usefulness.

Dank, Milton. *Red Flight Two*. New York: Delacorte, 1981. 185 pp.
Reading Level: YA/MA
Disability: Emotional Dysfunction; also orthopedic impairment

In this sequel to *Khaki Wings*, Edward Burton, an 18-year-old English pilot, emotionally exhausted by the strain of fighting for the British during World War I in inferior planes with deficient equipment, has recovered from a "breakdown" precipitated by the death of his best friend. He is assigned to work as an instructor for new pilots but is guilt-ridden over the War Office demands that the neophytes be shipped to the front with inadequate instruction and insufficient solo flying time. Edward is transferred to a home defense unit, where he successfully downs an enemy zeppelin headed for an ammunition dump. At a press conference arranged by the military to exploit the boy's heroic action, Burton is questioned by a reporter about his "nervous breakdown." He responds: "After twenty-two months in France I had given all I had to give. When they lifted me out of the cockpit of my plane, I was talking gibberish." He then speaks about his anger over the inadequate preparation young aviators are given and the life-wasting decisions of "blundering senior officers." The outspoken hero is promptly reassigned to an operational squadron at the front lines. He meets former comrades, including his commanding officer, who have been drastically changed by their experiences in the war. Burton's life becomes a bone-wearying series of raids and dogfights with enemy aircraft, and he is distraught as he watches the carnage increase and the ranks of his comrades diminish. The flyer learns his commander has committed suicide, breaking under the unremitting pressures of responsibility for a seemingly endless succession of deaths. The Kaiser's forces try a desperate push, which is initially successful but soon collapses. Burton is finally reconciled with his girl friend, who has been unable to accept his determination to return to combat. After hearing that the hostilities are over and he can return to her, Edward flies one last reconnaissance to pay a final visit to the war zone.

Analysis. The horrors of war are exhaustively chronicled in this account of a dashing young British flyer. The youth's visions of the glory of combat are swept away in a sea of broken bodies and disillusioned survivors. Maiming and psychological dysfunction are treated as a tragic and inevitable fact of combat, not a badge of honor: "Wounded men, the lucky ones, hobbled on crutches or were guided by nurses. An older man with an empty left sleeve and a black eye-patch gravely raised his hat. . . . The mutilated man smiled at Ann and passed on." Edward is distressed to see how the pressures of making life-and-death decisions had affected Major Fortescue, his old and admired mentor. Now he observes: "He looks like a corpse. . . . His hands are always shaking . . . his skin was an unhealthy yellow. His fingers kept up a nervous tattoo." More critically, "the major's behavior, his hysterical outbursts and contradictory orders had led to a lowering of squadron morale that was alarming." He is shocked, exclaiming, "Our lives are in the hands of that man," but it is the major himself who becomes an additional victim, apparently aware of his compulsive destructive behavior, and ends it the only way he can. The emotional disorders are seen as the result of unbearable pressures caused by the burdens of trying fruitlessly to protect underprepared neophytes while still serving the impersonal juggernaut of war. Edward's "breakdown" is presented as a disorder, also caused by intolerable stress, but one that has been overcome.

Danziger, Paula. *The Pistachio Prescription.* New York: Delacorte, 1978. 154 pp. Reading Level: YA
Disability: Special Health Problems

Her battling parents' concern about her appearance, asthma, and the natural crisis attendant upon entering high school combine to generate considerable turbulence in Cassie Stephens's life. She deals with both serious and trivial events in the histrionic manner characteristic of many of her contemporaries: trifling incidents are seen as cataclysmic, and hyperbole is her common mode of expression. For minor traumas or generalized states of anxiety, she relies on pistachio nuts for comfort, especially when Vicki, her best friend, who has ambitions to be a therapist, is not available for consultation. Serious stress, especially when precipitated by her family's increasingly acrimonious fights, is apt to trigger an asthma attack. Although the situation at home is rapidly deteriorating, Cassie's social life is improving: She has found her first boyfriend and she has discovered that insecurity is not her exclusive province. She works out a tentative truce with her older sister and, under the sage tutelage of Vicki, is even elected president of her class. Although the children's inept attempts to reunite their parents fail, at least they seem to have gained a modicum of insight and empathy into each other's problems. Cassie continues to translate her anxieties into imagined physical symptoms, but with her growing self-acceptance and maturity she is also developing more viable techniques of emotional expression. The reader is led to infer that the frequency and seriousness of her asthmatic attacks will probably be reduced.

Analysis. Cassie describes the onset of an asthmatic episode in a straightforward and realistic manner:

> The asthma's starting. It feels as if water is filling up my lungs and I'm going to drown. Opening my mouth to say something, I start to wheeze. I panic when that starts. That makes it worse, even harder to breathe, but I don't think I can control it. I put my head down to my knees. The pistachios spill on the pink carpet, but I don't even care. I feel as if I've got to fight to get even a little air inside of me.

Her disorder is seen as a serious and authentic somatic problem, but one that is adversely affected by emotional strain. It is a significant but not controlling factor in the character's life, another of those many and varied conditions she learns to manage as she grows up. The author's obvious affection for her mercurial, insecure teenage heroine will be shared by many readers. The witty dialogue and the focus on events and themes of compelling interest to adolescents will ensure the popularity of this title.

de Paola, Tomie. *Now One Foot, Now the Other.* Illus. by author. New York: Putnam's, 1981. unp. Reading Level: YC
Disability: Neurological Impairment

Bobby was named after his grandfather, who adores and dotes on him. One of the child's favorite stories is about how the older man taught him to walk. Shortly after Bobby's fifth birthday, his grandfather is hospitalized for treatment of a stroke. It is months before the paralyzed man is able to return home. The boy is warned that his grandfather has lost his ability to do many things and is cautioned: "Don't be scared if he doesn't remember you." Despite his parents' attempts to prepare him, Bobby is frightened, unable to accept the old man's radically altered condition. Bobby speaks to his grandfather and, despite the minimal response, becomes convinced that even if he cannot communicate, the man understands. The boy re-enacts some of their previously shared enjoyable experiences, and his grandfather gives further evidence that he does indeed know what is happening. Slowly he regains his ability to speak and feed himself. Then the youngster, in a loving exchange of roles, reteaches his grandfather how to walk, "Now one foot, now the other."

Analysis. With an unerring sensitivity to the comprehension level of his audience, de Paola has provided an on-target description of a stroke patient. The young hero serves as a stand-in for the child reader, who can share Bobby's distress as he comes to terms with the shock of responding to an older person who was once a source of strength and security in his life and who now is helpless and dependent. The restorative value of the youngster's love is given credible expression here. The illustrations are vintage de Paola—warm, tender, and uncluttered.

Delton, Jina. *Two Blocks Down.* New York: Harper & Row, 1981. 148 pp. Reading Level: YA/MA
Disability: Emotional Dysfunction

Star keeps herself aloof from the students in her new high school. Gestures of friendship are greeted with surprise, coolness, and, occasionally, panic. Despite her desire for solitude, Star finds herself involved with a few classmates. A beautiful loner, she thinks frequently of how happy she is and how content she feels when she visits her old friends at the Vagary Bar. In a desire to share her private happiness, Star invites some students to the tavern, but it is as deserted as it always has been. She accepts an invitation to a dance, but her discomfort is evident, and her date, who senses her distress, offers to return her to the Vagary, where she is greeted enthusiastically by her nonexistent friends.

Analysis. This is a strange and unsatisfying portrait of an adolescent who prefers a fantasy world to the real one. The stimulus for her behavior is never made clear in this murky, surrealistic novel, whose intent and meaning elude even the most careful reader.

Dengler, Marianna. *A Pebble in Newcomb's Pond.* Illus. by Kathleen Garry-McCord. New York: Holt, Rinehart & Winston, 1979. 160 pp. Reading Level: YA
Disability: Emotional Dysfunction, special health problems

Unable to tolerate the attention of other people or exert control over either her emotions or her behavior, Mara is becoming estranged from family and friends. The troubled girl feels compulsively drawn to a pond on school property from which a turtle seems to be calling out to her. These auditory delusions are compounded by perceptual ones: She has difficulty picking up or holding onto objects; stairs and ladders seem to tilt away from her. When Mara's food begins to taste bitter, the irrational girl is convinced she is being poisoned by her mother. On probation at school for excessive class cutting and with the quality of her schoolwork declining drastically, it seems unlikely Mara will pass any of her courses.

One night she is irresistibly drawn to the pond, only to find the entrance padlocked. Desperately frustrated at not being able to reach her goal, she swallows some pills in an unsuccessful suicide attempt. Still in a state of acute distress, Mara finds a piece of paper in her pocket (previously given to her by a worried friend) with the address of a psychiatrist on it. She makes her way to his office, where she is later found collapsed against his door. The doctor calls her parents and tentatively reports that he suspects there is a physical basis for their daughter's bizarre behavior. The girl's father is skeptical, but her mother, a diabetic, knows firsthand of the effects of disturbed body chemistry on perception and behavior. Without much hope, the girl's parents consent to the administration of tests, which confirm the psychiatrist's suspicions. A dietary regimen, supplemented by vitamins and drugs, appears to promise relief from Mara's schizophrenic behavior.

Analysis. The behavioral deterioration of the heroine, her intermittent episodes of depression, her diminished periods of lucidity, her irrational overreaction and irritability, her inability to concentrate, and a constellation of other symptoms add up to a credible picture of a tormented adolescent. Particularly well done are descriptions of intervals in which Mara does try to make sense of the disturbing events in her life and diagnose her own illness. The proposition that the dysfunctional girl has a vague understanding of what is happening to her and that this realization generates hopelessness and anxiety is especially sensitively developed. This is seen, for example, in Mara's fear of publicly acknowledging her problem, a fear exacerbated by a troubling recollection of a visit to a psychiatric hospital. The depiction of concerned parents and friends who remain supportive, although puzzled and frightened, is an important addition to the story. The adolescent's terrifying delusions are effectively communicated in the well-rendered, black-and-white illustrations. One serious criticism, however, must be leveled against this work: Its primary intent seems to be to endorse orthomolecular psychiatry as the treatment of choice for adolescent schizophrenia. A junior novel is an inappropriate arena for the presentation of a partisan argument in a hotly contested medical controversy.

Dexter, Pat Egan. *The Emancipation of Joe Tepper*. Nashville: Thomas Nelson, 1976. 159 pp. Reading Level: YA
Disability: Intellectual Impairment; also special health problems

Even without his alcoholic mother's constant nagging, Joe Tepper would be anxious to find a job. However, little work is available for a 15-year-old boy with only an eighth-grade education. Joe is offered employment by Delores, the manager of a bowling alley, after she observes him disperse a crowd of teenagers harassing Bayne, an employee. The grateful woman confides: " 'Bayne is kind of slow' . . . pointing to her head. 'Retarded,' she whispered softly. 'He's good about cleaning up and organizing simple things, but we don't expect him to handle problems.' "

Joe is outraged when he learns his mother has arranged for one of her many boyfriends to jettison his dog in the Arizona desert. The animal is rescued, but the teenager's long-smoldering resentment against his parent threatens to erupt. After Mrs. Tepper is mortally injured by a hit-and-run driver, Joe's ambivalent feelings are resolved, and she is reconciled with him shortly before she dies. Mrs. Hilton, a novice social worker, is determined to find the orphan a suitable home, but Joe is adamant about managing his own life, especially when he learns that foster home placement would mean giving up his dog. Bayne invites his new friend and mentor to share the janitor's quarters he occupies in an apartment complex. The teenager accepts with alacrity, recognizing the need for refuge, safe from the well-intentioned but misguided social worker. The evil apartment manager, although willing to exploit the desperate adolescent's need for housing, repeatedly threatens to get rid of Joe's noisy animal. An attractive tenant, admiring Joe's relationship with Bayne, offers to care for his pet even though her infant daughter has asthma. Mrs. Hilton relentlessly pursues the youth, finally bringing the boy to court, where, to her surprise, he is declared an emancipated minor. Efforts to have Bayne committed are likewise frustrated as Joe, frantic to help his friend, researches the rights of retarded adults, enlists the help of a sympathetic police officer, and solicits the assistance of the American Civil Liberties Union; then, armed with their support, successfully convinces a judge to approve Bayne's current living arrangements. The janitor does not share the general surprise or relief, having always believed he would be provided for. The overeager social worker belatedly admits her error and congratulates the self-sufficient, mature, and thoroughly admirable teenager for his accomplishments.

Analysis. This heavy-handed melodrama features stock characters walking through a series of set pieces for the apparent purpose of delivering a miscellany of messages on temperance, tolerance, faith, kindness to animals, diligence, and perseverance. Joe's comments reveal his initial contempt for Bayne and a willingness to exploit him: "Just bcause I was nice to this stupid guy, I might walk into a real good deal," and later: "What a good guy Bayne was, even if he was a dumbbell." Inevitably these perceptions are transformed into protectiveness and affection. This change in attitude and behavior, like his forgiveness of his mother and his efforts to protect his independence, is used as an index of the hero's increasing maturity.

Bayne's characterization is right on target—the man's naiveté and candor, his competence when the demands of a job have been carefully explained by a concerned employer, and his direct and inappropriate response to affection, such as kissing Joe's hand after a perceived kindness are all credible. An unusual aspect of this work is the religious bond between Bayne and a woman, now deceased, who had adopted him when he was a youngster. He was encouraged to believe that he had been "sent" to his "aunt" so she could provide him with love and guidance and that ever after Providence would watch out for him.

Dickinson, Peter. *Annerton Pit.* Boston: Little, Brown, 1977. 175 pp.
Reading Level: YA
Disability: Visual Impairment

When their grandfather unaccountably stops mailing postcards home, Jake, who is blind, persuades his older brother, Martin, that there is much cause for concern. Motivated by affection for their iconoclastic relative, prodded by Martin's restlessness following rejection from the university, and angered about the trial of some other members of the Green Revolutionaries, an environmentalist group, the two set off on the old man's trail. They track him as far as Annerton, an apparently abandoned coal mining area. The boys are stopped in their investigation by some adherents of the ecology group, ostensibly conducting historical research. The boys' suspicions that they are being lied to prove correct when the jittery group leader takes them prisoner. Jake is locked in a trailer with his seriously ill grandfather, who has been the prisoner of this renegade faction since his disappearance, while Martin is taken elsewhere for questioning. The gang underestimates the blind boy's abilities, and he is able to escape, but, after a futile struggle, is soon recaptured. The three intruders are confined in a dark corner of a mine with the exit wired to explode if they attempt to escape. Martin reveals that their captors are using the mine to store explosives they plan to employ in the imminent seizure of an oil rig. Martin is unnerved by the dissidents' willingness to risk the lives of innocent people and confesses he had once been a member who sincerely believed in their cause. Realizing that their grandfather's rapidly worsening condition could be fatal, Jake and Martin desperately search for an escape route. Using ingenuity, persistence, and tremendous physical effort, they clear a path that allows the older brother to escape and alert the police. Jake, left to guard the ailing man, finds his fears conjure up a suffocating and disorienting presence, which he is barely able to bring under control. The prisoners are ultimately rescued, the gang's plan is blocked, and all but one of its members are captured.

Analysis. The author has written a compelling cliffhanger with an admirable, bright, responsible, and caring adolescent who also happens to be blind. Jake's character is superbly developed and accurately demonstrates how an astute, sightless person uses his or her senses to understand his or her world. The youth's blindness does not dominate his other attributes, nor is it treated with false heroics. There is not one vestige of pity allowed him: His vision loss creates inconveniences and limitations, but his native intelligence and adaptive behaviors mitigate the effects of his disability. The boy is sufficiently self-confident to joke about the matter, a response that makes his brother uncomfortable. The difference in reaction is echoed in the brothers' contrasting personalities—Martin is the impetuous Catherine wheel, Jake the stable balance wheel. The close and interdependent relationships among the three family members are sensitively developed.

Another theme of major interest concerns the paradoxical actions of an alliance whose humanitarian objectives deteriorate into violent and destructive means, precipitating an agonizing moral dilemma for one of its devoted adherents. The interweaving of the various thought-provoking issues marks this as a memorable work.

Dickinson, Peter. *Tulku.* New York: Dutton, 1979. 286 pp. Reading Level: YA/MA
Disability: Visual Impairment

Theodore Tewker barely escapes with his life when his father is killed and his mission destroyed during the Boxer Rebellion. Wandering lost and alone, the 13-year-old orphan encounters Mrs. Jones, an ardent botanist who allows him to travel with her entourage. Although the mountainous countryside is filled with brigands, the clever and dauntless woman is able to evade or outwit them. Some of the corrupt men serving her set up an ambush, but she outfoxes them. Her only companions now are Lung, her Chinese guide, and Theo. They hurry

onward, hoping to escape the robbers pursuing them, when they encounter the Lama Amchi, who is searching for the child who will be
the Tulku, the holy leader of his people. At first the Lama believes
Theo is the anointed one but soon reassesses the signs, deciding they
really point to the unborn child of Daisy Jones and Lung. The party is
escorted to the Tibetan monastery to await the baby's birth. Accepting
this offer of a temporary haven, the botanist nevertheless plans to flee
with Lung and Theo at the first opportunity.

Lung is directed to locate dissidents who will help them, and
Theo is instructed to begin learning Tibetan, knowledge they will
surely need if they are to cross the countryside safely. The boy locates
a potential tutor, a self-effacing, almost blind, ex-British officer who
has joined the community to seek enlightenment. Achugla, formerly
Major Price Evans, at first demurs, explaining that silence is better
than speech, but is persuaded to help the youth in his studies. The
apostate's presence in these remote parts and his rambling conversations are disconcerting to the devout youngster, who has been scan-
dalized by the brazen manner of Mrs. Jones and the "heathen" behavior of everyone he has met since leaving the Christian mission. In
the meantime, Lama Amchi has become the guru of the Tulku's
mother-to-be, instructing her in her role and his religion. Lung is
frantic when he realizes his lover has become a convert and, in an act
of desperation, tries to shoot the Lama. He is captured and then, due
to Mrs. Jones's intercession, given safe passage from the country with
Theo. The lad, on instructions from the woman he has come to respect, journeys to England to the home of the man she once loved,
where he recounts his adventures with that unique and memorable
person and presents his host with a rare, exotic, and exquisite lily she
had collected.

Analysis: An intriguing, original, and wonderfully literate story,
Tulku features an absorbing cast of characters and a fast-moving plot.
The virtually sightless former soldier is just one of several converts
who has found his destiny in this remote locale. He regards his vision
loss with the same mixture of acceptance and wonder with which he
confronts a world that has proven to be simultaneously expected and
full of surprises.

Dixon, Paige (pseud. for Barbara Corcoran). *Skipper*. New York:
Atheneum, 1979. 103 pp. Reading Level: YA
Disability: Neurological Impairment; also auditory impairment

Skipper continues to mourn for his older brother who died a half
year ago. He is inconsolable, unable to excise his feeling of emptiness.

To work through his grief and anger and to compensate for his deeply felt loss, he impetuously decides to go to North Carolina to locate the father who abandoned him and who has shown little interest in the welfare of his progeny. At first, his older siblings are astonished at his quest, but soon they agree to help by paying his air fare from Colorado. With only a minimum of trouble, he tracks down his relatives, a motley collection who greet his arrival with mixed emotions. His initial encounter is with Mary Gwyn, whose hopes for a musical career were destroyed when a spinal injury received at a horse show left her partially paralyzed. Skipper had learned how to behave toward people who are disabled when his brother was dying and consequently is able to act naturally toward this cousin. His sensitivity undercuts her initial hostility, transforming it into affection. The boy learns he has a half brother who, with the connivance of another relative, is plotting to secure the ancestral lands and turn the area over to a developer. Skipper becomes embroiled in machinations to oppose the change, all of which prove superfluous when the venerable patriarch dies, leaving a more equitable division of the estate than was anticipated. Skipper's father, who continues to elude his son, is currently living with a black woman, a situation that allows the family to display an array of responses ranging from noblesse oblige to unreconstructed bigotry. Incomprehensibly, these family shenanigans give the sojourner sufficient peace of mind to return home, reconciled at last to the loss of his beloved brother.

Analysis. Situated in a swampy Southern backwater, this family seems suspended in an antebellum world, using language and engaging in practices that are anachronistic. Mary Gwyn personalizes this sense of being cut off from the mainstream: The wheelchair she uses acts to confine her—a prison within a prison. Skipper and Mary Gwyn play mutually supportive roles. He is startled by her provocative and caustic comments: "Are you scared of us? . . . And of me especially, because you don't know how to treat me. 'Shall I pretend she's running around on two legs?' you wondered. 'Or shall I offer sympathy and clichés? Hope on a platter, along with iced tea?' . . . Now I really am being embarrassing. Pay no attention. . . . Usually people act as if I've died and they're trying not to notice."

The boy is able to demonstrate that she has no need for the psychological defenses she has been using. For her part, Mary Gwyn helps the boy accept his father's irresponsibility and allows him to drain off some of his debilitating preoccupation with his deceased brother. The patriarch's presence is felt in the story, but his deafness and the results of his stroke have diminished his participation in the family.

The dialogue is, unfortunately, ridden with clichés: People named Mama Maeve and Papa Rhys are "right proud" to do things and speak the word "Yankee" as if it were an epithet. The heroine is a composite of intelligence and bitterness, sensitivity and hostility. As such, she has some substance, but all the other characters are plastic and unconvincing, a sad contrast to those in the novel's masterful predecessor, *May I Cross Your Golden River?*

Dixon, Paige (pseud. for Barbara Corcoran). *Walk My Way.* New York: Atheneum, 1980. 139 pp. Reading Level: YA
Disability: special health problems

When 14-year-old Kitty LeBlanc is attacked by her father's drunken friend, she knocks him to the floor, causing him to lose consciousness. Afraid he might be dead, she runs away, in fact relieved to be free of her unloving, abusive father. The youngster sets out through the woods, heading for the home of Aunt Lee, her dead mother's best friend. Along the way, she meets a basenji, who trails behind her, and an elderly man traveling on foot with his grandson and dog. Delaware, a retired sea captain, explains that his heart condition has deteriorated so that he knows he does not have long to live and has decided to settle Jody with the boy's Aunt Mary. They all journey together through backwoods trails, with Kitty taking responsibility for their welfare, arranging for food and shelter, and pulling the old man in the wagon when he is too weary to walk. It is clear that Mr. Delaware is at the end of his strength, and when he dies, the adolescent buries him among the trees as he had requested. She continues with the boy and dog to Aunt Lee's house, where they are lovingly received. Soon afterward, she calls her father and announces her determination to stay where she is, a decision the man realizes he must accept. The trip to take Jody to his new home fills them all with trepidation, but it is soon apparent that Aunt Mary and her new husband will give the boy the love and care he needs. A call from a former employer reveals that a recording executive has heard a tape of Kitty's voice and has confidently predicted that she will be admitted to a prestigious music school and will have a successful career as a singer.

Analysis. This slight effort includes an elderly man whose damaged heart offers the excuse for the unlikely encounter that permits some modest complications of the simple plot. The old man apparently suffers little, and his death is abrupt, neat, and clean. Characterizations are bland, and the plodding narrative moves slowly to an uninspired and unbelievable conclusion.

Donahue, Marilyn Cram. *The Crooked Gate*. Elgin, Ill.: David C. Cook, 1979. 208 pp. Reading Level: MC
Disability: Auditory Impairment

Because of a family emergency, Cass and her brothers Ted and Benjy are left with their eccentric Aunt Mathilda for the summer. The old woman's solitary house is on the seacoast, offering the youngsters little prospect for excitement. Cass's expectations improve when she meets Hal, a boy about her age. After their encounter, Ted comments on their new acquaintance: "Being deaf isn't any big deal. I mean, I'm glad I'm not, but it doesn't seem to bother him. He can do anything we can do, except hear." Aunt Mathilda cryptically adds: "He hears the most important way of all."

On an errand into town, Cass speaks with Tina, who offers her friendship to the newcomer. Cass intuits that Tina is not a proper companion but is nonetheless eager to develop some social life. As her price of admission to Tina's group, Cass is ordered to steal the glass eye from her aunt's prized cigar store Indian. The girl is successful but immediately feels remorseful. Retreating to a lonely cave on the sea cliffs she had discovered earlier, the youngster enters it to contemplate her reprehensible actions. While she is thus engrossed, the water rises, flooding the grotto and endangering her life. In her distress, the transgressor turns to God for help. Soon afterward, Hal arrives to save her. Realizing how insubstantial her values have been, the now enlightened girl begins to reassess her life.

Analysis: The difficulties of adjusting to deafness are minimized, and the character with an auditory impairment, rather than being a believable person, is a plaster saint. The description of how Aunt Mathilda talks to the boy would not be recommended by speech therapists: "She said each word in a special kind of way. She didn't make any more noise than usual, but her mouth seemed to work harder." More a sermon than a story, all events are contrived in order to deliver the moral lesson. The author's obvious good intentions far outstrip her writing ability, and the result is a plodding, leaden, sterile effort.

Duncan, Lois. *Killing Mr. Griffin*. Boston: Little, Brown, 1978. 243 pp. Reading Level: YA/MA
Disability: Emotional Dysfunction, special health problems

The students in Susan's high school class are simmering—frustrated and angered by what they regard as the unreasonable behavior of their English teacher, Mr. Griffin. He adamantly refuses to accept late papers, no matter what excuse is given; he demands technical excellence from his pupils; and he is scathing in his criticism of both content and form in his students' writing. Articulating the feelings of the group, Jeff angrily remarks that he could happily kill Griffin, and Mark, in all seriousness, endorses the idea. Mark tactically withdraws his declaration when his suggestion is greeted with horror, but he insists that their teacher should be taught a lesson. Dave, the class president, Betsy, a vacuous cheerleader, and Susan, an unhappy loner, are recruited for the task. Susan detains Griffin after school until the grounds are empty. When the teacher goes to his car, the youths overwhelm him, taking him, still bound, to a deserted spot. Mark tries to force the man to beg to be released but is unsuccessful. They decide to leave him there alone until he is sufficiently humbled. Having second thoughts about this escapade, Susan and David intend to release their victim, but they discover that he has died. The boys clumsily bury him and try to conceal their tracks, but their amateurish cover-up comes apart. When Dave's grandmother appears to threaten their alibi, Mark murders the old woman, trying to make her death appear an accident. He is observed but not identified; however, Susan deduces who is responsible. After a meeting in which she insists that they cease these outrages and inform the authorities, Mark sends the others away, ties her up, and sets her house afire. Luckily Susan is rescued, Mark is apprehended, and the whole sordid story is revealed.

Analysis. Mr. Griffin's heart condition is a minor one, but he is not strong enough to stand the stress resulting from his kidnapping. Without access to his nitroglycerine tablets, which are out of his reach, he dies. Mark is specifically identified as a psychopath:

> This individual has a behavior pattern that brings him repeatedly into conflict with society. He is incapable of significant loyalty to individuals, groups or social values. He is selfish, callous, irresponsible, impulsive and totally unable to experience guilt. His frustration level is low; he cannot stand to be thwarted. He tends to blame others or offer plausible rationalizations for his behavior. . . . This individual is unique among pathological personalities in appearing, even on close examination, to be not only quite normal but unusually intelligent and charming. He appears quite sincere and loyal and may perform brilliantly at any endeavor. He often has a tremendous charismatic power over others.

The youth's behavior is consistent with that diagnosis. He has a strong and forceful personality and is able to manipulate others into acting out his power fantasies. Mark is presented as a totally unsympathetic character, except for a passing reference to his feelings of being deserted as a child. He lies, brutalizes, and kills totally without conscience. However, the author seems to be focusing not so much on Mark's behavior as on the ready manipulability of the other students, who are essentially weak and characterless. Duncan has crafted her usual tight, well-designed, suspenseful story—in this case, a morality tale for our times.

Duncan, Lois. *Stranger with My Face*. Boston: Little, Brown, 1981. 250 pp. Reading Level: YA
Disability: Emotional Dysfunction, Cosmetic Impairment

Laurie has only recently become friends with the other island adolescents who form an exclusive, snobbish clique within the local high school. Jeff, a handsome boy but now disfigured from burns, is a loner, having rejected the tentative gestures of friendship offered by his neighbors after the accident. "The left side of his face was fine. . . . If you saw him from the right, you had to stop and swallow hard. That side of his face was welted and purple with the eye half closed and the mouth pulled up at the corner like a Halloween mask."

Laurie senses a specter in her house and begins to hear puzzling reports of her alleged actions. Lia, a ghostly presence and virtually identical in appearance to the teenage girl, makes herself known to Laurie. Anxious for some explanation, the girl forces the information from her resisting parents that she and an identical twin sister were born to an outcast Navaho woman. Her mother initially considered adopting both infants but, for reasons she is unable to articulate, found the other baby unacceptable. Lia, the twin, becomes a dominating force in her sister's life, exerting a magnetic, obsessive attraction and causing the teen to lose interest in social activities, family, and school. Laurie learns from her friend Helen, a newcomer to the community, about "astral projection," a technique that allows the soul to leave the corporeal body and travel vast distances. Helen, who lived in the Southwest where such rituals are commonly practiced, believes that this psychic process is the cause of the mysterious events and warns her friend that she is tampering with dangerous forces. Soon after the girl from Arizona is the victim of a nearly fatal accident, for which her distraught mother unreasonably holds Jeff accountable.

Lia tries to extend her power over her twin, insisting she too must learn to master this mystical means of teleportation and further demands that Laurie abandon her growing involvement with Jeff. Resenting this pressure, Laurie invites the boy for dinner. He accepts but, inexplicably, does not arrive at the appointed time. When a search is mounted, Laurie spots some books he had promised to bring her close by a dangerous, rocky shelf. While investigating, she too falls into the hidden cavern in which Jeff has been trapped. The youth realizes he mistook Lia for her sibling and was deliberately lured by the malevolent apparition onto the dangerous rocks from which he fell and broke his leg. Laurie projects her spirit body to the surface, where she is seen by her brother, who summons rescuers. Determined to locate her sister, Laurie traces her to a locked room in a psychiatric hospital. She is shocked to hear that Lia has been tried for the murder of her foster sister, after which she was hospitalized indefinitely after the court accepted her insanity plea. In the meantime, the diabolical Lia enters her sister's empty body, claiming it for her own. Laurie, realizing she has been tricked, watches helplessly as the imposter usurps her identity. She holds realistic fears that her younger sister is in danger because the child voiced suspicions of the interloper's behavior. When the girl joins Jeff in a confrontation that exposes Lia's evil acts, Laurie's twin becomes furious and violently attacks them. Jeff propitiously throws the Indian fetish that Helen claimed was a "defense against evil spirits" at her. Lia is jarred loose from her hold on Laurie's body, enabling its rightful owner to regain possession.

A short time later, Jeff undergoes plastic surgery paid for by Laurie's parents. He reports: "I'll never be a pretty boy, but, thanks to your folks, I'll have a crack at looking human."

Analysis. Such standard occult ingredients as twins separated at birth and supernatural practices of "exotic" cultures combine with a lightweight teen romance to produce this facile work. Jeff's disfigurement and other characters' reactions to it are extreme, as exemplified in the hysterical assertion of Helen's mother that her daughter "didn't have to settle for a boy with a face like that, a boy who looks like the devil himself." The willingness of comparative strangers to pay for major surgery strains credulity, and the boy's statement that the operation will result in his looking "human" shows insensitivity. The hero's appearance is posited as a major factor in shaping his personality, but his characterization is so shallow that this premise cannot be treated seriously. The most unfortunate aspect of this work is the coupling of emotional dysfunction and evil, a commonplace equation found in the gothic genre, but hardly excusable on those grounds.

Dunlop, Eileen. *The House on Mayferry Street.* Originally published in England as *A Flute on Mayferry Street* by Oxford University Press. Illus. by Phillida Gile. New York: Holt, Rinehart & Winston, 1976. 205 pp. Reading Level: MC/YA
Disability: Orthopedic Impairment

Soon after Mr. Ramsey died of a heart attack, his teenage daughter was hit by a motorcyclist. The physicians reported that Marion's spine was damaged, but they expected, in time, that she would recover completely. She has since adopted the role of an invalid in the house she shares with her mother and brother, Colin, in Edinburgh. Home tutoring and the few domestic activities in which she participates have done nothing to relieve the boredom of the girl, who has become alarmingly passive and apathetic. While cleaning the bookcase for their mother, Marion discovers a letter written prior to World War I, addressed to "My dear Charles" and signed "Alan A. B. Farquhar," which piques her interest. Logically following several obscure clues and aided by some fortuitous accidental discoveries, the clever children slowly move closer to resolving the mystery of the identity of the letter writer. Both Colin, a talented flutist, and Marion begin to hear ghostly flute music, which convinces them that they are on the right track in their detective work. Ultimately, their deductive powers and dogged determination provide an answer to the location of a trunk mentioned in the tantalizing old letter. When the casket is opened, it reveals a major musical composition alongside an excellent flute, which Colin is able to play with surprising skill: "Perhaps only Colin really knew that it was not Colin who was playing . . . while the music . . . lasted, the hands and brain that made it did not belong to him, but to the man who last played the flute." Equally enchanted by the treasure, Marion envisions herself in a romantic setting, and for the first time in years, under the force of her fantasy, sees herself walking. She soon recovers the use of her legs and is able to walk with confidence. The trunk, along with its contents, is forwarded to the descendants of Alan Farquhar, and after a nerve-wracking wait, the man's grandson appears at their doorstep. To her astonishment, he is the object of Marion's dreams and the fantasy episode during which she seemed to walk. He tells them that the person to whom the letter was addressed, Charles Ramsey, a relative, is living in Australia, wants Colin to have his flute, and plans to visit them all soon.

Analysis. The nature of Marion's injury is not explained, but full restoration of her mobility is predicted by her doctors. She spends three years completely immobile and then, within a very short interval, is walking unassisted. It is a peculiar ailment that tolerates years of nonuse without any atrophying of muscles and then permits almost instantaneous amelioration. The major part of this story involves a compelling but leisurely pursuit of an intriguing mystery and the development of interesting and appealing characters whose thoughts and feelings are more significant elements than their actions. The resolution is overly abrupt and neat, and consequently disappointing. This low-key gothic romance does not seem directed to any readily identifiable level of reader. The illustrations and the early chapters of the story seem most appropriate for elementary school youngsters, but the romantic resolution, although platonic, would only be of interest to a slightly older audience.

> Dunnahoo, Terry. *Who Needs Espie Sanchez?* New York: Dutton, 1977. 138 pp. Reading Level: YA
> *Disability:* Neurological Impairment, Special Health Problems

Following her father's abandonment, her drunken mother's rejection, and an abortive attempt at running away to Mexico, Espie finds refuge in a foster home with Mrs. Garcia. The 15-year-old girl needs considerable savvy to cope with life in the Los Angeles barrio, but she is greatly helped by participation in a police-sponsored youth program. The adolescent's life is affected by several events: the automobile accident that left her close friend Denise with spinal damage; her encounter with Allison, a rich, lonely alcoholic roommate; Mrs. Garcia's asthmatic condition, exacerbated by fatigue and worry about Denise; and Espie's growing attraction to Rick, choir leader in the local church. The independent teenager, although occasionally restive under the discipline imposed by her foster mother, feels both comfortable and wanted within an orderly surrogate family structure. Given her sense of control and the obvious efforts exerted by Denise and Mrs. Garcia to address their own predicaments, Espie becomes increasingly contemptuous of Allison's inability to manage her drinking problem. She collects information about Alcoholics Anonymous for her friend and makes an initial contact, but it is not clear at the conclusion whether the abuser will pursue this solution. Also unresolved is the extent of Denise's recovery from her spinal cord injury, although the physicians have said that she will not be crippled and "it will be months from now before she is all better."

Analysis. Dunnahoo gives a vivid sense of the barrio lifestyle in this simplistic, fast-paced junior novel. Drinking is involved in Denise's accident and Allison's family conflicts and worsens the teenagers' personal and social problems. While these situations mirror a major contemporary concern, this presentation resembles tract literature. The quality of the depiction of disability varies. Mrs. Garcia's asthmatic condition, although treated only briefly, is presented credibly. Worry, overwork, and unaccustomed physical effort could reasonably be expected to precipitate the kind of breathing problems she exhibits. Additional rest, elevation of her head and upper body following an attack, and pleasure received from hearing about the recovery of a loved one are properly seen to engender relief. The adolescent's recovery from a spinal injury is harder to accept. Little information is presented about the therapy, but the complete cure that is hinted at would appear to depend more on the need for a literary resolution than medical likelihood.

Dyer, Thomas A. *A Way of His Own*. Boston: Houghton Mifflin, 1981. 154 pp. Reading Level: MC
Disability: Orthopedic Impairment

Before recorded history, Shutok, a young Plains Indian, lived with his family as part of a small nomadic tribe. Pain, his constant companion, makes walking difficult, and his obvious disability leads the others to regard him with suspicion. His mother warns him if any misfortune befalls their people he will undoubtedly be blamed. Although determined to stay with them, the lad can scarcely keep pace with his people as they travel in search of game. In the aftermath of a hostile encounter with another tribe, a girl is captured and made a slave. She fashions a crutch for the limping boy, which he initially regards with suspicion but then grudgingly uses. During a hiatus, a shaman is summoned to ensure the success of their hunt as well as to accelerate the birth of a baby whose belated arrival is slowing the travelers. When the infant is born dead, Shutok, as his mother had foretold, is held responsible and exiled. Uita, the slave, is given to the medicine man in payment for the charms, but she escapes, returning to the cave where the abandoned boy now lives. She fashions a new crutch to replace the one destroyed by the shaman, and the two children apportion such survival chores as hunting and gathering wood. The spoor of a jaguar terrifies them, but Shutok constructs a barrier of sharpened sticks, and shielded by the fortification, he wields his spear sufficiently well to injure and kill the beast. As spring approaches, Uita makes plans to leave, intending to be gone before Shutok's people return and once more enslave her. She hesitates too long because of her concern for her companion, and her fears are realized. Shutok is beaten by the tribal chief, but he is rescued and dragged across the river to safety by his mother.

The marsh people approach with the shaman leading them, expecting to overcome the outnumbered nomads easily. The injured outcast boy cloaks himself in the jaguar pelt and rejoins his people. The would-be attackers are stopped by the evidence of the boy's power in overcoming the fearsome beast, withdraw from the confrontation, and return Uita to the tribal elders. Shutok and his arrogant elder brother are reconciled, paving the way for his acceptance back into the good graces of the tribe.

Analysis. Shutok's stigma condemns him to a leperlike role outside the core group as his people instinctively impute magic and evil power to his impairment. His astonishing accomplishments in overcoming the enemy and walking without his crutch are also attributed to supernatural forces, as the combination of luck, ingenuity, hard work, intelligence, and tenacity of both children, which made these achievements possible, are ignored. His subsequent ascribed potency, however, gives him a position of respect among his people, but, as the new shaman, Shutok still stands apart from the others. The linkage of disability and a special destiny is credible in a tale set in prehistoric times. The perception of impairment arising from evil sources and the corresponding reaction of punishment and banishment is tied to a preliterate, prescientific attitude toward natural phenomena. Thus, the boy's disability marks him for a special fate: first to be disparaged, then to triumph—a pattern common to such stories. The narration moves quickly and maintains interest, principally by virtue of its appealing leading characters and its imaginative recreation of a social order that can only be inferentially known.

Engel, Beth B. *Ride the Pine Sapling.* New York: Harper & Row, 1978. 199 pp. Reading Level: YA
Disability: intellectual impairment

Ann Randall's security is threatened as the Great Depression overtakes her small Georgia town. To compensate for the loss of the father's wages, the Randalls have been obliged to take in roomers. The girl is further upset about her mother's pregnancy, perceiving it as a threat to her mother's frail health as well as to the financial status of the family. A revivalist preacher, whom Ann instinctively fears, becomes their longest-staying lodger. The man's provocative sermons arouse prejudices among their neighbors as he unceasingly spews out his hatred for blacks, Jews, and foreigners. When Ann's Finnish friend is attacked by some local bigots, she must come to his rescue. In that melee, her mother is severely injured and must be rushed to the hospital, her own life and that of her unborn child in jeopardy.

Ann remains in the house alone one night when her father visits his wife in the hospital. The preacher drags her to watch a fire burning in the black community, presumably started by Willie, a young man influenced by the preacher's venomous exhortations. "There's talk that poor Willie was the one who set the fire. Pore addlepated critter—he was just a tool of the Devil and he probably didn't even know what he was doing." Hallie, who is a domestic in the household, comments that Willie "paid" for doing the devil's work when a fiery timber fell on his head. The evil minister tries to assault Ann, but she is saved through the efforts of another tenant. Ann sneaks into the hospital to confirm that her mother has successfully survived the birth of Ann's new brother.

Analysis. The picture of a young girl growing up in this stressful period is sensitively etched, in contrast to the stereotyped depiction of the maid. Willie is a peripheral character, but acts as a catalyst for the crucial scene in the story. He is depersonalized, and we know little or nothing about his family or their status. Although he is generally tolerated by the community, Willie is seen as someone who creates burdens for his neighbors.

> Willie was feebleminded. He joined the church fresh every Sunday. When, at the end of each sermon, Reverend Small invited all those who wanted to be saved from sin to step forward, poor Willie would always step forward. . . . Special church meetings were held about Willie, but nobody had figured out a solution. As Grandmother Peterson said, "He is a cross we have to bear, at least until he decides to be a Baptist or Presbyterian again."

The insensitive mayor speaks about the fraudulence of the religious service:

> I can't see that the halt and the blind . . . are any less afflicted now than when the snake handlers started their revival. . . . Take that poor crazy Willie, for instance—I understand he's gone forward for the laying on of hands every night, but he didn't seem one whit brighter when I saw him yesterday. If anything, he seems more addled with each passing day.

Neither the political nor the religious community provides for Willie's needs. In his innocence and ignorance of the motives of the manipulative churchman, as alleged, Willie acts as a tool of destruction but pays for his gullibility with his own life. The boy dies a horrible death, and the community members are as unhelpful at that moment as they were during his lifetime.

Eyerly, Jeannette. *The Seeing Summer.* Illus. by Emily Arnold McCully. New York: Lippincott, 1981. 153 pp. Reading Level: MC
Disability: Visual Impairment

Although she earnestly wants the new family in her neighborhood to include another ten-year-old, Carey Cramer's delight at her wish coming true is marred by the discovery that Jenny is blind. Jenny assertively demonstrates her competence to her neighbor and shows how she is able to use other senses or techniques to accomplish what her peers depend on sight to do. Carey learns that many of the assumptions she had accepted about the helplessness of blind people are totally incorrect. On one of their excursions, the girls stop to buy ice cream, and Carey reports that Jenny's father's picture appears on the front of a popular magazine on display. The inside story reveals that the cover portrait is of a fabulously wealthy man who is also a famous scientist. Carey is overheard by a disreputable-looking character, who engages her in conversation to confirm Jenny's relationship.

After the girls go to the park to run, Carey leaves Jenny on a bench while she goes on an errand for her housekeeper. Although absent only briefly, she returns to find her friend is no longer there. Jenny is not at home either, and it soon becomes clear that the child has been kidnapped. Later, Carey sees the man who had spoken to them at the ice cream store and, keeping in mind her admired fictional detective, follows him. The intrepid girl accuses him of "stealing" Jenny, which he denies. Nonetheless he claims he can take her to her missing friend. Foolishly Carey accompanies him to a deserted building, where she is locked in an abandoned loft with her friend. In a few days, the police track them down and rescue them.

Analysis. During the course of the story several popular misconceptions about the abilities of blind people are shown to be erroneous, and the awkwardness or reluctance that strangers often display toward them is explored. There are many editorial lapses, the plot is blatantly contrived, and characters are burdened with cute names such as Pansy Prugh and Aunt Richard as well as sitcom identities.

Ferry, Charles. *O Zebron Falls!* Boston: Houghton Mifflin, 1977. 213 pp. Reading Level: YA
Disability: Visual Impairment

The early days of World War II have little impact on Lukie's life in Zebron Falls, Michigan, except that her father's work, expediting army contracts, demands longer hours away from home. His absences cause her little regret since the two have a distant and mildly abrasive relationship, exacerbated by the 16 year old's closeness to Uncle Farnie, her father's estranged twin. Lukie's best friend is Billy Butts, the only black youth in town and captain of the high school football team. Harvey Toles, a talented young musician with vision problems, has recently become interested in her, but their modest romance is marred by his total immersion in his music (an enthusiasm she does not share) and by his tenseness before a concert, which she does not know how to handle.

The regional football championship in which their local high school will participate is the focus of tremendous community excitement. Billy plays brilliantly, leading his outmatched team to a thrilling victory. Despite the town's adulation, the black youngster is conscious of his precarious social position, never overstepping his "place" or behaving in class, at parties, or at dances in a manner others could consider "pushy." His decision to enlist makes the war a reality for Lukie, and the determined young man becomes a fighter pilot in an all-black squadron. When the airman returns home, he tells the naive girl that he still cherishes their relationship, but his experiences in a race riot in Detroit, an ugly incident with the local police chief, and his fight against prejudice in the military have forced him to reassess his life goals. He has decided that he will become a lawyer after the war and actively fight the discrimination he knows blacks must contend with.

A reconciliation between Lukie's father and uncle is barely initiated when Farnie is killed in a factory accident. He had recently deeded his orchard to his niece, a gift that thrills her. Lukie loves the land, although it had been a source of resentment to her father. Her parent has mellowed considerably, and she has grown sufficiently in understanding enough that their differences are now rightly seen as far less important than their love for each other.

Harvey's vision problems persist: He has had to change his glasses three times during his senior year, and recurring irritations plague him. When he walks into the path of a slowly moving car after a successful concert, although he is only slightly injured, it is obvious that his sight is rapidly failing. Mr. Toles tells Lukie that his son developed glaucoma after an accident in which he was pushed over a dam. The man says that the youngster's impending blindness still leaves him with two options: Harvey could become a music teacher at Zebron Falls High School, or he could pursue a career as a concert pianist. His father observes: "The next few weeks will be critical. . . . He must accept his failing eyesight not as a handicap but simply as an obstacle that can be overcome." Distraught with remorse since it was through her horseplay that Harvey got knocked into the water and thrown against the rocks, Lukie considers marrying him and selling her property so she would be able to support him during his studies. Lukie is relieved when she realizes that marrying Harvey to expiate her guilt is an unreasonable response. Still friends, they decide to part in order to follow their separate paths.

Analysis. O Zebron Falls! is a sentimental, bucolic, engaging study of gentle people living in more innocent times—not quite as innocent in actuality, however, as they are presented here. Ferry understates the depth and viciousness of the bigotry that persisted in small Northern

towns in which interracial semiromantic relationships would have precipitated a far more hostile response from the community. The reaction
to Harvey's blindness both by the boy and his father seems equally
underplayed. Each accepts it with an equanimity bordering on causal-
ness. Lukie's feelings of guilt are well handled, and the selfless manner
in which she proposes to assume responsibility for the care of a boy
she inadvertently injured is shown to be a disservice to both.

Filson, Brent. *The Puma*. New York: Doubleday, 1979. 112 pp.
Reading Level: YA
Disability: Speech Impairment

Sonny and his widower father, an ex-space scientist, move east,
where Dr. Street finds work teaching in a college and coaching the
school's perennially losing wrestling team. Sonny, a loner who stam-
mers, has an ungovernable temper. Although the 16 year old is a star
wrestler, he is suspended from the squad after a particularly obnoxious
tantrum. When the kids taunt him about his speech and call him
Monster, he tries to formulate a devastating retort, but "no words
come out. Just noises." Unable to respond to his chief tormentor or to
best him in a verbal duel, Sonny resorts to violence. He is comforted by
a wise, 70-year-old woman who manages a rundown pizza parlor and
is a wrestling aficionado. The adolescent becomes friendly with the
owners of the restaurant, but his attempts to help his new supporters
are in conflict with his desire to be active on the team.

Harry Jim, now a roomer at the Streets' home, was once a petty
criminal. He has renounced his sordid past, mastered his own temper,
and achieved self-control through his practice of Zen. When Sonny is
defeated again, he recollects all the advice he received about conquer-
ing his feelings of anger, reflects on how Harry Jim has been able to
adopt a life of restraint and self-mastery, and after a brief set-to with
his father, accepts counsel about changing his combative lifestyle and
finally becomes reconciled with his parents.

Analysis. "Simple" is the key word for virtually every aspect of this
novel. The vocabulary is limited and the motivations are obvious. Action
is all; characterizations, plot, dialogue, and resolution are developed at
the most basic level. As an example of the attempt to solve a plot dilemma,
Filson has the hero receive sudden enlightenment about the power of
self-control as he crashes into a wall. The treatment of the speech disorder
is equally ludicrous. Speech dysfluency is employed in the opening
segment to reflect Sonny's inner tension, and this disorder surfaces
randomly and erratically during the unfolding of this cautionary tale. The
writing style can be noted in the 16 year old's self-description:

I guess you could call my stuttering a handicap. Some people do. I don't. Having done it all my life, I feel it's not my problem. It's other people's. I mean it's their problem if they let it be. If you don't mind hanging around for the words to get out of my mouth, it's nobody's problem.

Fine, Anne. *The Summer-House Loon.* New York: Crowell, 1978. 127 pp. Reading Level: YA
Disability: Visual Impairment; also auditory impairment

Ione Muffet is startled by the sudden appearance of a distraught young man in the summer house. He introduces himself as Ned Hump, a graduate student and the unsuccessful suitor of her father's reader, Caroline Hope. She is the exceedingly helpful but unreliable transcriber of braille as well as general secretary to Professor Muffet. Although sympathetic to Ned's distress, Ione is amazed to find that Caroline could be the object of anyone's affection. Caroline had declared she would not marry Ned unless he were assured of employment, a condition that hinges on passing his final exams. Unacceptable views about the early Sardinian trade routes, which Ned tenaciously harbors, are the major stumbling blocks to receiving approval for his dissertation from Professor Muffet and the rest of the department. The inebriated professor, discovering Ned in the kitchen, where Ione has taken him, tries to persuade the young man of the error of his argument. In the meantime, Caroline, angry and worried, shares the cooking sherry with Ione, and before the night is over, all four are well potted. Ione, who is up first the next morning, maneuvers Ned into reconsidering his position on the trade routes. He returns later in the day victorious, having passed his exams and subsequently been offered a faculty appointment at the college. The entire examining committee descends on the Muffet house, including the professor emeritus of ancient history, an old man whose confusion is compounded by his hearing loss. Ecstatic, Ned presents Caroline with a curtain ring, the object closest to the real thing available in town. She happily accepts the modest token as well as the triumphant giver.

Analysis. Although the structure of this work suggests it is targeted for a junior high readership, the subject matter and the colorful asides focus on the arcane arguments, the pompous and mannered encounters, and the petty squabbles of academia. The games played with names, such as "Muffet," "Hope," and "Hump," are both infantile and adult, and the inclusion of an amusing drunken sequence may be unique in junior novels. All major characters are wittily rendered and display a variety of both admirable and deplorable traits. Although leader dogs are unusually sacrosanct objects, the obese and recalcitrant mutt introduced here is the recipient of considerable contempt. While poking sly fun at a professor who is blind is a dangerous game, Fine manages to bring it off successfully and humanize the man in the process. This romp achieves its goal since the author's basic assumption appears to be that the world is ridiculous and her characters as a part of that world are inevitably enmeshed in absurdity, blindness notwithstanding. This is a situation in which the disabled character, in effect, blunders into the mainstream. However inadvertently he has arrived, he is indisputably there.

Fleischman, Paul. *The Half-a-Moon Inn.* Illus. by Kathy Jacobi. New York: Harper & Row, 1980. 88 pp. Reading Level: MC/YA
Disability: Speech Impairment

Aaron's mother sets out for town, leaving him alone for the first time in his life. She is concerned for "though she's taught him to read and write as soon as he was able, she'd still feared to let him stray out into the world alone, afraid that he'd stumble into danger without a voice to call for help, or that he'd be mocked for his muteness or even stoned to death as being devil-possessed." She warns her son not to stray from the house, but when she does not return after two days, Aaron sets out in search of her. The 12 year old meets a ragman who first mistakes him for a thief, then appreciating what a nice, quiet boy he is, offers him a ride in his wagon. They arrive at the Half-a-Moon Inn, where the villainous Mrs. Grackle realizes the possibilities for exploiting the defenseless lad. She steals his boots and socks and forces him to work for her. Among his chores is lighting the fire in the grate, a task that can be accomplished only by an honest person. Since she drugs her guests, steals their purses, and reads their dreams, Mrs. Grackle cannot perform this task. Aaron's efforts to escape are thwarted, and he is severely punished when he is caught.

One day his mother arrives at the inn, but the lad has been locked in a closet by his evil captor and is unable to reveal his presence. The boy has been instructed in dream reading and is terrified when he sees that one of the guests is dreaming of murdering him. He discovers the would-be murderer is Lord Tom, a notorious thief. Fearing for his life, the clever boy devises a daring scheme. Aaron pantomimes to Mrs. Grackle that Tom is actually a king in disguise. After the avaricious crone lures Tom down into the cellar, Aaron flees, finding refuge in the back of the ragman's wagon. When the man finds his money gone and discovers the boy, he accuses him once again of being a thief. The lad demonstrates how Mrs. Grackle deceived him, and the furious traveler returns to the hostel to confront the thief. A terrible blizzard blows up, and the two arrive at the Half-a-Moon Inn to find Mrs. Grackle and Lord Tom frozen stiff before the fireplace, neither qualified to light a fire that could have saved them. There, waiting for him, is Aaron's mother, who had noticed his handkerchief in the wicked woman's possession and had returned prepared to rescue him from a dreadful fate. The reunited family happily heads for home.

Analysis. Aaron's muteness is essential for the development of the plot in this superb fantasy. It causes misunderstandings that even his ability to read and write (skills not shared by many in those parlous times) cannot overcome. He is a brave, resourceful, and intelligent lad who is primarily responsible for his own rescue. The writing is exceptionally vivid, colorful, and absorbing, resulting in a rousing tale of adventure. Black-and-white illustrations marvelously capture the plight of the silent hero.

Fleischman, Sid. *The Bloodhound Gang in the Case of the Cackling Ghost.* Illus. by Anthony Rao. New York: Random House, 1981. 63 pp. Reading Level: MC
Disability: Orthopedic Impairment

Feisty Mrs. Fairbanks stares incredulously from her porch at what appears to be a ghost in the garden of her estate. Simultaneously, her stereo broadcasts a cackling noise. The 70-year-old woman, restricted to her wheelchair, summons her nephew, Edmund, who suggests she is hallucinating. Unintimidated but curious, she calls in Vikki, Ricardo, and Zach, the youthful team comprising the Bloodhound Detective Agency, to solve the mystery. The old woman tells them that she does not believe in curses, but shows them her valuable Darjeeling necklace, disclosing that it reputedly has the power to cause insanity in its possessor. Handing the jewelry to Edmund, she fails to notice that her nephew only pretends to lock the safe after replacing the necklace. Vikki, however, has observed his behavior and factors it into her plan to investigate the apparition.

The trio checks out the garden spot where the ghost appeared and asks the head gardener for an explanation of all the dead moths they see there. The puzzled horticulturalist tells the detectives that she has eliminated the use of poisons and seems genuinely surprised to discover that a jar of synthetic insecticide is virtually empty. Ricardo notes the odd fact that moths have adhered to a few drops of the chemical that fell on his sleeve. Upon returning to the estate, the children learn the safe is empty—as Vikki had guessed it would be. In the showdown, Edmund's carefully staged alibi is exposed as a sham, and he is revealed as a thief and a charlatan, having cleverly staged the ghostly image with the moth-attracting purloined chemicals and tampered with his aunt's stereo to generate the cackling noise. The man admits he tried to make his aunt appear incompetent so he would be granted authority over her assets, explaining that his gambling debts made him desperate for money. Mrs. Fairbanks, unsympathetic to his plight, sends the villain packing.

Analysis. This easy-to-read piece of juvenile detective fluff features an elderly, intelligent, and competent woman who is the intended victim of her weak and unscrupulous nephew. Being in a wheelchair precludes the possibility of investigating the ghostly phenomenon herself, a mobility restriction essential to the plot. The unexceptional illustrations are entirely compatible with the mundane quality of this formula story.

French, Dorothy. *I Don't Belong Here.* Philadelphia: Westminster, 1980. 102 pp. Reading Level: YA
Disability: Neurological Impairment; also special health problems

Mary's parents suddenly leave on a business trip to the jungles of South America, sending their shallow, self-centered, petulant daughter to stay with her grandmother. Distressed at the prospect of spending her senior year suffocating in an unexciting small town, the 17 year old is further dismayed to discover that her relative has become senile. The woman is suspicious, forgetful, and stubborn, a far different person from the affectionate, active, supportive individual she had once been. When Mary realizes that no one will wait on her or cater to her whims, the teenager reluctantly and ungraciously assumes some household responsibilities. With the assistance of an elderly, arthritic housekeeper, the girl begins to manage the shopping, cleaning, and cooking. When her grandmother is hospitalized after a fall, Dr. Jasper sagely counsels the confused teenager, after which "much of her fear was gone." The makeover from a selfish person to an understanding, caring one is noticed by Ken, a poor but hardworking young man who plans to spend more time with the attractive newcomer.

Analysis. This easy-to-read romance combines tiresome characters, a silly and predictable plot, hackneyed writing, and a warmed-over theme to produce a book whose one virtue is brevity. The ridiculous heroine reacts to all incidents—from the loss of her luggage to the recognition of the drastic change in her grandmother's behavior—at a hysterical level: "But to spend a whole year with her? Mary's heart cried no. Somehow, somehow, she would get out of it. Somehow! She set her jaw." Although the older woman is depicted sympathetically, the soap opera treatment ensures that this aspect of the work will not be taken seriously.

Gackenbach, Dick. *A Bag Full of Pups*. Illus. by author. New York: Clarion, 1981. unp. Reading Level: YC
Disability: visual impairment, auditory impairment

When Mr. Mullin's dog delivers a litter of 12 puppies, he places them in a large sack and takes them to the city to find homes for them. The first 11 irresistible creatures are taken by people who have a special purpose in mind for the animals. These new owners include a blind man who proposes training the pup as a guide dog and a deaf woman who explains her pet "will tell me when someone knocks at my door." The last one is loaded on a skateboard by a little boy who wants a "pup to play with and be my friend." "That's what I call a lucky pup," observes Mr. Mullin.

Analysis. The dozen recipients of pets are a motley crew—idiosyncratic in their goals, their dress, and their comments. The two new dog owners who intend to use the animals to compensate partially for sensory loss are not notably different from their peers. This casual treatment of disabled characters is a delight. The appealing illustrations add enormously to the story, a simple and amusing romp.

Gage, Wilson (pseud. for Mary Q. Steele). *Down in the Boondocks*. Illus. by Glen Rounds. New York: Greenwillow, 1977. 32 pp. Reading Level: YC
Disability: Auditory Impairment

A farmer, "deaf in one ear . . . [and] deaf in the other for most of the year," lives in a remote rural area with his wife, hens, mule, and watchdog. Without an ear trumpet, he is unable to understand anything. He does not hear his mule, a squeaky wagon, the dog growling, or other nearby loud sounds. Although he finds his quiet world a blissful place, a thief who intended to rob the farmer is deafened by the noise and leaves in alarm.

Analysis. Told in verse form, the humor of this brief tale is dependent on the assumption that deafness makes people oblivious to the world around them—a premise that is neither funny nor accurate. The renowned illustrator whose lively sketches fill this book deserves a better showcase for his considerable talents.

Garcia, Jose Luis, and Miguel Angel Pacheco. *The Boy with Two Eyes*. Originally published by Ediciones Altea as *El Niño Que Tenia Dos Ojos*, Madrid, 1978. Illus. by Ulises Wensell. New York: Methuen, 1978. unp. Reading Level: YC
Disability: Visual Impairment

A two-eyed child is born on a planet of one-eyed people. His parents love him, but he has problems associated with his "anomaly": unlike other children, he is unable to see in the dark and he has trouble reading. He must wear special lenses if he wishes to see objects at a distance. Although no one else can see colors, he has this ability and, because of it, is able to regale the people he meets with wondrous and intriguing stories. Ultimately, he meets and marries a girl who "didn't mind that he had two eyes," and when they have a son, their only child has only one eye. "And that was all right, too!"

Analysis: This title, part of the Rights of Children Series, specifically states its intention is to address Principle 5 of the United Nations Declaration of the Rights of the Child on the rights of handicapped children to special education and care. The result, however, is a compendium of non sequiturs, irrelevant associations, and contradictions. No reason is offered as to why a two-eyed child should have difficulty in reading, and the attribution of such a deficiency seems capricious. Yet the child is depicted as being able to see colors, suggesting that disabled persons have unique or compensatory talents denied to the rest of the population, a myth without foundation. The birth of an offspring with only one eye like all babies implies the "impairment" is not congenital and supports the notion that conformity, in this case the disappearance of a deviant trait, means a return to "normalcy."

Garden, Nancy. *Fours Crossing.* New York: Farrar, Straus, Giroux, 1981. 198 pp. Reading Level: MC
Disability: Emotional Dysfunction

After her mother's death, Melissa moves to her grandmother's home in the New England village of Fours Crossing. Arriving in the midst of a fierce snowstorm, she is met by young Jed Ellison, who delivers her in a sleigh to Mrs. Dunn. Ulfin, a stray dog, appears soon after her arrival, and when Jed and Melissa enter the forest searching for firewood, the animal forces them to follow it to the house of a hermit, whom they see has possession of the silver plate stolen from her grandmother. While the hermit is momentarily distracted during the annual tree-cutting ceremony, the children hurriedly search his home, hoping to discover where the missing property has been hidden. They are unsuccessful, but as they leave Melissa grabs some loose pages from a mysterious book. She deduces that the notations on the pages match markings on the three other plates from the set her grandmother still retains. When the code is broken, the children learn the platter representing spring is the missing one and suspect that the hermit's curse consigning them all to eternal winter derives its potency from this object. When the dog summons the youngsters from school, they excitedly follow it to the hermit's empty house. This time their search is successful, but the man returns, trapping them and injuring the animal. Obsessed with his grievances against the town, the recluse conceals the children in a cave and forces Jed to participate in arcane pagan rites that keep spring in abeyance. Ulfin recovers sufficiently to struggle back to town, and when Melissa's father returns from his prolonged business trip and Jed's father sobers up enough to help, the two desperate parents follow the dog's lead and rescue their children. With the plate restored to its rightful setting, belated signs of spring appear at last in the beleaguered village. As a result of this frightening experience, the two self-absorbed and neglectful fathers appear ready to assume their parental responsibilities.

Analysis. The mixture of realism and occult is successful in this juvenile adventure novel, and the inclusion of a cipher, a reincarnated dog, appealing children, and mysterious events make this an engrossing tale. The hermit, however, is a "stage lunatic" whose bizarre and dangerous actions nonetheless add tension and excitement to the plot. The man's delusions derive from his identification with an ancestor he considered ill treated by the community. His desire for vengeance is bound up with religious rites that give legitimacy in his mind to his strange behavior. Melissa concludes: "It's as if it maybe isn't all his fault—how he is, I mean. It's as if he let himself get all—twisted inside because — because he couldn't accept the truth . . . that things change."

Garfield, Leon. *Footsteps.* New York: Delacorte, 1980. 196 pp.
Reading Level: MC/YA
Disability: Orthopedic Impairment

Every night young William Jones hears footsteps and fearful groans from the room of his dying father. Unable to keep away any longer, the lad enters the forbidden chamber, is given the man's watch, and is told a deathbed secret: his father cheated his former partner, Alfred Diamond. Without further explanation, the father mentions the names "K'Nee" and "Foxes Court," then dies. The day of the funeral, William's arrogant and conniving uncle accuses him of stealing the dead man's timepiece. When the boy says it was given to him and rashly repeats his father's last words, he is accused of being a liar as well as a thief. There seems nothing for the discredited child to do but go to London, find Mr. Diamond, clear his own name, and put his father's conscience to rest. He sneaks away at dawn, boards a coach, and after much confusion, finds himself in Foxes Court, where he is at last directed to the disreputable offices of one Mr. K'Nee, solicitor.

There the adventurer is informed that although Alfred Diamond is dead, the deceived colleague is survived by a son. Mr. Seed, so named "because [he] might have grown if [he'd] fallen on better soil," is a canny dwarf who runs the elevator in the solicitor's building. He takes charge of the innocent and bewildered boy, bundling him to his own home (for a fee), then, for another, delivers him to a tavern where the clerk has arranged a meeting. Jenkins, in the company of a stranger, arrives late, as he had intended, to discover the boy in a befogged state attributable to his unaccustomed consumption of alcohol. The friend, introduced as Mr. Robinson, is, in truth, John Diamond, the ne'er-do-well son of the ex-partner. The conspirators are convinced that William can lead them to a fortune, and in the pursuit of this goal, the hapless youth is led on a wild goose chase during which he is almost killed by band of hooligans. Saved by Shot-in-the-Head, one of the ruffians, the innocent lad is temporarily secreted in a garret hideaway. Intent on completing his mission, William returns to the street, where he discovers the true identity of Mr. Robinson and also learns, to his amazement, that Alfred Diamond is not dead. In the meantime, the scheming son has determined the location of the boy's home and has hastened there to take possession of the ten thousand pounds he is convinced is hidden on the premises. Alfred Diamond, K'Nee, Mr. Seed, and William hastily decamp, desperate to reach the Jones home first, but arriving too late, they find the house in flames. After a brief but dramatic reunion with his family, William charges into the conflagration to rescue John Diamond. The prodigal son, unchastened but presumably ready to reform, is reconciled with his father; William is joyfully reunited with his mother and sisters; Uncle Turner, "in a state of purple indignation," is sent packing; and Shot-in-the-Head, arriving late and apparently intent on making what is left of their home as his permanent residence, is unenthusiastically accepted into the fold.

Analysis. A typical Garfield extravaganza, *Footsteps* is filled with wild coincidences, plot twists and turns, colorful Dickensian characters, and some of the best metaphors currently at large in juvenile literature. Mr. Seed is the pivotal character in this adventure. His literary function is to rescue the young hero when he is confused or uncertain and start him in a new direction that will advance the convoluted plot. He is self-satisfied ("four times William's age and forty times as clever" by his own reckoning), blustering, astute, and avaricious. Seed's style of dealing with others' reactions to his short stature is to "get in there first" with some aggressive or diversionary comment. He asserts, "I've got nothing to hide. . . . All me deformity's out in the open and on public show. So why should I hide the best?" William sees through some of the man's bluff, believing his tricks to be childish and his need to bewilder people in order to distract them from too close a focus on his size pointless and ineffectual.

Garfield, Leon. *The Pleasure Garden*. New York: Viking, 1976. 198 pp. Reading Level: MA
Disability: visual impairment, orthopedic impairment, cosmetic impairment

Mrs. Bray is the proprietor of Mulberry Pleasure Garden, a popular trysting place for young and not-so-young couples. She is also the employer of a gang of ragamuffins whose duty it is to spy on the frequenters of the garden, reporting conversation or behavior that may later be used for extortion. Such information is ceremoniously recorded in a special ledger, after which the nefarious Dr. Dormann visits potential victims, offering to sell them a medallion symbolic of the garden and a token of his silence. One dark night, murder interrupts the revelry. The corpse is quickly attended to by Martin Young, a priest-magistrate, who surreptitiously removes from the body a scrap of fabric that he fears belongs to a girl whose advances he scorned, but whom he believes is innocent of this crime. After a frantic search, Martin locates the girl in question, Fanny Bush, only to learn that the fragment of cloth he destroyed in an effort to shield her did not come from the dress she wore that fateful night. In the meantime, Briskett, a poor urchin in Mrs. Bray's employ who witnessed the homicide, has been blackmailing the murderer.

Out walking, Martin unconsciously turns toward the garden, where he encounters a blind beggar whose face "was cobbled with lumps, like the street itself, and he wore a filthy rag around his eyes to advertise his disability." The young man gives the poor stranger a few coins, noticing with surprise that he has a medallion like those Dr. Dormann distributes. Martin explains the symbol embossed on it and, complying with the mendicant's request, directs him to the garden entrance, returning home with "curious forebodings."

Relieved that Fanny is indeed innocent, Martin searches for the real murderer. He seeks out the dead apprentice's former employer, hoping to find the slain youth's jacket, which apparently has been missing since the night of the killing. There he discovers all jackets are accounted for, but a dress made of the very material clutched in the corpse's hand has disappeared.

On the night a masquerade is to be held in the Pleasure Garden, Briskett insists that his victim pay him a considerable sum immediately or face exposure. The murderer panics and tries to choke the young blackmailer, but is interrupted by Dr. Dormann before the deed is finished, and both men hurriedly leave, finding temporary refuge in the killer's home. There the murderer removes his mask, revealing "the ugly man who always sat alone." His face "appeared to have been wrenched out of shape; it was unequal in everything and created a sense of sickness and revulsion in the beholder"—the result of "an injury sustained at birth." He confides to his companion that he stabbed the apprentice because the lad had humiliated him by dressing as a woman and pretending to seduce him. Dormann takes the man's money, assuring him that his confession and the purchase of the medallion are adequate atonement. The extortionist leaves, encountering Martin who had trailed him from the garden. The wicked doctor tells the lovesick young man that Fanny remains in danger of hanging since all evidence exonerating her has been destroyed. The murderer just then rushes over to them and, despite Dormann's efforts to silence him, continues his cathartic recounting of the crime. Martin struggles with Dormann and both tumble into the river. Martin is fished from the waters, having suffered injuries that leave him delirious for days and result in a permanent weakness in one leg, which causes him to limp. Fanny visits him during his convalescence, comforting him by reading verses from "The Song of Songs." Yet again, the blind beggar searches for the entrance to the park, but is deliberately misdirected by a patron who exclaims haughtily, "One has to protect the garden." The pauper promises his dog that someday they shall nonetheless enter the mysterious, haunting, and elusive place.

Analysis. The sights, sounds, and smells of Dickensian England are recreated in this audacious, lusty tale. The characters are scarcely disabled by chance—the blind man is both portent and modified Greek chorus; the disfigured murderer is the prototypical outcast, distressing to all who see him whose one hope for love turns out to be a cruel mockery; the lame hero is marked by his limp for, as his housekeeper explains, one cannot "expect a mon to cast down the de'il and come off scot-free." The convoluted plot, the pell-mell pace, the archetypical characters, and the rich metaphorical language mark this masquerade as a complex and compelling Garfield work.

Garfield, Leon. *Rosy Starling.* Illus. by Faith Jacques. London: Heinemann, 1977. 48 pp. Reading Level: MC/YA
Disability: Visual Impairment; also orthopedic impairment

Rosy is an apprentice bird-cage maker, "pretty as a picture and blind as a bat," who comes to a fair to sell her wares to the crowds assembling for a Maypole dance. She has been warned about the deceptive ways of opportunistic young men, and she has her own audacity and saucy tongue for further protection. After she hears a male voice singing, a man seats himself next to her on the steps, easing his approach with a whispered compliment, but she cools his ardor by turning "to show him her stone-dead eyes." Turtle, the startled wigmaker's apprentice, finds himself in a state of turmoil, "seized by an uncanny sensation that the blind birdcage seller was watching him from some invisible vantage point inside her head." Having been taught by his master to use his considerable charm to obtain hair for his trade, the youth is bewitched by Rosy's lovely tresses and covets them "as a madman covets a sun beam," but is so smitten he cannot pursue his mercenary goal. A passing Jewish peddler, accompanied by his lame assistant, tries to sell Turtle some brass jewelry for Rosy, which he brazenly proclaims is "better than gold, on my life and soul." The infatuated young man rejects the deception, choosing instead a silver chain he can scarcely afford. Rosy is pleased, and the two chat emotionally about the beautiful gift when Turtle sees he is being observed approvingly by his master who assumes his assistant is about to purchase the raw material for a future wig. Abruptly her frantic admirer begs her to dance. At first she uses his hand to guide her, but heady with excitement, she releases it to dance alone. Turtle sees his drunken employer stare at Rosy's hair and begs the greedy man to have pity, leading him away from the vulnerable girl. When Rosy asks an urchin about the whereabouts of her absent partner, his reply prompts her to believe the young man did not care for her but only wanted to buy her tresses cheaply: "I knew it all the time . . . I weren't that blind," she claims. The lad further reports that Turtle was crying when he left, an observation Rosy dismisses contemptuously, shaken to think she was so grievously deceived. She reconsiders when her employer comments on the value of the lovely jewelry. After a futile search for his partner of the day, Turtle returns to the shop to find two braids that could only have come from the woman he sought. His master said she had given him the hair, saying "it wasn't much to give for what she'd got." The desperate apprentice runs off to search for her to reveal his true feelings.

Analysis. This tale vibrates with a sense of seventeenth-century London working-class life. The blunt, often cruel descriptions of the blind heroine reflect linguistic conventions and common perceptions of disability. The title character, however, is presented as a proud, beautiful, and spunky young woman who seems to dare anyone to pity her. For all her prickliness, she is a vulnerable romantic who yearns to be loved yet fears a faithless lover. The brief anti-Semitic incident is both unnecessary and unacceptable. That the peddler's origins are broadly hinted at rather than overtly stated does not reduce the offensiveness of the stereotype.

Garner, Alan. *The Aimer Gate*. Illus. by Michael Foreman. New York: Collins, 1979. 79 pp. Reading Level: MC
Disability: Orthopedic Impairment

The Aimer Gate, the third title in the Stone Book Quartet, focuses on young Robert, a descendant of the family of stonemasons introduced in the first work. Among the lad's responsibilities is providing transportation in a homemade wagon for Faddock Allman, a legless veteran of the Boer Wars. Allman "dresses" rocks from the fields, which are brought to him since he cannot gather them. His work, although of low status, is nonetheless useful.

Robert discovers a place high in the clock steeple where his great grandfather had chiseled both his name and mason's mark with care. The boy is awed to find the man's standards of excellence were not compromised by the inaccessibility of the stone or the unlikelihood that his hallmark would ever be revealed. The youth, despite feeling as though he had communicated directly with his ancestor, tells his father he must break with family tradition and seek employment as a smith. Much to Robert's suprise, the man endorses his son's decision.

Robert's Uncle Charlie, a British soldier now serving in World War I, is home on leave to help with the harvest. The men in the community are fascinated with Charlie's rifle, which he polishes obsessively. Captivated by what he thinks is the romance of military life, his nephew suggests soldiering might be a proper trade for him as well. But his uncle disparages the medals the boy so admires: "Your father calls them bits stuck on the outside of one chap for sticking bits on the inside of another." Allman's tragic injury and Charlie's oblique allusion to the possibility of dying in battle successfully contradict the glamorous image the boy had at first envisioned.

Analysis. Faddock Allman depends on young Robert for his mobility and on the tolerance of others for his social position. The veteran's talk is full of references to fighting, and he still wears the helmet from his army days. Although Allman lives alone, the community willingly provides transportation, and on occasion he is invited to eat and drink with the other men. When the men play at soldiering, he participates in this tomfoolery as well. He is treated with contempt by Robert's father, who, when he finds the man eating outside his house, closes the window to shut out his conversation. Attempting to save face, the exsoldier comments: "I'd best be going . . . now as Master's having his dinner." Charlie intrudes, reminding his brother: "being as how it hadn't used to matter so much when Faddock Allman was shot to beggary by them Boers."

As with other titles in this series, Garner hints at far more than he says. The several names of the various characters, the extensive use of words and expressions indigenous to rural Cheshire, England, but unfamiliar to contemporary American children, combined with the tight, compressed, intellectually demanding style will make this book inaccessible to many young readers.

Garner, Alan. *The Stone Book.* Illus. by Michael Foreman. New York: Collins & World, 1976. 60 pp. Reading Level: MC
Disability: auditory impairment

Mary takes lunch to her father, a stonemason who is working on the tower of a church under construction. Although afraid, she climbs to the very top and then allows her father to place her on the weathercock at the tip of the spire. As she spins around, now completely free of fear, she can see the countryside all about her. She returns home to where her uncle, Old William, works as a weaver. The man "wasn't old, but he was called Old William because he was deaf and hadn't married." Her father, having completed his labor, arrives home and examines the stones Mary cleared from the field. He chooses one, breaks it, polishes it, and muses: "Tell me how these flakes were put together and what they are. . . . And who made them into pebbles on a hill, and where that was a rock and when." The two men argue, upsetting Mary, who hides under the table. "Father thought shouting would make Old William hear, and Old William didn't have Father's words."

Mary is unhappy that she will not be allowed to learn to read and asks her father if she cannot at least have her own book. He sends her to get some candles, matches, and a bobbin of thread and takes her to an old mine. They descend together into the earth, but then he sends her on alone with the candles for light and the thread to help her find her way back, with instructions to follow veins that can be seen on the walls of the cave. If after she arrives at her destination and returns and she still wants a book, her father promises she shall have one. She proceeds alone following her father's directions until

Mary saw Father's mason mark drawn on the wall. It was faint and black, as if drawn with soot. Next to it was an animal, falling. It had nearly worn itself away, but it looked like a bull, a great shaggy bull. . . . And near the bull and the mark, there was a hand, the outline of a hand. . . . She lifted her own and laid it over the hand on the wall. . . . She touched. . . . The hand fitted. Fingers and thumb and palm and a bull and Father's mark in the darkness under the ground. . . . All about her in the small place toes, shallow ones and deep ones, clear and sharp as if made altogether, tramping each other, hundreds pressed in the clay where only a dozen could stand.

Mary returns and tells her father what she has seen and done and asks him why he left his mark there. He tells her he found it there when his father took him—the only time he went, when he was Mary's age. He says the experience is passed from generation to generation in their family, but since the malachite is being mined, Mary may be able only to tell her son when she has one rather than show him; their secret place may no longer be accessible. They return home and, after working a bit, her father "gave Mary a prayer book bound in blue-black calfskin, tooled, stitched, and decorated. It was only by the weight that she could tell it was stone and not leather. . . . And Mary sat by the fire and read the stone book that had in it all the stories of the world and the flowers of the flood."

Analysis. In this deceptively simple tale, Garner has created a flaw-less, exquisite story of a family tied through generations by the stones of their craft to each other and to the timeless earth itself. The language is as archaic and remote as the setting and as sturdy and spare as the characters. Old William's hearing loss is an incidental factor in his makeup. His peevishness is explained by Mary's father: "He's as good as me but can't ever see the end of his work. And I make it worse by building houses for the masters who've taken his living."

Garrigue, Sheila. *Between Friends.* Scarsdale, N.Y.: Bradbury, 1978. 160 pp. Reading Level: MC/YA
Disability: Intellectual Impairment; also speech impairment

Jill Harvey describes her new home in Massachusetts as "Dulls-ville" and bemoans her lack of friends. Soon she has a job walking Squeak, a pet of elderly Mrs. Lacey. On her solitary jaunts, she meets Dede Atkins, who "was dumpy, with eyes that slanted. The back of her head was sort of flat." Jill thought, "She's like one of those re-tards." Dede's dog and Squeak enjoy each other's company, and soon the girls become friendly. But when Dede comes to visit, Mrs. Harvey, who is pregnant, retreats from any contact with her. Jill's father later explains that Jill had had a multiply disabled sister who died soon after her birth. Mrs. Harvey discloses that she is "spooked" by Dede's pres-ence, afraid that her unborn child may also have Down's syndrome, adding with some embarrassment that she knows that this is just su-perstitious nonsense.

Eventually the newcomer makes other acquaintances, including her next-door neighbor, Marla, a self-centered girl being groomed to follow her family's show business tradition. Marla pokes fun at Jill's continuing relationship with Dede, and others are puzzled over what the two girls could possibly have in common. Jill's friendship is put to the test when she is invited to attend a presentation at Dede's special school on the same day that Marla's debut as a ballerina in *The Nutcracker* is to take place. At first, the heroine tells the Atkinses that she will not attend, but later she informs the furious Marla that she must miss her performance since she has a prior commitment. Jill is ill at ease at the prospect of encountering so many impaired youngsters but soon becomes so intrigued at what the children have accomplished that she determines to become a part of the squad of seventh-graders who volunteer at the school.

Dede falls sick with pneumonia, and after her recovery, Mrs. Atkins concludes that they must move to a warmer climate. Following the precipitous but unremarkable arrival of her baby sister, Jill sadly bids goodbye to the Atkinses. When Marla comments: "I never could figure out why you liked her so much. I mean . . . like, she's pretty strange. You have to admit that. And she doesn't know anything about anything." Jill responds loyally, "Dede Atkins may never be a ballerina . . . but she knows more about being a friend than anyone else I know."

Analysis. Garrigue honestly reflects common attitudes toward retardation, including aversion, hostility, and irrational fears, but balances this constructively with feelings of admiration and affection. Considerable information about intellectual impairment is incorporated into the narrative, and a positive, plausible relationship based on shared interests and valued qualities between youngsters of vastly differing intellectual abilities is proposed for the two girls. The departure of the impaired child is an unfortunate, although common, plot device, and here it is not central to the development of the story. Such a tactic obliquely suggests that this friendship is only a brief interlude in the life of the heroine, who will now be able to return to a life with more "conventional" companions.

Gerson, Corinne. *Passing Through.* New York: Dial, 1978. 193 pp.
Reading Level: YA
Disability: Neurological Impairment

Devastated by her brother Paul's suicide, Liz Jordan retreats from all contact with friends and shuns her family, bitter over their seeming insensitivity. Although aggressively adopting the new role of loner, the high school girl nonetheless volunteers for the French tutoring program. At first she is repelled when she learns the student assigned to her is Sam Benedict, a fellow sophomore with cerebral palsy, but she is gradually won over by his warm and generous personality: "He was really pleasant and quite charming, but every once in a while she would notice how helpless he looked, how the lower part of this body lay like a sack in his wheelchair." Sam's matter-of-fact attitude toward his impairment gradually thaws her feelings of repugnance, and a friendship begins to develop. The Jordans are furious when they learn of their daughter's involvement with Sam; they are contemptuous of his Polish, lower-class origins and speak disdainfully of the "spastic kid." These disparaging remarks intensify the estrangement between Liz and her parents, who see their daughter as a selfish, uncaring child. She, in turn, considers her family coarse, pretentious, and materialistic, especially when compared with the warm, loving, and generous Benedicts. The teenage girl becomes aware of the importance of Sam in her life when he misses several tutoring sessions and it occurs to her he might be sick. She "practically flew to his house," where she finds he is recovering from a cold. He appears "in the doorway . . . looking pasty and very thin. . . . For Liz it was like seeing the first fragile crocus braving the gusts of early spring."

When Sam comes to Liz's house, she reads him her brother's last letter, in which Paul reveals he cannot handle the problems that his homosexuality will cause, convinced that *"there's just no way Mother and Dad are going to be able to accept me for who I am."* Some time later, the Jordans return home to discover Liz and Sam have fallen asleep in each other's arms. Finding conditions at home now impossible after her mother's intemperate attack, Liz moves out, staying temporarily with friends. She hopes both her parents and her hosts will allow her to remain permanently. Her parents pay a surprise visit, announce they have read Paul's letter, which Liz forgot to hide, and, humbled by remorse and unaccustomed self-doubts, are ready to begin the process of reconciliation with their daughter. They all return home ready to work out their differences. Soon the teenage girl reestablishes contact with former companions, and she and Sam agree that, although they will remain friends, it is necessary to reduce their mutual dependence and "start coming out of [their] nice little cocoons into the real world."

Analysis. This lightweight, overwritten junior novel caters to adolescents who tend to see issues, situations, and people in extreme terms. The author hints that relationships will be the major focus of this work but shies away from serious treatment of this topic. Paul's alleged reason for his suicide offers sensationalism rather than a believable rationale and serves primarily as a device to discredit his parents. Although all the elements exist for a romance to develop between Liz and Sam, this never happens, and the sole possibility of this work achieving any distinction is carefully avoided. The inference that the teenagers' relationship is artificial, that is, not "part of the real world," subtly suggests that closeness between an attractive girl and a disabled boy is not quite "normal."

Gezi, Kal, and Ann Bradford. *The Mystery of the Blind Writer*. Illus. by Mina Gow McLean. Elgin, Ill.: Child's World, 1980. 32 pp. Reading Level: YC
Disability: Visual Impairment

Mr. Rubin, a writer who lives near the school, is coming to visit the primary grades to tell the children about his occupation. The students question their principal about how the man will get there, but Mr. Johnson assures them that their guest, accompanied by his guide dog, will undoubtedly arrive. After the author completes his talk, one child asks: "How do you recognize people?" In response, he shakes hands with each child once and then identifies them on contact, explaining he is able to distinguish each "by the shapes of your rings and the feel of your hands." He then has Bingo demonstrate how a guide dog works. Before he leaves, the visitor asks the children to close their eyes for a few moments. "Are each of you the same person now as when your eyes were shut?" he asks. When all answer affirmatively, he declares, "I'm the same person now as when I could see. . . . We blind people do not want you to pity us. Just treat us as you treat other people." Soon after he leaves, the children are startled to see the German shepherd at the classroom window alone but are relieved to learn his master is safe at the police station. On their way home, the author's tape recorder was stolen, and Bingo, when released, ran after the crook but was unable to catch him. The youngsters accompany Mr. Rubin to the park where the theft took place and begin questioning people. They are directed to Cedar Street, where the dog suddenly leaps on a man just coming out of an apartment building, knocking the brown bag that contains the missing property from his hands. While the police put handcuffs on the disgruntled robber, Mr. Rubin invites the children to his house to celebrate.

Analysis. This silly and contrived story includes a positive portrait of a blind professional. The classroom visit allows the presentation of some useful information on mobility. The title character suggests he uses his tactile rather than his auditory sense as the primary means of identifying new acquaintances—a highly unusual choice for someone with intact hearing. Nondescript illustrations are in keeping with this modest and undistinguished effort.

Gillham, Bill. *My Brother Barry*. Illus. by Laszlo Acs. London: Andre Deutsch, 1981. 96 pp. Reading Level: MC
Disability: Intellectual Impairment

Barry Oakley "was mentally handicapped, so everything came slowly with him: not being able to talk was just the most obvious thing." The 11-year-old boy's younger brother James has much of the responsibility for his supervision. One day the 9-year-old boy notices young strangers throwing stones at the family's sheep. He runs toward the boys but is hit by a stone thrown by one of the ruffians and knocked unconscious. The kindness of a gypsy man and his son Tommy forces James to reevaluate the prejudiced statements he has heard about these itinerants, and soon a friendship develops between the boys. When some fires are deliberately started, causing considerable damage to farm property, gypsies are blamed. The real culprits are apprehended and are discovered to be the same boys who maliciously injured the Oakley sheep.

On the first day of the new school term, Barry gets off the special bus at the wrong stop: the route has been changed, the driver and helper are new, and so no one is aware of the problem until the youngster fails to arrive at his destination. All are alarmed since Barry's health is very fragile and he could be in considerable danger if not found quickly. The police are called, but despite a massive community search, no trace can be found of the missing lad. Tommy tells his father he has seen Barry on the moor, and the man reports this crucial information to Mr. Oakley. The boy is subsequently found and returned to his home. When asked what happened: " 'Got lost,' said Barry matter-of-factly. 'C'dn't find you,' he added." His family realizes that the complete story of Barry's adventure will inevitably remain unknown to them.

Analysis. In the context of a small, cohesive rural community, a youth like Barry, whose impairment is quite apparent, can be accommodated readily. Most adults are understanding, compassionate, and concerned about him, in contrast with their attitude toward the gypsies camped nearby. In this instance, the outsiders become the object of community suspicion rather than the boy, who although different is perceived as one of their own. The briefly described but on-target accounts of language, posture, and behavior reflect considerable knowledge about severely intellectually impaired youngsters. The incident involving the youngster getting off the bus at the fourth stop even though the route had been changed shows the persistence of learned behavior that such children would be apt to demonstrate in similar circumstances. However, the heavy-handed plea for tolerance articulated in an implausible speech by the headmaster, the unidimensional characters, the awkward phrases, such as "a gently-spoken man" or "whilst," and the illogical narrative (after seeing Tommy only once before, James remarks that the gypsy youth is "unlike his usual self") seriously diminish the book's utility.

Gilson, Jamie. *Do Bananas Chew Gum?* New York: Lothrop, Lee & Shepard, 1980. 158 pp. Reading Level: MC
Disability: Learning Disability

Sam reflects on his dismal reading skills as he heads for the orthodontist: "I couldn't read . . . any . . . long words without a whole lot of wheels burning rubber in my head." He recalls his family's many moves, his poor showing in first and second grades, his teacher labeling him "lazy," his parents' unsuccessful attempts at tutoring, and finally, his identification as a learning disabled student. The youngster, convinced that he is retarded, is unsettled by his parents' resistance to further testing and their arguments over who should do his homework. Sam sees himself as the least competent learner in school and decides Alicia, a classmate, must be the smartest. One day he offers her unsolicited advice on how to increase her popularity: he suggests the road to acceptance requires that she not always show off her intellect. In turn, the self-satisfied girl asks him about his inability to read. She sees the boy as a desirable friend but is curious about his lack of competence in this area.

The sixth-grader gets a job sitting with two younger children after school, hoping that the calamities that always seem to beset him will not sour this opportunity also. Mrs. Glass, his new employer, soon surmises that something is amiss when Sam doesn't follow the instructions on the note she left and when she sees his almost illegible printing. After a tornado rips through their community, Sam and his charges explore the area around the fallen tree in the boy's yard. They discover some artifacts in the roots and, in an excess of imagination, decide they must have belonged to Viking explorers who long ago sailed to Illinois. A young archeologist from a nearby university accepts Mrs. Glass's invitation to visit the site. She discounts the youngsters' claim but unearths a tool that is over one hundred years old as well as some other pieces of "garbage," which she identifies as objects of local Indian origin of historical value. Sam is excited about archeology as a profession and asks the woman if it is necessary to be smart to do her work. When she shows him one of her reference books, the size of it is so intimidating that tears of frustration cloud his eyes. Mrs. Glass forces him to discuss his problem with her, after which she reveals that her sister has a different kind of learning disability that caused the girl endless academic problems, adding, "Excuses were her lifestyle." She convinces the reluctant youth to take the assessment test he has been avoiding. The special teacher diagnoses his problem, assures him that he actually is intelligent, and prescribes a course of action that capitalizes on his superior memory and listening skills. She tells him about famous people who endured similar difficulties and, to his delight, shows him a technique for decoding the word *archeology*. The youngster is enormously pleased when Mrs. Glass takes him to the local historical society to see a display of the treasures he unearthed. An identifying card states: "Found in the roots of a sugar maple tree by archeologist, Sam Mott, age twelve."

Analysis. Sam is an original and very attractive character whose behavior is typical of that displayed by bright children with learning disabilities. He is self-deprecating, willing to believe his academic failures are the result of low intellectual ability. He has developed a repertoire of tricks, including feigning misunderstanding, pretending he did not hear instructions, relying on his memory to cover his inability to decode, clowning, and other diversionary tactics to draw attention away from his inadequate school performance. Despite these measures, his poor reading skills, including letter reversals, labored writing, and incorrect and unsubmitted papers and tests result in constant classroom embarrassment. The boy's enthusiasms outstrip his ability to carry through projects as his disorganized behavior propels him into trouble time after time. The author hints that Sam's disorder may be hereditary as his father claims to have had persistent school problems and the man's restlessness is echoed in his son's impulsive behavior. The characterization of Sam is excellent, the dialogue shows an ear attuned to the idiosyncratic argot of 12 year olds, and despite the seriousness of the topic, the tone of this engaging work is consistently upbeat.

Girion, Barbara. *A Handful of Stars*. New York: Scribner's, 1981. 179 pp. Reading Level: YA
Disability: Neurological Impairment

Julie Meyers is a sophomore in high school when she has her first seizure. She "just walked around in a circle talking about algebra equations and started banging on the door." The teenager is distressed and confused since she has absolutely no recollection of the behavior her friends report to her. They attribute it to her getting high from the fumes of the wine that spilled out of a broken bottle and casually dismiss the incident as unimportant. Subsequent incidents are not so easily explained, and Julie's classmates begin to regard her as peculiar. Her family, however, worries that she may have a serious medical disorder, and when a visit to her pediatrician is inconclusive, an appointment is made with a neurologist. After an EEG and a CAT scan, the specialist diagnoses epilepsy and prescribes a regimen of anticonvulsant pills for the distraught girl. As he had predicted, establishing the proper dosage is a matter of trial and error, and her episodes continue. These happenings are a source of intolerable embarrassment and seem, to the despairing adolescent, destined to occur at the most inopportune moments. Her boyfriend severs their relationship, other students make fun of her, most avoid her, and she alienates others because of her increasingly defensive attitude. When she confides her fears and frustrations to her drama coach, this mentor whom she has idolized suggests she withdraw from the class play instead of offering her the reassurance Julie desperately seeks. The solitary girl reaches out from her cocoon of self-pity to accept a job at a recreation center working with preteen youngsters. Disgusted at their lethargy, she prods them into an active project that brings all participants, including herself, considerable satisfaction.

During a visit with her sister, who is a student at Duke University, Julie meets David, an attractive freshman with whom she develops a friendship. Hoping to avoid the humiliation of being discovered, she tells him about her disorder. He not only fails to react negatively, he doesn't find the subject terribly interesting. Abetted by brief visits and long letters, a romance blossoms. In her senior year, Julie's application is accepted by Duke, and her family is relieved to know that her entrance into college life will be smoothed by David and her sibling. The now more confident girl decides to enter school elsewhere, determined to succeed through her own efforts.

Analysis. Particularly useful is the author's development of epilepsy as a familial, social, and personal problem as well as a medical one. The changes over time in the family of dismissal of the symptoms, of bewilderment, of growing discomfort, of the search for physical causes, of puzzlement, then of overprotection of Julie, all follow a familiar and even predictable path. The course of Julie's coming to terms with this disorder is bumpy and includes outrage and self-destructive behavior, as well as a childlike hope for a magical solution. At a time when adolescents seek avenues for their energies, when conformity is a social necessity, when control and mastery over their world is of primary importance, Julie is stonewalled in her growth. That psychological support to the patient and family is as much a necessity as medical treatment is underscored in this junior novel. Girion denounces the persisting misunderstandings and insensitivities that have followed those coping with epilepsy to this day. Much less impressive is the literary aspect, due in large measure to the cast of characters, who never seem to come to life, and the intent to persuade that lies just below the words.

Glasser, Dianne. *The Diary of Trilby Frost*. New York: Holiday House, 1976. 189 pp. Reading Level: YA
Disability: Cosmetic Impairment; also special health problems

Trilby's best friend is Saul Edwards, a half Native American youth whose mother died and whose father has not been allowed to return to the small turn-of-the-century Tennessee community in which his son lives. Although indifferent to Saul's birthmark, Trilby is aware of her neighbors' hostile interpretation of its significance:

> I guess I will describe my best friend in this temporary world, Saul Edwards. He has longish hair which is coal black, really white teeth, and he is skinnier even than me. Oh, and I almost forgot. He has this purplish birthmark down the whole right side of his face. I hardly notice it, we been bosom friends for so long. But just today when we passed two gossipy old women cutting through the fields, I heard one of them say in her crow-whispery voice, "It's that half-breed boy who's been marked by the devil! Sins of the father visited on the child."

When Trilby's father, desperate to support his impoverished family, tries to earn more for his dependents, he dies, his heart weakened by the stress of overwork. Their boarder, taken in to help with expenses, becomes engaged to Trilby's sister, but upon discovering Katherine is pregnant, he dishonorably abandons her. Tragedy dogs the Frost family and when Caleb, Trilby's brother, dies after a fall from a horse, they unwarrantedly blame Saul for permitting the accident to happen. Crushed by their rejection, the unhappy youth runs away from home. Despite the brutality he experienced there, Saul is forcibly returned and, to Trilby's great relief, ably defends his innocence in her brother's death. In addition, he announces his intention to marry Trilby one day.

Because of his great skill with horses, Saul becomes the protégé of a wealthy man who plans to train the youngster to take over his business and eventually become his son-in-law. The young man, however, remains faithful to Trilby. One evening, he is injured while taking his girl friend home from a party. Tetanus spreads through his body and the severity of the infection combined with its neglect result in Saul's untimely death. Once bright and optimistic, Trilby is crushed by these multiple bereavements.

Analysis. This rapidly moving novel poignantly demonstrates the pain suffered by the victims of a bigoted, self-righteous community. Saul, the vulnerable scapegoat of the ignorant and superstitious townspeople, seems relentlessly pursued by ill will and misfortune. The unrelieved series of tragedies that comprise the plot, especially those linking socially condemned behavior and retributive personal tragedy, such as the death of Katherine's illegitimate baby, the death of Caleb after he apparently disobeys orders and goes horseback riding alone, the death of Trilby's mother while giving birth to an illegitimate infant, leave the reader exhausted and depressed.

Goldreich, Gloria. *Lori.* New York: Holt, Rinehart & Winston, 1979. 181 pp. Reading Level: YA
Disability: Orthopedic Impairment

When Lori is caught smoking marijuana, the otherwise laissez-faire administrator of the private high school she attends feels compelled to suspend her. As is his custom, her grandfather takes charge, informing the defiant teenager that he has already made arrangements for her to spend the remainder of the school year with the Eron family in northern Israel. The old man explains that he and Mrs. Eron's father were childhood friends. With the rise to power of the Nazis in Germany, both were forced to flee their homeland. His friend escaped to Palestine to take up farming; Lori's grandfather went to America, where he became a successful businessman.

At the farm community, Lori makes friends instantly with Rina Eron, a girl her own age, but is unable to exchange a civil word with the Israeli girl's brother, Udi, an embittered veteran of the Yom Kippur War. The Erons are very concerned about their son's spinal injury but are even more worried about his debilitating depression. Although they are careful not to pressure him, they look for signs that Udi will end his purposeless behavior and complete his doctoral studies. Lori's days are filled with her work in the moshav greenhouse, visits to a kibbutz where she learns of Rina's maturing love for an Ethiopian Jew, her involvement with Danni, Rina's other brother, an unexpected friendship with an Arab girl trying to break with her family's traditionalism, and the care of a baby camel with a broken leg. The American girl's experiences with physical labor, unaccustomed responsibilities, friendships that are complicated by loyalties and tensions inherited from preceding generations, and the ever-present possibility of terrorist attacks force the spoiled, self-centered adolescent to gain a better perspective on herself, her studies, and her relationship with her loving but immature parents.

Prodded by the attentions of a desirable woman, Udi returns to the university and completes his dissertation. He explains to Lori:

Pnina and I were never lovers although when we first met that was what I wanted. And for a time she made me think that it was possible. Or rather I let myself think that it could be possible. It was what started me on the way back—back to myself, to a life that would count for something.

Aware that under similar circumstances the woman's brother had committed suicide, Lori concludes that "Pnina had teased . . . Udi back into feeling. She had provoked him into going to Jerusalem. She had teased him into coming alive again, using the only weapon she had." Now that the former soldier has excised his feelings of self-pity, he and the American are able to become good friends. Her relationship with Danni is less platonic, and they make plans to meet again after she completes school and he is discharged from the Israeli army.

Analysis. The life of Israeli immigrants, the strained relationships between Arab and Jew, the difficult adjustments that victims of the Holocaust must make, the conflicts between pioneers and newcomers, and the commotion that surrounds the ubiquitous tourists combine to provide a colorful setting for what is only a shallow melodrama. All characters are stereotypes, and the rationale for Pnina's behavior is blatantly sexist. Lori's growth in insight, Udi's turnabout, and the happy resolution of all romantic conflicts are predictable. The veteran's rehabilitation is swift and notable as he quickly moves from a wheelchair, to crutches, and then to canes. Comments on his adapted car, his use of specially designated parking spaces, and his increased mobility provide a record of his progress. The book ostensibly features a romance between a sabra and an American girl; the far more interesting love affair is the one between the author and the country she so affectionately describes.

Goldreich, Gloria. *Season of Discovery.* Nashville, Tenn.: Thomas Nelson, 1976. 156 pp. Reading Level: MC/YA
Disability: Intellectual Impairment, Special Health Problems; also orthopedic impairment

Lisa Robinow's eighth-grade year is going to be a busy and exciting one. Dr. Rothenberg, a scholar who survived the Holocaust, will be the teacher who assists in the preparation of her bat mitzvah. It is clear he expects her class to become knowledgeable about their heritage and concerned about ethical issues. As her youth group service assignment, the 12 year old has accepted responsibility for making regular visits to the terminally ill wife of her religion teacher. To Lisa's surprise, she begins to look forward to her meetings with the wise, kind, and gentle woman, with whom she shares not only a love of literature but other interests as well. In addition, the preteen works on the staff of the school newspaper and is infatuated with its editor, Carl Richardson. The boy's mother has recently remarried, and Carl's new father is a hate-filled, brutal man who has defiantly painted a swastika, a symbol of his beliefs, on their house.

Lisa's twin, Donny, lives in a residential center for moderately retarded persons. The boy's eyes "were wide and vacant . . . and his mouth . . . sometimes drooped as though the boy could not make the effort to manage his own expression. . . . He was what the doctors called 'brain damaged.' " His sister's next visit to him marks an important milestone for it "was the first time Donny had recognized her at once and called her by name." Mrs. Robinow devotes much of her time reading medical texts in a vain effort to discover some remedy for her son's disability. The woman finds any discussion of Donny's condition unbearably painful and the sight of other sets of twins an intolerable reminder of her boy's problems.

Mrs. Rothenberg suddenly becomes very ill and must be hospitalized. During Lisa's last visit before her death, the patient expresses her gratitude to her young friend. Their rabbi's words of consolation to the congregation cause the bereaved girl to rethink her attitude toward her brother. "It was better to have her . . . unfortunate twin, even with the sadness of his handicap, of his poor damaged brain, than for Donny to have died at birth." That night, she sneaks over to Carl's house, where she obliterates the hated Nazi symbol. She is caught, but Carl intercedes, holding off his irate stepfather until the frightened girl can escape.

Mrs. Robinow's plans for her daughter's bat mitzvah seem extravagant to her family, but the woman feels she must compensate somehow for her son's inability to participate in the traditional ritual. Unknown to her parents, Lisa, in cooperation with her brother's therapist, has arranged for Donny to learn the prayer of thanksgiving, which he recites in Hebrew with his sister before the ceremony.

Analysis: Donny, the developmentally disabled youth, is perceived in maudlin and pitying terms. Descriptions of his achievement level are wildly inconsistent: after he is over 12, he is finally able to recognize his sister on sight and can call her by name; one-half year later, he is able to recite a complicated sentence in a foreign language, the meaning of which is beyond his comprehension. The depiction of his mother is equally extreme: she had made so minimal an adjustment that any allusion to her son sparks a crying session. Events are manipulated for didactic purposes, and characters are without dimension in this novel in which the messages drown the story line.

Gordon, John. *The Ghost on the Hill*. New York: Viking, 1976. 171 pp. Reading Level: MA.
Disability: intellectual impairment, orthopedic impairment

Grace Jervis returns with her son Ralph to their newly purchased home in the village where she had lived before she married. She meets Betty Judd, once her closest childhood friend, and Mrs. Goodchild, an old woman whom she presumed had died long ago. The aged villager promises to tell her son Tom that "Gracie Jervis have come back." Actually, Tom, "a cripple" and "never right in the head," had hanged himself one evening after Grace promised to meet him but failed to appear. After his suicide, Mrs. Goodchild visited the graveyard regularly to "converse" with her son. The elderly woman's presence is disconcerting to Grace, who believed that this unhappy episode in her life was over and forgotten.

Over the years, Betty Judd had become dowdy and careless about her appearance and is now, moreover, in poor health. To her son's girl friend, Jenny, she reveals her dream in which "Tom Goodchild had come back and me and Gracie Jervis was going to meet him." That night she dies in her sleep, presumably the victim of Tom's long-delayed revenge for her cruelty to him in their youth. Ralph pursues a friendship with young Joe Judd, who becomes a regular visitor to the Jervis house, where he is seduced by Grace. Now infatuated with his friend's mother, Joe flees to the cemetery after he is rejected by the exploitive, fickle woman. Jenny follows her boyfriend, but when she believes she sees Tom reenacting his suicide, she screams and collapses in Joe's arms. In the morning, Jenny takes flowers to Tom's grave as Ralph and his mother drive out of town.

Analysis. This particularly murky and illogical gothic novel offers confusion and vagueness instead of tension and suspense. Mrs. Goodchild seems more befuddled than ominous, and Gracie is equally unconvincing as a temptress—first as the unintended catalyst in the disabled youth's suicide and then as the seducer of the son of her former friend. The inclusion of a disabled character is apparently intended to heighten the reader's revulsion over the rejected suitor/suicide victim while introducing a macabre element into this unfocused and meandering work.

Graber, Richard. *Pay Your Respects*. New York: Harper & Row, 1979. 234 pp. Reading Level: MA
Disability: Emotional Dysfunction, orthopedic impairment

Ray Decker's last year as a senior in a small Minnesota high school just prior to World War II is coming to a close. The sudden death of his beloved grandmother has unsettled him since she was the only stable, supportive, and caring adult in his life. The ease he felt in her home contrasts sharply to the battlefield his own house has become. His mother's nagging about his father's former alcoholism and her incessant, near-hysterical accusations of infidelity keep family life unpleasant. Ray had looked to a new, young teacher for attention, but she was dismissed, partially in reaction to his obviously ardent feelings toward her.

Ray's relationship with his best friend, Floyd Benson, is turbulent. The youth's father had committed suicide by hanging himself in the basement of his home, an incident that continues to torment his son. Although Floyd's actions are generally within acceptable bounds, the tension that builds in the volatile adolescent is increasingly manifested in such bizarre, hostile, and dangerous acts as a midair leap from a ferris wheel. Miraculously, he misses falling into the machinery, although he tears some ligaments in his leg and permanently damages his foot. In addition to his limp, Floyd has considerable pain and is more irritable and confrontational than ever. His roughhousing with his buddy now borders on the sadistic. He seeks further medical attention, but the surgery fails to improve his mobility and increases his anger. When Mrs. Benson returns home after having visited her son in the hospital, she finds Ray completing stoking the furnace, as she had requested. They speak briefly, then the lonely widow seduces her son's pal.

Sick and feverish, Ray leaves work early and discovers Mrs. Benson waiting for him with the message that Floyd is missing. Despite his own illness, Ray scours the town, finally locating his drunk and belligerent buddy and hauls him home. When the disturbed youth begins to insinuate that Ray was actually responsible for his fall, his sister interprets this as a sign that Ray is seriously out of touch with reality. Overwhelmed with his inability to cope with his battling family, his increasingly disordered friend, or the decisions to be made after graduation, Ray impulsively leaves town to seek work and some respite in the big city.

Analysis. Erratic plot development and inadequate insights into motivation sabotage this original novel. Despite some very effective passages, this small-town, slice-of-life story turns to unsatisfying melodrama. The depiction of Floyd is particularly disappointing since he is the catalyst for most of the action. Although his father's suicide is hinted at as the pivotal event in his life, his interpretation of the incident and the reasons for his own suicidal behavior are not clarified.

Green, Phyllis. *Walkie-Talkie*. Reading, Mass.: Addison-Wesley, 1978. 96 pp. Reading Level: MC
Disability: Emotional Dysfunction, Neurological Impairment

Richie's apparently complete lack of impulse control has interfered with his schoolwork, has precipitated his banishment from most neighborhood homes, and has been financially and emotionally expensive for his parents. His father periodically makes restitution to those whose property his son has destroyed, and his mother is haunted by the memory of Richie deliberately lying down on a railroad track in front of an onrushing train. Pregnant once again, she is also afraid to bring another child like her son into the world. To her, the boy's erratic behavior seems purposeless and frequently sadistic.

With the walkie-talkie he received for his fourteenth birthday, Richie eavesdrops on a conversation between a young woman and a boy with unintelligible speech. Impulsively he interrupts, insulting the unknown youngster who is, oddly enough, vastly amused. One day, Patty, the young woman studying to be a speech therapist whose voice he heard, invites him into the house to meet Norman, a 13-year-old boy who has always been housebound because of the seriousness of his cerebral palsy. Richie is appalled at the physical manifestation of the boy's condition but soon overcomes his initial dismay. Norman is overjoyed at having a friend at last and being joshed and insulted like other boys his age. Patty, responsible for Norman during his parents' absence, warmly welcomes Richie to the house, hoping a friendship will develop between the two boys. Norman has a constructive effect on his young neighbor's behavior: the boy seems to be acting in more caring ways than he ever did before. His techniques remain abusive as he browbeats his baseball teammates into letting Norman coach third base, although his speech cannot be understood by the other boys. The team is kept in line by Richie's threats and strange behavior but also by his glib tongue and freewheeling imagination:

> "Why did you bring that cripple?"
>
> "Oh, did you fall for that?" I said. "See he's really a normal-looking kid like you and me. He just puts on the act to fool his parents."
>
> "Why would he do a dumb thing like that?" Friedkin said.
>
> "It's not so dumb. He's already got a giant stereo, his own color TV, maid service, a trip to Europe, a private tutor. He's never been to school. That Norman! He's not so dumb, he's a good actor."
>
> Friedkin shook his head and stared at Norman. "I don't see how he could keep it up all the time though," he said.
>
> "Norman's persistent," I said. "It's his best quality."

Richie's verbal abuse and minor cruelties please Norman, drawing forth rare praise. Patty tries to explain:

Listen, Richie, you will probably never understand what you're doing for Norman. He was all closed up in a shell, inside himself. But you make him laugh, and you probably don't know this, but sometimes you make him cry. Listen, I'm not saying this to make you feel bad. Norman has to cry. He has to feel. You really make him come alive.

Richie hopes that this may be the summer during which he will discard his outlandish and self-destructive behavior, but in an emergency, when left alone to care for Norman, their relationship is sundered by Richie's cruel impulsivity. Precipitated into an irrational state by his fear of thunder, the frenetic youth threatens to leave Norman alone in the house, turns off all the lights, and begins a campaign of psychological harassment. But later, the chastened Richie rescues his frightened friend, who, in desperation, had tried to escape through the window of his second-story bedroom. Both Patty and Norman are completely repelled by Richie's reckless insensitivity and reject the boy completely. Richie sees Norman at the junior high school, but their association is over, and Richie once again spends almost all of his spare time alone.

Analysis. Green's considerable skill and insight are demonstrated in her portrayal of Richie as a boy completely in the grip of a compulsivity he cannot understand or control. He is shown as being neither indifferent to the results of his behavior nor unaware of their potential danger to himself and others. Despite the boy's reprehensible actions, the author manages to picture him sympathetically:

The whole evening made me reel. I knew if I didn't watch it I could be one of those creeps you read about in the papers who go around hurting people just for the kicks they get out of it. I held my stomach. It was churning. "There's nothing wrong with me," I told myself. "I just think differently from other people. I gotta get control before I do something stupid."

Norman's neurological involvement is seen as extremely severe, affecting both speech and mobility and drastically restricting his opportunities for socialization. However, the boy's language is inconsistently transcribed, causing some confusion. Presumably his therapy allowed him finally to be comfortably mainstreamed. Of particular interest is the relationship between these two youths. Richie is shown, at least initially, treating Norman directly and without condescension:

As shaky as Norman is, he does really great at ring toss. He won two of the games. And when he wins, he really wins, because

Patty told me . . . that one of the things I must not do is let him win anything. I guess that's the best way because Norman isn't dumb, and he'd know it if you were throwing the game. Of course, in all the games we play, he hardly ever comes up a winner, but when he does, he knows it's for real, and he's so happy it's worth going through all the times he lost. Norman has to get used to losing because that's what life will mostly be for him. But he will win a little, and when he does, Patty and I will know maybe we helped.

Of additional interest is the sympathetic depiction of Richie's parents: sensitive and aware people who are frustrated, discouraged, and occasionally terrified by their son's behavior. Green paints a world without heroes or villains, without judgment or condemnation, where children who are fettered by their disabilities struggle to achieve some mastery over their lives.

Greene, Constance C. *Getting Nowhere*. New York: Viking, 1977. 121 pp. Reading Level: YA
Disability: neurological impairment

Mark deliberately nurtures the hostility and resentment he feels toward Pat, his new stepmother. The boy's unreasonable and uncontrolled outbursts have resulted in an atmosphere of escalating tensions and conflict within his family. By contrast, his responsible behavior while working at odd jobs bolsters his self-confidence and has some moderating effect on his anger. One of his customers, Mrs. Baumgartner, solicitously attends to the needs of her husband, who, apparently because of a stroke, is currently confined to a wheelchair and unable to speak or move by himself.

The 14 year old's efforts to behave decently are repeatedly sabotaged. When he tries to rescue a young girl being bullied by a gang of toughs, they turn on him, beating him up and branding him as a likely new target. In a humiliating episode, Mark is asked to a nonexistent party at the home of a girl he admires, only to find that the invitation was a hoax.

After vandalizing Pat's new car, Mark takes her old one without permission, seriously injuring his brother and a friend whom he cajoled into going along for a joyride. Mark's father confronts his son, lambasting the rebellious youngster for his reckless actions. On a last visit to the Baumgartners, the boy learns the paralyzed man is going to be hospitalized at his doctor's insistence. There he meets for the first time the couple's boorish son and hears the old woman voice her dislike for her own child. In an inconclusive and unconvincing final scene, Mrs. Baumgartner, in contrast, expresses her faith in Mark, assuring him he will ultimately be all right.

Analysis. Although the disabled man has only a cameo role, he is a significant character. His wife's virtues are revealed through the care, love, loyalty, and dedication she displays toward him. As Mark learns to esteem these qualities in his employer, it is presumed he will learn to recognize them in others, specifically his stepmother, and ultimately develop them in himself. The parallel between Mr. Baumgartner's situation and Mark's is simultaneously inherently weak and poorly developed. The essential man is imprisoned in an immobile, unresponsive shell; the real Mark is trapped by his self-defeating provocative behavior. The characterization of the young hero elicits more annoyance than compassion, and his actions make sense neither as a plea for recognition nor as an expression of frustration.

Greenfield, Eloise. *Darlene.* Illus. by George Ford. New York: Methuen, 1980. unp. Reading Level: YC
Disability: Orthopedic Impairment

Darlene, a disabled young girl, is left at the house of her Uncle Eddie and cousin Joanne. Although impatient for her mother to return, the youngster is gradually distracted from this single focus by her relatives' attempts to entertain her. The two girls play a board game and an adapted version of jump rope and join Uncle Eddie in singing while he plays his guitar. When her mother returns, Darlene, now thoroughly enjoying herself, is reluctant to leave, "and they all sat down and sang songs."

Analysis. The story line—a disabled child visits her relatives and enjoys herself—is almost too insubstantial to describe. The attractive, naturalistic drawings reveal a girl in a wheelchair, but neither text nor illustrations provide identification, description, or information about her impairment.

Gripe, Maria. *In the Time of the Bells.* Originally published in Stockholm by Albert Bonniers Forlag, 1965, as *I Klockornas Tid.* Illus. by Harald Gripe. Trans. by Sheila La Farge. New York: Delacorte, 1976. 208 pp. Reading Level: MC/YA
Disability: Orthopedic Impairment

Arvid grew up thinking that his castle was a monster bent on devouring him. Now 16 and the reigning king, he is convinced of the reality of that metaphor. He is ceaselessly racked with doubts about his role in life and what purpose it may have. Arvid's withdrawal from the conventions of court life and its inflexible demands and his continual questioning and flouting of ritual, of religious doctrines, and of the expectations of his subjects alternately generate anger and despair in his parents and in the learned monk responsible for his education. After consulting the astrologers and interpreting the message within the spiderwebs in the royal tower, the former king, temporarily setting aside his obsessive search for the philosopher's stone, decides that he may reform Arvid's behavior by obtaining a whipping boy for his son. Helge, the orphan nephew of the court executioner, comes to the castle to fulfill that role. Through the process of symbolically accepting the young monarch's "guilt," Helge becomes mystically bonded to Arvid through the public whipping exhibition in ways unintended by Arvid's father. Meanwhile the queen has her own ideas: interpreting the stars, she believes romance will resuscitate her melancholy son, and she begins arrangements for him to marry his cousin, Elisif. The boy is totally oblivious to the girl's charms and becomes even more consumed by despair at the thought of the impending wedding. Helge, however, has been smitten by the would-be bride, but the orphaned youth is overwhelmed by the impossibility of resolving the situation in his favor and is unable to explain his distress to the puzzled girl.

The dark secrets of all the players in this medieval drama are observed and sometimes revealed by Atlas, the sinister dwarf, who shrewdly and brilliantly acts the fool. "Arvid had received him as a present for his fifth birthday. . . . With animal cunning, he ferreted out King Arvid's weaknesses, saw how tormented he was, that he was not and perhaps never would be the right person to be king." At the Midsummer Festival, Arvid, to everyone's surprise, places Helge instead of Atlas in the traditional role of the Fool King. The dwarf is infuriated, and the crowd is puzzled as Helge's unprecedented regal behavior cheats the multitudes of their malicious and cathartic fun. In a confrontation, Helge publicly humiliates Atlas and later verbally abuses the court councilors, who have come, according to custom, to taunt the Fool King. After Helge breaks the fake noose in the charade that marks the end of his reign, Elisif rushes to the simulated gallows and embraces the whipping boy, to everyone's further dismay. During the Dance of Death that follows, Elisif's sister, Engelke, speaks to Arvid of life, death, and love, subtly revealing her feelings about him. After once again consulting the heavens, the old king discloses to both boys that they are actually brothers, thus explaining and validating their profoundly felt mutual affection. Seizing this opportunity to put aside his onerous responsibility, Arvid announces that he will abdicate in favor of his brother, but Helge says he will not assume the throne, since he would always feel the intruder. The old monarch, infuriated, reluctantly concludes that he must again assume authority and become the ruler of his rudderless kingdom. Arvid leaves in a brief ceremony, retreating into a life where his behavior is not controlled by rules he perceives as arbitrary, perverse, and dishonest.

Analysis. This highly charged existential novel contains themes and dilemmas unique in juvenile literature. It questions the purpose of life and love; it deals with illusion and reality and whether the latter can be known with certainty; it concerns problems of personal need and philosophical commitment in conflict with socially imposed destiny, of public expectations, and of private, idiosyncratic needs.

While the story is compelling in its thematic treatment, it is even more so in terms of literary structure. The author's manipulation of symbols and incidents with myriad meaning is skillful and complex. Atlas plays a particular part: acting the fool, he can say what others dare only think. Maliciously, he mocks Arvid, revealing the boy's unsuitability to be king. His behavior, while villainous, makes dissembling impossible. Arvid regards him with fear and horror, but after he abdicates he suddenly, unexpectedly, encounters his nemesis. This time, he notes an expression on Atlas's face "that basically concealed fear and loneliness." Now, relieved of his own terrible burden, "the sickly disgust which the dwarf had always caused him was transformed into compassion."

This gripping, somber, and overpowering work can be expected to have a limited audience—in part because of the unresolved and unresolvable questions it poses but also because of its relentlessly depressing tone. The dark and haunting illustrations perfectly complement and amplify this unusual novel.

Grollman, Sharon Hya. *More Time To Grow.* Illus. by Arthur Polonsky. Boston: Beacon, 1977. 39 pp. Reading Level: YC
Disability: Intellectual Impairment

Five-year-old Arthur amuses his older sister Carla with the scribbling lines he makes as he draws in his coloring book, but he does not understand her sudden anger when he similarly marks all over her new puzzle. When her parents report the doctor's assessment that her brother is retarded, the nine-year-old girl finds this diagnosis difficult to understand, much less to accept: "The sound of the word made something hurt inside Carla. . . . Sometimes at school the kids called someone a 'retard' if he did something wrong, something stupid. She knew it was a bad word. And it buzzed in her head, making her dizzy. And she got angry at Arthur because he was retarded. It was because of him that everyone was unhappy."

Overcoming their own distress, Carla's parents try to help their daughter by discussing the implications of retardation: "They told her it meant different. Not worse, but different. 'He will learn and grow more slowly than you and your friends. We'll have to help him more. . . . But don't think we love you less. You'll always be very special to us.' " Despite their assurances and explanations, Carla feels alienated from her sibling until the neighborhood druggist engages her in conversation. Sam tells the girl that he has a retarded daughter who has enriched his life in unexpected ways. Carla returns home to find her brother singing an odd song. Intrigued, she asks him where he learned it and he states he made it up. To his delight, she asks him to teach it to her as they both find the shared silliness rewarding.

Analysis. In addition to this brief story, the book includes an interpretation of the text by Robert Perske addressed to parents and teachers as well as suggested discussion questions, activities, and resources for adults to use with youngsters to explore the topic further. The narrative has few literary pretensions, functioning primarily as a device for exploring familial response to an intellectually impaired member.

Guy, Rosa. *Mirror of Her Own.* New York: Delacorte, 1981. 183 pp.
Reading Level: YA/MA
Disability: Speech Impairment

Plain Mary, nearly 18, has always stood in awe of her glamorous sister. Roxanne is determined, self-confident, and assured of herself, and when the 22 year old comes home for the summer, it is inevitable that she dates the town's most eligible bachelor, wealthy, handsome, debonaire, dashing John Drysdale, Mary's secret passion. Mary's feelings about her sibling fluctuate from envy to admiration and from hatred to love, but her evaluation of her own personality is fairly constant—she considers herself unattractive, spiritless, and wishy-washy. The last two attributes she also sees in her father, who is content with his modest house and moderate income and is unwilling to fight the Drysdales for some disputed property that abuts his land. Mary wallows in masochism as she takes abuse from her presumed friend, Gloria, who cruelly taunts her about her speech dysfluency.

Mary manipulates her sister so as to wrangle an invitation to a sailing party where many wealthy guests will be present. She meets Anikwi, an African, Fatima, an Egyptian, and Emma, a black student in her high school, and is aghast when Gloria embarrasses her by making racial slurs. An argument over the evils of colonialist exploitation ensues, and Mary, whose stuttering compounds her sense of social isolation, is ignored. John, high on marijuana and angry about

Roxanne's absence, flirts with her sister. Mary is subsequently invited to another party, where she not only smokes pot but drinks and then is given cocaine by John. Roxanne discovers them and, with the African's help, manages to drag her stoned sister home. Despite her condition, Mary surreptitiously leaves the house and stumbles onto the road, barely escaping John's speeding car. He jumps from the crash unhurt and guides the bewildered adolescent to his bed for further drug indulgence and sex. Furious, Roxanne arrives at the Drysdale estate the next morning, but her former boyfriend hides Mary and denies he has seen her. Disillusioned, the teenager rushes home, stumbles into "quickslime," but miraculously she is able to grab onto a vine and, Tarzan fashion, pulls herself to safety. She is sick and feverish for two weeks: her recovery of health and lucidity incredibly signals the end of her speech dysfluency as well. Roxanne prepares to leave for study in Paris and assures her younger sister that her own future will work out, too.

Analysis. Mary is described as stuttering "only when very upset," but she seems troubled by this disorder frequently. The central premise that emotional trauma combined with physical danger would provide a cure for this disorder is romantic nonsense. Stuttering in this novel appears to be a costume effect, a means to contrast the two sisters even more: Mary has the common name and dingy brown hair, is so homely that she is mistaken for a "retarded" child, is withdrawn and masochistic in her choice of a friend, and stutters; Roxanne has the glamorous name, blue eyes, and blond hair, is talented, vibrant, and articulate. The writing is awkward and overblown: "Was what she had done so horrible that she deserved such an end? John? She had been mad! Mad on moonlight and drugs." The characters in this soap opera are flimsy and completely predictable caricatures. The narrative serves mainly as a vehicle to deliver unsubtle sermons against speeding, drinking, drugs, colonialism, and racism.

Hallman, Ruth. *Breakaway.* Philadelphia: Westminster, 1981. 92 pp.
Reading Level: YA
Disability: Auditory Impairment, Neurological Impairment

Since the diving accident, which left Roby Cory with a profound hearing loss, his mother has been smothering him with attempts at providing protection. His girl friend, Kate, realizing that he must be rescued from his oppressive and stultifying home atmosphere, persuades him to run away with her. They travel by bus to another state, where they rent rooms in a boardinghouse owned by Mzz Gogan, a sharp-tongued old lady whom Rob recognizes immediately as a "big bluffer." He explains this instantaneous insight to his companion:

"Since I can't hear, I'm learning to read everything else about a person." Soon after their arrival, their landlady has a stroke. Rob feels the vibrations as she pounds on the floor for help, correctly diagnosing her medical problem, and has Kate call for help. Guided by his helpful but uninformed girl friend, the adolescent boy begins to learn signing and lip reading. She has borrowed library books to aid in this rehabilitation project and forces Rob to watch soap operas, through which he is supposed to learn to interpret body language and facial expressions. Mzz Gogan returns from the hospital, continuing her recovery at home under the care of her two concerned but untrained lodgers. Now aware of the boy's auditory deficiency, she arranges for a trained dog to alert him to those sounds he cannot hear.

While Rob is out exercising, a gang of kids chase and taunt him, and he is demoralized when he realizes how vulnerable he is. Kate forces him to confront his tormentors. During this encounter, he quickly wins them over and cements the alliance by offering to coach their basketball team. When two men enter Mzz Gogan's store intending to rob her and take Kate hostage, Rob, his new street companions, and the dog outwit and capture the crooks. In the meantime, Mrs. Cory has traced her son to his new address, determined to take him home and sever all contacts with Kate. When the woman sees how the boy has taken control over his life and adjusted to his hearing loss, she is convinced of the error of her ways and the three are reconciled.

Analysis. In addition to the bubble-gum plot, the hackneyed characterizations, and the insipid writing, the presentation of the ramifications of hearing loss is absurd. The teenage girl, with the help of daytime television and a couple of library books, in just a few months brings about marvelous improvements in her boyfriend's functioning that would be the envy of a highly skilled therapist. The arduous process of learning communication techniques is accomplished with lightning speed and with little difficulty. Psychological aftereffects resulting from auditory loss are presented first in melodramatic terms and then shown as subject to ready remediation. The praiseworthy goal of demonstrating competence and social skills in the disabled protagonist is sabotaged by the facile treatment of his remediation.

Hanlon, Emily. *It's Too Late for Sorry.* Scarsdale, N.Y.: Bradbury, 1978. 222 pp. Reading Level: YA
Disability: Intellectual Impairment; also neurological impairment

Kenny's and Phil's friendship changes when Harold Havermeyer moves into their neighborhood. Phil finds mental retardation terribly amusing and spends much time mocking or imitating the newcomer.

Kenny is occupied on the gridiron and soon becomes infatuated with Rachel, a teammate's sister. Rachel, in turn, becomes concerned about Harold and devotes a great deal of attention to the young man, including him, to Kenny's growing resentment, in many of their social activities. When Phil taunts his buddy about his involvement with the "mental," Kenny comes face to face with Phil's cruelty but resists abandoning their relationship. Irritated and upset, Kenny argues with Rachel over her excessive interest in Harold's teacher and accuses her of having an obsession about retardation.

To rescue his pal from his melancholy state, Phil introduces Kenny to the wonders of marijuana, after which, when sufficiently recovered from the smoking interlude, they head for the Fourth of July picnic. Kenny confronts Harold, whom he insults and pushes. Subsequently, Kenny learns that Harold followed him at first but then disappeared into the crowd. After several days, he is found, needing hospitalization after having been badly assaulted by some junkies. Remorseful, Kenny is persuaded to visit Harold, who, clearly harboring no grudge, greets him warmly.

Because of Mr. Havermeyer's stroke, his wife concludes she cannot care for her husband as well as her son, and so Harold is placed in foster care, where he makes a good adjustment. Rachel tells her boyfriend that Harold has gained greater independence in this new situation, and despite his guilt, Kenny understands their crucial contribution in providing Harold with sufficient skills and opportunities for social and personal growth. It is now unlikely that he will ever be institutionalized again.

Analysis. The ominous title announces the onset of a message in a fictional format in such an unsubtle tone that one waits with trepidation for the calamity to happen, a technique that dampens anticipation. Further, the characters are drawn in extremes, and the plot is manipulated to deliver two major sermons: be nice to persons with impairments and avoid drugs. The latter homily is reminiscent of the old Woman's Christian Temperance Union tracts, and the description of the stoned youths is unbelievable. Motivation is reduced to a single dimension, and character is directly correlated with attitude toward retardation. Mr. Havermeyer's disorder is used to advance and add complexity to the plot, but the irony of his wife's situation is not emphasized. While her husband will actually require a good deal of her care, her ministrations to her son have had the effect of worsening his ability to cope, and the institutionalization he endured dissipated his abilities even more. This is yet another well-intentioned book where the author has allowed that objective to dominate and overwhelm literary considerations.

Hanlon, Emily. *The Swing.* Scarsdale, N.Y.: Bradbury, 1979. 209 pp. Reading Level: MC
Disability: Auditory Impairment

Because of Beth's deafness, her overprotective mother tries to discourage her child from participating in activities that other children engage in without much thought. Surprisingly, the reluctant woman gives her daughter permission to explore some nearby mountains by herself, and there, by chance, she comes upon the awe-inspiring sight of a mother bear and her cub. Correctly assuming she would be forbidden to return if her parents learned of the animals' presence, the girl wisely refrains from mentioning the incident at home. When Danny, a 13-year-old neighbor who is walking through the woods, accidentally discharges his stepfather's gun, the mother bear angrily charges at the terrified youngster. Paralyzed with fear, the boy is rescued when Beth intervenes and leads him to safety in a tall tree. Unwilling to admit that he was saved by a younger girl who, moreover, is deaf, Danny allows his family to conclude that he was the hero who saved the endangered girl.

Unhappy at the tension that exists between them, Danny's stepfather sees this as an opportunity to mend their growing rift. He organizes a hunt to track down the creatures he believes are a menace to the children. Beth, nearly hysterical with worry that the bears will be shot, angrily confronts the embarrassed boy, accusing him of lying, and of breaking his promise never to reveal the animals' whereabouts. On the second day, the elated hunters return triumphantly with the carcasses of the dead mammals.

Inconsolable at this slaughter, Beth retreats to the swing she uses as a haven. She is shocked to find the cub's bloody body tied to it in a grim and gruesome parody. Sensing she is not alone, the heartbroken girl glances up to see Danny watching her, and she attacks the helpless boy in fury and frustration. When her energy is drained, the boy tells her he is not responsible for that cruel joke and unburdens his remorse over his role in the slaying of the magnificent beasts. He further communicates with her his feelings about his father and gives his new companion a flute the man made for him. Beth accepts the gift as well as the offer of friendship, after which the two cooperate in burying the cub's body.

Analysis: Hanlon's presentation of the implications of profound hearing loss in a preadolescent girl is accomplished with extraordinary insight and empathy. Beth is shown able to communicate with her family, Danny, and those townspeople who take the time to be friendly, look directly at her when speaking, and treat her in ways that minimize her discomfort. Since she can not monitor pitch, articulation, or even rate of speech, these abilities tend to deteriorate when she is excited. Beth's communication training experiences and her reaction to them are recounted with wry humor. The extreme mood swings characteristic of her developmental stage are exaggerated by her deafness as she feels her striving for independence is being thwarted by her family's excessive anxieties about her welfare. Within the context of a compelling story, the author has created a heroine who is sensitive, admirable, likable, and deaf.

Hasler, Eveline. *Martin Is Our Friend*. Originally published as *Dann Kroch Martin durch den Zaun*. Illus. by Dorothea Desmarowitz. Nashville: Abingdon, 1981. unp. Reading Level: YC
Disability: Intellectual Impairment; also orthopedic impairment, visual impairment

Martin "looks different. His mouth is open most of the time. When Martin walks, he makes little limping steps. And he holds his head with the thick glasses sideways." The neighborhood youngsters ostracize him, but he does know others his own age in a class of multiply handicapped children. On a field trip, Martin discovers a beautiful horse. The owner offers the child a ride and, when she sees its effect, decides to make the animal available to all the children in that special class. When the corral gate is mistakenly left open, the horse wanders out to the street, where it becomes disoriented and panicky. No one is able to calm it until Martin appears. Recognizing him, the creature allows itself to be led back to safety. The local children who witnessed this event now wait for the young hero to return so he can tell them about the horse.

Analysis. Both style and conception of this work are simplistic. The improbable sequence of events climaxes with an unlikely incident—the rescue of a frightened, powerful animal by a seriously impaired little boy. The story resurrects the nature-child thesis, that those who are disabled are calmer, gentler, more in tune with the natural world than the common run of humanity. The illustrations, depicting an idyllic European cityscape, are gorgeously colored but primitive.

Hautzig, Deborah. *Second Star to the Right*. New York: Greenwillow, 1981. 151 pp. Reading Level: YA
Disability: Emotional Dysfunction

Fourteen-year-old Leslie Margolee Hillar attends a private school in Manhattan. Her middle name was given in memory of a cousin who died in a Nazi concentration camp. Although cousin Margolee might have avoided that fate, she chose to accompany her mother to the gas chambers, unable to abandon the doomed woman even to save her own life. This story, reverently retold in the family, has haunted Leslie, who feels that equally noble commitments are expected of her. Although apparently having the requisites for a contented life—a cultured, loving family, success in school, security, friends—she grows increasingly dissatisfied with herself. Mrs. Hillar's ambitions are seen by her daughter as creating unbearable burdens and intolerable pressures.

After a bout with the flu during which she sheds a few pounds, Leslie finds the impetus to continue losing the slight excess of weight she carries. Seeking to find one area that she can successfully manage by herself, the teenager focuses all her energies on dieting and contrives elaborate stratagems to disguise her avoidance of food. Her parents do not become alarmed until it gradually becomes clear to them that Leslie is endangering her health. Any threats to her regimen are greeted with outbursts of temper or with wily tricks aimed at obscuring her actions and the extent of her self-imposed starvation. Her visits to a doctor and therapist, who are unfamiliar with anorexia nervosa, are unsatisfactory, but she is subsequently taken to a specialist, who hospitalizes her. She meets other anorexics on the ward and is surprised to discover that her aberrant behavior is not unique. The psychiatrist helps the dangerously sick girl discern that excessive dieting is a device for gaining control over her life rather than the search for the unreachable goal of a body "thin enough" to be beautiful. Although Leslie accepts the explanation that this illness is not her conscious objective, she is reluctant to give up the life-threatening behaviors associated with it. The specialist promises the girl: "If you want to get well badly enough, you can." Finally, Leslie is able to free herself of some of the demands imposed by her loving but oppressive mother and concludes: "Well, it's not winning that counts; it's how you don't play the game, right? I think, at this point, I'd give myself a C+. And if anyone asked me, right this second, whether I'd go to the right [i.e., choose life] or to the left [i.e., choose death as her cousin did], I'd say—to the right. And straight on till morning."

Analysis. Mrs. Hillar's behavior does not seem to be sufficiently oppressive to precipitate her daughter's obsession, although it is its putative cause. The ascribed motivation seems weak and unconvincing, a criticism equally applicable to Leslie's actions, which appear more petulant than compulsive, as well as to her quick and relatively painless recovery. The author does present symptoms typical of this condition—amenorrhea, weakness, lightheadedness, difficulty in sitting, for example. The heavy-handed inclusion of ethnic components, the contrived plot development, and the overblown writing diminish the authenticity of the presentation and the empathy the author would otherwise generate for her main character.

Haynes, Henry Louis. *Squarehead and Me.* Illus. by Ben Epstein. Philadelphia: Westminster, 1980. 143 pp. Reading Level: MC
Disability: Learning Disability

When Robert Palmer, contemptuously known as "Squarehead," learns he will have to attend summer school again, he decides to run away. His mother sends their neighbor, David, to look for him and bring him back. The missing boy is readily located, but David sees there is no point in trying to influence him, for Robert is adamant about avoiding his fate. Squarehead has been invited to visit Sharon Van Pelt, one of the few students who does not make fun of him. He has a map for finding her home, but his map-reading skills are as deficient as his other academic ones. With David's help, some luck, and persistence, the boys finally arrive at the Olsen farm, where the girl is staying. Unprepared for visitors, Uncle Gregory greets them with his rifle, but their presence is satisfactorily explained, and Sharon subsequently invites them in.

Uncle Gregory takes a special interest in Robert. "He had Robert Squarehead read off many more numbers, and Squarehead got some of them wrong. . . . Then Uncle Gregory had Squarehead write down numbers . . . . [He] was able to read Squarehead's numbers well enough, and could understand Squarehead's talk, which most strangers couldn't manage to do the first time around." The boy understandably becomes restless with these academic activities, and the old man, now satisfied, ends them. David learns the reason for Sharon's coolness toward him: she resents his passivity in allowing other black youngsters to make life miserable for her and the rest of the newly integrated white students. She suggests it is part of the same weakness of character that keeps him from defending Robert from the taunts of his classmates. Sharon confesses that the school year has been too frustrating, and she has reluctantly decided to transfer to a private school. David, stung by her criticisms and ashamed of being maneuvered by others into a neutral and uninvolved stance, is startled at this blunt and uncomplimentary assessment of his behavior.

Further conflict arises when David teases a younger child, unaware of the boy's disability. "What's a matter with you, Jimmy. . . . And answer up sometimes, dumb-dumb. . . . And don't slobber on yourself, you big baby." Not unreasonably, the visitor defends his actions by pointing out the members of the household precipitated the incident by their unwarranted secrecy. When the two boys return home, Sharon's mother and Uncle Gregory prevail upon Mrs. Palmer not to send her son to summer school, where he is destined to fail. They are convinced the boy is bright but has a specific language disability that can be remediated in Mrs. Van Pelt's school. Reluctantly, but without much hope, the woman agrees to allow the placement, a decision that proves to be a constructive one.

Analysis. Squarehead and Me highlights two serious problems that prevent adequate response to children with learning disabilities: it is not uncommon for black children to be overlooked in the screening process, and misdiagnosed students are often subject to "more of the same," that is, an intensified repetition of procedures that have already failed with them. The Van Pelt school is posited as an ideal one in which corrective and compensatory strategies are employed that will allow youngsters to successfully return to regular classes. The image of its model teacher is discredited by her manner of dealing with an unwelcome visitor: "She broke off two swabs [of cotton] and placed them in her ears. Then she took the rest and jammed it in [her critic's] big mouth." Further inappropriate behavior is demonstrated when she conceals, babies, and overprotects the child identified as having developmental aphasia who lives in her home.

Incidents are improbable, professional references outdated, for example, "word blindness," and phrasing clumsy, such as, "Then it got all grueling, sure enough. My arms were getting stiff and frozen and bloodthirsty and suchlike. My mind took to wandering on me and my body seemed to be wilting and letting me down. My legs started to tremble under such a strain. And my eyes started looking straight downward, 'cause I was dejected." The language patterns of some characters vary without apparent reason: sometimes the boys speak a dialect and under similar circumstances sometimes use standard English. Although the obvious thrust of this work is to provide information about and develop positive attitudes toward children with specific learning disabilities, as well as to explore issues of integrity as they relate to friendship and race relations, the excessive and gratuitous instances of verbal and physical aggression counter this benign intent. The illustrations, which fail to give any individuality to the characters, are particularly poor.

Heide, Florence Parry. *Growing Anyway Up.* Philadelphia: Lippincott, 1976. 127 pp. Reading Level: YA
Disability: Emotional Dysfunction

Florence, racked by the guilt she harbors over her father's death, tries to bring some sense of security into her loveless life through compulsive, ritualistic acts and eccentric language behaviors and by withdrawing from her cold, insensitive mother and her sterile environment. Panicked by the announcement that they will soon leave their home in a Florida resort area to live in a distant northern suburb, the girl retreats even further into the seeming safety of her fantasy world. Although academically competent, her participation in classroom activities in her new school is minimal and her social isolation is total. Her mother's new boyfriend, whom the woman treats with demeaning obsequiousness, is a stodgy, self-centered bore. The one bright spot in Florence's life is Nina, her father's engaging, sensitive, and outgoing sister. The vibrant woman is able to penetrate her niece's obsessive, protectionist acts by relating warmly to her and speaking openly and lovingly of her dead brother. Prodded by her admired aunt's obvious esteem, the youngster makes some modest progress toward perceiving herself as a worthwhile person. Her growth in self-respect is cut short when Nina's business necessitates an abrupt separation. Florence is devastated by feelings of being abandoned once more, so she transforms a favored doll into an imaginary companion with whom she plans to run away. Nina's return prevents her departure, and when they speak, the distraught girl reveals the source of her compulsive behavior. She confesses: "It was my fault . . . that he died. . . . The good luck kiss, the one he wanted me to put in the suitcase. I hadn't put it in at all. I was angry and hurt because he was going away, leaving me again." Articulating the source of her distress is cathartic, and her aunt's continuing love and support are remediative. Florence's mother remarries, and the young girl transfers to a boarding school, where she manages to sort out the conflicts in her life and adopt a more tolerant attitude toward others as well as toward herself.

Analysis. Heide effectively communicates the intolerable stress that drives the tormented heroine of this story to adopt behaviors as self-destructive as they are eccentric. However, Florence emerges as a sympathetic character who is salvaged by honesty and love and who finally learns that both the pains and pleasures of one's past must be accepted. The youngster's rapid recovery from such profound distress and her facile identification of the origins for her anxiety are difficult to swallow, but these provide the only false notes in an otherwise insightful and sensitive work.

Heide, Florence Parry. *Secret Dreamer, Secret Dreams.* Philadelphia: Lippincott, 1978. 95 pp. Reading Level: YA
Disability: Emotional Dysfunction

I run to the basement stairs. I race down, up, down, the words I must say locked in me. My sister sighs and turns away, my mother wrings her hands, holds her breath, my father calls to me quietly, tenderly, and Brumm barks helplessly, his voice as unintelligible as my own, his message and mine undelivered.

Thirteen-year-old Caroline thus narrates her world as she knows it: she is aware of events but perceives them selectively and interprets them in limited, particularized, and sometimes bizarre ways. She remains mute; speech is too painful, too costly. When she wishes to communicate—to her parents, or to someone in the park with whom she feels a sense of communion—she cannot. Even at her special school where other students have serious emotional problems, Caroline is isolated. Her new teacher, an insensitive woman, is unable to detect the special fears or secret worlds of her charges.

Caroline's distorted perceptions cause her to behave inappropriately, resulting in actions that exasperate her mother and anger her sister. Only her father is endlessly loving, patiently reciting again and again the gentle little rhymes he makes up for her, excusing and explaining her behavior as best he can. The girl's lack of contact with reality causes her to spill and break objects, which her sister Amy must then take care of. Amy's need for her father's attention often waits on her sister's more immediate demands. When Caroline brings home a stray dog from the park, she is allowed to keep it despite her mother's mild protests for her father cannot deny his isolated daughter anything he thinks may bring her some happiness.

The family plans an excursion to the aquarium to celebrate Amy's birthday. All goes well until Caroline sees a turtle in a showcase, whose being she begins to incorporate into her irrational world. Agitatedly, she starts to beat on the glass walls, then falls to the floor. Amy is understandably mortified and angered that yet another trip has been spoiled, and she joins her family in their hasty departure.

In a calmer and more reflective frame of mind, Amy acknowledges that such behavior on her sister's part is not deliberate, and she accepts its inevitability. She assures her sister of her love, setting aside her resentment. The family is ultimately able to recapture its earlier festive mood, and after a modest but pleasant celebration, the day ends peacefully. Caroline feels she will surely now be able to express herself, but her words remain, as before, unspoken. Unable to communicate, she is as isolated as ever from those who, although loving, are excluded from her world.

Analysis. Heide takes a daring risk in viewing much of the plot from the perspective of her autistic character—a "gamble" that works admirably in literary terms. In this original and lyrical novel, she manages the difficult task of creating a sympathetic portrait of a child whose behavior exceeds reasonable limits. Because of the nature of

Caroline's disorder, it is impossible to assess the validity of her depiction. However, by postulating that the child responds to a different
symbol system, the author makes apparently inexplicable actions assume their own logic.

Hermes, Patricia. *What If They Knew?* New York: Harcourt Brace
Jovanovich, 1980. 121 pp. Reading Level: MC
Disability: Neurological Impairment

As a consequence of her parents' decision to remain in London,
Jeremy is obliged to extend her summer vacation and begin the fall
semester in a school in her grandparents' community. Twins Libby and
Mimi are enthusiastic at the prospect of being in the fifth grade with
their new chum. However, Jeremy panics, desperately afraid that the
tension and stress of the new situation might precipitate a seizure,
causing her dreadful embarrassment. These worries are heightened
when she sees Mimi's secret notebook—a compendium of unflattering
evaluations of her classmates that reveals low tolerance for any actions
perceived as unconventional. Her fears are further exacerbated when
Carrie, the most disliked girl in the room, first tries to force herself on
the newcomer and, when rebuffed, threatens to reveal a shameful
secret about the youngster. The outcast subsequently discloses she
found one of the pills Jeremy must take and then nastily informs her
avid listeners that their new classmate is obviously a drug addict. Having been careless about taking her medication, Jeremy has a seizure,
and Carrie tries to exploit the incident, focusing attention on herself by
exaggerating the details of the episode. Disgusted at this reprehensible
ploy, some girls determine to get even with Carrie. One part of their
retaliatory plan is to conceal some dead mice in her papers, a sure-fire
trick calculated to disrupt her speech on Parents' Night. The plan backfires when the distraught girl refuses to take part in the proceedings.
Jeremy is designated as her replacement and nervously considers
whether the topic of friendship would be a suitable one for her speech.

During a get-acquainted activity in school, the newcomer had been
paired with Andrew, a boy described by Mimi as "weird. He's got a
funny disease that makes him walk like a drunk." To Jeremy's surprise, she discovers that he is sensitive and sympathetic, qualities unaffected by his cerebral palsy. Reflecting on her chosen theme, the
speaker admits how concerned she had been about finding friends and
how relieved when everything worked out well. Jeremy emphasizes
her belief that friends can and should be accepting of nonconformist
behavior. She is calm enough during her presentation to monitor her
own responses. "I looked up, all of a sudden, I was looking straight at

Andrew. I hadn't really planned to say it, but suddenly I was saying, 'Like, a friend doesn't *really* care if you—talk or *walk* different from the way everybody else does.' "

Analysis. Hermes's book effectively depicts a young girl's concerns about the probable impact on her peers of the knowledge that she has seizures and the strategies the heroine employs to conceal her condition. Also well done is the portrayal of discomfort the family members suffer in dealing with the situation: particularly interesting are the contrasts between the girl's grandparents and how their personalities affect their perceptions. The downplaying of the "dramatic" aspects is admirable, and Jeremy's reactions are credible. In low-key, nondidactic fashion, the author imparts information about the importance of the medication regimen and develops a picture of an active heroine, growing in intelligence, empathy, and strength.

However, in addition to the melodramatic title, the quality of the writing is quite uneven. Characterizations of the twins are good, but Carrie is a flat, predictable villain, and Andrew serves only as a means of delivering the message that disability should not interfere with acceptance. This theme is stated with sufficient lack of subtlety that the obvious and heavy-handed homily that ends the story only functions to belabor a point already more than adequately made.

Hicks, Clifford B. *Alvin's Swap Shop.* Illus. by Bill Sokol. New York: Holt, Rinehart & Winston, 1976. 143 pp. Reading Level: MC
Disability: Cosmetic Impairment

Called on to come up with a plan to hold off the summer doldrums, Alvin, the Magnificent Brain, involves Daphne, his sister, and Shoie, his friend, in establishing a swap shop. The astute boy trades items so well that he and his friends are able to use an abandoned gas station acquired in a swap for their rapidly growing stock. One day they encounter Pim, a Bahamian boy, who is trying to escape from a scarred killer determined to steal the boy's treasure or kill him in the attempt. Pim appeals to his new-found friends for help, and under Alvin's inspired guidance, they outwit the criminal and locate the treasure. Its sale will provide Pim with enough money to return to the islands and build a real library for the other children who live there.

Analysis. This flimsy tale could easily follow its predecessors to the Disney studios. The plot is as thin as celluloid, and the dialogue, striving for archness, is unlike anything real children say to each other, such as using "old bean" as a form of address. The killer's scar is used principally as costuming to intensify the devilish character of the evil pursuer. It also provides the means by which Daphne locates the criminal in the mug book at the police station and the descriptive identifier for the children; when the children spot a man with a prominent scar, he immediately becomes known as "Scarface." It is a shabby device but all of a piece with the other components of this lightweight effort. Oddly enough, the only illustration of the criminal depicts him with a mark unlike that described in the text.

Hightower, Florence. *Dreamwold Castle*. Boston: Houghton Mifflin, 1978. 214 pp. Reading Level: MC/YA
Disability: Special Health Problems; also auditory impairment

Phoebe moves with her widowed mother to a small town, where she is very lonely. Doing poorly in school and unable to make new friends, she is pleased when Constance invites her home to meet her twin brother, Harry. The children share a passion for mountain climbing and fantasize about their own future ascent of the Himalayas. Harry, severely asthmatic, is confined to his house, in which he isolates himself from his parents. The twins speak adoringly of their elder brother, Tony, who also is estranged from his parents and whom they have been forbidden to contact. Phoebe shares books, the construction of models of Himalayan peaks, and hours of fun with her new friends. Their ally in the house is a Finnish housekeeper who has a hearing loss. She conspires with the children to conceal their activities from her employers. Phoebe is pressured to act as a conduit for communication with Tony, who, the twins claim, is coming back one day to rescue them. Tony does return, moody, vacillating between affectionate concern for his younger siblings and hostile, near violent, aggressive behavior. Phoebe's mother, involved in a romance, is oblivious to her daughter's behavior and relieved that her previously solitary child is busy with her new companions. Tony takes the children on nature walks, which have a salutary effect on Harry. A police officer discloses that Tony is wanted for murder because of a man who died during an armed robbery he allegedly committed. Nevertheless, Phoebe is persuaded to help Tony escape and returns to find that her home, where he had been briefly hiding, has burned to the ground. Soon afterward, she and the twins learn that Tony killed himself, preferring death to a life of imprisonment. Constance and Harry turn from her, absorbed both with grief and their own future plans and seemingly indifferent to Phoebe, discarding her after having used her. The distressed girl is able to relate the whole story to a friend of the family, a cathartic experience that helps her regain her perspective and emotional equilibrium.

Analysis. Ironically, worry about their son's health has led Harry's parents to keep him from the kinds of experiences that would increase his strength and stamina and lessen the debilitating effects of his asthma attacks. His brother's casual approach is more therapeutic, although Tony's wild escapades and the emotional stress he causes the boy are damaging. The deafness of the Finnish housekeeper, mentioned only in passing, seems an unnecessary attribution since her lack of fluency in English sufficiently establishes a rationale for the misunderstanding that ensues. This communication barrier, replicated in the various relationships, is a central motif underscoring the theme of each character's isolation. There are more subplots than usual in a book addressed to immature readers, but the tightly constructed narrative makes the action easier to follow. Phoebe's painful maturation is convincing, and after a slow start, this original and disturbing story gradually evolves into a gripping tale.

Hirsch, Karen. *Becky.* Illus. by Jo Esco. Minneapolis: Carolrhoda Books, 1981. unp. Reading Level: YC
Disability: Auditory Impairment

In order to attend a school for the hearing impaired so that she can receive proper instruction, Becky must leave her farm home and stay with another family, a situation that saddens the girl. Not having had any lessons in signing, Becky is unable to communicate with her foster family, but as she learns to lip-read and use sign language, her life becomes easier. Nevertheless, she has bouts of frustration when her need to communicate outstrips her still modest ability. At the end of the year, Becky's parents decide to enroll their daughter in a boarding school, where they expect her rate of learning to accelerate. Becky's foster "sister" is unhappy over their imminent separation, but her father reassures the girl that their friendship will survive.

Analysis. Becky provides a superficial look at some problems faced by a hearing-impaired child. The fictional youngster is remarkably unaffected by the break from her family, and the emotional implications of such a move are ignored. Problems are raised but never explored in any depth, and the girls never seem credible. The illustrations fail to amplify the text and are inadequate esthetically—those involving human figures are badly proportioned, with representation of hands and feet particularly amateurish.

Hirsch, Karen. *My Sister.* Illus. by Nancy Inderieden. Minneapolis: Carolrhoda Books, 1977. unp. Reading Level: YC
Disability: Intellectual Impairment

The speech and behavior of his sister, intellectually impaired since birth because of brain damage, are described by the young narrator, who also articulates his ambivalent feelings toward her. The girl is immature but because of her docile and gentle demeanor is included in neighborhood activities. Her brother admits that he sometimes resents her needs superseding his own and is both embarrassed and saddened when strangers are fearful or mocking. Frequently he wishes she could be different but honestly admits: "I know that she will always be special no matter how hard I wish. And I know that I love her the way she is."

Analysis. My Sister is a quasi-fictional attempt at honestly portraying a sensitive child's reactions to a severely impaired sibling. The family is supportive of both children, accommodating the exceptional needs of one while compensating the other as much as is practical for the inconveniences and inevitable difficulties that arise. The impaired child is anonymous, and no insight is given into her feelings, motives, or desires. None of the other characters are named either, an unfortunate decision since that omission substantially diminishes the depth of identification possible. The gentle black-and-white drawings contribute greatly in setting the tone of this work.

Holland, Isabelle. *Alan and the Animal Kingdom*. Philadelphia: Lippincott, 1977. 190 pp. Reading Level: MC
Disability: Speech Impairment; also special health problems

Ever since his parents' death when he was very young, Alan has been shuttled between a succession of relatives. When the boy learns of the death of his current guardian, he decides he is unable to face another change and determines to prevent the authorities from finding out he is now living alone. When last forced to move, all his pets were put to death, and he is adamant about protecting his present menagerie, which consists of a cat, dog, rat, and gerbils. Having lived in various countries, the boy has developed an idiosyncratic accent, which makes him, in the words of one teacher, "a focus of amusement." Alan comments: "I started to stutter when I was about nine, which just made the focus more amusing than ever. It's less of a hassle to be called stupid because you don't talk than to have everybody holding their ribs together while some stand-up comic talks about l-l-leaving the d-d-d-door cl-cl-cl-closed."

Inevitably, Alan runs into money problems. His nervousness is exacerbated as the building superintendent makes increasingly persistent inquiries about his now deceased great aunt. After the boy's cat takes sick, he locates a veterinarian whose office is open evenings. Alan sees that Dr. Harris, although drunk, is sufficiently in control of himself to treat Muff properly. The 12 year old cannot pay for his services, but the doctor continues to care for the animal, following up the office visits with a house call. Once in the apartment, he readily deduces the boy's situation and decides to help him out by cashing checks, buying food, and fixing dinners. The man stops drinking but warns Alan his sobriety is likely to be temporary. When the boy's dog is hit by a car, he cannot reach Dr. Harris and takes the injured animal elsewhere. In need of cash immediately, the youth seeks out his mentor but finds him drunk. The desperate youngster steals some money from his school. The headmaster easily figures out who the thief is, learns the truth about the boy's situation, and moves the youngster into his own home, promising that all the animals will be provided for. Hoping to ease the transition, the headmaster gives Alan a poodle pup, the only dog that does not precipitate an asthma attack in his wife. Unhappy with his new living arrangements, the youth visits Dr. Harris after learning the man is attending a rehabilitation program. Alan hints he would like to live with the veterinarian but is told that is impossible at this time. The man offers some hope for the future, "*if* I can stay sober, *if* the various authorities can be reassured enough by my staying clear and clean for a reasonable length of time to consider me as a foster parent."

Analysis. Considering that he spent his entire childhood shuffled from one temporary home to another, living with often unenthusiastic relatives who reluctantly accepted responsibility for his care, the young hero of this novel is remarkably stable emotionally. He is, however, a loner whose tension is manifested through speech dysfluency. Holland rarely uses the common technique of repeating initial letters to signal her character's impairment. Instead, she alludes to it in the narrative when evidence is needed of Alan's anxiety. The story, although far-fetched, moves quickly, and there are enough sure-fire ingredients to sustain interest: a child defying convention by living alone, a large, unruly collection of appealing animals, and a series of crises.

Holland, Isabelle. *Dinah and the Green Fat Kingdom.* Philadelphia: Lippincott, 1978. 189 pp. Reading Level: MC/YA
Disability: Neurological Impairment, Speech Impairment

Retreating as often as she can to the protective branches of a giant oak tree, Dinah fantasizes about the Green Kingdom, where everybody is fat and therefore beautiful. This is not the general opinion at school or in her home, where the girl is subjected to constant tirades about her obesity. Dinah's situation is worsened by having to share her bedroom with "beastly Brenda," her cousin, whose smarmy obsequiousness derives from her own insecurity. Moreover, the girl is extremely thin and self-disciplined, characteristics that, by comparison, draw further unfavorable attention to Dinah.

One day, Dinah impulsively adopts a puppy who would otherwise have been scheduled for an early demise at the local pound. On the way home, she meets Mrs. Van Hocht, a very overweight neighbor, who takes her home and gives her a leash for the pup. The woman's nephew, Sebastian, whose speech and mobility have been impaired by cerebral palsy, lives with her. The boy has an extensive collection of animals and also looks after another menagerie at school. His teacher reports that when "the hamsters and gerbils are all excited and upset, Sebastian walks in and they just calm down like that. It's astounding."

Dinah and her new pet get a frigid reception when they arrive home, but the heroine is allowed to keep Francis provided she agrees to abstain from sweets and regularly consult with Sister Elizabeth, a nutritionist. The nun, who is on the staff of Sebastian's school, is surprisingly sympathetic. She lends the girl a book on diets and another volume on dog training. They discuss the book's author, a graduate of the special school who is now a prominent veterinarian, and Sister Elizabeth reveals that she had polio as a child. She confides that she and the writer, trying to overcome the effects of cerebral palsy, had studied about exercise and diet, believing that "healthy eating is essential to make the best of whatever you have." The woman suggests that Dinah might assist Sebastian in caring for his animals but adds that the boy is very determined "about doing things the way everybody else does. He hates having special favors. . . . He likes to get that straight with everybody right away. He's very bright, and he pretty much knows what he does with the rest of his life depends on him. That's why he takes the hard line he does, and I respect him for it."

Dinah's doctor confirms that she has lost five pounds, but before she can announce her triumph, her mother announces that Brenda has had some very bad news and everyone must be particularly kind to her. Dinah is angry because, although she is finally addressing a problem she has been nagged about for years, no one even listens to her, so she vents her feelings about her family's insensitivity by running off, sobbing uncontrollably. After hours of solitary and unsatisfactory attempts to deal with her problem, she arrives at Sebastian's house asking for refuge. Her father is notified and arrives to take her home, where her parents at last acknowledge their errors and begin to develop some sensitivity to her needs.

Analysis. Sebastian is the agent through which Dinah achieves insight and learns self-acceptance. As she learns to recognize Sebastian's virtues (something his animals could do instinctively), she also gains in maturity. Other people, focusing on the boy's obviously different appearance and movements, have rejected and harassed him. Their abuse has exacerbated his symptoms and reduced his functioning to such a degree that "almost no one, including a lot of teachers, could see he was bright and quick." This hostility caused the youth to retreat from a mainstreamed setting to a more restrictive environment in order to regain his self-confidence. Mrs. Van Hocht comments on the similarity in attitudes toward disabled and overweight persons:

> Two hundred years ago Sebastian here might have been stoned. He would certainly have publicly been made fun of. Did you know that in the eighteenth century in London people used to go on Sundays and holidays to laugh at the poor, deranged inmates of Bethlehem Hospital—known as Bedlam? Laughing at others, or mocking them or making them feel uncomfortable is what makes some people feel superior. At least in one respect society has improved—laughing at the mentally ill or crippled is not considered socially acceptable today. But fat people are still thought of as fair game.

Holland's plot moves briskly but predictably, and her characters, although attractive, are never more than two-dimensional. In this instance, the story is definitely subservient to the message.

Hopper, Nancy J. *Secrets*. New York: Elsevier/Nelson, 1979. 138 pp. Reading Level: MC/YA
Disability: Emotional Dysfunction

Traumatized by having witnessed her father's death and hoping to protect herself from further emotional distress, Lenore has retreated into a private inner world. The unhappy girl's academic work declines rapidly in the exclusive school she attends, but her mother is able to pressure the institution to tolerate her poor performance. Occasionally a class is sufficiently challenging that she allows herself to become interested, but ordinarily the eighth-grader regards such forays into the external world as dangerous and jealously holds on to her reputation as a "loony." The solitary teenager accidently overhears a plot to kidnap Sammy, a classmate. She obliquely drops hints of the planned crime to her psychiatrist and a teacher, but both ignore her ambiguous warnings. Sammy, too, discounts her suspicions, pointing out the man identified as a plotter is actually his bodyguard.

Lenore discovers the time that the abduction is to take place, and when the intended victim is sent on an errand alone, the concerned girl follows him. Disconcerted by her unexpected appearance, the kidnappers seize both children, conceal them in a jaillike enclosure, and force them to tape-record a message that will be used in a ransom attempt. When the kidnappers learn that their plans have been thwarted, they force their prisoners to swallow some pills. Realizing that this could be a tactic to silence them forever, the children make themselves throw up, after which they await their inevitable rescue. Freed at last from this physical prison, Lenore decides to abandon the self-imposed confinement of her emotional bondage as well.

Analysis. An exciting plot is sabotaged as critical incidents take place without sufficient foreshadowing or apparent reason. Deficiencies in story development accumulate: the choice of Sammy as the victim, the neglect of the teachers to note the disappearance of the children, the failure of the ransom attempt, the fortuitous arrival of the police, and the rationale for the kidnappers' confession are never adequately explained. The murder attempt is strangely passionless—as though nothing extraordinary were transpiring. Although Lenore's behavior is depicted as dysfunctional in the early chapters of the book, her emotions and actions appear to be consciously, purposefully, and deliberately under control—evidence of self-mastery that those in a most robust state of mental health might well find enviable.

Hull, Eleanor. *Alice with Golden Hair.* New York: Atheneum, 1981. 186 pp. Reading Level: YA
Disability: Intellectual Impairment, auditory impairment, speech impairment, neurological impairment; also orthopedic impairment, emotional dysfunction, and special health problems

Uncertain even of what the word *graduation* means, Alice nonetheless awaits this seemingly important event in her life. Afterward, Mrs. Hones, her welfare worker, takes the 17 year old to an "interview" at a nursing home, explaining that Alice has been placed there to work as an aide for $50 a week. This new setting seems horrible to the bewildered adolescent, but she decides it is marginally better than living at home with her father and older siblings. Alice quickly becomes involved with the patients, but is confused by the multitude of names, duties, and problems with which she is confronted. She wants to quit, but doesn't know how to go about it, so she stays on more through inertia than deliberate choice. But to her surprise, she manages quite well when she is on her own. Although Alice has a run-in with Appolonia, she secretly admires the black woman's sense of self-respect, assertiveness, and purposefulness, qualities the novice knows she lacks. Alice is also drawn to Mrs. Daniels, who recites poetry and comments favorably on her aide's lovely hair. The patient, partially recovered from a stroke, tells Alice about Jim, the assistant physiotherapist who is "deaf and dumb." She observes it is "good to know someone who overcomes a handicap. . . . Because we all have them, handicaps, I mean." The girl is shocked to hear this tired old cliché repeated by someone she respects. "Alice hoped Mrs. Daniels would realize she had said something dumb and would take it back." Then the woman explains that she includes in that category her son who killed himself. Before Alice can react, this discussion is interrupted by news of the disappearance of one of the girl's charges, who sneaked out of the building while momentarily unattended. Dismayed, the new aide rushes outside, finds her patient, and wheels her back. She is surprised and pleased when Appolonia defends her against charges of negligence and prevents her from being dismissed.

Alice begins to assert herself in small ways. When she is notified that she will be shifted from the floor housing the senile patients and Mrs. Daniels, she unsuccessfully seeks help. She resorts to pleading with Browny, an orderly, but he comes to her room only to take advantage of her. By deliberately acting "crazy," she scares him off. To the girl's relief, Mrs. Hones reinstates Alice. The residential center experiences a plague of robberies. At a meeting called by the manager, Appolonia comes under suspicion, but Alice reveals that Browny had a key to the room where the losses were reported and thus suggests that he could be the perpetrator. Thereafter, she takes on new status with the other workers and is even acknowledged as one of those responsible for the discharge of the inept and unpopular director. Despite persisting problems, Alice appears to have found a place where she is needed and where she can make a useful contribution.

Analysis. Alice, whose IQ is reported to be 75, is described as "retarded" and displays characteristics common to those who are slow learners but who can, with support, manage adequately in society. Her unstable home life, combined with several traumatic incidents during her institutionalization, have exacerbated her difficulties in functioning, perhaps accounting for the hospitalization of such a relatively high-functioning child. Alice is depicted as a unique and admirable individual with a variety of distinctive traits only some of which are attributable to her intellectual limitations. She is concrete and literal but responds to Mrs. Daniel's poetry. She is naive and gullible but ingenious enough to cleverly deceive her attacker. Additionally, she is reliable and compassionate. She accepts not being able to understand some things, but devises pragmatic strategies to solve some of these problems:

Often Alice could see plainly what was going on—like lighted platforms that flashed by when you rode the subway, to be swallowed up in darkness the next moment. But she didn't know where those places were, or when she was to get off. The best she could do was to try to imitate people who did know.

Curious about her deceased mother, she is vastly relieved when the social worker tells her that her mother was retarded and gave her away only when she realized she was dying of tuberculosis. She is comforted to know her mother loved her and was a good and re-spected person, just as Alice has become.

In a compelling, realistic, well-written novel, Hull has created a memorable heroine and provided unsentimental insights into the lives of people with reduced intellectual abilities who contribute economi-cally and socially to society.

Hunt, Irene. *The Lottery Rose.* New York: Scribner's, 1976. 185 pp.
Reading Level: MC/YA
Disability: Cosmetic Impairment, Intellectual Impairment

A beautiful garden he has once seen in a book is the only haven known to Georgie Burgess, whose alcoholic mother has allowed her lover, Steve, to abuse her son viciously. One of the man's rages left the boy "scarred by a deep burn on the left side of his head which left him partly bald, with a crumpled ear and a streak that looked like fire running down the back of his neck. One night, Steve again goes out of control, breaking Georgie's arm and knocking him unconscious. When the police arrive to take him to the hospital, he piteously pleads with them to take along a rosebush he has won in a lottery.

Ultimately, the court sends Georgie to a school run by Sister Mary Angela. His one possession is temporarily placed under his window, where it "leaned crookedly against the wall, wondering why Georgie was so slow in giving it the bed it needed, in giving it a chance to grow the scarlet roses that the tag tied around it had promised." The kindly nun tries to dissuade Georgie from his decision to plant his bush in the garden across from the school, a flowery sanctuary Mrs. Harper has dedicated to the memory of her dead son and husband. The boy has stubbornly decided that that particular locale is the one perfect spot, and one night he surreptitiously places his beloved bush among the other plantings. When the owner discovers it, she is furious. The woman, feeling the shrine has been desecrated, uproots the greenery and threatens to incinerate the rosebush if the boy dares to repeat that act. In the confrontation, the boy's shirt slips off, revealing his back, which is a mass of "mutilated flesh." Mrs. Harper, horrified at the evidence of such brutality and ashamed of her own excessive reaction, rushes to locate Sister Angela. The two women find the boy, who has collapsed, and take him to bed, where his "fever ran high for five full days and during most of that time he tossed about in delirium, unaware of the need to protect the unhealed wounds on his back."

While the child is recovering, he is visited by Mrs. Harper's father and her son Robin, a developmentally disabled child who has "curly blond hair and blue eyes that somehow looked lost and all alone." As the old man teaches Georgie to master reading and to believe in himself, the boy is able to reach out to Robin with affection and, in turn, begin to teach the child new skills and expand his restricted vocabulary.

One day when Robin is briefly unattended, he heads for the lake to see the ducks. The creatures, which had seemed so lovable when he was with Georgie, now frighten him as they swarm around clamoring for the bread he is holding. "They pushed against him relentlessly, and when he tried to run from them he fell face downward in the water." Georgie is devastated at the loss of someone he has come to regard as a brother. During the night after the funeral, he uproots his rosebush, places it in a wheelbarrow, and walks with it three miles to the cemetery, where be begins to replant it on the child's grave. He is interrupted by Mrs. Harper, who helps him with this painful chore. In an emotional reconciliation, Georgie pathetically inquires: "Did you born me a long time ago and I forgot?" The bereaved woman cups his face and answers: "I didn't 'born' you, but you're mine."

Analysis. Hunt has written a very sentimental story about a battered child who is redeemed by love: love he receives from selfless, caring adults and love he is able to give to another. Many of Georgie's external scars are permanent, but the internal ones, although potentially more devastating, heal. Robin is much adored by his family, and his modest abilities flourish under the attentions of another child. The story consists of a sequence of unlikely events and is populated by characters who are either saintlike in their goodness or completely villainous. Nevertheless, it will be vastly enjoyed by readers who relish a good cry.

Hunt, Irene. *William: A Novel.* New York: Scribner's, 1977. 188 pp.
Reading Level: MC/YA
Disability: Visual Impairment, Special Health Problems

Mrs. Saunders has a debilitating illness that diminishes her ability to provide adequate care for William and her other two children. A teenage orphan comes to live in the temporarily empty house next door to the black family, and the eight-year-old boy, in a gesture of neighborliness, takes her a newborn puppy. Delighted with her present, Sarah engages the youngster in conversation, confirming the gossip that she is pregnant and adding that she will give the baby away when it arrives. However, a hurricane drenching the Florida coast prevents her from getting to the hospital when the baby is due. Elizabeth is born at home, and Sarah realizes she cannot part with her infant daughter. Since the Saunders' house has been badly damaged, they move in with the young mother. Soon after, Mrs. Saunders dies, leaving Amy, William, and Carla, who is blind, in the care of their adolescent neighbor. Carla

> knew when it was daylight or when the lamps were turned on at night. She could see the movement of an arm being lifted and lowered; she could see that a refrigerator was big and a step stool small. But let William and Amy sit side by side without speaking and Carla could not tell one from the other.

To William's relief, Sarah, with much help from the community, manages their finances, exchanging one of her paintings for a car so the family can have transportation. Amy, the oldest, becomes restive under the supervision of one who is only slightly older than herself. William worries that his sister's wildness will precipitate intervention by the authorities and threaten his fragile security. The headstrong girl dates someone with an unsavory reputation, gets drunk, and leaves home following a bitter argument with Sarah.

After a neighborly physician consults with a reknowned pediatric ophthalmologist about Carla's cataracts, he offers to arrange for an operation and organize a campaign to raise the funds needed for travel and other expenses. To everyone's relief, the surgery is successful: "There was a difference in Carla. William noticed it immediately. It was not just the unfamiliar glasses or the brown eyes that glowed with life—it was something joyous about her as if a caged little girl had lately been set free."

In an emotional reunion, Sarah relents, and Amy returns to the bosom of her family. With William's ambivalent approval, Sarah leaves to study art for a brief time in Chicago while the children are cared for by Amy, her new husband, and their mother's old friend, who has returned to reoccupy the house where they all had been staying.

Analysis. This homey little story is set in rural Florida, where no one in the community shows the slightest concern over the presence of a racially mixed family headed by an unmarried adolescent mother! Other components to the narrative are equally unlikely: William's mother's death, although handled with great sensitivity, is remarkably untraumatizing for her children; Carla is unbelievably compliant and docile, free of frustration or conflict; Sarah forgoes any personal ambitions, devoting herself entirely to the care of her infant daughter and three other children whom she has known for less than a year. Only Amy shows any rebelliousness, but she quickly reforms and marries a steady, reliable young man who will clearly keep her on the right path. Although pleasant reading, this work is far too idealized to be regarded as an accurate presentation of the people or the problems it considers.

Hurmence, Belinda. *Tough Tiffany*. New York: Doubleday, 1980. 166 pp. Reading Level: MC/YA
Disability: orthopedic impairment

Tiffany Cox, the youngest of six children, is "a gangling young girl with rather large ears and beautifully plaited corn rows." The news that her 15-year-old sister is pregnant throws the family into an uproar. Tiff persuades Dawn to accompany her to Aunt Sister's home, where their loving relative provides comfort and a refuge for the troubled older girl. The foster mother proposes that Dawn visit her daily and help with the children in her care so that when her own infant arrives she will have some experience. Joe, the baby's father, has accepted responsibility for the costs of the pregnancy and is eager to offer whatever support he can.

At a family reunion, Tiffany sees her cousins, including Tiny, who "had a withered arm with a twisted hand, and limp ribbony fingers. When other cousins younger than she were already walking, she sat silent in her stroller. Her brother, Kenneth, looked after her. Otherwise she was so quiet nobody paid her much attention." Tiffany observes Kenneth "fold Tiny's little lame hand in his" and "with a thrill of revulsion, Tiff imagined those ribbony fingers touching her own." Their cantankerous granny is angered by Tiny's poor table manners and wraps her switch around the offender's legs. Before she can do any harm, Kenneth rescues his sister and races out of sight with her. Later Tiffany joins them in a nearby woods and is there to pull Tiny out of the stream into which she had tumbled. "Tiff took her boneless fingers in her hand. . . . This morning she had shuddered to think of those queer, ribbony fingers touching hers. What had she feared? The limp little hand was warm, trusting. Tiff encircled her protectively, and together they floated back to the sunny side." While the out-of-town visitors remain, Tiff is told to stay with Granny. Unhappy at this arrangement at first, the youngster develops an affection for the irascible old woman. When Tiffany is able to help her relative locate money she had secreted, then persuades her to place her savings in a local bank, Granny is grateful and even approving of her grandchild. The old woman's gift of a check is just in time to keep the furniture company from repossessing the children's beds and dressers.

Tiffany is home alone with Dawn when her sister's labor begins. The frantic child spots a scout car down the street and convinces the policeman to take them to the hospital. In appreciation for her help, Dawn names the infant "Tiffany" and allows her to select a middle name for her new niece as well. When all the excitement dies down, the youngster muses: "You were always running up against new situations that nobody told you how to handle, and something always happened, you could always figure a way."

Analysis. In *Tough Tiffany*, the bright, resourceful, and compassionate heroine has a full and satisfying life despite the poverty in which she lives. Her relationship with Tiny, in which her initial aversion is replaced by a protective affection, is replicated in her association with Kenneth and Granny and reveals her increasing maturity. Of special note is the role of guardian that Kenneth assumes toward his sister. It is not clear whether Tiny's name is one that was given at birth, is a nickname, or is attached to her because of her developmental problem. Hurmence has written a pleasant, homey little story about an aspect of rural American life inadequately represented in juvenile literature.

Hutchins, Pat. *One-Eyed Jake.* Illus. by author. New York: Greenwillow, 1979. unp. Reading Level: YC
Disability: Visual Impairment

A wicked one-eyed pirate captain steals from the many ships he intercepts on the high seas. Although his own vessel is dangerously overloaded, he still craves more plunder. Finally his ship sinks under the weight of his stolen treasure and as a direct result of his own insatiable greed.

Analysis. The title character's missing eye, along with his "horrible face," are part of the costuming that marks his villainy. The story is obvious and frivolous, and the use of the pirate's eye patch is a tired, unimaginative device.

Jacobs, Dee. *Laura's Gift.* Illus. by Kris Karlsson. Portland, Oreg.: Oriel, 1980. 58 pp. Reading Level: MC
Disability: Orthopedic Impairment

Thirteen-year-old twins Catherine and Laura reluctantly attend St. Hilda's so that Laura, in a wheelchair due to muscular dystrophy, can avoid the insurmountable steps at the local public junior high. Both girls come down with a virus, but since the consequences of a respiratory infection can be fatal for Laura, she remains in the hospital for observation while her sister is permitted to recuperate at home. Her family is distraught when they learn that Laura has pneumonia. Cath is particularly irritable, neglecting schoolwork, canceling piano lessons, and being aggressively uncooperative. Her teacher speaks with her, articulating Cath's unspoken fear that her sister might die. The teacher adds that Laura has already learned the value of self-discipline, a quality notably lacking in her twin. When Cath hears from her parents that her sister will recover, she is profoundly relieved and for the first time asks the questions that have been troubling her: "Why does Laura have to have dystrophy? Why is it Laura who has to be in a wheelchair?" Her father responds that no one has the answers to such questions, but he points out that Laura has "dealt with [her] anger and lives every day to its fullest," even accepting the possibility of her death "as something that happens." Comforted by the news from the hospital and her father's explanations, Cath begins to put together the disparate strands of her own life.

Analysis. The descriptive language, dialogue, tone, content, and lack of thematic subtlety make this brief novel seem anachronistic. Although Laura has a very serious disorder, the proposition that her care is so demanding that her mother must live a life of denial ("The extra duties required of her because of Laura's handicap left her little time to concern herself with fashion") is an extravagant overstatement. The best parts of this book are the scenes in which the girls counter the pitying remarks and behaviors of a stranger and the presentation of the disabled child's interest in morbid topics (such as Sarah Bernhardt's practice of sleeping in a coffin, Felix Mendelssohn's untimely death and the despair felt by his friend Schumann, and St. Hilda's sickness and canonization) as a means of coping with her own mortality. Unfortunately, illustrations are muddy, depressing, and completely lacking in interest.

Johnston, Norma. *A Striving After Wind.* New York: Atheneum, 1976. 250 pp. Reading Level: MA
Disability: Intellectual Impairment, Emotional Dysfunction

Bedelia Vandever has not spoken since the night two drunken men raped her, but "even before that she spoke only in rhyme. 'Dummy!' the Culhaine boys always mocked her, but she's not stupid, only—different—ever since she fell from a horse when she was two." Although unable to use words, the young woman communicates with gestures to her devoted family.

There are two romantic interests in her sister Bridget's life: Clu, the younger, thoughtful, gentle brother of the brutes who attacked Bedelia; and an aging thespian who takes refuge in a hut in the nearby woods. Using the pseudonym of Mr. Odysseus, the actor has temporarily become a recluse while examining his life goals. He and Bridget become increasingly attracted to each other, provide mutual support, but ultimately part before their relationship escalates beyond what the proprieties of 1861 would permit.

Bedelia's pregnancy can no longer be concealed, but her parents will not allow her to be questioned about the identity of the child's father. She is therefore excluded from church rites despite the vigorous objections of her socially prominent family. A soldier, recuperating from war wounds, had been a visitor in the Vandever home. Romantically drawn to Bedelia, he proposes to marry her and adopt her yet unborn infant, but the man dies before the propriety and wisdom of such a solution can be determined. When Bedelia finally gives birth after a difficult delivery, the physician insists that no one interfere with the new mother's attempt to indicate the baby's name. With great effort, she is able to pronounce the name of her fallen love, the very name she wants her child to carry. All are overjoyed at this restoration of her speech, but their happiness is shattered by the censorious attitude of their congregation. The new mother does not understand the church's demand for her repentance, a condition that must be met if the baby is to be baptized. Innocently, she protests: "Yes I do bad things. . . . Everybody do. I not ashamed, stand up and say I sorry. Try be better. It right. For baby." This announcement, along with her parents' solemn avowal that the father is not a congregant, is acceptable to the church elders.

When Clu's two brothers, intoxicated again, attack the Vandevers' housekeeper, Indian John, her boyfriend intervenes and in the struggle kills one of the villains. Fearing that an innocent could be punished if the truth were known, Clu contrives another account, which attributes the death to a fight between siblings. In the meantime, his surviving brother is advised, when he sobers up, to hasten away from the scene of the fatal accident. Although the experience is a shattering one for Clu, Bridget, having drawn the necessary wisdom and steadfastness from her encounters with Mr. Odysseus, gives her friend the emotional support he needs. Having just learned of her daughter's relationship with the older man, Mrs. Vandever demands that it be terminated. Reluctantly, Bridget bows to convention and her mother's command. In their farewell meeting, Mr. Odysseus explains to Bridget that their friendship has helped them both, but he must now answer the insistent call of his muse and move on.

Analysis. This historical romance combines a seemingly endless series of clichés, a stock plot, impossible characters, and grandiose declamations masquerading as dialogue. When Mrs. Vandever confronts her daughter, she cries out: "Don't speak to me of loneliness . . . . Loneliness is part of the human condition. You'll always be lonely, unless you're willing to give up thinking and feeling and asking questions and reaching for the farther star." The impaired woman's characterization is equally unrestrained: Bedelia's disability is romanticized and her skills magnified to outrageous proportions: "In some ways she's stronger than the rest of us put together. . . . Bedelia my sister had taught me the language of those who cannot speak, and I had learned from her too that this silent language went far deeper than words." Another character observes: "Bedelia always does know more than all the rest of us put together," and "She's like a child in so many ways that we don't realize she has a wisdom of her own." This unexpected deduction is certainly not warranted from the artificially constructed dialogue attributed to the disabled young woman. Johnston resurrects a popular, naive mystical connection between impairment and divine purpose: "Persons afflicted like Bedelia are thought to have been given gifts of divination by the gods." Yet, in another context, a church representative, referring to her status as a "sinner" and an impaired person, asserts, "[Her] mental and emotional condition rendered her unfit to live in society in the ordinary way." The pretentious discussions of philosophical matters are as vacuous as the theme that great good—a new life and the restoration of speech—can come from seeming disaster, the rape and traumatizing of the innocent and vulnerable woman.

Johnston, Norma. *The Swallow's Song*. New York: Atheneum, 1978. 192 pp. Reading Level: YA
Disability: neurological impairment

Allison Standish has mixed feelings about spending the summer at her grandmother's home in a small waterfront town in New Jersey. She had hoped that her sixteenth birthday would usher in a glorious new life, but her parents' concerns about her grandmother's senility dampen prospects for a carefree future. While the elderly woman's rationality deteriorates, Allison watches helplessly as her family is torn asunder. Her life seems drab and lackluster so when she meets the gay, wealthy, and worldly Farradays she is dazzled by their glittering lifestyle, seemingly so much more desirable than her own. Forced by events to abandon her naiveté, the adolescent discovers that their riches conceal a profusion of vices: adultery, alcoholism, drug indulgence, and unrestrained contentiousness. The innocent's lingering illusions collapse when her brother and her perfidious boyfriend, Dirk Farraday, are arrested. The spoiled scion of the affluent clan buys his way out of his predicament, unconscionably leaving his companion to accept both the blame and the consequences of their joint act. Ultimately, her brother is released from incarceration, tensions are resolved, and responsibility for the matriarch's care is freely accepted by the Standish family, newly cognizant of their familial obligation.

> "Summer's almost over, and what are we going to do with Gran?"
>
> "Bring her home with us, of course," Dad said matter-of-factly.
>
> Naturally. We'd really known we'd have to do that, all along. It wouldn't be easy, of course, but then neither had this summer, and we had survived. And in a strange sort of way, it might actually be nice having Sara Dale [the grandmother] around.

Analysis. The portrayal of the old woman, her inconsistencies, her faulty sense of time and place, and her erratic behavior is the only credible component of this insipid teenage romance. Although the grandmother has moments of relative lucidity, most of the time she acts as though she were a young child, inappropriate behavior that is reinforced when her family addresses her by her childhood name. The family's selfless assumption of her care is less convincing. The literary function served by this character is to precipitate crisis, reveal aspects of the other characters' personalities as they interact with her, and structure a resolution permitting the family's reintegration. *The Swallow's Song*, with its use of Hollywood names, its characters with plastic emotions, and its jerry-built plot, is an example of supermarket fiction.

Jones, Adrienne. *The Beckoner.* New York: Harper & Row, 1980. 243 pp. Reading Level: MA
Disability: Emotional Dysfunction, orthopedic impairment

Determined and extraordinarily self-reliant, Kate prefers using her own resources rather than the ministrations of a psychiatrist to cope with the emotional turmoil she is currently experiencing. Since her adored father deserted his wife and children, she has reluctantly assumed the role of head of the family, striving to hold them all together, a task her ineffectual but manipulative mother sidesteps. After Kate's boyfriend leaves her, critical of the time and energy she devotes to her family, the young woman becomes alienated and depressed, loses weight, is unable to concentrate, and suffers night terrors and insomnia. Urgently needing relief from her responsibilities, she returns to a place in Oregon she had once visited with her father. There they had spent an idyllic interlude during which she recovered from her grief over her grandmother's death.

On her first walk along the coast, she sees a mysterious, compelling figure who seems to beckon her to return to the sea with him. She reports a drowning, but an investigation fails to turn up evidence of anyone missing. To her astonishment, Kate learns that her footloose father had purchased land in the region and had begun to develop a prosperous farm before he mysteriously vanished again. This discovery galvanizes her energies, and the city-bred woman moves into his abandoned home and begins to restore the land and orchards. She notifies her family of this change in her plans, announcing that she must address her own needs at this time. She is assisted by Bill, a friendly and concerned neighbor, who lends her equipment, moral support, and a guard dog to protect her from some local rowdies who have vandalized the property and threatened her. Bill's disability, the loss of his leg in Vietnam, where he served as a conscientious objector in the medical corps, has made him a local outcast since he had been an outspoken critic of U.S. involvement in Southeast Asia.

Hard work and freedom from pressure begin to revivify Kate, and Bill becomes convinced that she is who she claims to be, the intended heir to her father's property. Kate is finally able to sort out her highly ambivalent feelings about her father, set aside her childhood fantasies and resentments, and accept him despite his faults, knowing that he cared dearly for her. She is determined to make a new life for herself, more compatible with her hopes and abilities, in this setting. It seems likely that she and Bill will become more than just friends.

Analysis. The central character's need to feel loved is given substance in the hallucinatory figure who resembles both her father and a character from her grandmother's tales who beckons those who are living to join their dead relatives. The author proposes some old-fashioned therapy for her overworked and emotionally drained heroine: temporary removal from the reminders of her distress, a break in her unsatisfying routine, and the start of a new venture characterized by contact with nature and physically hard but psychologically gratifying work. Because Kate's depression is relatively mild and her will so strong, she is soon able to achieve a sense of self. The problems of coping with a prosthetic leg are minimized, and the disabled veteran is portrayed as a strong, attractive figure. Their love is natural, unforced, and inevitable in this upbeat adolescent romance.

Jones, Rebecca C. *Angie and Me.* New York: Macmillan, 1981. 113 pp. Reading Level: MC
Disability: Special Health Problems

In recent weeks, Jenna's knees have become swollen and walking has become very painful; a decision is made to hospitalize her for treatment of what is diagnosed as juvenile rheumatoid arthritis. Her terminally ill roommate, Angie, adopts the new patient, acting as advisor, commentator, interpreter of hospital routines, canny student of staff and patient psychology, and general forecaster of medical prognoses. After Jenna's friends visit, Angie advises that their expressions of concern indicate pity, and she cautions Jenna against permitting anyone to display such an attitude. Angie disdains any efforts to gloss over the seriousness of her own condition or to pretend that she will improve. She is fully aware of her own imminent death and properly interprets the head nurse's increased tolerance of her provocative behavior as a bad sign. Nevertheless, the self-possessed, plucky girl reveals her fear of dying when she discusses with Jenna the prospects of an afterlife. As Angie's health precipitously worsens, she is at first confined to bed, then moved to a private room where, soon thereafter, she dies. Jenna, anguished at the loss of a treasured friend, is comforted in her grief by the staff who share her sorrow.

Analysis. Angie and Me provides an abbreviated, but honest look at juvenile rheumatoid arthritis, although the emphasis is on the psychological rather than the physical aspects of this condition. Learning to adapt to hospitalization, to severely reduced functioning, and to the many options hospitalized youngsters select to deal with their medical problems—withdrawal, aggressiveness, passivity—are all empathically explored. Also examined are the ways patients deal with confinement and boredom. The writer reveals a sensitivity to the special problems of teenagers who must cope with demeaning and privacy-invading medical routines at a time when they are most vulnerable to such humiliations. Further, Jones provides a picture of a wide spectrum of reactions to illnesses demonstrated by various relatives of the patients. Although some of the vignettes featuring Jenna's mother reduce her to a caricature, the language and actions of the professionals and patients and the latters' responses to hospitalization all ring true. An especially interesting and unusual aspect of this work concerns how doctors, nurses, and parents, with all good intention, may lie to and cozen children about the nature, progress, or severity of their ailments. Certain literary deficiencies—uneven writing and instances of unconvincing dialogue—detract from the overall quality of the story.

Josephs, Rebecca. *Early Disorder.* New York: Farrar, Straus & Giroux, 1980. 186 pp. Reading Level: YA/MA
Disability: Emotional Dysfunction

Fifteen-year-old Willa Rahv, the middle child of cultured, well-to-do, high-achieving parents, is self-absorbed, indecisive, and unassertive. Restless and discontented, she interrupts a family vacation on

Long Island to return home to New York City, using a nonexistent New Year's party as an excuse. Instead of making the evening a celebration, she and her only friend, Ellen, drink to excess and use the occasion to ventilate their bitterness. Rather than being cathartic, their conversation intensifies their unhappiness, and subsequently Ellen tries to kill herself.

Although she had dieted casually in the past, Willa now becomes fanatically dedicated to the idea of becoming thinner, limiting her food intake drastically while craftily concealing her new regimen from her parents. A visit to her pediatrician reveals a precipitous decline in weight, which he correctly attributes to anorexia nervosa, but despite his warnings, the troubled adolescent adamantly refuses to eat enough to maintain her precarious health. Obsessed with food and more narcissistic than ever, Willa discovers that her self-starvation is a powerful tool by which she can control her family: they docilely accept her abuse and temper tantrums and bow to her whims in a futile effort to coax her to accept nourishment. After an unproductive visit to one psychiatrist, she begins sessions with a different therapist, to whom she can relate. He interprets her behavior as a tactic by which she releases her accumulated anger and resentment. He tries to help her drop the suffocating role she used to play of the perfect tractable daughter, discard the self-destructive script she is now using, and develop instead a viable and unique identity. Willa reflects: "I've been denied my inalienable right to unhappiness. Been cheated of my right to fight. They never heard me. They never heard what I didn't say. Dr. Jordan says that it's necessary to express one's conflicts. . . . But I'm not in the habit of fighting."

Despite garnering some insights into her situation, the now emaciated teenager becomes increasingly hysterical, erratic in her desires, and punitive toward her parents, particularly toward her mother. An invitation from her gentle, beloved French teacher to spend the summer in Provence seems to offer a desperately needed refuge from the despair that engulfs her. Her psychiatrist withholds permission until she promises to add enough pounds to her fragile frame to ensure her survival. The adolescent girl reviews the distressing elements in her existence, considers her options, vacillates, reconsiders, and then moves haltingly toward an affirmation of life.

Analysis. The classical elements of a typical anorexic case history are all evident here, but the story never seems more than an attempt to breathe life into a clinical report. Told from the perspective of the dysfunctional girl, her total self-preoccupation soon becomes tedious as redundant episodes accumulate and ever more refined accounts of her increasingly narrow world are detailed.

Judd, Denis. *Return to Treasure Island.* New York: St. Martin's, 1978. 209 pp. Reading Level: YA/MA
Disability: Orthopedic Impairment; also speech impairment

Having heard the tale from Long John Silver's own lips, Jim, now Dr. James Hawkins, has "sought to illuminate the events that occurred after he quit the *Hispaniola* on the homeward run . . . how Long John returned to that accursed island where lay the rest of Flint's ill-gotten treasure and what happened to him thereafter." Escaping from the *Hispaniola* through guile and treachery, Silver rejoins his faithful wife on a plantation in Granada. A slave revolt, fueled by the dispossessed French, leaves his wife dead, his home burned, and him imprisoned on the mainland. Released in a prisoner exchange, the pirate leaves for Boston, determined to assemble a crew and locate the treasure that has eluded him for years. Pretending to colonialist sympathies, Silver takes part in the Boston Tea Party, but steals a ship that he outfits with provisions, mans it with a gang of ruffians, then sets sail for Kidd Island. The adventurers discover the bars of silver and the elaborately decorated weapons that made up Flint's trove, load their bounty on board, then head exultantly for New York harbor, but most of his men are killed when a British man-of-war intercepts their vessel, and Long John and the other survivors are locked below decks. After inciting a mutiny, Black Dog, Silver's old crony, frees the prisoners, who seize control of the ship. They set adrift its captain, Horatio Nelson, then sail for Savannah harbor. There the bars are sold to Colonel Oglethorpe, who betrays the pirates, confiscating their ship and its treasure in the name of the patriots and throwing Silver and his cohorts into prison once again. However, the brigands are freed as the British approach, and they travel north on the trail of their booty.

The indefatigable Silver is received by General Howe's lisping aide-de-camp and given provisions that they take to Valley Forge as a cover for a pretended alliance with the colonial rebels. There the pirate discovers the ingots in Washington's quarters, but is able to steal only a handful, barely escaping with his life when a sentry becomes suspicious. From there the outlaw flees to Philadelphia, only to be betrayed by his mistress, who makes off with the bulk of his ill-gotten fortune. He and Isaiah Meek, the last of his companions to survive these adventures, journey circuitously to New Brunswick, where his investment in land at last yields him great wealth. Silver's final journey is to England, where the physician attends him, learns his story, and writes it down for all to know.

Analysis. This tale of derring-do outrageously and amusingly interweaves the adventures of the infamous pirate, Long John Silver, with historical figures and events. Its plot consists of a series of wild encounters, narrow escapes, and bloody battles—all in keeping with the character of the curmudgeonly old brigand. The disability of the villainous hero is treated with surprising realism: he has difficulty riding a horse since he cannot grip the creature's body with two legs, his crutch sinks into soft ground, preventing him from crossing parts of Kidd Island, and he is defeated in a fight when his crutch is knocked out from under his arm. Unlike most sequels, *Return to Treasure Island* is a witty, satisfying, tongue-in-cheek romp.

Kelley, Salley. *Trouble with Explosives*. Scarsdale, N.Y.: Bradbury, 1976. 117 pp. Reading Level: MC
Disability: Speech Impairment, emotional dysfunction

Because he is a "rising young executive," Mr. Banks and his family have never lived for long in any one community. His daughter Polly has seen several psychiatrists, but it is not until they move to Atlanta and she meets Dr. Maxie that the girl is able to talk about things that are important to her and gain some control over her stuttering. After they are settled in their new home, Mrs. Banks enrolls her daughter in a private school. She explains the 11-year-old's speech problem to the principal, who, despite her apparent understanding, assigns the new student to a class taught by the tyrannical Miss Patterson. When Polly is asked her name, she begins to stutter badly but is saved from further embarrassment when Sis Hawkins deliberately causes a disturbance, deflecting attention from the newcomer's distress. Polly considers herself a "freak," an image reinforced on the playground when she and the other outsiders are the last ones chosen for teams. However, her critical contribution to the kickball game is acknowledged as Sis bluntly comments: " 'Your mouth doesn't work worth a plugged nickel, . . . But your foot is fine.' 'D . . . D . . . D . . . Darn right,' I said. 'D . . . D . . . D . . . Darn right,' she mocked me. For some reason I laughed." As their friendship grows, Sis becomes mildly envious of Polly's ordered and conventional life, while Polly is attracted to the colorful Sis Hawkins and her casual, unorthodox lifestyle. Once Polly sits in on a women's awareness group with her friend and hears an exconvict's wife talk about how prisoners used Gandhi-like methods to subvert the terror tactics of a brutal prison guard.

When Polly is called upon to lead the Pledge of Allegiance, she becomes so nervous that her speech is unintelligible. Angry at the humiliation she sees her friend experiencing, Sis yells for the class to stop, pushes over the flags, and causes their sadistic teacher to become infuriated over this reaction. Miss Patterson seizes on this provocation to assert her authority and assigns the writing of the Pledge 700 times to her rebellious student. Aghast at the unfairness of the punishment visited on her friend, Polly describes the incident to her parents, who declare their outrage. Mr. Banks starts to phone the offending teacher but is stopped by his daughter, who convinces him that both the problem and its solution belong to the two girls. Sis, emulating the passive resistance model of the prisoners, accepts the unfair assignment and begins the laborious process of copying the oath. Incensed at the prospect of being bested by her despised student, Miss Patterson tears up the pages on which the diligent child had completed over 200 copies of the Pledge. Polly is galvanized into action by this latest abuse of her friend and organizes the other members of the class into planning some retaliation. Ignoring all other work, refusing all pleas to stop and threats of reprisals, each child begins to copy the Pledge. The unnerved woman, realizing she has been outmaneuvered and has lost face, is unable to continue teaching. Sis and Polly regret the obvious pain their former nemesis is experiencing and, going to the office where she now works, generously compliment her on her instructional skills and give her the names of several psychiatrists. The young heroine's speech problem has nearly vanished. She reflects: "Dr. Maxie taught me a lot. I know now when I stutter it means either I'm not feeling too good about myself or I am afraid to speak up."

Analysis. The dialogue is polished, clever, and witty in this fast-moving, coming-of-psychological-age novel. The contemporary characters are well developed, although the brevity of the narrative forces some stereotyping and the conclusion is excessively neat. Common childhood perceptions that "different" means "deviant" are explored by the author, whose heroines conclude that each person is unique in some ways and understanding, not exclusion, is the more mature approach. The author's view that the heroine's speech problem derives from unexamined fears and feelings of inadequacy is manifested as she has her character's growth in maturity and control over her life parallel a reduction in her stuttering. Although the title is a catchy one, the use of the term *explosives* rather than *plosives* echoes a common lay error that the author never corrects.

Kemp, Gene. *The Turbulent Term of Tyke Tiler.* Illus. by Carolyn Dinan. London: Faber & Faber, 1977. 118 pp. Reading Level: MC
Disability: Speech Impairment; also intellectual impairment

Tyke has been Danny's friend, protector, and personal translator of his incomprehensible speech for as long as she can remember. The boy is an inveterate mischief maker whose innocent, waiflike appearance invites his victims to be transformed into his champions. As Tyke, who is frequently blamed for Danny's misdeeds, observes: "All the people who come to see him at school to give him tests, the deaf lady, the talk lady, the shrinko chap, like him and take more trouble with him than anyone else. 'He looks bright (they say). There must be a block.' "

Tyke is aghast when she learns Danny has swiped a ten-pound note from a teacher's purse. Since he cannot safely return it, she takes charge, hiding the money until she can anonymously restore it to its rightful owner. When the money is discovered by chance, the headmaster concludes that Tyke must be involved since she is the only student athletic enough to have achieved entry to the attic hiding place. Using his friend as an interpreter, Danny admits his role in the theft, also revealing that the riot during morning assembly was caused when he let his mouse loose.

Tyke overhears a discussion among the faculty concerning the advisability of transferring Danny to a school "where they have facilities to deal with children of that type." Some of the staff argue for retention, claiming that Danny should remain near Tyke, the only stable influence in the boy's chaotic life. Both sides agree to be guided in their decision by the results of the upcoming annual examination. Angry at what she considers cavalier treatment of her friend and afraid the boy would be unable to manage without her, Tyke brazenly steals a copy of the test. She drills her reluctant protégé, cajoling, bribing, and threatening him into cramming his head as full of information as his restless and impatient personality allows. As a result of her efforts, Danny will continue at the neighborhood school, but Tyke scores so high that she is now eligible for a special facility for gifted youngsters. Angry and frustrated, Tyke impulsively climbs to the roof of their school and rings the old bell in the tower, a feat previously recorded in a book of local history as accomplished once before by an ancestor of the impetuous child. The vibrations are damaging to the old structure; the tower collapses, sending Tyke crashing to the ground. She is hospitalized with broken bones, bruises, and a concussion, injuries that only temporarily slow her down.

Analysis. Danny is a slow-learning child whose home life has inhibited intellectual development. His incomprehensible speech, which appears to consist mostly of substitutions, such as "Dyke dit dit, dedase de ded di did dit," seems to be a greater source of frustration to others than to him. The youngster is lovable, willful, loyal, immature, and stubborn. Although some students see him as a deviant: "It was probably him as he's not right in the head, a brick short of a load . . . barmy, nutty as a fruitcake, round the twist," others vigorously defend him. He has been tested and seen by a host of professionals, but no description of his therapy is included. The story is lighthearted, playful, and amusing, although some of the language and allusions may be missed by American readers.

Kennedy, Richard. *The Dark Princess.* Illus. by Donna Diamond. New York: Holiday House, 1978. unp. Reading Level: MC
Disability: Visual Impairment

Although the beautiful princess grows lovelier with each passing year, her ability to see diminishes until, while still a young woman, she becomes totally blind. The court physician, pretending to a competence he does not have, tells her royal parents that their daughter's vision loss is only temporary. She has many admirers, but none dares look directly at her: It is safe to observe her only through colored glass, for to do otherwise would cause immediate blindness to the viewer. When suitors declare their love, she insists they gaze upon her, but all fearfully decline. The princess interprets their refusals as evidence that their protestations of love are merely empty words.

One day the melancholy young woman sets out for a picnic by the sea. The court fool, who had already arrived at her chosen spot, warns the princess of a dangerous precipice nearby. As they converse, the jester seizes this moment of intimacy to inquire why she never laughs at his antics. She then dares him to make her laugh, to which he replies: " 'I will do it with words alone. Be ready to laugh, now, for here it is that will amuse you greatly, and only three words will do it.' He took a double gulp of wine and then said, 'I love you.' " The princess bitterly denies that love exists, declaring that he has confused admiration of her beauty with feelings of love. When he protests, she informs him that not one of her suitors has been willing to sacrifice his sight to gain her hand. She has therefore concluded that love is an illusion and she is doomed to a life of emptiness and sadness. The jester avers that he would eagerly give up his vision if it would restore her faith in love. He takes the protective colored glass from his eyes and places it in her hand. Now blind, the young man staggers over the edge of the cliff, falling into the waters below. Distressed, the princess dives after him. The two touch briefly before they drown, achieving, through this desperate act, eternal life.

Analysis. In this murky tale of unrealized metaphors and spurious associations, the author demonstrates some highly questionable attitudes about both blindness and love. Although apparently intending to grapple with ideas of character, sacrifice, illusion, and selfless devotion, the assumptions are so baseless, the connections so tenuous, and the conclusions so unwarranted that the work invites dismissal. Diamond's illustrations are far more successful than Kennedy's words in evoking a mythic world of beauty and darkness.

Kent, Deborah. *Belonging.* New York: Dial, 1978. 200 pp. Reading
Level: YA
Disability: Visual Impairment, Emotional Dysfunction

After much discussion, her parents reluctantly agree to their blind
daughter's entry into her first mainstreamed environment. Although
strong-willed and seemingly self-confident, Meg privately experiences
moments of trepidation about enrolling in the local high school. She
yearns to be treated like other teenagers and fantasizes about her ready
acceptance into the social life of the school. Instead, the teenager finds
pity, exaggerated concern, appalling ignorance about her disability,
and, fortunately, two genuine offers of friendship. Lindy, a loner, and
Keith, an opera buff whose spontaneous renditions of arias at odd
moments embarrass the newcomer, become her loyal companions.
Miss Kellogg, Meg's favorite teacher, pushes her students to stretch
their minds, but the educator's increasing paranoia interferes with her
work and causes her supporters considerable anxiety. The woman and
the three adolescents plan to attend a performance of the opera, but at
the last minute Meg is invited to a party and deserts her friends. The
longed-for event is a disaster. She is disappointed at the shallowness of
the crowd, angry at their insensitivity and exploitation of her, and
made uncomfortable by the presence of alcohol and marijuana. Now
more appreciative of her real friends, she joins them in protesting the
victimization of Miss Kellogg by the other pupils and the principal. The
stinging editorial they compose results in their suspension, a punishment Meg insists on sharing with her sighted friends. Although she
had decided to transfer to a special school for blind students at the end
of the semester, Meg changes her mind, determined to succeed in this
integrated setting.

Analysis. The author confronts several serious subjects: the difficulties of a disabled youngster in adjusting in a mainstreamed environment, the problem of maintaining individuality and integrity despite
pressure to conform and compromise, and the dilemma of a gifted
teacher whose emotional disorders interfere with professional demands. The characters, however, are too dimensionless to serve as
vehicles for the expression of complex issues, events are too manipulated to be credible, and the statement and resolution of problems are
too simplistic. Miss Kellogg's emotional instability is of long standing.
She has lost credibility with students and consequently her ability to
manage a class; she is delusional, perceiving all events as the result of a
campaign of persecution. To interpret her dismissal as the act of a
repressive administration is ridiculous. Meg's difficulties seem to arise
almost exclusively from the attitude of others toward her blindness.

Although this is of overwhelming importance, the implication that the first blind student in a totally unprepared and unadapted setting would not experience severe problems is excessively optimistic.

Kerr, M. E. (pseud. for Marijane Meaker). *Gentlehands*. New York: Harper & Row, 1978. 183 pp. Reading Level: YA/MA
Disability: auditory impairment

Buddy Boyle lives in an area that draws the very rich each summer. The behavior of Skye, one of the regular seasonal visitors, the other Penningtons, and their friends demonstrates to Buddy the inadequacies of his own gauche and lower-class values. The Penningtons' world of travel and high culture, which they take for granted, dazzles the youth. On their first date, Buddy takes Skye to visit his grandfather, Frank Trenker, a recluse whom his mother had never known as a child and toward whom she harbors deep resentments. But Trenker is as cultured and suave as Skye's social crowd; he is as knowledgeable as they about classical music, art, literature, fine foods and wine, and the other accoutrements of the "good life." Buddy's family is furious about his associations with Skye and with his grandfather. His parents sense his feelings that the lifestyle of his new companions is more valuable than their own. After an especially bitter confrontation, the adolescent leaves home to stay with his grandfather, whom he wishes to emulate.

One of the current visitors at the Penningtons' is Nick De Lucca, a journalist who is hearing impaired. His cousin died in the concentration camp at Auschwitz, and he is tracing rumors that the man responsible for her death—"Gentlehands," as he is called—is living somewhere in the community. De Lucca's investigation leads him to believe that Trenker is the notorious Gentlehands. The writer's evidence and conclusions are printed in newspapers, and the contents are widely discussed. Buddy asks his grandfather why he does not confront his accuser and deny even being near the concentration camp. Deliberately misleading the boy, Trenker responds: "A man who listens because he wants to hear that he is right, cannot hear that he is wrong. . . . Perhaps that's why Mr. De Lucca needs his hearing aid."

Trenker becomes the object of much abuse: he receives hate letters and angry phone calls; his dog is deliberately killed. When the number of such incidents increases, the old man insists that Buddy stay away from him. Later, Trenker sends a note to his grandson confessing that he was, indeed, the Nazi who committed those deeds, but he denies any connection with his former identity! Devastated by the horror of this assertion and the perfidy of the man he had so admired, Buddy gives the immigration authorities information about his grandfather's probable destination. A much-chastened youth returns to his family.

Analysis. Kerr has written a complex novel about illusion and reality, the ironic title providing a clue to this theme. The two protagonists typify the conflict. On the one side, Kerr holds up the evil Gentlehands, his vile past concealed by a cloak of culture and respectability. His opponent is the underdog, a member of a minority, a nonconformist, a man with a disability. Several aspects of De Lucca's character are unattractive or ludicrous—his use of the non-smoking cigarette substitute, his toupee, which seems ridiculous even to him. He is a man of honesty, persistence, and great integrity. In the combat, it is De Lucca who overcomes. He pierces Trenker's disguise and brings the remote, untouchable giant to his knees. Kerr embeds some vital lessons into her novel. She reveals the insidiousness of anti-Semitism and demonstrates a connection between its apparent innocuousness in a social situation and its inevitable climax in the Holocaust. Further, she reveals how the innocent or naive can be swayed by superficialities, assuming that individuals are what they seem to be. The context is heavy. The concepts are important and complex. Yet, despite the seriousness of the theme, Kerr takes time for word games. Skye is the perfect choice for the vacuous object of Buddy's infatuation, and the choice of the young hero's Everyman name serves to reinforce Kerr's message. As with many books with a message, there are some incidents that strain believability—Buddy's conversion and subsequent actions, for example. Despite this, *Gentlehands* conceptually and literarily is a masterful and unusual book.

Kerr, M. E. (pseud. for Marijane Meaker). *Little Little*. New York: Harper & Row, 1981. 183 pp. Reading Level: YA/MA
Disability: Orthopedic Impairment

Looking into the mirror, Sydney Cinnamon observes

> an orphaned dwarf . . . three foot four and a half, [with a] hump . . . Legs too short for my body. My face could pass for normal. Light blue eyes, fair teeth except for one that hung like a fang longer than the others, bucking out from the row, sandy-colored hair, good skin . . . but the rest of me was like God'd gone mad when he started making me from the neck down.

His future seems precarious until he is "discovered" by Palmer, the owner of an exterminating company who transforms the talented adolescent into "The Roach," star of a television commercial and popular performer at football games during halftime. When his generous but manipulative boss asks Sydney to make a suprise guest appearance at the eighteenth birthday party of Little Little LaBelle, he readily consents.

Neither wealth nor social position has brought Little Little much happiness. Her affected and ineffectual mother and her domineering but overprotective father have not quite succeeded in suppressing their headstrong daughter, and their home, consequently, is a frequent bat-tleground. Reverend LaBelle, another family combatant, takes his favo-rite granddaughter to a convention of TADs (The American Diminu-tives) and PODs (Parents of Diminutives), where the 3' 3" girl meets others her age, including Dora, The Dancing Lettuce Leaf, star of a television commercial for mayonnaise, with whom she immediately forms a relationship based on mutual contempt.

Reverend LaBelle is promoting an engagement between Little Little and Opportunity Knox, a self-proclaimed preacher who has dubbed himself "Little Lion." Sydney, now infatuated with Little Little, realizes that her fiancé is his old childhood buddy from the orphanage. Even then, Sydney recalls, Opportunity had been a hustler who knew how to maximize his situation.

Our hero is unwilling to abandon his interest in Little Little whom he rightly suspects is lukewarm in her enthusiasm for Opportunity. Despite her parents' hostility—Mr. LaBelle considers Sydney a totally unsuitable companion for his daughter, and Mrs. LaBelle is contemptu-ous of anyone not "p.f.," or perfectly formed—The Roach diligently pursues a friendship with the attractive young woman. Their first date to see the movie "The Incredible Two-Headed Transplant" is uncere-moniously interrupted when Little Little's irate father charges into the theater and bodily removes his daughter. Undaunted, Sydney, dressed as The Roach, makes a dramatic entrance at his would-be girl friend's party. There he learns that, despite his unofficial engagement, Oppor-tunity is ardently attracted to the seductive Dora. Wishing to claim Little Lion herself and at least embarrass Little Little in the bargain, Dora tips the birthday cake over on her hostess and the chagrined Little Little

> tripped over [Sydney's] roach shell and landed on the linoleum, where she sat with pieces of cake, and sticky frosting, and a single candle stuck to her.
>
> "Has anyone got a match?" [Sydney] said, and a waiter handed [him] an oven match.
>
> [He] struck it, reached down and removed the candle from the front of Little Little, wiped the wick clean with [his] fingers and lit it.
>
> "Make a wish," [he] said.

In addition to his work as Roy Roachers in a new commercial, the resourceful Sydney finds local employment as a dragon in a newly opened gambling parlor. Happy at being settled at last, the young man enrolls in the same high school that Little Little attends. Their romance is abruptly terminated, however, when his first essay upstages his girl friend's best effort in English class. Upon closer examination and reflection, Little Little decides that her mother is right: "That tooth of his sticks out too far."

Analysis. In this biting, satiric, outrageous, and hilarious story, Kerr explores how individuals, disabled or otherwise, use denial, exploitation, fantasy, vacuous slogans (Little's better, less is more), self-mockery, and humor to defuse the indignities and insults of the "real world." She contrasts the avoidance approach inherent in the euphemistic language of Mrs. LaBelle and the Diminutives with the aggressive directness of Sydney's friends at Miss Lake's school for disabled orphans where Wheels Potter, Bighead Langhorn, Wires Kaplan, Pill Suchaneck, and Cloud, calling themselves "Mistakes," in a parody of awards ceremonies, hold a "Monsters" competition with prizes for the contestant "Most Likely to Scare Little Children" or "Most Likely to Be Refused Service in a Restaurant." *Little Little* is peppered with attacks on such sacrosanct topics as special education and advocacy groups, as the author examines the different worlds of Little Little and Sydney as seen from their perspective and from the vantage of those of average height, showing how her hero and heroine struggle to cope with the pressures, biases, and occasional goodwill of the absurd universe they inhabit.

King, Clive. *Me and My Millions.* New York: Crowell, 1976. 180 pp.
Reading Level: MC/YA
Disability: Learning Disability; also auditory impairment

Ringo's half-brother, Elvis, involves the younger boy in a theft of a million dollar painting from a London Museum. Ringo's assignment is to wait at a designated place and receive a bag of laundry containing the purloined picture that he is to deliver to someone waiting at a laundromat across town. Decoding the bus name erroneously, the youth hops on the wrong vehicle. Lost, he retreats to a subway station from which he hopes to get a ride home but is locked in when it closes at night.

Ringo, passed on from one group to another, is taken to the home of a wealthy underworld character who decides the stolen picture is too hot to handle, then to a gang of thieves who instruct him to hide his booty in an apartment owned by Mrs. Tomkins in a building with the number 99. Instead, the boy arrives at 66, the residence of a Mrs. Smotnik. The elderly lady's hearing is faulty and she cannot understand Ringo's questions, but is overjoyed at the beautiful oil he has brought her. Ringo soon realizes his mistake and grabs this opportunity to escape the clutches of the gang. He climbs down the apartment drainpipe, but is spotted. Desperate to escape the criminals' wrath, Ringo jumps off the ledge that borders a canal, landing on the roof of a passing barge. The boat is owned by Big Van, a frustrated painter who has in his possession, by coincidence, a perfect likeness of the stolen painting. When they dock, a policeman takes them to the station where, after some confusion, the alleged masterpiece is proved a facsimile. The sailor and the boy return to Mrs. Smotnik's room for the original oil where the boy surreptitiously exchanges the pictures, then escapes, narrowly avoiding the gang members who have deduced the location of the missing treasure. Ringo is eventually located by Elvis and his partner in the robbery who trap the fugitive in a tunnel. At the other entrance are two gang members who are planning some mischief involving snakes. Ringo eludes both groups and flees to the nearby zoo where he foils a plot to blow up the reptile house and once again rescues the work of art.

Analysis. Me and My Millions is a slapstick adventure narrated by a streetwise, canny young character. Although the ethics involved in the heist are totally ignored and the coincidences shamelessly manipulated, King provides a compassionate and knowledgeable portrait of a hero with specific learning disabilities who uses his native intelligence to sidestep the myriad and prolific problems caused by his disorder. Ringo has form constancy and reversal problems, for example, "99" and "66," and "Tomkins" and "Smotkin"; and left-right confusion; auditory confusion, i.e., interpreting "Caracas" as "crackers"; and, in a key insightful phrase, complains about "nothing but words to tell you where to go." The boy's actions reflect many behaviors—memory deficits, simplistic thinking, skipping consideration of specifics while holding fast to the grand idea—behaviors familiar to the teacher who encounters many children with such learning disabilities. These attributes in no way diminish the characterization of the intrepid hero. They are simply facts, in addition to circumstances, which make his achievement all the more remarkable. The old woman's impairment functions to intensify the communication breakdown.

Kingman, Lee. *Head Over Wheels*. Boston: Houghton Mifflin, 1978. 186 pp. Reading Level: YA/MA
Disability: Neurological Impairment

As the result of a traffic accident, Terry Treddnick suffers a broken neck; his twin brother, Kerry, is only bruised in the collision. The physicians inform the family that Terry's paralysis is extensive; his spinal cord has been irreversibly damaged and there is no hope that he will ever walk again. When the patient regains some strength, they propose to fuse his neck so that he will be able to sit upright. What little use Terry has of his arms is maximized by physical therapy. However, his legs are without feeling or motion, except for uncontrollable spasms that occasionally seize them.

The Treddnicks are supportive but racked by grief over their son's devastating injuries and distressed by Terry's attempts to exclude them from his life. The youth's medical bills far outstrip the family's resources so his mother and twin find jobs and his younger sister seeks regular baby-sitting opportunities so she can contribute. Nevertheless, family tensions increase under the continual financial strain and uncertainty over Terry's future. Kerry feels painfully estranged from his brother. Once they had been very close, almost like two halves of a single unit, but now Terry's resentment of his brother's wholeness and Kerry's unreasonable guilt about his escape from injury seem to be driving them inexorably apart. Further exacerbating the situation, Terry's former girl friend, Roxy, finds endless excuses to avoid visiting the hospital, redirecting her attentions to Kerry, who reminds her of what Terry used to be.

Friends and neighbors are enlisted to adapt the house so it is usable by the boy. Although all look forward to his return, his abrasive attitude alienates Terry further and further from his family. When Kerry's girl friend in turn seems to be transferring her affection to his disabled brother, Kerry's jealousy causes him great anguish, and he decides to escape these pressures by joining the Coast Guard. Finding relief in this decision, Kerry returns home, heading directly for bed and ignoring his brother's request for a visit. During the night, he is awakened by the sound of Terry's laborious attempt to climb the stairs so they can talk. At this juncture, the twins are able to put aside their anger and feelings of rejection, warmly and honestly acknowledging their mutual need for each other.

Analysis. This book examines the dislocations in family life when a major accident permanently injures one of its members. Such variations in reaction as shock, depression, and guilt are realistically portrayed as the characters come to terms with this devastating event. The importance of counseling as a necessary rehabilitative component is explored as problems resulting from adventitious paraplegia are bluntly and explicitly examined. However, such devices as identical twins to provide contrast, the positive model of a successful, similarly disabled physician, and the negative model of a maladaptive room-mate, along with the melodrama of a faithless girl friend, are obvious and overly convenient.

Kirkegaard, Ole Lund. *Otto Is a Rhino*. Originally published by Gyldendalske Boghandel, Denmark, 1972. Illus. by author. Trans. by Joan Tate. Reading, Mass.: Addison-Wesley, 1976. 96 pp. Reading Level: MC
Disability: auditory impairment

Topper finds a magical pencil with which he draws a rhinoceros on the walls of his apartment. The creature comes to life immediately and begins munching on the furniture. The quick-witted youngster sends his friend Vigo off to find food for Otto, his new huge, docile, although insatiable pet. Directly below the hero lives Mrs. Flora, who owns "a long yellow ear trumpet, because she was dreadfully hard of hearing." No matter what is said to her, she interprets statements as requests for a cup of coffee, a beverage she reputably brews with exceptional skill. The rhino's weight is too much for the structure, and he crashes through to the lower level, accompanied by an assortment of observers, whereupon the imperturbable hostess offers her visitors some examples of her famous refreshment. Her floor, also unable to bear the mammal's extraordinary weight, cracks, causing Otto and his growing entourage to plunge through to the cafe below. Topper's dad arrives back from the sea and claims he can find a home for the rhino with a chieftain of some exotic isle whom he met on a sailing trip. Otto is dispatched to his new and presumably more supportive abode, and Mrs. Flora, unable to remain in her own badly damaged residence, pragmatically accepts the landlord's proposal of marriage.

Analysis. This thoroughly silly story, which depends on slapstick conventions for its humor, includes an old woman whose hearing loss is treated in lighthearted fashion. There would seem to be less comedic possibilities than the author is willing to admit in a character who interprets each and every statement as a request for coffee. This self-indulgent effort has much exuberance and a sense of spontaneity, but the outrageous events lose their impact due to an absence of wit and the unpleasant drawings that accompany the labored narrative.

Klein, Norma. *A Honey of a Chimp*. New York: Pantheon, 1980. 152 pp. Reading Level: MC
Disability: Orthopedic Impairment

Emily is surprised and excited when her parents agree she can have a chimpanzee for a pet. Olivia is a docile, clever, gentle creature whom Emily immediately and immoderately loves. The girl teaches the animal some tricks, which it demonstrates during talent night at her school, and a repeat performance on a children's television show is subsequently arranged.

The girl's grandmother had polio as a young woman and since then has been obliged to use a wheelchair. She has managed to cope with her disability extraordinarily well except for her intermittent regrets that she can no longer participate easily in sports. Nonetheless, the woman travels and pursues various interests and hobbies, remaining cheerful most of the time. She frequently uses an indoor swimming pool for pleasure as well as therapy and surpasses her physician's gloomy predictions that the results of her rehabilitation regimen would yield only minor improvements. Her reaction has always been better than that of her husband: he was so devastated by her paralysis that he collapsed under the strain but has long since recovered.

When Emily's mother learns she is pregnant, she tells her daughter they will have to get rid of Olivia since the apartment is too small for both a chimp and a newborn. She reminds the shocked girl that no long-term commitment was made to keep the animal. After considerable investigation, the family decides the San Diego Zoo would provide the best quarters, and a despondent girl and her grandfather fly the creature out to her new home. Despite a girl friend's dire predictions, the new baby's presence is not a disaster, and, in fact, Emily finds her a decidedly acceptable addition to the family. At Christmas, they all fly out to visit the chimp, who, to Emily's joy, has not forgotten them.

Analysis. Emily's grandparent is treated as a talented, interesting, active woman who has had to adjust to the consequences of a disabling illness. A brief vignette demonstrates her self-sufficiency and independence: her life preserver floats away, and after a moment of panic she realizes she can swim without it. Her impairment had its greatest impact before Emily's birth, causing distress to her husband, who, among other reactions, found his religious convictions no longer tenable. He still speaks of the days before his wife's illness but, like her, does not dwell excessively on what might have been. In addition to the central story line, Klein interweaves a number of side issues—a homosexual uncle who questions his lifestyle, a young friend of Emily's who has learned of her mother's affair, Emily's mother's miscarriages and yearnings for another child, children's discussions of the propriety of parents having intercourse—topics that are not standard fare in novels for schoolchildren. The author treats her attractive characters with wit and compassion, is sympathetic to the confusions and needs of pre-teenagers, and presents a believable, upbeat picture of the adjustments a pragmatic family might make to impairment.

Konigsburg, Elaine L. *Father's Arcane Daughter*. New York: Atheneum, 1976. 118 pp. Reading Level: MC/YA
Disability: Neurological Impairment, Auditory Impairment

Caroline Carmichal, presumed dead after being kidnapped 17 years earlier, unexpectedly returns to her father's home to claim her inheritance. The second Mrs. Carmichal is restrained in her welcome to this interloper, suspecting that Caroline is an imposter. Winston, her son, plans to act aloof toward the stranger, but the adolescent boy is soon completely won over by his newly found half-sister. Ten-year-old Heide, who is burdened by a cerebral palsylike condition as well as a hearing loss, is hostile to the intrusion the newcomer brings into her safe, if restricted world. The spoiled, infantile, and petulant girl's boorish manners and uncorrected social behavior, deliberately ignored by her parents, are extremely offensive, and Caroline determines to change them. The young woman is equally concerned for Winston, whom she sees as trapped in a complex relationship with his sister because of what he perceives as his responsibility for her and his consequent feelings of incompetency and guilt. Angry and frustrated, the boy is alternately cruel, protective, resentful, or supportive toward his sibling.

Caroline begins to suspect that Heide is neither as ignorant nor as incompetent as her behavior would seem to indicate. This assessment is confirmed when Caroline surreptitiously arranges to have the girl tested. Heide panics upon hearing the results: she has exceptionally high potential. Now she must choose between remaining in her constrained but secure world and acquiring the skills that would allow her more control over her destiny, a course of action that would necessitate leaving the home that has been both her refuge and her prison. Caroline applies for admission to a college program that would provide her with the knowledge to help her half-sister. Many, many years later, at Caroline's funeral, Heide, now a competent, intelligent, sensitive adult, and Winston, a practicing artist, disclose their awareness of the critical role that their fraudulent "sister" played in transforming their lives.

Analysis. Told as a series of flashbacks by the now mature Winston through the words of the caustic child he had once been, the narrative is interspersed with a dialogue between the adult Winston and an unidentified person, eventually revealed in the climax to be the ma-

ture, self-confident Heide. Characterization is surprisingly sophisticated as the unsuspected and conflicting purposes of various persons
become clear. Discrepancies between appearance and reality and the
play of contradictions among superficial and profound motivations are
recurring themes in this first-rate novel. The responses of other characters to the disabled girl are more complex and subtle than generally
found in stories addressed to middle-school readers. Heide's mother
provides endless care and protection, smothering her child with the
accoutrements of normality while preventing her from learning the
intellectual and social skills that would render her able to function
independently in society; the mother thus disguises her unutterable
shame as protective love. Winston deliberately speaks softly and insult-
ingly to his sister, whose deafness permits this safe expression of his
hostility. He thinks of her and describes her to himself in disparaging
and contemptuous terms, yet, in a sad and painful way, his feelings of
love are discernible. Although accepting responsibility for Heide, the
youth simultaneously devises elaborate means to keep her at the greatest possible distance. In the scene where Winston is overtly mean to
her, loudly insulting and poking her, he has for the first time treated
her in a normal way—acting as any provoked brother might to an
annoying sibling. Caroline, disgusted and repulsed by the girl's undisciplined actions, realizes that to rescue Winston she must first save
Heide. In the process, she moves successively from revulsion to pity to
profound affection in her relationship to her presumed half-sister.

Kropp, Paul. *Wilted*. New York: Coward, McCann & Geoghegan,
1980. 111 pp. Reading Level: YA
Disability: emotional dysfunction, speech impairment

Danny's home life is less than ideal: his father drinks excessively
and fights with his nagging wife, and his sister is often inaccessible
after bouts with marijuana. His younger brother, Bud, upset by these
behaviors, must frequently be comforted by Danny. School is beset
with traps, the most treacherous one consisting of being identified as a
"wilt," an all-purpose epithet denoting someone whose dress, mannerism, attitude, or behavior mark him as a loser. Danny is afraid that
wearing his new glasses may precipitate this undesirable status, but
aside from the obligatory derogatory remarks made by the would-be
toughs in class, nothing changes. The youth is pleased to learn that the
much-admired Samantha doesn't find them objectionable, and when
he hears from his best friend, Bloop, that this attractive girl is interested in him, he decides to make his move. Despite his bumbling
opening, the more sophisticated girl invites him to her house, where

his first lesson in sex education begins. However, the boy's stupefaction and elation at this unexpected social coup is eroded when his father terminates his stormy marriage by an abrupt and apparently permanent departure.

On the way to school the next morning, Danny is intercepted by the town character, a harmless derelict usually treated by the boy and his friends in a condescending but unmalicious manner. Crazy Charlie stutters a greeting, but the distraught youngster, angered over the turmoil at home, lashes out: "The one thing I don't need is more of your philosophy. You're crazy, Charlie. You know what I mean, crazy. Up there. I don't need crazy advice." A few days later, he apologizes, a gesture that is graciously accepted by the eccentric old man. When Danny leaves school for Samantha's house on the day a favored teacher dies in school, he is set upon by another youth who has been spoiling for a fight. Danny's frustration focuses on his attacker, and he is narrowly prevented from seriously injuring the boy. He heads for his girl friend's home, where his cuts and bruises are tenderly cared for while he considers in wonderment the vicissitudes of his young life.

Analysis. This very clever, witty story is written by an author who holds very few illusions about pubescent youngsters. The language demonstrates a level of realism lacking in comparable stories, and the characters are more complex and interesting. "Crazy Charlie" is a common enough type, a person who lives on the fringes of society, whose actions are outlandish but harmless. The other characters treat him with affectionate contempt, affirming their own distance from such a state by their ambivalent interaction.

Lasker, Joe. *Nick Joins In.* Illus. by author. Chicago: Albert Whitman, 1980. unp. Reading Level: YC
Disability: Orthopedic Impairment; also learning disability

Nick is getting ready to finish homebound instruction and enter a mainstreamed school. He questions his parents about the building's accessibility and the probable effects of being physically different from other pupils. In preparation for mainstreaming, Nick's school has constructed a ramp for his wheelchair, obtained a teacher's aide, and had a special desk built for him.

The noise and confusion of the first day frighten the newcomer, and he becomes shy when bombarded with the children's questions. They ask about his wheelchair and braces and, after their curiosity is satisfied, they plunge into their schoolwork. Nick plays comfortably with the other children but becomes a special friend of Timmie, a boy with a learning disability. One day a ball gets stuck in the gutter of the gym roof, and the kids are upset when they cannot retrieve it. Nick remembers the long pole used to open tall windows, fetches it, and is able to jostle the ball down, thereby becoming the hero of the day.

Analysis. Lasker's book on the integration of a young child with orthopedic problems is accomplished with warmth and affection. Two clichés mar the book's impact: pairing children with special problems undercuts the idea of mainstreaming; and the boy's timely solution to a sticky but minor problem is immoderately applauded. The illustrations are generally appealing, but two are outstanding: the front cover displays Nick with his class, and the final page depicts the hero imagining himself as Superman.

Lee, Benjamin. *It Can't Be Helped.* Originally published in Great Britain in 1976. New York: Farrar, Straus & Giroux, 1979. 155 pp.
Reading Level: YA/MA
Disability: Emotional Dysfunction

Even his father's funeral becomes an occasion of monumental absurdity as Max Orloff, discomfited by a painfully constricting suit, stumbles into his parent's grave on top of the coffin. Less than a week after the burial, Bernard, a long-term secret friend of his mother's, arrives at the widow's home intent on marrying his childhood sweetheart. Max makes a quick exit to stay with his relatives, the Lanskys, but he has barely settled in when his uncle informs him that his mother has been institutionalized. Not at all surprised, Max recalls the behavior that signaled her initial need for psychiatric care: "My mother was in the kitchen, but standing in the middle of the room, staring out the window, gripping her hands tightly together and twisting them about. She was not looking at anything. She had forgotten to comb her hair, and when I spoke to her, did not hear me."

In response to a request from the institution, Max visits his mother. Bernard arrives while the boy is there, and because there is evidence of improvement, he arranges to take the patient home. Max nevertheless returns to the Lansky home, but is immediately evicted by his irate uncle, who accuses him of responsibility for the pregnancy of his libertine daughter. Having nowhere else to go, the bewildered youth goes home. His mother is very agitated when he arrives, worried about a pearl necklace she left in the hospital. Max is dispatched to retrieve it, but instead of giving it to his mother, he decides to turn it over to Rebecca to pay for an abortion, even though there is no possibility that he could be the father. But his plans to contact his cousin are interrupted by his forced participation in "games day" at school, where he manages to make a colossal fool of himself. Bleasdale, the resident school Marxist, coerces Max into joining a demonstration against administrative repression. The distracted boy is swept up into the whirlwind event that culminates in a bizarre confrontation in the headmaster's office. The confusion is mind-boggling: the administrator believes the topic is Mr. Lansky's accusations regarding his student's alleged paternity, while Bleasdale discourses about the political protest. His remarks are highly suggestive in that chaotic setting, and the headmaster somehow concludes that an orgy involving the students has taken place.

After a further series of catastrophes, Max locates his mother's doctor and speaks to him about the situation. Dr. Patel telephones the adolescent's home and learns from Bernard that Mrs. Orloff is worse and she must be readmitted. The would-be bridegroom, now anxious to disengage himself from the situation, announces his intention to abandon the family. Max returns to the empty house, and his cousin soon arrives to announce that her suspected pregnancy was only a false alarm. The two cousins are reconciled, and she invites him to stay at her home once again.

Analysis. The death of the hero's father, the intermittent rehospitalization of his mother, an abortive Marxist demonstration, and an accusation of incest would not seem to be the likely elements of a farce for youngsters, but these are the key plot crises in this junior British novel. The treatment of Mrs. Orloff is not particularly sympathetic in this intermittently hilarious work that combines black comedy and slapstick. The troubled woman is perceived as a shrew by her sister-in-law, who holds her responsible for the untimely demise of Mr. Orloff, but is regarded ambivalently by her son, whose fond early memories had been diminished by his vivid recollections of the incessant family fights that lasted until his father's death.

Lee, Mildred. *The People Therein.* New York: Houghton Mifflin, 1980. 269 pp. Reading Level: MA
Disability: Orthopedic Impairment, speech impairment, cosmetic impairment, neurological impairment, special health problems

Under doctor's orders, Drew Thorndike leaves his wealthy Boston home and travels to Dewfall Gap, North Carolina, in an attempt to rid himself of an increasing dependence on alcohol. He rents a rundown cabin from Laban Farr, hoping to use it as his base from which to explore the mountains and pursue his studies as a naturalist. Ailanthus, called Lanthy by her family, develops a crush on the stranger, a novelty for her since she considers herself unsuited for marriage. When Drew asks her age, she responds: "I'm eighteen. . . . I know I look younger than what I am. It's because I never rightly got my growth. It took me close to three years to learn to walk." She explains that her limp was the result of her pregnant mother seeing a calf with an extra hoof. "I was borned a few nights later . . . my hips wasn't lined up right an' one of my legs was shorter than the other one. . . . It's not ever held me back, though. Leastways, not much. I'm as stout as the rest when it comes to field or housework, either one." Nevertheless, Drew tells her that she is as beautiful as her name.

Because her feet are different sizes, she cannot wear ready-made shoes, but has moccasins made for her by an Indian hermit, Silent Mary. "There was a tale told in the mountains that when she was a young girl she had loved a white man and betrayed some secret the Cherokee held sacred; for this, the story went, she had been tortured—her tongue burned or some such awful thing—and made unable to speak ever again." Returning from a visit to the Indian woman, Lanthy meets Drew, and the two, under the ledge of a rock, find partial refuge from a sudden downpour. There he holds her close to warm her and calm her shivering. Unable to ignore her feelings for him, she stops by his cabin soon after this chance meeting. He seduces her, then contrite over his loss of control, drinks until he passes out. Laban finds him in this state and is furious, considering his drunkenness a violation of their friendship. Lanthy persuades her father to forgive him. Subsequently the older man endorses the community's offer of the post of schoolmaster to the outsider. Ailanthus and Drew continue to meet; he proposes, but she is not ready to make public their engagement. He answers an unexpected summons back to Boston to care for his critically ill sister, unaware that Lanthy is pregnant. Drew writes, reaffirming his intentions and expressing regret that he did not ask Laban's permission to marry his daughter before he left. When Lanthy answers, she does not tell him that he has fathered her child because she is unwilling to oblige any man to marry her. Having been told at her birth that their daughter would be unable to bear children, her parents are stunned as well as shamed when they learn of her condition. Because she was considered an unlikely prospect for marriage, her mother had never thought to warn her against becoming pregnant. Laban is outraged when he learns who the father is—incensed at being twice deceived but concerned over the future of his beloved daughter.

After a difficult delivery, Lanthy anxiously asks: "His legs—his feet—do they match? Is he made crooked?" But the child is a healthy, fully formed girl, red-headed like her father. The mountain folk now disparage the absent "furriner," commenting he was "amongst our innocent little ones an' all the time tomcattin' around, gettin' that pore crippled girl in trouble."

Lanthy's kind aunt takes in a stray girl who has a large strawberry mark on her cheek. The teenager appears to forget her shyness with Lanthy, who "wondered if the girl felt free with her because Lanthy too bore an affliction."

Following his sister's death, Drew returns to the Smoky Mountains, unable to fathom the frosty reception he encounters. He arrives at Laban's home aghast to learn of the events that have taken place since he left. Lanthy realizes her father, consumed by fury, is intent on killing Drew. She deliberately falls, injuring her hand so badly that Laban is diverted from his murderous intent. The two men are ultimately reconciled. The wedding of Lanthy and Drew is a modest affair, but it succeeds in restoring the couple to a place of respect among their neighbors.

Analysis. Although the events in this story are melodramatic, Lee nicely captures the turn-of-the-century speech, manners, and mores of this isolated, hardy, and lively community. Their beliefs about disability, as about most other things, are colored by a lack of knowledge and shaped by superstition and misinformation. The origins of the Indian woman's muteness are explained through an absurdly romanticized tale that becomes part of the local folklore. Her mother's attempt to correct Ailanthus's injury involves such ritualistic actions as "standing [her] behind a door and sweeping [her] dress with a broom nine mornings in a row." Lanthy is undervalued as a woman despite her other obvious qualities. The midwife presumes her disability extends to an incapacity to have children, an assessment that goes unchallenged. The heroine rejects pity and pushes herself to prove that even if she is not as "good" as others, she can compete with anyone in accomplishments. Despite dire warnings of spinsterhood, she refuses the attentions of her cousin and later those of a preacher who is willing to marry her and adopt her child. The senile grandmother is an honored, revered member of the household, profoundly mourned when she dies. The attentions she requires as a result of her failing health are given generously and without complaint; she is too beloved and important a family member for it to be otherwise. The writing is literate, the characters well developed, and the time and place skillfully recreated.

Leggett, Linda Rodgers, and Linda Gambee Andrews. *The Rose-Colored Glasses: Melanie Adjusts to Poor Vision.* Illus. by Laura Hartman. New York: Human Sciences, 1979. 31 pp. Reading Level: MC
Disability: Visual Impairment

After the usual welcome-back-to-school speech, Mrs. Davis informs Deborah's class that Melanie, a new student who is recovering from an automobile accident, has been assigned to their room. Mary tells her friend that she waved to the newcomer but was ignored and concludes the girl is "a snob." When Melanie arrives, she walks slowly to her seat, banging noisily into her desk, much to the amusement of some class members. Ignoring the poster made to welcome her, the youngster sits down and silently begins to weep.

Later, Deborah eavesdrops on a conversation between Melanie and their teacher during which the girl is told that she must wear her glasses in class. Mrs. Davis is aware they embarrass the child and listens sympathetically when Melanie complains that they are ugly: "I know they make me see more clearly. But I'd rather have to stare and not see well than wear these glasses and have people stare at me." The perceptive instructor, recruiting Deborah as a collaborator, devises a plan to facilitate understanding by the other students of Melanie's condition. When the two girls walk home, they discover they have much in common. To her new confidant, Melanie reveals her fantasy:

> At night sometimes, I turn on the light, put on my glasses, and look into the mirror. . . . I pretend that I look beautiful, and then I pretend that the whole world wears the same kind of glasses, and then I pretend that nobody notices the glasses, and then I stop pretending and I start to cry. . . . I wish everything could be the way it was before my accident.

At school the next day, Mrs. Davis announces a film. At first, the children are excited, but soon become irritable when no adjustments are made to the unfocused images. Afterward they justifiably complain that watching the movie made them nervous and uncomfortable, whereupon Melanie reveals that they have just experienced a simulation of her vision problem. After this demonstration, all the students agree that Melanie should wear her glasses.

Analysis. Considerable information about the special kind of corrective lens the heroine must wear is presented. The authors are sensitive to a child's concerns about appearance and her rejection of the comparison with children who wear commonplace glasses. The immediate, wholesale acceptance of the child by her classmates following the simulation is not credible, and the presentation of children's behavior in this story bears little resemblance to that of real youngsters. However, the truly appalling feature of this work is its total disregard for literate expression. The text is replete with simple grammatical errors, non sequitors, sentence fragments, run-on sentences, and some of the clumsiest assembling of words in contemporary juvenile literature. The following complete "paragraph" is typical:

To hang around the hallway between the auditorium and the water fountain, its four cracks near the drain, like N-S-E-W on a map, and look cool talking with Jan and Mary maybe, Eleanor (if *she* wants to join in), and ignore obnoxious Raymond, and ask Matthew a question so he'll have to stop and talk (remember: figure out what to ask Matthew before leaving the house).

Levenkron, Steven. *The Best Little Girl in the World*. Chicago: Contemporary Books, 1978. 196 pp. Reading Level: YA/MA
Disability: Emotional Dysfunction, orthopedic impairment

From Francesca's perspective, it seems as though her parents are preoccupied with their own lives, with that of her older sister, who has moved across the country to live in a commune in California, and with that of her brother, who has apparently fulfilled parental hopes for the perfect son by being admitted to Harvard. Mr. and Mrs. Dietrich consider their youngest child with casual gratitude, an adolescent who has given them "no trouble." While fantasizing in dancing class, the 15 year old thinks about the life of a performer, particularly the slim body essential for such a career. To achieve the desired thinness, she embarks on a near-calamitous dietary regimen. She privately renames herself Kessa, assumes a new identity as an aspiring professional dancer, and soon becomes helpless before the demands of her obsessive fasting.

After the fruitless pleas of her parents and the inadequate intercession of several physicians, Kessa must be hospitalized and force-fed. On the ward she meets another anorexic girl and is both attracted and appalled by her behavior. Kessa's roommate, a savvy, outspoken black girl, immobilized by her leg cast, tries to point out the stupidity of the games being played by the "skinnies." The pathetic girl's defenses are finally breached by a concerned psychologist, who is able to see through her machinations. He calls the parents to a conference, and they learn, to their intense discomfort, that their daughter has so manipulated events that she now has their almost undivided attention. Kessa begins to acknowledge her own fears, to express anger in more constructive ways, and to articulate her needs. She starts on the long road to recovery from a body weight of 73 pounds and a feeling of worthlessness to a position from which she assumes a healthier, more assertive stance in her dealing with others.

Analysis. Given the generally gloomy prospects for recovery of anorexics, the rapid turnaround in Kessa's condition is probably atypical. Nevertheless, with a potent and chilling sense of authenticity, the novel does chronicle the near-suicidal course of this emotional disorder in an adolescent girl having many of the attributes of the "typical" patient. *The Best Little Girl in the World* has a quasi-fictional tone, for the heroine appears to be a synthesis of many case studies. Despite this, Levenkron's skills as a storyteller are considerable, and he has assembled the narrative ingredients necessary to provide insight into this condition and compassion for its victims. He includes extensive information on some of the arcane machinations and professional disputes involved in treating this disorder—insights that are probably of only ephemeral interest to adolescent readers. The choice of the family name "Dietrich," which can be read ironically as "diet-rich," seems forced and unnecessary. These are very minor flaws in a work that reveals how family dynamics can contribute to and support emotional dysfunction, convincingly relates the increasingly bizarre, ritualized, and driven behavior of an anorexic adolescent, and explores the remediative possibilities in a fascinating, nondidactic style. The author also provides one of the most direct and simple definitions of such problems to his audience. When Kessa, deprecatingly and desperately, says she's "screwed up, nuts, bonkers," her therapist interprets: "Crazy means your feelings aren't working right. Crazy means your head is playing tricks on you, giving you false information about yourself and false fears that can never be allayed because they are false."

Levinson, Nancy S. *World of Her Own.* Illus. by Gene Fuller. New York: Harvey House, 1981. 123 pp. Reading Level: YA
Disability: Auditory Impairment

Annie is angry and frightened when she learns that her father can no longer afford the tuition for the special school she has been attending for children with hearing impairments. Furthermore, without her knowledge, he has arranged for her to participate in the mainstreaming program at the local high school, where, unfortunately, the special education teacher has made only minimal and inadequate arrangements for her. No student mentors have been provided, and Annie has been assigned to two classes taught by a hostile, unsympathetic teacher whose beard and mustache block the newcomer's speech-reading efforts. When Annie complains, her advisor says "You'll run into plenty of teachers like him," and suggests that the anxious girl needs to learn better coping skills, although she does offer to "see what I can do about making sure you get assignments in advance and getting your seat changed. . . . But . . . you know we can't make these changes in every class every semester."

Overtures from her peers are rebuffed by the unhappy girl, who is afraid to rely on her communication skills or the seemingly good intentions and actions of others. Annie's very presence arouses the wrath of

Rita and her group, who take pleasure in making fun of the new student. Incorrectly believing that her auditory loss is complete, they speak openly in front of her of their plans to vandalize the school. Afraid that she may have misunderstood their conversation, but equally torn by the possibility that she may have correctly comprehended their plans for Larchmont High, the young woman tries to alert the authorities. When her warnings are dismissed by the police as well as by a schoolmate she has come to trust, she bravely goes to the school by herself, observes some movement within the building, and prevails on a neighbor to call for help. When a squad car arrives and the youths are caught redhanded, Annie is vindicated.

Analysis. This easy-to-read adolescent romance promulgates some unfortunate assumptions about who is responsible for the success of mainstreaming. The school authorities in this novel offer virtually nothing in the way of support services for the hearing-impaired teenager. The one adaptation grudgingly offered was accompanied by the warning that this was a special case. Far from being critical of this attitude, the author appears to endorse it, in effect indicating that the burdens of integration lie almost exclusively on those who sustain the disabilities. Major plot incidents involving the heroine's crime-stopping actions and the blossoming of a romance with a school leader, as well as the vignette in which Annie is able to comprehend an angry conversation that takes place on the other side of a closed door, are equally improbable. The illustrations accompanying this shallow effort reveal neither skill nor imagination and are generally muddy and unattractive.

Levitan, Sonia. *A Sound to Remember.* Illus. by Gabriel Lisowski. New York: Harcourt Brace Jovanovich, 1979. unp. Reading Level: YC
Disability: Intellectual Impairment, Speech Impairment

The villagers look upon Jacov with derision, and their children mock his slowness, awkwardness, and stuttering speech. Even though everyone knows their beloved rabbi is the boy's particular friend and protector, the community is aghast when they learn that Jacov has been chosen to blow the ram's horn on Rosh Hashanah. In disbelief, they come to check the rumor and suggest more suitable candidates for such a great honor, but their spiritual leader assures them that all will be well. As the congregation had predicted, Jacov's notes come out "weak and trembling," and the congregation is furious at being "cheated out of its Rosh Hashanah call, because of the clumsy, halting Jacov." The country folk insist that another more appropriate member of the synagogue be selected for the honor at Yom Kippur, but the rabbi does not even answer them. As the holy day approaches, the peasants are greatly agitated. Just before the shofar is to be blown, the wise rabbi says: "There are times when God wishes us to be silent, that we may listen to that soft small voice inside us that tells us what is right and pure and just. . . . Our friend Jacov gave us such a moment. . . . Who can say that this silence was not pleasing to God?" The rabbi then brings out another shofar, and he and the boy joyously, in unison, proclaim the new year.

Analysis. In this lovely, gentle tale, Jacov is seen as a lonely, isolated child. His impairments are known to all, and he is consequently treated with scorn and mockery. The revered spiritual leader, whose wisdom and goodness are unquestioned, provides the message of love and acceptance in his role of interpreter to his flock. The simple, stiff line drawings lack the charm and warmth this story needs and deserves.

Levoy, Myron. *Alan and Naomi.* New York: Harper & Row, 1977. 192 pp. Reading Level: YA
Disability: Emotional Dysfunction

Except for his father's preoccupation with Hitler's advance through the countries of Europe, the war seems far away for Alan Silverman. The youth had determined to develop his meager physical strength in stickball games and thereby secure the admiration of his non-Jewish peers. The likelihood of that improbable goal being achieved is diminished further when he is asked by his parents to establish communication with Naomi, a withdrawn and virtually uncommunicative refugee, newly moved into Alan's New York apartment building. She has been severely traumatized as a result of watching her brave father beaten by the Nazis. Panicked at first that such involvement might be found out by his friends, the ingenious boy nevertheless succeeds in initiating contact with the silent girl. Over time, and despite many setbacks, Alan is able to wean her away from her psychotic behavior. The reluctant hero is amazed at his ability to accomplish more than her doctors could. Alan gains the strength to defy the rigid social taboos of other 12-year-old boys by being seen with Naomi in public and, to his surprise, actually enjoys her company. Finally, he is able to persuade the mute girl to speak, and she painstakingly begins to slough off the sequelae of the repressive memories that have haunted her. One day after the two friends left school together, they are taunted with anti-Semitic remarks, and in the ensuing fight, Naomi sees Alan attacked and bloodied. Stricken by this reenactment of her recurring nightmare, the girl runs away. Although the brawl cements the friendship of Alan and his Irish Catholic friend, Shaun, it has sabotaged Naomi's psychological improvement, and she returns to her private hell. The unfortunate girl is hospitalized, and little hope is proposed for her ultimate recovery.

Analysis. Despite the heavy reliance on ethnic stereotypes, Levoy's novel is a powerful one in which the author successfully utilizes the pain and suffering of an individual child to symbolize the human devastation wreaked on the survivors of the Holocaust. The narrative and dialogue, while capturing the innocence and naiveté of the period, reduces the story's plausibility for contemporary readers. The hero's use of puppetry is a credible therapeutic technique that allows the fragile child a shield behind which she can safely hide as she slowly emerges from her shell. The use of Naomi's rapid recovery and her instantaneous retreat to a virtually catatonic state serve the author's literary purposes. In actuality, however, it is unlikely for a recovery to be so radically accelerated or a retreat so final.

Levoy, Myron. *A Shadow Like a Leopard*. New York: Harper & Row, 1981. 184 pp. Reading Level: YA
Disability: Special Health Problems, emotional dysfunction

Fourteen-year-old Ramon writes in his diary: "Got my book in my left pocket, knife in the other. Book is my sister, knife is my brother. I need them both." The Puerto Rican boy considers his switchblade essential to his survival—a weapon he uses skillfully for defense or flaunts challengingly to proclaim his "manhood." His prudently hidden journal, filled with crude but potent poetry, is another matter—a violation of the macho facade demanded by his absent father. Although he helps a punk mug a helpless woman, he is considered too young and green to join the ranks of the neighborhood gang. Ramon decides to commit a burglary on his own, finagling his way into the apartment of Arnold Glasser, a 76-year-old artist living on welfare. Bitterly the man taunts him: "I'm not going to give you any money, you two-bit bum. You've got a knife. I'm a cripple. What more do you need? Kill me! Go ahead. Then you can take everything. Money. Paintings. My underwear. Who cares? Do it already!" Disconcerted, the youth takes the $12 from Glasser's wallet and escapes. Mocked by members of the gang who insist he stupidly overlooked other treasure, the boy returns. Convinced this time that the man really is poor, Ramon proposes he hustle his paintings on the street and split the take. The glib youngster sells all but one, realizing $160; the remaining picture he takes to his mother, who is in a psychiatric ward, but the woman is too depressed and disoriented to respond. To Glasser's amazement, a jubilant Ramon returns, laden with groceries. The neophyte agent enthusiastically tells the old man, "You ain't no flop . . . you would've been as big as Pedro Picasso." His defenses momentarily breached, the artist shows him a book, *Despair and Hope: Painters of the 1930's,* containing reproductions of his murals. Prodded from his gloomy state, Glasser persuades the youth to push his wheelchair to the Metropolitan Museum, where they talk, argue, separate, and make up, agreeing about the irresistible power of Rembrandt's works.

After an unsuccessful day trying to sell more paintings, Ramon discovers the art galleries and tries to persuade the owners to stock Glasser's works. All refuse until one dealer finally agrees to hang some paintings the following week. Ramon is ecstatic at the results of his brazenness and gleefully informs the old man that he has a surprise for him. Deep in thought, he is caught off guard by four toughs who knife him. After being treated in the emergency room of the hospital where his mother is a patient, he visits the woman, relieved to see she is more attuned to reality and no longer requires intravenous feeding.

Ramon takes Glasser to the Madison Avenue gallery where the painter becomes enraged, deciding that the exhibition of his paintings is an act of charity. In an emotion-laden confrontation, the old man and the youth force each other to admit their lack of faith in themselves, and each, fearfully and reluctantly, agrees to risk failure—and success. Glasser allows his pictures to remain, and Ramon puts aside his need for vengeance and his dependence on the gang. When his father comes home on parole, talking of honor and machismo, Ramon rebels, declaring his right to define his own standards.

Analysis. Despite the thoroughly unlikely sequence of incidents, this story has a gritty, compelling charm. Images are simple but striking, for example, "Ramon's mind raced in and out of each argument like a rabbit searching for a hole," and the two major characters are attractive and original. Despite their superficial differences, they both combine hope and cynicism, qualities revealed in their abrasive yet warily affectionate conversations. The neglect Ramon's mother suffers in a hospital staffed with an overworked and resentful crew is starkly conveyed. Cut loose from her native land and ground down by the brutal pressures of life in a New York slum, the woman withdraws into a private world. Despite the arthritic condition that confines him to a wheelchair, disillusionment about his environment, and public indifference to his work, Glasser is a tough, tenacious, indomitable character. His disability increases the likelihood that he will be victimized by the neighborhood punks but does not diminish his sense of self or his pride.

Lillington, Kenneth. *Young Man of Morning.* London: Faber & Faber, 1979. 173 pp. Reading Level: YA
Disability: Speech Impairment

Phillip lives with his uncle's family where, despite his dependent status, he is grudgingly given the same opportunities as his favored cousin, Alexis. The boy spends many hours in the Athenian studio run by Cimon, the sculptor. When the artist gives the youth some clay, suspecting he may have some talent, Phillip, instead of responding, "stared at him helplessly, as though he were in the grip of one of the Furies. He tried to speak, but no words came. His eyes bulged, his face went purple." However, after seeing his work, Cimon is impressed, and although such labor is considered declassé by his relatives, Phillip is apprenticed to the artist. The boy is exceedingly pleased with his instruction and with such new-found friends as the great Pericles, but rumors of an imminent invasion by Xerxes' army cause him and others much anxiety.

The novice deduces that his master was once a Spartan, and Cimon, who had taken pains to conceal his origins, confesses that he did grow up in that despised culture. He tells his assistant how Poleon, the famed potter, helped to promote his talent, even funding a workshop so his protégé could become independent. Thus, when Cimon hears that some Persians have casually murdered his one-time benefactor, he decides to abandon his art and return to the life of a warrior to avenge his beloved mentor.

Bewildered by these events, Phillip wanders out of the city and encounters Lucy, a flute girl, in the woods. He tries to speak, "but his stammer caught him in a positive seizure. He bent double and panted a few breaths to relax the muscles of his stomach." The girl proposes a startling remedy: "You want to *make* yourself stammer. Do it on purpose. Every day, practise stammering as hard as you can. Then when you want to talk normal, you'll find you can do it." As they travel to Thermopylae, the youth is astonished to learn how knowledgeable Lucy is about problems of health. Phillip sets his companion up as a healer, renames her Lukeia, and negotiates with sick people who seek her salutary ministrations. Tales of her therapeutic prowess precede them, including "a legend that she cured [Phillip] of dumbness with one miraculous stroke."

On the way to join in the battle against the invaders, Cimon encounters a traitor who intends to betray the Hellenes by revealing a secret passageway through the mountains to the enemy. Hampered by the pain from a leg injury, the furious Spartan is unable to prevent the evil man from escaping. When the two adolescents catch up with the artist, Lukeia, through massage, assuages the man's agony. Unhappily, Phillip's speech difficulty returns. Cimon is determined to pursue his vow but forbids his apprentice to follow him, sadly forecasting that their cause is doomed because of the traitor's perfidy. Although the

Greek armies battle bravely, the Persian horde sweeps through the land, overcoming the defenders. The artist dies in the conflict, but Phillip lives to carry on his mentor's teachings.

Analysis. Pre-Periclean Greece is the backdrop for this adolescent novel rich in information on domestic and military life, cultural variations, and the role of art in that society. Phillip's poor speech, in a setting where fluency and eloquence are so esteemed, sets him even further apart from the status enjoyed by his uncle's family than his fatherless situation alone would cause. The boy's dysfluency is seen as exacerbated by tension and stress and alleviated by those circumstances in which he is able to control certain aspects of his life. Although the author offers an exciting historical drama, his lapses into contemporary slang are jarring. Expressions such as "What do you think you know about it, chum?" and references to "poor kid" unhappily disrupt otherwise successful efforts to evoke a sense of ancient Greece.

Lipsyte, Robert. *Summer Rules.* New York: Harper & Row, 1981. 150 pp. Reading Level: YA
Disability: Intellectual Impairment

Bobby had envisioned his sixteenth summer as one fabulous event after another—girls, money, freedom, a car—uncountable adventures featuring himself in classic Hemingway roles. His daydreams are rudely destroyed when Mr. Marks informs his son that arrangements have been made for him to be a counselor at Happy Valley Camp, an obvious ploy to get him away from the influence of a gang of punks led by Willie Rumson, who has routinely been terrorizing their community. Bobby's father has given him an ultimatum: no camp job, no driving lessons. His older sister, Michelle, is even less thrilled when she learns her brother will join her on the staff. Bobby's horror at being assigned to guide Harley, the director's incorrigible son, is counterbalanced by his meeting with Sheila, a cousin of Harley's who works in the kitchen. When the teenager stops his charge from setting a fire, the ten year old climbs to the roof, refusing to return to safety until Bobby scares him with a story of predatory birds. The novice counselor's days are filled with efforts to protect the victims of Harley's malicious taunts, but his nights are devoted to the pursuit of a summer romance with the beautiful, green-eyed Sheila. Bobby convinces the camp manager to compel the sports coach to give Harley a place on his team and the drama coach to devise something the boy can do on the stage. While earning the hostility of these two instructors, he is compensated by now having his nights free and his days less harried. Before long, however, he begins to tire of his girl friend's mindlessness and, to his surprise, becomes concerned about Harley's obvious exhaustion caused by his nonstop schedule.

One day, Willie Rumson shows up at camp in the care of his cousin, Jim. Bobby is shocked to note that the "pointed rat face I remembered was now a dopey moon. Willie Rumson's eyes were glazed. His fat cheeks were smooth as a baby's. That blond hair he used to wear in a duck's ass was chopped down to a crew cut. His body, once lean and wiry, looked swollen and soft." Jim says he has a job locally and asks Bobby to keep an eye out for Willie in case he wanders off. Clearly he is no longer a problem to anyone, Jim reports, since when he was in jail "they gave him electric shock treatments and injections" and now "Willie's sweet as pie."

The adolescent hero finds Willie unconscious and smelling of alcohol the night his girl friend finally agrees to accompany him to a nearby island where he hopes to finally lose his virginity, but their tryst is interrupted by the sight of flames coming from the campsite. When Bobby expresses his belief that Harley set the fire and not the accused Willie, the adults try to persuade him to lie. The director advises him to forget what he saw, saying Willie is "trash, an animal. You want to take the responsibility of setting him free? To kill somebody next time?" But the teenager cannot accept their rationalizations and decides to tell the truth. He provides an alibi for Willie and reports to the police some details about Harley's past flirtations with arson. Although the 16 year old bemoans the waste of a summer—"No license yet, not a single new muscle, still a virgin"—he recognizes he has discovered a code of ethics he can live by—not an immodest achievement for a maturing youth. As he says, "There are no summer rules."

Analysis. Lipsyte has written a breezy, funny, irreverent novel featuring a hero aching to emulate his macho ideals. Bobby's relationship with Willie, a minor character, is one of the barometers of his maturation. He had been terrified of the brute and was relieved to hear that the man was under lock and key. Reports of Willie's transformation are disconcerting, and when he sees the fellow he once feared he is unnerved, then relieved, then full of pity for the man. It is unlikely that Willie's delinquency was treated by such a regimen, but reports of abuses still surface periodically: Since so little information is provided as to the precise cause of Willie's lowered functioning, it is not possible to comment on its validity. When the adolescent agrees to watch over his former nemesis and defends him against unwarranted attacks, it is an indication of his growing sense of responsibility. Finally, his refusal to let the man be blamed for an act he did not commit is, in effect, his moral rite of passage.

Litchfield, Ada B. *A Button in Her Ear*. Illus. by Eleanor Mill. Chicago: Whitman, 1976. unp. Reading Level: YC
Disability: Auditory Impairment

Unable to hear properly, Angela generally fails to understand what her friends, her teacher, or members of her family say to her. Inevitably this leads to confusion and hard feelings. Her parents consult a doctor, who refers the child to an audiologist. After testing, the young girl is fitted with a hearing aid and given instruction in its care. Her teacher asks her to demonstrate its use to her classmates, who are impressed. The child observes: "Some of them even wished a little they could try a hearing aid also." She is happier now that she knows what others are saying and is a little smug about her ability to tune them out when she doesn't want to be bothered.

Analysis. This low-key, quasi-fictional story offers primary-level readers a satisfactory introduction to the problems of diminished hearing ability and the compensatory function of a hearing aid. Illustrations, in both black-and-white and color, support the text, clearly showing an initial medical examination, testing equipment and procedures, and an aid with its batteries and harness.

Litchfield, Ada B. *A Cane in Her Hand*. Illus. by Eleanor Mill. Chicago: Whitman, 1977. unp. Reading Level: YC
Disability: Visual Impairment

Valerie becomes alarmed over the recurring pain in one eye and her diminished ability, even while wearing glasses, to discern objects that are quite close by. Her parents take her for an eye examination during which the youngster expresses her fear that she will become totally blind. Her physician responds: "We're going to do all we can to keep that from happening." Valerie returns to her regular classroom, where her teacher continues to make special accommodations. The girl is also assigned to work with a peripatologist, who instructs her in cane travel and sensory training so that she may become more alert to her environment. After some initial resistance, Val adapts to her situation but is irritated at the lack of understanding toward her disability that some people display. She wishes others would learn that "there are lots of ways of seeing. Seeing with your eyes is important, but it isn't everything."

Analysis. This is a pleasant, upbeat, quasi-fictional effort about a child whose already impaired vision suddenly deteriorates even further. The girl, now legally blind, learns she may lose her sight completely, but the ophthalmologist's obvious concern and his assurance that everything possible will be done to prevent such an eventuality provide some comfort. Although the style and illustrations are unexceptional, the book is useful in offering an informative, constructive portrayal of a child with a severe disability, aided in her adjustment by an intelligent, sensitive family and capable, supportive school staff who respond with practical help and appropriate guidance to her academic, social, and psychological needs.

Litchfield, Ada B. *Words in Our Hands.* Illus. by Helen Cogancherry. Chicago: Albert Whitman, 1980. unp. Reading Level: YC
Disability: Auditory Impairment

Michael discusses the presumed causes of his parents' deafness:

Nobody knows for sure why, but it might be because Grandma Ellis had measles before my mother was born and Grandma Turner was in a car accident before my father was born. Sometimes when a mother who is expecting a baby has some disease or is in an accident, the baby is born blind or deaf or is hurt in some other way.

He also explains why their voices don't sound like those of other people: They "have never heard other people talking or even their own voices, so they don't know how voices sound." Michael and his sisters have learned sign language, finger spelling, and speech reading and can select which way to speak with their parents, although communicating is not always easy. Some special devices are utilized in the boy's home to change auditory messages into visual ones, and Polly, their hearing ear dog, alerts the children's parents to situations requiring their attention.

If Michael's father is to keep his job as editor of a journal, the family must move to a new town. His mother is particularly uneasy since she will have to establish new contacts with shopkeepers and clerks, who will predictably have difficulty understanding her. Michael is acutely aware of the stares of strangers and tries, not altogether successfully, to ignore the mimicking behavior of some of the boys at his new school. One day his sister's teacher sends the family an invitation to a performance of the National Theater of the Deaf. At first, Michael doesn't want them to go, fearing it would be just another occasion for embarrassment, but he is persuaded that it could be an enjoyable experience as well as an opportunity to meet new people. After the performance, one of the teachers signs to his mother, and the youngster realizes "there were many friendly people in our new town who could talk with our parents. . . . This place wasn't going to be so bad after all."

Analysis. Much useful information is transmitted in this quasi-fiction book about the adaptations deaf persons must make, the basic communication techniques they use, the socialization problems they face, and the responsibilities that need to be assumed by hearing family members on their behalf. The parents are presented as ordinary people who have made appropriate accommodations to their disability. The extra demands made on their children are seen not as a burden but as a necessary response resulting in closer family relationships. Numerous illustrations extend the text, providing additional information and revealing some affectional components of various situations.

Little, Jean. *Listen for the Singing.* New York: Dutton, 1977. 215 pp.
Reading Level: YA
Disability: Visual Impairment

Anticipating the repressive measures of the Nazi government and fiercely opposed to its trampling on human rights, Mr. Solden moves his family to a new home in Canada. Ironically, once there, they become the target of anti-German sentiment when their adopted homeland enters the war. Vicious remarks are directed at them, and their business is boycotted by former customers as mobilization of the nation begins. Anna's more immediate concerns involve her transition from the security of a sight-saving room in a lower school to the impersonality of an integrated but unadapted high school where she will not know anyone in the class. Despite her anxiety, she makes friends with several girls and, by choosing a front row seat in her classroom, using her well-developed memory skills, and extrapolating from gross color cues, she copes with the academic demands. One of her teachers, a man universally disliked by the other students, types out her exams in large print and makes other accommodations that enable her to function more easily in the classroom. She is startled to learn that this haughty and seemingly unfeeling instructor has a disability similar to her own. He uses sarcasm and aloofness to avoid appearing weak and vulnerable. Rudi, her older brother, who had been her greatest antagonist when they were younger, now helps her with homework, soon becoming her friend as well as mentor. Rudi is angry at the prejudice he experiences and worried about a beloved aunt imprisoned in their native Germany. He is impelled to action by the tragic news from abroad and enlists to fight in the war. While still in the country, he is blinded in a bizarre accident. Embittered, depressed, and ashamed of what he anticipates will be a life of dependence, Rudi returns home to brood, living in self-imposed isolation. Anna refuses to allow her brother to surrender to depression. She obtains some brailled materials and, guided by instructions from her former teacher, begins the young man's reeducation. She persuades him to leave his room and venture beyond the protecting walls of their home. Rudi is uneasy during their brief excursion and when they return demands to know if others were staring at him. "How would I know?" Anna asks, reminding him that she has lived all her life with limited vision. "Talk about the perfect squelch!" Rudi responds. The two work to improve his new reading skills and demonstrate them to his anxious family in an emotion-charged scene that signals the youth's readiness to accept his blindness.

Analysis. In this sequel to *From Anna,* themes of freedom and prejudice reappear in a more intensified form. The author succeeds in capturing the ambiance of Canada just prior to World War II and in communicating the problems of refugees fleeing from oppression and trying to establish a new home. Despite the strained coincidence of three vision-impaired characters and the improbability that Anna's teacher could successfully conceal such a severe disability, the story moves quickly, engagingly, and believably. The depiction of the minor daily problems and the major adjustments of a young woman with extensive vision loss is forthrightly and compassionately presented.

Long, Judy. *Volunteer Spring.* New York: Dodd, Mead, 1976. 126 pp. Reading Level: MC/YA
Disability: Intellectual Impairment

After hearing an occupational therapist speak about her job at a state hospital for mentally retarded persons, 14-year-old Jill and two of her friends volunteer to work there on Saturdays. Their introduction to the institution begins with a visit to the infirmary, where "each bed and cart had some—some creature in it who was drooling, screaming, or lying there vacant eyed. . . . It was impossible to turn without being confronted with a misshapen mass of humanity." Miss Robinson, their guide, points out the sights to them: "Now, this is Susie . . . Susie's known as a hydrocephalic, or more commonly, a waterhead. . . . Now, here's an interesting case. . . . Due entirely to prenatal brain damage, she is frozen in the fetal position."

Although her friends readily adjust to the center, Jill is upset by the extent of the residents' disabilities, the institutional odors, and an unexpected and misunderstood encounter. When she arrives home, drained by the experience, her mother is alarmed at her daughter's obvious distress and refuses to allow her to return, a decision Jill greets with relief. The therapist, aware of the girl's unhappiness, visits her at home and persuades her to face her fears and attempt to master them. On her second visit, Jill assists with the residents' band and becomes involved in instructing a child with Down's syndrome. She soon sees that her efforts as a volunteer enrich the emotionally and socially sterile lives of the residents, and this insight promotes increased enthusiasm for her work. She is upset when she learns that the man who drove her to the institution will be absent for several months but eagerly awaits resuming her charitable chores in the fall when he returns.

Analysis. Volunteer Spring is an extended, naive, and inaccurate discourse on how those designated as severely and profoundly retarded are treated in state hospitals. It is only lightly papered over with a fragile story line. The narrative is static, lacking tension or climax. Jill thankfully contrasts her abilities to those of the residents of the institution and learns a lesson in humility and appreciation for her own good fortune—a literary approach to character improvement that would be more at home in children's trade books of the last century.

> Jill was suddenly, overwhelmingly, ashamed of herself. Here she'd been moping because she couldn't help decorate the gym. But she could go to the dance. She could *dance*; a lot of Overton residents could not even walk, could not move a muscle. She'd been complaining about having to spend a Saturday here, just one Saturday. And practically everyone she encountered at Overton would end up spending the greater part of his or her life here. Some were literally strapped to beds and carts, like the infirmary residents, while others could do no more than roam from building to building. Miss Robinson had told her that a few privileged residents could go to town on short visits. But all had to have special permission to step out of the fixed routine. Jill might spend one short Saturday at Overton, but she could leave when she wanted to. It had never dawned on her how important "freedom" really was; now the lesson struck home with frightening clarity.

But more important than the book's literary failure are the attitudes expressed toward persons sustaining these conditions and those who work with them. Long's insensitivity is epitomized in the scene depicting the youngsters' introduction to the hospital. Their visit begins in the infirmary, where patients with the most extreme and unusual forms of physical and intellectual anomalies are warehoused. This combination medical rounds inspection and freak show approach is an outrageous depiction of how volunteers are initiated into their roles. The reprehensibility of the behavior of the professional staff is exacerbated in their vocabulary, which is dated and demeaning, for example, "mongoloid" is used to refer to a person with Down's syndrome, "waterhead" is used to mean hydrocephalus, "custodial" is employed instead of "profoundly retarded." The inappropriateness of such a tour and the treatment of the "cases" as though they were members of a sideshow does not seem to bother any of the staff. The heroine's preceptions are shown to be artless, but the patronizing attitude they accompany appears to have the writer's approval: "And Jill would love them, love them regardless of their 'lower intelligence level' (that sounded so much better than stupidity), love them despite their ugliness and deformities, love them because nobody else would."

In a final display of naiveté, condescension, and pretentiousness, she wonders: "Wouldn't it be exciting to take a mentally retarded child by the hand and show him the beauty of a rose?"

Lowry, Lois. *Anastasia Krupnik*. Boston: Houghton Mifflin, 1979. 113 pp. Reading Level: MC
Disability: neurological impairment

Anastasia is indignant to discover her mother is pregnant, a situation she is confident can only lead to unpleasant consequences. Hoping to placate their ten-year-old daughter, the Krupniks impetuously promise her that she can name the new baby. Taking advantage of the opportunity for revenge she has been offered, Anastasia writes in her secret book the epithet she overheard some boys utter, which she has chosen for the intruder's name. She relishes the regret her parents will feel when they learn their infant is to be called One Ball-Reiley.

The youngster's 92-year-old grandmother leaves the nursing home where she has been living to spend some time with her family at Thanksgiving. The girl is repelled by her elderly relative: "The wrinkles on the side of her mouth were scabby. She talked with her mouth full, and what she said usually didn't make any sense, and there were food spots on the front of her dress." Moreover, the old woman cannot remember her granddaughter's name and is even confused about who Anastasia is. She speaks frequently about her son, Anastasia's father, as though he were still a child and constantly asks for Sam, her long dead husband. The girl's mother explains that Mrs. Krupnik has returned in her mind to times long past, when she was a young woman. One day the youngster accompanies her father to the university, attending a literature class he teaches. Afterward, he is pleasantly surprised to discover that his daughter has garnered a great deal from the poetry discussion. The perceptive girl concludes that her grandmother has an "inward eye," like the one spoken of by the poet in the lecture, an insight that generates a feeling of affection toward her grandparent. Soon after, the old woman dies, and Anastasia shares her parents' grief. When her brother is born, the youngster, now reconciled to this addition to her family, announces his name will be Sam, a decision she is confident would have pleased her grandmother.

Analysis. Lowry has created an engaging and witty story featuring a quirky, independent, and admirable title character. Her parents are nonconformists unencumbered by concern for appearances who provide models of understanding and tolerance. Their acceptance of non-standard behavior extends to their elderly relative, who is now disoriented and unable to care for herself. The use of a literary metaphor to interpret the seemingly bizarre behavior of the senile woman permits the youngster to come to an understanding of the woman's actions, which leads to empathy for her situation. They wisely allow their sometimes prickly daughter the room she needs on her stormy route to maturity. The combination of compassion and humor is successful, although some scenes that adults will find hilarious may slip by youthful readers.

Lowry, Lois. *Autumn Street.* Boston: Houghton Mifflin, 1980. 188 pp. Reading Level: MC/YA
Disability: Neurological Impairment, Emotional Dysfunction, orthopedic impairment

The time is the early 1940s and the narrator, just six, moves with her mother and sister to her grandparents' home after her father is drafted. Young Elizabeth finds many things frightening and confusing—the sudden silence when she mentions her cousin David, now hospitalized; the startling realization that her beloved father may die in the war; her young neighbor's warning that giant people-eating turtles live in the woods at the end of Autumn Street. Her main source of comfort is Tatie, her grandparents' housekeeper. Her best friend is Charles, Tatie's grandson. The black youngster is slightly older than the heroine but in her eyes seems far more worldly wise than she. From her sister, Jess, she hears of Ferdie Gossett, a filthy, unkempt man who talks to himself, rummages through trash barrels, and can often be seen waiting near the schoolground watching the children at play. Elizabeth asks: "Did he look at you as if he was friendly, or mean?" Jess answers: "Neither one. As if he didn't even see us. It was really scary."

One day her grandfather collapses from a stroke and, after a brief hospital stay, is brought home to be cared for by Elizabeth's imperious grandmother. In attending her newly helpless husband, the elderly woman reveals an unsuspected compassion as she tenderly ministers to his many needs. Elizabeth tries to communicate with the now inarticulate man, stroking his legs "as a comfort and apology for his infirmities." Later, wanting to share Christmas with the old man, she "sprinkled cinnamon on his damp fingertip and lifted it to the wet black shape that had once been his fine proud mouth. It touched his tongue, and with his mouth he shaped what [she] understood to be a smile."

The youngster enters first grade and is upset when she sees Ferdie Gossett near the school, discomfited by the perception that "his vacant eyes made me think of my grandfather." The other children ignore the derelict or occasionally "pelt[ed] him with pebbles, the tiny weapons as casually cruel as the small insults that we inflict on each other at play."

The "lunatic" comes to their home for a Christmas meal, and Elizabeth's grandmother coolly gives him ten dollars as an "act of Christian charity," saying afterward to the girl: "He is a tasteless, impolite, and demented man." Charles and Elizabeth take the girl's new Christmas sled to a hill, where some older white boys humilate Charles and take away the sled. The girl, feeling the early stages of what will be pneumonia, begs her friend to take her home, but his pride is wounded and he insists on entering the forbidden woods at the end of the street. She staggers home, desperately sick. Despite the delirium brought about by her raging temperature, she overhears that Charles was killed in the woods by Ferdie Gossett: "With their different angers, their different terms of innocence, the two had met in the woods that I had always feared for the wrong reasons."

Her father returns while she is still ill. "Part of his leg was gone. He had a new lower leg, made of wood and metal in fascinating, complicated combinations. After the first, startling sight of the place where his real leg ended and the new one began, it didn't seem terrible any more." Her father promises that bad things won't happen again. "Probably my father and I both knew, even then, that it was not true, what we told each other, that bad things would never happen again. But we needed that lie, that pretending, the spring I was seven."

Analysis. This gentle, reflective tale exquisitely explores the mellow, strained, loving, evolving, conflicting relationships between a young girl and her family and friends. It accurately recreates a child's attempt, inevitably restricted by innocence and immaturity, to understand a complex, often brutal world. The murderer of her friend stood outside of the society they shared, seen but ignored as though he were some unattractive aspect of the scenery. He is an object of ungracious and begrudging charity, of fear because of his strange and incomprehensible behavior, of abuse by the children who attack him with stones, but mostly of indifference. Her grandfather is loved and respected as ever, but many relationships alter because of his helplessness. In her naiveté, Elizabeth thinks that the "stroke" the old man is said to have had is tied in with the time of the onset of his paralysis—just at the "stroke" of eight o'clock. In a similar manner, she stares uncomprehendingly at a shell, wondering how her beloved cousin could have become "shell-shocked." After the initial impact, her father's impairment is casually accepted, its significance all but lost in the joy of his homecoming. The implications of disability are seen across many age groups, placed in high relief by contrasting the security inside the home on Autumn Street with the horrors of war and of discrimination outside it. Lowry has infused vitality and compassion into her sensitive story and, despite the problems associated with severe distress, provided a sense of the indomitability of life.

Lutters, Valerie A. *The Haunting of Julie Unger.* New York: Atheneum, 1977. 193 pp. Reading Level: MC/YA
Disability: Emotional Dysfunction

Julie is shattered when her beloved father dies suddenly of a heart attack. This totally unexpected event paralyzes the 12-year-old girl, who is able neither to mourn for him nor to cope with the painful vacuum in her life. The loss is particularly devastating since she has only a distant, abrasive relationship with her mother, few friends, and little satisfaction in her life. When Julie's family moves to Maine permanently to live with her grandmother, the girl seeks relief and solitude at the remote cove where she and her father used to photograph Canadian geese together. Her loneliness and intense need combine to evoke his presence, and she converses with this manifestation of her deceased parent, ventilating her resentment about her situation and trying to recapture the closeness and lightheartedness of their relationship. The wild birds trust her and approach when she offers food. However, Julie has unwittingly been a party to their destruction since they no longer fear people and consequently are easy targets for hunters. Frustrated and angry at the loss of the creatures she has invested so much in, she turns on her "father," throws his camera at him, watching in horror as both the image and the camera disappear. A concerned neighbor rescues her and is able to redirect the girl's energies. Now released from her unhealthy obsession, Julie is freed to participate in less self-centered occupations.

Analysis. Julie's determination, deriving in large measure from guilt, to isolate herself from family, classmates, and friends and her obsession with her dead father result in a life dependent on hallucinatory visions for satisfactions. The kindness, patience, and understanding of a neighbor, the realization that her behavior has caused harm to the wild geese she loves, and the opportunity to help someone else now in need are shown to be remediative. Although the story ends on an optimistic note, it is clear that the heroine has some reconstruction of her life yet to accomplish. The plot is unique, but Lutters keeps the reader at a distance from the action, a style that generates a feeling of some sympathy for the heroine but discourages much involvement.

Mace, Elizabeth. *Out There.* Originally published in England as *Ransome Revisited* by Andre Deutsch, 1975. New York: Greenwillow, 1978. 181 pp. Reading Level: YA
Disability: Intellectual Impairment

In the time after the destruction and great sickness caused by the war, children are gathered together in schools and then, after completion of the seventh-level class, are assigned to various work crews. One nameless boy is told to care for his older brother, whose intellectual impairment makes him unable to fend for himself. When the two youths reach the resettlement area, they are given numbers no longer in use and are henceforth known respectively as Eleven, or Leven, and Thirty. The boys are sent to join a mining crew, where the work is hard, rations are short, and the overseer is brutal. Leven grudgingly protects his brother as best he can from the teasing and abuse of the other boys. The newcomers are befriended by Susanna, one of the few people with a name, who shares her secret hideout with Leven and warns him against Will, a boy whose surface friendliness masks a cold, exploitive, and self-serving interior.

One day Susanna and Leven find two runaway sisters, whom they conceal in one of the mines. Will, notified that he is to be sent away, arranges for a cave-in, trapping the cruel overseer but also killing the older fugitive. Susanna and Leven realize they must leave immediately if they are to save the younger girl, and Susanna reminds her companion of his responsibility toward Thirty.

The desperate youngsters head for Scotland and the fabled "Colony" where they believe they will find refuge. After many miles, they reach a forest and are befriended by a hunter who, after feeding and clothing them, leads them toward the sea. Unknown to the travelers, Will has trailed them and tricks a young hunter into shooting at the escapees. Thirty is hit and dies instantly. Will comes forward to help Leven and Susanna bury the body, then joins the wayfarers, who finally reach the shore. They find a young boy who speaks an unfamiliar language but who is willing to take them in his boat to safety. Susanna remains, selecting this place as her destination, Will leaves to search for the stars (!), and Leven and the youngster whom he has named A.B. continue until they find the Colony, where they will presumably find a haven.

Analysis. The imprecise, ambiguous, and vague title seems particularly apt for this doomsday science fiction tale since its passionless tone and abstruseness match the lack of involvement and unempathetic response readers will feel toward the dimensionless, forgettable characters. Much of their behavior is incomprehensible, as in the group's ready acceptance of Will despite the fact that he has been responsible for the death of the siblings of two members of the party. Even though there appears to be little affection shared by the brothers, the total lack of concern caused by Thirty's death seems extreme. There are no further references to him once he is buried, but that death should have completely eradicated him is consistent since he was not valued much in life either. The disabled youth is drawn as a thoroughly passive person—responding placidly to insistent demands, exhibiting as few emotions as he inspires. That no anger is directed at his murderer's accomplice is further evidence of his worthlessness.

Little is explained in the story. There is no exploration of why his brother's impairment should preclude Leven's obtaining the occupational training he desires. Will and Susanna have names, but why they are so privileged is equally unclear. Neither their respective motivations nor their chosen destination has discernible meaning. A further mystery is the purpose of the quarry, a place unlike others since it seems to have no function other than to provide a locale to generate useless labor. This general confusion is compounded by the quality of the writing, which ranges from vague—"There was no one anywhere, but of course they must either be a long way away by now, or hiding somewhere as they had done"—or unfathomable:

> Never mind death and the stars, Will; never mind the glory and the forever; this will do the rest of my life. He walked the length of the School Room, a little boy in Class 3, and it was a muddy yard leading to a thick stone farmhouse, an old man, a stinking dog and Swallowdale sheep waiting like white stars for his hands on the green universe, the mountain.

McHargue, Georgess. *The Horseman's Word*. New York: Delacorte, 1981. 259 pp. Reading Level: YA
Disability: Neurological Impairment

Aunt Connie and Uncle Will welcome their American niece, Leigh, to Kinloch Farm in Scotland. Will's recent stroke "had cost him most of the use of his right leg and weakened his right arm, and Leigh felt an embarrassing impulse to look away whenever he tried to do anything that needed two hands." The man pointedly ignores his wife's assurances that he will undoubtedly fully recover and their life will soon resume its former patterns. Col, their six-year-old son, has made a more accurate appraisal of his father's capabilities, frequently alluding to activities in which the man can no longer take part.

Leigh, drawing on her skill with horses and wishing to make a contribution, assumes responsibility for leading tourists on pony rides to a local monument commemorating the deeds of a Scottish hero. In her explorations of the brooding but lovely countryside, she meets a lad named Rob, who is a ward of Young Tam, the general handyman at Kinloch Farm. The laborer harbors a fierce but unwarranted animosity toward the American, a feeling the visitor reciprocates when she learns how the man has exploited and abused Rob. In town on an errand, Leigh impulsively follows someone she mistakenly thinks is her new friend into a tavern, where she overhears Young Tam speak of "The Horseman's Word" and discuss plans for a secret meeting during the upcoming festival of Common Riding. Rob later explains that the term is a supposedly magical gypsy expression known only to those who have been initiated into a secret society during a special ritual. The intrepid foreigner decides to participate in the rites, although the ruse involves danger and she will need to prepare a careful disguise. With Rob's help she manages to conceal her identity and lose herself among the legitimate initiates. After a frightening devil-worshiping ceremony, Leigh is discovered, and when confronted by Young Tam, she inadvertently reveals a confidence entrusted to her by Rob. In doing so, she causes the boy to be humiliated, an outcome that delights Tam.

When Rob is reported missing, Leigh correctly assumes he is hiding in the remote, abandoned castle where they originally met. The adolescent brings him supplies as well as an apology, and, in the reconciliation, he reveals his painful secret: his mother had callously abandoned him when he was a baby. When Leigh returns home, Will tells her that Rob's guardian had reported the boy's absence to the police, demanding that the runaway be returned to his care. Despite her fear, the teenage girl tells Tam he must allow Rob his freedom or she will give the police evidence that he tried to kill her. Leigh further threatens to inform the fanatically religious woman on whom the tyrant depends for support that he is a participant in pagan rituals, a revelation that would undoubtedly result in his eviction. Furious, the man acknowledges defeat and accedes to Leigh's demands, after which Rob finds a temporary haven with her relatives. Connie at last admits that her husband's impairment has resulted in irreversible damage and accepts the necessity for accommodation. The American returns home, content in the knowledge that she has made a constructive difference in the lives of people she has learned to love and respect.

Analysis. The one aspect of this novel that lifts it above the ordinary run of teenage romances is its sensitive treatment of a family adjusting to the consequences of serious neurological impairment in one of its members. Although many stories explore the psychological and physiological aftereffects of disability, this author examines economic trauma as well. The popularly held idea that willpower and determination are sufficient to overcome any obstacle is shown here to be a damaging rather than a productive attitude.

McKay, Robert. *The Girl Who Wanted to Run the Boston Marathon.* New York: Elsevier/Nelson, 1979. 188 pp. Reading Level: YA
Disability: Special Health Problems, neurological impairment

Chris has run only for the pleasure of the experience, but one day she impetuously decides to become an entrant in the Boston Marathon. While training for the contest, she collides with Skip Malone, who aggressively pursues a friendship with the independent, headstrong girl. When Chris learns that her new acquaintance is a world-class runner who refuses to compete in the marathon, she is both angry and disappointed; when he discovers that her father is the successful and respected author, Martin Cole, he is elated and nervous at the prospect of meeting someone he has long admired. Skip offers to coach Chris, a proposal she initially rejects since she is reluctant to give up control over this aspect of her life. Later she reconsiders because she is determined to be ready for the event. Unhappily, the young woman develops soreness in muscles and joints, a mild rash, and some other seemingly innocuous ailments, which, while annoying, are not of sufficient intensity or duration to cause alarm.

Skip visits his grandfather, a wealthy, dynamic businessman, now semiretired after a stroke left him unable to walk. The elderly man lives in an opulent Victorian mansion, attended by a small staff of loyal servants. He tells his grandson that in a few months, when Skip is 21, the young man will have to take over the management of the inheritance left by his father. Skip is astonished to learn that he will be a millionaire several times over and ponders the warning that, in addition to the many opportunities it offers, the responsibility of the estate carries with it many obligations. The young man tells his grandfather about Chris, confiding his deep feelings for her to the old man.

During a training session, Chris suddenly collapses, obviously seriously ill. The initial diagnosis is systemic lupus, an assessment later confirmed by a specialist, who prescribes aspirin, bed rest, and a stress-free lifestyle. The doctor in charge admits that knowledge about the disorder, lupus erythematosus, is incomplete and treatment protocols are untested. Mr. Cole, on another of his alcoholic binges and unable to make any serious decisions, abdicates responsibility to his daughter's boyfriend, who uses his wealth to provide a private room and nurse for Chris. When the girl feels better, the two young people discuss their mutual love and Skip's decision to enter the marathon. The next morning, he makes arrangements for another specialist to consult on the case, trains for a few hours, takes a brief nap, then heads for the hospital. Mr. Cole intercepts him in the parking lot to tell him that Chris is dead. The frantic youth is furious, convinced that his informant is too drunk to be trusted. From the physician, he discovers that the grim news is true: during a psychotic episode, Chris imagined the room was on fire and jumped through the fourth-floor window in a tragic reenactment of Skip's own father's death.

Analysis. This novel has a promising beginning, but it soon loses momentum. The writing becomes increasingly weighted down with clichés: "I've got a hunch this might be a turning point," and "Nobody ever told you it was going to be easy." In addition, the shocking climax seems unwarranted, and the abrupt and arbitrary conclusion is extremely unsatisfying. However, readers can obtain considerable information about lupus, which is introduced through the device of a special lecture to interns on the hospital staff, discussions between the consultant and admitting doctor, and an exposition made during hospital rounds. The elderly relative employs a wheelchair, indicating his stroke affected his mobility, although his sagacity and business acumen remain very much intact.

MacKellar, William. *The Soccer Orphans.* New York: Dodd, Mead, 1979. 157 pp. Reading Level: MC/YA
Disability: orthopedic impairment, auditory impairment

Football is the sole sports focus at affluent Orkney High School where Jamie is newly enrolled, but he cannot make the team because, although sufficiently talented, he is not big enough for the bruising style that is the team's hallmark. Practicing soccer skills alone, he is observed by a group of boys, who commend him for his ability in handling the ball. The group decides to form a soccer team, and Jamie is elected captain. This is an unlikely crew: Coach Huntley is a female French teacher; the other members are Manny, a street fighter from New York's Lower East Side; Sy, a boy using a prosthesis for the portion of his right arm lost in an automobile accident; Charlie, an obese youth; Horace, a quiet, undersized son of a former football hero; and Mark, who has a hearing loss. Their late start and outcast status at the school preclude getting uniforms, and when their unexpectedly tough mentor arranges for them to participate in the regional soccer conference, they play in makeshift outfits.

Coach Huntley is undismayed at their losses, and the valiant group, working together, learns how to overcome their deficiencies and manages to spring back from their early defeats. Jamie's outlook is cheered by some victories, a budding romance with a sportswriter on the high school paper, and the results of a car wash fund raiser that nets enough money to purchase team uniforms. Just before the crucial playoff, an anonymous caller challenges the legality of allowing a boy with a prosthesis to play, alleging that his device is "ineligible equipment." Although Jamie suspects that quarterback Gil Larue is responsible, when the football star's father is injured in a hunting accident, he donates his own rare type blood to save the critically ill man. The next morning, the complaint is withdrawn, and although the soccer team loses the conference finals, the exuberant team members celebrate a victory—"a game that was a lot more important than the one we just lost . . . the game of facing up to adversity. Of refusing to accept a handicap or a disadvantage as an excuse for failure." At the celebration, the football coach reveals that next year's budget will include expenditures for the "orphans" and that his personal plans include marrying Coach Huntley.

Analysis. Even though the boys with impairments play secondary roles, they are crucial to the key theme in the book: athletics (and life) is enriched by accommodating diversity. The team made up of outsiders is shown to be a collection of obvious winners. Mark, whose determination and enthusiasm are emphasized, typifies this outlook:

> He was clumsy and awkward at times but he never stopped rushing the ball like an enraged bull. Twice he charged Jamie, lost his balance, and went hurtling to the ground. Each time he had grinned, reassured himself that his hearing aid was still there, then flung himself back into the action.

Typical of the genre, the pace is fast, there is considerable description of sports action, virtue is rewarded, and prose is unabashedly overblown and replete with clichés, as "Just us and a crazy dream," or "But sometimes there were no winners. No acclaim. And it had taken a quiet kid with one arm to tell him so."

McKillop, Patricia A. *The Night Gift*. Illus. by Kathy McKillop. New York: Atheneum, 1976. 156 pp. Reading Level: MC/YA
Disability: Cosmetic Impairment, emotional dysfunction

Claudia is concerned about her upcoming operation:

> She was born with a cleft palate, and every once in a while she got very depressed about her face, which the doctors still hadn't finished. Her upper lip was flat and pulled up towards her nose, and

you could see more of the underside of her nose than you would ordinarily expect. Her voice sounded hollow, and honked a little sometimes like a goose's voice, so in her classes at school she never said anything.

Barbara Takaota's brother, Joe, is returning home from the hospital, where he had been sent after slashing his hands on a window glass in a suicide attempt. Confused and saddened by her brother's actions, the girl reflects: "I wish I knew why he did it. . . . I wish I could make a place for him, just for him, where he could go when he was depressed, that was so beautiful, that just being in it would make him happy."

Determined to help the despondent youth, Barbara and her two best friends, Claudia and Jocelyn, search for such a place. They locate an abandoned house, which they intend to convert into a refuge before Joe comes home. Jocelyn is consumed with jealousy when Neil, who joins the project, becomes increasingly attentive to Barbara—an act that jeopardizes the girls' friendship. She is further disconcerted when her usually abrasive older brother behaves with unexpected thoughtfulness toward Claudia, using banter as a means to break through the reserve of the painfully shy girl. To her friends' surprise, Claudia speaks openly with him and later even shares her concerns about her scheduled palate reconstruction and cosmetic surgery with Jocelyn, confiding:

> I hate the part where they give you a shot to put you to sleep, and I get sleepier and sleepier but I make myself wake up because I don't like that kind of sleep. I hate hospitals. I hate having to be like this. I don't see why I was born this way instead of someone else.

When Jocelyn tries to console her friend with the promise that she will be prettier after the operation, Claudia casually and pragmatically responds that she will simply be more normal, and the two discuss strategies to improve her appearance in other ways.

The secret room is finished by the time Joe arrives home, but when his well-wishers bring him to the lovingly decorated hideout, he disappoints them with his passive, seemingly disinterested response to their labor of love. Later, indifferent to the terrible physical pain, Joe deliberately mutilates his hands on a steel fence, and arrangements are made to rehospitalize the troubled youth. Anguished over their failure, the youngsters plan to dismantle the room, discovering to their surprise that the plants have been tended, presumably by Joe. They are relieved and gratified to know that, however indirectly, Barbara's brother has acknowledged the love and concern expressed through their efforts.

Analysis. Issues of familial ties, friendships, emerging adolescence, facial disfigurement, and attempted suicide are interwoven in this sensitive and subtle novel. Although loving and anxious to help, Joe's family and friends are unable to combat the youth's acute depression. The youngsters' attempts to help are admirable, even though they are inevitably inadequate to combat a problem as complex and intractable as Joe's. There is no clear reason offered for his despair, and although he suffered racial slurs, these are not proposed as the explanation for his dysfunction. Claudia's questioning of why she was born with a cleft lip and palate is neither answered nor, in a sense, answerable, obliquely suggesting that some situations exist without apparent reason and must simply be accommodated as well as they can be. Her withdrawal from verbal and social interaction is perceived as plausible but neither desirable nor ultimately useful. *The Night Gift* is unusual and thought-provoking, the characters are credible and interesting, and the style demonstrates respect for both the complexity of the problems addressed as well as the intelligence of the audience.

MacLachlan, Patricia. *Through Grandpa's Eyes.* Illus. by Deborah Ray. New York: Harper & Row, 1980. unp. Reading Level: YC
Disability: Visual Impairment

On a visit John learns to experience the world in the way his blind grandfather does. He learns that there is nothing mysterious about the way his grandfather knows what is happening; the man simply depends on senses other than vision to tell him about the world. His nose tells him that eggs and buttered toast are for breakfast and his wife has picked marigolds for their table. His sensitive fingers inform him that the likeness of John's grandmother that he has sculpted is a true one, and the wind he feels tells him the breeze is blowing from the south. His keen ears identify the red-winged blackbirds and sparrows in the meadow and the geese flying overhead. John, newly inspired to activate his own senses, hears the smile in his grandmother's voice when she bids him to go to sleep that night.

Analysis. A lyrical story of love and experiences is shared by a grandfather and his grandson. John is full of wonder at the way his grandfather manages and, in a demonstration of affection and curiosity about his style of discovery, wants to emulate him. The old man is a tender, kind, loving person who has learned to let his other senses substitute for vision loss. There is nothing mystical in this: it is just an instance of necessity and adaptation. John is admiring but not thunderstruck—in other words, his interested response is both reasonable and credible. The gentle, warm tone of both text and illustration is admirable.

MacLeod, Charlotte. *King Devil.* New York: Atheneum, 1978. 212 pp. Reading Level: YA
Disability: Intellectual Impairment

After finishing school, Lavinia Tabard is invited to stay with her wealthy, self-indulgent cousin, Zilpha, who has recently purchased a house she is in the process of renovating. However, Zilpha's companion, Tetsy, finds the newcomer's presence an unwelcome intrusion into their well-ordered life. Lavinia first encounters Peter, a boy with developmental disabilities, swinging a bladeless scythe. Their next meeting is at a cemetery, where Lavinia is making a grave rubbing and selects for her artwork the headstone of Jonah Jenks, a man whose name has been used by successive owners of the property on which Zilpha's house stands. The young woman meets two architects, one a highly desirable mate in the eyes of her cousin, and the other, Hayward Clinton, a rude, unmannerly, but talented and hard-working young man. The last Mr. Jenks has disappeared, and the two architects whom he employed stand to inherit his business if the missing man can be declared dead.

Exploring an abandoned mill, Lavinia finds Jenks's remains. She panics and, in her precipitous exit, is trapped by some rickety stairs, which collapse. After her rescue, the trauma and head injuries she sustains prevent her from remembering the incidents that led to her accident. She does recall enough to alert Clinton that she may need protection, and he advises the town constable. The story of the cover-up of Jenks's demise is soon revealed: Peter's mother had found the body at the bottom of a flight of stairs. Assuming that her son, then six, had pushed the man and was therefore the unwitting agent of his death, she did not report her find. Subsequently, it is learned that Zilpha and Tetsy had visited Jenks earlier on that fateful day, pressuring him to sell his land. Although Zilpha undoubtedly killed him, Tetsy is taken into custody, and, it is implied, her unswerving loyalty to her employer will keep her from divulging the truth. Lack of concrete evidence will enable the lawyer to clear his client. A romance will inevitably flourish between Lavinia and Hayward Clinton.

Analysis. The image of Peter harvesting nothing, the unsubtle implication of a lesbian relationship, the allusions to a deaf character, which are never developed, are all unsuccessful attempts to flesh out a spare and insubstantial narrative. The youngster is presented as a child with a severe intellectual impairment who is also a mathematical wizard:

Oddly enough, the child has an uncommon ability for doing sums. He doesn't even know how to tie his own bootlaces, but he can read off a string of numbers, add them up in his head, and multiply by anything you please. His mother claims he's never once been caught in a mistake. . . . He had the answers almost before we could finish writing down the sums, much less cipher them out.

Real-life counterparts of the *idiot savant* can occasionally be found, but the only use of the syndrome here is to prop up a weak plot line. This shallow costume drama offers stock characters, unlikely situations, and a dull romance—ingredients that add up to a trite and forgettable effort.

Maguire, Gregory. *Lights on the Lake*. New York: Farrar, Straus & Giroux, 1981. 214 pp. Reading Level: YA
Disability: Emotional Dysfunction

Daniel Rider is at the rectory when Nikos Grishas, a young poet, is unceremoniously dumped on the doorstep by his furious, nearly hysterical sister, who claims she will have nothing more to do with him. The withdrawn, sickly man is helped into bed, where he will be allowed to remain until Father Petrarkis returns. The curious youngster hopes for an opportunity to talk to the poet, but the man, weakened by his emotional ordeal, is incapable of responding. Susan Barrey becomes Daniel's first friend in this community, and they talk about Nikos's puzzling arrival. The children learn from local gossip that the stranger and a companion had recently been camping and, during the night of their outing, Nikos got lost and was unable to find their tent until the next morning. To his horror, he discovered that his friend had frozen to death in his absence. Unreasonably blaming himself for the disaster, Nikos has been overwhelmed by feelings of guilt. The tormented man has withdrawn into his private world, shutting out all attempts at communication. Hallucinations cause him to cry out in anguish, but he is unable to articulate his grief.

One day, Daniel unsuccessfully tries to investigate a strange luminous mist that seemingly rises from the lake. When the puzzling cloud appears again, a large ebony bird emerges from it. Risking considerable danger, the children follow it and are able to retrieve a single black feather. This talisman transports Daniel into the dreams of a villager searching for his dead wife, of Susan's grandfather seeking his infant son, and of Nikos looking for Mark, his dead companion. When it is learned that Nikos is missing, the community mounts a thorough search and ultimately he is discovered, alone and shivering on the ice, further exhausted by this traumatic odyssey. Father Petrarkis returns to the rectory for Easter services, and the relieved Daniel recounts the enigmatic events that have transpired, showing his trusted confidant the dark feather. The priest examines it, asserting: "This is not ours . . . not ours at all. Not of this world." The feather is then given to the almost lifeless poet, who is escorted to a boat that hurls them at breakneck speed toward the mysterious cloud hovering over the lake. Suddenly there is an explosion of light, and an image of the deceased man materializes. When Nikos begs for forgiveness, "Mark" rejects its necessity but bestows it when his friend continues his desperate pleading. The boat turns, the mysterious light fades, and the travelers return to shore. The next evening at dinnertime, the revived Nikos appears— alert, hungry, and enormously relieved to be able to function again without his suffocating burden.

Analysis. Although there are many passages of graceful writing and the pacing and unusual topic arouse interest, the allusions, imagery, and symbolism lack coherence. The setting in a rectory on Lake Canaan at Easter, the references to church practices, rites, and dogma, and the themes of guilt, death, resurrection, and absolution demand a religious interpretation and resolution rather than magical ones. The central role of the ebony bird and its ice-melting feather, Mark's imperfect and confusing Christlike function, and Nikos's obsessive insistence on forgiveness where no fault exists are unsettling and unsatisfactory elements. Neither a rational, theological, nor mythological basis for the imagery is developed with consistency. Moreover, the attribution of hallucinatory visions, psychotic withdrawal, and suicidal behaviors deriving from relentless, all-consuming feelings of guilt is not credible in this context.

Mark, Jan. *Divide and Rule.* New York: Crowell, 1979. 246 pp.
Reading Level: MA
Disability: Visual Impairment, emotional dysfunction

Reluctant to inform his family of his diminishing vision, Hanno disappoints them in their hopes that he follow some scholarly pursuit or join their pottery business. He reflects on his decision to work on the river, an occupation his family disparages:

He had taken the boat to save his sight. Much as he disliked to deceive, this was one secret he would never reveal to his family. Sitting with his tutor, day after day, surrounded by scrolls and books, he had discovered that each day seemed to bring his face closer to the manuscript, while other faces around him turned into approximate sketches. He could see his way about, clearly enough, but all the dear details of life began to escape him. He foresaw, with real terror, a day when the whole world melted before his eyes and he would be dependent thereafter on the eyes and hands of others;

so when the tutor walked out of the house for the last time, he closed his books and began instantly to look round for a means of escape, and the river offered him one. He missed reading more than he would admit, but since he had given it up his sight had become no worse and he reckoned that he was safe for the time being.

With full understanding of the consequences of doing otherwise, he vigilantly guards his secret, for "if anyone had once suspected [Hanno's] trouble he would have been seized and subjected to treatment; incantations, ointments, evil lotions, bandages round his eyes and hands to lead him where he did not want to go. He knew of people who had died of being cured." Although rebellious and a loner, his good nature has earned him the tolerance of his neighbors. "His precaution of waving to anything that moved in case it recognized him was regarded as charmingly friendly, and his habit of poking his head forward as if peering over a high fence was thought to be simply one of his many eccentricities, along with his talent for tripping over."

Despite his agnosticism, Hanno succumbs to family pressures to attend the annual church festival, where, to his utter dismay, he is selected to be the community's religious shepherd for the coming year. Since it has been written that the shepherd chosen this particular year would be the most unwilling of all, the young man's angry protestations are seen as confirming what was foretold. Even though resistant and contemptuous of the charade in which he unwillingly participates, Hanno's days within the temple compound evolve into a routine, and having no means of escape, the prisoner gradually lessens his overtly hostile behavior and his contemptuous confrontations. Hanno is watched constantly by a priest and a cohort of guardians, who use force to compel compliance from the lad. More insidiously, the guards attempt to humble him, withholding food and blankets during the freezing winter, and deceive him with psychological tricks, which cause him to doubt his perceptions and his memory.

The temple authorities allow a harmless old man, Aram, to wander about the walled compound. Dow, one of the guards, tells Hanno: "He's mad—you probably guessed. . . . The gods look kindly on lunatics. . . . It's bad luck to cross a madman, everyone knows. The book says, the god is tenderest to those whose wits he has taken." When Aram dies, his bizarre and nonsensical ravings are elevated to prophecy by the church authorities, who see them as a device to recapture the interest of lapsed parishioners and lure converts to their creed. The formerly apathetic community becomes energized, overwhelmed with piety in the presence of new shrines, ecstatic at visiting the sites of supposedly wondrous and holy events. Hanno is aghast at the cynicism with which the church manipulates the gullible populace and fabricates happenings in order to gain wealth, power, and prestige. The youth discovers that the priest has exploited his knowledge of Hanno's near blindness by altering the report of Aram's "miraculous" death, claiming the shepherd witnessed the fulfillment of a prophecy. The youth now fears he will never be allowed to leave the temple grounds alive. He fervently denies that his frequent nosebleeds are a sign predicted by the martyr, but the guards discount his protests. Now, his vision nearly gone, weakened by an extended fast and psychologically exhausted, Hanno doubts that he can participate in the festival that will presumably release him from his bonds. He objects to lying about events but knows he cannot tell the people a truth they will refuse to believe. Obsessed by his dilemma, he begins to interpret various activities as evidence that he will be killed as a ritual sacrifice in the coming ceremonies. In the middle of the rites, the desperate lad blurts out that he killed the prophet himself. The priest twists his false confession to the church's own purposes, and Hanno is removed from the sanctuary and deposited outside the gates. The ordeal has devastated him, drained him of energy, will, and identity, and made him an outcast—rejected and scorned by his family and the community.

Analysis. Mark has written a disturbing, compelling story of venery, corruption, and lust for power. The hero's loss of vision serves a practical as well as symbolic purpose. His diminished eyesight makes him vulnerable to physical danger and psychological pressure as he is led to doubt what his senses have told him. Hanno, as a manifestation of the blind seer, is the only one who perceives that the authorities' theology is fraudulent, their profession of belief a sham, their manipulation of events and people cynical and exploitive. The shepherd is reluctant, although the people are fatally sheeplike. The delusions of Aram, the false martyr, become another instrument for deception as the linking of madness and divine providence makes possible a new mythology.

Mark, Jan. *The Ennead.* New York: Crowell, 1978. 306 pp. Reading Level: MA
Disability: Speech Impairment

On the inhospitable planet of Erato lives a harsh, oppressive community. Theodore, one of its wealthiest inhabitants, employs his half-brother, Isaac, as his steward. Issac, whose stutter worsens under pressure, arranges for the importation of a sculptor to adorn Theodore's house so that it may be distinguished from its neighbors. When Eleanor Ashe arrives, she turns out to be a talented but stiff-necked individualist. She and Moshe, the gardener, become lovers, a situation known to all in the neighborhood but Isaac. Moshe's philosophy—to be one's brother's keeper—is unsettling to the steward and highly offensive to the community. When the gardener, chafing under the repressive establishment, defiantly leaves the church, making clear his opposition to its totally secular purpose of fostering conformity within the populace, he is marked for exile. Eleanor is imprisoned to await her expulsion as well. When the deportation squad arrives, Theodore tells the artist that she will not be allowed to travel with Moshe but must leave separately on a flight she will probably not survive. Using her handcuffs as a weapon, Eleanor overcomes her would-be captors, calling for help from the citizens. However, they are furious at her behavior and not only ignore her entreaties but attempt to stone her.

Eleanor escapes to the desert, where Isaac waits, and surprisingly, he joins her in exile. He has changed from a cringing, craven character who stutters to one who has, however reluctantly and in fact almost inadvertently, taken responsibility for his own actions and in the process overcome his dysfluency.

Analysis. Mark has postulated a futuristic society permeated with biblical characters, incidents, and morality. However, it will take a remarkably astute adolescent to translate her obscure allusions and confusing symbols into a coherent story. The name of the planet on which the action takes place is Erato, in Greek mythology the muse of erotic poetry. "Ennead" of the title, referring to "nine," suggests the ninth planet, Pluto, known as "hell" in another context. Such unique and particular names are certainly suggestive, but their meaning is far from clear in the novel. The association of Eleanor with "light" or artistry is acceptable, but why that is tied to her last name is puzzling. The obviously biblically inspired names of Isaac and Moshe (Moses) recall persons whose behaviors have little in common with their literary descendants. According to tradition, it was Moses who stuttered, and the attribution of this speech disorder to another character in this drama is baffling. Isaac's impairment is used to reinforce his "weak" image: When he casts off his indecisiveness, his speech disorder disappears. Like many novelists who write about the future, Mark touches on a serious social issue: the survival of the artist in a "hellish," nihilistic environment. Such a crucial topic ought not to be buried under unnecessarily diversionary rhetoric.

Mayne, William. *Max's Dream.* Illus. by Laszlo Acs. New York: Morrow, 1977. 88 pp. Reading Level: MC
Disability: Orthopedic Impairment

Max, confined to bed in considerable pain, lives with Mrs. Veary, where he is lovingly attended by Katie, a young household helper. The neighborhood children arrive to inform Max that he has been chosen king of the village midsummer festival. Katie and the other girls each hope they will be chosen as his partner, but in a dream Max travels a great distance until he sees a young girl whom he says is the one he wants for his queen. The local girls are distressed to find none of them has been selected for this role, and the boys become fearful that they have made a poor decision in naming Max their king.

Katie retraces the route in Max's dream until she comes to a house she knows must be the right one. Helen, the girl of Max's imaginings, is there, but she cannot travel to meet him. Instead, the man who lives there announces that Max must come to him to be fitted with braces. When Katie sees the prosthetic devices, she is terrified but senses she must return there with Max. The girl persuades her father to pull the sick lad in a cart, and accompanied by the other children, they set out. The journey is very taxing, and even the white powder that Katie has brought for her charge does not relieve his agony. The delegation arrives at their destination, leaves Max there, and returns home. Mrs. Veary is overcome with worry when she is told about their travels and leaves the next day to assure herself that the youth is all right. No one hears from Max until the festival, when he arrives with the man who has promised to help and the young girl of his dream. Max sits up for the first time without support and is able to preside over the dancing. The three children stand together for the next dance. Max and his consort eventually marry, and Katie remains with them as a serving maid throughout their lives.

Analysis. Narrated by Katie in an archaic dialect, *Max's Dream* is a surrealistic story whose opening lines cue the reader that the logic of more traditional stories will be irrelevant here. The opiate the boy takes to relieve his suffering is frequently mentioned, underscoring the imperative to understand this narrative as though it were a dream. Although the writing is precise and replete with striking imagery, this work will predictably be understood and enjoyed by only a few readers. The unusual construction, mythological allusions (such as Helen and Troy Town), localisms, idiomatic speech patterns, and other nonstandard word usages will make it inaccessible to many youngsters.

Ambivalent and ambiguous feelings about disability find expression here. Childish, irrational fears about leg braces are expressed in the initial reaction of Katie, the character embodying innocence. The local children maintain a distance between themselves and Max, but whether this is because the boy is an orphan, in fragile health, disabled, or from different social class origins is unclear. Nonetheless, he is selected by them for the position of honor at the festival. He is strong enough to accept his role, but the change from a pain-wracked, bedridden youth to the reigning monarch at the celebration only makes sense within the fantasy. Helen, whom he ultimately marries, appears to be similarly disabled, a situation hinted at obliquely and thus of little significance.

Mazer, Harry. *The War on Villa Street*. New York: Delacorte, 1978. 182 pp. Reading Level: YA
Disability: Intellectual Impairment

His father's frequent bouts of drinking cause financial problems at home and repeated instances of public humiliation. Willis tries to protect himself from derogatory remarks by keeping aloof. He is particularly careful to keep out of the way of Rabbit and his gang of bullies, but also avoids kids like Richard Hayfoot:

> One of the retards from Special Ed class . . . Richard was 15, maybe even 16. But he might as well have been six months, Willis thought. He wasn't a real person. Just half a person, or maybe one quarter of a person. Retards like Richard bugged Willis. Some of them knew their place and stayed in it. They didn't try to mix with the normal kids. But Richard didn't even have that much sense.

Cruising for trouble, Rabbit's gang corners Willis one day, taunting and beating him, when the sudden appearance of Richard interrupts them. They disperse, vowing revenge. The retarded youth considers his timely arrival and the boys' rout irrefutable evidence that he and Willis must become bosom buddies. The avowed loner tries desperately to get rid of his new companion: "He spoke in a slow, loud voice so the retard would get it. 'I don't have any friends. And if I did, you'd be at the bottom of the list.' "

Later, manipulated into an impromptu basketball game with Richard against two of Rabbit's gang, Willis derives considerable satisfaction from beating his enemies handily. Contemptuously, he tells the losers he is going to give Richard special lessons since it is clear his teammate, among all the competitors, has the most potential. During the practice that follows, he is observed by the boy's father, who offers to pay Willis three dollars an hour to coach his son in the skills needed to participate in Field Day. Mr. Hayfoot explains:

> I don't want him left out of the normal events of a boy's life. . . . Taking part in things is important for his feeling about himself.

The more he does, the more confidence he should have. And he needs confidence badly. Now I think a normal, well-coordinated, confident boy like you can do a lot for him. Someday, I hope he'll be able to hold down a job and live a semblance of a normal life.

The money is too tempting to refuse, so Willis reluctantly accepts the man's offer. As he anticipated, being able to help his mother with expenses is satisfying, but teaching his inept pupil is almost unbearably frustrating. Richard forgets directions, loses his concentration, lacks coordination, and employs a variety of ruses to distract his young coach from enforcing his rigorous schedule. When the boy fails at simple tasks, Willis becomes furious and calls him an idiot. Frustrated and ashamed, he is surprised when Richard tells him he knows he is retarded: "Yes, I'm retarded. I know about it. It's not nice. It means I'm stupid." Willis insists that he is only slow but is capable of learning, and he teaches the boy, at long last, to tie his shoelaces. When he tells his mother of the incident, she suggests he could consider going to college to become a teacher. This idea is endorsed by Richard's father, who praises the youngster's natural athletic abilities, suggesting the possibility of a scholarship and encouraging him, as a first step toward that goal, to participate in the upcoming Field Day. Willis runs a strong race, challenging the school's champion, until he sees his own father, drunk again, at the finish line being bodily removed from the race. Heartbroken, he fights with his father, runs away from home, but returns in despair. He is relieved to be reconciled with his parent, accepting the man's overtures at reestablishing a relationship. Willis is afraid of the humiliation he will face at school and is astonished and relieved when he is not teased about his father's behavior. He is further surprised to discover that his actions have earned him considerable respect and the attention of one of the more attractive girls in his class.

Analysis. The characterization of Richard is excellent in this original, fast-moving, coming-of-age junior novel. The youth is seen as slow to learn, naive in social encounters, ingenuous, good-hearted, eager to please, and vulnerable. He is one of the targets of neighborhood bullies, but he is also befriended and protected by other peers. A supportive family and a mainstreamed school help him to function well in a far from perfect world.

Melton, David. *A Boy Called Hopeless.* Independence, Mo.: Independence Press, 1976. 231 pp. Reading Level: YA
Disability: Neurological Impairment

This quasi-fictional story concerns Jeremiah, a child described as brain-injured, and the efforts of his family to remediate his problems.

For years doctors have dismissed his mother's fears and counseled patience in waiting for the child to develop certain skills. Intuitively she rejects their diagnosis that her son is hopelessly retarded and becomes incensed at the school's failure to improve his functioning. The family learns of a program in Philadelphia that claims success in treating children like Jeremiah. Using their vacation time and money, they travel from their Indianapolis home to learn patterning, a technique that it is hoped will compensate for the midbrain damage they are told he has: "Congratulations, Mr. and Mrs. Rogers. You have a brain-injured child." This diagnosis means Jeremiah is a candidate for special treatment by the staff. Family life is totally reorganized to accommodate a daily schedule that begins at 7:15 A.M. and continues, with only very brief interruptions, until almost 4:45 P.M. The routine is exhausting, but the family perseveres, despite times of despair, and finally sees dramatic progress. On their return visit to the institute, the doctor proposes: "The goal I would like to set is for Jeremiah to be well by this time next year." The family returns to the center with renewed vigor, and despite experiencing a discouraging extended plateau, their objective is achieved. Jeremiah is able to attend a regular classroom, where no one will suspect his former difficulties.

Analysis. The "story" derives from case studies of children who have been patients at the Institute for Human Potential. The worshipful adulation for Glenn Doman, its director, and the unconvincing use of an older sister's diary to narrate events make the reading of this effort tough slogging. Written in a patronizing manner, it nonetheless tells its tale with a feeling of respect and commitment to parents who undertake such a demanding regimen. None of the conversations in the book approach real dialogue; they are simply one speech after another:

> "Mr. Doman," Mother said quietly, "I know why parents do it. They do it because no matter how rough your program may be, it can't possibly be as difficult as watching your child, day by day, and seeing that he isn't able to do the things other children his age can do. I've looked out our living-room window and watched the children across the street as they run and play their games. I realize that Jeremiah is not like those children. Every day those children are growing and learning. Every day the differences between them and Jeremiah are wider. Every day his chances for catching up with them or ever being able to do the things they can do are getting less and less. Don't tell me what is rough. No program in the world can be as difficult for a mother as having to stand by and watch her child left out and behind."

The doctor's description of some of the children is highly unorthodox and offensive: "Some of them are blind as bats, deaf as doorknobs,
and some of them can't even move their little fingers." Unfortunately,
such descriptions from the mouth of a physician unwarrantedly legit-
imize them. While apparently meant to be direct, its effect is callous
and shocking. It is questionable whether a juvenile novel is the place,
under any circumstances, to argue the virtues of a treatment regimen
that remains highly controversial and whose claims are questioned by
much of the medical establishment.

Milton, Hilary. *Blind Flight*. New York: Watts, 1980. 138 pp. Reading Level: MC
Disability: Visual Impairment

Debbie, visiting her aunt and uncle for the weekend, tries to avoid
thinking about her upcoming eye surgery. To divert his 13-year-old
niece from dwelling on the operation that would restore some vision,
Uncle Walt takes her for a ride in his small plane. She had flown many
times with him and has some knowledge of how to handle the controls. Debbie listens to the radio, senses the movements of the tiny
aircraft with her body, and generally accommodates herself to the
flight. Suddenly a goose collides with the aircraft, shattering the wind-
shield, plunging into the cockpit, and causing her uncle to lose consciousness. Debbie is alone in the freezing cold, strapped into the
copilot's seat. After several frantic attempts, she makes radio contact
with an astonished captain of a commercial craft, who, in turn, reveals
her plight to local airport officials. Rescue plans are hurriedly formulated while the erratic movements of the stricken airplane are meticu-
lously monitored.

An expert in "talking down" pilots who have encountered emer-
gencies is contacted, a plane similar to her uncle's is obtained, and the
girl is given practice instruction in how to maneuver the aircraft. She is
understandably terrified by the circumstances, but gains a modicum of
confidence as she directs the plane's movements and is praised by
pilots dispatched to fly in formation with her. The girl makes an unsuccessful pass at the local runway, and the authorities decide she should
be diverted to a major airport, where foam is available to cushion a
crash landing. Debbie balks at going over the mountains and appears
to be in shock when her brother's voice penetrates her panic and, in a
familiar, challenging tone, calls out, "Hey, stupid—I'm the one that's
scared of planes. You're not." Overcoming his own dread of flying, her
brother Rick takes the controls in a plane like his uncle's, accompanied
by a pilot who is determined to guide Debbie down safely. The man

commands Debbie to listen closely and follow the exact instructions her brother receives so that the motions of the two craft will be precisely the same. When the flyer gives orders, Rick translates them for his sister: "It's as far from the edge of [your] doorway . . . to the light switch." They simulate landing procedures, aided tremendously by Rick's skill in translating spatial measures so that his sister can interpret the orders she is given. The girl brings the plane down to a bumpy landing, ripping a wing from the fuselage, but otherwise doing admirably. She refuses a ride to the hospital for a checkup, declaring that she will be there for surgery soon enough.

Analysis. The heroine has been blind for only a year, presumably from cataracts, and the surgical procedure alluded to appears to be commonplace. The impression is conveyed that the operation will, of course, be successful. Parallels between orientation training at home and in the cockpit are well drawn, and that instruction becomes the facilitating factor in Debbie's rescue. The heroine's dilemma is inherently dramatic, and Milton further adds to her problems by including elements of freezing weather and diminishing fuel reserves. The blind girl is seen as a competent, intelligent child whose fear under the circumstances is perfectly normal. Her vision loss critically compounds the danger, but past experience, trust in her brother, and her proven ability to translate instructions into actions make the unlikely story exciting and, under the circumstances, credible.

Milton, Hilary. *November's Wheel.* New York: Abelard-Schuman, 1976. 186 pp. Reading Level: MC
Disability: orthopedic impairment; also visual impairment

Every aspect of Billy Bob's life is affected by the Depression—his restricted diet, his constant alertness to unnecessary expenditures, his worn out shoes, and his make-do clothes. Yet the 11 year old knows that he is luckier than most: he has food and shelter, a loving grandfather, and two hard-working parents. The poverty, starvation, and degradation he sees all about him have a profound impact on the child, as do his parents' compassion for those even more in need.

Billy Bob longs to own a beautiful new bicycle he sees in the window of a grocer's shop. Since his family cannot patronize that store, he offers to work for the owner in return for lottery slips, which will enable him to compete for the bike. The youngster willingly delivers groceries, runs errands, and exchanges his labor for tickets, finally collecting enough slips to give him five chances for the coveted prize. At the last minute, however, the boy changes his mind and converts some of his entries into the food drawing as well—a decision triggered by the hunger-wracked faces of a family his father has been helping.

During the time Billy Bob has been working, he has become friendly with an elderly lady humiliated at her dependence on relief and a mechanical genius whose workshop excites the boy's admiration. On a trip with his father to deliver firewood to Dr. Gillis, the youth meets the man's son, Steven, who cannot walk. The disabled boy's father reports that his son's initial recovery from his illness was satisfactory, but now "he won't even try to use his legs. He made an effort one time . . . and fell flat." Billy Bob's attempts to be friendly are greeted with hostility, and finally, in desperation, after all his overtures have been refused, he tells the bitter invalid: "Then I guess you won't ever do anything but sit there, all wrapped in that blanket, looking at fires and staring through windows." Steven is stung by having his worst fears articulated, and his visitor remorsefully says, "If I could do it, I would give you one of my legs to walk on." Later, on a shopping expedition with his grandfather, Billy Bob notices a blind beggar and questions whether the disability is real. The old man assures him the mendicant is not faking, explaining that he can tell by the way the beggar is dressed—he's "put together by feel." The grandfather passes some coins to Billy Bob, telling him: "Drop that in. . . . And say a prayer you're not in his shape."

Although the boy misses the lottery when he insists on accompanying his father on an errand of mercy, his grandparent stands in for him, reporting later that he has won an electric train and a basket of food, which the lad intends to donate to a hungry family. Because they cannot spare the electricity costs to run the toy and because he has little interest in it, Billy Bob lends the train to Steven, who is greatly intrigued by the mechanism. Dr. Gillis, pleased at his son's emergence from what he thought was a state of intractable apathy, is grateful to the young boy. He has further cause for gratitude when the hero introduces him to an inventor who has devised an exercise machine that has the potential to increase the functioning of the child's atrophied leg muscles. The winner of the bicycle sells his prize to the doctor, who then thoughtfully trades it to Billy Bob for the electrical train, thus allowing the child to attain his heart's desire.

Analysis. Milton paints a vivid picture of the trauma and pain endured by many during the Great Depression. However, the major characters are so noble and pure of heart that the central story begs credibility. Billy Bob, selfless and generous, brightens people's lives, provides food to the needy, hope to the discouraged, comfort to the bereaved, and remedies to those ailing in mind, body, and spirit. At the end he is rewarded, although by a circuitous route, for his extraordinary goodness. This saccharine effort presents a theme offered to readers with sledgehammer subtlety and plot and characterizations that seem holdovers from another century.

Minshull, Evelyn. *The Steps to My Best Friend's House.* Illus. by Unada. Philadelphia: Westminster, 1980. 142 pp. Reading Level: MC

Disability: Emotional Dysfunction, special health problems

Carrie is delighted when Trish moves into her neighborhood. The newcomer reports that her family's disorganized life has forced them to move many times and predicts that this current location will be temporary also. Trish alludes to her mother's emotional problems, which she hints were intensified after her father's death and are mysteriously connected to their turbulent past. Although unnerved by these revelations, Carrie is enthralled by her new companion, whom she finds imaginative, exciting, and full of wonderful ideas and unusual talents. Trish is initially reluctant to share Carrie with anyone else, but soon becomes the leader of Carrie's group of friends, overwhelming them with the force of her personality and the range of her intellect. There are, however, a few dissenters, who see Trish as a threat and suspect she is untrustworthy.

Carrie's mother soon learns that the child's stories are all untrue; Trish has been under psychiatric treatment for some time and has woven her elaborate tales to cover her inability to face her father's desertion. Carrie refuses to believe that her friend's stories are fabrications, and when the girl comes to her house in the middle of the night saying that her mother has beaten her and she must escape, the credulous youngster agrees to accompany her. Cold, wet, and miserable, the two runaways find a hiding place where they are able to sleep fitfully. Trish begins telling more stories, but these contradict her previous ones, and Carrie, in shock, realizes that her new friend is a compulsive liar. After Trish is hospitalized, Carrie becomes morose, feeling that she has been deceived and betrayed. Her grandmother admonishes her: "Trish, bein' the magic kind of girl she is, just lied to herself better than most people can. I don't think, most of the time she knew she was lyin', it had become that real to her. And what she did was much, much better than drownin' in self-pity." This observation jolts Carrie, propelling her out of her self-absorption and into resuming her former carefree ways.

Analysis. That profoundly dysfunctional people can be charismatic, brilliant, convincing, and manipulative is certainly true. However, none of the descriptions of Trish's behavior are convincing. The other characters also are flat and unremarkable, their responses and conversations contrived. The woman's arthritic condition is frequently mentioned and causes her much suffering:

> Grandma, with little pain wrinkles across her forehead and pain in her eyes, fumbled the violin into its case. . . ."You go ahead. My hands—" She held them before her, turning them, rubbing them harshly. "Sometimes I hate them." There was an edge of desperation to her voice, but her expression softened into helplessness, and she leaned back, eyes closed, crippled hands rigid in her lap.

The sketchy cartoonlike illustrations are unattractive and inappropriate, being more suited to a light, humorous work.

Moeri, Louise. *The Girl Who Lived on the Ferris Wheel.* New York: Dutton, 1979. 117 pp. Reading Level: MC/YA
Disability: Emotional Dysfunction; also auditory impairment

Most of the week Til Foerster spends in the confines of a drab San Francisco home with her tyrannical mother. Her release from the angry woman's dominion comes each Saturday, when her divorced father rescues her for a holiday at a local park, where he can play his violin and they can ride the ferris wheel. Although Til is deathly afraid of the ride, she is willing to pay this price to enjoy her father's company and seize this brief interlude of happiness. Her mother's behavior has become more and more bizarre since the divorce, and the woman finds an outlet for her ungovernable rage by incessant, unnecessary, ritualistic housecleaning and physical, verbal, and psychological abuse of her terrorized 11-year-old daughter. Til senses that, although her father dearly loves her, if she describes her home life to him it will spoil their times together, so she remains silent. Her only respite comes from her contact with an elderly neighbor. "There was no use to try to talk to Mrs. Fundy—she couldn't hear a single word—so Til made some general, friendly motions, smiled, nodded, blew some kisses, and stood out of the way so the old lady could take her pet and go back into the house."

Til tries to make sense out of her mother's irrational demands, tentatively inquiring from other schoolmates what punishment they receive for infractions. Her distracted behavior and body bruises soon attract the attention of her teachers and the school nurse, but they mistakenly conclude these have been caused by an abusive father. Realizing the enormity of their mistake, feeling defeated and abandoned and unable to communicate her desperation, Til begins to doubt herself. The confused girl believes that since mothers always love their children, she must somehow be the one at fault. Nevertheless, Til is profoundly startled when she sees a row of butcher knives set at her mother's place at the table. Panicked, Til runs out of the house. Convinced that her assumption could not possibly be correct, she returns but conceals herself when she observes her mother waiting for her, talking aloud to herself, and holding a large knife in her hand. The dark covers her escape as she sneaks away, desperately hoping that her complacent father will protect her. After some harrowing experiences, Til finds his apartment, but when she sees a woman there, she bolts. After alerting Mr. Foerster at work, the woman, who is her father's friend, tries to follow the fearful girl. Til by now is almost reduced to a trancelike state and going home, beckoned by her mother, walks robotlike up the steps, hypnotized by the shining blade in her mother's hands. As Gertrude lifts the weapon, the police arrive, interrupting her assault on the youngster. Safe at last, Til asks her father whether her mother would have been all right if they had only loved her more. He reassures her that the roots of her aberrant behavior were too deep to be modified by such actions.

Analysis. This story is a powerful one, not only because of the potency of its theme but because of the vividness and dimensionality of the characters. Adults are seen as imperfect and variously motivated. Gertrude's excessive and bizarre behavior, seen in progressively more horrible acts, derives from the woman's desperate need for self-preservation. She had always wanted "a place of her own . . . where *she* would come first," but "Helmut and Til kept trying to take it away from her—kept trying to take possession of bits and pieces of it, sometimes even whole rooms. It was like they were trying to take her very skin away from her, and thrust their own arms and legs into it, fasten it around them, leaving her exposed and dying in the cold." Moeri gives some insight into the illogical perceptions that Gertrude is subject to and that she uses to justify her actions. The deaf neighbor is a convenience for the story and also serves to accentuate the heroine's loneliness and isolation from social contact. The metaphor of the ferris wheel, of moving and going nowhere, of being out of control of one's destiny, is imaginatively developed.

Mohr, Nicholasa. *In Nueva York.* New York: Dial, 1977. 192 pp.
Reading Level: MA
Disability: Orthopedic Impairment, special health problems

Old Mary eagerly awaits the arrival of her son from Puerto Rico. She has not seen him in the 40 years since she moved from her birthplace to New York's Lower East Side. She fantasizes he will rescue her from her dreary and impoverished existence. When William arrives, the old woman is dismayed to see his dwarfed stature, but after her initial shock, she absorbs him into her family and the routines of their life. William takes a job at Rudi's diner, where he befriends Lali, the owner's lonely young wife. When Rudi breaks a leg, Federico, William's handsome, irresponsible brother, takes over in the diner and becomes Lali's lover. The two plan to run off with Rudi's money, but Federico takes only enough to buy himself a car and leaves alone. One of their neighbors is drafted, but distressed at the prospect of abandoning his asthmatic, homosexual lover without any financial support, the prospective soldier arranges a marriage with a woman with the understanding that her support payments will be turned over to his friend.

When two young hoodlums hold up the restaurant, William is wounded. Enraged, Rudi, now recovered, angrily grabs his gun and runs after them, fatally wounding the leader. The dead boy's mother demands that her son's killer purchase a headstone for his unmarked grave, but Rudi swears he will never agree to her outrageous request.

Analysis. This mature episodic novel centers on the life of impoverished Puerto Rican immigrants who, in their various ways, are attempting to survive in an often hostile environment. William is sympathetically developed; his disability is an impediment to his full functioning, but he persists and adjusts to its demands. Others can hardly fail to notice his size and, at times, allude disparagingly to it, but they become used to him and he soon garners affection and respect in the neighborhood.

Montgomery, Elizabeth Rider. *The Mystery of the Boy Next Door.* Illus. by E. Gold. Champaign, Ill.: Garrard, 1978. 48 pp. Reading Level: YC
Disability: Auditory Impairment

Neighborhood children are distressed by the apparently unfriendly behavior of the new boy on their block. He rejects all their friendly overtures and does not return a baseball hit into his yard or answer the door even though obviously at home. When the youngsters see his T-shirt with the manual alphabet on it and note his unusual gestures, they correctly conclude that he is deaf. Realizing they have misinterpreted his seeming aloofness, they accept him into their company. Excited by the challenge of communicating with the newcomer, each decides to learn finger spelling.

Analysis. Intended as an easy-to-read book, *The Mystery of the Boy Next Door* contains the stilted prose and simplistic plot typical of the genre. The illustrations fail to show any hearing apparatus being used by students attending a special school. However, the depiction of the manual alphabet that concludes the book is particularly clear. An unusual feature is the inclusion of a child and parent similarly disabled signing to one another.

Morganroth, Barbara. *Demons at My Door*. New York: Atheneum, 1980. 145 pp. Reading Level: YA
Disability: Emotional Dysfunction

Aly Canzler chronicles the events that contributed to and supported her delusional state. On the surface, her adolescent life seemed ideal: her family was close-knit and caring; the family income allowed a very comfortable lifestyle; she was an attractive, intelligent, well-liked girl and had a boyfriend with similar attributes with whom she planned to attend an Ivy League school. The students and faculty at her high school think of Aly as a model of competence and make demands on her organizational and academic skills. The girl feels she must maintain her all-A average and participate in activities, not for satisfactions they bring, but to ensure her acceptance at a prestigious college and because a stellar performance is expected of her. She accepts the job of editor of the school literary magazine but is contemptuous of all the manuscripts submitted, insisting they are "mostly pompous drivel." Unable to manage this responsibility, she maneuvers a friend into doing most of the work and then suspects her of trying to "steal" credit for the publication.

Aly spends more and more time daydreaming, avoiding responsibility, and pursuing pointless and futile activities. She is convinced that demons are harassing her, disturbing her sleep, mocking her, and sabotaging her ambitions. Their sudden manifestation outside the testing room causes her to panic during SAT exams, and her consequent sudden departure invalidates the test. As is her custom, she tries to deal with her fears through an intellectual approach and finds a book in the library that confirms her belief in the existence of the creatures that plague her. Aly persuades her sister to visit the library with her to check the reference in question, but no such volume can be found, and the panicked girl explains to her sibling that the demons must have stolen the evidence. On the drive home, she becomes almost hysterical and deliberately crashes her car into the one in front of her. The damage is slight, but this behavior is evidence of her increasingly unpredictable moods. The teenager's behavior at this juncture vacillates between irrational rage and surface calmness. She asks her boyfriend to take her to a "different time-space continuum," a request he does not understand. In an abrupt and confusing conclusion, the pathetic girl reveals a scheme for confronting the creatures that torment her.

Analysis. Morganroth attempts to depict the torment of an adolescent so overwhelmed by pressures that she retreats into hallucinatory behavior, but neither the pressures nor the hallucinations are convincing. Although the girl sees herself as an adolescent suffering from parental misunderstanding and excessive demands, the characterizations reveal a loving and supportive mother and father whose expectations are well within the capability of their child. The school's stance seems equally moderate, particularly since the girl is involved in a program that allows considerable freedom and individualization. The "demons" are present but not threatening, and the girl's paranoia does not spring from any sources revealed by the author. In addition, the heroine is a most unsympathetic character, petulant, whining, self-absorbed, and uninteresting.

Morganroth, Barbara. *Will the Real Renie Lake Please Stand Up?* New York: Atheneum, 1981. 164 pp. Reading Level: YA
Disability: Auditory Impairment

Renie Lake has worked out the rules for surviving in the blackboard jungle: be street smart, join a gang, keep a boy around for protection, and above all, never reveal your true feelings. The high schooler has plenty of reasons for despair. Her divorced mother has brought a man even more immature than she into their apartment, and the girl's life in this squalid setting is filled with animosity and confrontation. When the police overtake her boyfriend's speeding car, they discover it is loaded with drugs. He is not carrying a weapon, but after they report to the court that they found a knife concealed on the belligerent girl, she is remanded to her father's custody in a suburban Connecticut community.

Gretchen warns her interloping stepsister to keep out of her life, but Renie informs the spoiled adolescent that neither has a choice in their new living arrangements. The former delinquent has decided that the way to get along is to be as unobtrusive and uncontentious as possible, but Gretchen is frantically determined to dislodge the unwelcome newcomer. Needing relief from her stepsister's relentless persecution, Renie leaves the house and later discovers an injured deer alongside a road. Seeking assistance, she locates a young man, who brings the creature back to an improvised veterinary clinic he has built in his home. His mother, Mrs. Redner, talks extensively with Renie about her son, Jan, and his hearing loss. The girl is intrigued by the process of communicating with him and checks out a book on finger spelling, from which she learns the manual alphabet. Quite quickly, she realizes that this is too burdensome a process and she must acquire proficiency in signing as well.

Mr. Lake informs his surprised daughter that she will be going to a psychiatrist, and although initially resistant, the girl is able to communicate some of her anger to the sympathetic woman. Fearful of any entanglements, she deliberately does not pursue a friendship with Jan. During a subsequent visit, she tells him about her background, adding a warning that he could be hurt as a result of their association. Jan says he thought she had been avoiding him because he was deaf and knows that underneath her tough facade there is a kind and worthy person. Her psychiatrist is interested in their relationship, seeing the boy as someone whom Renie could trust. Sensitive to his new friend's insecurity, Jan tells her that he is upset that "you still think you have to protect yourself from me." The girl discovers that he is seeking entrance to a school of veterinary medicine, but his teachers fear he may not be accepted since they assume communicating with his patients' owners would be viewed as an insurmountable problem. When Jan learns that Renie carries a switchblade, they quarrel, a confrontation the insecure girl views as a rejection.

Gretchen, obsessed with getting rid of Renie, frames her by putting marijuana in her school locker. Fearful of being sent to reform school and feeling hopeless about her situation, Renie contacts her old boyfriend, persuading him to help her run away. She is reluctant to leave without saying goodbye, so she stops at the Redners', where Jan convinces her that giving up is no solution. Renie decides to stay and fight for her newly won security and stability.

Analysis. Some of the social difficulties accompanying profound hearing loss—isolation, peer rejection, dependence on an intermediary to communicate in certain situations—are honestly, although briefly, depicted. In addition, Jan's misinterpretation of the cause of Renie's absence brings into high relief how deafness may complicate personal relationships and set up barriers to resolving them satisfactorily. Limited information about Ameslan and hearing ear dogs is accurately conveyed. The characterization of Jan, however, is seriously deficient. Qualities are more often ascribed to him rather than revealed through the unfolding of the plot or by his interaction with others. The psychiatrist and Mrs. Redner both act as conduits channeling information about many critical events and the characters' reactions to them. This secondhand approach has the effect of diminishing the vitality of the major characters.

Moskin, Marietta. *Adam and the Wishing Charm.* Illus. by Joseph Scrofani. New York: Coward, McCann & Geoghegan, 1977. 61 pp.
Reading Level: MC
Disability: Orthopedic Impairment

Reacting to the sounds, smells, sights, and excitement of New York harbor in the early nineteenth century, ten-year-old Adam yearns to become a sailor. His father tries to squelch such ambitions, telling his son it was "hopeless to dream about being a sailor when your left leg is too short and you limped when you walked." Titus, a black youngster apprenticed to Adam's merchant father, consoles the boy and reluctantly lends him his African wishing charm, which he says has great powers. Hoping to keep the memento safe and also undetected by his father, Adam hides the magical object in a lantern. When he realizes his father has sold the lamp, he attempts to follow the buyer, trailing the man onto a mercantile clipper ship that sets sail for England. The unlikely explanation of his presence to the captain is proven true when the charm is discovered. The bemused skipper gives the stowaway the option of continuing the voyage or returning to shore on the pilot's boat that guides them through the Narrows. The child's decision to go back home pleases the captain, who suggests the lad might consider shipping on his vessel in a year or two. When Adam reminds the man that he has a limp, he is admonished: "A good man doesn't let a limp or anything else keep him from what he wants to do!" Titus and Adam's father row out to the boat at anchor and bring the boy home.

Looking back on his adventure, Adam is satisfied at having been faithful to his friend's trust and having proved himself capable of climbing rope ladders and narrow steps and keeping his balance on a sloping deck despite his limp. The youth realizes his father has been witness to his performance and can no longer doubt his son's abilities.

Analysis. Adam's disability is a minor element that adds modest complications to his escapades. His limp, more an inconvenience than an obstacle, provides a legitimate occasion for the articulation of one of the story's messages: steadfastness and determination will overcome difficulties. The illustrations that accompany this pleasant, low-key work ably convey the excitement of sailing ships. Unfortunately, the human characters are stiff and awkward and, in contrast to the stately vessels, seem incapable of graceful motion.

Myers, Walter Dean. *The Legend of Tarik*. New York: Viking, 1981. 185 pp. Reading Level: YA
Disability: Orthopedic Impairment, Visual Impairment, Emotional Dysfunction

The land around the Niger River is devastated in a war waged by the most brutal and murderous of conquerors, the infamous El Muerte. After a battle, when his bloody appetite is temporarily slaked, he enslaves those captives who are left alive. Horrified, young Tarik watches El Muerte kill his father for sport, then witnesses a ferocious attack on the women and boys by the despot's soldiers before he loses consciousness. Left for dead, the black youth is rescued by a priest named Docao and Nongo, a scholar from his tribe, who together nurse him back to health, then groom him to avenge his father's death. Docao shows his protégé his arm, revealing "a stump where his hand had been," and tells him Nongo was blinded by their mutual enemy. His tribesman cautions the boy that if he wishes to rid the world of El Muerte, he must learn an iron self-discipline, prove himself worthy of the mission, and channel his anger into a cold, unswerving determination, "for hatred will make your eyes as blind as mine. . . . There is evil within him that is larger than his body. To defeat such a man you must learn much." During his rigorous training, he is observed by a silent and aloof girl. Docao explains her demeanor: "When El Muerte's men destroyed [Stria's] family, she ran away, not from fear—as they imagined—but rather possessed with a certain madness from which she may never recover."

Nongo guides Tarik in preparation for the three tasks he must complete before confronting El Muerte: he must take the Sword of Serq from a giant monster, seize the Crystal of Truth from the open-eyed beast that guards it, and capture the magnificent, spirited horse known as Zinzinbadio. After gaining possession of these objects, the lad sets off on his quest, with Stria, uninvited, following behind. On his travels he rescues Capa, the baker, from El Muerte's minions, and as a result, the grateful man enlists as his aide and his reputation as a black knight with magic power spreads. With Stria's help, Tarik defeats a small contingent of soldiers, one of whom is the tyrant's cousin. Hoping to force Tarik into the open, El Muerte captures Nongo and Docao, then publicly executes them. The concealed youth, cued by the dying blind man, realizes the time is not yet ripe for him to take his stand. Tarik devises a trap, and the evil one goes to meet his challenger. In a fierce hand-to-hand battle, the notorious murderer is finally vanquished, but "there was no sweetness in his victory over El Muerte, no satisfaction in vengeance gained." Their mission completed, the companions separate: Tarik returns to his people, Capa to his wife, and Stria, alone, to an unknown destination.

Analysis. Medieval Africa provides the backdrop for this absorbing tale of blood and gore, of violent times and violent people engaged in a classical struggle between good and evil. The characters whose wounds were caused by the arch villain symbolically attain power in their area of loss: Nongo, the blind scholar, is a visionary who helps Tarik perceive his mission with clarity; Docao, of the brutally amputated hand, endows his student with strength; and Stria's disorder infuses here with a singleness of purpose, an unswerving drive for revenge.

Newman, Robert. *The Case of the Somerville Secret.* New York: Atheneum, 1981. 184 pp. Reading Level: MC
Disability: Intellectual Impairment, Cosmetic Impairment, Orthopedic Impairment

Young Andrew Tillett, having once before played an important role in solving a criminal case, visits his erstwhile "colleague," Inspector Wyatt at Scotland Yard. They are joined by Sergeant Major Polk, who informs them that he has retired from the army but suspiciously conceals the name of his new employer. Interrupting their chat, he speaks to a "gypsy-looking" fellow with "yellow eyes and a scar on his cheek that ran from the corner of his eye to his chin." On the way home, Andrew observes the scar-faced man waving to a scarecrowlike chimney sweep, who is accompanied by a frightened French waif named Pierre. Later, when he is threatened by some local toughs, Andrew, his friend Sara, and a coachman rescue the hapless lad, earning his everlasting gratitude.

The children next meet Wyatt while he is investigating Polk's murder, a crime presumably perpetrated near the Somerville estate, where the body was discovered. During the interrogation, Mrs. Severn, the lord's housekeeper, identifies the man with the scars as her husband, a nefarious felon who had spent much of his life in jail. However, the detectives are chagrined to learn from Dr. Owen, a neighborhood physician, that Severn, their prime suspect, had a fractured leg, and was incapacitated during the time of the homicide. Pursuing another lead, the investigators drive to the Somerville country house, where they discover barred nursery windows, some curious facts about the Somerville heir, and the odd news that Severn's nickname was "Sixty." While being questioned, Somerville reveals his tragic family history: when his beloved wife died in childbirth, the heartbroken man consulted a doctor about his son's condition and was told: "The boy would never be normal and, as time went by, he would become even abnormal—a creature of more than human size and strength, but of no intelligence." Although the housekeeper had repeatedly assured her master that the boy "was always good, never threatening or dangerous," Somerville ignored Mrs. Severn's pleas and kept him locked up on his own grounds. When Mr. Severn learns of the child's situation, he first considers blackmail but ultimately decides to kidnap the boy.

Pierre is found unconscious on the lawn of Andrew's home. When the youth awakens, he tells his friends of his adventure: he had surreptitiously followed his master, Severn, to a barge, where he saw a "monster." Startled by the sight, the boy was incautious; he was noticed, clubbed, and callously thrown into the canal to drown. The youth guides the authorities to the vessel where the victim he saw was held. Their rescue is accelerated by a scream. On the barge they see Dr. Owen, who directs their attention to a carmine hatchet, the body of Severn, and some bloody footprints. The person Pierre spotted is nowhere in evidence. The physician hypothesizes that the injured creature killed his jailer, then completed his escape. All take up the chase, but when Sara sees the presumed killer, she decides he looks more frightened than belligerent. She approaches him calmly and is able to lead him back to the band of rescuers.

Dr. Owen reveals that he has been practicing medicine under an assumed name after he broke both his legs in a carriage accident and accumulated many unpayable debts. He also reports that long ago he attended her ladyship at her delivery and knew about the fact that the housekeeper's disabled child had been switched with that of the dead child of the peer. When Severn found out that the child he kidnapped had six toes (the birth anomaly he also had), he deduced the parentage of the victim. He tried to chop off the extra toe on each foot and so disguise his origins. However, the inspector is not deceived about this yarn about "Sixty" and concludes that the mendacious doctor is the brains behind this villainous scheme. His lordship, relieved to know the child is not his, announces his plan to remarry, but magnanimously accepts responsibility for the lad and agrees to pay for a lifetime of institutional care.

Analysis. All the events in this pseudo-Victorian melodrama are drawn in extreme terms, as the genre demands. Thus, the birth anomaly provides the obvious clue to unravel the mystery: the malefactors are physically marked—one by a limp and the other with a scar—and probability plays no part in the action. Further, the child is described in classic Lombrosian terms and is referred to as a "monster," although, in actuality, he is portrayed as harmless and even pitiful. The lord's reaction, one of relief and the acceptance of responsibility, are also consonant with the facts and attitudes about developmental disability held at the time this story takes place.

Newman, Robert. *Night Spell.* Illus. by Peter Burchard. New York: Atheneum, 1977. 189 pp. Reading Level: MC/YA
Disability: Neurological Impairment, Emotional Dysfunction, Auditory Impairment, Speech Impairment

Since his parents' death, Tad Harper has been enrolled in a boarding school, presumably on a scholarship. He is dismayed to learn that his fees have actually been paid by Martin Gorham, a distant relative and former friend of his grandfather. The headmaster notifies the youngster that his benefactor has requested that Tad spend his summer with him. Realizing he has little choice, the 14 year old reluctantly accedes. He is met at the train station by Hugo, Mr. Gorham's chauffeur, who can neither hear nor speak. The man brings him to his employer's dreary Victorian mansion, the only residence on a private island. There he is greeted by Rosa, Hugo's wife, who shares her husband's disorder.

It is several days before Tad meets Mr. Gorham, who, because of a stroke, now uses a wheelchair. His host is grouchy, critical, and demanding, causing the youth to wonder what purpose was served by his being sent for. The summer promises little pleasure until the lonely youth meets Karen, the best friend of Mr. Gorham's granddaughter, Nonny, who died in a boating accident after which her mother disappeared. Karen and Tad rapidly become friends, sharing a love for swimming and sailing. One day when Tad returns home, he finds his self-appointed guardian has experienced an "episode," which had been precipitated by the boy's actions. Years ago, the old man had accused Tad's father, an artist, of having improperly taken back a portrait he had painted of Nonny. He said that a pattern he saw Tad replicate with shells, starfish, and pebbles on the beach had appeared in the painting, and he concluded the boy must have seen the original (presumably stolen by his father) to be able to reproduce the image so accurately.

Dr. Warren removes the agitated man to the hospital, leaving Tad confused and distraught. When he speaks with Karen, she tells him that, despite being dead, Nonny communicates with her, although her messages are not completely clear. Tad reports he has sensed a strange presence both awake and asleep. Karen accompanies him to the attic of the Gorham house, where they discover the missing portrait Nonny had hidden. At Karen's urging, the two travel to a psychiatric hospital in a nearby community. Following the omniscient Nonny's instructions, they ask to see a "Mrs. X." The doctor in charge presses them for information, but they are evasive and insistent. He is reluctant to allow strangers near the woman, who has been in a catatonic state since she was admitted, but concurs when Dr. Warren attests to their integrity. Considering that he has little to lose, Dr. Rosso permits the children to enter the room of the severely withdrawn woman. Karen presents her with photographs of the portrait, which instantaneously causes "a change . . . as if somewhere in the darkness that lay behind those empty eyes a candle had been lit." The patient speaks Nonny's name and then begins to weep. The psychiatrist learns that she is Gorham's daughter and speaks at length with her. He predicts a recovery: "When a patient comes out of a catatonic state in this particular way, the prognosis is usually very good." The teenagers return home, eager to reveal their astounding news. Karen is concussed in the hurricane that sweeps over the island, but by attending to Nonny's directive, Tad manages to save her from drowning. After making sure she is cared for at the hospital, the boy searches out his erstwhile mentor. He explains the mystery of the missing picture and the circumstances surrounding his daughter's whereabouts. The old man is ecstatic at hearing she is safe and earnestly implores the boy to remain with him, an offer the orphan realizes is made out of genuine affection, not gratitude.

Analysis. The disabilities in this story are as contrived as the events are unconvincing. The restricted communication abilities of the chauffeur and housekeeper are used to deepen the sense of isolation the young hero feels. Mr. Gorham's stroke provides a rationale for his irascible temper, "evidence" of his consuming sense of guilt and sorrow at the loss of the two people he loved the most, and later, the impetus for those actions leading to the denouement. The psychotic behavior attributed to Nonny's mother and her miraculous recovery are equally preposterous. Although the initial chapters are quite promising, the use of dreams and occult devices is hackneyed and arbitrary. The careless illustrations depict Mr. Gorham, described as "having a closely trimmed beard," with only a mustache.

Ney, John. *Ox under Pressure.* Philadelphia: Lippincott, 1976. 253 pp. Reading Level: YA/MA
Disability: Emotional Dysfunction, speech impairment

Ox Olmstead's father abruptly decides to leave his Palm Beach, Florida, home, temporarily establishing residence on Long Island, New York, from where he plans to assist a long-time friend in straightening out the financial mess he created as head of a philanthropic foundation. To the boy's dismay, Mr. Olmstead insists his son accompany him. The relocated household consists of a cook, butler, Sally, an attractive friend of Ox's father, and Ted, a pretentious, stuttering tutor, who is perpetually confused by the sophisticated game playing of the residents and visitors to this unorthodox establishment. Ox meets Arabella Marlborough, the bright, tense, formerly anorexic daughter of a toadying financial consultant for their fabulously wealthy neighbor, Lizzie Revere. The girl is mimicking Mrs. Revere when the old woman suddenly appears, having witnessed enough of the performance to be enraged. Ox tries to brazen out the escalating confrontation but is threatened with arrest. While preparing to leave, he is attacked by Mrs. Revere's employees, one of whom hits him in the back of his head with a shovel. The powerful, ordinarily phlegmatic youngster heaves his assailant into the branches of a tree.

Arabella's father arrives at Ox's home, alluding to his employer's anger and making vague threats. Mr. Olmstead, relishing a fight with an obviously inferior opponent, makes a fool of the man, announces Arabella will remain with them, then floors Andy Marlborough with a haymaker. Warming up to the conflict, he then calls the police and charges his visitor with assault. Ox's father suggests the girl must eventually return home, but she and Ox decide to go to New York City to see if she could manage to live by herself. Their brief, unlikely experiment is a failure, and the youngsters return to their respective homes.

When his friend doesn't phone the next morning as promised, Ox, accompanied by Sally, goes to Arabella's home, where they find her mother incoherent from tranquilizers, obviously her usual state. Now anxious for the girl's safety, they force their way in to see Mrs. Revere, from whom they learn the youngster has been bundled off to a sanatorium. Ox is arrested, but his father arrives at the jail with a couple of aggressive lawyers. Mr. Olmstead, now committed to fight his son's battle, has assault charges filed against Mrs. Revere's gardener and engages in some Machiavellian maneuvers against the Olmsteads' enemies. The battle now joined, Mr. Olmstead instructs his helicopter pilot to fly him to where Arabella is confined, later reporting back to his son that the girl insisted on remaining where she is. After Ox is released from jail, he rides the chopper to the hospital to find his friend apparently relaxed but determined to remain. She calmly explains she wants to see the experience through and must work out what she calls her constant need for "diversion." "I *am* sick to the extent that I have this diversion problem. . . . I hate it, . . . it disgusts me. I've got to get rid of it." Ox seeks out the psychiatrist's opinion before he leaves, and the man admits his patient probably should not have been admitted. The boy is at first confused, then angry and resentful. The more he thinks of Arabella's explanation, the less sense it makes and the less acceptable it is to him. In the meantime, his father's friend's financial problems have been righted, the relationship with Sally has soured, and the man decides to return home with his son.

Analysis. Ney combines wit, absurdity, and outrageous situations with deadly serious issues to yield a story alternately hilarious and disturbing. His characters are invariably more complex than they initially seem and are unfailingly interesting. Arabella, although no longer anorexic, is a very neurotic young woman; she is self-dramatizing, manipulative, self-flagellating, and vulnerable. She likens her self-imposed food deprivation to the emotional starvation that characterized her upbringing. Of particular interest is her ability to rationalize her behavior: she offers superficially valid accounts and interpretations of her irrational actions. Ox, wanting to understand, begins by tentatively accepting her behavior as a constructive, assertive act, then completely rejecting her convoluted decision to accept the sanctuary offered by the hospital. Ted's stuttering, an uncontrollable mannerism, makes his affected British accent seem ludicrous and is used here as the overt clue to his inner vacuity.

Nichols, Ruth. *Song of the Pearl.* New York: Atheneum, 1976. 158 pp. Reading Level: MA
Disability: Special Health Problems; also visual impairment

Asthma had restricted Margaret's 17 years of life and is the cause of her early death. The most important person during her life was her dashing uncle, who cultivated her love and then, when she was 15, raped her. "As a child she shrank from judging her uncle; as a woman she realized in abject shame, that the rape had heightened not destroyed her longing for him." After her death, Margaret is transported to a small island, where she encounters Paul, an Oriental youth who guides her search for self-knowledge and perfect love. She observes young women from exotic cultures trapped in various relationships with abusive or repressive men. She finally realizes she has been seeing herself and her uncle in other incarnations bound in a union that is perpetuated by her hatred for "one poor, selfish man." Margaret visits Paul's family, where she learns that only through forgiveness can she attain happiness and that love and hate are simply aspects of the same condition. Enlightened and at peace with herself, the girl returns to her now blind uncle and forgives him, kissing him as a sign of her love. She then rejoins Paul, with whom she begins a journey toward a new life in which she will be his lover.

Analysis. In addition to pompous and pretentious writing ("Death, like life, is for learning. I know I must find my own wisdom"; and, "[In her existence after death, she began] to explore unwillingly the pain that had . . . been born with her, for she did not know its source. Because self-knowledge lay potential beneath her childishness, she had recognized even in life that misery had caused her asthma, not resulted from it") and ludicrous images ("The violet shadow of the ocean drew nearer, its remotest reaches curved against a turquoise sky"), this work

displays a convoluted morality. Margaret, at 15, is portrayed as a temptress, inviting the assault by her middle-aged uncle. The act increases
her longing for him, and *she* seeks *his* forgiveness! The victim thus
becomes the transgressor, and the sexist cliché popular in cheap pulp
novels of the rapist as lover rather than brutal exploiter is resurrected.
In addition, the author proposes that the girl's fatal health problems
were actually a form of punishment that persisted through her various
incarnations and from which she would never be free as long as she
harbored hatred in her soul.

Nixon, Joan Lowrey. *The Seance.* New York: Harcourt Brace Jovanovich, 1980. 142 pp. Reading Level: YA
Disability: Emotional Dysfunction

Sara Martin has been removed from her mother's care and placed
by the courts in the home Lauren shares with her Aunt Mel. Although
the same age, the girls have little in common and maintain a barely
civil relationship. When a seance is held at Roberta's home, Sara, who
plans to use the occasion to cover her disappearance, persuades
Lauren to support the deception. The runaway's body is discovered
drowned in the swamp. Soon after, Roberta's corpse is found in the
same area, and the community can no longer pretend that the first
death was accidental. Lauren fears she may be the next victim. Carley
Hughes, a handsome senior, visits her home, admitting that he had
planned to meet Sara on the night of her disappearance and run off to
the city with her. After the youth leaves, the terrified girl realizes she is
not alone in the house. She escapes to the garden but is trapped there
by Carley's grandmother, who claims responsibility for the other
killings and announces her intention to murder Lauren. She explains
she was determined to save her grandson from the seductive, wicked
Sara, who would have interfered with the boy's plan to attend college.
Forced at gunpoint to drive the old woman's car, the resourceful adolescent crashes it into a house, injuring herself slightly but making her
rescue possible.

Analysis. The rationale for the murderer's behavior is stated by Aunt
Mel: "There are a lot of sick minds in this world. . . . Some of them are
inside people who look very normal on the outside, people you live next
to and work with every day in the week. When something fearful happens to disrupt the pattern of their lives, they react." Since Mrs. Hughes's
collection of bird skulls, allusions to morbid superstitions, and ominous
mutterings about evil forces round out the common stereotypical perception of a "crazy" person and provide the literary justification for her
villainous role, to describe her behavior as normal seems excessively

obtuse. The story creates some tension, but the resolution is arbitrary and unsatisfactory, and the image of a woman of 60 physically overcoming two healthy adolescents strains credulity.

O'Dell, Scott. *The Captive*. Boston: Houghton Mifflin, 1979. 211 pp.
Reading Level: YA
Disability: Orthopedic Impairment

Against his will, Julián Escobar is ordered to prepare himself to accompany his protector, Don Luis, to the New World. The young seminarian suspects he has been selected because the local priest is vehemently against slavery, and as a mere student, the youth is expected to be less troublesome. Under the direction of Captain Roa, the caravel sails west with the expectation that it will return to Seville with its hold crammed with gold. During the course of the voyage, it becomes increasingly apparent that the youth's role is to provide a respectable facade for his mentor's avarice: under the guise of establishing Christianity, Don Luis intends to plunder the islands and enslave the natives. He is encouraged in his schemes by Guzmán, an evil, unscrupulous miner who contracts with the local chief of a small island to use the Indians as laborers to locate and extract the precious ore. The natives are first ruthlessly exploited and, in the end, betrayed and enslaved. After the gold is loaded on board along with some captured Indians, the ship sets sail but founders during a violent storm. Julián, swept overboard, swims to an apparently abandoned island nearby.

He is discovered by an adolescent Mayan girl, who assists him to survive and teaches him her language. Both try to persuade the other of the correctness of their respective religious beliefs, but without success. One day, Guillermo Cantú arrives on the island and reveals to Julián that he was formerly a law student in Spain. He recounts that out of 21 passengers lost in a shipwreck, all were sacrificed to the gods except himself "for dwarfs are venerated here among the Maya, unlike Seville, where they're the butt of many a scurrilous joke." Cantú devises an ambitious scheme, proposing that Julián pose as Kukulcán, the former lord of the island who promised to return one day and govern his people. Similarities between the youth's appearance and that of the legendary god are striking, and Cantú pragmatically points out that Julián should either prepare himself to participate in the charade or ready himself for the inevitable ceremony of sacrifice, in which he would surely be the victim. Seeing no real choice, Julián agrees to the scheme, and the two set about stage-managing the ex-seminarian's arrival so that it will have the most convincing and dramatic impact on the populace. His masquerade persuades two out of the three priests that he is Kukulcán, and he is accompanied to the godhouse for the welcoming ceremony. In horror, he watches the sacrificial rites, aghast at the realization that 15 people have been killed to honor him. Close by his side is his conspirator, ready to be the youth's guide and share in the riches he is convinced will be forthcoming.

Analysis. Cantú is an intelligent, cynical pragmatist, motivated, as were so many of his contemporaries, by an obsessive lust for gold. Eschewing a central role, he plans to control events from behind the scenes, exploiting the opportunities fortune throws his way: the veneration accorded him because of his stature, the appearance of a naive young man who can be made to seem the embodiment of a prophecy, and access to untold wealth for those clever and unscrupulous enough to seize it. This first installment of a projected series, City of the Seven Serpents, is an unusual and compelling narrative. The time and place are vividly evoked, and the introduction of an exotic and little-known culture is masterfully handled.

O'Dell, Scott. *The Feathered Serpent.* Boston: Houghton Mifflin, 1981. 211 pp. Reading Level: YA
Disability: Orthopedic Impairment

This sequel to *The Captive* continues the adventures of Julián Escobar as he attempts to consolidate his power over the Mayan community that has accepted his claim to be the god, Kukulcán. The youth, nevertheless, aspires to bring Christianity to the Indians and re-establish the former grandeur of their city. His ambitious plans necessitate the enslavement of natives and his acquiescence in the human sacrifices that are a central component of Mayan religious ceremonies, behaviors his increasingly compromised conscience allow. He determines to visit the fabled city of Tenochtitlán and meets its ruler, Moctezuma. Julián forces his reluctant mentor, the dwarf Cantú, to accompany him. They narrowly escape disaster and leave the Aztec capital, encountering Cortés during their attempted return. Pressed into his service, they flee after an indecisive battle between the forces of the conquistador and the Indians and continue their journey home.

Analysis. Cantú's role and personality remain virtually unchanged in this second installment of O'Dell's projected multivolume work, City of the Seven Serpents. Cantú's frail constitution, unequal to the rigorous demands of his protégé's escapades, is the cause of some of the plot complications. Considerably less satisfying than the original, in this novel, one violent, dramatic event follows close upon another with little attention paid to character development or cultural and historical insights.

Ogan, Margaret, and George Ogan. *Green Thirteen*. Philadelphia:
Westminster, 1978. 126 pp. Reading Level: YA
Disability: orthopedic impairment

James, also known as J.J., looks in the rearview mirror of his speeding sports car, sees a competitor approaching too fast, and suddenly
feels himself airborne. His next memory is of hearing a doctor tell his
mother that he is ready for surgery. Upon awakening, he discovers that
Dennis Johnson, the driver who crashed into him and then pulled him
unconscious from his burning car, is being treated for burns and is
sharing his room. J.J.'s recovery is facilitated by the attentions of his
mother and cousin Voncil, who both work at the hospital, and by Mr.
Johnson, who insists on paying for the teenager's medical expenses and
eventually offers him a job working on automotive engines in the factory
he owns. James reports to Bill Kelly, a master mechanic crippled years
ago while competing in the Daytona race. The former driver not only
plans the engineering details of the Johnson cars but shares his extensive automotive know-how and information about competitive race car
handling with Dennis and J.J. After the two boys, now good friends,
prove themselves, Johnson makes them an offer to drive his entries in
the All-American race. The novices, gaining important experience and
growing more mature with each contest, are traumatized when one of
the other competitors is killed on the track. This tragedy haunts Dennis,
and he determines to return to his premed studies at Tulane. Shaw, a
laconic loner with an irrepressible desire to win, replaces him, and the
two drivers, after working out their initial incompatibility, manage to
justify their backer's faith in them. Several romances begin to flourish:
Mr. Johnson and James's mother, Dennis and Voncil, James and Sonia.
J.J.'s girl friend, however, has misgivings about involvement with a race
car driver. After the big race in Ontario, another driver takes over the
narrator's role, recounting the final moments of James's life as he
crashes the green car with the unlucky big 13.

Analysis. Race car driving is alternately presented as an irresistibly
exciting sport and a lethal obsession. Extensive descriptions of engines,
carburetors, drive shafts, and aggressive, on-track action are loosely
held together by a flimsy and carelessly written story line featuring
stock characters and silly events. The mother of one character is reported to have died soon after his father's death and then again 15
pages later after several years of a second marriage. Kelly is the race
track Cassandra: his injuries and constant pain are reminders of the
danger of the sport to which he dedicates his life; his knowledge and
experience allow him to express his misgivings and issue warnings to
the unheeding novices.

Oneal, Zibby. *The Language of Goldfish*. New York: Viking, 1980.
179 pp. Reading Level: YA
Disability: Emotional Dysfunction

Hospitalized after a suicide attempt, Carrie is prodded by Dr.
Ross, a psychiatrist, to discover the roots of her maladjustment. She is
aware that her problems were not precipitated by a single traumatic
event but have been developing over the past several years. In sharp
and painful contrast, Moira, her older sister, has put away their childish games and enthusiastically embraces the excitement of adolescence.
She disdains Carrie's reminders of a game they used to play together in
which they spoke "magically" to the goldfish in their garden pool. The
mother programs her daughters for social events, fashion, school
dances, and the like, all of which bore Carrie immoderately. Being an
obedient child, however resentful, she is compliant. Completing the
household are a younger brother, totally absorbed in sports, and their
father, a physician.

Carrie's two passions are her drawing lessons and mathematics.
Mrs. Ramsey, her art teacher, believes she has much talent, and Carrie,
advanced in math, finds security and success in dealing with the certainty she perceives as a core attribute of the discipline. In addition to a
general malaise, Carrie soon begins to have hallucinations, dissociating
herself temporarily from her milieu, then returning to a normal state of
awareness. After one such incident, she recalls:

> It seemed as though things suddenly slipped sideways. . . . Inside
> my head colors—queer colored shapes—began to tumble around
> like the colored glass in a kaleidoscope. There was a kind of roar-
> ing noise. My head began to float. I thought I was sick. I thought I
> was going to faint. I held onto the doorframe and shut my eyes.
> Behind my eyes I saw the colors all beautiful and tumbling. And
> then it was over.

These episodes increase in frequency, and Carrie is forced to use
the excuse of "dizzy spells" as a cover for her behavior. She becomes
almost mesmerized by the lines in a drawing she sees with Mrs.
Ramsey on a visit to the art museum. She panics later when they
discuss its sexual connotations, suddenly begins to scream, and runs,
covered with paint, to her father's office. She tries to tell him of her
fears, but he insists she is only anemic. After a walk in the snow
during which she loses all track of time and place, Carrie is returned
home by a helpful motorist to discover her house occupied by guests at
a party. Overwhelmed, she retreats to the bathroom, where she tries to
find oblivion by swallowing some pills.

During her recovery, she often thinks about her past, the beautiful golden fish, and their immutable island, deriving much comfort from these lovely, reassuring images. After her discharge from the hospital, she is scheduled for daily therapy sessions with Dr. Ross. There is an awkward time of adjustment and intermittent moments of anxiety, which Carrie musters the will to overcome. She is initially unable to make sense of her obsessive painting of the island with the goldfish, but finally she intuits that it symbolizes an unmoving solid object, a desperate desire for an unalterable world, a conclusion Dr. Ross supports. She realizes that she has been fearful of growing up and begins, albeit irregularly, to accept this incontrovertible fact. Symbolic of her new awareness and status, Carrie shares her game of pretending to be able to communicate with goldfish with a young child, acknowledging its appropriateness for someone at that stage of development and its inappropriateness for herself.

"Magic!" said Sara.
Carrie nodded. "That's what I used to think."
"Not now?"
"Not anymore."

Analysis. This extraordinary work combines literary excellence with honest, compassionate exploration of the turmoil experienced by a youngster unable to cope with the changes in her life. Oneal's writing is crisp, sensuous, and insightful; characterizations are outstanding, and the plot is absorbing and credible. The heroine is seen as a basically "normal" child whose behavior is adaptive to a world she perceives to be threatening. Her responses, however, are destructive rather than protective, and she requires help to work her way through to a better accommodation. The role her art talent plays in the expression of her distress and as a barometer of her recovery is particularly interesting. Her therapeutic sessions are recorded in much detail, and the seemingly passive psychiatrist is sensitively depicted as he interacts with his patient. The reactions of members of her family and others involved in her life are realistic and create a vivid picture of the only intermittently supportive environment to which the teenager must return and adapt.

Owen, Wendy. *The Education of Winnie D.* Originally published in England by Owen, Ltd., 1968, as *Whatever Happened to Ruby?* New York: Taplinger, 1979. 183 pp. Reading Level: YA/MA
Disability: Neurological Impairment, Emotional Dysfunction, intellectual impairment

Although her parents believe that boarding school will be both socially and educationally beneficial for their daughter, Winnie finds her life there hellish. Most teachers are remote, caring little for their students. The dormitory is austere and the food deplorable. The nonacademic life of the girls is dominated by a trio of smug, despotic, sadistic adolescents. Ruby, a girl of lower-class origins, few social skills, fewer academic abilities, and a high degree of emotional instability, becomes their natural victim. Desperate for friends and social acceptance, she is, instead, the constant object of rejection or, occasionally, outright abuse. The unhappy girl is further distressed by her parents' marital problems, which culminate when her mother runs off with an uncle. She is, however, able to form some alliance with Maureen, "a gawky unattractive girl with a substandard intelligence."

While at home, Winnie experiences some mild convulsions but is able to conceal them from her unperceptive parents. Similar episodes occur at school: "my right arm twitched suddenly and I had a momentary lapse of consciousness followed by a strange trancelike sensation." She tries to hide such incidents, but inevitably the other girls notice, and she is cruelly nicknamed "Twitchy Win." The preadolescent's seizures, often precipitated by anxiety, increase in frequency and severity. When the girls startle her by dragging her blankets off the bed at night, her "left arm twitched violently and [she] experienced a momentary aura followed by a sickly pang of fear in [her] stomach." Later, during a fire drill, she falls twice, experiencing dizziness and a sense of drowning and imagines she hears bells. She awakens with a headache, grogginess, and a desperate thirst. The physician casually dismisses these symptoms as "war nerves," and the matron suggests these fainting spells may be a result of growing too fast.

Winnie is shocked when she hears the news that her brother has been killed while serving with the British forces in North Africa. When she returns home, she finds her parents are far too distracted by their grief over their son to notice her worsening condition. Back at school, Winnie has another seizure and loses consciousness again. This time, upon wakening in the infirmary, she is told by the matron that she has "a slight brain disorder" and has had an "epileptic fit," statements that suggest to the panicked girl that she is "going mad."

Ruby returns to the school after the holidays in a state of acute distress. She, too, is sent to the infirmary, where her bouts of weeping are punctuated by periods of withdrawn, almost trancelike behavior. Winnie discovers that the girls have been assigned to neighboring beds and that both families have been summoned to retrieve their daughters. Bitterly, Ruby tells her roommate that she has been raped by her uncle, an accusation Winnie believes since the man had once behaved improperly toward her when the two were, by chance, alone. When the concerned Winnie reports Ruby's charges to the school authorities, it is treated as the irresponsible ravings of a "filthy minded," disturbed girl. Soon afterward, much to the amusement of the other students, Ruby's mother arrives to take her near-comatose child home. Meanwhile, a neurologist confirms that Winnie has a seizure disorder. The medication he prescribes virtually eliminates her grand mal seizures, but petit mal ones persist "like a guardian demon" throughout her young adult life.

Analysis. Using a mature woman to describe events that happened years ago in boarding school provides a barrier to emotional involvement. The reports seem of historical rather than immediate interest, and although preadolescent passions, cruelties, fears, and insecurities are graphically recounted by the narrator, they are not deeply felt by the reader. The confusion and anxiety caused by the first evidence of epilepsy in the young heroine, the awkwardness of the girl's parents, the ignorance of both matron and physician, and the social opprobrium that attaches to the condition are well handled. The trauma of rape is shown to be exacerbated by the unwillingness of adults to provide support to the young victim, a lack that acts to precipitate severe psychological problems for the vulnerable child. Maureen, a lesser character, is, as a result of her impairment, readily manipulated by her heartless peers and equally scorned by her teachers.

Pahz, Jim, and Cheryl Pahz. *Robin Sees a Song.* Illus. by Cheryl Pahz. Silver Springs, Md.: National Association of the Deaf, 1977. unp. Reading Level: YC
Disability: Auditory Impairment

Robin is one of those young "people it has been found/who simply cannot hear any sound." She wonders "how does it sound when somebody sings," but her search for an answer is unsatisfactory until a "song" embodiment appears at the foot of her bed one night. The song creature explains that sound is not essential for a song—touch, color, or smell can convey its essence equally well. It then transports the eager child to where she discovers an apple tree, the sun, and a butterfly cloud all "singing" in their own special way. Robin is elated to learn that she can "smile" a song. "She smiled all the way back to her bed/She smiled as the song put the hat on its head." Upon awakening, Robin greets the day zestfully and informs her mother she is "going outside to see the world sing."

Analysis. This very long sequel to *The Girl Who Wouldn't Talk* uses atrociously rhymed, often ridiculous couplets to impart the message that a positive attitude and employment of other senses can readily compensate for hearing loss. The saccharine story and the simplistic and sometimes anatomically incorrect illustrations add little substance to this effort.

Parker, Mark. *Horses, Airplanes, and Frogs.* Illus. by Dan Siculan. Elgin, Ill.: Children's Press, 1977. 32 pp. Reading Level: YC
Disability: Visual Impairment

Nick enjoys his life in the city—playing in the park, romping with his dog, listening to and dancing along with his records. When he wants to read, he uses braille. Dissatisfied with his mother's spare descriptions of objects because they yield only incomplete and errone-ous images in his imagination, the blind youngster longs for someone who can better interpret the world to him. At the playground one day, Nick meets Seth, who shows him how to use the steps to the slide. Nick asks his new friend for a clearer explanation than his mother gave him of a horse, a frog, and an airplane. He is delighted when Seth shows him actual models, for "by touching things, Nick could imagine what they looked like." That night the boy "dreamed wonderful dreams of horses, airplanes and frogs."

Analysis. This lightweight, innocuous effort hints gently at the value of interracial mainstreamed friendships. Information and story line are of minimal interest and the illustrations only adequate.

Paterson, Katherine. *The Great Gilly Hopkins.* New York: Crowell, 1978. 148 pp. Reading Level: MC
Disability: Visual Impairment

Gilly is cynical about her latest foster home placement with Mamie Trotter, confident she will again be in complete control before long. The other foster child there is William Ernest, called W.E., an under-sized, perpetually terrified boy whom Gilly plans to keep in line through intimidation and other forms of manipulation. To the new-comer's distress, the household is visited nightly by their neighbor, Mr. Randolph, an elderly, blind black man. Further disgusted to find that her new teacher is also black, Gilly slips the woman a homemade card that contains a racial slur. Mrs. Harris coolly comments to her privately that the two of them have something in common—each car-ries a tremendous load of undischarged anger. Much of the 11 year old's frustration and orneriness stems from her rootlessness, a situa-tion she hopes to rectify by locating and rejoining her mother, a woman she has idealized but not seen for seven years.

The unhappy girl writes to her mother, informing her she is being exploited and begs her for a reunion. On an errand to Mr. Randolph's house, Gilly discovers some cash and takes it, planning to come back at a convenient time and search for more. However, afraid the theft will be revealed, she runs away, taking some of her foster mother's money with her as well. At the bus depot, she tries to buy a ticket, but her nervousness causes the agent to become suspicious, and he notifies the police. Mamie persuades the authorities to drop the charges and allow the girl to return home. Gilly's social worker then tries to have the troublemaker transferred, but Mamie will not countenance it. The failed mission sets in motion the investigative arm of the state, and a relative is contacted. Upon her return, the irrepressible youngster, beginning to gain a sense of security, agrees to tutor W.E. and decides that an equally urgent need for him is self-defense instruction, a skill in which she has already demonstrated her own competence.

Mr. Randolph becomes ill, and his concerned neighbors carry him into their home to provide better care for him. Soon Mamie and W.E. are stricken, and even though exhausted, Gilly manages to care for them all. When the girl's grandmother unexpectedly arrives, having just learned that she has a granddaughter, she is aghast to see Gilly exclusively responsible for what she regards as an odd assortment of characters. The woman leaves hurriedly but promises to return and rescue Gilly. When Trotter recovers, the wise woman convinces the now reluctant child that she must leave, for she belongs with her normal family. The meeting with her mother, a selfish, spoiled, over-age flower child, is disillusioning, but the resilient girl, after an emotion-laden conference with Trotter, agrees to start life over with her concerned grandmother.

Analysis. This is an expertly written story about a bright, tough, and calculating youngster. Gilly at first decides that her mannerly, literary, blind neighbor will be no barrier to whatever schemes she decides to develop. Her attempts to disparage and distance herself from those she believes are weaker than she is or outside what is considered the mainstream is a pathetic tactic for avoiding placing herself in these categories as well. Mr. Randolph's vulnerability, generosity, and affection, the latter qualities also found in W.E. and her foster parent, penetrate the barbed-wire defenses of the quasi-orphan: they respond to her needs for love, not her obnoxious behavior. Mrs. Trotter is totally matter-of-fact about her friend's impairment, an attitude embodied in her casual observation: "I 'clare, Mr. Randolph, sometimes it's a pity you gotta miss seeing things." Gilly at first claims that W.E. is retarded in her written appeal to her parent, but this description is inaccurate, an attention-getting ploy, deliberately selected to convince her self-centered mother to come to her rescue.

Paulsen, Gary. *The Foxman.* Nashville: Nelson, 1977. 125 pp. Reading Level: YA
Disability: Cosmetic Impairment

A knife attack by the narrator's mother precipitates a judge's decision to send the hero to live with his Uncle Harvey's family in a remote section of northern Minnesota. At first, the newcomer feels alienated by the vastness of the woods and his separation from city life, but he is warmly welcomed and made part of the family, and soon he contributes his brawn to the backbreaking but shared hardships of farm life. Successfully mastering these challenges matures the 15 year old, and he soon is as skillful and as self-confident as his cousin Harry.

When the deep snows arrive, the protagonist shares a winter family tradition: the two elderly Norwegian uncles recount their military adventures during World War I. Although they tell these stories in ways that elicit laughter from their listeners, the hero senses the bleakness and sadness that underlie these accounts.

One day, out hunting, the two youths lose track of time in their eager pursuit of a fox and, to avoid camping out in a snowstorm, seek shelter in a log cabin. The hero is shocked by the man who opens the door: "The face was scarred and twisted and kind of purple-paste looking and from the eyes down it wasn't really a face at all but like a nightmare with no nose and no lips so you could see teeth like a skeleton." Quickly, the man grabs a mask, with which he covers the lower part of his face, and makes a noticeable effort to reduce the boys' discomfort. The visitor thinks: "I wanted to ask him about a thousand questions, but they all seemed to have something to do with his face, or why he was living alone way out in the woods, and it didn't seem right to ask them," and then wonders: "What it was in war that could do that to a man's face and not kill him?"

Harry becomes infatuated with a local girl, leaving his cousin with much time on his hands, which he uses to visit the isolated cabin. The veteran plays some flamenco music and then promises to teach the 15 year old how to trap the wily fox. The boy returns every weekend, and the Foxman talks about the horrors of war as the youth tries to understand why his own relatives romanticize their combat experience. In many ways, the hermit becomes a friend, a mentor, even a father-figure for the youth. At one point, he rescues the adolescent from certain death when he becomes snowblind and loses his way in the woods. One cold day, the teenager arrives at the cabin to discover the old man hopelessly ill. He builds a fire, staying by his friend's side until the hunter dies. Following instructions, the boy burns the cabin "so there wouldn't be any trace of him to find and pity."

Analysis. A brutal act opens the novel, and other incidents of violence punctuate the narrative, specifically in hunting sequences, in the tales of war, and in the recounting of the Foxman's disfiguration. Paulsen contrasts the superficial with the substantive: the disfigured hermit's visage in no way reflects the man's sensitive, cultured, and intelligent nature. He plays the role of a sage, attempting to help the youth perceive how brutality emerges in one's personal life and examines and analyzes its manifestation on the international scene. Wearing a mask and requesting his body be consumed in a pyre are means the veteran uses to protect himself from the stares, and undoubtedly the revulsion, of the curious. This easy-to-read story is directed at a male readership and is hampered by a predilection for run-on sentences. These deficiencies detract only modestly from a thoughtful exploration of both aggression and its opposite, pacifism. Neither the narrator nor the Foxman are given names, presumably in an attempt at promoting the universality of the characters.

Paulsen, Gary. *The Spitball Gang*. New York: Elsevier/Nelson, 1980. 125 pp. Reading Level: MC/YA
Disability: orthopedic impairment

When the call comes in to the Denver police station that some children have robbed a bank, detectives Schaeker and Haldine are assigned the case. Incredulous at first, the evidence, including video tapes from the scene of the crime, forces them to accept the likelihood that school-age youngsters are involved. A second robbery yields additional information, and, from the clues, the police deduce that a Little League team may be implicated. A youngster caught during the stake-out lets slip some information that points to Sloan, the coach, as the guilty party. Under pressure, he admits that he led his boys into crime in order to make "real men" out of them. Although the case against the coach seems clear, the detectives are dissatisfied and continue their inquiry. Discussion with several of the players reveals that an older boy, Peter, masterminded the robberies. The 12-year-old youth, who must spend his time in a wheelchair, was able, through "manipulation of psyche" and "behavior modification in reverse," to compel his "gang" to hold up banks. The investigators decide to leave Peter alone. One man comments: "It wouldn't have done any good to bring him down. Kid in a wheelchair like that . . . it wouldn't have worked. . . . We'll just let Sloan have it all and be done. Sloan would want it that way anyway."

Analysis. In addition to pretentious, self-conscious writing, unnecessarily crude dialogue, totally unbelievable characters, and narrative more suited to adult pulp fiction than juvenile literature, this title's patronizing and ridiculous attitudes toward children, justice, the police, society, disability, and so on make it unacceptable in any context.

Peck, Robert Newton. *Clunie*. New York: Knopf, 1979. 124 pp. Reading Level: YA
Disability: Intellectual Impairment

Braddy Macon's days are filled with learning about the intricacies of his position as shortstop on the varsity team, helping his widowed mother, who washes clothes for the gentry in their small papermill town, and wondering why Sally Rowe, the most yearned-after girl in high school, finds him irresistible. Leo is the hero's antagonist. Through devious maneuvers, he has managed to become captain of the baseball team, but despite this coveted position, he is insecure and obsessed with jealousy and resentment toward Braddy. A ne'er-do-well like his father, Leo lusts after Sally, who haughtily rebuffs his crude attempts to attract her attention. The disappointed youth then turns his attention to Clunie, finding her a convenient target for his vicious jokes.

Clunie's father worries constantly about his only child: "Sixteen, and a woman. . . . But her mind'll ever be childish. Only the Almighty knows why. . . . Because I was drunk on gin. Shirttail drunk, when I come the road home and fell to bed with Bess. I deserve my torment, Lord." Father and daughter live alone since he found his wife "hanging in the barn, her bare feet high in the air . . . Bess knew that Clunie wasn't right. Not for the first two or three years. But after that they both knew. They'd begot a simple child."

One day, frustrated by the knowledge of his inadequacies and failures, Leo decides to follow Clunie and rape her. While protecting herself, she repels the attacker, killing him. The youth's body is discovered, and a search is started for his unknown assailant. Braddy deduces Clunie's involvement in the homicide and concludes that she must be hiding near the dam close to a dangerous stream. Following his hunch, he goes out to the dam, where he hears Clunie's cry. He plunges into the roiling waters to save her, but the strong current and freezing temperatures undermine the hero's resolve, and he fears he will not have the strength and endurance to complete his mission. Clunie blurts out her fear that she will be locked away for hurting Leo, a fate her rescuer wants to avoid. She asks him, "Do daisies grow in Heaven?" He assures her that they do. With that he decides her fate, releasing her to the water. Braddy consoles himself with the knowledge that now, "Nobody will lock her up. She'll always be free." As she slips away from him, Braddy could see, "Clunie wasn't struggling anymore. She was smiling."

Analysis. In this crude and shabby imitation of Steinbeck's *Of Mice and Men*, Clunie—huge, powerful, intellectually impaired, fond of animals, and an inadvertent killer—is a stand-in for Lennie; Braddy, compassionate, loving, loyal, willing to risk the contempt of his peers, takes the role of George. *Clunie* suffers in any comparison between the novels, not only lacking the grace, style, and sensitivity of its model, but also because of glaring deficits in logic and credibility. That the poorly coordinated, slow-thinking child, even though she was strong, could so readily overpower an outstanding high school athlete is quite unlikely; that Braddy would be so insightful that he could immediately understand every element of the fateful confrontation and intuit exactly where the frightened girl would flee is equally improbable. Far more pernicious are the innuendos that run through the story: that Clunie's limitations are tied to her father's alcoholic state at the time of her conception, that retardation is a punishment for such behavioral lapses, that the child's retardation is a sufficient motive for a parent's suicide, that one human has the right to make life-and-death decisions about another, and perhaps the most reprehensible, that freedom and peace for Clunie can be found only in death.

> Pelgrom, Els. *The Winter When Time Was Frozen.* Originally published by Oitgeverij Kosmos in Amsterdam, 1977, as *De Kinderen van het Achtsts Woud.* Trans. by Maryka and Raphael Rudnik. New York: Morrow, 1980. 253 pp. Reading Level: MC/YA
> *Disability:* Intellectual Impairment; also special health problems

When the Germans invade Holland during World War II, Noortje Vanderhook and her father flee their home in Arnhem, finding refuge at the Everingen farm. In addition to Evert, who becomes Noortje's close friend, the family also contains a younger boy and Wilhelmina, a severely retarded child, nicknamed "Baby Sis," who was

> small and fat and couldn't walk. She sat the whole day in a crib pushed against one of the walls of the kitchen. Baby Sis had round red cheeks and a small puny nose. Her little blue eyes were always filled with tears, and she was always drooling. She had thin fine hair, cut off straight in front. Baby Sis made her noises all day long. "Ug! Uh! Ugg! Ugg!" she cried, and "prr *rrrlll!* Then she would bubble and sputter with her lips so that the saliva splattered all around.

Henk, the hired hand, and Theo, a former Resistance fighter now sick with tuberculosis, also live with the family. Somehow room is found in their desperately overcrowded house for four additional refugees, one an elderly, arthritic woman, driven from their home by the invaders.

One night a man comes to the Everingens' seeking help. Mrs. Everingen and Noortje accompany him to a concealed cave in the woods, where they assist the man's wife in the delivery of her baby, whom they name Sarah. Afraid that the infant's cries may reveal their place of concealment to the Germans, the Meyers entrust Sarah's care to their benefactors when she is only a few weeks old.

Although more insulated from the war than city dwellers, there are times when soldiers are quartered in their stables or in the house, when their food is stolen, and when the Dutch men are forced to provide labor or transportation for the enemy army. Theo enlists the children's help in finding another place to hide, afraid that, if he is discovered, all will be punished. The children are exposed to strafing when they travel to town, and one night a rocket explodes nearby, damaging the house. Worst of all, Hank returns from one of his nightly visits to supply food to the Meyers to report that they are missing and their sanctuary has been ransacked.

The Allies finally liberate the Netherlands, but just when life seems to be returning to normal, Baby Sis contracts diphtheria, dying within the week. After the funeral, Noortje overhears some visitor remark: "It's a good thing the child has died. She was such a heavy burden." Her companion replies: "They never get to be very old usually. And it's just as well. It's really too much, taking care of them."

Mr. Vanderhook contacts the Red Cross to see whether Sarah's parents or other relatives can be located. Noortje had come to think of Sarah as part of her family and is dismayed at the prospect of losing her, but Mrs. Everingen explains: "No child is ever ours. . . . Sissy wasn't ours either. It was given to us to take care of her. The Lord has given, the Lord has taken away." One day a visitor arrives for the baby, reporting that all in the Meyers family died in a concentration camp and arrangements have been made to send Sarah to relatives in America. Noortje and her father leave the farm to build a new life in Amsterdam, but her thoughts continue to pull her back to that vivid, emotion-packed year that seems more real and vital than the humdrum world she now inhabits.

Analysis. Pelgrom provides a moving, powerful picture of the dislocations caused by war as seen through the eyes of a sensitive child. Despite the inevitable loss of innocence, the heroine does not understand fully the implications of the many traumatic events and is able to find comfort and satisfaction in the supportive environment created by the loving, compassionate, and thoroughly admirable Everingen family. The mother's response to her baby echoes her reaction to the other unexpected stresses in her life: a rational, willing acceptance of life's vicissitudes, free of self-pity or excess emotionalism. In this same manner, she offers a haven to Theo, despite the danger he poses, and finds useful work for the arthritic grandmother who came to them as a refugee. On the one hand, the farm woman seems detached from ties with both Baby Sis and Sarah, but this is rooted, oddly enough, in her religious beliefs and in her stoic pragmatism. She, in contrast to the critical neighbors, does not see the two babies as burdens but as responsibilities she cannot shirk.

Petersen, Palle. *Sally Can't See*. Originally published in Denmark by Borgens Forlag A/S, 1976. Trans by A. and C. Black. New York: John Day, 1977. unp. Reading Level: YC
Disability: Visual Impairment

Sally attends a residential school for blind children, where she learns skills that will enable her to function in and out of the classroom. Through her intact senses, she develops the ability to read braille and use a white cane effectively. The 12-year-old participates in music and sports activities, takes responsibility for her pet parakeet, enjoys horseback riding, takes pleasure in social gatherings, and, in general, wants "to be treated as much like other people as possible."

Analysis. Despite the obvious benevolent intentions of the author of this photographic essay, this book has numerous problems that drastically limit its usefulness. The central character, although attractive, is considerably older than the prospective audience. The implications that blind individuals see "blackness," that blind children must, of necessity, attend a segregated school, and that such students are extraordinarily dependent not only are inaccurate but perpetuate misperceptions about other blind children. The references to adults always being "close by" are excessive and seem pointless since supervision—during swimming, for example—is essential for all children. The colored photographs are both handsome and informative, but this asset is undercut by the condescending tone and stilted writing in the narrative.

Pevsner, Sheila. *Keep Stompin' Till the Music Stops*. New York: Bradbury, 1977. 136 pp. Reading Level: MC
Disability: Learning Disability; also speech impairment

Richard's clumsiness, letter reversals, concrete thinking, poor word memory, and distractability have all contributed to his academic failure, social immaturity, and damaged sense of self-worth. Consequently, his home has become a battleground as his parents argue over the cause, seriousness, and remedy for his problems. An enigmatic note from his cousin, Alexandra, alerts the sixth-grade youth to be on the lookout for some devious attempts to manipulate events at their upcoming family gathering. Because of his perceptual problems, Richard has trouble understanding the message but is confident clarification will come as the extended clan assembles at his great-grandfather's house. To his dismay, his mother insists he take his schoolwork with him and devote part of each day to his lessons. As the clever Alexandra had surmised, a scheme has been hatched by one of Richard's aunts to uproot the old man, sell his house and property, and pack him off to a "trailer village for senior citizens" in Florida, where he can be supervised by other relatives. Respectful of his attachment to his home, the four great-grandchildren, led by Alexandra, determine to foil this plot. Desperate to think of some solution for the old man he loves, Richard suggests to his seemingly indifferent and self-absorbed father that all the family problems might be simultaneously resolved if his parent returned home with the youngest sibling while he and his mother remained with Granddad. This idea appalls the boy's father, moving him to criticize the family's insensitive machinations and asserting that he intends to support their elderly relative's independence. The old man, showing some signs of age, still has his wits about him and, on his own, concludes a deal whereby the local historical association rents part of his old house for its headquarters in exchange for cooking and cleaning services. All are relieved at this resolution, particularly Richard, who "picked up his books and found a place for them in his suitcase. In the meantime, he had to do the best he could. Maybe he'd make it. If not, he'd go to the special school. He wasn't a hopeless case. He was just a little different."

Analysis. Pevsner has devised a remarkably accurate picture of a child with a severe learning disability, showing how his disorder complicates daily functioning and how its manifestations affect school, family, and social relationships. Richard is an attractive, sympathetic character, fully aware of his problems, exasperated by the confusion they cause him, resigned to being different, and pleasantly and continuously surprised by his favorite cousin's obvious approval. He ultimately adopts his aunt's attitude that no matter what vicissitudes life holds, his best gambit is to "keep stompin' till the music stops."

Peyton, K. M. *The Right-Hand Man.* Illus. by Victor Ambrus. Oxford: Oxford University Press, 1977. 218 pp. Reading Level: YA/MA

Disability: Orthopedic Impairment, Special Health Problems

Watching Ned Rowlands coolly and skillfully manage a coach and four under difficult and dangerous circumstances, Lord Ironminister senses he has found a horseman to match his exacting standards. The wealthy landowner suffers from consumption and, since the amputation of his right arm following an accident, is unable to participate in the major passion of his life, driving his team of horses. He offers Ned a job at twice his present pay, but the 19 year old declines. Unaccustomed to being refused and unscrupulous in the pursuit of his desires, the lord causes the youth to be fired. Forced to accept Ironminister's offer, the young man soon learns to respect and admire his employer and becomes caught up in his mania for racing.

Ned learns that the lord's two conniving cousins impatiently await the ill man's demise since, without wife or child, his lands will become theirs at his death. Ironminister has wagered a goodly sum that his horses can outrun those of his cousins, and with Ned schooling his team, the sick man is revitalized at the prospect of his relatives' incipient defeat. The brothers, aware of Ned's prowess, boobytrap a bridge, causing an accident that results in the death of one of Ironminister's horses and terrible injury to three others. The peer and his friends, infuriated by this vicious act, arrange a grudge boxing match in which Ned is set up to fight one of the cousins. Intensive but all too brief instruction is provided for the youth. He is brutally pounded in the ring, but a lucky punch gives him the victory. When sufficiently recovered, Ned joins his jubilant employer at an inn to celebrate, where the boy is tricked into meeting a hired thug in the courtyard. He defends himself, but in the melee, one of the cousins is killed. Despite Ironminister's help, Ned is tracked down and imprisoned pending trial. Finally, with the aid of bribery, paid witnesses, and perjury, the boy is acquitted. Ironminister pays dearly but gets his revenge: to assure a favorable verdict for Ned, he agrees to marry the judge's obnoxious daughter, who will undoubtedly provide him with an heir and so secure his lands from the further machinations of his remaining villainous cousin.

Analysis. Ironminister is a complex, fascinating character—unscrupulous and noble, brave and petulant, selfish and self-sacrificing, manipulative and honorable. His illness is debilitating, but, by almost superhuman efforts, he is frequently able to ignore its ravaging effects. He reacts to the loss of his arm with furious resentment, but seeks to compensate as best he can by vicariously experiencing the thrills of racing through the actions of his employee, who has almost literally become his right-hand man. This wonderfully literate story, set in early nineteenth-century England, is an action-packed tale peopled with original, intriguing characters whose perilous adventures make compelling reading.

Pfeffer, Susan Beth. *About David.* New York: Delacorte, 1980. 167 pp. Reading Level: YA
Disability: Emotional Dysfunction

Lynn Epstein can scarcely believe the startling revelation that David, her closest friend, shot both his parents before killing himself. After the initial shock wears off, she begins to react violently to the traumatic event: she is tense, irritable, her sleep is interrupted by nightmares, and she finds she is even unable to enter the school cafeteria, the place where she last spoke with David. When the girl is questioned by Lieutenant Donovan, she tells him: "David compartmentalized his life. And his rage could be quite cold." She acknowledges that his surface behavior was similar to that of his more stable, high-achieving peers but reflects that "you can be angry and still behave well." Underneath his calm facade, she knew her friend was an angry, hostile, vengeful youth whose "rages burnt . . . like dry ice." His basic fury focused on his natural parents, who gave him away, but his fiercest hatred was directed toward his adoptive parents, who constantly goaded him to ever greater accomplishments but who never praised him for his achievements or considered his needs when family plans were made. Silently he harbored grudges that he constantly and determinedly nurtured. When the policeman asks Lynn about David's frame of mind on that fateful day, she realizes that she has completely blanked the subjects of their lunchtime conversation from her memory.

Jeffrey, an outcast and David's best friend, is so devastated by the murder-suicide that he becomes hysterical and is subsequently hospitalized in a center for emotionally dysfunctional adolescents. The Epsteins arrange for Dr. Collins to see their daughter: he helps the teenager explore her relationship with her troubled friend, and gradually these therapeutic sessions begin to offer some relief from the distressing emotional trauma. Lynn learns that David willed her his notebooks. She is reluctant to read the contents at first but is driven by a need to discover the reasons underlying the youth's brutal actions. Dr. Collins suggests that when she finishes them she will be free to relinquish the repressive emotional bonds which tie her to her dead companion. The young man's last entry reveals his discovery that his mother is pregnant. Lynn feels she understands the profound sense of rejection he must have felt at this news but is even more shocked when Donovan tells her: "We did an autopsy and Mrs. Morris was not pregnant at the time of her death." Appalled, she responds: "But what David did . . . It was . . . dear God, it was crazy." Slowly Lynn begins to reassemble the elements of her own life, preferring to recall the good qualities of her friend rather than dwell on the anguish and pain he must have suffered.

Analysis. The author proposes that David's insecurity, his inability to live up to parental expectations, and the absence of love have left him defenseless to cope with the stresses of living. To the casual observer, he seems placid and self-sufficient, but underneath, he is a volatile, vulnerable adolescent without any satisfactory channels for expressing his fury and suffering. His two pals, Jeffrey and Lynn, from whose perspective the story is told, are apparently inadequate to the task. Jeffrey's stability is at issue since he "was having a rough time differentiating between reality . . . and fantasy," but is sufficiently helped by therapy that he is able to leave the institution where he was hospitalized and enter Princeton. Pfeffer demonstrates considerable sympathy for her characters and makes a strong case for the value of psychotherapy. However, the plot is excessively slick, and the explanations of disordered behavior are both facile and superficial.

Pfeffer, Susan Beth. *Starring Peter and Leigh.* New York: Delacorte, 1979. 200 pp. Reading Level: YA
Disability: Special Health Problems

Leigh Thorpe, ex-child actress on television, leaves the bright lights and glitter of show business with relief. Hoping her mother's remarriage to a Long Island, New York, businessman will mean a "normal" existence for her as a high school student, the 16-year-old girl is both anxious and excited at this prospect. Although she is uneasy about getting along with her new stepbrother, Peter, they quickly become friends. The 17-year-old youth has suffered all his life from various health problems, the most disabling being hemophilia. He explains:

"Bumping into things, which I do all the time can cause bleeding. So can tension. Or sometimes it just starts for no good reason. If I think I'm going to bleed, I take some stuff that helps ward it off. But most of the time, I can't predict, and I bleed and my father gives me transfusions. We keep the clotting factor I need in the house just in case."

"And you're never going to get any better?" I asked.

"Yes and no," he said. "I'll never be a professional wrestler. But the teen-age years are the worst because the body is still growing. And I'm a late bloomer. I keep getting taller. That puts strain on my joints, which is where I bleed the most: knees, elbows."

"But you won't be bedridden forever?"

"No," he said. "This is temporary. But there's been permanent damage to my knees, and I have arthritis, which doesn't help matters. Still, it could be worse."

"How?" I asked.

"At least I have my looks," he said grinning. "It's just a question of finding the right girl to be bedridden with."

This banter sets the tone for their relationship. Peter decides he will stage-manage Leigh's entry into "normalcy," a ploy that will enable him to vicariously enjoy high school life, from which he has been temporarily forced to withdraw. Classmates are hesitant about initiating contact, but soon Leigh begins to develop acquaintances. She side-steps pressures to assume the lead in the school play, well aware of the social consequences should she accept. Instead, the newcomer suggests that another friend audition for the main role. Abetted by her coaching, her chum is successful in the part. Leigh soon gains the attention of the class president, makes new friends, and generally blends into the mainstream of high school life. It seems to her that everyone is clear about future goals, while only she remains uncertain.

Despite Leigh's efforts to dismiss her past, it is obvious that acting has a hold on her, and when her father proposes that they work together in a revival of *The Diary of Anne Frank*, she is torn by conflicting emotions. She finally decides to accept the offer despite Peter's strong objections. In a turbulent reaction to the news, he bumps into a table and reactivates his hemophilic problems. The youth requires three transfusions, coagulants, ice, and bed rest, undergoing a night of agonizing pain. Leigh insists on talking to him, explaining that she must make her own life choices even if he doesn't approve. Peter confesses that he loves her. Leigh responds that she loves him too but is uncertain whether her feeling is sisterly affection or something more and predicts that being apart will allow her to gain a perspective on their relationship. He accepts her decision and begins his recovery.

Analysis. The dialogue and repartee are engaging in this lightweight, breezy junior novel. The writing is generally slick, fast paced, and likely to stimulate the daydreams of star-struck adolescent readers. The characters, by and large, have the same dimensionality as those in television soaps. This frothy romance is both enlivened and weakened by Peter's characterization, an unconvincing portrayal of a boy troubled by fears but with compensating qualities as well—tenacity, social savvy, and determination. Although compassion is generated for his problem, he is depicted as an attractive, romantic youth, his wheelchair notwithstanding. The hero's disorder is apparently serious enough to exclude him from school, but this presentation emphasizes his illness as inconvenient, rather than debilitating, and one that additionally gives him an aura of glamour.

Phelan, Terry Wolfe. *The S.S. Valentine.* Illus. by Judy Glasser. New York: Four Winds, 1979. 40 pp. Reading Level: MC
Disability: Orthopedic Impairment

Andy, anticipating that the new pupil will be yet another antagonist, is surprised when the principal pushes a wheelchair into their elementary classroom. Connie, the vehicle's "inhabitant," smiled and then "she did the neatest thing. She pressed a bunch of buttons and levers on the arm of her wheelchair . . . zoomed along the front of the room, made a quick turn, and stopped right next to Gary." Andy is uncertain about how he should react to her. "Gary asked me if I knew what was wrong with her. I don't know . . . and I'm afraid to ask. 'Me too,' Gary said. 'Wheelchairs are scary.' " Andy is curious about the mechanism (Does it have snowtires? he wonders) but also about why Connie comes late to class every day. Even though the child is main-streamed, he later learns she must have daily physical therapy as an outpatient at the local hospital.

The class decides on the topic of their upcoming February play, and although Andy considers it a disaster, the girls vote as a bloc for a Valentine's Day theme. Connie murmurs, "I was never in a play be-fore. And I'm not sure I can be in this play either." Andy's suggestion that they decorate Connie's wheelchair like a rocket ship to carry Val-entine messages appeals to the newcomer, and she throws herself enthusiastically into her part. Connie's absence during the days before the play is scheduled is due to her hospitalization for some tests. This causes anxiety among her fellow actors, but she returns in the nick of time, and the performance goes off splendidly despite a minor mishap. Andy hops on the back of the "space vehicle," assisting the "captain" in maneuvering it.

Analysis. Connie is initially portrayed as a shy child, but soon emerges as a sociable, creative, and competent youngster in this pleas-ant but overwhelmingly didactic story. Characterizations are forced, particularly that of the starry-eyed teacher, who incessantly tries to kiss her students. There are occasional instances of real dialogue, but these are submerged in the contrived plot and theme. Many illustrations pepper the book. The cast of the play is pictured in costume on the front cover, engagingly but nervously eyeing the audience. Connie is smack in the middle.

Phipson, Joan. *A Tide Flowing.* New York: Atheneum, 1981. 156 pp. Reading Level: YA
Disability: Neurological Impairment

Ominous signs precede their leave-taking when Mark and his mother sail from Tasmania on the first leg of their trip to visit her parents in England. In the night, the boy senses his mother's move-ment up to the deck but is too late to prevent her from slipping over-board. In the aftershock of agonizing whether the act was deliberate or not, he sees an albatross swooping over the waves and is somehow comforted—in his mind transforming his mother into the beautiful white creature. Sent to his paternal grandparents in Australia, Mark is further depressed when it appears that his father, now involved with a new woman companion, is not enthusiastic about retrieving him. The boy lives a passive, uninvolved existence in Sidney, tolerated by his cousins, who, under adult pressure, allow him to crew in their sailing races.

The water has a therapeutic effect on the lonely boy, and contemplating the albatross, the harmony of sea and sky, and the teeming life in each, Mark experiences a transcendental sense of unity with nature. The youth seeks out further information about the white bird and as a result ponders the meaning of solitude and loneliness, drawing easy parallels between his own anomic life and that of the bird.

On his daily route to the bus, he notices Connie Peterson, a taciturn girl in a wheelchair being pushed by her mother and, after ridding himself of some aversion, occasionally greets them with a hello. One morning he hears a scream, looks up to see the wheelchair speeding down the hill out of control, and blocks the vehicle with his body, decelerating its headlong plunge into the street. The car that hits them breaks Mark's legs, ribs, and collarbone; although badly injured, he is expected to recover fully. Mrs. Peterson tells the youngster that his bravery saved her daughter's life, and the girl's quadriplegia will not be worsened by this accident. She reveals that another collision was the cause of her daughter's condition and her husband's death. It is during their hospitalization that Mark looks at Connie closely for the first time:

> The . . . hollows between the bones and the pale almost grey colour of her skin turned the promise of future beauty into a premature indication of the same face in old age. . . . Her hair was straight, fairly short and a dull yellow—the hair of an invalid. It was hard to know whether she was tall or short. She had not quite finished growing when the accident happened. She had a little movement in her arms, but no co-ordination and her arms had a tendency to wave aimlessly like seaweed in an eddy.

The 17-year-old girl and the 14-year-old boy confide their feelings to each other about their absent parents, their pervasive solitude, and the mutual pleasure in their developing friendship. Impulsively, the youth invites her to go sailing, but his grandfather is skeptical that such a project can be safely undertaken. Knowing the risk, all nevertheless agree to try, and they are able, with much assistance, to get Connie aboard. She is ecstatic about the adventure, but on disembarking, she and the old man fall over the side as he tries to raise her up to the men waiting on the pier. Jolted into action, Mark dives overboard and, with help, is able to lift her to safety. Connie apologizes for the trouble she has caused and vows she will never sail again. In shock, Mark directs his unrestrained fury toward his grandfather, but the old sailor, instead of taking offense at the boy's insolence, is pleased that his grandson is at last able to display some spirit. When Connie recovers, Mark takes her for walks and they speculate about the albatross. The ailing heroine claims she sees the bird and says, "I think I know where I belong—not alone, still part of everything after all." The image correctly foretells her death, but she is now able to accept this fate with equanimity.

Analysis. The description of Connie prepares the reader for her premature death. She is presented as a girl with low self-esteem. She ruefully observes: "A person in a wheelchair is always a nuisance," and later bitterly comments that she is a "curse" to everyone. Connie is acutely aware of the fascinated and pitying reaction of strangers. Mark, too, learns of the "artificial tone in the voice of those meeting her for the first time." Despite her fragile health, Connie has a powerful impact on the lives of others. Sensitivity to her new friend and her willingness to respond to his profound and complex needs is literally a lifesaving gift; in this manner she reciprocates for the added meaning he has given her days. Her injuries in the auto accident had caused harm beyond the paralysis, and her mother had been informed then that the girl could not be expected to live long. Nevertheless, she consciously opts to help her daughter have richer, more satisfying experiences, even if they threaten her longevity.

Images of an imperative human need for harmony with nature and the cyclical quality of life pervade this work: Connie's first auto accident consigns her to a lonely existence; her second initiates the most important friendship of her life. Mark cannot save his mother from dying in the ocean, but he saves Connie from drowning in the sea and metaphorically from drowning in isolation. The water is the most important element in the boy's life—in it he loses one parent and miles of ocean separate him from the other. His sailing skills give him immeasurable comfort, connecting him with his grandparents and cousins. His lack of interest in their sailboat racing ambitions sunders this fragile relationship. This is a story rich in complex characterizations, vivid images, and persistent symbols. The albatross, with the sea, provides a unifying symbol, simultaneously suggesting birth and immortality, solitude and connectedness.

Phipson, Joan. *When the City Stopped.* New York: Atheneum, 1978. 177 pp. Reading Level: MC/YA
Disability: Orthopedic Impairment

In response to an announcement that a nuclear reactor will be constructed near the city, a general strike engulfs Sydney, Australia, bringing urban services to a standstill: there is no electricity, public transportation has ceased, schools are closed, and garbage collections are suspended. In the ensuing confusion, Mrs. Lorimer is injured in an automobile accident on her way home and loses consciousness for several days. The hospital staff is unable to find any identification and so cannot notify her 13-year-old son, Nick, and his 11-year-old sister, Binkie, of their mother's whereabouts. With their father abroad, the children are left on their own. After a few hectic days, the youngsters realize that the city is becoming unlivable and decide to locate their housekeeper and ask her to leave the city with them. They meet Digby Todd and Tilly, a dog he has rescued, who join forces with the Lorimer children. When they arrive at Mrs. Piggott's, she is unenthusiastic about their plan; however, her husband, Jo, crippled from injuries suffered breaking horses, insists that the city is an inappropriate human environment at the best of times but will soon become downright dangerous. Mrs. Piggott reluctantly agrees, and the boys retrieve a cart that Jo will use as a vehicle for himself. The two boys pull, Mrs. Piggott and Binkie push, and Jo, although weak, directs their evacuation from his perch inside the wagon. They pass a young girl whose suitcase has been stolen by a gang of looters, and she joins them on their journey out of the beleaguered town.

Law and order have completely broken down, and gangs of toughs begin looting, brutalizing anyone who interferes with their thieving. Homeless dogs roam the city and rats and scavenger birds, attracted by the growing mounds of uncollected garbage, forage freely. The little band becomes increasingly apprehensive until they finally reach a highway, where they hope to flag down a truck hauling freight. When a car stops to pick up the young girl they befriended, to the group's surprise, she gets in without a backward glance or a word of gratitude for her former protectors. Finally, a compassionate truck driver stops and takes the weary travelers to his home. Anticipating his death, Jo leaves his bed that night, making his way painfully to the mountains, where he is found the next day. Now alone and heartbroken, Mrs. Piggott generously offers Digby a permanent home with her. The local constable finds the recovered Mrs. Lorimer and makes arrangements for the family to be reunited.

Analysis. Before the disaster, Jo's once keen intelligence seemed to be atrophying, but during the exodus, he assumes command. He is thoroughly admirable—intelligent, sensitive, practical, brave, determined, and persevering, obviously in harmony with nature and resistant to the destructive potential of technology. In this role, he established rapport with the dog, who quickly accepts him as master; he speaks against the incursion of nuclear power; and he seeks the open air in which to die.

When the City Stopped seems more a story fragment than a complete and fully developed novel. The tale is curiously uninvolving, despite the dramatic potential inherent in the chaos and devastation that form the backdrop of this doomsday scenario. Moreover, the pacing is slow and the action sparse. The final moral does not arise inevitably from the story, but seems obviously and clumsily appended.

Pieper, Elizabeth. *A School for Tommy*. Illus. by Mina G. McLean. Elgin, Ill.: Child's World, 1979. 32 pp. Reading Level: YC
Disability: Orthopedic Impairment

Seven-year-old Tommy overhears his mother trying to persuade the principal of the local school to admit him into a mainstreamed class. The reluctant administrator tries to put her off: "Schools are just not built for crippled kids. It's not easy for a child to get around in a wheelchair. . . . What if he were to get hurt?" He ultimately agrees to the integration on a trial basis. It is clear that neither the teacher nor the children have been prepared for Tommy's arrival since he is greeted with expressions of curiosity and concern. His new classmates question him directly, and his straightforward responses relieve their discomfort at his physical differences. His teacher tries to protect the boy by limiting his activities, but the newcomer prefers to join his peers during recess. While watching a baseball game, Tommy has the ingenious idea of disassembling the arm of his wheelchair and using it for a bat. After designating a substitute runner should he connect, he slams the ball, but in doing so, he tumbles from his chair. Although he is slightly hurt, Tommy puts on a brave front so as not to appear fragile before the fearful teacher. The boy urges her to allow him to attend gym with his class, where he suggests a wheelbarrow race to his physical education instructor. He and his partner come in first, convincing his home-room teacher of his ability to function in a competitive setting. As the gym teacher remarks: "Well, Sport . . . it looks like you're a winner."

Analysis. This quasi-fictional work suggests that disabled youngsters should not be kept from risk taking—that such minor mishaps as falling may be no more dangerous for them than for their ablebodied peers and are, indeed, far less damaging than exclusion. In the afterward, directed to child readers, Pieper elaborates on this theme, discussing the implications of an impairment and how it affects the person sustaining it. The author implies that some mainstreaming failures may be caused by administrative and staff attitudes and ignorance, an argument not without merit. The illustrations add little to the story and would be more at home in a primer than in a trade book.

Platt, Kin. *The Doomsday Gang*. New York: Morrow, 1978. 185 pp.
Reading Level: YA
Disability: Intellectual Impairment

Five boys, rejected as incompetents by other gangs in their Los Angeles neighborhood, are prodded by Coby into forming the Doomsday Gang, thereby nominally giving themselves some visible identity, protection, and mutual support. Coby is their leader and Gooch is their faithful follower. He "was six feet and, at fifteen, weighed two hundred ten pounds. Incredibly strong, without a mean bone in his flawless body, he was perfectly coordinated everywhere except in his head. . . . The psychiatric report . . . was that he was a disturbed child, mentally arrested and potentially dangerous if provoked. He was classified as retarded with the mentality and IQ of a five-year-old child." The enterprises the boys devise inevitably end in disaster. After they plan a break-in to vandalize a junior high school, Joker deserts to make his drug connection and the other four are delayed for hours, sabotaged both by bad luck and their inability to carry though any venture requiring organization or discipline. When they finally reach the school, it is late. They mindlessly ravage the classrooms but are halted by an accident in a chemistry lab when some chemicals ignite, slightly injuring the adolescents. They escape and return to their hideout intent on castigating Gooch for his thoughtlessness in lighting a match, but they are mollified when they learn the boy had found $50, which he selflessly turns over to the club treasury.

When the leader of a notorious black gang is seriously wounded by some Chicanos, Coby helps him to escape to his own turf, where, to his astonishment, he is rewarded with a gift of an arsenal of weapons. After their disappearance, Joker deduces they have been stolen by his drug connection. He and Coby threaten the thief with a gun, taking almost $2,000 of his money as an advance against the presumed value of the weapons. Dimby, Hinch, and Gooch travel across town to watch a gang war between some Anglos and Chicanos. The confrontation results in a massacre, and when the enraged Chicanos spot the Doomsday members, they attack, fatally stabbing Gooch. Joker and Coby spend their recently acquired cash for some motorcycles and race over to the fight, hoping to catch some of the action. The inexperienced drivers rack up their bikes and end up in the hospital, but assert that their brief moment of glory was worth it.

Analysis. Although Gooch's infantile and erratic behavior and speech infuriate the gang at times, he is tolerated because of his loyalty, honesty, openness, strength, and selflessness. His final act, in which he dies trying to save his buddies, illustrates his dedication to his friends but expresses the too common literary convention of the final sacrifice of the impaired character. The boy's mother, a petty thief, who is awkwardly described as "hard of hearing and had a stammer speech defect," is an example of an attributed problem that needlessly complicates the picture of a burdensome existence. The author swamps his gritty narrative with invective, and this poverty of language aptly reflects the emotional and economic poverty of the characters. Page after page of these relentlessly repeated obscenities inevitably has a desensitizing effect on the reader. Through this device, however, Platt underscores his message that the language, perceptions, and goals of the school, the courts, the social workers, and other agents of authority function in a totally different world from that of a gang member. The appallingly hopeless, pointless lives led by the characters should elicit compassion, but they are such callous, repellent, stereotypical hoodlums that little identification or empathy is possible.

Platt, Kin. *Flames Going Out.* New York: Methuen, 1980. 167 pp.
Reading Level: YA
Disability: Emotional Dysfunction

Tammy is literally experiencing an identity crisis:

> The image she had of herself would dissolve, fragmenting so that she had no clear conception of who she was. It was an anonymous and obscure identity without conformity, sometimes filling the interior landscape of her mind, or else vanishing completely, leaving her with the desolation of having disappeared somehow from her own life.

Conversations with herself, phantom lovers, her other persona, and rituals involving the lighting of matches occupy Tammy's lonely days, but none of these reduce her anxiety or provide her relief from tormenting thoughts. Her wealthy parents recognize some improvements from her three years of psychotherapy but continue to find her incessant cursing disturbing.

One day she meets Jonathan Greengold, her psychiatrist's son, and she is immediately attracted to the drug-addicted youth. Although concern for another human being is a constructive move for the totally self-absorbed girl, the Berkeley student's obvious pathology promises complications. Jonathan claims he isn't "into relationships," but she persists, observing both his compassion and his passivity. The teenager tries to dissuade him from his drug dependency, aware that his "euphoria was short-lived, followed immediately by depression." When Dr. Greengold hears about his patient's attraction to his son, he warns her, "He's an irredeemable junkie."

Whether in school, on the street, on buses, at parties, or on her ill-considered visit to a disco club, almost all of Tammy's encounters with males have a sexual element. She believes her status as the "last sixteen-year-old virgin in Beverly Hills" is another of her problems and tries in erratic and awkward ways to alter that condition. Tammy is attracted by thoughts of sex but repelled by the crudeness and exploitiveness of the men she encounters; she typically flees in panic at the prospect of contact actually being made. The adolescent persists in feeling withdrawn from the rest of the world and is highly sensitive to her own lack of substantiality.

Tammy is ecstatic when Jonathan calls her, and they plan a consummation of their physical feelings. On the way to a friend's home, borrowed for the evening, they are stopped by a police car and searched, a frightening incident that puts a damper on their passion. Their date is a fiasco, and the youth swallows more pills, which he believes will allow him to survive the trip back to Oakland.

In a nightmare in which her two selves again separate, Tammy thinks she hears Jonathan laughing from behind a gray shroud. She asks herself why she persists in such an unsatisfying relationship: "He's incapable of maintaining any emotional or physical level for long, with drugs or without. He falls apart and takes me with him. He's doomed and so am I." On an impulse, she flies to the campus to see him but finds his dead body. The troubled youth had violated his doctor's injunction not to mix drugs with antibiotics, with the predictable result. Tammy first becomes hysterical at this horrendous scene, then extremely depressed. When she returns home, she begins to swallow a random collection of pills, intent on ending her own life.

Analysis. With the exception of the brilliant Dr. Greengold, all the characters in this depressing novel indulge their hedonistic whims or selfish personal goals. The preoccupation with self-indulgence, particularly exploitive, impersonal sex, while contributing to the story's theme, ultimately becomes tedious. The incessant profanity, although a valid reflection of the speech of their real-life counterparts, has an equally numbing effect. The heroine's distress is vividly portrayed, as are the physician's attempts to help the young woman rid herself of self-defeating behavior. *Flames Going Out* is a skillful cautionary tale about the dangers of drug abuse, but it also conveys the message that for substance abusers and nonusers, for both selfish and caring people, for adjusted and nonadjusted alike, there is little in the world to hope for.

Polette, Nancy. *Katie Penn*. Illus. by Charles Molina. St. Louis: Concordia, 1978. 111 pp. Reading Level: MC/YA
Disability: Cosmetic Impairment, Emotional Dysfunction

Despite her alcoholic mother's vague but ominous warnings, Katie Penn accepts work from Miss Addie, a formerly wealthy woman who now lives a solitary and apparently impoverished life. When the adolescent arrives at her employer's home and sees the woman for the first time, she suspects "the Lord . . . must have gotten distracted for a minute" for "the eyes that stared at the girl could not focus in a direct line—each pupil stared in an opposite direction across the bridge of the woman's nose." Katie feels great sympathy for this proud lady since "knowing the superstitions of the hill folk [she] was sure that the woman had suffered a great deal because of her deformity."

Before long, Katie discovers a bedraggled, forlorn woman chained to a bedpost hidden away on the upper floor of the once imposing mansion. Miss Addie unexpectedly enters and explains: "This is only for her protection when I can't be with her. . . . My sister, as you can see, has the mind of a five-year-old child." In addition to her other responsibilities, the teenager now assists with the care and entertainment of Miss Emily, who had been presumed dead by her neighbors.

When a visiting preacher comes to their hardscrabble Ozark village, Katie asks him to try his healing powers on her mother. Reluctantly, Mrs. Penn permits a delegation to her home to pray for her deliverance from drink. Apparently deeply affected by the service, the woman suddenly stiffens, points to the doorway, and screams: "The devil woman's come for my soul," then faints. Katie makes sure her mother is taken care of, then leaves in search of Miss Addie, whose sudden presence so terrified Mrs. Penn.

Katie is distressed to hear that Miss Emily is missing. She and Miss Addie continue searching until they locate Miss Emily at Hangman's Tree, where some vandals have hanged her beloved cat. The overnight experience in the woods leaves Miss Emily chilled, and, now ill with a debilitating cough, the helpless woman requires increased care. Katie has meanwhile given sanctuary in the huge, sprawling house to a runaway hiding from his brutal stepfather. Miss Addie investigates a noise she hears in the night made by this youth, trips over a kitten, and falls down the staircase, breaking her neck. Katie finds her former employer's body the next morning, rushes home to enlist her mother's help in caring for Miss Emily, then leaves for town to notify the authorities. The doctor diagnoses the sick woman's ailment as pneumonia and sends her to a hospital, from which she will be transferred to a nursing home. Arrangements are made for Miss Addie's funeral, an event that draws an unexpectedly large crowd. At first, Katie is indignant, suspecting that those assembled are merely curiosity seekers. But Doc explains that Addie's money paid for an operation to repair a cleft lip for one child and plastic surgery for another, who consequently now "look[s] like a human being instead of a freak." The parents of these children helped by Miss Addie had just been informed of the identification of their benefactor and have come to the funeral to pay their respects. Doc offers Katie a job in his office to replace the one she just lost. The girl hopes her mother will remain sober from now on but realizes that one's destiny is a matter of individual control.

Analysis. This mountain soap opera features such stock characters as a once wealthy recluse with a dark family secret, a town lout and his long-suffering wife, a kindly town doctor, and a noble adolescent heroine. As is common in such scripts, action, too, tends to be extreme and melodramatic. Although life was difficult during the Depression, a killing, an animal hanged, an accidental death, an attempted murder, a false imprisonment, and a forced confinement of an adult woman seem an excessive amount of drama for a tiny community. The language employed to describe disability is equally overwrought and lacks any moderating interpretation. To label someone with strabismus as "deformed" or a "devil woman" or to refer to a burned child as a "freak" as part of local ignorant speech is one thing; to allow that image to stand is quite another.

Polette does capture a sense of time and place in this story, weaving into the narrative the archaic and superstitious beliefs that shape her characters' responses to disability as well as to other facets of life. However, the subordinating of literary imperatives to the promotions of an ethical tenet has a constricting effect on this junior novel.

Pollowitz, Melinda. *Cinnamon Cane.* New York: Harper & Row, 1977. 154 pp. Reading Level: MC/YA
Disability: Neurological Impairment

Cassie is upset because her parents have finally convinced her grandfather that he can no longer maintain the old family homestead alone. The house, fields, and barn are sold, and the old man is transferred to a small townhouse apartment. Although the 12-year-old girl is well aware of how disheartening the move has been to her grandparent, she is nonetheless jealous of the friendly attentions he receives from a widow who lives next door. Cassie's growing involvement with a junior high school group and a school poetry club eats into her free time, leaving her fewer opportunities to spend with her grandfather. Signs of decreased functioning begin to appear in the old man: he now regularly uses a cane carved from a cinnamon tree and experiences an alarming dizzy spell, which he begs Cassie not to reveal to her parents. Unfortunately, this episode is an antecedent to more serious central nervous system dysfunction, and after a severe stroke, he is left with a partial paralysis. Cassie's guilt-ridden father begins converting a section of their home for the old man's use and, over his vigorous protestations, takes him there. Objecting to the role of invalid, he fires his nurse, walks before permission is given, and one afternoon while unattended, wanders outside where he collapses in the snow. At the hospital, he is disoriented, confusing Cassie with his deceased wife. The child is increasingly distressed to see the deterioration wrought in her beloved grandparent. She continues to share poetry, reports on her social activities with him, and nibbles on pieces of his cane, a tool he predicts he will never use again. She cherishes this object as a memento of the happy times and the love they shared.

Analysis. Cinnamon Cane is the story of two difficult passages: Cassie's is from the security and seeming permanence of childhood to the turbulence and uncertainty of adolescence; her grandfather's is from the independence and vigor of adulthood to the declining powers and dependence of old age. The child's resistance echoes and is intensified by her grandfather's as each initially resists, but eventually accepts, the inevitable. The confusion and forgetfulness that often result from cerebral accidents are portrayed realistically and compassionately, and their effect on loved ones is movingly depicted. Responses of others to the old man provide a measure of their character: the nurse's reference to him as "a bad boy" shows her callousness and unsuitability for her work; the son's initial insensitivity, then overcompensation, reveal his self-absorption, guilt, and finally his devotion.

Posner, Grace. *In My Sister's Eyes.* New York: Beaufort, 1980. 160 pp. Reading Level: YA
Disability: Intellectual Impairment, Neurological Impairment

Billy Roster, also known as Bilbo, is a high school tennis ace. He can hardly believe that Chrissy Ockham, co-captain of the cheerleaders, wants to be his girl friend. Moreover, she wants him to coach her in tennis since she has been considering breaking with family tradition by leaving "cheering" and becoming an athlete. Because of a developmental disability, compounded by a seizure disorder, Jeanette,

Bilbo's older sister, has been institutionalized, and the youth is relieved when Chrissy is not upset by this news. Jen comes home for a visit but must stay longer than planned due to an epidemic at her special school. Billy and Chris take her for a ride to the beach, and while the two are momentarily distracted, Jen slips away unnoticed. After a night of frantic searching, the young woman is discovered, fast asleep. Chrissy confesses that her accepting behavior of Bilbo's sister is partially based on curiosity about what such a person is like, and after this admission, the ex-cheerleader is properly contrite. However, she is assured by her tennis mentor and boyfriend that such interest is normal. When the crisis at Jen's permanent residence is over, her family is ambivalent about their daughter's return: They have enjoyed her visit but are cognizant of its effect on the household and are aware that Jen no longer considers the Roster home her real residence.

Analysis. From the misleading title to the insipid conclusion, this plodding work is an admixture of misinformation, anachronistic narrative, and offensive commentary about the disabled. Additionally, it is burdened by a lightweight, jerry-built plot and sitcom characterizations. The assumption that events will be viewed from Jen's perspective is erroneous since that outlook is rarely used. The girl's eyes are referred to in the text as "empty windows," an overworked figure of speech that reflects lack of knowledge about individuals diagnosed as retarded. The statement, "She also had epilepsy so she couldn't be handled by the family," is an insupportable non sequitur, which is subsequently contradicted by events in the story. The implication that the alternatives for her care are only those of institutionalization or family living and the lack of reference to vocational training suggest that the author is unfamiliar with current community-based programs.

The language is consistently patronizing and frequently insulting: "She was really a pretty girl . . . even if she was retarded," "Jeanette wore no makeup, *of course*" (emphasis added), "There's someone [a character refers to Jen] locked up in there, a real, living, thinking, feeling person." Jeanette's mother is described as feeling guilty for not having "given" her son a normal brother or sister. When Billy is nervous and speaks incessantly, he adopts his mother's perception and says of himself: "You're beginning to sound retarded yourself." These demeaning attitudes are not countered by the writer of this novel. The descriptors used to picture Jen are inconsistent and sometimes capricious. The young woman is credited with minimal verbal skills, but, on occasion, she is shown to have complex thoughts. Some unspecified surgery is alluded to, but its intent and nature are unclear. A reference to those who wear glasses as "owls" is another outdated absurdity. Near the conclusion of the story, going to a prom is equated with "participating in life fully and meaningfully," demonstrating with its own language the banality of this vapid, anachronistic, and tasteless effort.

Potter, Marian. *The Shared Room*. New York: Morrow, 1979. 192 pp.
Reading Level: MC
Disability: Emotional Dysfunction

The small western New York town knows the secret of her mother's hospitalization, and Catherine, in anger and frustration, fights with her schoolmates over the teasing she receives about her missing parent. A fifth-grade assignment to write her autobiography again stirs uneasiness in the girl. Since her well-meaning grandparents have concealed from her the specific circumstances of her father's disappearance and the whereabouts of her "sick" mother, the youngster is beset with anxiety and curiosity. She concludes that her mother's continued absence is a form of rejection: "It was strange she's stayed in the hospital so long. If she had really tried hard, she wouldn't be sick. After all, she didn't have tonsilitis or flu or a broken arm." Catherine spends much time fantasizing, trying to reconstruct images and memories of the past or wondering what life will be like when her mother comes back to her. When, at last, she learns where her mother is institutionalized, she begs to be allowed to visit. This request upsets her grandmother, who is adamant about prohibiting contact between the two; however, the child manages to send her mother a Christmas present. Mrs. Doyle writes, thanking her daughter and reporting that other patients are being discharged and that she also hopes for such an opportunity.

Mrs. Doyle's social worker informs the family that a new drug regimen has been effective and pressures them to permit a brief return. Catherine opens the letter from the hospital addressed to her grandparents and forges a response accepting the recommendation. The visit begins smoothly enough, and the woman seems sufficiently in control of herself to function outside the institution, but soon realizes she does not have the strength to respond to the needs of others or to the emotional demands they would make of her. Catherine's grandfather is aware that the silence they have maintained with the youngster has increased her distress rather than lessening it. He then explains the circumstances of his daughter's "breakdown." Almost immediately after her unsuitable marriage, the 18-year-old bride began to demonstrate highly erratic behavior, moving from apathy to hyperactivity without apparent cause. Her husband, too immature to cope with the situation, abandoned his wife and child. After several suicide attempts by their daughter, the young woman's agonized parents hospitalized her and accepted the fact that her impairment was a permanent one. Catherine responds: "You told me sad things, but I'm glad you've told me. I feel like one piece now, not a bunch of wonderings."

Previous improvements had always been short term, and Mrs. Doyle's parents have steeled themselves against false and futile hopes. Now at their home, the woman seems to be entering a depressive phase again, and they are concerned that their fears will be realized. Catherine is able to penetrate her mother's self-absorption briefly but comes to realize that her mother still has major adjustments to make. Mrs. Doyle is assigned to a halfway house in the community, where there will be less pressure, a plan ultimately all accept as providing the best hope for the future.

Analysis. Told from the naive viewpoint of a ten-year-old, *The Shared Room* is an honest, if simple, look at the family dislocations that can result when one member must be hospitalized. The ramifications of suppressing information and refusing to discuss a problem with a concerned child are seen to confuse the girl and exacerbate her worries. Adults are shown to have coping difficulties—afraid to invest overly in hopes for improvement in the face of innumerable disappointments, unsureness in what course of action to take with curious neighbors, and worry over the future of their offspring. The young protagonist's wishful fantasies, her shame, guilt, love, and anxieties, are given respectful treatment in this low-key, yet involving story.

Rabe, Berniece. *The Balancing Girl.* Illus. by Lillian Hoban. New York: Dutton, 1981. unp. Reading Level: YC
Disability: Orthopedic Impairment

Even though Margaret must use aluminum crutches to get around, she excels in balancing objects—blocks, magic markers, books atop her head—even herself! Tommy, her nemesis, belittles her accomplishments, but when the first-grade girl challenges him to match her feats, he declines, accompanying his refusal with the retort: "I still say it's simple." When her castle is toppled during recess, Margaret thinks she knows who the culprit is.

The principal announces a fund-raising carnival and solicits ideas for booths. Margaret considers ways she can exploit her skill to earn money for her school. She begins work on a construction made from dominoes, which she and the teacher carefully monitor so that Tommy does not "accidentally" destroy it. When the elaborate project is completed, the proud youngster proposes that the name of the person who will have the privilege of knocking it over be pulled out of a hat. "*And* you will have to pay to get your name in that hat." Tommy's name is selected and "*Click, click, click,* a thousand times *click* the dominoes took their turns falling. It seemed it took hours for them all to fall." Everybody cheers the Balancing Girl, including her former antagonist.

Analysis. Rabe's story features a youngster whose heavy, full-leg braces and wheelchair are obvious, yet do not figure prominently in the story. Margaret must clearly make adjustments to function in her class, but her disability, while apparent, is not highlighted. Warm and whimsical illustrations reinforce the text of this amiable story about a perky child who achieves a small but satisfying personal victory.

Radley, Gail. *Nothing Stays the Same Forever.* New York: Crown, 1981. 148 pp. Reading Level: MC
Disability: Special Health Problems

Still aching from her mother's death four years earlier, Carrie Moyers bitterly resents her father's interest in Sharon. Moreover, she considers her older sister's friendship with the woman a betrayal and determines that she will be as uncooperative as possible, hoping in this manner to retard the progress of the romance. Carrie's best friend, Bridget, urges her to attend an art workshop in New York City, an idea Mr. Moyers discourages. He hints that other events will sufficiently enliven their summer, and the payment of her sister's college tuition is a higher priority. Carrie expects that if she earns the necessary $200 by mid-August, her father will relent. Her first employer, Mrs. Stebbins, an elderly widow, has Carrie help her with weeding, replanting, carting, and a host of other chores that have taxed the woman's back, heart, and general stamina. As the two become friends, the sensitive widow helps her young neighbor explore and articulate some of her painful memories and feelings about the loss of her parent.

Carrie leans even more on her new companion after her father clumsily but persistently badgers her in an attempt to force a friendship between his daughter and his bride-to-be. He is impatient with her talk of the workshop and suggests she attend a local art class. After some subtle encouragement from Mrs. Stebbins, Carrie agrees, surprised to find it a worthwhile experience. The widow involves Carrie in a project to build a greenhouse, which she sees as a memorial to her husband, further helping the girl to understand that change is essential for the living and not evidence of disloyalty to those who have died.

When Carrie learns that her elderly friend has had a heart attack, she is distraught. Her visits to the hospital, where the seriousness of Mrs. Stebbins's illness becomes apparent, are upsetting. Too weak to return home, the patient is transferred to a nursing home. Responding to Carrie's desire for continued contact, Sharon drives the youngster to Mrs. Stebbins's new residence. The woman has adjusted to the alterations of her life with equanimity and recommends that pragmatic attitude to her visitor. Bridget returns from the workshop to report that a similar program will be offered next summer nearer their home, and Mr. Moyers, pointing out that the family will soon have two incomes, hints that attendance may be a possibility. Appreciative of Sharon's support and reconciled to her father's desire to remarry, Carrie ungrudgingly accepts the inevitable changes that are taking place in her life.

Analysis. Radley has written a sensitive, intelligent, well-constructed novel about a youngster's maturation. Mrs. Stebbins's declining abilities are seen in her lapses of memory, occasional instances of poor judgment, reduced stamina, and ultimately her poor cardiac functioning. The depiction is realistic and empathic, providing a model of acceptance and accommodation. The theme of this work, succinctly expressed in the title, addresses the need to cope with the inevitability of change.

Raskin, Ellen. *The Westing Game.* New York: Dutton, 1978. 185 pp.
Reading Level: YA
Disability: Neurological Impairment

Samuel Westing, an eccentric millionaire with a gigantic ego and an equally outsize sense of the dramatic, fakes his own death to observe and enjoy the reactions of carefully selected individuals he has chosen as eligible to inherit his substantial estate. Using the astute planning skills that made him a fortune and a world class chess player, he brings all the would-be inheritors' families together in one apartment building overlooking the Westing home. Then, disguising himself as one of the potential beneficiaries, he joins the others in a macabre game, the object of which is to successfully interpret various cryptic clues and thereby prove themselves worthy of Westing's fortune. The 16 participants are divided into teams of two and given a confusing message containing a partial solution to the conundrum.

One of the prospective heirs is 15-year-old Chris, whose lonely existence is considerably enlivened by the excitement of the challenge and by his treatment, despite his use of a wheelchair, as an equal player, in this adventure. Although "his head jerked, his body coiled, lashed by violent spasms," his speech is labored and sometimes difficult to understand, Chris's mind functions extraordinarily well.

The process of deduction is complicated by the tangle of family and personal conflicts as well as the shenanigans of a thief, a bomber, and the dramatic scenes staged by one of the other players. Ultimately the competitors decide to work together, sharing their clues with each other. Immediately following his collaboration, the partner of Judge Ford dies and the woman's assumption that he was the guilty party is dashed. New evidence suggests that the cleaning woman, revealed to be the former wife of Sam Westing, now suspected of poisoning the latest corpse, may actually be the object of their search. Turtle, the homely, undervalued niece of Westing, finally separates the false leads from the real ones, decodes the mystifying and misleading messages, and solves the puzzle. She persuades the judge to hold a mock trial in which her uncle's multiple identities are exposed and the mysterious limping stranger is unmasked. Turtle then locates Westing who has assumed still another disguise. They become close friends and when he at last dies, she is ready to take over the direction of his industrial empire, entering the last stage of the millionaire's elaborate and convoluted game plan.

Analysis. The inadequacies of the various members of the cast are revealed, in part, through their reaction to Chris. The young man's difficulties are described with a notable lack of sympathy: "Chris's arm flailed the air, his accusing finger pointed here, no, there; it pointed everywhere. His exaggerated motions acted out the confusion shared by all but one of the heirs as they looked around at the stunned faces of their neighbors to confirm what they had heard." The same absence of affection seems to characterize the author's attitudes toward most of the players in this charade. In the windup, it is revealed that Chris, still in a wheelchair, becomes an ornithologist and includes in his activities a bird-watching excursion to the South American jungles. This action is only one of a conglomerate of improbable events that suffuse this work. Except for some minor logical leaps and some capricious events, the challenge of untangling the clues should appeal to many young readers, especially those who are susceptible to the numerous word games, double meanings, and verbal legerdemain that are the heart of the book.

Ray, Mary. *Rain from the West.* London: Faber & Faber, 1980. 175 pp. Reading Level: YA
Disability: Orthopedic Impairment, Cosmetic Impairment

It is the first century, and Roman soldiers are extending and securing their domination of Britain. All the major characters in this drama converge on Glevum, now Gloucester, at the height of the resistance by Velpomulus, a native brigand who is trying to undermine the invaders' rule as his men pillage and despoil the countryside. Flavius is elated at the prospect of being posted there since he will have the opportunity of coming into contact with Camillus, his mentor and a hero whose military career he hopes to emulate. To his further delight, he encounters Hylas, whose "face was shadowed in scars" received when he was "pegged out in the desert in the sun" by Roman soldiers who captured him as he was attempting to flee with some fellow Christians. He was rescued by a stranger, but not before he was permanently marked. Hylas, now secretary to Zeno, is a scholar and herbalist who travels with his son, Nico, and his wife, Pyrrha, once a Greek slave whose life had been saved by Camillus. Flavius is nearly overcome with joy upon hearing that his old friend is nearby.

The three are reunited, but their pleasure is interrupted by news of assaults by rebellious raiding parties. Camillus is injured in a freak accident, and the medical help he receives is inadequate to restore full control to his sword hand. The wounded man, accompanied by Zeno's party, repair to a nearby farm, where they are warmly welcomed by a family of Britons —Tincommius, Hedwych, and their newborn infant. Soon after settling in, Flavius warns them about a marauding party heading for their refuge. All leave for the safety of a Roman encampment except the farmer, who hopes to save his livestock. Zeno dies of a fever soon after Velpomulus is captured, and it is learned that the brave Tincommius has been murdered and his property destroyed. The two young widows comfort each other, wondering what will become of them and their families. Camillus is voluntarily discharged from the army and, according to the promise he gave to his now deceased host, returns to the farm, which he will try to restore. Pyrrha is startled to discover that Hylas wants to marry her, a prospect she looks on with favor.

Analysis. The wound Camillus receives disqualifies him from active service, and he is too energetic to accept a mere administrative post. His move from a military life to an agrarian one is consistent with his growing doubts about the rights of stronger societies to subjugate weaker ones. Hylas's scars, the result of persecution for his beliefs, are frequently alluded to, but this does not cause him distress and does not result in others shunning him. These marks are evidence of the violence of the times and, along with his discussion of conversion to a nascent religion, set him apart from his fellows. Although setting and events create a potent sense of first-century life in Britain, the perspectives and sensibilities of the major characters often seem discordantly modern.

Ray, N. L. *There Was This Man Running*. New York: Macmillan, 1981. 151 pp. Reading Level: MC/YA
Disability: Auditory Impairment

O'Mara, visiting this planet again, has taken human shape in the belief that this will facilitate his covert investigation of Earth's primitive metallurgy. He becomes extremely distressed when he discovers that his ank, a portable energy unit shaped like a disc, has somehow disappeared. A microdot supposedly containing industrial secrets has been stolen and coincidentally hidden, along with the space traveler's disc, in a matchbox. The industrial thief turns over the small package to his collaborator, a Mr. Bywater, who is trailed by O'Mara, alarmed about his survival without the energy source. The crook panics and finally collapses in front of the Mackens' grocery store. The fallen man hands over his tiny parcel to Cass Macken, whom he begs to keep its whereabouts a secret. The teenager deduces that that package is somehow related to the rash of recent neighborhood break-ins.

The spaceman, in the meantime, has been courting Alanna, the oldest Macken daughter, hoping by that ploy to uncover the location of his disc. Cass realizes his sister's new admirer is not an earthling when he observes his pet cat pass through the man's body and then senses the stranger's attempt to penetrate his own mind. Cass's other sister, Clare, "had been born with defective hearing because of German measles" but is exceptionally skilled in interpreting individuals' characters or moods and is able to sense their "auras" as well as to communicate telepathically. Clare and her brother seem to be the only ones who suspect O'Mara, who has now ingratiated himself with the other family members.

Cass is worried when his pet disappears, but his distress is eclipsed by Clare's kidnapping. Clare, alone and imprisoned, steels herself to prevent O'Mara from reading her thoughts. Startled by the touch of an animal in the basement of the abandoned house where she is held captive, she is relieved to discover it is her brother's missing pet, Seville. Quickly deciding that she can use the feline as a courier, the quick-witted child

> took one of the batteries from her hearing aid and rubbed it over the mossy part of the rock, then wrapped it in a scrap of paper from the cake bag. She slid the package under Seville's flea collar and bound it in place with a shoe lace. It seemed firm enough and the cat didn't mind: he was used to her dressing him up in ribbons.

Clare is able to lob the animal through a small window high in the wall. When his bedraggled pet finds his way home, Cass comprehends his sister's communication and, acting on other information he has gathered, figures out where she has been held and races to her rescue. Acting on a premonition that the building is on fire, Cass redoubles his efforts to reach Clare. A priest helps him break in, then dashes off to summon the fire brigade, which, happily, arrives in time.

Meanwhile, Bywater has been released from the hospital, and he locates the Macken home so that he can retrieve his stolen microdot. But he and his accomplice, the kidnapper, are identified by Clare, and the police arrest the malefactors. The child, pitying O'Mara despite his responsibility for her scrape with death, returns the ank, allowing him to meet the space vehicle that will safely transport him to his own galaxy.

Analysis. Ray portrays a warm, loving, religious Australian family who are devoted to their youngest member.

> Clare had started special schooling when she was three, each word repeated hundreds and hundreds of times before she mastered it. She needed to practice her speaking all the time to gain tone control. Now she was a pupil at a private school and competing with children whose hearing was normal. It was constant work for Clare and for every member of the family, but no one grumbled. Alanna Caterina shrugged off thoughts of university and helped in the shop. Cass gave up his afternoons and Saturday mornings. Mr. Macken gave up his leisure hours.

Although much is given to Clare, she is expected to assume her share of responsibilities, which include working in the family business. The science-fiction plot maintains interest, although too many events rely on the foolish behavior of characters who eschew simple, practical, or even likely actions that would precipitously shorten the story.

Rees, Lucy. *Horse of Air.* New York: Methuen, 1980. 211 pp. Reading Level: YA/MA
Disability: Emotional Dysfunction

When Julie's gregarious, generous, selfish, unreliable, but adored stepfather leaves his family, she is heartbroken. She has never gotten along with her rigid, austere mother, and when the woman announces that they must leave their home on the moors for a flat in Eastbourne, depression overwhelms her daughter. The adolescent's older brothers do not accompany the family, and the loss of their support combined with the bleakness of her new life create a sense of hopelessness, causing Julie to withdraw from a world she cannot tolerate. Later she recalls:

> I found it increasingly difficult to know how to behave, for there was no rhyme or reason in human behaviour. I would stare for

hours at the blotches of colour that were my school uniform until Little, exasperated, handed me each garment in turn to put on. Several times I walked into the wrong class at school and was unable to work out what had happened, nor what to do next. Quite often I found myself wandering along with tears running down my face. But in strict sense of the word I was not *crying*, there was no agony or mourning. . . . I did not know who I was. There was nothing as I looked inwards, searching for a sign, nothing but a body without a person in it.

Her brother Kevin comes to visit, his evident concern penetrating the protective armor she has created. Although Julie begs him to take her away with him, he proposes instead that she accompany him to a cottage in Wales for his vacation. There the girl gradually begins to relax, to relate, to participate in the life around her, but the prospect of having to return home terrifies her. Kevin returns to school but suggests she could stay on if she really wanted to. Surprised at her own nerve, she borrows a tent and a horse, sustaining herself in the salubrious environment. Julie's encounter with an untamed Welsh cob gives new direction to her life. No one else seems able to control the undisciplined creature, which she is convinced will someday belong to her. The animal's custodians are happy to relinquish their responsibility over the unruly creature. The owner's brother arrives intending to sell it, but the horse is too abusive and hostile to attract a buyer. Unwilling to see the cob killed, the man turns over the ownership papers to Julie. However, arranging for the care, feeding, and stabling of the Welsh pony becomes an unceasingly frustrating process.

Julie learns that her mother has a new boyfriend, a man she considers contemptible, and their relationship worsens. Upon being told she must go to France with the rest of the family, the girl, finding this prospect intolerable, takes her horse and dog and heads across England toward Wales. The journey is difficult and dangerous, but despite near disaster, the experience propels Julie into asserting more responsibility for her actions and restores a sense of the potential wonder and joy of life.

Analysis. Julie's psychotic withdrawal is attributed to her feelings of abandonment and her perception that she has no control over her destiny. Everyone she loves chooses a path that leads away from her. Then, bereft of human support, she is forced to move from an environment both familiar and sustaining. Her recovery begins when she finds a compelling focus outside of herself. She is bolstered in self-confidence by successfully meeting every challenge. Although the rapidity and extent of her improvement exceed realistic expectations and the ameliorative power of animals is undoubtedly exaggerated, the story is compelling reading. Characterizations are interesting, the depiction of Julie's anomie is sensitively etched, and the plot moves well, but the outstanding quality of this work is its evocation of a sense of place:

> Round the top of one hill we stopped with a gasp, for two huge tractors were ploughing the side in tandem, with a cloud of crows and seagulls tossing around them and the yellow sun behind. Earth creamed from the shining blades as the birds flashed and swooped, and the timelessness of the scene swept us up and carried us with it, as if we were riding a wave: past ploughman and walkers, recreationists and truant lads, through the miles, through the centuries.

Reuter, Margaret. *My Mother Is Blind.* Photog. by Philip Lanier. Chicago: Children's Press, 1979. 31 pp. Reading Level: YC
Disability: Visual Impairment

The youthful narrator recalls his mother's depression when she first lost her sight. However, after a rehabilitation counselor gives her instructions in how to accomplish her homemaking tasks, she readily resumes her former activities and makes the appropriate adjustments. With additional training, she is soon able to travel independently throughout the neighborhood and to read and write using her braille apparatus. The boy is happy that his mother is now a fully functioning person but reveals his regret at her inability to see.

Analysis. Told from a child's perspective, this unpretentious work provides a simple account of how a mother's daily household chores are performed capably despite vision loss. It is especially useful in focusing on the pleasures available to the adult who has had to make accommodations to a situation that has radically altered even her most mundane routines. Although ending on an unexpected note of wistfulness, the easy text and superior photographs are informative and free of excess emotionalism.

Riskind, Mary. *Apple Is My Sign.* Boston: Houghton Mifflin, 1981. 146 pp. Reading Level: MC
Disability: Auditory Impairment

Harry knows his father has sent him to a boarding school to learn much needed skills; nevertheless, the hearing-impaired child feels lonely and abandoned until he is befriended by Landis, one of the older students. The newcomer's skill in drawing is noted immediately, and he is assigned to the tailoring shop, where his ability in design can be extended. The humming vibrations of the machine he so capably uses delight him, and the youngster decides "Singer" is an appropriate name for it. He gets into a fight with Cowlick, but is soon forgiven: "I know you not mean for hurt. I first ask fight. Anyway, we all same. Important, deaf must together." A bystander adds: "Right. Deaf never tattle. Always together."

One morning, on the way to the "hearing church," Harry sees his first motorcar. Landis informs him that he has seen other even greater wonders such as the Liberty Bell in Philadelphia. Upon questioning, Landis confesses that he does not know what that object is for or even why it is kept in an honored place, Harry affectionately puts him down: "You knock-head. For history. For remember begin America." Obsessed with the desire to see another car, the ten-year-old clambers over the school wall, later wanders into a church where he plays the organ, just barely escaping the wrath of its guardian. The boy notices how oddly people regard him when he tries to communicate with them, using gestures to tell them he cannot hear and is lost. Back at school and on restriction for his unauthorized leave, Harry regales his buddies with his adventures, including finding a library and seeing a blind man. All his friends agree that they prefer deafness to blindness. The headmaster tries unsuccessfully to teach Harry to speak until he ingeniously tempts the boy into saying "whoa" and leads him to note its reaction on the school's ancient horse.

The hero and his young friends become ardent football enthusiasts, but when they challenge a hearing team, they are easily outplayed. Harry climbs a tree during a timeout from which he observes why his team's maneuvers were unsuccessful. With this knowledge, he devises a counterstrategy and, pleased with its effectiveness, concludes that the deaf are as smart as the hearing.

Harry returns home for vacation but is uncomfortable, afraid that he is now an outsider. The boy looks forward to meeting his hearing pals, whom he begins to instruct in finger spelling. Later, when he locates them at the fair, he is crushed to see that they are using the manual alphabet as a code to cheat in a spelling bee. When the culprits are exposed, Harry's father is furious, accusing his son of complicity and interpreting the entire affair as a typical example of how exploitive the hearing world is. Humiliated, Harry runs away but is followed by his guilty friend, who is uncertain about how to apologize and make amends. In a brave act, the boy tackles Harry, throwing him from the path of an approaching train, which the youngster had not heard. Harry delightedly anticipates the excited reception the account of his vacation adventures will receive when he returns to the attentive, eager audience back at school.

Analysis. Within this turn-of-the-century novel, Riskind recreates the lives of a family who all have auditory disorders and affectionately explores the problems and accomplishments of a boarding school for youngsters with profound hearing loss. The author successfully transcribes the substance and structure of a signed language and demonstrates how some auditorily impaired youngsters solve intellectual, communication, and social problems. The struggles of the hearing and nonhearing characters to understand each other, including the well-intentioned, helpful, but patronizing actions of the minister, are vividly presented. Insights into the efforts of boys to make sense of their world, for example, such wondrous inventions as the horseless carriage, the purposes of a gigantic cracked (and therefore seemingly useless) bell, abstract words such as *academy*, the process of producing sound one cannot hear, allow readers to understand the usual as well as the special difficulties encountered by deaf people. Although considerable information about deafness is incorporated in the narrative, the book's main appeal lies in the absorbing adventures of its engaging, enterprising, and admirable young hero.

Roberts, Willo Davis. *Don't Hurt Laurie.* Illus. by Ruth Sanderson. New York: Atheneum, 1977. 166 pp. Reading Level: MC
Disability: Emotional Dysfunction, orthopedic impairment

After being abandoned by her first husband, Laurie's mother, Annabelle, married Jack. The girl's life is an unrelieved nightmare: periodically, Annabelle goes into uncontrollable rages during which she brutally abuses her helpless, innocent daughter. Laurie futilely dreams of rescue by her natural father, but only her younger stepbrother, Tim, offers her the understanding and compassion she so desperately needs. Just when she has made some friends for the first time, a staff member at the emergency room at the hospital remarks on the frequency of Laurie's injuries, causing Annabelle to fear that inquiries might be made. The woman convinces her husband that the family must leave, and the children are downcast at the prospect of yet another move and starting anew in a different neighborhood and school.

In the adjoining duplex, Laurie discovers a seventh-grade boy who reveals he has a "bone disease" that has necessitated four operations so far. She and George become good friends, concealing their relationship from Annabelle by spending most of their time together unobserved in a nearby ravine, which the youth is able to negotiate despite his braces and crutches. He finds an injured puppy and takes it to their secret place, where the two friends begin its training. When George unexpectedly must return to the hospital, Laurie accepts responsibility for their pet. One day, the lonely animal finds its way to her home, where Annabelle becomes hysterical upon seeing it. First she kicks, then beats the creature with a broomstick. Terrified, Laurie and Tim protest, provoking the enraged woman to turn upon them. She strikes her daughter repeatedly with a poker until the child collapses upon the floor. When Laurie regains consciousness, the children run away to Jack's mother, where their grandmother comforts the children, feeds them, and treats Laurie's bruises. She confronts her son with details of the abuse, and he is at first skeptical, but when faced with the unassailable evidence that supports the children's accounts of the events, he becomes convinced of the truth of the claims. Jack arranges therapy for his wife, after which he attempts to explain her behavior to Laurie:

> Many parents who mistreat their kids do it because they, themselves, were mistreated by their parents, years before. And it makes a sort of sickness in them that they can't control. It doesn't mean that she hates you, or that she doesn't care what happens to you. It just means she's unhappy and she can't help it, the things she does.

Analysis. Annabelle's violent behavior is explained on the basis of similar traumatic incidents in her own childhood, which have been intensified by feelings of rejection. Unable to exact revenge for her husband's desertion, the woman takes out her frustration on her own offspring. Her recurring headaches are a further contributing factor and generally signal the onset of a state in which she loses control. Despite his serious problems, George shows remarkable agility in being able to negotiate the ravine, and his pale depiction as a selfless, supportive, uncomplicated character underscores his function as more of a prop to Laurie than as a person to be regarded seriously. The illustrator has portrayed Annabelle with effectiveness and restraint. The angry woman is always shown unsmiling, watchful, smoldering, and ready to erupt. The anticipation of violence and abuse is powerfully revealed in Laurie's fearful eyes as she sees her mother approach and anticipates the results. George only appears once in the illustrations, and neither his braces nor crutches are shown.

The author has bravely selected an unlikely villain as a central character and shown her to be a victim who has internalized brutality and repeated those horrible childhood scenes with the heroine (as her stand-in). Although there are countless children who have endured experiences such as Laurie's, the story, directed at a grade-school audience, seems the stuff of which nightmares are made.

Robinet, Harriette G. *Jay and the Marigold.* Illus. by Trudy Scott. Chicago: Children's Press, 1976. 47 pp. Reading Level: YC
Disability: Neurological Impairment

Although he has many moments of frustration and guilt about his inability to speak or walk, Jay's basic outlook is one of optimism and enjoyment of the pleasure of the moment. During his eighth summer, he notices a small marigold plant that has sprouted in the crack of his porch step. The boy reflects on the unlikelihood of the plant's chances for survival but nevertheless waters it daily. Ignored by the neighborhood children, Jay is approached by Pedro, a newcomer, who is also shunned by the other youths and so presumably is sensitive to the problems of social isolation. Somehow Pedro becomes involved with the daily games and manages to introduce Jay into the activities. To the other children's surprise, they discover Jay's skill is umpiring, and he is soon in demand in that capacity, a modest acceptance that slowly extends to other activities. As the vacation wanes, Jay determines that he will exert maximum effort to achieve more in the coming semester. On the way out of his house to meet his special school bus, he sees the marigold has flowered and remembering his speech therapist's instructions, is able to say "boom." His twin sister understands immediately that he meant to say "bloom."

Analysis. In this parable of the persisting flower and the persisting child, Robinet describes some major physical limitations and frustrations associated with cerebral palsy. She presents the familiar hypothesis that those who are outsiders are consequently aware of the rejected status of others and suggests that competence in a needed or admired activity can be the route to social acceptance. The comparison between the boy and the flower is strongly hinted at and finally overtly stated: "In spite of its limitations, in spite of its handicaps, Jay's marigold has bloomed." Jay too, "in spite of limitations, in spite of handicaps, in his own way, in his own time—he, too, would bloom." The generally unattractive illustrations, which occasionally distort body shape, attempt to show the extent of Jay's physical limitations and the accommodations in posture and hand movement he must make. Unfortunately, the story is a sermon, and this detracts from its potential appeal.

Robinet, Harriette G. *Ride the Red Cycle.* Illus. by David Brown. Boston: Houghton Mifflin, 1980. 34 pp. Reading Level: YC/MC
Disability: Neurological Impairment

A viral infection at the age of two has left Jerome Johnson with impaired mobility, poor physical coordination, and severely dysfunctional speech. The consequent frustrations have caused him to be impatient, temperamental, and often angry. Now, at 11, he wants more than anything to own a tricycle. His mother worries about expenses and her son's seeming ingratitude, but his father realizes how important the tricycle is to the boy, and after he is informed that the exercise involved may be therapeutic, he is convinced that Jerome must have his wish. When the youngster finally mounts the three-wheeler, he finds his legs are too weak and uncoordinated even to work the pedals. Undeterred by this obstacle, the determined boy enlists his sister's aid and arranges to practice in secret. Through unremitting effort, Jerome learns to move the vehicle forward, a skill he demonstrates to family and neighbors at a Labor Day block party. Before the astonished eyes of the onlookers, the black boy dismounts and takes the first unaided steps of his life.

Analysis. The author tries to provide insight into the psychological as well as physical demands of cerebral palsy, including its effect on family life. The young hero's emotional distress and related negative behaviors are clearly conveyed, but other than his triumph over adversity, no positive aspects of character are apparent. Thus, while his achievement is laudable, his literary characterization precludes involvement. Additionally, the plot is so contrived that the story does not succeed as a work of fiction. The illustrations are unexceptional, with all characters displaying a mannikinlike stiffness rather than the fluid motion of live people.

Rodowsky, Colby. *P.S. Write Soon.* New York: Franklin Watts, 1978. 149 pp. Reading Level: MC
Disability: Orthopedic Impairment

Her older sister Courtney, whom she calls "the Zilch," and the leg brace contemptuously named "Fenhagen" that she must use since being permanently injured in a car accident, are the banes of Tanner McClean's existence. The unhappy sixth-grader is furious when she learns that Jon, her favorite brother, has married Cheryl, a woman unknown to the family, in a ceremony to which they were not invited. Determined to dislike her new sister-in-law, Tanner makes little effort to conceal her contempt for the awkward, poorly dressed, mousy bride. The girl's letters to her pen pal, however, describe a highly idealized family relationship and an active sports life distinctly at odds with reality. Even though Cheryl is patient and sympathetic, the preteen's relationship with the newlyweds deteriorates drastically through a series of misunderstandings. When the new sister-in-law reads a letter Tanner has composed to Jessie Lee, she tells the girl it is not necessary to lie, that her correspondent would like the actual person as much as the invented one. Tanner, furious that her charade has been discovered and her privacy breached, tells Cheryl that the letter is just a joke. Soon after, Jessie Lee writes the exciting news that she and her family plan to travel to the area, allowing the writers to meet for the first time. Cheryl advises the girl to tell Jessie the unvarnished truth about Fenhagen, her crutches, and her relationship with the newly-weds—in short, to correct the fabrications of herself and her family she has devised. In desperation, Tanner follows this suggestion, and, to her surprise, Jessie Lee still wants to be her friend.

Analysis. Although the story line is plausible, the technique of using the child's letters to her friend to end each chapter is effective, and the message that the cover is not necessarily the book is a commendable one, slick and shallow characterizations unfortunately diminish this work. Motivations, while not unlikely, are never adequately developed, so Tanner's behavior generally seems capricious. The author has clearly attempted to treat her heroine's disability in a casual, natural manner—an admirable, if only intermittently successful approach.

Rodowsky, Colby. *What About Me?* New York: Franklin Watts, 1976. 136 pp. Reading Level: YA
Disability: Intellectual Impairment, Special Health Problems

The emotional turmoil of adolescence is exacerbated for 15-year-old Dorrie Shafer by the intensity of her feelings toward her younger brother, Fred, a child born with Down's syndrome and a serious cardiac defect. "Fredlet was eleven—and a really big eleven—but he had a little mind. From the back he looked like he should play football; from the front you knew why he played blocks. My stomach lurched again and I tried to swallow the bitter taste of guilt." The necessity for constant supervision of the boy means that Dorrie's plans are often postponed or canceled, and her own needs frequently take second place to his more pressing ones. Angry and resentful, she strikes out at her parents and finds herself growing increasingly more intolerant of the person she feels is ruining her life. Torn by her awareness of her ambivalence and growing insensitivity to her brother's needs, the teenage girl volunteers to teach art at the special school Fred attends. There she learns more about retardation, but nevertheless fluctuates in her attitude toward her sibling, feeling both affection and bitterness. For diversion, inspiration, and comfort, she seeks out a nonconformist neighbor, Guntzie, who is a well-known artist, a talented teacher, and a sympathetic mentor.

News that her family plans to leave New York City for her mother's hometown, where other relatives can assist her mother with Fred's care, causes the heroine much distress. She is relieved and grateful when Guntzie generously offers to let her stay in her apartment until the end of her senior year. However, just before the move, and while Fred is in Dorrie's care, he becomes cyanotic. Dorrie rushes with him to the hospital, but his condition is beyond help. Depressed and exhausted after the funeral, Mrs. Shafer starts to withdraw from social intercourse but, with the help of her family, slowly begins to regain her emotional stability. In a conversation that is restorative to them both, she discusses with her daughter the love both felt for Fred despite their frustration and occasional displays of hostility.

Analysis. Rodowsky has successfully shown how problems arising from coping with a severely retarded, multiply disabled child can lead to unmanageable familial stress, especially when few demands are made on the impaired individual. In this story, the impaired youngster is seen as loving but demanding, necessitating unceasing supervision, care, comfort, and reassurance. Mrs. Shafer's physical and psychological energies are drained by this task, and Fred's sister, often unable to control her jealousy, explodes in anger and verbal abuse. It is surprising to see the obsolete term *mongoloid* repeatedly used in an otherwise sensitive and sensitizing work. During the course of the story, the youth is given an infantile nickname, which he carries until his death, when his original name is restored to him.

Rosen, Lillian. *Just Like Everybody Else.* New York: Harcourt Brace Jovanovich, 1981. 155 pp. Reading Level: YA
Disability: Auditory Impairment

Until the bus accident in which her skull was fractured, Jenny's existence was fairly conventional. During the subsequent weeks, the 15 year old's worries about her hearing loss are confirmed: the physician tells her that her auditory nerve has been destroyed, and no hope for restoration of hearing should be harbored. Further, he explains about the difficulties she experiences during walking: "Severe hearing loss caused a loss of balance as well." Although her parents try to overprotect her and Jenny has outbursts fueled by her frustration and anger, the family members begin to make adjustments to the girl's sensory deprivation.

When lipreading at last is proposed, Jenny muses:

Maybe lipreading might work. I have to understand people somehow. I have to! Because when it came right down to it, most of all, I missed understanding. Hearing means knowing and understanding. Knowing what others thought, questioned, and felt. Knowing people were sad, pleased, joyful, or irritated and angry, and why. I could figure out a little of the way people felt from their faces, even in the way they moved sometimes. But why they were angry or sad, laughing or gay, I couldn't know. The words were gone. The sounds were gone. Inflections, tones, stress, intensity, volume—all things that conveyed different meaning were gone. Now there were only faces and lips, which moved soundlessly. They were guessing instead of knowing and understanding so little unless someone wrote the words out for me. More and more I was left out.

Encouraged by her progress in mastering this technique, she goes on to learn finger spelling and teaches it to her friends. Rallying round in her hour of need, a cohort of loyal students organizes a committee to visit the still homebound girl, prepare her for a return to class, and keep her informed about the events at Stevens High. Moreover, one girl friend tells her about Joe Benton, who has a similar disability. They meet and talk about coping with their problems, achieving despite their impairments, and the communication network within the community of the deaf. Their first dates start with this focus but soon they branch out to other concerns. In this closer relationship, the two young adults are able to share their deep emotional reactions to hearing loss with each other and to discuss their resentments about the social exclusion they endure. While at the Benton home, a call comes in from the police asking someone to act as an interpreter for a runaway deaf child. The child has been abused in her foster home, and Jenny infers that the fugitive's impairment worsened an intolerable situation. This incident dramatizes the profound impact that hearing loss can superimpose on relationships. Soon her parents become concerned about the intensity of her involvement with Joe but are relieved to learn that he will be going off to college and she will, at last, be returning to high school.

Analysis. As the title suggests, this junior novel informs the adolescent reader how the onset of deafness impinges on the lives of capable teenagers who at the same time are struggling with typical needs, hopes, and ambitions. Readers are also able to gain knowledge about some of the tasks involved in the reentry into mainstreamed life. The writer concentrates more on dressing up the incidents in fictional clothes than in creating credible dialogue or convincing characters. A heated comment by Jenny's father is a typical example:

There are thousands of towns all over the country doing the same thing. Mainstreaming without really knowing how to go about it!

We'll put on all the pressure we can. If all that doesn't work, we'll sue! Take our lawsuit right up to the Supreme Court if necessary. We'd have plenty of backing and help from the National Center for Law and the Deaf *and* the deaf community.

The easy-to-read work squeezes in much useful information, such as what a TTY is and how captioned films work, and perhaps most importantly, provides insight into the familial, academic, social, and career concerns of individuals who are adventitiously deaf.

Ross, Marianne. *Good-Bye Atlantis.* New York: Elsevier/Nelson, 1980. 172 pp. Reading Level: YA/MA
Disability: Neurological Impairment, Emotional Dysfunction; also special health problems

By his senior year, Jonathan is an acknowledged leader at Wilson High School. Although a nonconformist in appearance, mannerism, and style, he is charismatic, and others, even if sometimes reluctantly, follow his lead. His concept of Atlantis, a world where "you always do your best," is adopted as an ideal by his class, and Ann, with whom he has an intense but platonic relationship, is its staunchest advocate. When Ann shops for a formal for the school dance during class hours, then lies to her teachers about her absence, Jonathan is profoundly disappointed and insists that she must be punished. Some minor inconvenience is proposed, but Jonathan is not satisfied until Ann suggests that she will forgo the eagerly anticipated dance. Later, when the youth permits another student to copy from his paper during a test, he is filled with guilt and remorse at his own betrayal of the precepts of Atlantis. He confesses his role as a cheat, suspends himself from the basketball team, then, feeling these penalties are still inadequate, shaves his head. Ann, who admires his constant striving for perfection, his impressive intellect, and his compulsive goal-directed behavior, realizes that she loves him. However, uneasy about the completely asexual nature of their relationship, the adolescent girl periodically suspects him of being homosexual.

Jonathan decides to hold a farewell party for the senior class, which promises to be the social affair of the year. The gathering begins pleasantly enough, but undercurrents of bitterness and jealousy begin to surface. The host, hoping to dispel the growing tension, tries to distract his contentious guests and restore the party's carefree atmosphere. Grabbing the school's most obviously gay student, Jonathan begins dancing frenetically until Ann forces them to stop as the others look on "filled with silence and shame." The next night Jonathan tries to commit suicide. Unable to swim, he throws himself into the river, but Ann dives in after him and with difficulty manages to drag him to the surface. Panicky, he begins to flail about hysterically, causing his rescuer to be swept onto the rocks.

The teenage girl awakens in the hospital, partially paralyzed from "a blood clot on the brain stem" and is told she must remain quiet for a few weeks. Warned about the "possibility of further damage," Ann learns of plans to move her to a nursing home. She is unable to prevent the transfer and hates the facility, being frightened by the condition of the other patients, some of whom are terminally ill and all of whom she regards as hopeless. Her parents—superficial, frivolous, and self-absorbed—offer little support or comfort. They find visiting painful: their stays are brief and unsatisfactory since her father is primarily concerned about protecting his wife from further distress. Jonathan visits his friend regularly, urging her to cooperate more with the therapist and strive for the ideals of Atlantis. Ann falls while he is helping her to walk and she turns on him angrily, demanding: "What are you trying to do? Kill me again?" He leaves, devastated by her accusation, but returns repeatedly, postponing his entry into college, while doing everything possible to further his friend's recovery. The two make plans to enter the local university, but, while home for a Christmas visit, Ann suddenly becomes very ill. She is rushed to the hospital, where she overhears her doctor tell a nurse: "It looks like another blood clot. . . . Aphasia, I think. The loss of speech. And probably most motor coordination. We'll have to try using an alphabet board for some sort of communication." Immediately thereafter, Jonathan arrives with the device, determined to work on this problem as well.

Ann is moved to another section of the nursing home, ostensibly to facilitate her care, but the 19-year-old girl suspects that the area is "where they put people who are going to die." When her friend returns, she announces that she knows her death is imminent. Jonathan denies this, responding that there are no nursing homes in Atlantis and nobody dies there except the very old. Ann vacillates between hope and despair, resenting anyone robust, particularly her devoted companion. Some speech returns, and with it a brief optimism, which she knows is unwarranted. Ann persuades Jonathan to continue his schooling, realizing that it is an admission that she will never improve. She instructs him not to visit her anymore for now she is prepared to die alone without anyone or anything except "the image of a shining, splendid island that thousands of years ago sank into the sea."

Analysis. Jonathan is an obsessed, driven person, acutely sensitive in some areas and startlingly callous in others. A perfectionist, he deals with unpleasantness by denying its reality so emphatically that he convinces himself and others of the validity of his perceptions. Ann's physical problems—the pain, paralysis, medical regimens, and rehabilitative therapies—are of no significance in this novel: what matters is the heroine's psychological state. She experiences a variety of emotions: anger, resentment, despair, hope, and finally resignation, but none of these is deeply felt by the reader. The narrative, although related in the first person, projects a sense of detachment from the unfolding events, as though their raw edges had all been rubbed smooth.

Rossman, Parker. *Pirate Slave.* Nashville: Thomas Nelson, 1977. 146 pp. Reading Level: MC
Disability: cosmetic impairment; also orthopedic impairment, visual impairment

Twelve-year-old Sandy Short bemoans his mother's reluctance to let him go to sea. He is thrilled when she finally allows him to sign on as a cabin boy on a ship leaving Salem for the Persian Gulf. On his first voyage, the vessel is waylaid by Arab pirates, who brutally murder all the American crew except Sandy, who has hidden in the rigging. The terrified lad watches in horror as "the older of . . . two half naked boys took his knife and slit the [American] captain's neck." When discovered, the cabin boy is taken on board a dhow, joining other black and white children headed for the slave markets dotting the North African and Middle Eastern coasts. His captors consider Sandy a particularly valuable property because of his fair complexion and blond hair. Even though he abhors slavery and works to ease the agony of his fellow victims, Sandy soon comes to admire Khalil, the scarred pirate captain, on one occasion even saving his life. In gratitude, the captain frees the youth, converting him to Islam and giving him a new name. Now called "Skander," the adolescent takes a black slave girl for his wife and convinces Khalil to abandon his inhumane trade and join him in a commercial venture uncontaminated by the exploitation of other human beings. The youth achieves fame when he obtains medicine from Italy to cure a prevalent disease that is responsible for causing blindness in the populace. Despite tremendous obstacles, Skander is able to get a message to his mother informing her that he is safe but unable to return home. The letter gives credence to the legend circulating in America of a white sheikh who "passed out medicine to the sick and fought slavery."

Analysis. Presumably based on an amalgam of several sea journals, *Pirate Slave* abounds with exciting and horrifying incidents. Although chronicling the brutality of slavery, it also romanticizes the institution through the relationship of Skander and Khalil. The ruthless killer is almost instantly rehabilitated: a short time after the captain has murdered all the youth's friends, the young hero, upon observing the slave trader, "found it difficult to hate him at all, even to be afraid of him. He sang with his men and seemed to ask them rather than command them." This camaraderie is evidently seen as sufficient evidence of innate goodness to negate his other actions. Khalil, initially indifferent to the suffering he causes by kidnapping children and forcing them into slavery, is inspired by the youngster's example of goodness into abandoning his trade. The pirate exhibits the cosmetic signs common to literary depictions: he is a "tall, well built man with a sword mark across one cheek. One eye also drooped from an old wound." The practice of deliberately crippling children so as to increase their worth as beggars, alluded to in the story, has historical validity. Other stereotypical portrayals include a blind storyteller and another scarred villain. Foreshadowing is excessive so few incidents are surprising and the writing is often awkward, as in the description of the desert community: "It was as if the town were continually broiled in a frying pan."

Roth, David. *The Hermit of Fog Hollow Station*. New York: Beaufort, 1980. 96 pp. Reading Level: MC
Disability: Special Health Problems; also auditory impairment

Since moving to the country, Alex has become a loner. Fritz and Benny, the only neighbors close to his own age, are cruel and brutish louts. Reluctantly, the 12-year-old newcomer agrees to go fishing with them. As they pass Fog Hollow Station, Benny explains it is now the home of a hermit and warns his naive companion if "old man Turner catches you there, he'll fry your heart for supper." The youths speak knowingly of a hoard of silver the recluse allegedly guards. When the man angrily approaches them, Fritz throws a rock at their pursuer, who falls insensate into the stream. Abandoned by the other boys, Alex pulls the injured man out of the water, then frantically runs for help. He finally persuades a neighbor with deficient hearing of the urgency of the old man's plight, and she calls for assistance. Chief Bicks arrives and asks Alex to lead him and the ambulance attendants to the victim, who is rushed to the hospital. While driving the boy home, Bicks tells him: "Mr. Turner, he's what we call around here a real peculiar character. . . . And people like him, who are different . . . don't make out so good, even away out here in the boondocks. They attract troublemakers the way a lightning rod attracts lightning."

The concerned boy asks his father to inquire at the hospital about the hermit's condition and learns that the old man has suffered a heart attack. Alex sneaks into the hospital, locates his room, but is unable to speak with the weakened patient. Soon after, he is angrily accosted by Fritz and Benny, who beat him up for rescuing Turner. Alex's parents express their anxiety about his lack of friends, his fighting, and his preoccupation with the hermit, but their son tries to downplay their worries. After several months, the weakened man returns home, becoming a mentor to the boy by teaching him to love and respect their natural surroundings. Alex is "commanded" to read *Walden,* and subsequently the two often discuss Thoreau's philosophy. Despite Turner's frequent need for medication to ease his chest pains, he and the boy attempt a difficult and lengthy hike to retrieve some objects the recluse had buried long ago. Alex, exhausted, arrives home at 2 A.M. to find his parents justifiably furious.

One day, after a particularly pleasant expedition in the woods, Alex and Turner return to find the man's cabin has been ransacked and his strongbox stolen. Although Fritz and Benny damaged some letters and pictures in their frustration at not finding treasure, Alex is able to recover some of the hermit's memorabilia. But with the destruction of his mementos, Turner seems to have lost his desire to live: his health declines rapidly and he dies soon thereafter. Alex remembers their shared experiences, their companionship, and the wonders of nature his friend taught him to see and cherish.

Analysis. This gentle, delicate, and leisurely story explores the development of an unusual friendship between a sensitive youth and a headstrong, wise, and sickly old man. Roth disposes of the idea that someone who elects to live alone should automatically be presumed to be troubled. Alex asks: " 'You mean he's not' . . . Alex searched for a word that wasn't cruel. 'He's not all there?' The chief responds: 'He's sharper than you and me put together.' " Turner's heart attack, recovery, relapse, and death are realistically portrayed. His strenuous activities are seen to put an insupportable burden on his heart, and the wanton destruction of his photographs and papers precipitate his final, irreversible decline. The narrative maintains tension until the old man's death and then seems to disintegrate rather than conclude.

Rounds, Glen. *Blind Outlaw.* Illus. by author. New York: Holiday House, 1980. 94 pp. Reading Level: MC
Disability: Speech Impairment

The boy drifted onto the ranch in the wake of an itinerant buggy salesman and stayed on, earning his keep by doing chores. Because the young stranger was competent and diligent, he was readily accepted by the other ranch hands, who were amused by the menagerie of pets he collected. "While the Boy could hear and understand what was said to him, for some reason or other he was unable to speak. He could make some sounds, but nothing more. However, he seemed to understand animals and birds, and in some fashion was able to communicate with them."

The horsebreaker begins to tame the wild horses that have been brought into the corral. He is surprised when one horse furiously and frantically resists all his efforts to gentle it, until he discovers the recalcitrant captive is blind. The boy wordlessly requests that he be allowed to try his hand at training it. The ranch owner agrees and generously offers to give him the outlaw horse if he is successful. Separated from the other animals and placed in an unused corral, the frightened creature skittishly reacts to the strange sounds and smells of this new environment. Slowly and with infinite patience, the boy begins a campaign to accustom the wary animal to his presence. The once skeptical men observe: "The Horse can't see, and neither one can talk, yet they really seem to understand each other." By mistake, the animal is released from its enclosure and returns to the wild, but the boy's assiduous search locates the runaway, and he leads it back to the ranch. When the youth gets restless and wants to accompany a horse trader to Oklahoma, the ranch owner makes out a bill of sale: "Sold this day, one unbranded blind horse, blue-gray in color and about five (5) years old, to a boy of small size whose name and age are unknown because of the fact that he cannot speak." Just before he crosses the ridge, "the Boy turned in his saddle and raised a hand to the ranch owner and the cowboys still standing by the gate. And that was the last they saw or heard of either the Boy or the Blind Outlaw."

Analysis. The young hero is a plucky, smart, and tenacious character whose extraordinary ability to relate to wild creatures—not only the outlaw horse but a magpie and coyote as well—derives from limitless patience, sensitivity to the animals' instincts, and native intelligence. The style, tone, and use of unnamed characters add a timeless, mythic quality to this gentle, low-key story. The superlative miniature sketches that are liberally sprinkled throughout the narrative perfectly complement and interpret the text.

Ruby, Lois. *What Do You Do in Quicksand?* New York: Viking, 1979. 199 pp. Reading Level: YA/MA
Disability: Emotional Dysfunction

Leah lives with Moe, her deceased mother's third husband, who, although old enough to be her grandfather, dotes on the solitary, gawky 15 year old, providing structure, affection, and companionship for the troubled girl. Leah struggles to repress recollections of her other stepfather, who secretly abused her sexually but who left their home after a divorce. She often asks about the biological father she never knew and her mother, dead seven years, but such inquiries are stonewalled by her grandmother and discouraged by her adoptive father.

A new family moves in next door, and Leah becomes a regular visitor to the Russell household despite their increasing impatience with the girl's repeated unwelcome intrusions. Mrs. Russell is appalled by the news that her 16-year-old son is about to become a father and, furthermore, plans to raise the infant himself. Supported in this decision by his father, Matt, accompanied by his parents, takes the baby from her indifferent mother and returns home. The youth is soon overwhelmed by the amount of time and energy the newborn takes and the change in his status from an unencumbered adolescent to a responsibility-ridden father.

When Leah arrives to inspect the baby, she instantly develops an obsessive need to mother her. She tries to bargain with Matt to take the new arrival to her house, but the disconcerted youth adamantly refuses. Nevertheless, the teenager fantasizes: "I had plans to make. I had our future to plan for, Barbara's and mine." The new father tries to juggle going to classes in the mornings, studying in the afternoons, and working evenings in the post office, but this regimen soon exhausts him. When his exams are over, Leah convinces him to take a brief vacation while she watches over the infant. Although he accepts, the youth worries about her offer: "Leah wasn't all *there*. . . . You could tell at a glance she wasn't like other girls. . . . She wasn't feminine, but not exactly masculine, either. Neuter. Maybe that was what made her so strange. Like my mother says, 'neither here nor there.' "

Being with a baby whose mother abandoned her engenders a sense of rootlessness in Leah. Persistent in her search for information about her past, Leah finally discovers the whereabouts of her paternal grandparents, only to learn, during an emotional phone conversation, that her father has died. Moe has met a widow his own age and begins courting the woman, a situation that aggravates his stepdaughter's anomie.

One day when the teenager talks to Matt about Barbara's mother, Matt is shocked to discover that Leah "couldn't sort herself out from Barbara." Even the brittle and self-involved Mrs. Russell notes that the teenager is not behaving normally and suggests she needs therapy. When Matt angrily tries to sever their relationship, he notices "she didn't act like a normal person. She should have been insulted, furious, hurt. But she kept that same stupid smile, like it was drawn across her face with a crayon, and she said, 'We have a right to know about

Barbara's mother.' " Worming her name from Matt's sister, she calls the newborn's mother to report on Barbara's growth and development. Shocked at the woman's apparent indifference, Leah invents a horrible disease, which she claims the baby has, then, losing control, begins to sob. Later, Matt warns Leah that the baby does not belong to her, advising her to quit "living in one of your own weird stories." The desperate adolescent kidnaps Barbara, locking herself and the infant in her room. She ignores pleas to return the child, but the pressures on her are too great and she passes out. After her temporary hospitalization, she at last begins to obtain information about her past, expunges the terrible experiences with her abusive stepparent, and under the guidance of her therapist, begins to restructure her life.

Analysis. Leah's delusional behavior has its origins in a turbulent childhood, marked by what she perceived as repeated abandonments and betrayals, exacerbated by sexual abuse and consequent feelings of guilt and fear. The appearance of an infant whom she sees as beginning a similar journey acts as a catalyst in breaking the adolescent's shaky hold on reality. The untimely appearance of a rival for her adoptive father's affection accelerates the process of melding fantasy with reality. Although the cause and progress of the character's emotional deterioration are credible, the implied speed of movement toward recovery seems wildly improbable. The girl is released only four days after her hospitalization, makes astonishing progress in the "fourteen hours I talked around it all" to her psychiatrist, and has a rational, coherent conversation with Matt concerning his departure with Barbara only a few weeks after her release. The author's skill is manifest in the crackling dialogue, in the presentation of teenage perceptions and concerns, and in the creation of a sympathetic, original character who fights desperately for identity and a sense of connectedness.

Sachs, Elizabeth-Ann. *Just Like Always.* New York: Atheneum, 1981. 160 pp. Reading Level: MC/YA
Disability: Orthopedic Impairment

Irrepressible Janie Tannenbaum checks into the hospital to be treated for scoliosis. Her roommate, Courtney-Ann, a pale, dreamy child, completely opposite in appearance and temperament, is undergoing treatment for the same disorder. Courtney refuses to reveal her secret invented name, unwilling to allow her boisterous new companion access to her private world. The timid child risks sharing a small pretense with Janie and is appalled when her confidence is casually passed on to a nurse. She is further vexed when Janie confesses that she has read her roommate's diary. After a confrontation the two girls settle their differences, and a warm friendship begins to blossom between the impulsive, adventurous youngster and the subdued, cautious one.

Courtney is frightened at the prospect of having to wear a body cast to remediate her spinal curvature, and the young patient's dismay is heightened by her extremely active imagination. She appeals to Janie for an explanation of why she has been singled out for this fate and is reminded that the pair obviously share the same condition, an observation that calms her considerably. The girls talk about Greno, the magical land Courtney devised, and this entertains them and provides much comfort.

After they are each encased in plaster, their discussions continue, allowing an escape from the feelings of frustration and helplessness their immobility imposes. To relieve the tedium of daily routines, Janie engineers a series of original diversions. The two patients design a questionnaire on the topic of love and, encouraged by the responses, plot a romantic rendezvous between their adored doctor and favorite nurse. The girls have psychologically prepared themselves for their medical procedures, but Courtney becomes acutely depressed upon learning that her operation must be delayed because of unforeseen complications. Janie recovers from her surgery but is upset to learn she will not be able to say goodbye to her friend. She writes a loving note to Courtney and includes her address. Although Janie has matured and become more sensitive as a consequence of her contact with Courtney, she has retained some of her old style. On the ambulance ride home, she directs the driver: "Put the siren on, will ya? I want my friend Harold to know I'm coming home."

Analysis. Sachs has created an original, well-crafted novel featuring two memorable characters. The youngsters are seen coping with the inevitable tedium of hospital routines and the fear and pain of recovery, and readers are led to see how their personalities affect that reaction. The author has created a staff containing repressive, punitive people as well as caring, supportive ones, and these workers provide the rich background for the main theme—the emergence of an unlikely but wonderful friendship.

Salassi, Otto L. *On the Ropes.* New York: Greenwillow, 1981. 248 pp. Reading Level: YA
Disability: Orthopedic Impairment; also cosmetic impairment

To avoid being adopted by his straightlaced aunts after his pious mother's death, Squint sends a fake telegram to himself, signed by his long lost father, which indicates the man will soon return to claim his children. The 11-year-old boy and his 17-year-old sister, Julie, track down their wayward parent, whom they persuade to return home with them. Squint, recognizing a fellow opportunist in his father, Claudius Gains, is confident that the flimflam artist can launch a scheme to prevent the imminent foreclosure on their Texas ranch. Claudius packs up his wrestling troupe, which includes Panzer Kaufman, who "had a scar that ran from his cheek to the middle of his forehead," the Baron, their wives, the Masked Marvel, and the Claw, a burly wrestler whose right hand has been replaced by a hook. They are soon joined by other professionals currently indebted to the promoter and by Seymour, a reluctant wrestling bear. Living up to his reputation, Claudius devises a surefire, failproof plan to save the family homestead. He advertises a contest and offers ten thousand dollars to anyone who successfully outwrestles his fighters, simultaneously making arrangements to ensure that the winner will be one of his own people. He intends to use the money collected from admissions and the concession stands to pay off the bank note and launch the Claudius Gains Wrestling College.

The community has never seen such excitement, and people gather from miles around—including the shrewd and villainous Louis Karp. This unscrupulous fight manager brings with him the Angel of Sorrow, a competitor of immense size whose obvious brute strength intimidates the regulars, who had always considered their performances more show business than athletic contest. Karp describes the Angel's prowess:

> No man has ever been able to beat him. . . . He's a killer . . . with no conscience and no remorse. The woman who gave him birth, to this day, lives in a mental home in Baton Rouge. He snapped the spine of an alligator and ate him for dinner when he was only twelve years old. . . . The Angel of Sorrow [is] visiting your lives because you've been bragging too much.

To confirm this appraisal to his anxious audience, Angel bites the wheel of a motorcycle, smiling when it explodes in his face. The evil promoter warns, "They'll be needing wheelchairs and Seeing Eye dogs" when his protégé finishes with the other wrestlers, but makes a secret deal with Gains to increase the theatricality of the event by promising no serious injuries will occur until the last round, when Angel will fight four men simultaneously.

During the match, Claudius tries as many stratagems as his devious mind can invent, but none even slows the powerful giant. Squint, alarmed at the impending failure of his father's plan, decides to scout out the enemy's camp. He brings some potent home-cooked chili to Angel's trailer, which the underfed and lonely wrestler gratefully consumes, revealing to his would-be friend that his real name is Arthur.

The ingenious youngster locates a slippery concoction that his father had once used in a clown act and brings it to the ring. Karp seizes the bucket containing the clear liquid, mistaking it for water, and throws it on Angel and Claudius, who are participating in the final match. They drop to the mat, where Angel remains, unable to get to his feet. Claudius had hammered carpenter's tacks through the soles of his own shoes so he now has enough traction to enable him to stand. In desperation, Karp tosses his fighter a towel to dry off the gooey mess, an act the referee interprets as his acceptance of defeat. After the match, Angel joins the troupe, Julie marries the Marvel, and the Claw is promised "a real claw, one of them mechanical hands like the army wanted to give you in the first place" to replace the one Angel destroyed during the contest. The veteran objects, claiming, "They look like lobster pinchers." Undaunted, Claudius says, "How 'bout we take it over to Neiman-Marcus and have it gold-plated? Then we call you the Golden Claw," a prospect appealing to the wrestler and one he readily accepts. When things get too tame around the homestead, Claudius takes off once again, but Squint, now grown up, soon after leaves for Florida "where he had wanted to go in the first place."

Analysis. Disability is treated in casual ways in this witty, tongue-in-cheek romp. The wrestlers' obvious impairments are distinguishing qualities that are exploited to help give them a fierce and memorable identity. The naive Claw is both vain about his hook and embarrassed by it: "I figured if I had a big diamond ring on my hand, people wouldn't notice the hook so much." Claw eventually gets married, raises a family, and becomes a potato farmer, "snipping off sucker buds with his golden claw." Squint, disgusted by his sister's romance with the Marvel, remarks that the only worse thing he could think of was "three little babies with steel hooks on their arms." The self-righteous minister who tries to shut down Claudius's arena recounts the horrible things found there: monsters, criminals, and men with "claws for hands." These outlandish descriptions only make the foolish man appear even more ridiculous.

Salassi's absurd world of bombast and fakery also includes simple, naive folk who "conceal" their disabilities while at the same time exploiting them for their commercial value. Despite Squint's disparaging remark, the comedy points out the ambivalence the public (and the two vain wrestlers) hold about such conditions.

Sallis, Susan. *Only Love.* New York: Harper & Row, 1980. 240 pp.
Reading Level: YA
Disability: Neurological Impairment, Orthopedic Impairment, Special Health Problems

Fran, a 16-year-old English girl, enters Thornton Hall, a residence for disabled persons. Her exuberance has not been dampened by her orphan status, her paraplegia, or her impaired cardiac and respiratory functioning. Her first act at the center is to steal Mrs. Gorman's false teeth, a trick the undiscriminating old lady finds vastly amusing. Although Fran is at first contemptuous of the couple who are assigned to assume the roles of surrogate aunt and uncle, she gradually learns to love them. The irrepressible girl is convinced she should become involved in helping Luke, the newest resident, emerge from his self-imposed solitude, eschew his self-pity, and adjust to life despite the loss of both legs in an auto accident. The resourceful teen convinces him to share her project to ignite a romance between the staff nurse and doctor and to participate in the coming Fete Day celebration. Caught up in the excitement, the formerly depressed boy suggests that the site of the program be moved to the swimming pool: "Come on, Franny! The pool! Water! You all swim, and the light there is interesting. You've got the changing rooms right behind—quite enough space at the end and side for seating—you can have loads of comedy pushing each other in."

The program is a huge success (how could it fail?), and Luke and Fran promptly fall in love. At her insistence, he learns how to use artificial legs, making remarkable progress in a short time. Dr. Beamish warns her of the unsuitability of this romance, reminding her that her health is very fragile and her life expectancy brief. Although initially angry, Fran realizes the soundness of the physician's advice and tries to terminate this love affair with her boyfriend. Luke is understandably resentful and furious. After a brief separation, the two tragic lovers are reunited and serenely spend Fran's last declining days together.

Analysis. This book is not only an empty-headed romance, it is a melodramatic and patently absurd work. Although it ostensibly attempts to explore the options available to and the limitations imposed upon a multihandicapped adolescent, the absurdity of the treatment undermines these objectives. Enlightenment descends on characters, causing sudden reversals in their attitudes and behavior. Luke's abrupt transformation from self-imposed exile to center stage in a romance, from adamant refusal to participate in his own rehabilitation to successful maneuvering on artificial legs, is typical. For a novel that seems to have as its major purpose sensitizing readers to the problems of an undervalued population, it is inexcusably callous. When the heroine is adjusting to her new home, she observes: "There was even a pair of mentally deficient dogs. At least they acted mentally deficient what with drooling and flopping about all over the place. . . . This old girl must have just had new teeth fitted, because she had a grin like a Jap officer in an old American war movie."

These gratuitous and irrelevant remarks are evidently intended to demonstrate the wit and cleverness of the main character. They obviously fail. The author's treatment of death is equally distorted: descriptions of the surrogate aunt initially dwell on her unattractive physical appearance; however, after her death, her loving, generous qualities are exclusively recognized. The heroine, aware that she has little time left, observes, "I knew with calm certainty that it was a privilege to die young." Such offensive drivel characterizes the abysmal quality of this exploitive work.

Sallis, Susan. *An Open Mind.* New York: Harper & Row, 1978. 139 pp. Reading Level: YA
Disability: Neurological Impairment

Angry over his parents' separation, David Winterborne is unwarrantedly hostile toward his father's new friend, Margaret Daly. The woman does volunteer work at Underwood, a center providing instruction for physically disabled children. She invites Mr. Winterborne, who brings his reluctant son to see a performance by the students. The experience has a profound impact, and David arranges to visit again, using a class assignment as a cover for his true intention—to obtain "evidence" that will tarnish the reputation of his father's presumed paramour. There he becomes involved with Bruce, a boy with cerebral palsy who, coincidentally, happens to be Mrs. Daly's son.

During Mrs. Winterborne's hospitalization for surgery, David had planned to spend his time with some friends. Stopping to say goodbye to Bruce, he discovers the boy outside the walls of the building, alone in his wheelchair and in a high state of agitation. The youth is determined to run away and insists that his new buddy help him "escape." Seeing no other course, David takes the now chilled and obviously sick boy to his own empty house. While out seeking food for them both, he bumps into Jasper, an old acquaintance, whose unwilling help he enlists. Jasper, however, informs the authorities of the whereabouts of the fugitives. Bruce recovers from the ordeal, all is forgiven, and David is encouraged to write about his adventures.

Analysis. An Open Mind provides useful information about some of the physiological and emotional problems that might arise as a result of serious and multiple impairments and also gives insights into some of the motivations of those who work with these children. However, institutionalization for adolescents like Bruce, who are mentally competent but who also have complex but manageable physical problems, seems anachronistic in a contemporary setting. Some of the language— for example, "genned"—will be unfamiliar to American readers; most meanings can be deduced from context clues, but some others may remain puzzling. Dialogue attributed to some of the young characters frequently seems awkward, such as "Miss Ruskin came up and asked us what we thought of Gilbert and Sullivan now, and we had quite a chat, which made old Nanki-Poo look a bit down-in-the-mouth." Moreover, the novel's structure is too obvious and the conclusion overly contrived. Of most concern, however, is the implication that able-bodied persons are motivated in their relations with the disabled by a sense of guilt. "But I was beginning to feel guilty. Like Miss Ruskin had said back in November, did I owe something to Bruce? Because my body worked and his didn't?"

Sallis, Susan. *A Time for Everything.* New York: Harper & Row, 1979. 218 pp. Reading Level: YA
Disability: Intellectual Impairment, speech impairment, neurological impairment

Because of the threat of Nazi bombing raids, Aunt Flo and Cousin Philippa leave their home and accept refuge with Lily's family in Gloucester. Lily's father suggests it would be "better for Philippa to stay in London and take her chance," explaining that the girl's death would mean little for she's "a mongol. All she can do is take." But when enemy planes strafe the beach where the cousins are relaxing, Phil, keeping her wits about her, saves them both by pulling her cousin under the waves with her.

Mavis, an evacuee, joins the crowded household, causing additional consternation because of her lice, her lack of familiarity with lavatory training, her extremely limited expressive speech, and her thoroughly unpleasant and vengeful personality. One evening, Mavis and Lily overhear a conversation that reveals that the latter's impending birth prompted her parents to marry. Her father, seeing the war as a means to escape family obligations, enlists with no intention of ever returning. Lily's life is further marred by the death of her beloved grandfather and the initial rejection of her scholarship application.

Lily is later embarrassed and mortified by the gossip concerning an alleged affair her mother is carrying on with her daughter's favorite teacher. The man, who did not enlist, is considered a coward by his neighbors who assemble intending to drive him from their community. Philippa, intuitively understanding the angry crowd's need for a violent confrontation, diverts the attention of the vigilantes and defuses their fury, thus saving the endangered teacher. Uncle Bart, Philippa's peripatetic father, brings home an American who eventually becomes the lover of Lily's mother. Unaware of this latest complication, the youngster develops a crush on the handsome, romantic, and kindly visitor. The girl's mother discloses she is once again pregnant, but before the Yank learns he is to be a father, he is killed in combat. The conservative community is outraged to hear of the incipient birth and begins to gather signatures on a petition to drive the mother of the illegitimate child from their midst. Aware of the danger to her aunt, Philippa runs off so the neighbors will dissipate their energies into a diversionary search for her. Lily picks up her cousin's trail at the home of the village sage, who reports: "I couldn't have stopped her if I'd tried. But I didn't try all that hard. It's maybe for the best."

The missing girl is eventually located in the snow and taken to the hospital, desperately ill. The heroine and her mother are told by a nurse: "Mongoloids of that particular type rarely live far into puberty." The girl's aunt responds: "Philippa has never been diagnosed as mongoloid. . . . She has slight cerebral palsy, of course, but . . ." A contrary view surfaces after the child dies, and one neighbor comments that she "was one of those people who generate . . . good feeling . . . love. . . . She generated love." Lily, now at loose ends and unsure of what to do with her life, is astonished and relieved when her father returns home to stay. After the birth of the baby, she and her parents discuss the wrongs that have been committed and determine to avoid such meretricious and painful behavior in the future, choosing instead to emulate Philippa's admirable example.

Analysis. The information about Down's syndrome is distorted and misleading. Philippa is initially identified as having this disorder, an impression that is reinforced until the climax, when she is described as having "slight cerebral palsy." This confusion as to her condition is unwarranted, and it is unclear whether she sustains both of these disabilities or not. Since there is little similarity, such a depiction is unjustifiably obscure. Moreover, the child's mouth malformation is described in offensive terms: "The words were strained through the cleft palate into nasal nonsense."

Many hints presage Philippa's demise. When Lily's father comments that his niece's death would be no significant loss, it acts to establish him as an unfeeling person, but when the "wise woman" implies that death would be a reasonable sacrifice to save her aunt's life, no opprobrium attaches to such vile sentiments. Despite repeated references to her limited intellectual ability, Philippa is credited with saving the lives of several other characters, although these incidents lack believability. The thoroughly unpleasant child who is taken in transposes into a martyred, saintlike character, but neither of these extremes has credibility. What is certainly reprehensible is the frequent inclusion of gratuitous remarks that are rife with bias, for instance:

"Mum . . . hung on to the bitter end, which was a couple of wheel-chairs. The occupants looked half dead. Surely they would have pre-ferred Hitler's bombs to the indignity of flight." The plot is marked by melodramatic twists and turns, the characters are thin as pasteboard, and the writing style is pure suds.

Savitz, Harriet M. *Run, Don't Walk*. New York: Franklin Watts, 1979. 122 pp. Reading Level: YA
Disability: Orthopedic Impairment; also special health problems, visual impairment

Samantha tries to repress memories of a fateful dive made the year before last that left her with no sensation in her lower limbs. Unwilling to admit the permanence of her condition or to identify with other disabled people, she becomes angry when Johnny Jay, the only other student in the school who uses a wheelchair, tries to enlist her in his strident, aggressive campaign to make the lavatories accessible. Saman-tha obviously faces the same barriers he does, but she finds the issue embarrassing. Through great effort and with considerable discomfort, she trains her body to retain fluids until she can utilize her own bath-room at home.

At first, the lonely girl's only companion is Mandy, "a dog who could fetch: an extra set of legs." But later, Sue Jenkins, a teacher, becomes friendly with Samantha after being interviewed for the school newspaper for an article on jogging. Soon the teacher, the high school student, and her pet are a familiar sight as they move through the streets of the town. The teenager, whose stamina increases daily, re-veals to Sue her decision to enter the upcoming marathon and confront the challenge of the steep and pitted incline the contestants call "Heart-break Hill." In her mind, that barrier "stood for the stares and obsta-cles, and everything she had never dared to cry out against before."

Although the adolescent girl feels that Johnny has made a specta-cle of himself over the issue of toilets, this does not interfere with their growing relationship. Her father, whose "heart attack had left him with a scar, a weakness that came over him suddenly," warns her that the boy means "trouble," but she has become more assertive and per-sists in seeing him. One day, Johnny connives to involve her in a rally to demand benefits for blind persons. She is furious both at his decep-tion and at the obvious elation the youth feels at the opportunity to articulate the group's demands over television during media coverage of the protest. With the support and participation of members of the advocacy organization, Johnny plans a demonstration at his school, but the administration expels the youthful leader and evicts his supporters.

The act awakens Samantha, who, having been rejected by the marathon committee, now acknowledges that disabled people must band together to obtain their rights. "She had the tool, her writing, and the power to write it the way it would be understood." Her formerly unaccepting father reads her "fiery words" and rushes out to have "a couple of hundred" photocopies made. Samantha hands out the leaflets to students, urging them to spread the news about the planned walkout she has called for noon. A reporter arrives, noting the crowd with interest, and enthusiastically records the heroine's account of the school's violation of Section 504 of the Rehabilitation Act. The dispute is ultimately arbitrated, and the financially pressed school board is informed of possible inexpensive modifications by Johnny Jay's advocacy group. Buoyed by their victory, the protesters pressure the racing committee to change their rules so that Samantha may be allowed to participate. Of the 1,500 who enter, she is one of only 50 who complete the 26-mile course. Samantha's boyfriend congratulates her warmly, then turns his attentions to a new campaign to make public transportation available to those would-be riders who are disabled.

Analysis. Run, Don't Walk is an extended tract on society's neglect of the disabled. It consists of many expository paragraphs outlining these crucial matters interpersed with a pastiche of such worn-out conventions as a noble dog saved from certain death, the blossoming love affair of two apparently incompatible characters, and the successful completion of a herculean task by an unlikely participant who overcomes incredible odds. The matter of accessibility to toilets, although a matter of vital seriousness, is thoroughly devoid of any dramatic possibilities, and a novel that uses this as its focus inevitably diminishes its potential effect. The tone of rebuke in this work as well as the topic argue for a lectern or a soapbox for the message rather than a literary medium.

Savitz, Harriet M. *Wait Until Tomorrow.* New York: New American Library, 1981. 149 pp. Reading Level: YA
Disability: Speech Impairment, emotional dysfunction

The presence of Shawn's father at his wife's funeral makes the experience even more painful for the sorrowing boy. The long absent man's hollow insistence that his son come to Arizona with him sounds insincere to the adolescent, whose overwhelming sense of loneliness and anomie prompts an abortive suicide attempt. The physician suggests counseling, but the youth is resistant, opting instead to spend what he hopes will be a restorative summer with his grandfather. The year before, the 70-year-old man had undergone a laryngectomy, and since his speech lessons have been without result, the man must communicate through written messages.

On the bus to his grandfather's beachfront home, Shawn notices an attractive, purple-eyed girl distributing flyers for an upcoming anti-nuclear rally. The teenage girl's energies have become increasingly focussed on the dangers of a nuclear accident, and she devotes her free time and energy to persuade those who live in the community of the potential for disaster that the facility represents. When Robin is at last introduced to Shawn by a resident of the town, the newcomer has conflicting feelings: Robin is a very attractive girl, but he cannot accept her point of view on the issue. Their budding romance is frequently threatened by arguments about nuclear energy. One day, seeking respite from these problems, Shawn toys again with the possibility of suicide but finally rejects self-destruction as a solution to his dilemma. The caring youth tries to help his relative by working with him on speech lessons and giving him much praise for even the most modest of achievements. But after a particularly embarrassing encounter in town, the elderly man angrily concedes defeat and, in his frustration and rage, turns his hostility toward his grandson. Their comfortable, loving relationship markedly deteriorates, causing them both frustration and anguish. Shawn meets a man who uses an electronic larynx and tries to convince his grandfather to purchase one, but the elderly man is too depressed to risk another failure.

At the rally, Shawn sees that Robin has defied the authorities and is trespassing on the grounds of the nuclear plant. He gallantly tries to rescue her but is arrested along with his girl friend and other protesters. To the youth's surprise, he hears his grandfather's voice, distorted through an artificial larynx, but clearly recognizable, demanding their release from jail. There is a happy reconciliation, and the adolescent youth, with his girl friend at his side, looks to the future with optimism.

Analysis. Neither good literature nor good propaganda, *Wait Until Tomorrow* fails to offer credible plot development, interesting characters, likely dialogue, or reasoned argument. The images are jarring: "The aroma of hot things baking in the oven drifted across the room like an expensive perfume"; the heroine's proclamation of her beliefs has the effect of a harangue; her boyfriend's opposing views are devoid of interest, and thus little tension is generated. The hero's attempted suicide is unconvincing, and his grandfather's initially immature behavior, then sudden conversion to the virtues of the prosthesis, seems highly improbable.

Shreve, Susan. *Loveletters*. New York: Knopf, 1978. 217 pp. Reading Level: YA/MA
Disability: Emotional Dysfunction; also special health problems, neurological impairment

Kate Leuthi suffers from a growing emotional separation from her parents; her father is a workaholic, preoccupied with his writing, and her mother is totally absorbed with her role as a college student. The child uses up her lonely days with conversations with her occasionally lucid grandmother or by creating theatricals. The eight-year-old girl's life is dramatically changed when a foster child moves in across the street. Tommy's reputation as an incorrigible troublemaker has preceded him, but so far his behavior has been limited to "racing . . . bicycles, climbing the highest trees," sneaking a swim in the mayor's pool, smoking, and other acts of bravado. Tommy brings a hopeful joy to his temporary caretaker and is, in turn, cautiously reponsive to her uncompromising devotion to him. When the woman suddenly dies, the boy sees this as but one of many betrayals, and it provides him with further evidence that it is dangerous to trust others. Rejected by his ill foster father, Tommy has social contact only with Kate, whom he inducts into a secret club in a cave in the woods, which becomes their private hideaway during the next few years.

The boy allows his smoldering anger to surface only when he is teased about his relationship to the girl: he trusses up a six-year-old youngster on one occasion, holding her incommunicado in the cave, and then beating up Kate when she arrives. Despite an apology, their friendship is riven when Kate, motivated by her emerging 13-year-old sensuality, impulsively kisses the boy, who withdraws in revulsion. Kate, still lonely in high school, becomes infatuated with a married cleric, and their liaison results in her pregnancy. When she adamantly resists pressure and maintains her intention to keep the baby, Kate is sent to a home for unwed mothers. After a traumatic delivery, Kate precipitously decides to give up the child. She returns home, haunted by thoughts of Tommy. Abandoning an obnoxious date one evening, she is accosted by the youth. He forces her to accompany him back to their cave, where he assaults her and compels her to remain there as his prisoner.

The Leuthis, now obliged to turn from their self-absorption and focus on their daughter, are in shock over her disappearance. Her grandmother, momentarily alert, suggests that Tommy may be the key to locating her. Kate's parents rummage through her memorabilia and, in addition to finding some unpleasant, revealing material about themselves, come upon messages from Tommy that enable them to determine the location of the cave. There they find her, bound and gagged, and her captor whimpering uncontrollably in a corner. The young man is sent off once again to a psychiatrist, and Kate returns to her parents' house, where it appears they will all make a concerted effort to learn to communicate with each other.

Analysis. Although not narrated by one of the adolescent characters, events appear to be seen from that perspective. All adults but one are shown to be self-serving, insensitive, and grievously inadequate. Kate's pregnancy, her insistence on keeping the child, then her abrupt and impetuous decision to give up the infant for adoption are all treated in a judgmental vacuum, although contempt for the behavior for those past the teen years is obvious. No clear distinction is made between those actions of Tommy's that are demonstrations of defiance and those that reveal a profoundly distressed youth. There are serious literary flaws as well. Kate's mother appears to be directing all her energies toward college studies during the entire nine years covered in the book—a situation that needs some explanation. The grandmother has a sudden and convenient interlude of insight that permits a positive resolution of the crisis. The insistence on the Scrabble game as a metaphor for the family's inability to communicate becomes tedious, and some of the writing is overdone: "The blood rushed to their necks, the wild pulsing like a pendulum gone mad. Their legs suspended over the earth, bloodless as crushed carcasses, they clambered up the hill."

Shreve, Susan. *The Masquerade.* New York: Knopf, 1980. 184 pp.
Reading Level: MA
Disability: Emotional Dysfunction

When Edward Walker is arrested for embezzlement, the fragile structure of his family collapses. The Walkers had lived comfortably in opulent surroundings, but the cost of the trial and the outlays for reimbursement to his victims reduce the family to poverty. They sell almost all their possessions and move to a flat above a drugstore. Alicia Walker, the mother, a woman who had always been emotionally vulnerable, is reduced by these devastating events to irrational behavior. Although she does make one brief attempt at work, her behavior is so erratic that her employer, although sympathetic, feels he cannot afford to have her on the premises. Alicia retreats into a much kinder fantasy world and is sometimes found by her children, or occasionally the police, wandering about, dressed as though for a prom date.

Eric, her oldest son, is a medical student, a choice of professions that allows him ample opportunity to give play to his hypochrondria.

He immediately imagines he is the incurable victim of each new disorder he reads about or observes in a patient. Cynically, he tries to persuade Rebecca, the most mature sibling, that her beloved father is actually guilty and not someone whose life has simply been confounded by circumstance. Rebecca dismisses his accusations until the evidence against her father is so overwhelming that she must finally yield to the truth. In a fury, she undergoes a complete transformation, turning hostile, vicious, and unforgiving toward her father. Sarah, their sister, who had shown promise as a dancer, runs away to New York, but mysteriously returns after a brief interlude—morose, refusing either to practice or to reveal her experiences there.

In the meantime, Eric has moved back into the family home with his Pakistani girl friend whose excessive ministrations foster a dependence that he relishes. This interloper is ultimately ejected from their home by his two sisters who realize that Eric's passivity has so dominated his life that it is verging on a behavioral disorder. Mrs. Walker is hospitalized and is slowly able to exert a tenuous hold on reality. Rebecca, too, demonstrates more mature actions: she is able to cease her self-destructive behaviors and visit her father.

Analysis. Alicia is depicted as a person so protected from the normal vicissitudes of life that she never developed the skill needed to cope with any demanding situation. Her retreat from the cares of daily living, surrounding herself with fragments and mementos of a more desirable past, is effectively and movingly portrayed. The responses of the small-town police to one they consider an "old money" eccentric is also well done. When tragedy strikes, she adopts a pattern of undemonstrativeness, and her learned helplessness now takes on devastating dimensions. The sudden change in family fortunes affects the others as well: Eric's self-absorption degenerates into alarmingly unstable behavior; the sisters experience personality alterations, although they are able to draw on untapped resources, work through some of their concerns, and return to a functioning state. Unfortunately, the book reads like a soap opera script. Readers are offered descriptions of behavior, but no evidence or background is presented to give substance or dimension to the characters.

Shtainmets, Leon. *The Story of Ricky the Royal Dwarf.* Illus. by author. New York: Harper & Row, 1976. 48 pp. Reading Level: MC
Disability: Orthopedic Impairment

When the princess of the royal court of Spain was young, she played happily with the court dwarf, Carlos Juan Pedro Miguel Rodriguez de Irrabera, known as Ricky. "She told him all her secrets [and] she loved him more than her toys—even more than her favorite poodle." As she grew older, she rejected the companionship of her former friend, but Ricky continues to love her from afar. The dwarf does not see any reason why he should be the constant subject of court ridicule. He looks at his portrait in puzzlement and asks himself: "Can I really be so ugly?" observing, "I'm just smaller than everyone. But I have such a beautiful lace collar. And my little sword is just like a real one."

During the visit of the French king, Ricky is ordered to entertain the assembled guests. He panics when his sovereign, smoldering with anger, loses a chess match to the visiting ruler. The reluctant performer, observing the increasingly antagonistic mood of his master, begins to play the flute, a talent he has kept secret. The music embodies his most tender thoughts, causing all within hearing to be overcome with emotion. The Spanish king, responsive to this transcendent experience, offers to reward the musician, but the French king interrupts, claiming Ricky as his chess trophy and declaring his intention to add the flautist to his palace orchestra. Ricky prepares to leave, dismayed at this precipitous move to a foreign land, but aware that the Spanish monarch and his daughter at last understand that he, too, has human feelings. As the procession moves off, the musician wonders sadly what the future holds.

Analysis. This maudlin story, more a literary fragment than a fully developed tale, introduces a character whose nobility of spirit and finely tuned sensibilities persist despite the contemptible behavior of others toward him. The use of dwarfs as court entertainers is historically accurate, and the powerlessness of their status is effectively portrayed. However, the presentation here is patronizing, and the insubstantial nature of the narrative, combined with the anemic-appearing sketches, yields a work that is unenduring.

Shura, Mary Francis. *The Gray Ghosts of Taylor Ridge.* Illus. by Michael Hampshire. New York: Dodd, Mead, 1978. 127 pp. Reading Level: MC
Disability: Visual Impairment

Ten-year-old Nan Miller pressures her older brother Nat into returning to the site of her class field trip so she can recover their father's compass, which she had carelessly left behind. The youngsters are alarmed by a blind old man who threatens them with a gun. They later learn from their father that Boomer is a harmless local character given to telling tall tales. The children return to the area to resume their search, but they stop by Boomer's cabin to introduce themselves and explain their purpose. He warns them of the gray ghosts who haunt Taylor Ridge. Nan does not find the compass, but she discovers an antebellum gold coin, which the elated hermit claims is evidence that the fabled Taylor treasure does exist. Determined to recover her father's property, Nan, accompanied by Bubba, Boomer's dog, resumes her search. When she does not return, her brother tracks her down, finding her trapped in the root cellar of what had been the old Taylor house.

A few days later, Mrs. Miller receives a call for help from Boomer. She collects her children from school and quickly drives to the anxious man's cabin. There they learn that Bubba has been missing for some time, and the intrepid children rescue the dog from the same cellar. The excited animal leads them to an abandoned well, from which they hear a man's agonized groans. Nat stands guard while his sister runs for help, returning with the sheriff and his men. They lower the boy into the well, where he secures a rope around the now inert body. The two are pulled to safety, after which the stranger recovers sufficiently to announce that the treasure Boomer has been searching for is hidden in the well. Nat descends once again, recovers gold coins and silver plates, stuffs them into a bag, and returns to the surface. He is startled to find that the man he rescued is Boomer's estranged foster son, Perry, who relates the disagreement that led to his leaving. Boomer, his eyesight failing, had inadvertently started a fire. When the latest evidence of his diminished ability is remarked upon by his foster child, the angry man heatedly accuses Perry of responsibility for the fire. Perry explains: "He couldn't face his own blindness and getting old and helpless." The young man had surreptitiously returned to look for the treasure, intending to use the wealth to provide either medical help or a caretaker for his father. "It was for Boomer. He's blind, Sheriff. If he doesn't get help he's going to kill himself wandering around out here."

The rescue party returns to the hermit's home, where Perry tells the old man that the money is for his care. Boomer becomes furious at the insinuation that he is blind. Nan tells him not to be silly: "You can't make yourself see just by saying that you can." He protests the label saying that if he *were* blind, he would be forced to move from his home. Mrs. Miller suggests his vision loss is probably the result of cataracts and predicts that surgery will undoubtedly restore his sight. Perry and his foster father are happily reconciled, and the young man hands over to a grateful Nan the compass he discovered while on Taylor Ridge.

Analysis. The coupling of blindness and helplessness is a repeated strategy of the author. Described as "walled in by his blindness," the old man seems far less astute than he should be: he cannot tell when it is snowing and is unable to deduce from the voices who is in his presence when the rescuers return. Several false issues are raised—blindness does not deprive one of civil rights, that is, Boomer could not be forced to leave the house he owns. In addition, basic medical care is available for indigent citizens; therefore, the proposition that help for cataracts would be unavailable without the treasure is misleading, although the old man's fear that he would become dependent is credible. The story creates some mild tension but contains many formula elements, and the resolution is far too pat. Realistic black-and-white illustrations are adequate.

Shyer, Marlene F. *Welcome Home, Jellybean*. New York: Scribner, 1978. 152 pp. Reading Level: MC/YA
Disability: Intellectual Impairment

Mrs. Oxley decides it is time to bring her 13-year-old daughter home from the state training school where she has been living for years. Geraldine's coordination is poor, she eats only with a spoon, she has neither intelligible speech nor minimal social skills. Her younger brother, Neil, the narrator of the story, is basically a compassionate youth, and his sister's presence initially causes him only mild annoyance and embarrassment. Mrs. Oxley devotes herself full time to her daughter's care and education, but her husband undermines her efforts by his unsympathetic and unsupportive behavior, absenting himself when any crisis arises. When he is unable to concentrate on his work as a tunesmith, he becomes very upset with Geraldine. His daughter not only interferes with his work during the day, but at night she bangs her head against the wall of her bedroom, keeping her family as well as the neighbors in the adjacent apartment awake. The 12-year-old boy gets into trouble at school as a result of the sleep he loses at night, his sister's destruction of his homework, and the fights he has with the other students over her. Their father leaves home and invites Neil to join him, but although the boy is tempted, he feels he must be of help to his mother, whom he cannot abandon, especially since his sister is showing some improvement. Meanwhile, the neighbors have circulated a petition demanding that the Oxleys be evicted, but the kind building superintendent is reluctant to execute it. When the man comes to the apartment to discuss their departure, he is convinced that Gerry's behavior is much more acceptable and, declaring that he must live with his conscience, tears up the eviction notice.

Neil is featured in a school program in which he will play the piano. That evening, the sitter who promised to stay with Geraldine does not arrive, so Mrs. Oxley, unwilling to miss her son's performance, takes her daughter to the rear of the auditorium, hoping to remain inconspicuous. When Gerry spots her brother, she shrieks in delight, escapes her mother's restraining hand, dashes up to the stage, and, to her brother's mortification, stops the show. Neil decides the situation is intolerable and calls his father to come and get him. But by the time Mr. Oxley arrives, Neil has changed his mind again, realizing that he must accept some responsibility for his sister, to whom he owes loyalty and love.

Analysis. The state institution is depicted as a stultifying place where children such as Gerry will never learn self-sufficiency. The girl is fed only soft, mushy food that can be eaten with a spoon, and this is an analogue for the other aspects of the hospital to which she is exposed. Inevitably, she is educationally, socially, and physically undernourished. In desperation, her mother precipitously decides to dedicate herself to her daughter's needs, oblivious to the ramifications of this decision. Mrs. Oxley is seen as having no good options: the institution keeps her child at a level that precludes growth, but Geraldine's requirements are all-consuming, leaving the woman neither time nor energy for herself or the rest of her family. Neil is portrayed as ambivalent—ashamed of his sister's behavior but enormously proud of what she has accomplished. However, the boy's adaptability and flexibility are remarkable for a preteen, and Geraldine's progress after such a long period of stagnation seems exaggerated. The pressures used by neighbors to rid themselves of undesirables are potently revealed, but it is shown that these can be successfully resisted. Although some scenes lack credibility and dimension, the story has value both as an introduction to some of the dislocations and problems in caring for a low-functioning child, but also as an indictment of society in terms of how it deals with individuals with severe disorders.

Singer, Marilyn. *It Can't Hurt Forever.* Illus. by Leigh Grant. New York: Harper & Row, 1978. 186 pp. Reading Level: MC
Disability: General Health Problems

Eleven-year-old Ellie Simon enters the hospital to have a heart defect corrected. Her parents have tried to prepare her emotionally for the ordeal, but she is still anxious about the pain and the possibility of dying. Some of the other young patients help her by discussing their feelings, as well as their surgery, treatment, and recovery, but one terrorizes the young cardiac patient by emphasizing the dangers involved in the operation. Ellie's catheterization is traumatic and increases her distress even more. However, the procedure reveals no additional problems, so surgery proceeds as scheduled. There are no complications; Ellie recuperates easily and soon returns home.

Analysis. A tremendous amount of information about hospital procedures is explored, as well as the real concerns of children facing serious surgery. Ellie reveals her persisting fears of suffering and of dying, which are not completely alleviated by the many explanations she is offered. Her pain is intense, and the author clearly shows how traumatic it is for the young heroine. The best aspect of this work underlines Singer's contention that full revelation of medical and surgical procedures is essential even for youngsters and offers the greatest relief from the patient's anxiety. The problem with the book is literary: Ellie's speech is as natural as that of children on television commercials. For example, after an encounter with an elderly patient with leaky heart valves, the child's nurse tells her that she too will have an echocardiogram taken. Ellie protests and, in a minilecture on anatomy, informs the nurse: "But there's nothing wrong with my valves. My *patent ductus* is between my aorta and my pulmonary artery. It means blood that already got oxygen is being pushed into my lungs and . . ." Singer's constructive intention to include multiracial and nonsexist characters and to present positive female and ethnic models is undermined by the heavy-handed deliberateness of the effort.

Sivers, Brenda. *The Snailman.* Illus. by Shirley Hughes. Boston: Little, Brown, 1978. 118 pp. Reading Level: MC
Disability: Orthopedic Impairment, Cosmetic Impairment; also auditory impairment

The four months since Timothy's family moved from London to a rural village have been unhappy ones for the boy. Periodic fights or hairbreadth escapes from the bullying Payne brothers punctuate days of agonizing boredom. Home is not a peaceful sanctuary since Timothy's mother is angry about her enforced idleness in the remote countryside. Seeking escape, the boy finds himself at the cottage of the weaver Bob Mimms, known derisively as "The Snailman." The outcast's "nose has obviously been broken earlier in life and badly reset, giving him the belligerent expression of a prizefighter." One of his eyes was misformed, and it rolled around menacingly under a lowered lid. In addition, he had "some kind of a spinal deformity that gave him a lurching, one-sided gait." The country folk "suspected him of a thousand unnatural acts, none of which they could prove," and the youth, alarmed by the gossip, expected him "to be a raging maniac, frothing at the mouth and pulling babies limb from limb." Instead, Mimms is a gentle person who invites Timothy into his cottage, shows him his beloved loom, and takes him to the shed, where he keeps snails. When the boy's face reflects his discomfort at the slimy creatures, the man defends his pets: "They don't harm nobody. They ain't so pretty to look at, but neither are we. Leastways, I ain't."

One day, Timothy brings a bird whose wing had been broken when a tramp hit it with a stone. He discovers Mimms in bed, racked with pain. The boy

> found a blanket, which he threw over the Snailman, tucking it in the way his mother did when she wanted to feel particularly loving. Then he stood back, unsure. He wanted to do something to relieve the man's pain but he was afraid to touch the huge misshapen body. Would the Snailman resent it and lash out at him? Worse still, would he find some horrible lump or deformity on the man's back?
>
> Overcoming his fear with an effort, Timothy reached out and, as gently as he could, he began to stroke the Snailman's back. He wasn't sure where the injury was. Spinal . . . but that could have been anywhere from the shoulder blade to the tailbone, so he rubbed somewhere between the two and hoped he was relieving the Snailman's obvious distress.

Timothy's problems in school continue, but his one attempt to fight back when confronted and his friendly relationship with the feared hermit intimidate the local rowdies, and they refrain from outright attacks. The boy is heartbroken when he learns that Mimms's dog is accused of harassing some cattle, his weaver's loom has been deliberately destroyed, and all the man's snails have been killed. The ten-year-old, aghast at the cruelty of the attacks on his friend, decides to prove that the charges against the dog were unfounded. Timothy hides out in the field where the cows are pastured, which Mimms and his canine regularly cross on their way to visit an elderly, deaf, arthritic friend. He and the farmer who owns the cattle discover that the real culprit is a tramp who has been nursing a grudge. After the man is hauled off to jail and Timothy returned safely home, his parents, newly aware of the whole situation, permit their son to remain friends with their falsely maligned neighbor. Timothy diligently searches for a large snail worthy of beginning a new colony for the Snailman. Overwhelmed by the thoughtfulness of his young benefactor, Mimms names the giant snail in his honor.

Analysis. The man's disfigurement, his reclusive habits, and his unusual hobby make him a target for the little community's hostility. They consider him "crazy" and ignore their children's abuse toward him. His frightening physical exterior, which disguises a warm, compassionate nature, provides the young hero with his first lesson on the difference between appearance and reality—a lesson he relearns in several forms throughout the story. Characters are familiar, as is the theme, but the simple tale is well told and the illustrations depict the man's impairments in a manner consistent with their description in the text.

Skurzynski, Gloria. *Manwolf.* New York: Houghton Mifflin, 1981. 175 pp. Reading Level: YA
Disability: Special Health Problems, orthopedic impairment

Near the end of the fourteenth century, Reinman, a Teutonic knight, stops by the estate of Pan Lucas, a petty Polish landowner. The mysterious nobleman wears a leather mask, which together with his beard so completely covers his face that only his eyes are revealed. He insists that Danusha, a serf, be given to him to use as a servant for himself and his attendant, Marek. Despite her father's protests, the 16 year old is forced to leave home. The count buys her expensive clothes and treats her courteously but, ignoring his vow of chastity, sleeps with her. When her horse becomes lame, the knight considers the hardships that will undoubtedly ensue if she continues on their arduous travels and, confronting his conscience at last, decides to send the young woman home. She begs to be allowed to stay, but Reinman is adamant. Soon after her return, she gives birth to his child. The infant's pink urine is the first sign of his disorder. When Adam's first teeth appear, they too are discolored, ranging in shades from pink to deep red. His alarmed mother keeps her son hidden, fearing the superstitious peasants would mock and torment him. Soon she is compelled by Pan Lucas to marry another of his serfs, a drunken brute who gives her a second son, Marcin. Her husband is killed in a fight, and Danusha becomes a field hand, forced to take her sons to work with her. Adam's appearance becomes even more noticeable, the sun causes his skin to blister, his face becomes covered with hair, and scars form on his hands, causing them to tighten up and lose dexterity. The peasants' suspicion that Adam's father is Satan makes Danusha realize that her child's life is in danger, and after being stoned, she flees with her two boys to a religious sanctuary, where Brother Vincenty arranges for her to live in a secluded cottage in a forest belonging to the monks.

There is great excitement when it is announced that their beloved and pregnant queen will pass by the monastery. Rumors have circulated that the monarch is able to heal the sick and bring the dead back to life. Danusha and Marcin await her in the church, but Adam is counseled to hide so that his whereabouts will remain secret. At the approach of the queen's carriage, Adam springs forward to ask Queen

Jadwiga for a miracle. The weak and astonished woman faints at the sight of the disfigured youth. He escapes into the woods, but her attendants track down the hapless fugitive and confine him to a local jail. A princess is born who is too frail to survive, and the mother's death follows quickly after the infant's. The warden hopes to capitalize on these events by announcing that he has imprisoned the werewolf responsible for this dreadful tragedy. He beats Adam and directs a one-armed guard to place the weakened youth in a cage and exhibit him, rousing the public to acts of cruelty against the defenseless prisoner. Marek passes through the town and recognizes the boy's condition as one from which his master also suffers. When he confirms that the boy is the son of Danusha, he plans, with support from the compassionate guard, to deceive the cruel keeper and rescue Adam. The two stop at an inn where the youth, nearly dead from exposure and maltreatment, is restored sufficiently to continue their journey to a Franciscan monastery, where Adam recovers his health. Reinman appears to claim the patient as his son, but Adam is reluctant to leave a place where he has found not only security but purpose as a healer. His wealthy father persuades him to interrupt his life as a novice to become schooled as a physician and then return with more advanced training to his religious vocation. They leave so the young man can study in Italy but pause for him to bid farewell to his family.

Analysis. Adam is more the victim of the superstitious fears that cause the ignorant mob to see his disfigurement, his excessive hairiness, and his discoloration as a sign of the devil than from actual physical discomfort that his illness generates. He becomes the hostage of a petty official who would use the boy's impairment to boost his own political fortunes. Although depending far too heavily on coincidence, a romantic view of knighthood, and on the cliché of a woman falling in love with her rapist, the story conveys the harsh, brutish life experienced by the propertyless class at the dawn of the Renaissance. The author's afterword explains what little is currently known of erythropoietic porphyria, Adam's extremely rare hereditary disorder.

Slepian, Jan. *The Alfred Summer.* New York: Macmillan, 1980. 119 pp. Reading Level: YA
Disability: Neurological Impairment, Intellectual Impairment, speech impairment

Cerebral palsy has so severely impaired Lester's speech and mobility that he has had little opportunity to make friends. As he explains:

I want to say sure I'm okay, or that's all right, I'm fine. Something like that. Well, if he has an hour or two to spare I'll get it out. I

might in that time be able to tell him what's on my mind. In other
words . . . in other words I have no words. Or none that I can get
out without looking as if I'm strangling.

The lonely youth meets Alfred Burt, a neighbor whose physical condition and retardation upset Lester's fiercely protective mother, who discourages any further contact, insisting her very intelligent son has
nothing to gain from such an association. Both families are at Coney
Island when Lester spots Alfred trapped on some rocks. He manages
to raise an alarm, but the strangers from whom he tries to enlist help
cannot understand him. Fortunately his father arrives and, assisted by
Myron, a teenage neighbor, rescues the hapless boy. In the congenial-
ity which ensues, Myron shares his secret with them—he is building a
real boat. Alfred and Lester are impressed and offer to help. Myron at
first refuses, but reconsiders when Alfred mentions he knows where to
find wood and Lester volunteers the use of his wagon.

Assembling the boat becomes the focus of their summer, and the
bond of friendship grows among the construction crew. They are discovered in the basement by Claire, who is fascinated with what the
boys are fabricating there. She soon becomes the fourth member of this
unlikely quartet, vitalizing the group even more with her restless energy. One day they all picnic at Coney Island. While inspecting some
rental boats, Myron is thunderstruck with the realization that he has
not planned to include oarlocks on his own boat. Wanting to help,
Lester conceives the daring and preposterous idea of stealing a pair for
his friend. Using another picnic outing as a cover, he is able to maneuver Alfred into taking the coveted oarlocks. Overcome with emotion
as he leaves the scene of his crime, Lester falls but is helped to his feet
by a couple who invite the boys to share their lunch. Ex-vaudevillians,
they perform old routines for their appreciative audience. The man's
tracheotomy has destroyed his speech, but this diminishes neither his
enthusiasm for his performance nor his wife's adoration. The boys
return home by subway. Just before their stop, Lester notices that
Alfred has suddenly and obviously become very sick. Lester tries to
recruit assistance from other riders, but they all withdraw from any
contact. Desperate, he manages to drag his now-unconscious friend
out of the train and onto the subway platform, where aid is available.
Alfred is taken to a hospital, where extensive tests reveal he has epilepsy. No indication is given of how much help he can receive from
drugs in controlling his disorder, and for the first time Alfred's mother
is overcome by the problems with which her son must cope. Alfred's
friends are also distressed and decide to postpone the launching of
their boat until their absent companion can participate, but Mrs. Burt

implies she is uncertain when her son will be home again. Claire therefore proposes they hold the launching the next morning and that Alfred's parents attend and report the event to their son. On the way to the beach, the trio attracts considerable attention, and soon a large crowd has gathered to watch the spectacle. Myron takes the boat out on the calm water, where it promptly sinks like a rock. Ignoring the jeers and catcalling of the audience and scarcely believing what is happening, the shocked lad nevertheless raises his arms in a victory salute; the surprised crowd responds to this gesture of indomitability and begins to cheer.

Analysis. Narrated in part by Lester, the story presents a picture of a sensitive, bright, frequently bitter, and self-deprecating youth who nonetheless discovers that "sometimes life just knocks [me] out." His ironic comments are effective in revealing both the pain and resignation with which he manages his disability. Alfred is an open, trusting, and innocent boy who emerges as an admirable and dependable friend. The fiery defensiveness of Lester's mother at first almost seems a cliché, but is later revealed to encompass a more complex relationship. Mrs. Burt's assessment of her son's problems combines realism with wishful thinking. The diagnosis of epilepsy reveals that she is more vulnerable than she had previously appeared; this latest problem strains her coping abilities to their limit. The author's evocation of New York in 1937 is superlative; her characters are complicated and credible; her language is vibrant, witty, and perfectly suited to the subject. Her message—that the winning is in the trying—is offered in the boat episode, echoed in the scene with the ex-vaudevillians, and seen again in the development of the hero.

Slepian, Jan. *Lester's Turn.* New York: Macmillan, 1981. 139 pp. Reading Level: YA
Disability: Neurological Impairment, Intellectual Impairment, Orthopedic Impairment

Since his mother's death, Alfie has been living in a residential hospital for multiply handicapped individuals. Lester is heartbroken when he visits his friend, a boy once curious and full of life who now "sits . . . like a bundle in the Lost and Found." Impulsively, the 16 year old decides to "kidnap" his former companion, but their getaway is stopped by a guard. Mrs. Brenner, the director of the institution, bluntly but compassionately explains to Lester the difficulties involved in caring for Alfie, urging the youth who has cerebral palsy to attend to his own schooling and thus prepare himself for a reasonably secure future. The woman suggests a weekend visit as an alternative to

Lester's plan, which, she reasons, would be beneficial to both her patient and his friend by allowing the youth a more realistic look at the implications of his rash proposal. Unwilling to abandon his original scheme, Lester cannily agrees to the woman's idea as an interim step and then seeks ways to get enough money to support both himself and Alfie in the future.

Their mutual friend, Claire, enlists the help of her talented neighbors in staging a benefit, with the proceeds to go to "The Alfred Fund." The weekend of the concert, Claire's family brings Alfie to their home, but after a day spent with Lester that seems to capture their former happier days, Alfie suddenly becomes sick. The visitor is rushed to the hospital, but his appendix has ruptured and he dies during the night. Lester, inconsolable, returns to the institution to unburden himself to Mrs. Brenner. The guilt-ridden youth confesses that he pretended to himself he was motivated by altruism, but, in truth, he used Alfie to fulfill his own needs. She perceptively responds: "So what's the difference? What's the contradiction? You can use and need love at the same time. You think people are simple like a glass of water? We all take things from one another. What's so terrible about that? We *need* one another!"

Mrs. Brenner again tries to convince Lester to return to school, warning that without an education, he could end up institutionalized too. As the bereaved adolescent leaves, pondering what he has heard, he stops to speak with Charlie, a resident with cerebral palsy who sells tickets and newspapers to visitors. Lester observes: "It was painful for me to see. I wasn't as bad as that, but it was close enough." To his surprise, the man, soon joined by others, expresses his love and admiration for Alfie and reports that it was his intention to make the boy a partner in his business. Lester is astounded. He had thought the man "was a dummy, retarded, way, way different from me. And then, listening to him, I could see that the only real difference between Charlie and me was that I was able to leave and he wasn't. That I had choices and he didn't. Only the wheelchair separated us. Only my determination to never, not ever, be in that wheelchair."

Analysis. This sequel to *The Alfred Summer* deals with complex issues in an original and compelling manner. Lacking its predecessor's cerebral wit and electric joyfulness, it is less a celebration of life's possibilities than a warning of its potential heartbreak. Even when not at the top of her form, Slepian is a writer of considerable power who can create memorable characters and raise haunting questions. In this work, she speaks through the sagacious, pragmatic, yet optimistic Mrs. Brenner, who reminds Lester of the astonishing intricacy and perpetual surprises to be found in human relationships. Disability is seen as a single facet of a person's life whose impact is moderated by determination, hard work, the support of families and friends—and luck.

Small, Mary. *And Alice Did the Walking.* Photog. by Lionel Jensen. Melbourne: Oxford University Press, 1978. unp. Reading Level: MC
Disability: Orthopedic Impairment

Scott, who attends a special school for disabled children, is surprised to find a Shetland pony in the paddock next to his house. He maneuvers his wheelchair close to the fence and sees the animal is covered with a rug with "Alice" on it. Scott offers Alice some bread, but his mother informs him that bread is not good for the tiny animal. He finds, however, that when he goes to the enclosure without food, the pony backs away.

On Saturday, he sees Jody, his new neighbor, playing with two other boys and the animal, but they ignore him. He fantasizes about having a creature like Alice to ride, but such a possibility seems utterly impossible. One weekend, he decides to approach the little creature by tipping himself out of his chair and crawling under the fence wire. He brings some forbidden food, attracting the curious pony, who now seems to tower over him. He is interrupted by Jody, to whom he explains that he cannot walk but adds that someday, if he is able to strengthen his leg muscles, he will be able to get around on crutches. Impetuously, he blurts out his dream of riding a pony. To his surprise, Jody's father and her brother come to his house to invite him to ride the horse. His parents agree, and he is ecstatic with the arrangements, eagerly looking forward to each weekend jaunt. The need for concentrating and maintaining his balance leads to improved muscle tone, but just when he is at the point of mastering some skills, Jody's family leaves for their vacation. When they return, they bring with them a younger, slightly larger pony for Scott. The boy is "pleased and proud . . . to have a pony of his own. Now Dusty would do the walking for him, and that, as far as Scott was concerned, was just about the greatest thing in the world."

Analysis. The homey black-and-white photographs, which include clear images of the hero's braces, wheelchair, and crutches, enhance this simple tale of a child's dream come true. Scott, who has an unspecified orthopedic impairment, has learned how to cope with the curious looks of strangers, has few fears despite his repeated tumbles from his chair, has managed his "leg irons" competently, and is, altogether, a curious, resourceful, resilient, and assertive child. His desire for a horse echoes the wishes of innumerable children his age, although for someone with weak lower extremities like his, the exercise is therapeutic as well as recreational.

Smith, Doris Buchanan. *Up and Over*. New York: Morrow, 1976. 224 pp. Reading Level: YA/MA
Disability: Intellectual Impairment

Their impending high school graduation has intensified feelings of unease about the future among Kim and his friends. As part of the annual spring hijinks, members of the track team vow to shave their heads, but only Kim carries through on this pledge. His friend Sapp, once a runner but now alienated from school, family, and society and heavily into drugs, duplicates this ridiculous act, reducing the other boy's feeling of isolation and making the mockery of schoolmates and anger of his parents easier to bear. Kim gets much pleasure from photography, his athletic achievements, and the comradeship of the loosely structured neighborhood gang, which includes Mitch, a retarded youth. The youth's development has been hampered by a mother who thinks of him as an infant, insisting on special treatment and the avoidance of any conflict. When the neighborhood children wanted him to wait his turn, she yelled at them: "If Mitchell wants to bat, you let him bat. You know he's not normal like the rest of you." She is also reluctant to let him participate in the Special Olympics and prevents him from traveling to national competitions. Motivated by affection and concern, Mitchell's friends try to compensate by avoiding unnecessary special treatment, providing encouragement and information, which they feel he needs. They discuss his sexual feelings and confirm his doctor's lecture to him on the subject, well aware that his mother considers this a forbidden topic.

One of their group, Devo, has become an ardent churchgoer. He is confident Sapp can find salvation through religion and urges Kim to pressure their friend to attend a meeting where an ex-addict will speak. The boy is unenthusiastic, skeptical about Sapp's response, and resentful of the pastor's hypocrisy in not defending Mitch against the derogatory comments of an "important" congregant.

Kim is worried when he discovers that his friend has finally carried out his threat to run away from home, knowing that since "Mitchell was easily confused . . . it would not be difficult for someone to take advantage of him," but the missing adolescent is found in Kim's room. Kim considers taking his friend with him to Atlanta after graduation: "They could get an apartment and Kim could help Mitchell get a job, talk to the employer and explain about Mitch. Mitchell was good at anything that required methodical attention, which was why he was such a good equipment manager." The youth eventually returns home and, with the support of his sister and his friends, asserts himself, demanding a measure of independence. Kim accompanies Mitch to the Special Olympics, where his buddy wins a medal.

To his surprise, Sapp insists they attend the last school social event of the year. Kim is not surprised when his friend disappears but is horrified to see him race across the dance floor, naked except for a ski mask. Although Sapp escapes, the authorities soon discover who the streaker is and threaten to withhold his diploma. The other graduates vigorously protest, and after a confrontation, the principal agrees to a compromise.

Analysis. Smith chronicles the turmoil faced by a youngster in conflict with his parents over his present behavior and future goals, who is distressed at the realization that his friends are growing apart from each other as well as growing older. He needs special consideration and strains the other boys' patience at times—but so does Sapp with his reckless use of drugs, Devo with his religious zealotry, and Waxy with his tiresome infatuation with the girl he left in Texas. Mitch's mother's efforts to overprotect her son are seen as not only unwise but dangerous: Kim is startled to realize he and his friends are guilty of the same behavior for they have been intervening on his behalf in potentially difficult encounters. There are a few problems in the author's treatment of retardation: when Kim, as a child, first asks about his new friend, his mother tells him the boy is sick. "Only much later did Kim learn that the sickness was of the mind rather than the body." References are made to a "mongoloid" child and others who are "grossly" retarded. These lapses are surprising in an otherwise discerning work.

Smith, Lucia B. *A Special Kind of Sister.* Illus. by Chuck Hall. New York: Holt, Rinehart & Winston, 1979. unp. Reading Level: YC *Disability:* Intellectual Impairment

Sarah, seven years old, narrates this brief essay about life with her retarded younger brother. She alludes to Andy's limitations and her family's efforts to love him, accommodate his needs, and help him to develop. The girl admits to feeling resentment as well as affection toward him, distress at the negative reactions of strangers, and anxiety that she too could suddenly become like her brother. Nevertheless, Sarah accepts responsibility for helping Andy with his exercises. She is aware of her need to learn to deal with social rejection and acknowledges that she finds comfort and happiness in her brother's love.

Analysis. The problems of a child with a severely retarded sibling are given abbreviated and superficial treatment in this slight work.

Issues are raised and resolved in a few sentences, and then other topics are abruptly introduced without adequate transitions. The tone is didactic and the writing frequently awkward: After noting Andy's poor health, the heroine observes, "With all that is the matter with him, I could get hurt or sick once in a while." The illustrations are terrible: the central character's appearance is different in every scene; many of the portraits are indistinct; and there is not a single clear picture of Andy, the character who provides the rationale for the text.

Smucker, Barbara. *Runaway to Freedom*. Illus. by Charles Lilly. New York: Harper & Row, 1977. 152 pp. Reading Level: MC/YA
Disability: Orthopedic Impairment

When the Virginia plantation on which Julilly and her mother live is dismantled, the child, along with other slaves, is sold to a ruthless plantation owner. Although terrified at the prospect of never seeing her parent again, the 12-year-old girl nonetheless comforts the younger children bundled into the wagon with her and offers what assistance she can to the chained men walking behind the vehicle on the trip to their new home in Mississippi. There she meets Liza, a girl her age who bears the scars of the overseer's whip on her malformed back. Unable to reach the high bolls of cotton they must pick, Liza is grateful to Julilly for doing this work for her. When an abolitionist visits the plantation, the two girls and two men plot an escape to Canada. But after traveling several days, the men are captured, and the girls are left to complete the dangerous journey alone. Traveling north becomes increasingly difficult for Liza, whose injuries cause her considerable pain and push her to the brink of exhaustion. With the help of both blacks and whites, the youngsters are passed along via the stations of the Underground Railroad, narrowly missing being apprehended several times. At last they reach Canada, where they are greeted by Lester, the original leader of their group, who managed to escape from the slave catchers. Julilly is ecstatic when she discovers her mother, also fled from bondage, living safely in the same border town.

Analysis. In this exciting work of historical fiction, the nightmare of slavery and the dream of freedom are made real and immediate to young readers. A strong sense of time and place, the intermixing of actual historical figures and fictional characters, and the vivid descriptions, enriched by authentic details, are successfully united. Only the final chapter is seriously flawed as Julilly is reunited with her mother and fellow escapee in a forced and melodramatic conclusion. Liza's disability, caused by a vicious beating after her unsuccessful escape, is realistically treated. Julilly's compassionate response contrasts with the overseer's sadistic one, highlighting the admirable qualities of the compassionate girl and the brutality of the representative of the slaveholders. Liza's disability causes realistic problems. Julilly's responses to these are depicted as acts of friendship, not of pity. Julilly is clearly the leader but is not seen as heroic at Liza's expense. Although the difference in size of the two girls is emphasized many times in the text, the final illustrations show the heroines of comparable height.

Snell, Nigel. *Peter Gets a Hearing Aid.* Illus. by author. London: Hamish Hamilton, 1979. unp. Reading Level: YC
Disability: Auditory Impairment

Peter's inability to hear well causes many problems at home and at school. Since he cannot monitor his own voice, his communication problems are severe, and Peter becomes disheartened by the insensitive reactions of the other children. When the youngster is taken again to the clinic for an otological and audiometric examination, he is told he will soon receive a hearing aid, which will assist in resolving some of his difficulties. The new appliance, worn behind his ear, makes a big difference in his life.

Analysis. Snell's engaging illustrations depict a young boy, at first overwhelmed by his inability to communicate, then later overjoyed at the improvement made possible by his hearing aid. Illustrations that provide simple but accurate information about the evaluation process and the soundproof room where such examinations are done help to diminish fears a child might harbor about such diagnostic settings or procedures. The charming picture book portrays an ordinary boy who has a not-so-ordinary problem that is satisfactorily resolved.

Snyder, Anne. *Goodbye, Paper Doll.* New York: New American Library, 1980. 155 pp. Reading Level: YA
Disability: Emotional Dysfunction

On the surface, Rosemary Northon's life appears ideal, but there is tension between her parents, and the teenager feels ugly, awkward, lonely, and unfulfilled. She decides that her essential problem is obesity and is determined to control at least some portion of her life by dieting. Jason, an attractive, intelligent, sensitive senior, beomes interested in her, but she is alarmed by his attentions and her own ambivalent attitudes about sex. The youth takes her to meet his grandmother at their estate, and the two vastly dissimilar women form an immediate bond.

Rosemary quarrels with Trudy, her only girl friend, exchanging angry words about each other's weight. Later, Jason prepares dinner for

Rosemary, but when he tries to become intimate, affectionately calling her a dumpling, she recoils from him in horror and forces herself to regurgitate. In the meantime, Mrs. Northon notices her daughter's weight loss and makes an appointment for her with their family physician. Dr. Feinstein immediately recognizes his patient's disorder and tries, albeit clumsily, to discuss reasons for her behavior, warning about the potentially catastrophic results of self-starvation. However, the 17 year old is very proud of her weight of 91 pounds and, heartened by her dramatic success, accelerates her regimen for losing even more weight. Rosemary increases the number and strenuousness of her exercises, disciplines herself to maintain some form of constant motion, skips meals, or after the binges that she occasionally allows herself, forces herself to vomit.

By chance, she sees her father in the company of an attractive young woman, and the strife and discord at home begin to make sense. When she is obliged to return to the doctor, he is alarmed at her emaciated body and carefully explains the ramifications of anorexia nervosa to her. Rosemary soon exhibits the classical symptoms of the condition—loss of scalp hair and concomitant growth of body hair, headaches, soreness at bone ends—but she disciplines herself to ignore these danger signals, expending a great deal of energy to further regiment her life. Soon the ploys and ritualistic devices she uses to disguise her drastically lowered caloric intake become apparent to others. One day she collapses, and her physician arranges for her hospitalization, informing the weakened girl that a psychiatrist will be called in on her case. The therapist challenges his patient's conceptions about herself, ultimately breaking through the adolescent's defenses.

Jason comes to see her, sharing his delight in the imminent visit of his father, a world-renowned photojournalist who is rarely able to be with his adoring son. Unfortunately, Rosemary misunderstands the youth's motives, and they argue. Trudy's visit is more satisfactory, and the estranged girls are happily reconciled. After the teenager gains some weight and some insight about her condition, she is allowed to leave the hospital. She immediately goes to see Jason and discovers that he is acutely depressed following the news about the sudden violent death of his father. She apologizes to the bereaved youth for her irrational, selfish behavior, offers him her understanding, and consoles him with some food.

Analysis. Although there is some information about the psychological motivations prompting anorexic behavior and a brief glimpse at the physical treatment as well as the necessity for patient and family counseling, this problem novel offers only the most superficial understanding of the disorder. The author communicates her obvious awareness of the potentially fatal nature of anorexia nervosa but repeatedly describes her emaciated, scarecrowlike heroine as extraordinarily attractive, thus inadvertently reinforcing the perception of excessive thinness as desirable! Even though Rosemary has never displayed any particularly admirable traits, Jason becomes infatuated with her; her employer finds her sexually irresistible; and when she is hospitalized with only 90 pounds on her five-foot-six-inch frame, her doctor introduces her to the psychiatrist by announcing "this beautiful child is Rosemary."

Snyder, Zilpha Keatley. *Heirs of Darkness.* New York: Atheneum, 1978. 248 pp. Reading Level: MA
Disability: Emotional Dysfunction, Intellectual Impairment, orthopedic impairment, cosmetic impairment, neurological impairment

After her husband's death, Beth is barely able to support her young son, Paul. The widow is surprised to discover that her in-laws, whom she had been told were dead, are still living and want her and Paul to join them. With relief and some trepidation, Beth accepts their offer and travels with her son to an isolated, rambling farmhouse dominated by Eva, her husband's aunt. Eva has two sons: Carl, who is severely retarded and Miles, who is a vicious, brutal tyrant. Beth is shocked when she meets Carl for she "had never been good with the mentally deficient, never knew how to separate her response from . . . pity and revulsion." She finds the young man's uncanny resemblance to Jon, her deceased husband, a cruel mockery. Carl's father, a drunkard who limps as the result of an accident; a housekeeper with a cleft lip who is slavishly devoted to Eva; Jon's mother, Rachel, a meek, almost hysterically frightened woman; and Margaret, Paul's senile great grandmother, round out the cast of characters.

Paul's behavior, much absorbed with fantasy characters, becomes increasingly more so in this bizarre household in which he seems to be influenced by his dead grandfather's evil presence. His mother, filled with apprehensiveness, tries to deny the dangers she senses from both human and spectral sources. She becomes panicky upon learning that Carl is the incestuous progeny of Eva and her brother and that Beth's husband's death had been caused by his own family. After being attacked twice by Miles and seeing her son wooed from her by the wicked Eva, Beth belatedly realizes she must leave. Miles says he will help her, but he is killed in an accident and immediately thereafter she is imprisoned in the wing of the house where Jon's father's ghost resides. With help, Eva ties and gags her and sends Paul into the room with a gun to shoot his mother. The robotlike Rachel, galvanized into action by this dreadful scheme, frees Beth and allows her to escape. She returns home where she is comforted by a former friend and lover and soon sees evidence that Paul's behavior is returning to normal.

Analysis. As in many semioccult novels, the story can only proceed when abetted by the phenomenal obtuseness of a central character—in this case, the stupid and marvelously dense Beth. Although avoiding graphic descriptions, the author includes several incidents and allusions to brutal and aberrant sexual encounters. Only the heroine's boundless passivity allows Miles to escape being branded a rapist. Disability is likewise exploited: Eva's wickedness appears to derive from her pathological obsessiveness through which she controls other members of the household; Margaret's dysfunction is partially attributable to age, but equally to the family "curse"; Carl's impairment is arbitrarily blamed on his incestuous origins; the housekeeper's scarred face seems to account for her ties to this strange family.

This novel has nothing to recommend it. It is tedious, illogical, poorly developed, and features one of the most insipid heroines in contemporary juvenile fiction.

Southall, Ivan. *The Golden Goose.* New York: Greenwillow, 1981. 180 pp. Reading Level: YA
Disability: Intellectual Impairment; also orthopedic impairment

In this continuation of *King of the Sticks,* Preacher Tom, hungry for gold, drags 13-year-old Custard across the Australian desert, searching for the precious ore. The boy insists he has no special power to divine its presence, but his protests are ignored. Rumors of Custard's supposed talent race through the countryside, and the two travelers are quickly pursued by a motley assortment of renegades, drifters, and easy-money prospectors, all hoping to get their hands on the boy. Rebecca, his mother, sets out to locate him too, leaving her elder son and disabled daughter at home.

The former minister and his victim are soon tracked down by the gold seekers, and in the ensuing fray, the apostate is fatally shot. Custard joyfully greets Tom's sons, even though they are the ones responsible for all his woes. The boy, assisting at Tom's hasty burial, recognizes the stone on the man's grave to be gold. The cursory ceremonies soon dispensed with, Tom's progeny begin shouting out their plans for the wealth they expect will soon be theirs. Drowning out their noise is "something like a cattle stampede," as wild men, inflamed with gold fever, descend upon them like an invading army, grabbing and digging. Into this frenzy rides Rebecca, accompanied by two lawmen, who rescues her son. The adolescent first heads for a large lump of gold to take home but changes his mind, leaving, empty-handed, with his mother.

Analysis. Southall continues his series with an uneasy combination of an outlandish tall tale and a partly comic, partly bitter commentary on human foolishness and greed. Custard's mental limitations have been demonstrated, but here he plays more the classical *naif*— uncomplicated and untouched by the villainy that surrounds him.

Southall, Ivan. *King of the Sticks.* New York: Greenwillow, 1979. 177 pp. Reading Level: YA
Disability: Intellectual Impairment, Orthopedic Impairment

Ever since her husband's death, Rebecca has lived with her older son, Seth, her 15-year-old daughter, Bella, and her youngest child, Cuthbert (known as Custard), trying to deflect greedy suitors who covet her humble cabin and her acres of farmland. When Seth goes off on a routine market trip, ruffians descend on the widow's property, intending to kidnap Custard. The slow-thinking child manages to alert his mother and hold off one rowdy with his whip while his disabled sister retreats to the safety of their cabin. The family members barricade themselves inside, perplexed at this totally unexpected attack. Bella wonders:

> How tall would she stand if the fist of some roughneck started crashing at the door or beating at the shutter? What could anyone do, whose legs were props for swinging on? Whose legs went nowhere unless sticks were there to balance them? Who couldn't run and couldn't hide and couldn't fight with sound and fury like Mum in a fever?

When the hooligans demand that Custard be turned over to them, Rebecca is as furious as she is astonished that anyone would want her seeemingly incompetent child. When they storm the house, she fires at them with her rifle and Bella attacks with her grandfather's sword, but they are overpowered, trussed up, and left helpless, while the gang flees with their victim. The crew is as inept as it is misguided: they explain to the child that he has been taken because of his reputed power to divine hidden sources of gold. Custard is astonished at this news but is, on the other hand, pleased to learn that he is to be sixth in command of this ragtag band of five kidnappers. Their plans for exploiting Custard's alleged talents are interrupted by Preacher Tom, father of four and uncle to the fifth thief, who roundly condemns the men for their villainy, trounces his oldest, and then takes off with the lad. As the two leave, the erstwhile preacher announces that he has abandoned his religious calling and will henceforth be known as Prospector Tom.

Analysis. This first book of a projected trilogy introduces an unusual cast of characters for purposes that are unpredictable, in a style that is lively and original but confusing, creating scenes of extreme tension, which are nonetheless silly. Although no permanent harm is done, the attack on the family is brutal and frightening, while subsequent events in the desert are pure slapstick. Custard is depicted as a classical, simple innocent, but his captors are great fools and Preacher Tom is a familiar charlatan. Bella is portrayed as a courageous adolescent, frustrated by her useless legs and angered by her mother's presumption of her helplessness. The narration of *King of the Sticks* seems more appropriate to an oral format than a written one, exhibiting strong rhythms, extravagant, repetitive constructions, and elements more at home in legends and ballads than in contemporary fiction.

> Spence, Eleanor. *The Devil Hole.* Originally published in Great Britain in 1976 as *The October Child.* New York: Lothrop, Lee & Shepard, 1977, 215 pp. Reading Level: YA
> *Disability:* Emotional Dysfunction; also special health problems

The Mariner family lives a pleasant, low-key life on the coast of Australia, where the father runs a small shop-cum-post office. Their tranquility is interrupted by the birth of Carl, the fourth child, whose slow development, irrational behavior, and uncontrollable rages disrupt every aspect of the family's existence. The only sibling Carl responds to is 13-year-old Douglas, whose outstanding singing voice has a soothing effect on his younger brother. No longer bothered by his childhood asthma, the boy nonetheless remains shy and uncertain of himself. After Carl is tested, the Mariners move to Sydney, where the baby, now three, can receive specialized education. Douglas is admitted to a music school, gaining great pleasure from his studies and his new friends. One of his music teachers has an acquaintance who plans to work in Carl's school. She interprets the child's autistic behavior to the older boy, helping him gain insight into his brother's needs and allowing him to shed his feelings of guilt.

Analysis. Spence accurately and compassionately describes the potentially devastating impact an autistic child may have upon even a loving and dedicated family. The initial confusion of the boy's disorder with mental retardation, the unhelpful reaction of misguided neighbors, a sibling's desperate hope that a faith healer might help where educators and doctors have failed, are all plausible situations. Characters are well drawn, and each family member's manner of coping with Carl's aberrant and disturbing behavior is convincing. However, the abrupt and contrived upbeat ending, the ambiguous title, and such awkward phrasing as, "It had been a pleasant and short-lived dream, to have Tessa around occasionally to share the burden of Carl's presence—he should have know [sic] that it could never eventuate," are serious flaws.

Spencer, Zane, and Jay Leech. *Cry of the Wolf*. Philadelphia: Westminster, 1977. 144 pp. Reading Level: YA
Disability: Emotional Dysfunction, auditory impairment

Sixteen-year-old Jim Tyler was at the wheel the night the family truck flipped over, killing his father. After weeks in the hospital, depressed and discouraged, he returns home in a wheelchair. Although his doctor insists that there is no medical reason for Jim's lack of mobility, the boy's legs fail to support him. He has physical therapy weekly at the hospital, supplemented at home by his mother's efforts. As Mrs. Tyler assumes responsibility for much of the heavy physical labor on the ranch, Aunt Martha takes over many domestic chores. After the physician implies that Jim is a quitter, Monty, the ranchhand, calls him a coward, and his guilt over his mother's obvious weariness overwhelms him, Jim decides he must contribute to the general good. He cries out to the vehicle he used to ride: "No . . . I haven't given up. I'll prove it to you. I'll drive you, tractor. . . . I'll show you." He forces his wheelchair over the uneven ground; one wheel breaks a board covering an old abandoned well, and the boy is pitched into the freezing water. He yells for help, but knows "Aunt Martha would never be able to hear him, as deaf as she was." Hours later, he is rescued by Monty, an event that marks a turning point for the boy.

After Jim is given responsibility for keeping the ranch's financial records in order, he discovers the dire straits they are in. Although their future is at stake, no one suggests selling their prize horse, Lady Kate, now in foal. Trouble arrives with the news that a big winter storm is approaching, which will leave their herds exposed to murderously low temperatures, insufficient feed, and attack from a pack of famished and emboldened wolves. Monty bravely goes out into the blizzard in a desperate attempt to save the cattle. Jim and his mother take a pickup truck to a high ridge and light flares to guide the exhausted hand home, correctly assuming that the low visibility could cause Monty to lose direction and possibly freeze in the unheated tractor.

The local ranchers prepare to track and destroy the wolves. The youth is excluded for "this was a job for men who were whole, for men who had legs. . . . He wasn't a man. He wasn't even half a man. He was a cripple." The night of the hunt, Jim is awakened by the frantic sounds made by Lady Kate. The desperate youth grabs his gun, scrambles into his wheelchair, and rushes outdoors, afraid he may be powerless to save the threatened horse. He shoots one wolf, Lady Kate kicks another to death, and he bludgeons the third with the empty rifle stock as the predator tries to attack the newborn foal. Once both animals are safe, Jim becomes "consciously aware for the first time that he . . . was standing." Astonished, he observes: "I can stand. I can walk. I can run." The fully recovered youth and the two rescued horses return in triumph to the house.

Analysis. The major characters, quite familiar to fans of Western movies, include: the determined, endlessly patient, plucky mom, going it alone; the trusty, loyal ranchhand, once a drifter but now a part of the family; the seemingly simple but wise old aunt; and the youthful hero who, although apparently self-defeated, rises, literally, to his "manhood" during a crisis. Martha's impairment has two modest functions in the story: it provides the rationale for the interlude in the well, where Jim has time for introspection, and it is used as a model for the boy in which another member of the family makes a contribution unhampered by her disability. Neither the speed, the completeness, nor the convenience of Jim's cure are credible. The linking of masculinity to the state of able-bodiedness is a particularly unfortunate segment of this simplistic, easy-to-read novel.

Stanek, Muriel. *Growl When You Say R.* Illus. by Phil Smith. Chicago: Whitman, 1979. unp. Reading Level: YC
Disability: Speech Impairment

Robbie, intimidated by the reception his immature speech receives in his new school, tries without success to convince his mother that he is too ill to return. The unhappy boy avoids contact with other students so they will not have any opportunity to make fun of him. When he is taunted, he turns on his persecutor, thereby gaining sympathy from the onlookers. That night Robbie's teacher consults with his mother, recommending placement in a speech correction class. To his surprise, the class is fun. He discovers ways to practice the "r" sound by pretending to be a fire engine siren or a growling tiger. In the spring, Robbie's class visits the zoo, where the youngster and several of his pals get separated from the others. They locate the lost and found booth, where Robbie displays his self-confidence and hard-won skills by speaking clearly into a microphone that broadcasts his message over a loudspeaker system. His worried teacher hears him and arrives to claim her missing charges, publicly announcing her pride in the now articulate youngster.

Analysis. In this quasi-fictional effort, Stanek provides a pleasant, although simple view of remediation procedures for an articulation disorder. Readers will be able to see through the hero's pathetic defenses against ridicule and how these sorely affect his behavior. Detracting from the book are the poor, unattractive, slipshod illustrations, in which the characters look much older than the first-graders the text describes.

Steele, William O. *The Magic Amulet.* New York: Harcourt Brace Jovanovich, 1979. 114 pp. Reading Level: MC
Disability: Orthopedic Impairment, cosmetic impairment

Survival of the tribe is the paramount concern of every leader, so when Tragg is injured by a saber-toothed tiger, his father makes the difficult but inevitable decision to abandon his son. All alone and possessing only his flint-pointed spear and a bone bracelet presumed to have supernatural powers, the wounded youngster is nonetheless determined to survive. He locates a hot spring in which he soaks his infected foot, finding some relief from the pain and simultaneously initiating the healing process. The muscle damage is extensive, and although he recovers, Tragg is left with a "rolling limp." Despite his youth, he survives the hazards of wilderness life alone, including an attack by a vicious wolf.

The boy comes upon a small band of hunters, but before he can decide whether to approach them, he is spotted, then captured. Their leader, Odak, has "a bright-red scar [which] curved upward from a corner of [his] mouth and froze forever a false lopsided smile on his face." The shaman is summoned and, fearing the power of the boy's amulet, orders the stranger killed. The man's word is challenged, and at a ceremony to decide his fate, "a carved wooden figure with one eye, one leg and one arm" is used. The youth is spared, but he is treated little better than a slave. Game is scarce, and when Tragg offers to lead the group to the hot springs area for better hunting, they follow him, convinced the magical properties of the talisman will guide them. They are not disappointed, and Tragg's status radically changes as he is elevated to the position of one who can contribute to the general welfare. Odak resents this challenge to his authority and becomes Tragg's enemy. Under the man's bullying and incompetent rule, the hunters set off to a spot near a glacier where every winter they find game. On this trek, Tragg survives many dangers, including deliberate attempts on his life. He takes part in the mammoth hunt in which the

huge beasts are stampeded to their deaths over the edge of the precipice. In the confusion of the moment, someone crashes into him and
he falls over the edge of the cliff "into the mass of thrashing animals."
Miraculously, the terrified lad lands on the back of a still living creature, which extricates itself from the dying herd. It lumbers to safety
with the astonished, thankful youth on its back. As Tragg drops safely
to the ground, the onlookers "came running to meet him with cries of
happiness and praise—and with a kind of awe. Here was Tragg, a
special creature, owner of a powerful amulet, blessed with unbelievable luck, survivor of all terrors, rider of a mammoth."

Analysis. The Magic Amulet is neither grandiose enough to seem
mythic nor credible enough to be accepted as realistic fiction. The
hero's close calls are excessive: they include escaping from a tiger and a
wolf, quicksand, a charging mammoth, a spear attack, a kidnapping,
the negative decision of a tribal leader, and finally, a stampede of wild
beasts that climaxes in a chaotic plunge over a cliff. The attitudes displayed toward disabled characters are inconsistent: Odak alludes to the
special powers held by a "crippled shaman," but Tragg's disability has
a disquieting effect on his would-be persecutors. Odak's own severe
scarring is ignored, and the boy's limp is equally unimportant once he
has proved his value to the group.

Stern, Cecily. *A Different Kind of Gold.* Illus. by Ruth Sanderson.
New York: Harper & Row, 1981. 123 pp. Reading Level: MC
Disability: Emotional Dysfuntion

Their home in the Alaskan wilderness offers continuing satisfactions to the Leifson family. Nine-year-old Cara and Bart, one of her
two older brothers, find special pleasure in exploring the countless
wonders of the remote area. Only Eric, the other brother, is dissatisfied
and restless. Seeking isolation, he has moved to a nearby cabin, from
which he rarely emerges. Despondent and increasingly withdrawn, he
avoids others, stares off into space, and eschews those contacts with
the natural world that enrich the lives of his siblings. When Cara's
friend refers to Eric as "crazy," his loyal sister says: "I don't know . . .
what's wrong with him. I just know he's very unhappy. More miserable than you can possibly imagine." She ponders the possibility that
perhaps "the best thing to do was to give Eric the privacy he demanded and just wait and hope. . . . It seemed impossible that anyone
could stay depressed in a place as beautiful as this."

When an injured hawk is temporarily caged, the once apathetic
youth becomes agitated, insisting they cannot delay the bird's release
for any reason whatsoever. The young man sees a parallel between the

creature's captive state and the situation he expects will be forced upon him:

> Sometimes I feel as though I just can't function on that everyday level. But if that happens to a person, and you let it show, they take away your control over your life. They put you in a hospital or somewhere and keep you full of drugs so that you feel calm all the time. And they take care of things for you until they've trained you to think the way they do. When they let you out, you're just like everybody else. . . . I won't let that happen to me. . . . I'd kill myself first.

The depressed youth begins to allow some increased contact with his family. Soon after, he is able to describe the sense of powerlessness to his sister that led to his departure from school, his feelings of vulnerability, and his growing ambition to be a writer. In the meantime, a neighbor has informed the Leifsons that some land in their community is being sold to developers for a resort. Cara's parents are appalled, determined that if the project goes through they will move. Eric's isolation is penetrated by this threat to the fragile environment, and he is energized by the crisis. He suggests a cooperative of concerned individuals be formed to purchase the land. His proposal is acted upon, but the group, lacking a final contributor, seems destined to fail. At the last moment, an eccentric, semirecluse joins the consortium, deeding his share to Cara. The girl is surprised at this wholly unexpected generosity, but is delighted that her connection to the land and to a way of life she treasures will be sustained.

Analysis. Stern delivers a low-key, sympathetic depiction of an intense, seriously troubled youth who works through his sense of futility and despair with the help of loving, supportive parents and family and an open, liberating environment. His initiative in recommending a cooperative endeavor is somewhat surprising, but some prior moves away from total withdrawal increase the credibility of the act. The fairy godfather resolution diminishes the story's power, and the pacing is leisurely, demanding only modest reader commitment. Sanderson's naturalistic black-and-white drawings nicely complement the author's affectionate portrayal of a maturing child, her attempts at understanding her brother's behavior, and her intimate relationship with nature in many of its raw but achingly beautiful forms.

Stewart, A. C. *Silas and Con.* New York: Atheneum, 1977. 120 pp.
Reading Level: MC
Disability: Orthopedic Impairment, Cosmetic Impairment; also emotional dysfunction

When ten-year-old Silas is abandoned by his abusive parents, he pragmatically sets off with a stray dog, Con, and a stuffed monkey to find some alternative living arrangement. His street savvy is of little use in the Scottish countryside, and the child comes close to starving. His first encounter is with a tinker woman, whose irrational ravings terrify him. She forces him to spend the night in her tent, but at dawn he breaks away while she is logy with sleep. A farmer who needs another hand due to the inability of his pregnant wife to manage her chores then takes the wanderer in. Silas works conscientiously for his keep and, through his new association with animals, learns to care for other creatures, experiencing a sense of responsibility and a feeling of love for the first time. When the farmer decides he must market a cow whose calf was stillborn, Silas determines to leave the man he judges to be a hypocrite. With Con, the heifer, some chicks, and a rescued kitten, the youth leads his caravan toward the sea, where he hopes to find a haven. At low tide, they cross to an island deserted except for a man whose appearance fills the traveler with boundless fear:

> He was tall, a big man; on his head a great scar ran back and where it vanished into his thick, dark hair the hair grew white. He had only one eye, the eye on the side of the scar was gone and the face so disfigured no decent glass eye to hide the disfigurement could ever have found a place; nor had he a proper ear, just a fold against his head. The hand that gripped the stick had only two fingers, and it was not a stick, it was a crutch—the man had no legs below the knee; the other hand, spread wide on a boulder, was broad and powerful.

The man welcomes him, offering to trade shelter for some fresh milk and later board and lodging for help with the chores. He questions the boy about his life and in return reveals the source of his injuries, adding: "I thought I could go back . . . start life again as before—or as nearly as before as possible." When Silas asks why this could not be, he is told:

> It was the unconscious cruelty—and the unintentional cruelty of people who really meant to be kind—that set me for ever apart . . . the people in buses or trains, at the cinema, who, when they looked at me found an excuse to move away or stayed strained and distressed, too kind to go as they long to; the kindly people who went out of their way to help when I could have managed perfectly well on my own. It kept my disabilities forever before me: I realized I would never escape them there amongst men and so I came here where the birds and the fish and wild

things do not notice or care; man is just another animal to them, what matter if he has one foot or two, two eyes or one?

Silas abandons his plan to leave when the supply boat next arrives, preferring to stay with an adult whose kindness sets him apart from all the others the child has ever known.

Analysis. Rather than a fully realized story, *Silas and Con* seems a compilation of elements that are never developed into a cohesive work. There are hints that the stuffed monkey has supernatural powers: he seems to take a malicious delight in the misfortunes of others and may even be responsible for some calamities, but his role is abruptly discontinued just before the climax. The islander calls his youthful visitor "Moses" and sprinkles his speech with biblical allusions. The child adopts the name "Andrew," also suggested by his mentor, who remarks, "You promise well as a fisherman." Such references to the Old and New Testaments are both forced and frivolous, promising a weight and meaning to events that are not forthcoming. The disfigurements ascribed to the man seem excessive, and his accomplishments would require phenomenal agility—although legless, the man walks with his crutches through sand.

Stone, Nancy Y. *Dune Shadow.* Boston: Houghton Mifflin, 1980. 178 pp. Reading level: MC/YA
Disability: Neurological Impairment

Serena's parents have left their home in a small Michigan lakeside town to seek work elsewhere. After their departure, the sand dunes continue sweeping into the little community, driving more and more residents from their houses. The 13-year-old's brother, feeling his absent parents are unaware of the immediacy of the impending tragedy, leaves to locate them, promising to return with help for his grandmother and sister. All the other townspeople hastily depart, but the old woman stubbornly refuses to budge from the home she has known. Soon the two are the only ones remaining in the town except for Jody, a child left behind in the confusion of her family's precipitous exodus. Granny's frequent senile episodes frighten Serena, and when the old woman is injured in the collapse of a part of their house, the youngster realizes that she must assume responsibility for their survival and welfare.

The trio moves to the bank, the structure least damaged by the ever-encroaching sand. Food stocks diminish, and hunger becomes their constant companion. Desperate, Serena tries to catch fish with a makeshift fishing pole, and, although she is only moderately successful in her effort, her observation of the buildup of ice on the lake suggests a means of escape. After studying an old map, she decides that, as soon as the temperature drops sufficiently, the two girls will haul the grandmother on their sled down the frozen waterway to a nearby town, from which they may find a way to be reunited with their families. Cold, hungry, but determined, they begin the dangerous journey.

Analysis. This unusual story seems more focused on the awesome power of the juggernaut of sand than on the characters affected by it. The abandonment of the senile woman and the children by family and townsfolk alike seems farfetched—more a fictional convenience than a credible possibility. The old woman's aberrant episodes and the aftermath of her injury, while aptly portrayed, are also transparent devices to increase pressure on the young heroine while they intensify the drama. The result is a work that is only intermittently involving.

Sudbery, Rodie. *The Silk and the Skin.* London: Andre Deutsch, 1976. 144 pp. Reading Level: MC/YA
Disability: Intellectual Impairment

Guy is unhappy that his seven-year-old retarded brother will soon be starting school. He protests to his father that the boy might not like being there, but "what he really meant was that the other children might not like Simon. They would think he was funny. Guy didn't want to have a brother who was laughed at by everybody." The older boy has been a loner, rejected by the gang that dominates his class and unwilling to align himself with the two other outsiders. To his surprise, he is suddenly invited to join the group of rowdies. His initiation involves trying to call forth the spirit of a magician buried in the church cemetery, but his efforts are no more successful than the others. His search through the parish records, ostensibly for a school assignment, reveals the former dwelling place of the sorcerer. A hunt through his attic turns up a book that describes a spell to conjure up a creature that "will do [their] bidding." The boys, more bluff than bravery, are reluctant to tempt unknown forces and persuade Guy to use his brother as their cat's-paw. Simon, eager to participate, recites the charm, reaches into the urn over the conjuror's grave, and pulls out a bat. Some gang members immediately order the bat to exact revenge on those villagers they feel have wronged them. The creature follows their orders but in an unexpected way, causing considerable havoc. When one youngster threatens Simon, all quickly learn that the bat is his special protector. The child is emboldened by his new status, becoming smug and even callous toward his old friends. The animal's escapades become increasingly dangerous, but not until Simon's beloved housekeeper is injured trying to escape from it does he agree to its destruction. The conversion formula is discovered, and the bat is transformed into the harmless silk and hide from which it was created. When the gang learns that Simon is again vulnerable, some want to retaliate against him for their humiliation, but others help Guy defuse their anger, and the boys part amicably.

Analysis. This tightly woven tale of the supernatural offers excitement, suspense, well-developed characters, and more thought-provoking themes than are usually found in this genre. The depiction of Simon is convincing: he is stubborn, slow learning, loving, appealing, yet capable of craftiness. His character changes when he possesses powers beyond his ability to manage, but his innocence returns when he forsakes the magic, a convention often found in this type of story. Although a surprising choice for this role, the impaired boy's characterization is logical, credible, and nonexploitive.

Sutcliff, Rosemary. *Blood Feud.* New York: Dutton, 1976. 144 pp.
Reading Level: YA
Disability: Orthopedic Impairment; also visual impairment, auditory impairment

Jestyn is bought in the Dublin slave market by Thormod, a Danish Viking, and soon after proves his worth by defending his master from some cutthroats. Acknowledging his debt, Thormod frees the young man, and they become close companions. The killing of Thormod's father results in a blood feud between the murderers and the dead man's avengers. A blind harper sings about "two brothers against two brothers who will not turn back before all is finished." Thormod admonishes Jestyn: "Never forget what blind Thorn says. The eyes of his body do not see as other men see, but he has another kind of seeing." The two friends nick their wrists and intermingle their blood, symbolically becoming brothers and, following their predestined paths, set off for Constantinople to find their enemies. One of the murderers is killed in Kiev, but before Anders, the remaining brother, and Jestyn undertake combat, the khan insists their grudge be postponed so that he can be served. The Viking contingent is brave in battle and soon becomes part of Emperor Basil's barbarian guard.

Jestyn, on one assignment, pulls a royal hunting cheetah away from a girl's pet gazelle. He is too late to save the injured creature but rescues its unborn fawn, which he gives to Alexia, its grateful owner. The guard is ordered to Thrace to hunt Bulgars, where, in the midst of a bloody battle, Anders is able to ambush and slay Thormod and realize half of the prophet's forecast. Jestyn's leg is crushed, and after the festering wound heals and his fever subsides, he leaves his post, for there is "no room in the . . . Guard for a man with a smashed knee who must swing one leg stiff as a broomstick to the end of his days." The ex-soldier searches out Alexia, whose father, a physician, employs Jestyn as a helper. He is led into a trap by Anders, who is so weak that he collapses before either man is injured further. Jestyn, now committed to life, not death, tries unsuccessfully to save his erstwhile enemy. With the death of Anders, the bondage imposed by the feud is over and Jestyn is able to accept the physician's offer to learn his art and become a healer.

Analysis. Blood and gore suffuse the pages of this Viking adventure tale of friendship and enmity, love and hate, death and rebirth. Given the time and setting, the frequent allusions to disability are not unexpected—Hakon, who has only one eye, a farmhand who cannot hear, and others. Deliberate maiming was not uncommon at that time, and references to the blinding of survivors of a particular battle has historical validity. Jestyn's wound, described in some detail, allows him to move from a role of mercenary soldier to that of healer. Common stereotypes are found here, notably the musician who cannot see his harp but can see the future and Jestyn's observation about the farm woman's deafness: "I have noticed the same thing about some other deaf people, that they can hear none so ill when they want to." Sutcliff's writing is well researched and literate, vividly evoking a violent and turbulent time.

Ter Haar, Jaap. *The World of Ben Lighthart.* Trans. by Martha Mearns. New York: Delacorte, 1977. 123 pp. Reading Level: MC/ YA
Disability: Visual Impairment, cosmetic impairment, general health problems

When Ben regains consciousness in the hospital, he does not realize at first that he has been blinded as a result of falling "with his head on the sharp rake carried by a gardener who was passing on a motorbike." The boy's painful recovery is accompanied by fears for his future, only partially balanced by assurances from his parents that their shaky marriage will remain intact and has even been bolstered by the circumstances they all must now face. Nurse Win has been able to guide Ben toward a rational, serene acceptance of the consequences of his accident. The woman's personal trauma has presumably made her sensitive to her patients' distress: "The right half of my face was burned when I was fifteen. . . . I look very unattractive you know," she reports. The stalwart nurse insists: "My brown leather cheek is no great tragedy. It's a small tragedy, like millions of others in the world."

When the youth improves sufficiently, he is transferred to a ward where the camaraderie of the other invalids sustains him. One, a psychology student, is particularly supportive. After Ben discovers the young man is near death, their conversations about priorities and the meaning of life take on heightened poignancy. Upon returning home, Ben finds his friends, family, and neighbors have established a new relationship with him, and he begins to think about how his ambitions and interests must be reevaluated because of his vision loss: "As the other boys went on playing, he directed his life from all that is physical and visible to all that is spiritual and essential in human existence."

His parents deliberately avoid overprotecting their son, and his mother embarks on a campaign to teach him braille and touch-typing. Although the tutoring Ben has received from a friend and his progress in achieving independence are notable, the faculty at his school votes against readmitting the lad. At times he yields to despair for he "was still too young to realize that the way to the stars is always through darkness." A visit to an institute for blind youngsters convinces his parents that the skills their son must develop are too complex and extensive to learn without instruction from highly trained professionals. Ben concurs for "he saw the way to the future ahead of him," and as he moves to the residential school, "he took the first steps along it as he walked into his second home."

Analysis. Although there are some scenes in this work that deal effectively with the emotional trauma attendant upon adventitious blindness, the absurdity of the events and the fatuousness of their interpretation render this effort unacceptable. In addition to the many grammatical lapses, the story is replete with literary clichés, such as the name "Lighthart" for the brave, blind boy, the name "Win" for a nurse who urges the hero to struggle and win his battle for independence, a watch given to Ben by a dying young man whose time has run out. Among the seemingly endless supply of platitudes, those asserting that loss of sight can be a boon are the most ludicrous: Ben is advised that "our eyes often distract us from the important things . . . that mistake won't be yours from now on. Can you understand that it can be an advantage?" and "Because if death can be a loving friend, blindness can certainly grow to be a good companion." By so extravagantly overstating his claim, the author inevitably calls into question the validity of his judgment.

Theis, Dan. *The Education of Steven Bell.* Illus. by Ken Frank. Milwaukee: Roundtree, 1977. 80 pp. Reading Level: MC
Disability: Learning Disability

At the age of six, Steven had an accident that "scrambled his speech. . . . The fall left a scar that ran from the back of his head and curved around almost to his temple. Most of the scar was hidden by his hair. But something was visible that others could see and Steven couldn't. Whatever it was created *boys like him.*" Since then he has been in a special school, where, after three years of work, he finally learns to read. This achievement convinces him that he is not stupid, despite the cruel or thoughtless comments of others. After two more years in which he gains the proficiency he needs, the youth insists on transferring to a mainstreamed class in a regular school, where, because of his considerable athletic ability, he is greeted enthusiastically by the fanatical football coach. Although distorted speech makes him the butt of humor by many students, Steven becomes friends with Bill, the team's cynical quarterback. School is an ordeal both socially and academically as his isolation increases and his grades decline. Injuries during a game resulting in dizzy spells combined with his growing disillusionment about football cause Steven seriously to consider giving up the sport. He is maneuvered by Bill into playing one last game, where he is so badly hurt that he is hospitalized. Full recovery is predicted, but Bill is so distressed by what he feels is his culpability in his teammate's suffering that he decides to quit football, too.

Analysis. This portrait of a physically traumatized youngster is unclear and unconvincing. He and the other characters are dull and unbelievable, their conversations improbable, the writing choppy and trite ("He was shouting something as he ran up the stairs, two at a time, toward the field and the light"), the final scene confusing, the plot pointless, and the illustrations unattractive.

Thomas, William E. *The New Boy Is Blind.* Illus. with photographs. New York: Julian Messner, 1980. 64 pp. Reading Level: MC
Disability: Visual Impairment

Mrs. Conboy reluctantly leaves her blind son in his new classroom with sighted children. Although Ricky is very matter-of-fact about his blindness, his mother babies him, dresses him, takes him home every day for lunch, and causes him to miss school under any pretext. Ricky has difficulty in learning and in adopting the rules governing behavior in his new class and must be frequently reminded not to shout out, sing, or otherwise distract the other children. He has special teachers who help him with assignments, and he is provided a brailler and adapted materials when he needs them. The other children are fascinated by their new classmate and have to be taught to let him do for himself those things he is capable of. He also has to be protected from bullies on the playground. Gradually his mother, prodded by her husband, allows him to participate more fully in the school, and the other children learn to respond more naturally as the novelty of vision loss in a new classmate wears off.

Analysis. The problems of a young child adjusting to a mainstreamed situation are handled well in this quasi-fictional book. Ricky's behavior, although disruptive, is not unexpected in light of his mother's overprotection and his lack of experience in an integrated milieu. The author seems to have anticipated many of the kinds of questions children would ask if they could. Explanations of trailing and other aspects of mobility training, blindisms, the instructional materials commonly used by blind children, and the frustrations common to impaired pupils are presented in an understated but explicit manner. The text is a bit stiff, even didactic, but not intolerably so. The black-and-white photographs give a clear, naturalistic picture of appropriate situations and are without any particular artistic pretensions. On the whole, *The New Boy Is Blind* is a useful work.

Thrasher, Crystal. *Between Dark and Daylight.* New York: Atheneum, 1979. 251 pp. Reading Level: YA
Disability: Intellectual Impairment, Speech Impairment

Mr. Robinson promised his wife he would find his family another home away from the Indiana hills she hates, but before they are able to leave the area, their borrowed truck breaks an axle. Twelve-year-old Seely is sent to the nearest farm for water while her parents set up camp under the trees for the night. Linzy Meaders tells them of a nearby house for rent, but Zel, the girl's mother, refuses to budge, afraid they might be trapped there forever. Rain soon changes her mind, and the family moves into the most comfortable lodging they have yet known. Seely quickly becomes friends with Johnny Meaders and Byron Tyson, exploring the woods and visiting the town. Twins Schylar and Sylvester Fender, angry at a brutal remark made by Johnny's father, have become the boy's nemeses. Their desire for revenge has long since passed the point of mischief and degenerated into dangerous and reckless acts. When Seely first sees them, she is unnerved to note "their blank amber-green eyes staring back, but not seeing me. As if they looked always inward, not caring to see the outside world around them." Their mother, Nellie, who stutters, loves her sons, but acknowledges their serious limitations:

Seely, my boys can't reason, or they never would have come near you. . . . I knowed they wasn't right in the head, not from the day they were born, but I kept hoping that somehow they'd outgrow it. They're grown now, but their minds still ain't no bigger than when they were babies.

She tells Seely that her sons were the product of rape by her uncle and warns the girl about such dangers. Alerted, the girl is able to ward off an attack by the brothers.

After a fire in their house, the Meaders move in with the Robinsons. Johnny, who cannot get along with his boorish father, stays elsewhere when the man is at home. Leaving one night to meet Byron, he is ambushed by the twins, who tie him to the bumper of a car and drag him to his death. The community is aghast; his brokenhearted parents make arrangements to take his body to their family home in another state for burial. Nellie, overcome with grief and remorse, tells Linzy: "I should've . . . put them in a home when they were little, but I couldn't do it. . . . They were all I had in the world." Johnny's father admits responsibility for antagonizing the youths, but all recognize that attempting to place blame at this late date is a futile exercise.

Analysis. In this sequel to *The Dark Didn't Catch Me*, Thrasher provides a stark but compassionate portrait of impoverished families struggling to survive the Depression. They are benefactors of each other's kindness and support and victims of human weaknesses as well as of events beyond their control. The twins, born as a result of incestuous rape, are apparently brain-damaged and uncontrollable by their vigilant, loving mother. The hesitancy in her speech is shown to be paralleled in her delay or inability to take direct action in relation to her sons.

Tolan, Stephanie S. *Grandpa—and Me.* New York: Scribner, 1978. 120 pp. Reading Level: MC
Disability: Neurological Impairment; also auditory impairment

Her grandfather has lived with her family for as long as Kerry Warren can remember. When she and her brother were younger, he was their friend, mentor, and teacher, but in recent years they have become absorbed in their own interests and activities and have needed him less, at times even finding his presence inconvenient. Although generally the old man behaves with decorum, there are times when his actions are embarrassing, even bizarre: he wears his pants inside out, urinates in the yard, and talks to Kerry as though she were Sophie, his long dead sister. The adult Warrens, concerned about how to handle this crisis, call a family council. Matt, 14, becomes incensed when the possibility of placing the old man in a nursing home is raised. Mr. Warren tries to explain that their grandfather's senility will increasingly cause problems for himself and for everyone else as his cerebration deteriorates and the frequency of his irrational episodes increases. Matt insists that his grandfather be consulted in the decisions about how he will spend the rest of his life, but his parents explain that doing so may put too great a burden on the old man, who they think would selflessly set aside his own best interests and select what he thought was best for everyone else.

Early one morning, the old man awakens Kerry and, speaking to her as though she were his sister, presents her with a locket that once belonged to Sophie. After giving Matt a present of similar sentimental importance, the 80-year-old man leaves the house. Convinced that this time he was faking strange behavior, the children conclude he knew exactly who they were and what he was doing. As they are discussing this puzzling incident with their mother, a phone call reports that the old man's body has been found in a neighborhood pool. The state of his room shows that he had spent considerable time in organizing his possessions. Consequently, the family is persuaded he had consciously and deliberately taken his life. Kerry, although heartbroken, insists he had the right to make his decision:

> I've thought and thought about what Grandpa chose, and I'm not sure how I feel about it. I know there are lots of people who would say he chose wrong. It sure wasn't a choice that makes any of *us* feel good. . . . But maybe how bad we feel isn't really what's important. Maybe it's only important that Grandpa made his own choice.

Analysis. Tolan treats senility as a correlate of the advancing years of this particular old man. It is shown to cause distress to the person affected and to those who love him. The author's approach is both sophisticated and compassionate as she tries to capture the panic, guilt, anxiety, and love that characterize the emotional state of the man who is becoming increasingly aware of his mental lapses and of those who observe the grandfather's eroding abilities. Her presentation of suicide as a defensible option is surprising in a book addressed to a grade-school audience, but it is not the taking of one's life she endorses as much as the right to make decisions, no matter how drastic, that will profoundly affect one's future. The portrait of the family's turmoil devolving from their attempts to provide the most appropriate arrangements for the grandfather is undoubtedly the best aspect of this book. Although the characters of Matt and the old man are not sufficiently developed, the fluidity of the writing, the originality of the story line, and the disturbing nature of the theme combine to create a thought-provoking and memorable work.

Towne, Mary. *First Serve*. Illus. by Ruth Sanderson. New York: Atheneum, 1976. 214 pp. Reading Level: MC/YA

Disability: Cosmetic Impairment

When only a toddler, Dulcie Kane threw a jelly jar at her sister, cutting the older child's face so severely that even after extensive plastic surgery Pat remained permanently scarred. Without consulting either of them, the Kanes define specific roles for their daughters: Pat is the family tennis champion, excused from most household chores; Dulcie is the swimmer and housekeeper. Although usually docile and obedient, the younger girl secretly resents this domestic exploitation and suspects "the main reason [her parents] were always encouraging Pat and praising her achievements was their fear that she could never have a so-called normal life as a woman, because of her face." Over the mild objections of her parents, the summer she is 13, Dulcie takes a job baby-sitting. Exerting her independence even further, she accepts the offer of a former tennis star who has seen her play and proposes to coach her. Lessons proceed surreptitiously at first, but her mentor, Mrs. Trask, finally insists her protégé's parents be fully informed. When the family is invited to visit the Trask home, the woman arranges for her student to compete in a match that she knows will show the younger girl's exceptional talent. Dulcie's grueling practice sessions pay off in an obviously superior performance. But seeing the contest as a humiliation for her older daughter, Mrs. Kane insists that Dulcie ease up: "You've already proved your point. . . . You're better than Pat; in a few years you won't even be in the same league with her. But I will not let you go back out there and destroy her!" The girl refuses, knowing that to capitulate would be far more insulting to Pat. Readily acknowledging her sister's greater skill, the older girl is more than consoled by the attentions of a young man she has just met who is indifferent to her imperfect features. Under Mrs. Trask's imperious but expert tutelage, the now more assertive and confident heroine looks ahead to the likelihood of championship play and perhaps even a career in tennis.

Analysis. Although basically a simple sports-romance story, *First Serve* looks at issues of family dynamics, including sibling rivalry, parental assumptions about roles and goals, and adolescent rebellion. There are some allusions to feminist concerns, but the critical importance of Pat's boyfriend in establishing her validity as a woman undercuts the author's mildly stated support. The scarring is shown to be a determinant of relationships, and the youth's acceptance of Pat parallels his ability to see beyond the superficial in other areas as well:

Johnny's not the kind that cares anything about appearances—you have the feeling he just looks right through them to whatever's important underneath. His car is typical of him, a battered old Pontiac with a rebuilt engine under the hood. He spends a lot of time tinkering with it, but I don't think he's ever noticed the ugly dents and patches of rust. As long as it runs, it's beautiful.

The illustrations in this novel are realistic but commercial. Despite an excessively contrived conclusion—Dulcie arranges to continue her training, Pat finds romance, their younger brother gets his longed-for pet, Mrs. Kane resolves to quit her job and devote herself to homemaking—the extensive and exciting descriptions of tennis matches should provide absorbing reading for dedicated fans.

Townsend, John Rowe. *Top of the World.* Illus. by John Wallner. Philadelphia: Lippincott, 1976. 94 pp. Reading Level: MC
Disability: orthopedic impairment

The Barretts are superintendents of a downtown commercial building where there are no available playmates for their children in the immediate area. Ten-year-old Kathy is put in charge of her brother when both their parents are busy with errands: their mother must go shopping and their father has an appointment at the hospital for a checkup on his leg. Donald and Kathy speak frequently about going to heaven, by which they mean the top floor housing the executive suite and a rooftop garden tended by their father. Taking advantage of the moment when his sister is distracted, Donald decides to visit the penthouse, disrobes, and begins cavorting in the pool, where he is discovered by the astonished Mr. Swanson, president of the insurance company that owns the building.

Although he is ordered to remove himself at once, Donald, in a giddy mood, refuses. The seven-year-old eludes capture, escaping to a precarious catwalk on the roof. The child becomes paralyzed with terror as the walkway sways and he realizes he is suspended in space 21 floors above the street. Old Mr. Swanson cannot manage the climb, and so Kathy, despite her fear of heights, cautiously threads her way to her panicky brother. Vertigo overtakes her until she is calmed by hearing her father's reassuring voice and familiar limp, then feeling his arm protectively around her. Much relieved, Mr. Swanson makes arrangements for the conversion of the executive parking lot into an area "safe for children."

Analysis. The father's disability has a peripheral role in this modest tale. His "permanent limp, the result of a war wound he'd got in Vietnam," has limited his employment possibilities. He does his job well, however, and when he discovers his children in danger, "a man with two good legs could hardly have moved faster." Other than this positive depiction, there is little to recommend this slight tale.

Uchida, Yoshiko. *A Jar of Dreams*. New York: Atheneum, 1981. 131 pp. Reading Level: YC
Disability: orthopedic impairment

At 11, Rinko, a Japanese-American girl living in pre–World War II California, has already experienced the pain of bigotry. When her mother decides to supplement the family income by opening a home laundry, the Tsujimuras become the targets of vicious attacks: tires on the family car are slashed, bundles of clothes left for cleaning are stolen, and their dog is killed. Aunt Waka arrives from Japan in the midst of this turmoil, providing help for her sister and comfort for her troubled niece. Rinko knew her aunt has been born with a malformed foot and wonders if her disability has "gone away." When Cal, the older son, announces his decision to postpone college in order to help support the others, he causes further anxiety. Aunt Waka admonishes him, saying, "You must never give up on a dream," and suggests to her brother-in-law that the perpetrator of the crimes against them must be confronted before further injury is done to the family. After the encounter, from which he returns satisfied, Mr. Tsujimura declares he too must pursue his dream of opening a garage and engaging in the kind of work he finds most satisfying. Waka's impending departure causes Rinko to consider how the woman's ethnic identity has been a source of strength. The youngster tells her aunt about her feeling of shame at being Japanese and her resentment of the rejection and isolation she endures. Waka draws a parallel between the antagonistic feelings of Americans toward the Japanese and the experiences she had had as a child who was "different." She reports: "When I was young and couldn't run or play with my friends, they used to tease me and call me a cripple. They often made me cry." Rinko realizes that what makes her aunt so self-assured is that she is proud of who she is. The family is saddened by the departure of this strong and sensitive woman, but Rinko promises to visit her one day in Japan.

Analysis. This gentle, understated story recounts the real and psychological distress experienced by a child victimized by prejudice. A supportive, resourceful family, abetted by kind and generous neighbors, mitigate the damage to her self-worth. Waka's impairment, a minor element in her characterization, provides a rationale for overtly stating the theme: "Just because you're different from other people doesn't mean you're not as good or that you have to dislike yourself. . . . Feel proud of yourself, even the part of you that's different."

Uchida, Yoshiko. *Journey Home*. Illus. by Charles Robinson. New York: Atheneum, 1978. 131 pp. Reading Level: MC
Disability: orthopedic impairment

Yuki thinks longingly of her life in California before she and other Japanese were cruelly and arbitrarily interned in a detention center during the early days of World War II. The Sakanes have been permitted to live outside the compound, but the 12-year-old's grandmother, Emi, her closest friend, and other valued companions remain incarcerated. This painful separation, the family's worry about the safety of their son, Ken, who enlisted in the army and is now fighting on the European front, and their uncertain future all cast a pall over the Japanese family. Finally, the deportees are allowed to go back to Berkeley, where they refit their old church as a temporary hostel and haven for other returning Japanese. Several families pool their meager resources to buy a small, run-down grocery, which they work hard to restock and revitalize. Their efforts to reestablish some financial independence are endangered when a deliberately set fire partially destroys the store. This instance of racial hatred is balanced by the kindness of neighbors, who, despite their grief over their only son's death at the hands of Japanese military forces, offer the Oriental family and their partners the hospitality of their home and assistance in repairing the premises.

Ken returns home and, even after extensive therapy for his wounds, must still use crutches. More debilitating than his shattered leg is his deep depression over the heroic death of his best friend. Chastened by the depth of forgiveness demonstrated by his neighbors and with the help of his father's embittered partner, Ken is able to exorcise his own feelings of guilt and inadequacy and begin to plan a future.

Analysis. This novel looks at a neglected aspect of life in America during the war years. It explores the impact on a group of Americans who, because of their ethnic origins, were uprooted from their homes and imprisoned in concentration camps. The theme of starting anew is given repeated expression in this slim volume: despite personal and financial losses, despite dislocations, despite the destruction wrought by war, people must survive. When the cherry tree the Sakanes placed on the grave of their infant daughter is vandalized, they plant a new one. When the beleaguered community loses their businesses—first at the time of their internment and later through the actions of a hate-driven arsonist—they rebuild. When their neighbors lose a son and Ken's close friend is killed, they ultimately put aside their anger, forgive, and begin once more. Uchida contends that not doing so results in a self-destruction as terrible as that inflicted by any enemy. Ken's impairment is one of the inevitable costs of war, but his bitterness and apathy are attributed to his initial unwillingness to forgive—especially himself—rather than to the injury he has suffered. The author's message is delivered directly through the observations of her characters and underlined by their actions, but the message is always conveyed with a light touch. The gentle, softly focused drawings contribute markedly to the narrative's warm and humane tone.

Van Leeuwen, Jean. *Seems Like This Road Goes on Forever*. New York: Dial, 1979. 214 pp. Reading Level: YA
Disability: Emotional Dysfunction

Mary Alice's 17 years have been punctuated by a series of moves made by her father as he is called to successively poorer ministries. The genteel poverty in which her family lives has meant that her clothes and toys have always been handmade or hand-me-downs. Her childhood was empty of friends, associations, or passions. Her father, always a distant and imposing figure in her life, is developing an increasing fascination with a charismatic religious leader as his preoccupation with sin, punishment, and the pastoral concerns of his congregation consumes all of his energies. Her mother, equally remote, is absorbed with the social aspects of the church and is far more concerned with her neighbor's opinions than with the responsibilities of parenthood.

Pressures to succeed in school, to conform to her father's rigid standards, and to center her life on the church pile on Mary Alice unendurably. Her only protector, her brother, is at college, too far away to supply the daily support she needs. Although he has offered to help her, she is uncertain about how to respond and afraid to make demands. It is not until high school that she finally has a girl friend, but this desperately needed relationship is sundered when a boy to whom Mary Alice is attracted asks her friend for a date. Her parents insist she apply for admission to a religiously affiliated college, an institution that appears highly threatening to her. This fear is intensified when she sees the connection between the university and her father's sudden interest in making healing ceremonies a focus of his church services. The teenager begins to shoplift and, although terrified at the prospect of being discovered, is unable to control this urge. Feeling that she has "had no life" and is so insignificant as to be "invisible" and desperate at the prospect of her future being indistinguishable from her past, the young woman tries to run away. Leaving her house in a trancelike state, she drives to a store, where she steals a sweater admired by the boy she hoped would like her. Returning to the car, she speeds erratically away to an inevitable accident. During her hospitalization for her broken leg, Mary Alice is visited by a psychiatrist, who gently and patiently leads her to examine the elements in her experience that culminated in this self-destructive act. These sessions help the teenager see her problem more clearly, but whether she will find the strength to take control of her life when she returns home is unclear.

Analysis. Van Leeuwen offers an interesting and empathic account of the development of emotional instability in an adolescent. Although the central character's parents are not physically abusive, they are authoritarian and inflexible, allowing no deviation from their uncompromising standards of behavior or dogmatic perceptions and beliefs. Additionally, they are seen as preoccupied with their own concerns, creating a home void of tenderness and affection. The author shows that her heroine's two siblings are able to survive this stultifying environment—one by rebelling, the other by willingly conforming—but the middle child, who could do neither, gradually loses her sense of self and her feeling that she has any impact on her destiny. The antisocial actions of the teenager are seen, in this context, to be desperate efforts to escape the bonds of passivity with which she has tried to accommodate her parent's intolerable demands.

This novel, beginning just after the accident, uses flashbacks to recount critical incidents and a psychiatrist to interpret them. The consequent unhurried revelation of key events in the heroine's life evokes sympathy and promotes understanding, but in an uninvolving manner. The title suggests Mary Alice's sense that she is trapped on an interminable journey over which she exerts no control.

Vogel, Ilse-Margret. *Farewell, Aunt Isabell.* Illus. by author. New York: Harper & Row, 1979. 54 pp. Reading Level: MC
Disability: Emotional Dysfunction

The mother and grandmother of twins Erika and Inge decide to bring Aunt Isabell home from a residential psychiatric institution. The women are unhappy with the care their relative is getting and feel they can provide a healthier, more supportive environment. Since Isabell has been confined to her barred room with someone always in attendance, the girls are startled one day to find her outside alone. When they first spot her, she is lying in a stream with the water coursing over her, and the distressed twins assume she has died. She jumps to her feet, amused at the girls' mistake, and plays happily with them in the fields. After their childlike games, she takes them to the train station, promising that someday they will all travel together to exotic places. When at last they return home, the house is in an uproar over Isabell's disappearance. Although they guard her more carefully than ever, her family can do little to halt the increasingly erratic quality of her behavior.

Hoping to create another interlude of happiness, the girls make Isabell an apron for a present. She turns it backward, then, descending the steps backward, falls and injures herself. The twins confide in a young neighbor, Magda, their worries about their aunt, whereupon the curious child insists on being allowed to see this mysterious relative. The next day, the girls receive permission to take Isabell to the meadow again. Magda, who had been hiding in the bushes, steps forward, startling the unsuspecting woman. Distraught, Isabell turns on Magda, pushing and pummeling her, while bitterly accusing the youngster of killing her bridegroom. In the confusion, Isabell disappears but is found again at the railroad station. Later, despite increased attention, the wily woman manages to slip out of the house once more. This time she is discovered hiding in a cistern up to her neck in water. The adults in the family reluctantly conclude that they are ill equipped to care for their relative, and the woman is sent back to an institution. Although heavily sedated, she is able to say goodbye to her nieces.

Analysis. This story examines the impact of an emotionally dysfunctional member on a loving family, particularly on the confused, dutiful, and compassionate children in it. Of particular interest is the depiction of the disabled aunt as a woman who is sometimes lucid, although at other times completely out of touch with reality. She is seen as a person chafing at the restrictions imposed on her by a caring family, yet completely unaware of the danger in which she may be placing herself. A sense of sadness, sympathy, and inevitability infuses the low-key ending. This seems less the child's account it purports to be than a childhood remembrance narrated by an adult. As a consequence, the pastoral story has a fuzzy, uninvolving aspect, as though memories heavily filtered by time have been recalled; the gentle, tender illustrations compound this impression.

Wahl, Jan. *Jamie's Tiger.* Illus. by Tomie de Paola. New York: Harcourt Brace Jovanovich, 1978. unp. Reading Level: YC
Disability: Auditory Impairment

Jamie lost his hearing after contracting German measles. Distressed at missing out on fun with friends and upset by events at school and home, the boy clings to his stuffed pet tiger, pretending its growling drowns out all other noises. After a medical examination reveals his problem, Jamie begins to learn lipreading, signing, and finger spelling. When other children learn to communicate with him, he begins to experience some success again: the tiger's growl changes to a purr.

Analysis. This story looks briefly at the implications of hearing loss in a young child and suggests that the attendant problems can be remedied. Information at a very simple level is presented about signing, finger spelling, and the adapted education Jamie receives in his neighborhood school. The tone of both text and illustrations is gentle, supportive, and affectionate—in sum, an exemplary work to introduce primary-level children to peers who have auditory impairments.

Walsh, Jill Paton. *A Chance Child*. New York: Farrar, Straus & Giroux, 1978. 185 pp. Reading Level: YA
Disability: Cosmetic Impairment, Orthopedic Impairment

A child, known only as "Creep," escapes from the closet where his ashamed and neglectful mother has hidden him, seeking refuge in a boat that journeys back through time to the Industrial Revolution. He pulls to shore near a coal mine, where he rescues Tom, a young coal carrier who is regularly beaten by the miner for whom he works. The two youngsters drift down the canal, returning to land near a forge. Tom finds temporary work at a bellows, replacing a girl named Blackie, who then works on the anvil. One side of the girl's face had been badly burned when she fell into the fire: "A huge crinkled pink and black scar lay across her visage; her mouth was pulled crooked at the corner, her eye was drawn tight and half shut, and her eyelashes were gone."

In the meantime, Creep's brother, Christopher, has started to search for him, accompanied intermittently and reluctantly by his weary younger sister, who, echoing their mother's sentiments, sometimes feels it would be best if the missing youth were never found.

Tom finds the labor at the forge exhausting and the treatment no improvement over what he just escaped, so the boys, now accompanied by Blackie, continue their odyssey. The girl envisions a permanent future with Tom, but he tells her: "I'm not going to marry thee, Blackie. . . . Doubt if *anyone* 'll marry thee; but I know *I* won't." He later explains to Creep: "When I get a girl . . . she'll have a lovely kind face." Creep moves wraithlike among people, unseen by them, never eating, and surreptitiously helping his friends. There is work for the other two at a pottery yard, but when Tom breaks some plates, he is peremptorily fired. Blackie, loyal to her new friend, quits her job to return to the boat. Tom locates work once again in a mine, and the others sail on without him to a mill town. Hungry and desolate, Blackie insists she look for employment immediately and is taken on in the deafeningly noisy spinning room. Cotton lint fills the air and the lungs of the weary, ill-used laborers. Many children are employed to help keep the insatiable machines turning at full speed. Creep slips in, unnoticed as usual. Although beatings are common, one youngster is abused more than the others. After a particularly brutal whipping, the victim's outraged mother appears and sets upon her son's overseer. As she forces the big man to retreat before her blows, Creep begins to laugh, leading a wave of sound that sweeps through the room. With this, he takes on substance and is seen for the first time by the other factory hands.

Christopher's tenacious search leads him finally to the library, where he pores over rare old volumes containing interviews collected by commissions investigating working conditions in England during the Industrial Revolution. He comes across an account by a Nathaniel Creep, who reports he was injured working on the canals: "I fell beneath a barrow and had my hip and my back broken. They got a doctor for me after three days, but he could do nothing for me. The other men put a hat round for me, and got up a guinea to support me. From the day of this accident I have needed a crutch and stick." Creep worked thereafter for a printer and returned to the mill town to marry Blackie. Christopher is convinced that this is his half-brother's true story.

Analysis. Walsh's attempt to explore the evils of child labor through a time-travel fantasy is only moderately successful. The abrupt moves from one vignette to another and the use of an elusive, insubstantial central character have a distracting rather than a unifying effect. Although hampered by a slow and confusing opening, the story gathers momentum, plunging tenacious readers into scenes that are vivid and gripping. The judicious employment of eloquent primary source material, the juxtaposition of varying language patterns, and the vivid evocation of oppressive working conditions of the period all contribute to make setting the most powerful element in this literate and demanding novel. The permanent injuries suffered by the two children were not unusual penalties paid by exploited youth during the nineteenth century. In this novel, the importance and function of the two disabled youngsters are primarily symbolic, as they give visible form to the iniquities of a system that exploited children.

Walsh, Jill Paton. *Unleaving.* New York: Farrar, Straus & Giroux, 1976. 145 pp. Reading Level: MA
Disability: Intellectual Impairment

Madge Fielding inherited Goldengrove, her grandmother's home by the sea. She is persuaded to rent it for the summer to a philosophy professor and his students, who intend to use it as a retreat where they will combine seminars and recreation. Professor and Mrs. Tregeagle arrive, accompanied by Patrick, their adolescent son, and their young daughter, Molly. As their youthful hostess prepares to greet them,

> the child looks up. Its face is very ruddy, with almond-shaped pale blue eyes and hardly any lashes. It smiles, and as it does so the smile fills with spittle, which overflows and oozes down its chin. The eyes swim inward into a squint. Madge sickens for an instant, then realizes, then covers up and steadies her smile.

Patrick does not bother to conceal his contempt for his father's endless philosophical jousting. The professor considers his son's musical interest trivial, observing with asperity that the boy prefers the romantic Chopin to the more intellectual Bach. He comments, with bitter resignation, that the main focus of his life, the refinement of thinking, is beyond the ability of his younger child and outside the interest of the other.

When Molly wanders off, momentarily unwatched, the household begins an anxious search. She is found sleeping among the rocks, oblivious to the pandemonium she has caused. Soon after, her father confides to a friend: "You know, Hugh, quite a lot of time I wish she were dead. All the time. It seems the only way out for any of us. Have you *seen* an adult mongol? Or the kind of home we could put her in when she gets too much for us?" Then he recalls, with some surprise, the anguish he felt when she was lost.

Madge is alternately interested, confused, and repelled by the endless metaphysical discussions that overflow her home. One of the students engages her brother, Paul, and Patrick in an impromptu exploration of the moral dilemmas concerning means and ends. Patrick, to Madge's horror, proposes they consider the behavior of the doctor who cured Molly when he could have easily let her die—an outcome Patrick asserts would have been preferable. He is then challenged to consider whether some acts are unequivocably morally wrong: "Is there *anything* we must not do, regardless of the consequences? Are there absolute moral values?" It is a proposition the boy rejects.

To mock his father, Patrick teaches Molly to recite "Cogito ergo sum," which she articulates during an argument on the primacy of intellect just after Professor Tregeagle has asked his students to consider Wittgenstein's observation that "the human body is the perfect image of the human soul." While the assembled group tries to cover its embarrassment, Molly is led off by her brother to search for flowers. Madge, worried about her new friend's state of mind, persuades Paul to help look for him. They finally catch sight of them just as Molly tumbles over the edge of the cliff, falling into the turbulent sea below.

Paul assumes that Patrick reached out too late to save his sister, but Madge realizes that the boy deliberately pushed Molly to her death. Help is summoned and a boat launched in the choppy waters to recover the body. One of the men, known to the three youngsters, drowns—and Patrick is horrified at this unintended consequence of his act. He is wracked by feelings of guilt and despair, comforted at last by Madge's assertion that she knows what he has done and, despite this knowledge, loves him. Mrs. Tregeagle grieves for three days, "But then she is tranquil, and more than tranquil . . . she is slowly unfurling like a florist's rose freed from cellophane. She is more herself— well, more like somebody. . . . A great burden has rolled from her, and the future no longer hangs over her like death."

Interwoven within the main narrative is a parallel tale of Madge as an old woman, surrounded by her grandchildren. She reflects with satisfaction on her past and particularly her years as Patrick's wife.

Analysis. Molly is first introduced by the impersonal pronoun "it." Her demeanor and behavior are repellent, inspiring disgust in strangers, malicious imitation in children, guilt and hopelessness in her family. The child's very existence calls into question her father's obsessive rationality and mocks his passionately pursued petty arguments. Ironically, only Patrick seems to feel any deep affection, but this is mixed with pity, anger, and finally despair. Molly's family wishes her dead—for her sake and theirs. Her life is a burden to them, and they cannot refrain from gloomily speculating on her inevitably bleak future. Mrs. Tregeagle, at last relieved of responsibility, recovers quickly from her daughter's death. She grieved, "but grieving for Molly is a good deal easier than living with the thought of her there forever." Patrick is filled with guilt over the unexpected, unplanned death of the man who tried to recover his sister's body. Madge tries to help him put aside his feeling: "You didn't mean to hurt Jeremy. . . . And people usually feel guilty only about what they meant, don't they?"

The narrative never suggests that there is anything admirable, likable, or even tolerable about the retarded child. Her murder is important because of its impact on others; tragic because a more valuable life was lost in its aftermath. Patrick's guilt is quickly assuaged, and judging from the serenity of Madge's later life, she has hardly been haunted by feelings of remorse. The defining of a human life in terms of its inconvenience to others and the rationalizing of a killing as an acceptable means to obviate a painful future reflect an offensive, inhumane, intolerable value system. Such callousness toward disabled persons is, fortunately, unique in contemporary adolescent fiction.

Walter, Mildred Pitts. *Ty's One-Man Band.* Illus. by Margot Tomes. New York: Four Winds, 1980. unp. Reading Level: YC
Disability: Orthopedic Impairment

Seeking relief from the oppressive summer heat, Ty, a young black boy, wanders down to the pond flanking the small Southern town in which he lives. An odd sound disturbs the silence, and the boy is intrigued by his observation of a black man with a wooden peg for a leg who has come down to the water's edge. Hidden by some grasses, Ty watches the stranger eat and then suddenly begin to juggle his dishes. Finally the two speak, and the man tells the boy that his name is Andro and he is a one-man band. He bids the boy locate a washboard, some wooden spoons, a pail, and a comb, promising to return that evening to the town to "make music for you and your friends." Everyone to whom the youth turns for help points out that the objects requested serve more mundane purposes and are useless as musical instruments. Nevertheless, they agree to lend them for the evening. Just when Ty has about given up hope that Andro will reappear, he does. His melodies pull the people into the town's center, and all, black and white, old and young, rich and poor, join enthusiastically into a joyous frenzy of dancing, singing, and shouting. In the midst of the merrymaking, Ty observes Andro slip away into the concealing night.

Analysis. The lyrical narrative and the lovely, sensitive drawings combine to give a mythic, dreamlike quality to this gentle tale that subtly suggests the unifying spirit of music. Andro's wooden leg intensifies the boy's wonder at this unusual stranger so rich in spirit although lacking in material things. Clearly his generosity and talents far overshadow the importance of his disability.

Wartski, Maureen C. *My Brother Is Special.* Philadelphia: Westminster, 1978. 152 pp. Reading Level: MC/YA
Disability: Intellectual Impairment

The dominant mood at the Harlow house is characterized by discord between the two adults, who hold vastly differing perceptions about the capabilities of their intellectually impaired son, Kip. Noni, his sister, dreads mealtime, when her parents' antagonism often explodes into harsh, cruel taunts and wild accusations. Convinced that her brother could be a winner in the Special Olympics, the eighth-grade girl tries to figure out how to capitalize on the athletic abilities Kip already has demonstrated. She wants him to share the feelings of pride and elation she has known after excelling in track competitions. Noni sanguinely expects that if her parents could view their son as an achiever in one endeavor, they will be obliged to revise their all-encompassing negative assessment. To her dismay, they refuse to allow Kip to participate in the meets.

Noni still smarts over the snubs she received from Denise Baxly and her clique, who have not only denigrated her skills but also ridiculed those of her brother. But when Kip finds an injured bird coated with oil and insists on taking it home, it is Denise and her boyfriend, Neill, who help with its care. Mrs. Harlow becomes incensed when she reads a newspaper account about Kip's bird and discovers, with shock, that her son is training for the Special Olympics. Vituperatively, she rebukes her daughter: " 'I'm going to call the *Sun*. . . . I am going to tell them what I think of their comparing my Kip to a crippled bird. Hasn't Kip been hurt enough without people seeing him as some hopeless cripple!' Her finger stabbed. 'You did this to him, Noni!' "

Mr. Harlow also berates his daughter when he learns she has forged their signature on the medical forms required for Kip's participation. However, after their son demonstrates his athletic prowess, his formerly skeptical parents capitulate. When Neill says, "We all could help," Mr. Harlow responds: " 'Yes, by God!' [His] voice made Noni come around much faster than a whiff of ammonia. 'We can help Kip win.' The pride . . . in Dad's voice told her everything was going to be all right." News of Noni's efforts electrifies the small community, making her the recipient of much adulation from other students, but her euphoria is diminished by Denise's criticism characterizing her as a "glory hound."

Kip becomes hysterical the morning of the big race when he learns that some vandals have hurt his gull. Despite their daughter's protests, her parents administer a tranquilizer to their distraught son. Feeling that they must put in an appearance, the demoralized family goes to the track, although "Kip didn't even know where he was." Disoriented by the medication, the boy makes a late start, but once begun, the intrepid youth doggedly pushes on to the finish line. The crowd, rejoicing in the child's valiant effort, rewards him with their cheers for his determination and perseverance.

Analysis. Employing style and dialogue reminiscent of pre–World War II children's stories, *My Brother Is Special* is as bland and unimaginative as its title. All the key elements in the story are contrived: the parents are straw villains; the Special Olympics is proposed as a panacea for personal, familial, and social problems, and events are imbued with excessive emotionalism. Kip's problems are simultaneously exaggerated and minimized as the boy is initially seen as the prime source of family disharmony; then his single act of courage brings about a complete reversal of attitudes. In addition to a simplistic response to the complex problems attending disability, the author burdens her narrative with a plethora of non sequiturs. For example, it is reported that Georgie, whose ability to function in a special school is used as a rationale for Kip's possible matriculation, "was brain damaged, but certainly held his own," and in reference to other Special Olympians, "nearly all the other athletes were smiling, but their bodies didn't always obey them."

Weiman, Eiveen. *Which Way Courage.* New York: Atheneum, 1981. 132 pp. Reading Level: YA
Disability: Orthopedic Impairment

When Jason Kuntzler is born with spina bifida, his Amish father is reluctant to permit an operation, seeing such action as interfering with God's plan. The boy's spine is closed, but he is left with hydrocephalus and other problems involving bladder control and respiratory weakness. His father finally allows further surgery to relieve pressure on his son's brain but becomes more than ever convinced that such interference is both useless and sacrilegious when the boy's difficulties continue. Jason's oldest sister, Courage, helps him learn to walk and takes him with her as she does her chores. Courage is inept in the skills she needs as an Amish wife and is uninterested in wedlock, finding satisfaction instead in academic pursuits. As Courage approaches the last year of mandatory schooling, she increasingly yearns to enter high school. Although it is contrary to family custom, she implores her father to allow her to continue. He fears that she will learn worldly ways but promises to pray for guidance, after which, despite his misgivings, he gives his permission for one more year of secular education.

When Jason becomes sick, Courage surreptitiously takes him to a doctor, who provides medication that cures his infection. When the child gets sick again, the remaining pills Courage has secretly saved provide only partial relief, and she begs her parents to seek medical help. They refuse. One night the child becomes so ill that, in desperation, his sister rushes him to the hospital, deliberately attempting to deceive the doctors by claiming that she is his mother so they will be authorized to treat him. It is too late and Jason dies. Distraught, the young woman returns home to tell the family. They are shocked at the loss of their son but have been expecting his life would not be a long one. Her father is furious and her mother and siblings aghast at her disobedience and the violation of their religious tenets. Courage calls a cousin with whom she has been secretly corresponding. The girl is the daughter of her father's brother, who has been ostracized for leaving the community. The exiles arrive for the funeral, further angering Mr.

Kuntzler but providing Courage with some measure of comfort. She is forbidden to return to school and ordered to devote her energies to preparation for marriage. Her family seems engaged in a conspiracy to promote a dull Amish farmer as a suitor. The young woman cannot face the oppression and dreariness life seems to hold for her. She announces her decision to leave the community and calls on her uncle to help her make a start in a new life.

Analysis. The author reveals how theological and social perception of a sect can structure their response to disability. Jason's parents and the religious community to which they belong see his impairment as well as all other incidents in their lives as part of God's unchallengeable plan. The minister points out their willingness to use the skills of a veterinarian to heal animals and suggests that consulting a doctor to treat a person is a parallel situation. Mr. Kuntzler accepts this interpretation at the outset but returns to a more stringent view when his son's "cure" is incomplete. The boy is valued and loved, but there is little understanding of the ramifications or complexity of his disorder, a perception reflected in his mother's inability even to say "bifida" and his siblings' impatience with his incontinence. Although the child's difficulties are greeted with stoic acceptance, the father's coolness toward his youngest also hints at the man's conviction that his boy will not be a family member for too long. Jason's death acts as the catalytic element that forces Courage to make a decision about her future. Weiman has drawn a compassionate picture of an adolescent caught between irreconcilable forces and, as a result, confronted with a profound and painful decision.

Weir, Joan. *Career Girl*. Edmonton: Tree Frog Press, 1979. 139 pp.
Reading Level: YA
Disability: Orthopedic Impairment

Patti Maxwell, a senior in a residential ballet school, is determined to succeed in the upcoming tryout for a position with a professional troupe. But Yvonne's mother, on the center's board of trustees, manipulates the audition regulations to increase her daughter's chances. Patti has made friends with Sharon Boles, a younger girl whom she helps with dance exercises to strengthen muscles atrophied by polio. Although there is dramatic initial progress, the teenager reaches a plateau beyond which she seems unable to improve. However, she becomes interested in Benesh notation, a method for transcribing movement, and rescores *Swan Lake* using this technique. Patti is preparing the *pas de deux* from this famous ballet with Guy as her partner. The young man has never recovered from a gaffe he committed two years ago that undercut his partner's performance. Totally immersed in the relentless demands of exercise and rehearsals, the aspiring ballerina cancels a dinner prepared in her honor by Mrs. Boles and then neglects to phone Sharon as she had promised. Finally remembering, the distressed young woman calls but, to her puzzlement, gets no response. Patti is too worried to concentrate on her work and, after getting permission to leave school, travels to her young friend's home. There she learns the girl fell, broke her leg, and had to be hospitalized. The explanation proffered is that Sharon's legs had become "stiff and awkward" from waiting immobilized so long for the call from her friend and mentor that never came. The guilt-ridden dancer goes to the hospital, hoping to get permission to visit. Dr. Wadforth reports that Sharon's depression at her perceived desertion has left her resistant to mobility instruction and urges the visitor to help his patient. Greeted with hostility, the clever girl informs Sharon that her excellent notation, representing choreography "better than any of the standard scores," will be the basis for Patti's upcoming performance. Patti generously spends the next days helping the now energized girl walk instead of practicing her routines. When Mrs. Boles mildly protests, Patti responds: "If I'd devoted a little more time to her last weekend, this wouldn't have happened." Sure enough, Sharon makes sufficient progress to attend the audition, where she witnesses Guy being awarded the male position and Yvonne, despite her "plumpness," the female assignment with the ballet company. The judge tells the disappointed Patti that her sacrifice has been commendable and that the expected opening next year will almost certainly be hers. To round out the happy ending, Sharon is encouraged to enter the Institute for Choreography, where her talents will have an opportunity to develop.

Analysis. This thoroughly silly work puts forth the extremely unlikely proposition that the talents of a 16 year old with practically no training could surpass those of someone with years of experience and enable her to become a star choreographer. *Career Girl* also implies that the severely disabled adolescent's near-parasitic dependence is acceptable and that the moral obligation it requires from a friend to neglect a major career opportunity is entirely appropriate. The endorsement of the exploitation of a disability to manipulate others would be unfortunate in a serious novel; here it is just another naive component of a frivolous story.

Weiss, Joan Talmage. *Home for a Stranger.* New York: Harcourt Brace Jovanovich, 1980. 109 pp. Reading Level: MC
Disability: Cosmetic Impairment; also orthopedic impairment

On a routine visit to an impoverished Mexican orphanage, a doctor, Señor Don, inquires about Juana's malformed lip. The youngster knows nothing about how it happened, only that she was not born with it. Señor Don tells the administrator that his physician's association in the United States is willing to repair the girl's mouth but needs a birth certificate in order to bring her across the border. Although no official documents are available for the child, the determined doctor arranges for a 30-day visitor's permit, which would, at least, allow time for both surgery and recovery before the girl's return to Mexico.

The youngster is extremely anxious while driving to California, which Sr. Don ascribes to her lack of experience with cars and her general fearfulness. Juana stays temporarily with her benefactor, but the opulence of the surroundings intimidates her and she is mortified when she must be deloused, then again when yelled at for eating with her fingers and hoarding food. Juana is panicked by the alterations in her normal routines and the introduction of new expectations at a rate far faster than she can accommodate them. When the Mexican girl is examined by a specialist, it is learned that the scar tissue on her upper lip is the result of a postaccident repair and, moreover, her palate has been seriously injured, causing severe misalignment of her upper teeth. Juana becomes depressed: "I was more of a mess than everybody thought. Now I had a new fear. Maybe they could not fix my twisted mouth." Acknowledging her adjustment difficulties, Sr. Don transfers his charge to the home of a Hispanic family. Having been born in Ecuador under conditions of poverty even more severe than she experienced and sharing some aspects of her culture, Mr. Rodriguez seems to have a special understanding for her problems. As her surrogate father, he tells her he sympathizes with her fears and concerns, but she nonetheless must comply with the disciplines he maintains in his home. Despite his urging, she is unable to apply herself to the schoolwork, and her interim placement in first grade is a source of additional distress.

As a result of the preoperative exam, the doctors state that she will require the services of an oral surgeon as well as an orthodontist, and one man concludes from her physiology that she is of mixed heritage. In the excited, probing questioning that follows, the patient reveals that she attended kindergarten in "L.A." The medical team pieces together her probable story—an accident, her placement with a Mrs. Perez, beatings severe enough to raise body welts, after which "she ran away and was found wandering the streets and stealing food. The police took her to the orphanage."

Plastic surgery is performed and her front teeth removed so that the palate can be repaired and a partial plate made. Eager to keep Juana from returning to the destitute conditions from which he removed her, the California physician accompanies his patient to Mexico to the site where she was found by the police. The search for clues to her background appears fruitless until the child recognizes some landmarks that lead to the Perez home. Although the woman tries to deny any involvement, Juana remembers she "walked with one leg dragging." Later, the manager of the children's center gives up a St. Christopher's medal she took from the homeless child. On it is imprinted the girl's real name. With her identity established, Juana's real mother is located, and the two meet again in a joyful reunion. Both bear physical and emotional scars from the accident and their separation but are eager to build a future together. The woman explains that she was too badly injured in the accident to care for Juana properly and turned her over to Sra. Perez. When she could no longer pay for her care, Sra. Perez misinformed her that the child had died and she mourned her daughter's loss.

Analysis. Juana's disfiguring scars have magnified the shyness she feels around strangers. The terrifying accident and the passage of time have caused her to suppress memories of a happier existence. All the child's problems are exacerbated by the grinding poverty, which, except for the intervention of dedicated, compassionate outsiders, would have made proper medical care and the search for her origins impossible. There is a heavy reliance on fortuitous circumstances and the peculiar situation of a supposedly skilled doctor who cannot distinguish between a congenital disorder and traumatic injury, but the pursuit of help for the heroine and the uncovering of clues to her true identity keep interest high. Weiss is supportive of the values and benefits of living in American middle-class culture but also sympathetic to the problems of pressures of living in poverty in an underdeveloped country.

Wells, Rosemary. *Leave Well Enough Alone.* New York: Dial, 1977, 218 pp. Reading Level: YA
Disability: Intellectual Impairment; also auditory impairment, speech impairment

Fourteen-year-old Dorothy Coughlin is hired to sit for the summer with two wealthy but spoiled and neglected children. Their mother, Maria Hoade, recently gave birth to a baby with Down's syndrome who is allegedly being tended in a cottage away from the main house. Her other daughters are informed that the infant has a cold and are instructed that they must not try to see her. Dorothy is warned to keep away from the hut where Mrs. Borg, an elderly non-English-speaking woman, acts as nurse. The curious girl, frustrated in her attempts to learn more about the baby, dismisses the Hoades' "deaf-and-dumb" gardener as a source of information. When the infant's death is announced, the teenager becomes suspicious, recalling events that were inconsistent with her employers' account of what has happened.

Dorothy learns that it was actually Mrs. Hoade's mother who occupied the cottage. The old woman made a will leaving her estate to Mrs. Borg, but Mr. Hoade, her son-in-law, has hidden the document. When the nurse, unable to bear the suffering of her patient, decides, without consultation, to withhold life-prolonging medicines, Mr. Hoade, who has evidence of this, intimidates her, pays her a considerable sum of money, and sends her back to her native country. Dorothy finds the will and considers making its contents public, but she realizes that to do so would endanger the elderly woman. After deliberation, she decides to remain silent and goes home at summer's end considerably less naive than when she arrived.

Analysis. Characterizations are original but insufficiently developed in this slow-moving story and, although the action centers around a mystery, there is little excitement or suspense. The inclusion of an infant with Down's syndrome as a mere plot device seems both insensitive and contrived. The gardener's impairment, like the nurse's inability to speak English, makes possible the heroine's seeming isolation from adult assistance, forcing her to come to her own decisions. Dorothy is embarrassed at the revelation of the presence of an impaired baby; however, these feelings, as her other emotions, are talked about but never adequately explored.

Westall, Robert. *The Wind Eye.* New York: Greenwillow, 1977. 213 pp. Reading Level: YA
Disability: Cosmetic Impairment, Orthopedic Impairment

The second marriage for the pompous, opinionated, and dogmatically rational Bertrand Studdard to the impetuous, argumentative, vituperative Madeleine is inevitably explosive. Their combined families include three children, of whom the youngest, Sally, has a badly disfigured hand, burned when it was trapped in an electric space heater. At her father's insistence, the child wears a glove, even though the covering causes itching and considerable discomfort. During their vacation on the Northumberland coast in a house inherited from Bertrand's uncle, the children discover a boat, *The Ressure,* which is capable of transporting them through time. Summoned by St. Cuthbert, whose presence dominates the area, Sally sails back through the centuries to see the holy man who restores her hand. Bertrand is furious, insisting the miracle is a malevolent act whose specific purpose is to challenge his fiercely antireligious tenets. At first he denies that the children have journeyed through time, but when more and more evidence accumulates, the man declares he will study their claim scientifically and, despite his family's entreaties, obstinately sails off alone into the mist. Beth, his oldest daughter, tries to follow him, but is washed ashore on an island with the saint. Through St. Cuthbert's power and goodness, she learns more truly who she is and discovers that the name of their boat was originally *I Am the Resurrection and the Life*.

Professor Studdard lands at the island just before the Viking invasion. Finding the monks there despicable, he departs, hoping to persuade the Vikings not to fight. He is unsuccessful and, despite his often proclaimed hatred of violence, kills one invader and maims another. As a storm approaches, the foreigners flee, but it is too late: the tempest summoned by the saint destroys the vessels and washes them into the sea. As the academic drifts back to the present, he recalls a passage from an ancient book about the monks who attended Cuthbert at his death, realizing that one must have been his ancestor. Since the sterility of his purely rational approach to life has been demonstrated and concluding that denial of faith inevitably leads to futility, the professor decides to stay at Northumbria, where he can devote himself to a thorough study of the saint.

Analysis. Westall's tale is essentially an attack on rationalism and an endorsement of Christian faith. The child's impairment is used to demonstrate the inadequacy of mere logic and the superordinate power of belief. Sally is injured because her father stubbornly dismisses warnings and insists that the heater he purchased is both safe and necessary. The child's resulting deformity racks him with a guilt he will not admit. He forces her to cover her hand to protect her from the revulsion of others and to conceal his own shame. When the physician suggests discarding the glove, the father refuses, saying: "and have everyone staring at her? Or trying hard to be nice and not to stare? How could she make friends with everyone flinching away? Sometimes I think she'd be better off socially with a complete amputation of the hand." None of the medical specialists can help, but the saint is able to, after he makes her "believe he could do anything"; then "she trusted him absolutely. She *believed*." The narrative moves quickly, maintaining tension; the characters, although extreme, are skillfully drawn, but its message—rationalism is insufficient, only faith can provide meaning—is insistently reiterated.

Wilkinson, Brenda. *Ludell and Willie*. New York: Harper & Row, 1977. 181 pp. Reading Level: YA
Disability: Emotional Dysfunction; also special health problems

A poor, small, Georgia backwoods in the early 1960s is the setting for this low-key adolescent novel. Ludell has been staying with her strict, religious, elderly grandmother, who ekes out a marginal living doing domestic work. The youngster, now an adolescent, has become restless under the woman's rigid restrictions. However, Ludell is sustained by her plans for a postgraduation marriage to Willie, her equally impoverished neighbor. After considerable pleading, Ludell is allowed to attend the dance that follows the high school football game in which Willie is the quarterback. On the way, she meets Bobbi Jean, whose emotional disorder is manifested in compulsive talking and defiant, reckless behavior. Her preacher father punishes her for minor infractions of his tyrannical rules, and the youngster is becoming increasingly confrontational, leading to the speculation that she may be hospitalized soon again. Instead, Bobbi Jean is given medication, which induces a zombielike state that is ignored by her teachers, who are intimidated by her father and relieved to be free of an obstreperous student.

Ludell's grandmother's physical and emotional health rapidly deteriorates. She has had to quit work, has eliminated shopping and all other activities except for attending church. As the adolescent reports to an interested friend: "Mama aine been too well lately, you know—be talking to herself all the time—sometime I even hear her in there talkin like my granddaddy still alive and in the room with her." Although the woman's memory lapses and episodes during which she is disoriented become more frequent, she is still strong-willed enough to control her fractious granddaughter. Willie minimizes his girl friend's concerns, feeling she exaggerates their importance. He comments: "All she is is febbleminded." Ludell calls her mother long distance, painting a desolate picture of their circumstances, but her seemingly indifferent parent postpones returning to Georgia until after the old woman dies. Despite Ludell's anguish over leaving friends and the place she considers home, Dessa insists on taking her daughter back to New York with her. This decision brings on an asthma attack in the teenager: "She hadn't had an attack of asthma in years, so Willie was sure that it was the whole business of her having to go to New York that had brought it on." Her boyfriend's love and support and her expectation of their eventual reunion are all that Ludell has to bolster her during this distressing time.

Analysis. Wilkinson presents a sympathetic portrait of people struggling to maintain dignity and hope in the face of poverty and discrimination. The changes in the old woman from a lively, vigorous, determined matriarch to one who is confused, senile, and helpless is described from the perspective of a loving, loyal, but constantly frustrated adolescent. Both Bobbi Jean's aberrant behavior and Ludell's asthmatic episode are attributed to situational stress. Each is exacerbated by inappropriate responses. This slow-moving sequel to *Ludell* focuses on a high school romance between two naive youngsters. Its abrupt and inconclusive ending suggests subsequent novels may be planned. The narrative, in dialect, may offer some difficulties to readers accustomed to standard grammar and spelling.

Willard, Barbara. *Harrow and Harvest*. Originally published in England by Kestrel Books, 1974. London: Puffin, 1977. 203 pp. Reading Level: YA/MA
Disability: Intellectual Impairment

The political conflict between the King of England and Parliament has erupted into open warfare, resulting in widespread destruction and loss of life. Among the victims is Edmund's father, who, with his last breath, orders his son to journey to Mantlemass in Sussex. The boy arrives desperately ill. He is nursed back to health by Cecilia, whose brother is the steward for both house and lands. The heir apparent to the estate is nine-year-old Jamie, whose "wits would never be more than the wits of a troubled child." However, long-hidden papers reveal that Edmund's claim has priority, and all but Dorian, Jamie's mother, are pleased with this designated successor to the Medley wealth. Angry at the loss of what she considers her rightful property, Dorian conspires with Royalist forces to betray Mantlemass. A diversion is created, drawing the men out of the manor house, which is then set afire. The women and Jamie escape in time, finding shelter in a barn. Edmund is killed, and the discouraged survivors are persuaded to join a cousin in the New World. Jamie is left behind with caretakers. At the last minute, Cecilia changes her mind, finding she is unable to abandon Mantlemass, the still-frightened child, and the hope that the man she loves may yet come back safely from the wars.

Jamie shows her a book Edmund had brought with him that had been missing since his arrival. The volume reveals that the family are descendants of King Richard III. The soldier returns and asks Cecilia to marry him. He says news of her lineage confirms old rumors about a host of impairments in the Medley ancestors: "I did hear something of this once . . . Medley faults—such as backs and shoulders, I mean, and wits." At first unsure of what course to take, the woman decides to accept the proposal and "destroy the book. . . . It would be the first hard proof of her love for him."

Analysis. Harrow and Harvest is the final volume in a series of the fortunes of a family whose lives are intertwined with exciting historical events. Jamie is a catalyst in the tale, repeatedly redirecting the family fortunes: he finds Edmund and brings rescuers; he locates the genealogical book, hides it, and later delivers it to Cecilia; and he undermines his mother's acts of disloyalty. The boy is loved, abhorred, exploited, cared for, disdained, or ignored by various relatives and servants, who thereby reveal their own character. The theme of inherited disability, frequently alluded to, is confirmed in the revelation of descent from the Plantagenets: stammering, kyphosis, and retardation are part of the lineage—expected and accommodated by the descendants. True to its genre, this historical romance offers a convoluted tale of intrigue, perfidy, loyalty, violence, and splendor.

Winthrop, Elizabeth. *Marathon Miranda.* New York: Holiday House, 1979. 155 pp. Reading Level: MC
Disability: Special Health Problems

Miranda's best friends are Margaret, an older woman who lives in her apartment building, and Phoebe Livingston, a girl her age who is an inveterate jogger. Despite her doctor's suggestion that exercise could have a salutary effect on her asthma, Miranda thinks of herself as exclusively the sedentary type, recalling all too vividly those times of panic when exertion brought on an attack. Phoebe persuades her friend to try running, and much to the novice's surprise, she enjoys the activity and is troubled less by wheezing. One day, feeling pressured and angry at Phoebe's suspicion that her asthma is only a ploy, Miranda pushes herself beyond her limits and collapses, barely able to breathe. Much to her embarrassment, the police are summoned and she is rushed to the hospital, where a shot of adrenaline restores her.

Margaret has a new boyfriend, a younger, very attractive man who acts in daytime television. Soon after Miranda sees him in the company of another woman, she is not surprised to learn that her neighbor's romance has been abruptly terminated. As a gesture of kindness to cushion the shock, the youngster's parents agree to include Margaret on their vacation trip to Miranda's grandfather's home in Vermont.

Phoebe suddenly learns that she has been adopted, a revelation that shakes the 13 year old, who is already at odds with her parents. She leaves home, arriving secretly at the grandfather's farm. After talking to Miranda and her brother, she sneaks away, afraid her whereabouts will be disclosed. She is soon discovered hitchhiking on the highway and is brought back to the farm, where Margaret convinces the runaway's parents to allow her to remain with them and then helps the distraught child deal with her fears and anxieties.

When they all return to the city and the girls resume their preparation for the upcoming marathon, the pollution and heat leave Miranda gasping for breath after only two miles. Phoebe encourages her friend, reassuring her that they really do have time to get acclimated before the event. Both girls enter: Phoebe finishes a respectable forty-fifth and Miranda just finishes, but it is a victory for them both.

Analysis. Miranda's asthma is seen as a disorder that can be aggravated by emotional stress and overexertion, or improved by a regimen that increases her lung power and stamina. She is particularly sensitive both to untrue accusations that she is faking her attacks and to the partially true ones that she uses them to avoid troublesome demands. This pleasant work introduces some appealing characters and unusual situations, offering low-key solutions to some common problems.

Witter, Evelyn. *Claw Foot.* Illus. by Sandra Heinen. Minneapolis: Lerner, 1976. 66 pp. Reading Level: MC
Disability: Orthopedic Impairment

Claw Foot's misshapen foot, only partially concealed by a specially designed moccasin, does not prevent him from competing in the athletic contests in which young Sioux engage to develop their skills. Tradition and pride demand that the boy be tenacious, but his disability ensures he will never win. Ashamed of his name, he seeks an adventure that will allow him legitimately to change his name to one he deems more honorable. As a dream predicts, Claw Foot tames a wild horse, even though it had been cruelly abused by his nemesis, Red Duck.

The Sioux men set out to hunt buffalo, leaving the women and children behind. Claw Foot sees his chance to earn a new name by finding food for his starving people. He heads north toward territory controlled by the Crow tribe, his people's fiercest enemies. He is followed by Red Duck, who steals his horse, and his best friend, who hoped to be of help. The three boys are captured by Crow warriors and taken to their chief, Broken Wing. The man empathizes with the disabled youngster and admires his audacity and courage. The chief offers a single buffalo and safe return, but Claw Foot knows one animal is not sufficient to feed his tribe. He asks to be given all the land that the buffalo hide can cover. This seemingly frivolous request is honored, and the ingenious youth cuts the hide to pieces, spreading them over a considerable territory. Acknowledging the boy's cleverness in outwitting him, Broken Wing gives the land to the Sioux. A tribal elder aptly renames the boy "He Who Thinks."

Analysis. Claw Foot initially sees his disability as a sign of divine disfavor: "He was a claw foot who must bear the burden of shame all the days of his life. Why had the Great One chosen him to be so slow and useless?" Big Owl sagely puts this problem in perspective: "You cannot let one foot be more important than the rest of your body. You must use what you have and not feel sorry for what you have not." With these words, the tribal elder suggests the inevitable conclusion and the child's renaming. The behavior of Red Duck not only precipitates the resolution but demonstrates how others may mock physical differences as a means of gaining status for themselves. This story is a later version of such other tales as *Red Eagle* and *At the Mouth of the Luckiest River*, which involve Indian children with birth defects who surmount obstacles to achieve status and acceptance. The soft, indistinct drawings obscure the boy's foot and the Crow chief's malformed arm, hinting at but never explicitly showing these impairments.

Wittman, Sally. *A Special Trade.* Illus. by Karen Gundersheimer. New York: Harper & Row, 1978. unp. Reading Level: YC
Disability: Orthopedic Impairment

An elderly man named Bartholomew has a very young neighbor, Nelly, whose stroller he pushes. They have great fun companionably sharing such ordinary pleasures as petting friendly dogs, rushing through sprinklers, and commenting on familiar sights. The old man is particularly sensitive to Nelly's struggles at independence and is careful to provide only the help she really needs. When Bartholomew begins to have mobility problems, his young neighbor gives him the assistance he now requires, being equally careful to respect his desire to remain self-sufficient. One day he falls down some steps and, after a long hospitalization, returns home in a wheelchair. Bartholomew bemoans his inability to go on his strolls, but Nelly readily reverses their roles: now she is the one who does the pushing.

Analysis. Bartholomew's gradual debilitation, a not unexpected consequence of aging, is accelerated when he falls. His young friend responds to his new situation in a loving and appropriate way. *A Special Trade* is a warm, affectionate story, enhanced by charming, lively illustrations.

Wolitzer, Hilma. *Toby Lived Here.* New York: Farrar, Straus & Giroux, 1978, 147 pp. Reading level: MC/YA
Disability: Emotional Dysfunction

When their mother's increasingly erratic behavior finally culminates in complete psychotic withdrawal, the woman is committed to a psychiatric institution. Twelve-year-old Toby and her six-year-old sister, Anne, are placed with the Selwyns, a gentle, loving couple who have happily raised a succession of foster children. Anne accepts their affection readily, but Toby resists, tormented by anxiety over being disloyal. Toby frequently writes to her absent parent, hoping for a response that does not come. The patient's social worker is vague in her reports, mistakenly believing that this will keep the children from worrying. At Toby's thirteenth birthday party, when she still hasn't heard from her mother, the teenager can scarcely contain her anger at the woman, who she feels has deserted her. Aware of her foster child's distress, Mrs. Selwyn insists it is time the girl visits her mother.

The meeting is not at all what Toby expected. Fearful that her mother would be raving, incoherent, or, worse, unloving, she finds instead the woman she once knew but without her usual facade of false gaiety. Toby's mother says she is still not ready to return home for she must have more time to develop the strength and skills necessary to manage her life competently. Relief floods over the teenager, but it is not unmixed with disappointment that she must continue to wait. When Toby questions her foster mother about the likelihood of inheriting her parent's condition, she is assured that such fears are groundless. Mrs. Selwyn responds:

"I don't think so. What happened to your mother happened because she stored up her feelings for such a long time, because she was grieving but wouldn't let herself grieve, because she was angry and wouldn't let herself be that, either."

"Angry?" Toby asked. "Who was she angry with?"

"Well, it's a different kind of anger. But I guess she was angry with your father. For leaving her like that."

"But he didn't leave her, he *died*." Toby cried. "He couldn't help it."

"I know," Sylvia said. "And *she* couldn't help her feelings either. But she was ashamed of them, and they hurt too much. She pushed them down, kept them inside her, simmering, simmering away like a pot of soup, until it all boiled over. And she had that breakdown."

After the girl's mother leaves the hospital, she and her daughters move back to their old neighborhood. Toby wishes they could stay near the Selwyns, but her mother says *she* needs the security of familiar things and places. Toby is comforted by knowing that she can maintain a relationship with her foster family. Her mother explains: "The Selwyns were very good to you when you really needed somebody. They just won't drop out of your life, Toby. You'll see them, keep in touch." The youngster now understands that the Selwyns' role in her life did not diminish or negate her love for her mother.

Analysis. A warm and sensitive story, *Toby Lived Here* examines the problems of a child whose mother lives in a psychiatric facility. Toby has had much to endure: her father's death, her mother's bizarre behavior, culminating in a dramatic nighttime removal to a psychiatric hospital, her placement in a foster home, her grandmother's rejection, and her uncles' lack of interest in her future. The portraits of family members who shirk their responsibilities are effectively contrasted with those of the foster parents who welcome troubled girls into their home. The explication of the cause of Toby's mother's distress is at an appropriate level for an audience, some of whose members might also harbor fears about the inheritability of the behavior, and the term *nervous breakdown* used by Toby reflects a child's language usage. The adolescent remembers her mother as "super courageous," an image in conflict with the real woman who is "sensitive and fragile." Wolitzer encourages the assumption that the ex-patient has regained a large measure of self-control and is on the way to a functional recovery. Although the reader presumably will identify with the heroine, whose churning, volatile emotions and resentment ebb and flow throughout the story, the depiction of her mother, who is the most immediate source of her distress, is nevertheless sympathetic.

Wolkoff, Judie. *Where the Elf King Sings.* Scarsdale, N.Y.: Bradbury, 1980. 178 pp. Reading Level: YA
Disability: Emotional Dysfunction; also auditory impairment, speech impairment

Marcie Breckenridge meets Mrs. King, an elderly eccentric lady, in the cemetery and on impulse accepts an invitation to visit her. The sixth-grade youngster's home life is chaotic, especially when her father is in a "blue funk," an emotional state invariably succeeded by a drinking binge. Since he has returned home from Vietnam, Mr. Breckenridge has been unable to control his temper, keep away from alcohol, or hold a job. Marcie's younger brother, David, warily observes his father's erratic moods, alcoholic episodes, and generally depressed and withdrawn behavior and leans on his sister for an interpretation of these events and support for the anxiety they generate. Their mother, who now must work as a waitress to support the family, is frustrated by her husband's problems and her inability to help him. Marcie, in the center of these storms, is unsure whether "she hated him or whether she felt sorry for him." Even after the veteran destroys their home during a violent rage, Marcie's grandmother consistently makes excuses for her son's behavior, blaming the war, society, and an insufficiently helpful family. Their father's latest rampage has so terrified his children that, in desperation, Mrs. Breckenridge threatens to get a court order if her husband returns.

Mrs. Breckenridge forbids her children to see Mrs. King because of town gossip implying that the old woman is unstable and would be an improper influence. The reclusive woman provides so much comfort to them, however, that the usually obedient youngsters ignore their mother's prohibition. David especially is intrigued and intellectually challenged by Mrs. King, finding in her company some of the security he needs from an adult and gets from no other source since he no longer sees his father, grandmother, or even his working mother very often. Mrs. King tells the young boy about her gifted brother, Matthew, who could neither hear nor speak and who died at age 12, having, in Goethe's words, "heard the elf king sing." David, entranced by the youth's drawings, wants to draw birds like those of the dead boy and in wonderment asks Marcie, "Do you suppose Matthew saw more because he couldn't hear? I mean, do you think he just looked at things harder? To make up for not hearing? I guess he must have. Otherwise he couldn't have drawn like he had microscope eyes."

Mr. Breckenridge begins attending rap sessions at a church, where he shares his torment with other Vietnam veterans. On the anniversary of the death of a friend killed while trying to help him, he reaches a crisis point and, at last perceiving that he has little hope of recovery on his own, decides to enter a VA hospital. Initially, he is treated in their alcoholism unit but is later transferred to the psychiatric ward for additional therapy. A fellow soldier he met at the support group offers Mrs. Breckenridge a job more compatible with her interests and with hours that permit more time with her children. On the veteran's first leave home, his family sees the man they had once loved. They hope he can recapture once again his old self when the rage and frustration he accumulated during the Southeast Asian fighting have been spent.

Analysis. The unique problems of returned Vietnam veterans are sympathetically explored in this work. The acute family distress experienced by those whom society both used, then disparaged, and the self-destructive techniques for coping with untenable memories that many men adopted are treated with compassion. Because Mrs. King was misunderstood and had a brother who also stood outside the mainstream, she is seen as being especially sensitive to others similarly regarded. Both children have an emotional maturity far beyond their years, and the young boy's artistic talents seem inordinately exaggerated. Since their father's emotional disorders derive from the traumas experienced during the war, that is, they are situation-specific, their hinted-at remediation, while optimistic, is plausible.

Wood, Colin. *A Confusion of Time*. Originally published in England as *The Alabama Story*. Nashville: Thomas Nelson, 1977. 168 pp.
Reading Level: MC
Disability: Special Health Problems, Orthopedic Impairment

Raymond lives with his mother in a basement apartment in a building marked for demolition. When his physical condition worsens, he is confined to bed, where his window permits a limited view of the street. Just as the bored boy wistfully remarks to himself that he wishes he could see whole people, not just their bottom halves, the intrepid Wally, a man of child's size, appears, accompanied by his magical mongrel dog, Mullinger. In the presence of his new acquaintance, Raymond discovers that his kitchen has suddenly and inexplicably been turned into the Hamilton household of the 1860s. The boy is transported back and forth between the nineteenth century and the recent past. In the latter period, his health continues to decline and the wrecker's ball comes ever closer; in the former, he, Wally, Mullinger, and Laura Hamilton, a child his own age, are pulled into a daring adventure involving attempts by supporters of the American Confederacy to kidnap Mr. Hamilton, whose sympathies are firmly with the Union side. Laura's father is violently opposed to the sale of a powerful ship, the *Alabama*, to the Southern forces and is working diligently to interfere with a plot to smuggle the vessel away from Liverpool under the very noses of the customs agents. Wally leads the children, his dog, and the well-meaning but slow-thinking Constable Crumble through several completely improbable escapades and hairsbreadth escapes to rescue Mr. Hamilton and foil the evildoers' plans. Although Raymond is a full participant in these exciting enterprises of the past, in his other life his health deteriorates so seriously that he must be hospitalized. The weakened child is able to blend both worlds after Wally rushes him to Terminal Station by ambulance and all his friends gather around his bedside to express their mutual love and support.

Analysis. The youngster's mysterious ailment is never named in his fantastic adventures, and references to Wally, Mullinger, Laura, et al. are considered by his physician to be the products of delirium. Although the boy's tragic demise can be predicted from his rapid decline, this eventuality is never overtly stated, and optimistic readers can choose to ignore the evidence. Wally's reduced stature makes possible a compromise in his characterization that echoes a convention of folk literature: he combines the enthusiasm, effervescence, and adventurousness of a child with the resourcefulness, intelligence, and skills of an adult. The author has created in this work a witty and skillful parody of a Victorian's children's novel complete with extreme and outrageous characterizations (including villains named Smarling, Grimskill, Gooch, Sprage, and Harpoon Harry), a convoluted and thoroughly unlikely plot, and occasional impromptu moral observations delivered with a total absence of subtlety.

Wood, Phyllis Anderson. *I Think This Is Where We Came In*. Philadelphia: Westminster, 1976. 155 pp. Reading Level: YA
Disability: auditory impairment

Teenagers Paul and Maggie Johnson and their friend Mike pack their camping gear into a pickup truck and head for the Sierras. As they drive through the roasting flatlands, they pass an abandoned dog, nearly starved, whose paws are bleeding from walking on the blistering roadway. Mike adopts the animal and names it Fritzi; they tend its wounds and restore it to health. At one of their camping stops, Maggie sees "a small boy with hair like corn silk and eyes like the sky" who watches her intently but does not speak. Soon after, she learns from his mother that the boy, now lost, is deaf. Paul, Maggie, and Mike join the search but are unsuccessful and must wait until morning, when the bloodhounds arrive to continue their efforts. The next day a trainer arrives with the dogs, who follow the child's scent, find him unharmed, and make possible his return to his distraught parent. The adolescents move on to a new campsite, but during the course of the trip the relationship between Mike and Maggie has changed from childhood friendship to teenage romance. When the truck stops at a ranch, Fritzi displays her natural talent as a sheepdog, and Mike regretfully leaves his pet at a home he recognizes is more suitable than any he could provide. As they travel back through the valley, they see a sick, abandoned dog at the roadside. They stop and tend its wounds, and Mike ruefully comments: "I think this is where we came in."

Analysis. This shallow, very easy-to-read, teenage novel uses the device of a camping trip to tie together a series of vignettes. The child, who reveals the compassionate, caring aspects of the central characters, is treated with excessive sentimentality in the brief incident in which he appears: "Mrs. Jameson and Robbie visited Fritzi often because Robbie seemed to have some sort of communication going with her. It was a tearful moment for Robbie when finally he had to pull out."

Wosmek, Frances. *A Bowl of Sun*. Illus. by author. Chicago: Childrens Press, 1976. 47 pp. Reading Level: YC
Disability: Visual Impairment

Life is idyllic for Megan, a young blind girl who lives by the sea with her father, a sandalmaker. Mike encourages his daughter to learn through her other senses and shares his feelings that "nobody lives a better life than we do," an assessment she thoroughly endorses. But recognizing Megan's need for special instruction and socialization, Mike arranges a move to Boston. Traumatized by the change, the radically different environment, and her diminished independence, the child becomes apathetic and is unable to learn. Her father begins to doubt the wisdom of his decision because of his daughter's obvious distress, her lack of academic achievement, and her solitude resulting from his having to work much longer hours. Megan has a frightening experience in which she tries to cross a street alone, is rescued by a policeman, and returned home by Rose, a potter who lives in their building. The artisan comforts the distraught child and attempts to distract her by showing her how to work with clay, for which Megan seems to have a natural aptitude. She is eventually able to make a bowl good enough to give to Mike. Her enthusiasm for this new activity increases her self-confidence and improves her schoolwork dramatically.

Analysis. This story examines the problems involved in moving beyond the protective confines of a loving home into a more complicated world, problems precipitated and compounded by disability. The security offered by the former is recognized as inadequate for the future needs of the heroine, but the author suggests that there are caring, able people who can make the transition less painful. Megan's feelings and behavior are credible under the circumstances, and she emerges as a likable and admirable youngster. Illustrations and text are seamlessly joined in this gentle, lovely story.

Yolen, Jane. *Dream Weaver.* Illus. by Michael Hague. Cleveland: Collins, 1979. 80 pp. Reading Level: MC
Disability: Visual Impairment, orthopedic impairment

The blind Dream Weaver, pleased with her busy site near the steps of the Great Temple, calls out to the passing crowd: "A penny for a woven dream." When such a coin is safely pocketed, the old woman takes out her loom and threads and begins to weave a dream for her customer. This day, seven sets of listeners request dreams, which unfold from the woman's loom like ancient fairy tales. Characters change form and shape, becoming deer, cat, and tree, or are made of stone or clay, yet are humans who live, love, and sometimes suffer as their adventures are played out. In one dream, Princess Heart O'Stone is obliged to live an empty barren life until a poor woodcutter comes to the palace to rescue her from her cruel fate. The youth tells the maiden what the animals have said: "Heart of stone crack, ride on your back." The princess declares she will marry the young man over the objections of her mother, when all notice "his proud straight back was now crooked. A hump, like a great stone, grew between his shoulders." The king, approving the transfer of this terrible burden from his daughter to Donnal, her suitor, announces: "He is a man of courage and compassion [who] shall carry the burdens of the kingdom on that crooked back with ease." And "King Donnal never minded his hump, for the only mirrors he sought were the princess's eyes. And when they told him that he was straight and true, he knew they did not lie."

Some of the purchasers like their dream, some folks are skeptical, others are disappointed, but all leave behind the weaving produced by the old woman. At the end of the day, a couple give her a penny for her own dream. She is overwhelmed, and she conjures up an ironic parable on art and the artist. When she is finished, she is startled to learn that there is "no picture or pattern" in the threads of this or any weaving, for it was her words, not her fingers, that revealed the dreams. This pleases her since she knows that memory will preserve their essence far better than a piece of cloth.

Analysis. Both the weaver and King Donnal embody legendary stereotypes: the blind seer and the person chosen and "marked" for a special, exalted destiny. The fairy-tale quality and style of *Dream Weaver* make such usage expected and underscore the classical concern that distinguishes between the superficial and the substantive. The carefully crafted text invites readers to contemplate the subtle themes undergirding the familiar and obvious plot lines. Haunting illustrations, beautiful typefaces, and superior book design all add immensely to the pleasure of the story.

Yolen, Jane. *The Mermaid's Three Wisdoms.* Illus. by Laura Rader. Cleveland: Collins-World, 1978. 111 pp. Reading Level: MC
Disability: Auditory Impairment, speech impairment

Because she has been observed by a human, the mermaid Melusina is punished by the king of the merfolk by being banished from the ocean. Her lively tail is replaced by two awkward legs, and the unhappy creature is tossed up on the beach, where she is discovered by the girl responsible for her exile. After resuscitating her, Jess is outraged when the stranger reacts violently to her rescuer's incoherent speech. With the assistance of Captain A, a retired seaman who has a modest hearing loss and is the girl's only friend, the 12-year-old manages to take the former mermaid to the old man's shanty. Although he had originally dismissed the child's claim to have seen a mermaid, the old salt becomes convinced when he sees a crystal tear come from Melusina's eyes. The alien attempts to imitate the speech she hears but is unable to because she has no tongue—further evidence of her origins. They all despair of communicating until Jess suggests that since the fishgirl moves her hands, perhaps they might speak through the use of the gestures learned at the center for deaf children she once attended. Using hand signs, Melusina and the girl are able to understand each other.

One day, an obviously ill baby dolphin drifts dangerously close to shore despite the warnings the two new companions give. Dismayed at their failure, Melusina stays to comfort the now-stranded calf. A turtle has observed his former swimming partner's plea for help and summons some merfolk, who tenderly transport the sick mammal back to sea. Melusina, overcome with longing for her home, dives into the water and disappears. When Jess complains that the visitor left without even a message of farewell and that her departure has been a source of great pain, Captain A comforts the grieving girl with his fanciful suggestion that the mermaid came to teach them a lesson. He points out that they were fortunate that Jess's experiences with signing gave her the expertise to be capable of communicating with the silent exile from the sea. Then "Jess put her hands up to her ears and covered them. She had never thought of her ears as being a help. Only a burden. And certainly she had never thought they could get her a friend."

With sudden, surprising insight, Jess primly reminds the captain that further contact with Melusina should be avoided:

> Jess nodded solemnly. "We shouldn't *see* her again. It would be against the rules, the Three Wisdoms, really. And those Wisdoms, captain, why they'd work just as well here on land as down in the sea. Because they're true. Everyone should know them, not only where Melusina comes from. That much I know. And especially all the deaf kids. Because we are kind of like merfolk here on the land. Not really altogether fitting, speaking without tongues really. Knowing how much a touch means. And having that long patience.

Analysis. Yolen's story is unusual, and her idea of suggesting signing as a communication device between human and fantasy folk is an original one. However, the language employed is far too precious, the central metaphor is simultaneously pretentious and vague, and the frequent use of italics for emphasis or explanation is artificial. The kindly, knowing, old sea captain is surely a Hollywood product, and the "Wisdom of the Sea" philosophy is trite. Certain stereotypes about disabled individuals are perpetuated, such as that deaf people are unable to speak and are more patient than their hearing peers.

The story has some good qualities—particularly the portrait of a bristly girl whose defensiveness is at least partially attributable to her hearing loss. Descriptions are often pleasing, even lyrical: the fish's name, Wave Greeter, is felicitous, and the discussion of how to avoid graceless signing is admirable. Rader's drawings, although anatomically distorted, contribute to the fantasy mood. The story's most notable attribute is its portrayal of sign as a beautiful language capable of poetic as well as precise meanings.

Yolen, Jane. *The Seeing Stick.* Illus. by Remy Charlip and Demetra Maraslis. New York: Crowell, 1977. unp. Reading Level: YC
Disability: Visual Impairment

Long ago in Peking there lived an emperor who had a blind daughter. Although he offered a fortune to anyone who could cure her, all who came—magicians, priests, and doctors—failed to restore her sight. At last a poor old man whose only possessions are his walking stick and his knife seeks an audience with the monarch. As the sightless stranger is brought into the throne room, he is overheard by the princess as he describes his "seeing stick." Curious about this reference, the child listens carefully to the story of his journey to the palace and allows her fingers to be led gently over the wondrous scenes the old man has carved. Inspired, the girl begins to touch the faces of those around her and delights in what she is able to learn as "she grew eyes on the tips of her fingers and taught other blind children to see as she saw."

Analysis. An inescapable message of this book is that pity is the proper attitude toward blind persons and mourning the proper response to blindness. The child is without joy for "all the beautiful handcrafts in the kingdom brought her no pleasure at all." Yet her other senses are intact, and the things given to the child have textural as well as visual components. Her father did not cry for his blind daughter for he "had given up weeping over such things when he ascended the throne." Clearly, then, it is only his position that makes weeping improper. That her teacher is blind and she in turn becomes a teacher of other blind children perpetuates the bias society has toward keeping those with impairments among their "own kind." The illustrations are delicate, but flat and lifeless. They change from black and white to pale pastel colors when the princess first meets her tutor, unsubtly suggesting the increased richness of her life. The black-and-white pictures show both the emperor and his daughter dressed in white, shroudlike garments, once more equating blindness and death. The story, related as a legend, is more sentimental and maudlin and considerably less profound than it initially appears.

Young, Helen. *What Difference Does It Make, Danny?* Illus. by Quentin Blake. London: Andre Deutsch, 1980. 93 pp. Reading Level: MC

Disability: Neurological Impairment

Danny's epilepsy is fairly well controlled by medication by the time he enters school. The staff is informed of his disorder, and when he does have a seizure, his teacher, who had previously prepared the class, calmly discusses what is happening. Although absorbed in watching the event, the children are cued by the teacher's rational attitude, which dissipates their anxiety. When Danny recovers, he wants to know specifically what happened, and his classmates compete both in describing and simulating his actions. One imaginative, cool youngster reports: "You looked . . . like a disco dancer who has gone over the top." Danny's adjustment is exemplary until the new master decides it is not safe to allow the child to participate in any but the most innocuous sports. Disheartened, he becomes moody and uncooperative, capping his increasingly distraught actions with truancy. As he walks along the canal, an expressly forbidden activity, a toddler appears, predictably falls into the water, and sinks like a stone. Danny plunges in and, recalling his lifesaving training, pulls the child to safety and restores the tot's breathing. Not unexpectedly, he becomes a local hero, and the games master, now temporarily on crutches, belatedly but graciously, acknowledges his error: "It's a good job everyone didn't take my attitude, lad. . . . It's a good job *someone* taught you to swim."

Analysis. The English setting should offer few problems to American readers except for what may seem a quaint, naive representation of children's behavior. The irreverent description of the seizure is one of the best available in juvenile fiction. The term *fit,* more commonly used to describe a seizure in England, is generally considered unacceptable in this country. There is, however, repeated and appropriate insistence on calling Danny a boy with epilepsy, not an epileptic. This didactic but entertaining work is adamant about the importance of allowing children with epilepsy to participate fully in activities. However, its argument, presented through the timely rescue, is unsubtle and forced. More effectively, it proposes that adults can strongly influence the reactions of children through their own understanding and modeling behavior, and, in fact, some of the narrative seems directed to adult readers. The sketchy illustrations nicely support the breezy, upbeat tone of the text.

Zelonky, Joy. *I Can't Always Hear You.* Illus. by Barbara Bejna and Shirlee Jensen. Milwaukee: Raintree, 1980. 31 pp. Reading Level: YC
Disability: Auditory Impairment

Kim worries that she will be considered an outsider at her new school because of her hearing aid. The Oriental girl informs her teacher that she can hear his words most of the time so he doesn't have to shout. Kim has apparently been reading lips, and the first time she speaks in class, a misunderstanding occurs, which, because of her slightly incorrect answer, results in general laughter. Mr. Davis tells the class that Kim needs her aid to hear just as he requires his glasses to see, but some of the students continue to embarrass her. Mistakenly getting into the boys' line to go to the lavatory is the final straw, and the youngster announces to her teacher that she intends to leave the school. He promptly introduces Kim to the principal, who lifts a lock of her hair to reveal a hearing aid. Calling on the advice given by the empathic administrator, Kim discovers her classmates all admit to something "different" about themselves and concludes that these attributes do not interfere with friendship.

Analysis. This simple, extensively illustrated, quasi-fictional book bluntly but effectively delivers a message about the necessity for accommodation to a child with a hearing loss. Such paraphernalia as a harness and battery holder are depicted in a direct and straightforward manner.

Zelonky, Joy. *My Best Friend Moved Away.* Illus. by Angela Adams. Milwaukee: Raintree, 1980. 31 pp. Reading Level: YC
Disability: orthopedic impairment

Brian is sad when Nick, his best friend, announces his family is moving across town. When he visits Nick in his new home, the two youngsters are awkward with each other. A subsequent discussion with his father helps Brian accept the changed situation.

Analysis. Although it is never alluded to, Brian has a disability that necessitates the wearing of a leg brace. It is prominently depicted in the illustrations, including some pictures showing the boy in short pants. This didactic work focuses on coping with changes in a relationship between friends, but there is an obvious peripheral message about disability. By ostentatiously avoiding mentioning any impairment in the text, yet featuring it prominently in the pictures, the author and illustrator are, in effect, minimizing its importance as a factor in a relationship.

Zumwalt, Eva. *Sun Dust*. Illus. by Zenowij Onyshkewych. New York: McKay, 1976. 184 pp. Reading Level: YA
Disability: Orthopedic Impairment

After an auto accident leaves Laurie Campbell with a permanent limp, she accompanies her mother to her grandparents' ranch in New Mexico, where no one she knows will be able to stare at her uneven gait. Her grandfather gives her a newborn foal but also insists she choose a riding horse for use now. Impulsively, she selects Sun Dust, the wild filly of a dam so ferocious it had to be destroyed. The man shrewdly agrees to his granddaughter's inappropriate selection, realizing this is Laurie's way of avoiding learning to ride, but counters by directing his stable boy to begin her lessons on another animal immediately. David starts breaking the beautiful but rambunctious creature and instructing the city girl in the fundamentals of riding. Randa, a schoolmate, has a proprietary interest in David and, seeing the newcomer as a potential rival, tries to maximize her discomfort and undermine her shaky self-confidence. Nonetheless, with the young man's skillful guidance, Laurie becomes proficient enough to enter the upcoming Queen of the Rodeo contest. In the arena, she falls from her horse but remounts and takes her place in the competition. Randa is the winner, but to Laurie's surprise, she is named a runner-up.

Finally, Sun Dust is sufficiently gentled to be turned over to his new owner. David teaches her the precise, demanding maneuvers she must make with her horse if she is to compete in the exacting sport of barrel racing. At the next rodeo, she challenges and beats Randa in the more experienced girl's best event. Her happiness is complete when she learns that her journalist father had returned from a dangerous mission in time to watch her triumph from the grandstands.

Analysis. This formula teenage romance features a heroine whose impairment is used to inflate the significance of her accomplishments. Although the girl refers to herself repeatedly as a "lame duck," it is clear from the start that she is really a beautiful swan. The story's best features are the setting and the glimpses into ranch life, but the inevitability of the plot after the first few pages reduces any tension that might have been generated.

Title Index

This index provides access by title to the Chapter 3 annotations. The page references to any of these titles discussed earlier in Chapters 1 and 2 may be found by consulting the Subject Index.

Subject Index

References by title to the Chapter 3 annotations are separately listed in the Title Index. Page references to any of these titles discussed earlier in Chapters 1 and 2 are included here.